D0047410

LIFE APPLICATION® BIBLE COMMENTARY

Acts

Bruce B. Barton, D.Min.

Linda Taylor

J. Richard Love, D.Min.

Len Woods, Th.M.

Dave Veerman, M.Div.

General Editor:

Grant Osborne, Ph.D.

Series Editor:

Philip W. Comfort, Ph.D., D.Litt. et Phil.

Tyndale House Publishers, Inc.
CAROL STREAM, ILLINOIS

Visit Tyndale's exciting Web site at www.tyndale.com

Contributing Editors: James C. Galvin, Ed.D., and Ronald A. Beers

(No citation is given for Scripture text that is exactly the same wording in all four versions—NIV, NKJV, NRSV, and NLT.)

Library of Congress Cataloging-in-Publication Data

Acts / Bruce B. Barton . . . [et al.] ; general editor, Grant Osborne.
p. cm. — (Life application Bible commentary)
Includes bibliographical references and index.
ISBN-10: 0-8423-2861-0 (pbk. : alk. paper)
ISBN-13: 978-0-8423-2861-6
1. Bible. N.T. Acts Commentaries. I. Barton, Bruce B. II. Osborne, Grant R. III. Series.
BS2625.3.A26 1999
226.6'0-077—dc21
99-21515

Printed in the United States of America

10 09 08 07
12 11 10 9 8

CONTENTS

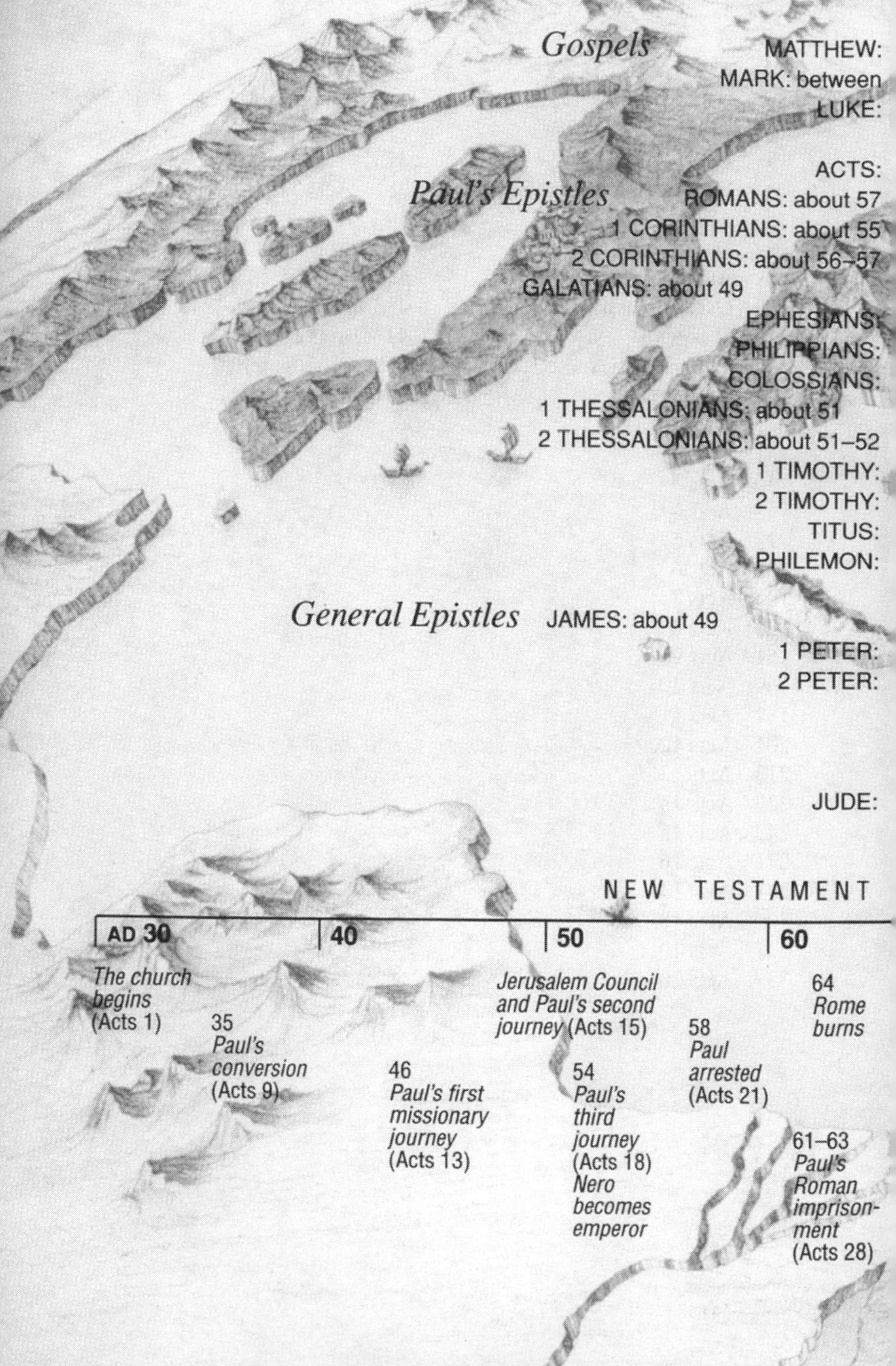
Gospels
MATTHEW:
MARK: between
LUKE:
ACTS:
Paul's Epistles
ROMANS: about 57
1 CORINTHIANS: about 55
2 CORINTHIANS: about 56–57
GALATIANS: about 49
EPHESIANS:
PHILIPPIANS:
COLOSSIANS:
1 THESSALONIANS: about 51
2 THESSALONIANS: about 51–52
1 TIMOTHY:
2 TIMOTHY:
TITUS:
PHILEMON:
General Epistles
JAMES: about 49
1 PETER:
2 PETER:
JUDE:
NEW TESTAMENT
AD 30
40
50
60
The church begins (Acts 1)
35 Paul's conversion (Acts 9)
46 Paul's first missionary journey (Acts 13)
Jerusalem Council and Paul's second journey (Acts 15)
54 Paul's third journey (Acts 18) Nero becomes emperor
58 Paul arrested (Acts 21)
61–63 Paul's Roman imprisonment (Acts 28)
64 Rome burns

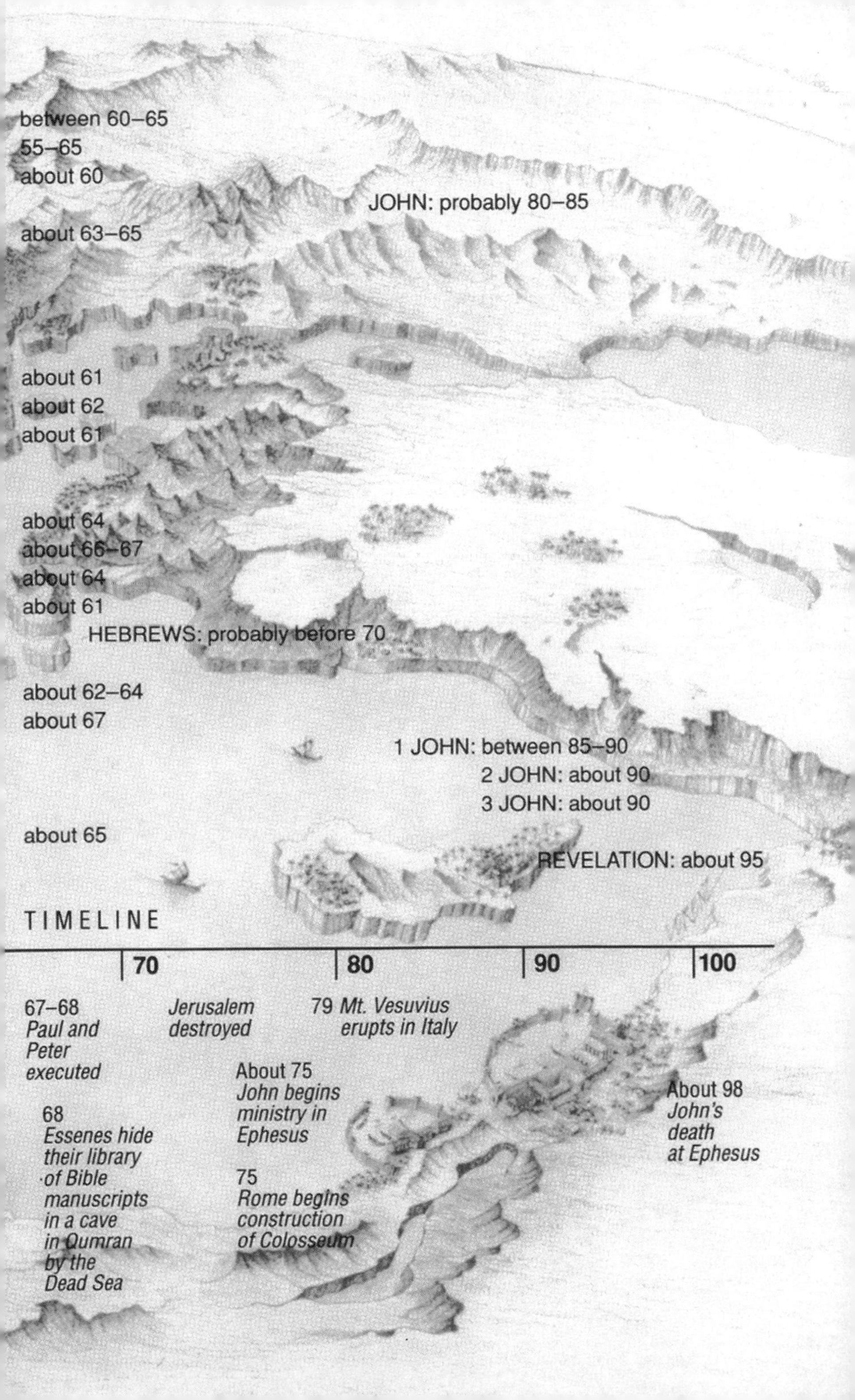

between 60–65
55–65
about 60

JOHN: probably 80–85

about 63–65

about 61
about 62
about 61

about 64
about 66–67
about 64
about 61

HEBREWS: probably before 70

about 62–64
about 67

1 JOHN: between 85–90
2 JOHN: about 90
3 JOHN: about 90

about 65

REVELATION: about 95

TIMELINE

70 **80** **90** **100**

67–68 *Paul and Peter executed*

Jerusalem destroyed

79 *Mt. Vesuvius erupts in Italy*

68 *Essenes hide their library of Bible manuscripts in a cave in Qumran by the Dead Sea*

About 75 *John begins ministry in Ephesus*

75 *Rome begins construction of Colosseum*

About 98 *John's death at Ephesus*

FOREWORD

The Life Application Bible Commentary series provides verse-by-verse explanation, background, and application for every verse in the New Testament. In addition, it gives personal help, teaching notes, and sermon ideas that will address needs, answer questions, and provide insight for applying the Word of God to life today. The content is highlighted so that particular verses and phrases are easy to find.

Each volume contains three sections: introduction, commentary, and reference. The introduction includes an overview of the book, the book's historical context, a time line, cultural background information, major themes, an overview map, and an explanation about the author and audience.

The commentary section includes running commentary on the Bible text with reference to several modern versions, especially the New International Version, the New Revised Standard Version, and the New Living Translation, accompanied by life applications interspersed throughout. Additional elements include charts, diagrams, maps, and illustrations. There are also insightful quotes from church leaders and theologians such as John Calvin, Martin Luther, John Wesley, and A. W. Tozer. These features are designed to help you quickly grasp the biblical information and be prepared to communicate it to others. The reference section includes an index and a bibliography.

INTRODUCTION

Acts has it all—supernatural intervention, astounding miracles, powerful preaching, breathtaking escapes, harrowing journeys, life-and-death decisions, courtroom dramas, thrilling rescues, action, mystery, and adventure! Acts will grab your attention, trigger your imagination, and tug at your emotions. It's a terrific story and a great read . . . and it's true.

As you flip through the pages, however, don't miss the story behind the stories. Underlying the stimulating sermons and the display of miracles, look for God at work in individuals. In fact, as much as Acts could be called the story of the early church, it could also be titled "The Miracle of Changed Lives."

Consider this: When last we saw the disciples, they were running scared and abandoning their Lord (Matthew 26:56). Fleeing, denying, disillusioned, and crying, these men seemed the least likely candidates to be boldly proclaiming the gospel. Yet that's what happened. Peter, James, John, and the rest had been transformed from cowardly to courageous, argumentative to articulate, and selfish to selfless. Then they were joined by Paul, whom God also miraculously transformed.

What made the difference? Acts reveals the profound answer. This is their story—the history of the early church and the changed men and women who changed the world.

As you read of the Holy Spirit, the gifts, persecution and power, Paul's dramatic conversion, and the rapid spread of the gospel beyond Jerusalem and Judea to the ends of the earth, look for yourself in the stories. Ask God to transform you into the kind of person he can use to change *your* world.

AUTHOR

Luke: doctor, Gentile Christian, traveling companion of Paul, and writer of the Gospel according to Luke.

Luke was a close friend and companion of Paul. He is listed as the writer of the gospel bearing his name by nearly all the ancient church fathers, including Justin Martyr (A.D. 100–165), Irenaeus (c. A.D. 120–200), and Tertullian (A.D. 160–230); all agree on Luke.

The text of the book of Acts clearly reveals the same author as the Gospel of Luke. Both books are addressed to "Theophilus" (Luke 1:1; Acts 1:1), and this opening sentence in Acts refers to a previous book that sounds very much like the Gospel ("Dear Theophilus: In my first book I told you about everything Jesus began to do and teach until the day he ascended to heaven after giving his chosen apostles further instructions from the Holy Spirit"—1:1-2 NLT). It makes sense, as well, in light of Luke's commitment to writing "a careful summary" of "the events that took place" (Luke 1:3, 1 NLT), that Acts be seen as a continuation of the story, a second volume detailing what happened subsequent to Christ's death and resurrection.

Although the writer does not identify himself by name anywhere in the book, he does use the pronoun "we" beginning with 16:10, thereby indicating that the writer had joined Paul in his journeys in Troas at that point. As such, Luke must have become one of Paul's coworkers, which is what Paul explicitly acknowledges in Philemon 1:24.

Although Luke had a major role in the formation of the early church through his writing and through his ministry with Paul, he is only mentioned in three of Paul's letters (Colossians 4:14; 2 Timothy 4:11; Philemon 1:24). It is significant that Luke was not a Jew but a Greek and not one of the original disciples of Christ. Thus he was not a member of the inner circle of Jesus' followers nor one who saw Jesus as his long-promised Messiah. Luke must have been a convert, convinced of the truth of the gospel message and determined to spread the message to others. Perhaps little is said of Luke because he chose not to give himself a prominent place in the text of his books.

According to Colossians 4:14, Luke was a doctor. The medical references and terminology in Acts, therefore, also point to him as the probable author. For instance, when describing the miraculous healing of the lame man by Peter, Acts doesn't just say, "He jumped up, stood on his feet, and began to walk!" (3:8 NLT). Instead, that description is preceded by the medical explanation, "the man's feet and anklebones were healed and strengthened" (3:7 NLT). And when describing Paul's snakebite in Malta, the writer took care to explain the possible results: "The people waited for him to swell up or suddenly drop dead" (28:6 NLT). Both descriptions are what would be expected from a doctor. Although the style and terminology of Acts cannot prove that Luke, the doctor, was the author, the literary style of this book, as with the Gospel, certainly suggests an educated writer.

As a physician and, thus, a scientist, Luke became a meticulous historian, researching the facts and paying attention to detail.

The beginning of his Gospel states: "Many people have written accounts about the events that took place among us. They used as their source material the reports circulating among us from the early disciples and other eyewitnesses of what God has done in fulfillment of his promises. Having carefully investigated all of these accounts from the beginning, I have decided to write a careful summary for you, to reassure you of the truth of all you were taught" (Luke 1:1-4 NLT).

Luke's research into what had already been written about Jesus gave him a start. And his close relationship to the apostle Paul (20:5-15; 27:1–28:16) undoubtedly gave him access to an abundance of information concerning Christ, thus helping him write the Gospel. Certainly there also could be no better person to record the history of the early church than an eyewitness of the tremendous spread of the gospel (himself a convert) and a close friend of the church's greatest missionary.

As mentioned above, Acts implies strongly that Luke had traveled with Paul. Acts 16:10-17; 20:5-15; 21:1-18; and 27:1–28:16 use the pronoun "we," apparently indicating that the writer was Paul's traveling companion. Some scholars have considered the use of "we" merely a literary device to give the impression that the author was an eyewitness, but most understand it as accurately reflecting the time when the author of Acts joined Paul in his travels. A careful study of these "we" sections of Acts reveals that the author was with Paul when he established the church at Philippi and when he returned to Jerusalem. The writer also accompanied Paul to his trial in Rome.

These details about the author's life fit well with what is known about Luke. His presence with Paul during Paul's imprisonment is well attested in three of Paul's prison letters (Colossians 4:14; 2 Timothy 4:11; Philemon 1:24).

Traditionally, Luke has been described as a Greek and, thus, a Gentile. Paul's final message of greeting in Colossians does not include Luke among the Jews ("These are the only Jewish Christians among my co-workers"—Colossians 4:11 NLT). Instead, Paul wrote, "Dear Doctor Luke sends his greetings, and so does Demas" (Colossians 4:14 NLT), implying strongly that both Luke and Demas were Gentiles.

Acts 1:19 provides another clue to Luke's Gentile identity. In this passage he took the trouble to translate an Aramaic name, referring to Aramaic as "their" language. This implies that Aramaic was not Luke's own language. Also a careful study of the Greek style of both the Gospel and Acts agrees with the conclusion that the author of both books was a Gentile. The text consistently avoids Aramaic expressions, such as *rabbi,* using in their place words that would be more familiar to Gentiles, such as "teacher."

Luke probably met Paul in Troas, after Paul had his vision of a Macedonian man pleading for help (16:8-9), for that is where the "we" section begins. Undoubtedly the small missionary band was energized with their clear call to preach the Good News to an entirely new group of people, the Greeks in Macedonia.

Philippi provided their first opportunity, and the simple gospel message rocked this affluent Macedonian city. But here the evangelists suffered as well—they were beaten after exorcising a demon from a fortune-teller. Bruised and bloody, Paul and Silas were thrown into the inner dungeon of the Philippian jail. There Luke's medical expertise may have helped. Perhaps he was allowed into the damp jail to nurse Paul and Silas's wounds and to pray with them. Whatever the case, Luke would have felt the great earthquake that rocked the entire city that night, leaving the prison in ruins. These miraculous events led to the salvation of the Philippian jailer and his household and to the Philippian judges' fearful pleading with Paul and Silas to leave town before anything else could happen to disturb the city's peace. If Luke hadn't been completely convinced of the power of the gospel before he joined Paul, he would have been by that time.

At this point in the text, "we" stops being used to describe the missionaries. It is uncertain, therefore, whether Luke continued traveling with Paul on the rest of this journey. The text makes it clear, however, that he joined Paul on the third missionary journey, even accompanying him to Jerusalem, where Paul was arrested. Luke stayed with Paul, now a Roman prisoner, and accompanied him to Rome, where Paul had to await trial. On the journey, Luke courageously faced a hurricane and a shipwreck in order to stay with Paul and serve him. Although not much is known about Luke, it is clear that he was Paul's faithful and true friend, supporting him as he courageously preached the Good News and then as he sat in prison. Later, when everyone else had deserted Paul, Luke was by his side, still supporting the apostle during his last days (2 Timothy 4:11).

DATE AND SETTING

Written between A.D. 63 and 65 from an unknown location.

The final event of Acts—Paul's ministry in Rome—provides a clue to the date and setting of the book. Christianity was recognized by the Roman authorities before A.D. 65, but then Nero began persecuting followers of the Christian faith. Yet Acts makes no mention of this persecution. It also does not comment on the destruction of Jerusalem in A.D. 70, something that would surely have been mentioned if Luke had written in the 70s. The Gospel records Jesus' words regarding the destruction of the temple (Luke 19:41-44; 21:20-24), so Luke certainly would have mentioned in Acts the prophecy's fulfillment. Noting that the gospel account, probably written A.D. 60–61, was the first of his two books to Theophilus (1:1), the two books probably were written within a short time of each other, possibly during Luke's stays with Paul while in prison in Caesarea (23:33) and Rome (28:14-16).

Biblical scholars suggest a number of possible places where Luke may have written Acts. Because Luke is traditionally associated with Antioch, some believe that Luke penned the book in that city, where the disciples were "first called Christians" (11:26 NLT). Rome is another option held by scholars due to the fact that Acts concludes with Paul's ministry there. A third option is the city of Ephesus because the book focuses on many events in that Greek city, including Paul's farewell to the leaders of the church. In summary, there is no consensus among scholars about where Luke actually wrote the follow-up to his gospel account.

AUDIENCE

Theophilus ("one who loves God"), Gentiles, and people everywhere.

Both the Gospel of Luke and Acts name Theophilus (Luke 1:1; 1:1) as the addressee. Because the literal meaning of "Theophilus" is "lover of God" or "friend of God," some have thought that the books were addressed generally and written to anyone who loves God, not a specific, first-century individual. Others note that "most excellent" is attached to "Theophilus" in Luke 1:3. In that day, this title was used only when addressing a Roman officer, thus leading to the conclusion that Theophilus was a Gentile and possibly someone of high rank in Roman society. Beyond those inferences, little is known—the name Theophilus appears nowhere else in Scripture.

Many biblical scholars think that Theophilus was a new believer who was having some difficulty with the Christian faith. Thus Luke wrote the gospel account in order to provide solid answers to Theophilus's questions, so he could "know the certainty of the things [he had] been taught" (Luke 1:4 NIV). (For more on Theophilus, see the introduction to the *Life Application Bible Commentary* on the Gospel of Luke.)

Luke also elaborated in Acts about a subject that he had mentioned in his gospel account—that the Gentiles are heirs of God's salvation together with the Jews. The Gospel records stories of Jesus healing non-Jewish people and proclaiming his message to them (Luke 7:1-10; 8:26-39). Acts describes the spread of Christianity among the Jews and then well beyond, to the vast Gentile world. Chapter 10 contains a dramatic turning point in the missionary enterprise as Peter preached to Cornelius and Gentiles received the Holy Spirit. When Peter reported this to church leaders in Jerusalem, he was met with skepticism because Jews believed that they alone would know the Messiah. But after Peter shared with them his experience at Cornelius's home (see 10:9-48), "all their objections were answered and they began praising God. They said, 'God has also given the Gentiles the privilege of turning from sin and receiving eternal life'" (11:18 NLT). Thus the gospel message spread across the world, to Ephesus, to Rome, and, eventually, to where you (the reader) live.

Clearly, then, Gentile Christians would have been eager readers of this book.

OCCASION AND PURPOSE

To give an accurate account of the birth and growth of the Christian church.

After reading what Luke had written in his gospel account, Theophilus may have had unanswered questions. So Luke wrote Acts to answer those questions and to underscore the truth of the gospel. By tracing the growth of the Christian church throughout the known world at that time, Luke demonstrated that God's good news of salvation applies to every person—from the lowliest slave to the most respected nobleman and from the Jews to the Greeks and Romans.

Luke probably had other purposes in mind for writing the book of Acts. These are mentioned below.

Historic. In writing his Gospel, Luke wanted to present "a careful summary" (Luke 1:3 NLT). Thus, he took great pains to verify the historical accuracy of the events he was recording, because his purpose was to write a careful and accurate account of what he had researched and seen. Evidence of his accuracy can also be seen throughout Acts. For example, the Roman famine prophesied by Agabus is confirmed and dated through a parenthetical note by Luke that the prophecy had come true during Emperor Claudius's reign (11:28).

These facts, along with the numerous details in Acts, reveal the careful and diligent research of a precise historian. In Acts, Luke was writing history.

Kerygmatic. The Greek word *kerygma* literally means "that which is preached"—i.e., the message. An important purpose of the book of Acts is to highlight the *kerygma,* the core of the gospel message proclaimed by the apostles. The good news of Jesus' death and resurrection, proclaimed fearlessly in streets, synagogues, and prisons, changed thousands of lives and the course of history. Paul's three missionary journeys and voyage to Rome provide solid evidence that the gospel was being proclaimed to the ends of the earth (1:8).

Apologetic. The word "apologetic" refers to a rational defense of the faith, a presentation of solid evidence that the gospel is true. Because of the rapid spread of the Way (i.e., Christianity) across the Roman Empire, Luke wanted to assure readers that Christianity was not a political movement or threat but the reality of God becoming flesh and the fulfillment of Israel's hope of a Messiah.

Roman law defined religions as either *licitia* (legal) or *illicita* (illegal). Even though Christianity was the offspring of Judaism, it was having difficulty acquiring *licitia* status because the Jewish establishment considered it a sect. Thus, Luke may have written this as an apology to the Roman government. Because Luke probably wrote this book while Paul was awaiting trial in Rome, the intended audience may have included Paul's trial judge. Acts includes several defenses presented both to Jews (see 4:8-12) and Gentiles (see 25:8-11).

Conciliatory. The early church contained two dominant factions—Jewish believers and Gentile believers. Paul had become the champion of reaching the Gentiles, while in many ways Peter had been leading the charge for ministering to the Jews. The council at Jerusalem was held to discuss the issue, and the matter was resolved amicably (15:1-35). But old ways are hard to change, so the same issues were raised again and again. Each time, Paul would write to the church to try to defuse the potential explosion and to keep believers focused on the truth (see, for example, Galatians).

The book of Acts presents a noteworthy parallel between Peter and Paul. Each conceded specific aspects of the church to the other. For example, Peter conferred upon Paul a second mode of apostolic authority as well as approval for reaching out to Gentiles, not on the merits of the law. At the same time, Paul conceded primacy in the church to Peter and apostleship to the Twelve, due to their earthly relationship with Christ.

In many ways, the church struggles today with the same issues: new believers need encouragement and assurance, nonbelievers need to know that the Christian message is true, and the church needs to avoid petty wranglings and unite around the core of the gospel message.

As you read Acts, recommit to unity in the church, working together with Christian brothers and sisters to spread the gospel throughout the world. And thank God for his grace, which extends salvation to all kinds of people, even you.

MESSAGE

Church beginnings; Holy Spirit; church growth; witnessing; opposition.

Church Beginnings(1:4-8, 12-26; 2:1–8:40). Acts is the history of how the Christian church was founded and organized as well as how the early church solved its problems. Led by outspoken and courageous apostles, the community of believers grew as individuals put their trust in the risen Christ. Filled with the Holy Spirit, they were empowered to witness, to love, and to serve. Although pressured and persecuted, they continued to preach, considering it a privilege to suffer for Christ. And the church thrived.

Importance for today. New churches are continually being founded, but true Christian churches preach the crucified and risen Christ. Although believers continue to be pressured to give up or give in, by faith in Jesus Christ and in the power of the Holy Spirit, the church can be a vibrant agent for change.

God wants to work in you and through you. Filled with his Spirit, as a courageous witness, you also can share the Good News with the world—with *your* world.

Holy Spirit (1:5, 8; 2:1-13, 17-18, 33, 38-39; 4:8, 25, 31; 5:3, 9, 32; 6:3, 5; 7:51, 55; 8:15-24, 29, 39; 9:17, 31; 10:19, 38, 44-47; 11:12-18, 24, 28; 13:2-12, 52; 15:8, 28-29; 16:6-7; 19:2-6, 21; 20:22-28; 21:4, 10-12; 28:25). The church did not start or grow by its own power and enthusiasm. The disciples were empowered by God's Holy Spirit. He was the Comforter and Guide promised by Jesus and sent when Jesus went to heaven. The Holy Spirit came upon the assembled believers at Pentecost and continued to fill those who trusted in Christ as Savior. Through the Spirit's power, the gospel was preached, and people were healed.

Importance for today. The filling of the Holy Spirit at Pentecost demonstrated that Christianity was supernatural. As a result, the church became more Holy Spirit-conscious than problem-conscious. Then, led and empowered by the Spirit, they changed the world. Everyone who trusts in Christ as Savior receives the

Holy Spirit. By faith, therefore, any believer can claim the Holy Spirit's power to do Christ's work.

Allow God to fill you with his Spirit; then follow the Spirit's leading as you live and minister in this world.

Church Growth (2:37-47; 4:1-4, 32-37; 5:12-16, 42; 6:1-7; 8:12, 40; 9:31-35, 39-42; 10:44-48; 11:19-21, 24; 12:24; 13:42-43, 44-49; 14:1, 21-28; 16:4-5, 13-15, 29-34; 17:1-4, 10-12, 32-34; 18:7-8; 19:17-20; 28:23-31). Jesus had told his disciples to take the gospel to all the world (Matthew 28:19-20). He also had said that they would be his witnesses in Jerusalem, Judea and Samaria, and to the ends of the earth. Acts shows the fulfillment of this prediction, presenting the history of a dynamic, growing community of believers from Jerusalem to Syria, Africa, Asia, and Europe. In the first century, it spread from believing Jews to non-Jews in thirty-nine cities and thirty countries, islands, or provinces.

Importance for today. The Holy Spirit brings movement, excitement, and growth. He gives believers the motivation, energy, and ability to spread the gospel. God still loves the world (John 3:16)—the whole world. And he wants men and women everywhere to hear his wonderful, life-changing message.

Consider how you are part of God's plan to expand the Christian gospel.

Witnessing (1:8; 2:4-40; 3:12-26; 4:8-15; 5:29-32, 42; 6:7; 7:1-56; 8:4-40; 9:20-22, 28-29; 10:34-43; 11:4-17, 20-21; 13:4-6, 16-47; 14:1, 6-7, 14-17, 21; 16:9-15, 25-34; 17:2-4, 22-34; 18:4-11, 19-20, 24-28; 19:8-10; 20:7, 20-27; 22:1-21; 23:1, 6; 24:10-21, 24-26; 26:1-23, 28-29; 28:17-31). Peter, John, Philip, Paul, Barnabas, and thousands more witnessed to their new faith in Christ. By personal testimony, preaching, or defense before authorities, they told the story with boldness and courage to groups of all sizes. Paul, in particular, took every opportunity to tell others about Jesus' life, death, and resurrection, and Paul told how God had changed his life. Whether in a synagogue (17:10) or lecture hall (19:9), on a riverbank (16:13) or in prison (16:31-32), in the public square (17:17) or on Mars Hill (17:22), in front of a mob (21:40) or in front of rulers (24:10), Paul courageously spoke the truth.

Importance for today. We are God's people, chosen to be part of his plan to reach the world. We have the truth, the good news about the only way to God, and the message of eternal life. Like the apostles and early believers, we must share this message with boldness and love. And God has promised that the Holy Spirit will help us as we witness or preach. Witnessing is also beneficial to us because it strengthens our faith as we confront those who challenge it.

To whom has God called you to share his message of forgiveness and hope? Who needs to hear from you about Christ? What can you do to take the Good News to the world?

Opposition (4:1-22, 29-30; 5:17-42; 6:8-14; 7:54-60; 8:1-3; 9:1-2, 22-30; 12:1-19; 13:50-52; 14:1-7, 19-20; 16:16-39; 17:5-9, 13-15; 18:12-17; 19:9, 23-41; 21:26-36; 22:22-29; 23:2, 7-10, 12-21; 24:1-9; 25:2-7). Through imprisonment, beatings, plots, and riots, Christians were persecuted by both Jews and Gentiles. Countless numbers suffered financial loss and physical and emotional pain, and many died. Although Christ's message focused on love and forgiveness, it threatened the pagan establishment and brought furious opposition. But this opposition became a catalyst for the spread of Christianity as believers, convinced of the truth of the gospel, courageously continued to hold on to the faith and to share it with others. This showed that the Christian movement was not the work of humans but of God.

Importance for today. Christ still threatens the establishment because he identifies sin and calls people to repent and to turn to him. And Jesus' claim to be the only way (see John 14:6) is said to be impossibly narrow and politically incorrect. So believers continue to be threatened and persecuted for believing in Christ and telling others about him. But God can work through any opposition, and persecution can help spread his Word.

When severe treatment from hostile unbelievers comes, realize that it is because you have been a faithful witness. Then look for the opportunity to present the Good News. Stay focused on Christ, and seize the opportunities that opposition brings.

VITAL STATISTICS

Purpose: To give an accurate account of the birth and growth of the Christian church

Author: Luke (a Gentile physician)

To Whom Written: Theophilus and all lovers of God

Date Written: Between A.D. 63 and 65

Setting: Acts is the connecting link between Christ's life and the life of the church, between the Gospels and the Letters.

Key Verse: "When the Holy Spirit has come upon you, you will receive power and will tell people about me everywhere—in Jerusalem, throughout Judea, in Samaria, and to the ends of the earth" (1:8 NLT).

Key People: Peter, John, James, Stephen, Philip, Paul, Barnabas, Cornelius, James (Jesus' brother), Timothy, Lydia, Silas, Titus, Apollos, Agabus, Ananias, Felix, Festus, Agrippa, Luke

Key Places: Jerusalem, Samaria, Lydda, Joppa, Antioch, Cyprus, Pisidian Antioch, Iconium, Lystra, Derbe, Philippi, Thessalonica, Berea, Athens, Corinth, Ephesus, Caesarea, Malta, Rome

Special Features: Acts is a sequel to the Gospel of Luke. Because Acts ends so abruptly, Luke may have planned to write a third book, continuing the story.

OUTLINE

A. PETER'S MINISTRY (1:1–12:25)
   1. Establishment of the church
   2. Expansion of the church

B. PAUL'S MINISTRY (13:1–28:31)
   1. First missionary journey
   2. The council at Jerusalem
   3. Second missionary journey
   4. Third missionary journey
   5. Paul on trial

Acts 1

THE PROMISE OF THE HOLY SPIRIT / 1:1-5

The book of Acts, written by Luke, picks up where Luke's Gospel left off, providing details of the birth and early years of the church that Jesus had promised to build. Together the two books, Luke and Acts, form a seamless account of how the followers of Jesus "turned . . . the world upside down" (Acts 17:6 NLT) by taking the good news of the life, death, and resurrection of Jesus Christ "to the ends of the earth" (Acts 1:8 NLT).

Before documenting this rapid spread of the gospel, however, Luke asserted two important truths in what serves as an introduction to the book of Acts: (1) the indisputable fact of Christ's resurrection; and (2) the indispensable presence of the Holy Spirit. Apart from these two strong foundations, the church would be without hope and without power. What was true in the first century is still true today.

1:1-2 **Dear Theophilus: In my first book I told you about everything Jesus began to do and teach until the day he ascended to heaven after giving his chosen apostles further instructions from the Holy Spirit.**NLT Luke's opening statement ties this volume to his *first book*, the Gospel of Luke. That book was also addressed to *Theophilus,* whose name means "one who loves God." While some scholars have argued that this is a general term for all believers, it is more likely a proper name. When addressing Theophilus in Luke 1:3, Luke called him "most excellent." A proper name with a title indicates that this was probably a real person, someone who belonged to the nobility, possibly as a high-ranking Roman official. Theophilus may have been Luke's patron who helped to finance the writing of both the Gospel and Acts. More likely Theophilus was a Roman acquaintance of Luke's with a strong interest in the new Christian religion.

Whether or not Theophilus was a believer, he had apparently learned some of the facts, but he may have needed further clarification. Luke set out to explain the entire gospel story to Theophilus, telling him *about everything Jesus began to do and teach until the day he ascended to heaven after giving his chosen apostles further instructions from the Holy Spirit.* The translation "began to do and teach" shows that the books of Luke and Acts give the accurate account of the beginning of all that Christ was to do on earth. The book of Acts would show the continuation of his work on earth through his church, his body.

The following verses provide a bridge between the events recorded in Luke's Gospel and the events marking the beginning of the church. Before he "ascended to heaven," the resurrected Christ taught his disciples for forty days. In that short period, he gave those "chosen apostles" the instruction that would radically change their lives and, through them, the world. The fact that the apostles had been chosen by Christ (Luke 6:12-16) is an extremely important point. With that choosing came apostolic authority to preach, teach, direct the church, and preserve the record of his life and teaching. (For more on the Holy Spirit, see 1:8.)

1:3 After his suffering, he showed himself to these men and gave many convincing proofs that he was alive. He appeared to them over a period of forty days and spoke about the kingdom of God.[NIV] "After his suffering" refers to Jesus' crucifixion. During the days after Christ rose from the dead, *he showed himself* to many of his followers (see the chart, "Jesus' Appearances after His Resurrection" on page 3). Christ showed himself and (as if more were needed) also *gave many convincing proofs that he was alive.* The word "proofs" *(tekmeriois)* refers to demonstrated, decisive evidence. Jesus' resurrection had not been sleight of hand or illusion, with Jesus being merely a ghostly presence. Instead, these were solid, visible, and undeniable proofs of the fact that Jesus was alive.

> The early Christians did not believe in the resurrection of Christ because they could *not* find his dead body; they believed because they *did* find a living Christ.
> *C. T. Craig*

These proofs would form the heart and soul of the forthcoming witness of the church (from Acts 1:8 forward). The apostles, and the church behind them, would spread the truth of Christ because they had seen him after he rose from the grave! If Jesus had not truly risen from the dead, then nothing that proceeds from this point on in the book of Acts (or the New Testament for that matter) would make any sense or make any difference in people's lives. (See Paul's comments in 1 Corinthians 15:13-14.)

Studying and using convincing proofs for the defense of Christianity (apologetics) is a valuable tool today. Not only does it help confirm the faith of Christians, but it also functions to help unbelievers come to faith. Many Christians today owe

JESUS' APPEARANCES AFTER HIS RESURRECTION

1. Mary Magdalene	Mark 16:9-11; John 20:11-18
2. The other women at the tomb	Matthew 28:8-10
3. Peter in Jerusalem	Luke 24:34; 1 Corinthians 15:5
4. The two travelers on the road	Mark 16:12-13; Luke 24:13-35
5. Ten disciples behind closed doors	Luke 24:36-43; John 20:19-25
6. All eleven disciples (including Thomas)	Mark 16:14; John 20:26-31; 1 Corinthians 15:5
7. Seven disciples while fishing on the Sea of Galilee	John 21:1-14
8. Eleven disciples on a mountain in Galilee	Matthew 28:16-20; Mark 16:15-18
9. A crowd of five hundred	1 Corinthians 15:6
10. Jesus' brother James	1 Corinthians 15:7
11. Those who watched Jesus ascend into heaven	Mark 16:19-20; Luke 24:50-53; Acts 1:3-9

their conversion, humanly speaking, to the work of C. S. Lewis, whose apologetic arguments in *Mere Christianity* led them to believe. C. S. Lewis himself was converted by means of these kinds of arguments.

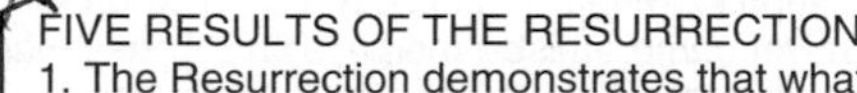

FIVE RESULTS OF THE RESURRECTION

1. The Resurrection demonstrates that what Jesus predicted about his being raised was true (Mark 8:31; 9:9, 31; 10:34; John 2:19).

2. The Resurrection proves that Jesus is the Son of God (Romans 1:4).

3. The Resurrection testifies to the success of Christ's mission of salvation (Romans 4:25).

4. The Resurrection entitles Jesus to a position of glory (1 Peter 1:11).

5. The Resurrection proclaims that Jesus is Lord (Acts 2:36).

During Jesus' post-Resurrection appearances, the main subject of Jesus' remarks was *the kingdom of God.* Throughout the Gospels the kingdom was always on Jesus' lips, for this unified his teachings and activities (see, for example, Luke 13:18-21; 17:20-37). When Christ came to earth, he brought God's kingdom, but it was not an earthly kingdom. The promised kingdom is present now only in part. The New Testament writers confirmed that through his death and resurrection, Christ bound Satan (Colossians 2:15; 1 Peter 3:22), provided forgiveness and holiness to sinners (Romans 3:21-26; Hebrews 9:11-12; 10:10), and is now enthroned as Lord over all (Acts 2:33-36; 5:31; Ephesians 1:20-22). Believers become participants of this kingdom through God's power (Matthew 19:24-26; John 3:3), by repentance and trust in Jesus (Matthew 4:17; John 14:6; Acts 8:12). His kingdom began in the hearts of his followers. When Christ returned to heaven, God's kingdom remained in the hearts of all believers through the presence of the Holy Spirit. God promised, however, that he would ultimately reign over all and bring about the end of all death and disease. The ultimate culmination of the kingdom of God will not be fully realized until Jesus Christ comes again to rule, defeat his enemies, and consummate the kingdom (Matthew 24:29-31; 25:31-46; John 14:1-3). Before that time believers are to work to spread God's kingdom across the world. Often the term "kingdom," at least in Acts, is used almost synonymously with the gospel message—see 8:12; 19:8; 20:25; 28:23, 31.

NO LEAP IN THE DARK

Jesus gave many proofs to the early followers. Today many people doubt Jesus' resurrection. But history records that Jesus appeared in bodily form to his disciples on many occasions after his resurrection, proving that he was alive. Note the change that occurred in the disciples' lives. At Jesus' death, they scattered; they were disillusioned and fearful. After seeing the resurrected Christ, they were fearless and risked everything to spread the good news about him around the world. They faced imprisonment, beatings, rejection, and martyrdom, yet they never compromised their mission. These men would not have risked their lives for something they knew was a fraud. They knew that Jesus had been raised from the dead, and the early church members were fired with their enthusiasm to tell others. We can have confidence in their testimony. Twenty centuries later we can know that our faith is based on solid, historical fact.

So we have the two aspects of Christianity that would soon spread like wildfire from the temple porticoes in Jerusalem: (1) convinced witnesses who had been with the resurrected

Christ; and (2) a clear message of Christ's desire to rule in people's hearts and of his promise to return (1:3-10).

1:4-5 **In one of these meetings as he was eating a meal with them, he told them, "Do not leave Jerusalem until the Father sends you what he promised. Remember, I have told you about this before. John baptized with water, but in just a few days you will be baptized with the Holy Spirit."**NLT As the risen Christ met with his disciples, here *eating a meal with them* (yet another of the "convincing proofs" mentioned in 1:3), he surely told them many things. Luke records only a handful of sentences from those forty days of instruction, so they certainly are important words. These statements of Jesus are loaded with significance, giving us not only the outline of the book of Acts, but the general outline of church history.

Christ first told his followers to stay in Jerusalem *until the Father sends you what he promised.* This points back to Luke 24:49. He had spoken *about this before,* at the Last Supper: "And I will ask the Father, and he will give you another Counselor, who will never leave you. He is the Holy Spirit" (John 14:16-17 NLT; see also John 14:26).

This would be a new kind of baptism. *John baptized with water,* said Jesus, but these believers would *be baptized with the Holy Spirit.* John the Baptist had baptized people as a sign of repentance. They had confessed their sins and had determined to live as God wanted them to live. Baptism was an outward sign of commitment. To be effective, it had to be accompanied by an inward change of attitude leading to a changed life. John's baptism did not give salvation; it prepared a person to welcome the coming Messiah and receive *his* message and *his* baptism. John himself had said, "I baptize you with water for repentance, but one who is more powerful than I is coming. . . . He will baptize you with the Holy Spirit and fire" (Matthew 3:11 NRSV).

The "one" who was coming was Jesus, the promised Messiah. The coming of the Spirit had been prophesied as part of the Messiah's arrival:

- "I will pour out my Spirit on your offspring, and my blessing on your descendants." (Isaiah 44:3 NIV)
- "The time is coming. . . . I will put my law in their minds and write it on their hearts. I will be their God, and they will be my people. . . . For I will forgive their wickedness and will remember their sins no more." (Jeremiah 31:31-34 NIV)
- "I will give you a new heart and put a new spirit in you; I will remove from you your heart of stone and give you a heart of flesh. And I will put my Spirit in you and move you to follow

my decrees and be careful to keep my laws." (Ezekiel 36:26-27 NIV)

- "And afterward, I will pour out my Spirit on all people. Your sons and daughters will prophesy, your old men will dream dreams, your young men will see visions. Even on my servants, both men and women, I will pour out my Spirit in those days." (Joel 2:28-29 NIV)

The Old Testament promised a time when God would demonstrate his purifying power among people (Isaiah 32:15; Ezekiel 39:29). The prophets also looked forward to a purifying fire (Isaiah 4:4; Malachi 3:2). This looked ahead to Pentecost (Acts 2:1-6), when the Holy Spirit would be sent by Jesus in the form of tongues of fire, empowering his followers to preach the gospel. All believers, those who would later come to Jesus Christ for salvation, would receive the baptism of the Holy Spirit and the fire of purification (in the Greek one article precedes these words, indicating that they were not two separate baptisms). This baptism would purify and refine each believer. When Jesus baptized with the Holy Spirit, the entire person would be transformed by the Spirit's power.

If Jesus had stayed on earth, his physical presence would have limited the spread of the gospel because physically he could be in only one place at a time. After Christ was taken up into heaven, he would be spiritually present everywhere through the Holy Spirit. The Holy Spirit was sent so that God would be with and within his followers after Christ returned to heaven. The Spirit would comfort them, guide them to know his truth, remind them of Jesus' words, give them the right words to say, and fill them with power. As promised by Christ in the upper room (John 13–17) and by the Father (see Peter's speech in Acts 2:17 and following), the Holy Spirit would be the next great event in the life of the church. Many believe it to be the very birth of the church.

BELIEVERS HAVE PRIVILEGES

In a series of meetings with the living, resurrected Christ, the disciples had many questions answered. They became convinced of the Resurrection, learned about the kingdom of God, and discovered the truth about their power source—the Holy Spirit. By reading the Bible, we can sit with the resurrected Christ in his school of discipleship. By believing in him, we can receive his power through the Holy Spirit to be new people. By joining with other Christians in Christ's church, we can take part in doing his work on earth.

THE ASCENSION OF JESUS / 1:6-11

When would the risen Lord set up his kingdom? This was the question uppermost in the apostles' minds. They were eagerly hoping for a glorious earthly kingdom free from Roman rule. Christ, however, sidestepped these questions about earthly kingdoms and divine timetables. Instead, he reminded his followers of their calling to be Spirit-filled witnesses who would take the gospel message everywhere. A spiritual revolution needed first to take place in the hearts and minds of people.

With this final charge on the top of the Mount of Olives, Christ ascended into heaven. Moments later divine messengers appeared and assured the apostles that the Lord would one day return in similar fashion.

1:6 **So when they met together, they asked him, "Lord, are you at this time going to restore the kingdom to Israel?"**[NIV] The average Jew of Jesus' day was looking forward with great anticipation to the literal coming of the Messiah's earthly kingdom and with it the restoration of the fortunes and military might that the nation had enjoyed under King David. Jesus had certainly taught a great deal about his coming kingdom in his ministry with the disciples. During this forty-day instruction period, the disciples had questions about the promised kingdom, for their anticipation had been heightened with their Master's resurrection from the dead. Fully expecting Jesus to bring in his kingdom on earth at that moment, the disciples asked: *"Are you at this time going to restore the kingdom to Israel?"*

The coming of the kingdom was closely associated with the coming of the Holy Spirit (as implied in passages such as Isaiah 32:15-20; 44:3-5; Ezekiel 39:28-29; Joel 2:28–3:1; Zechariah 12:8-10). When Christ told the disciples of the imminent coming of the Spirit, therefore, they were even more likely to assume the coming of the kingdom would also be at hand. During the years of Jesus' ministry on earth, the disciples continually had wondered about the coming of the kingdom and what their roles would be in it. In the traditional view, the Messiah would be an earthly conqueror who would free Israel from Rome. But the kingdom about which Jesus spoke was first of all a "spiritual" kingdom established in the hearts and lives of believers (Luke 17:21); behind it was the earthly kingdom that Christ promised to institute at his return.

Jesus' answer, disappointing to the disciples, was a rebuke and a gentle reminder that the apostles' role (like the role *he* had modeled on earth) was to desire to be in God's presence in prayer and worship and to faithfully follow the Father's sovereign lead.

TRUSTING THE FATHER'S PLAN
The disciples wanted to know Jesus' timetable for the restoration of the kingdom. Like other Jews, the disciples chafed under their Roman rulers. They wanted Jesus to free Israel from Roman power and then become their king. Jesus replied that God the Father sets the timetable for all events—worldwide, national, and personal. If you want changes that God isn't making immediately, don't become impatient. Instead, trust God's timetable. Remember that he is wise, good, and all-powerful. Even when things seem chaotic, he is in control. His perfect will ultimately will prevail.

1:7 **He said to them: "It is not for you to know the times or dates the Father has set by his own authority."**[NIV] Neither the *times* (*chronous*—referring purely to chronology) nor the *dates* (*kaipous*—more the character or circumstances of the era) were really any of the disciples' business. These are set by the Father's *authority,* and as far as the disciples were concerned, it was out of their jurisdiction. Later revelation through Paul and others would help clarify the issue (1 Thessalonians 5:1-2). What *should* concern and consume the disciples, however (notice the contrastive word "but" that begins 1:8), was the loaded statement that follows.

1:8 **"But you will receive power when the Holy Spirit comes on you; and you will be my witnesses in Jerusalem, and in all Judea and Samaria, and to the ends of the earth."**[NIV] This is the last recorded statement of Christ on earth. It is thus final, authoritative, and of utmost importance. The Holy Spirit is a major theme in Luke and Acts and is the major point of continuity between the life of Jesus and the ministry of the church.

Who is the Holy Spirit? God is three persons in one—the Father, the Son, and the Holy Spirit. God became a man in Jesus so that Jesus could die for our sins. Jesus rose from the dead to offer salvation to all people through spiritual renewal and rebirth. When Jesus ascended into heaven, his physical presence left the earth, but he promised to send the Holy Spirit so that his spiritual presence would still be among mankind (see Luke 24:49). The Holy Spirit first became available to all believers at Pen-

There is no believer whom the Son of God does not require to be his witness. In what place, at what time, with what degree of frequency, in what manner, and to what extent, we ought to profess our faith, cannot easily be determined by a fixed rule: but we must consider the occasion, that not one of us may fail to discharge his duty at the proper time.
John Calvin

tecost (Acts 2). Whereas in Old Testament days the Holy Spirit empowered specific individuals for specific purposes, now all believers have the power of the Holy Spirit available to them. For more on the Holy Spirit, read John 14:16-28; Romans 8:9; 1 Corinthians 12:13; and 2 Corinthians 1:22.

THE CHURCH'S VISION STATEMENT

- The *people* for the task: *you*—those who know Christ, who listen to him
- The *power* for the task: *the Holy Spirit*
- The *philosophy* of approach to the task: *my witnesses*—say what you saw
- The *plan* for the task: *to Jerusalem, Judea, to the ends*—begin where you are and move outward from there

---

Luke's Gospel emphasizes the role of the Holy Spirit in the ministry of Christ. Luke continued that emphasis here as he focused on the Holy Spirit's role in the early days of the church. The term "spirit" *(pneuma)* occurs nineteen times in Matthew, twenty-three times in Mark, thirty-six times in Luke, twenty-four times in John, and seventy times in Acts. Christ had just reminded his followers that they would soon receive the Holy Spirit (1:5). When the Spirit comes, he told his followers, *you will receive power.* To do what? To *be my witnesses.* Power from the Holy Spirit is not limited to strength beyond the ordinary; that power also involves courage, boldness, confidence, insight, ability, and authority. The disciples would need all these gifts to fulfill their mission.

POWER SOURCE

Jesus promised the disciples that they would receive power to witness after they received the Holy Spirit. Notice the progression:

(1) They would receive the Holy Spirit.
(2) The Holy Spirit would give them power.
(3) They would witness with extraordinary results.

Often we try to reverse the order and witness by our own power and authority. Witnessing is not showing what we can do for God. It is showing and telling others what God has done for us. When you tell others about Christ, rely on the power of the Holy Spirit. You can be a powerful witness.

The term "witness" *(martures)* provides remarkable insight into the nature of the disciples' task. A witness gives testimony based on what the witness knows, what he or she has seen—not hearsay, not rumor, not something someone else saw, but what *he* or *she* has experienced, seen, or heard. This witnessing theme is a repeated emphasis of the apostles' work—for example, see 2:32; 3:15; 5:32; 10:39; 13:31; 22:15. In effect, Jesus was saying to his followers: "There is going to be a period of witnessing by you about me between my two visits to your planet. Go out and tell people what you know—what you've seen, experienced, and learned. I'll be back."

They were to start right there in *Jerusalem* (1:4). *Judea* was the region surrounding Jerusalem (possibly including Galilee). *Samaria* was Judea's hostile next-door neighbor, a more difficult but equally important place to take the gospel. The "ends of the earth" is actually a singular form in Greek *(eschatou),* suggesting that perhaps the reference is to Rome or the Roman empire, the world power at that time. The direction was of primary importance: Beginning from where you are at this moment, take the message of Christ outward, like ripples caused by a pebble thrown into a pond, not stopping at just your city or state but moving on beyond regional influence to the very "ends" of the earth. In other words, reach it *all!*

The disciples took Jesus at his word and went about their task exactly as he directed: they began in Jerusalem (1–7), spread to Judea and Samaria (8–12), then filtered out across the world to the imperial capital, Rome (13–28).

AN EVER EXPANDING WITNESS

Acts 1:8 describes the manner in which the gospel would spread geographically, from Jerusalem, into Judea and Samaria, and finally to the whole world. It would begin with devout Jews in Jerusalem and Judea, spread to the mixed race in Samaria, and finally be offered to Gentiles in the uttermost parts of the earth. God's gospel has not reached its final destination if someone in your family, your workplace, your school, or your community hasn't heard about Jesus Christ. How are you contributing to the ever expanding testimony of God's mercy and grace?

1:9 When he had said this, as they were watching, he was lifted up, and a cloud took him out of their sight.NRSV After giving this important charge, Jesus was *lifted up, and a cloud took him out of their sight.* This cloud symbolized the glory of God. In the Old Testament, we read that a cloud led the Israelites through the wilderness (Exodus 13:21-22) and that God made his presence known to the people by appearing in a cloud (Exodus 16:10; 19:9, 16; 24:15-18; 33:9-10; 34:5; 40:34-35). A cloud also enveloped Jesus and three of his disciples at the Transfiguration (Luke 9:34-35) as a visible symbol of God's presence. So when Jesus returned to glory, he returned in a cloud that took him "out of their sight."

The disciples needed to see Jesus make this transition. The Ascension confirmed for them that Jesus truly was God. In addition, they witnessed the fact that he had physically left earth and had returned to his heavenly home; thus, the remaining work would be done by the witnesses he had left behind, operating in the power of the promised Holy Spirit.

1:10-11 **As they were straining their eyes to see him, two white-robed men suddenly stood there among them. They said, "Men of Galilee, why are you standing here staring at the sky? Jesus has been taken away from you into heaven. And someday, just as you saw him go, he will return!"**NLT While the disciples were *straining their eyes,* staring into the sky, two angelic messengers appeared *among them.* The angels confirmed what had just happened: indeed, Jesus had been *taken away . . . into heaven.* They also reminded the disciples of Jesus' promise: *Someday, just as you saw him go, he will return!* The question, of course, is what part of Jesus' departure will be reproduced upon his return: The cloud? The arrival on the Mount of Olives (see 1:12 and Zechariah 14:4)? Most likely, it refers to Jesus' coming in a cloud to show his glory. In the Olivet discourse, Jesus had described his return: "At that time they will see the Son of Man coming in a cloud with power and great glory" (Luke 21:27 NIV; see also Matthew 24:30; Mark 13:26). At his trial Jesus had told Caiaphas, "In the future you will see the Son of Man sitting at the right hand of the Mighty One and coming on the clouds of heaven" (Matthew 26:64 NIV).

> The great thing is to be found at one's post as a child of God, living each day as though it were our last, but planning as though our world might last a hundred years.
> *C. S. Lewis*

WORKING HARD UNTIL THE END

After forty days with his disciples (1:3), Jesus returned to heaven. The two men dressed in white (these were angels who appear to people in a humanlike form) proclaimed to the disciples that one day Jesus would return in the same way he had left—bodily and visibly. History is not haphazard or cyclical; it is moving toward a specific point—the return of Jesus to judge and rule over the earth. We should be ready for his sudden return (1 Thessalonians 5:2), not by standing around "staring at the sky" but by working hard to spread the Good News and help build Christ's church so that others will be able to share in God's great blessings.

There is no disputing the promise—Jesus is coming back, in a fashion similar to the way he departed that day. His followers would work in the power of the Spirit. They would walk out into the lost world, telling all they had seen and heard of the one whom they had watched ascend. Surely their attitude about the sky and clouds from that day on was never the same. Every tilt of their head upward would recall the poignant moment of his ascent and remind them of the angelic promise of his return: "As you saw him go, he will return!"

MATTHIAS REPLACES JUDAS / 1:12-26

What an exhausting, exhilarating six weeks! The disciples had witnessed the arrest, trial, and crucifixion of their Master, then his powerful and undeniable resurrection, and finally his awesome ascension into heaven. Surely they were reeling from all that they had seen, heard, and felt.

Having been instructed to wait for the coming of the Holy Spirit, the disciples withdrew to an upstairs room in Jerusalem. There they wisely spent time praying (and surely sharing and reflecting). It was during this lull that the apostles, under Peter's leadership, filled the vacancy in their ranks created by the defection of Judas. It was important for them to have twelve apostles, representing the twelve tribes of Israel, to position the church as the fulfillment of the righteous remnant (see 1:21). Practical and simple steps in organization often play an important part in God's kingdom plan.

1:12-13 **The apostles were at the Mount of Olives when this happened, so they walked the half mile back to Jerusalem. Then they went to the upstairs room of the house where they were staying. Here is the list of those who were present: Peter, John, James, Andrew, Philip, Thomas, Bartholomew, Matthew, James (son of Alphaeus), Simon (the Zealot), and Judas (son of James).**[NLT] Following the instructions of Christ (1:4), the disciples stayed in Jerusalem. The *upstairs room* seems to have been a specific and well-known place (the noun has the definite Greek article). In that day an upstairs room was the larger room of a house, since the downstairs rooms needed more walls to support the weight of the second story. This may have been the same room in which they had eaten the Last Supper with Christ (Luke 22:12), as well as the location of many of the post-Resurrection appearances. At this time it became the first meeting place of the church.

IN THE UPSTAIRS ROOM

Name	*Major Events in His Life*	*Selected References*
Simon Peter (son of John)	One of three in the core group of disciples; recognized Jesus as the Messiah; denied Christ and repented; preached Pentecost sermon; a leader of the Jerusalem church; baptized Gentiles; wrote 1 and 2 Peter.	Matthew 4:18-20; Mark 8:29-33; Luke 22:31-34; John 21:15-19; Acts 2;14-41; 10:1–11:18
James (son of Zebedee)	Also in the core group; he and his brother, John, asked Jesus for places of honor in his kingdom; wanted to call fire down to destroy a Samaritan village; first disciple to be martyred.	Mark 3:17; 10:35-40; Luke 9: 52-56; Acts 12:1-2
John (son of Zebedee)	Third disciple in the core group; asked Jesus for a place of honor in his kingdom; wanted to call down fire on a Samaritan village; a leader of the Jerusalem church; wrote the Gospel of John; 1, 2, 3 John; and Revelation.	Mark 1:19; 10:35-40; Luke 9:52-56; John 19:26-27; 21:20-24
Andrew (Peter's brother)	Accepted John the Baptist's testimony about Jesus; told Peter about Jesus; he and Philip told Jesus that Greeks wanted to see him.	Matthew 4:18-20; John 1:35-42; 6:8-9; 12:20-22
Philip	Told Nathanael about Jesus; wondered how Jesus could feed the five thousand; asked Jesus to show his followers God the Father; he and Andrew told Jesus that Greeks wanted to see him.	Matthew 10:3; John 1:43-46; 6:2-7; 12:20-22; 14:8-11
Bartholomew (Nathanael)	Initially rejected Jesus because Jesus was from Nazareth but acknowledged him as the "Son of God" and "King of Israel" when they met.	Mark 3:18; John 1:45-51; 21:1-13

This list of names of the eleven disciples parallels the lists in the Gospels (Matthew 10:2-4; Mark 3:16-19; Luke 6:14-16). Here, as in the other lists, Peter is named first, though John is listed second (John was fourth in the list in Luke's Gospel). Likely this is because of John's prominence as Peter's partner in the events recorded later in Acts. Simon is called a *Zealot.* A "Zealot" could mean anyone zealous for the Jewish law, or

Name	*Major Events in His Life*	*Selected References*
Matthew (Levi)	Abandoned his corrupt (and financially profitable) way of life to follow Jesus; invited Jesus to a party with his notorious friends; wrote the Gospel of Matthew.	Matthew 9:9-13; Mark 2:15-17; Luke 5:27-32
Thomas (the Twin)	Suggested the disciples go with Jesus to Bethany—even if it meant death; asked Jesus about where he was going; refused to believe Jesus was risen until he could see Jesus alive and touch his wounds.	Matthew 10:3; John 14:5; 20:24-29; 21:1-13
James (son of Alphaeus)	Became one of Jesus' disciples.	Matthew 10:3; Mark 3:18; Luke 6:15
Judas son of James (Thaddeus)	Asked Jesus why he would reveal himself to his followers and not to the world.	Matthew 10:3; Mark 3:18; John 14:22
Simon the Zealot	Became a disciple of Jesus.	Matthew 10:4; Mark 3:18; Luke 6:15
Matthias	Chosen to replace Judas Iscariot (who had betrayed Jesus and then killed himself).	Acts 1:15-26

generally it could mean an insurrectionist. The Zealots became a radical political party working for the violent overthrow of Roman rule in Israel around A.D. 60. All the lists vary slightly in order, but the groupings (of the more prominent leaders and of family relationships) remain essentially the same.

1:14 **They all met together continually for prayer, along with Mary the mother of Jesus, several other women, and the brothers of Jesus.**[NLT] Luke took special note of the fact that the disciples were joined by *Mary the mother of Jesus* and *several other women,* likely the ones who had been present at the Crucifixion and at the empty tomb (Luke 8:2-3; 23:49; 23:55–24:10). Also present were *the brothers of Jesus.* During his lifetime, Jesus' brothers

> Prayer is weakness leaning on omnipotence.
> *W. S. Bowden*

(Mary and Joseph's other sons) did not believe he was the Messiah (John 7:5) and actually thought he was out of his mind (Mark 3:21-35). But Jesus' resurrection must have convinced them otherwise. Jesus' special appearance to James, one of his brothers, may have been an especially significant event in James's conversion (see 1 Corinthians 15:7). This gathering may have included all of Jesus' other brothers—Joses (or Joseph), Judas (or Jude) and Simon (see Matthew 13:55-56; Mark 6:3). Jesus' sisters may have been there as well (Matthew 13:56). As believers, they joined the disciples during the time of prayer and waiting.

The main emphasis, however, is not who was present but what they were doing—praying! Prayer begins to appear as a mark of the early church. When they were fearful, they prayed. When they were confused, they prayed. When they were waiting for God to fulfill his promise to them, they prayed. When they needed an answer to a question (such as who was to be the twelfth apostle), they prayed!

WAITING ON GOD

Jesus had instructed his disciples to witness to people of all nations about him (Matthew 28:19-20). Before setting out, however, they were told to wait for the coming Holy Spirit (Luke 24:49). While the apostles waited, they were doing what they could—praying, seeking God's guidance, and getting organized. Waiting for God to work does not mean sitting around doing nothing. We must do what we can, while we can, as long as we don't run ahead of God. How are you using even mundane moments of your life for God? Ask God to show you today how to become better prepared for future service.

1:15-16 **During this time, on a day when about 120 believers were present, Peter stood up and addressed them as follows: "Brothers, it was necessary for the Scriptures to be fulfilled concerning Judas, who guided the Temple police to arrest Jesus. This was predicted long ago by the Holy Spirit, speaking through King David."**NLT The group was a little larger than the previous verses seem to indicate. During this "waiting" period, evidently, the meetings in the upper room were regular *(during this time),* repeated *(on a day when),* and growing in size *(about 120 believers* attended this particular meeting). *Peter,* who had taken a prominent role among the disciples throughout the Gospels, continued in that leadership role.

Peter pointed the gathered believers to the Scriptures. He showed that he had been paying attention during his training under Jesus. Peter put the events concerning Judas' betrayal and suicide into biblical perspective by explaining how *it was necessary for the Scriptures to be fulfilled,* and then he called the believers to the task of choosing Judas's replacement, something he likewise said was necessary (1:21). The Greek word used both here and in 1:21 is *dei* (meaning "it is necessary"); it is used to show logical or divine necessity. Peter and the disciples believed it was necessary for these verses to be fulfilled. They were regarded as prophecy. Peter gave a great lesson in healthy biblical leadership: it is a combination of insight from the Word of God and corresponding practical action. Peter's reference to *King David* refers to the Spirit-led predictions recorded in some of David's psalms, such as Psalm 69:25 and Psalm 109:8.

1:17-19 "Judas was one of us, chosen to share in the ministry with us." (Judas bought a field with the money he received for his treachery, and falling there, he burst open, spilling out his intestines. The news of his death spread rapidly among all the people of Jerusalem, and they gave the place the Aramaic name *Akeldama,* which means "Field of Blood.")[NLT] It is hard to believe that someone who had been with Jesus daily could betray him. Judas had received the same calling and teaching as everyone else. Though *chosen to share in the ministry* by Christ himself, Judas hardened his heart and joined in the plot with Jesus' enemies to put him to death. Judas remained unrepentant to the end, and he finally committed suicide. Although Jesus predicted this betrayal and bitter end, it was Judas's choice. Those privileged to be close to the truth are not necessarily committed to the truth.

The section set off by parentheses was not part of Peter's speech but rather was an insertion by Luke explaining the suicide of Judas, the resulting spread of the news, and the naming of the place where it happened. Matthew reports that Judas hung himself (Matthew 27:5); here Luke says that he fell. The traditional explanation proposed by Augustine of this seeming contradiction is that both reports are true: when Judas hung himself, the rope or branch broke, Judas fell, and his body burst open. As is so often the case, when two (or more) different writers record an event, they write from different perspectives, have different purposes in their writing, and have different sources for their information. When confronted by such seeming contradictions, we must remember that the eyewitnesses of the events (who were the first recipients of these records) evidently had no problem reconciling the differing accounts. If there had been a real contradiction that could not be cleared up by an unmentioned factor, the witness (that is, the writer and his book) would have been discredited and subsequently discarded by the church. Such is certainly not the case with the book of Matthew or the book of Acts.

1:20 **Peter continued, "This was predicted in the book of Psalms, where it says, 'Let his home become desolate, with no one living in it.' And again, 'Let his position be given to someone else.'"**[NLT] The psalms picture the Messiah as the ideal king. Thus the enemies of King David (addressed in certain psalms where curses are called on God's enemies) are a prototype or foreshadowing of the enemies of the Messiah. Peter applied the meaning in those psalms to the enemies of Jesus, particularly here to Judas. Peter saw Psalm 69:25 as a prediction of Judas's horrible end, the "desolate" name of the place of his demise. Peter then quoted Psalm 109:8 as the basis of the necessity of choosing someone to replace Judas. Thus Peter's Spirit-led application of David's Spirit-inspired prediction became the basis for the gathered believers' first significant decision—replacing Judas.

KNOWING SCRIPTURE

During the discussion about Judas, Peter quoted without fanfare two verses from the book of Psalms (Psalm 69:25; 109:8). To be able to do this, he obviously had read and studied the Scriptures extensively. Because he had hidden God's Word in his heart (Psalm 119:11), it helped guide him and the others when they faced an important decision. Likewise, if we are to think and act in a biblical fashion, we must be steeped in biblical truth. The only way to do this is to immerse ourselves in Scripture. We must read it, study it, hear it taught and preached, memorize it, and meditate on it. Be a person who truly lives by the Book.

1:21-22 **"Therefore it is necessary to choose one of the men who have been with us the whole time the Lord Jesus went in and out among us, beginning from John's baptism to the time when Jesus was taken up from us. For one of these must become a witness with us of his resurrection."**[NIV] The main reason for this process was to make sure that there were twelve apostolic witnesses. They also believed that a twelfth disciple would be necessary to fulfill such promises as Matthew 19:28 and Luke 22:28-30 (the twelve disciples sitting on twelve thrones in the kingdom government). The church was regarded as a fulfillment of the Old Testament righteous remnant, those faithful to God, and so must assure its rightful place. The Twelve were needed to lead. Because Judas betrayed Christ, he had to be replaced because twelve faithful leaders were needed. James was not replaced after his death (12:2) because he had not defected from the faith. Even after James's death, he still was regarded as one of the Twelve.

Peter pointed out the qualifications of the one who was to be chosen. Notice that it had to be someone who had been with Jesus and the other disciples *the whole time the Lord Jesus went in and out among us, beginning from John's baptism to the time when Jesus was taken up.* Such eyewitness involvement was absolutely necessary for the credibility of the person bearing witness to the words and the works of Christ. This one would join the other apostles in being *a witness . . . of his resurrection.* What this witness said would be a testimony to the credibility of the life of Christ and the words of Christ. It is clear that, in addition to the twelve disciples, many others had consistently followed Jesus throughout his ministry on earth. The Twelve were his inner circle, but many others shared deep love for and commitment to Jesus. It was now simply a matter of finding the one who would be elevated to the title of apostle.

> Our prayers unite us in God's concern for the harvest, make us of one mind, heart, and will with Him, partners of Jesus Himself. *R. C. H. Lenski*

WISE DECISIONS
In choosing a replacement for Judas Iscariot, the apostles outlined specific criteria for making the choice. When the "finalists" had been chosen, the apostles prayed, asking God to guide the selection process. Their deliberate actions serve as a good example of how to proceed when making important decisions. We should set up criteria consistent with the Bible, examine the alternatives, and pray for wisdom and guidance to reach a wise decision.

1:23 **So they proposed two men: Joseph called Barsabbas (also known as Justus) and Matthias.**[NIV] In answer to Peter's request, the eleven apostles *proposed two men* who met the qualifications of 1:21-22. "Barsabbas" means "son of the Sabbath." "Matthias" means "gift of God." Very little is known of these men, either from the Bible or from other historical sources.

1:24-25 **Then they prayed and said, "Lord, you know everyone's heart. Show us which one of these two you have chosen to take the place in this ministry and apostleship from which Judas turned aside to go to his own place."**[NRSV] As *they prayed* for direction in this decision, the apostles reminded themselves of God's omniscience. God had known that Judas would betray

Christ and subsequently take his own life. God also knew the hearts of all the people in that room. All these believers needed God to *show* them *which one*—either Matthias or Barsabbas—he had already *chosen.*

1:26 Then they cast lots, and in this way Matthias was chosen and became an apostle with the other eleven.[NLT] The final phase of this choosing process was that *they cast lots.* This casting of the lots was not done casually or flippantly, for the apostles had carefully chosen two candidates according to certain qualifications (1:21-22) and then had spent time in prayer (1:24-25). The final process of casting the lots was likely done by writing the two names on two stones and then placing them into a container. The first stone to fall out when the container was tipped would be considered God's choice. Proverbs 16:33 mentions this practice. It is also similar to the use of the Urim and Thummim in the Old Testament (see Leviticus 8:8; 1 Chronicles 26:13; Ezra 2:63; Nehemiah 7:65).

LOSER?
Luke wrote that in the contest to fill the vacant apostle's post, Matthias was chosen. What Luke doesn't say, but only implies, is that Barsabbas was *not* picked. How do you suppose he felt? Rejected? Inferior? Jealous? Angry? Or content and eager to serve in another capacity? One of the best indicators of our true character is when we get passed over for a prestigious place of service. In such times, our true beliefs and motives come into view. If we feel cheated, pout, become petty, or criticize and create waves, we are serving for the wrong reasons. If we trust that God is in control and quickly volunteer with a glad heart to serve somewhere else, we are on the right track. Ask yourself, "Am I more concerned that God be served, or that *I* be the one to serve him?"

As far as we know, this practice did not continue after Pentecost because the "Guide," the Holy Spirit, had come to indwell the hearts and minds of God's people. Later, the elders would select the leaders at the various churches, but not with lots. Christians—then as now—were encouraged to search the Scriptures and to know the will of the Lord (Ephesians 5:17-18; Colossians 1:9; 1 Thessalonians 4:1; 2 Timothy 3:16-17).

Matthias was chosen to be the twelfth apostle. That may seem odd because Paul (who is also called an "apostle") is not mentioned here. Remember that all of this occurred prior to Paul's conversion. As Paul himself put it, "Last of all he [Christ] appeared to me also, as to one abnormally born. For I am the least of the apostles and do not even deserve to be called an apostle, because I persecuted the church of God" (1 Corinthians 15:8-9 NIV). Paul's calling was unique. To begin with, he did not meet the qualifications spelled out by Peter. Thus, though Paul was not technically one of the Twelve, he clearly was designated an apostle with authority equal to any of them. Note, too, that the "disciples" have become "apostles." "Disciple" means follower or learner, and "apostle" means messenger or missionary. These men now had the special assignment of spreading the Good News of Jesus' death and resurrection.

Acts 2

THE HOLY SPIRIT COMES / 2:1-13

In Old Testament times, the Spirit of God came upon isolated individuals or smaller groups only on special occasions and only in a temporary way to help them accomplish God's purposes (Exodus 31:3; Judges 14:6; 1 Samuel 16:13). As the apostles were gathered together in Jerusalem for the feast of Pentecost, the time had come for the fulfillment of Christ's promise to send his Spirit completely and permanently upon all believers (Luke 24:49; John 14:16-17, 26; 16:5-15). This marvelous outpouring of God provided the supernatural power for believers to take the life-changing message of the gospel to the ends of the earth (Acts 1:8). This is the day Christ made good on his promise to send the Helper, the Comforter, the Holy Spirit who would take up permanent residence in those who put their faith in Christ. And what a day it was! God's individualized pouring out of his Spirit into the lives of 120 believers resulted in the effective pouring out of his story, changing the lives of three thousand people in one day!

2:1 When the day of Pentecost had come, they were all together in one place.[NRSV] The *day of Pentecost* was an annual feast celebrated on "the day after the seventh Sabbath" after Passover (Leviticus 23:15-16). Since the date was determined by the passing of a "week" of weeks (seven weeks), it was often called the Feast of Weeks. The word "Pentecost" means "fifty," so named because this feast was celebrated fifty days after Passover. It was originally the Feast of the Firstfruits of the grain harvest. By this time Jews had associated Pentecost with the giving of the Law (Torah) at Mount Sinai. Pentecost was one of three major annual feasts celebrated by the Jews (along with Passover, fifty days earlier, and the Feast of Tabernacles about four months later). Jesus was crucified at Passover time, and he ascended forty days after his resurrection. The Holy Spirit came fifty days after the Resurrection, ten days after the Ascension. The identification of Pentecost with "firstfruits" likely has a real significance here, since the three thousand who came to faith in Christ this day were the "firstfruits" of many thousands who would follow.

Those gathered were the 120 believers mentioned in 1:15. The *one place* where they were gathered was likely the same upper room mentioned in 1:13. Most likely the believers were praying, as had been their regular practice during the period since the Ascension (1:14). What happened this day would forever change the world.

2:2 **Suddenly a sound like the blowing of a violent wind came from heaven and filled the whole house where they were sitting.**NIV *Suddenly,* as the believers were gathered, they heard a *sound* or noise *like the blowing of a violent wind* (it was not necessarily movement of air, but perhaps a sound like that of wind). The word for "wind" *(pnoes)* is similar in sound and spelling to the word for "spirit" *(pneuma).* The wind is a good analogy for the Spirit: it is not seen, though its effects are, and it can be found everywhere in never-ending supply.

Some have made the connection here between this event and the dry bones of Ezekiel 37:1-14 as well as the discussion between Jesus and Nicodemus (John 3:8), where Jesus compared the Spirit to the wind. Jews believed that the wind of God's Spirit would precede and announce the coming of the messianic age.

The source of this sound is made clear: it *came from heaven.* It would affect everyone, for it *filled the whole house where they were sitting.* The "house" probably refers to the upper room mentioned in 1:13 where the believers had been meeting and praying.

2:3 **Then, what looked like flames or tongues of fire appeared and settled on each of them.**NLT To the great sound of wind was added a visual image: *what looked like flames or tongues of fire appeared and settled on each of them.* Why tongues of fire? It may be that "tongues" symbolized speech and the communication of the gospel. "Fire" symbolizes God's purifying presence, which burns away the undesirable elements in people's lives and sets their hearts aflame to ignite the lives of others. On Mount Sinai, God confirmed the validity of the Old Testament law with fire from heaven (Exodus 19:16-18). Elsewhere in the Old Testament, fire was used to portray the presence of God (Genesis 15:17; Exodus 3:2-6; 13:21-22; 24:17; 40:38; see also *Life Application Bible Commen-*

O Thou who camest from
above
The pure celestial fire
to impart,
Kindle a flame of sacred
love
On the mean altar of my
heart!
Jesus, confirm my heart's
desire
To work, and speak, and
think for Thee;
Still let me guard the holy
fire,
And still stir up Thy gift
in me. *John Wesley*

"BAPTISM IN THE SPIRIT" IN THE NEW TESTAMENT

The term (or concept) occurs only a few times in the New Testament. It is used in basically three different ways.

PROPHETIC	*HISTORICAL*	*DOCTRINAL*
Matthew 3:11	(Acts 2:1-4)	1 Corinthians 12:13
Mark 1:8 Luke 3:16 John 1:33 Acts 1:5	Acts 11:15-17	(Romans 6:1-4)

• In the Gospels, John the Baptist used the term in describing Jesus' ministry.

• In Acts 1:5, Jesus quotes John's prophecy looking forward to Pentecost.

• In Acts 2, the process was initiated on the day of Pentecost: the Holy Spirit came to make the church his residence, indwelling every believer.

• In Acts 11:16 the term is used by Peter who referred to Jesus' quote of John's prophecy.

• In Romans 6:1-4 and 1 Corinthians 12:13 Paul taught its significance.

---

taries, Matthew and *Luke,* notes in Matthew 3:11 and Luke 3:16). John said that Jesus would baptize the people with the Holy Spirit and with fire.

At Pentecost God confirmed the validity of the Holy Spirit's ministry by sending fire. And while at Mount Sinai fire had come down on one place, at Pentecost fire came down on many believers, symbolizing that God's presence is available to all who believe in him. This event certainly fulfilled John the Baptist's words about the Holy Spirit baptizing with fire (Luke 3:16). Peter declared that this event had been prophesied by Joel (Joel 2:28-29). Note, too, that every believer in the room received this blessing; no one was excluded. It was clear to all present that God was at work.

2:4 **And everyone present was filled with the Holy Spirit and began speaking in other languages, as the Holy Spirit gave them this ability.**[NLT] At this point in this wonderful scene, Luke recorded that *everyone present was filled with the Holy Spirit and began speaking in other languages.* The "filling" that occurred on Pentecost is called a "baptizing" (1:5 and 11:16) and a "receiving" (10:47). "Baptizing" or "filling" can be used to describe the basic act of receiving the Spirit. It can be understood to refer to the first occurrence of the Spirit's indwelling a believer. Acts 1:5 looks forward to this day; Acts 11:15-16 refers back to it. Here, four short verses record it.

In principle, the filling of the Holy Spirit can be distinguished from the term "baptism" of the Spirit. "Baptism" is the theological, objective term referring to the Spirit's initial work in a believer's life, beginning the relationship, and—like water baptism—is not a repeated act (Acts 11:15-16; Romans 6:3; 1 Corinthians 12:13; Colossians 2:12). The believer who has taken this initial step of Spirit baptism must, however, continue to take advantage of the Spirit's active work in his or her life. That phenomenon is described in the New Testament as the Spirit's filling (see Acts 4:8, 31; 6:3, 5; 7:55; 9:17; 13:9, 52; Galatians 5:16; Ephesians 4:30; 5:18).

At Pentecost (2:1-4), the Holy Spirit was made available to all who believe in Jesus. Believers receive the Holy Spirit (are baptized with him) when they trust in Jesus Christ for salvation. The baptism of the Holy Spirit must be understood in the light of his total work in Christians:

- The Spirit marks the beginning of the Christian experience. No one belongs to Christ without his Spirit (Romans 8:9); no one is united to Christ without his Spirit (1 Corinthians 6:17); no one is adopted as God's child without his Spirit (Romans 8:14-17; Galatians 4:6-7); no one is in the body of Christ except by baptism in the Spirit (1 Corinthians 12:13).
- The Spirit is the power for the new life. He begins a lifelong process of change as believers become more like Christ (Galatians 3:3; Philippians 1:6). Those who receive Christ by faith begin an immediate personal relationship with God. The Holy Spirit works in them to help them become like Christ.
- The Spirit unites the Christian community in Christ (Ephesians 2:19-22). The Holy Spirit can be experienced by all, and he works through all (1 Corinthians 12:11; Ephesians 4:4).

Was this phenomenon the birthday of the church? Some think this was the inauguration day for the church, whereby the Spirit made the church into a corporate body (1 Corinthians 12:13). Most likely the church did not begin at Pentecost but at the time of Christ's resurrection. The Spirit of the risen Christ began a new, more intense relationship with individual believers than ever before. The promise of John 14:17 that the Spirit "will be in you" was fulfilled. As a new instrument of service called into action with the mission Israel formerly had, the church did have its birthday at Pentecost. It was the beginning of a time of rapid growth for the church.

These people literally spoke in "other languages" (see comments on the following verse)—a miraculous attention getter for the international crowd gathered in town for the feast. All the nationalities represented recognized their own languages being spoken. Jews believed that spoken prophecy had ceased with Malachi, the last of the writing prophets. They believed that from that point on, God spoke through the Torah as interpreted by scholars and teachers. So this was truly a remarkable day for the church, fulfilling Ezekiel 37:11-14.

The believers could speak in these other languages because *the Holy Spirit gave them this ability.* This is the clear teaching of the New Testament—that the Holy Spirit sovereignly determines which gift(s) a believer will have (1 Corinthians 12:7, 11). Furthermore, these gifts are meant to be used to build up the body of Christ.

THE MIRACLE OF A CHANGED LIFE

Luke's record of the birth and early years of the church is mind-boggling. Some Christians read about supernatural events like the foreign languages spoken at Pentecost and wonder, "Why doesn't God still do miracles like this?" Sometimes, however, in our desire to see "signs and wonders," we forget about the miracle of a changed life. When an abusive father is genuinely transformed into a caring and gentle soul, is that any less wonderful than seeing a crippled person walk? Which is more impressive long term: the sound of a mighty rushing wind coming upon a group of praying Christians once or a self-centered woman changed into a compassionate servant who devotes the rest of her life to helping others? Don't downplay the significance of divinity changing human lives! Pray more for these kinds of miraculous interventions.

2:5-8 Godly Jews from many nations were living in Jerusalem at that time. When they heard this sound, they came running to see what it was all about, and they were bewildered to hear their own languages being spoken by the believers. They were beside themselves with wonder. "How can this be?" they exclaimed. "These people are all from Galilee, and yet we hear them speaking the languages of the lands where we were born!"[NLT] Such an event could not help but attract attention, and a crowd must have quickly gathered. The *godly Jews from many nations* [who] *were living in Jerusalem at that time* were the Jews among the *Diaspora* (the Greek word for "scattering"), whose families had been driven from

Jerusalem and forced to live in other nations but had since returned to Jerusalem to live. These people had been born and raised in other nations, so among them many different languages were spoken. Thus, *they were bewildered to hear their own languages being spoken. . . . languages of the lands where [they] were born!* As the international, multilingual crowd gathered, they were astonished to hear their native tongues spoken by these Galileans. The term for "their own languages" is *dialekto,* from which we get our English word "dialect." These were spoken, living languages. At this point, "tongues" was not the ecstatic or heavenly utterance to which Paul referred in 1 Corinthians 12–14; these were languages people understood.

This gathering of the nations was a perfect platform for launching the worldwide mission of the church. This event told the Jerusalem church that God intended the gospel for all the nations in their own languages.

2:9-11 "Parthians, Medes and Elamites; residents of Mesopotamia, Judea and Cappadocia, Pontus and Asia, Phrygia and Pamphylia, Egypt and the parts of Libya near Cyrene; visitors from Rome (both Jews and converts to Judaism); Cretans and Arabs—we hear them declaring the wonders of God in our own tongues!"[NIV] This list includes the many lands from which Jews came to Jerusalem—some living in Palestine and others who had been dispersed throughout the world through captivities and persecutions. The list begins from the east of the Roman Empire and sweeps to the south and west. Very likely, some of the Jews who responded to Peter's message then returned to their homelands with God's good news of salvation (for example, see Acts 8). Through this divine manifestation of languages, therefore, God prepared the way for the spread of the gospel across the world. Throughout the book of Acts, it is clear how often the way was prepared for Paul and other messengers by people who had become believers at Pentecost. The church at Rome, for example, was probably begun by such Jewish believers. The list of countries reads mostly from East to West geographically, but why they are cited and why in this order is not known.

The content of these speeches in each language was *the wonders of God.* The subject of discussion was not sin, repentance, judgment, not even the gospel, but rather the proclamation of the mighty works of God.

Some have called this event at Pentecost "Babel Reversed." They speculate that God seems to be saying: "I confused your languages thousands of years ago because you failed to obey me, but now I've got a message so important, I'll countermand that program to get this message out."

The important fact to remember about this first occurrence of "tongues" is its purpose: to get the message of Christ out to the world. It was a sign for unbelieving Israel that the Messiah had come. The promised Spirit had been poured out as foretold in Joel, Isaiah, Jeremiah, and others. It was also an effective sign for the propagation of the gospel message—an instant, Spirit-given gift of a foreign language with which to spread the glorious news of God's work in the world. And that is exactly the point of Pentecost. The faithful believers were waiting and praying. Then came the prophesied signal that something big was about to happen. When it occurred, God delivered his message to the world.

With all the misinformation available today, many believers tend to look at Pentecost in an entirely improper light. It is often viewed as only some tremendous outpouring of power—sound of wind, fire, signs and wonders. If believers will take a fresh and straight-forward look at the events of Pentecost, however, they will find that the focus is on the fulfillment of Old Testament prophecy and the beginning of the witness of the apostles to the world.

THE UNIVERSALITY OF THE GOSPEL
Christianity is not limited to any race or group of people. Christ offers salvation to all people, without regard to nationality. People in Jerusalem were shocked to hear the apostles and other believers speaking in languages other than their own, the languages of other nationalities, but they need not have been surprised. God works all kinds of miracles to spread the gospel, using many languages as he calls all kinds of people to become his followers. No matter what your race, color, nationality, or language, God speaks to you. Are you listening for his voice?

2:12-13 They stood there amazed and perplexed. "What can this mean?" they asked each other. But others in the crowd were mocking. "They're drunk, that's all!" they said.[NLT] These two verses describe a typical response of the crowd, leading up to Peter's speech. The crowd continued to be *amazed* (see 2:7), but their amazement led them to be *perplexed* and to try to figure out what was happening. Some *were mocking.* Others were speculating that the believers were *drunk.* Such confusion and the drawing of such wrong conclusions was just the prodding Peter needed to clear things up. There will always be those who misunderstand the working of God, who mock it and call into question its integrity. Christians can either wring their hands and worry or, like Peter, seize the opportunity to tell the watching world about the work of God in their midst.

READY
When the gathered crowds recognized that something supernatural was taking place, they naturally wanted explanations and answers. At this point Peter stepped forward and explained the truth about God. This should be the pattern in our lives as well. Hopefully we are living in such a way that people will see Christ in us. If we *do* shine and sparkle (Matthew 5:14; Philippians 2:15), if we are "salty" (Matthew 5:13), we will get the attention of others. They will surely want to know what is so attractive and different about us. Then we can explain our "Christian hope" (1 Peter 3:15). What is different about your life? What supernatural evidence would cause someone to stop you and say, "What does this mean?"

PETER PREACHES TO A CROWD / 2:14-41

In Luke's history of the church, there is always a close connection between the activity of God's Spirit and the proclamation of the gospel. Time and again those who experience the baptism or filling of the Spirit begin immediately speaking with others concerning the truth about God and his Son, Jesus Christ (1:8; 2:4, 17; 4:8, 31; 6:10; 10:44-46; 13:9; 19:6).

This was certainly the case when the Spirit of God was poured out at Pentecost. The people gathered in Jerusalem were astonished to hear the Spirit-filled Palestinian Jews speaking fluently about God in foreign languages they had never learned. Confusion reigned until Peter delivered a convicting sermon, challenging his audience: "Turn to God, and be baptized in the name of Jesus Christ for the forgiveness of your sins" (2:38 NLT). God used this sermon, rich with Old Testament references, to draw about three thousand men and women to himself.

2:14 Then Peter stood up with the Eleven, raised his voice and addressed the crowd: "Fellow Jews and all of you who live in Jerusalem, let me explain this to you; listen carefully to what I say."NIV Peter, the early spokesman for the Twelve, seized the opportunity. He *stood up with the Eleven, raised his voice and addressed the crowd.* Peter explained to the people why they should listen to the testimony of the believers: because the Old Testament prophecies had been entirely fulfilled in Jesus (2:14-21), because Jesus is the Messiah (2:25-36), and because the risen Christ could change their lives (2:37-40).

A FRESH START
Peter had been an unstable leader during Jesus' ministry; he had even denied that he knew Jesus (John 18:15-18, 25-27). But Christ had forgiven and restored him (John 21:15-19). This was a new Peter, humble but bold. His confidence came from the Holy Spirit, who made him a powerful and dynamic speaker. Have you ever felt as if you've made such bad mistakes that God could never forgive and use you? No matter what sins you have committed, God promises to forgive you and make you useful for his kingdom. Allow him to forgive you and use you effectively to serve him.

2:15-18 **"These men are not drunk, as you suppose. It's only nine in the morning! No, this is what was spoken by the prophet Joel: 'In the last days, God says, I will pour out my Spirit on all people. Your sons and daughters will prophesy, your young men will see visions, your old men will dream dreams. Even on my servants, both men and women, I will pour out my Spirit in those days, and they will prophesy.'"**NIV Peter answered the accusation that they were all drunk (2:13) by saying it was much too early in the day for that. He then proceeded to tie the event the crowd had just witnessed to the words of the prophet Joel, quoting from Joel 2:28-32. Not everything mentioned in Joel 2:28-32 was occurring that particular morning. The *last days* include all the days between Christ's first and second comings; it is another way of saying "from now on." Peter was reminding these Jewish listeners that from prophecies like this one recorded by Joel, *I will pour out my Spirit on all people,* they should recognize the event they had just witnessed as the work of the Spirit. It would be to all kinds of people—Jews and Gentiles, rich and poor—not just to kings and priests.

The "prophesying" mentioned by Peter is likely not only prediction of the future but also declaration of the nature and will of God. The *visions* and the *dreams* were common means that God used to reveal himself to all people. The point was that the insight into these visions and dreams would be the product of the Spirit's work.

At Pentecost the Holy Spirit was released throughout the entire world—to men, women, slave owners, slaves, Jews, and Gentiles. Everyone can receive the Spirit. This was a revolutionary thought for first-century Jews. Pentecost was designed to be a clear indication—to Jew and Gentile alike—that the messianic age had arrived. The Messiah had come!

2:19-20 **"'I will show wonders in the heaven above and signs on the earth below, blood and fire and billows of smoke. The sun will be turned to darkness and the moon to blood before the**

coming of the great and glorious day of the Lord.'"NIV Not everything mentioned in Joel 2:28-32 was happening that particular morning. This part of Joel's prophecy probably refers to the future period surrounding the second coming of Christ, placing the period of the church age (between Christ's ascension and his return) between verses 18 and 19 (see Revelation 6:12). These events bear more resemblance to the phenomena of the Tribulation period as spelled out by many other Old Testament prophets, as well as Jesus himself (see Matthew 24:14, 21, 29-30 and the judgments of Revelation 8, 9, and 16).

It is possible that Peter was quoting the entire prophecy from Joel—even some of the parts that are still future—in order to avoid being accused of improper use of Scripture (the crowd would certainly know the Joel passage) and to get all the way through Joel's passage to its final sentence, quoted in the next verse.

2:21 **"'And anyone who calls on the name of the Lord will be saved.'"**NLT This is Peter's punch line. This salvation is available to *anyone.* Any person *who calls on the name of the Lord will be saved.* God's special relationship with Israel will continue, but it has been broadened to include everyone who calls on the name of the Lord. God's plans for Israel had their climax in Christ. Access to God—for all people—now comes through Jesus Christ. With these words Peter witnessed to the crowd, as Jesus had predicted (1:8).

It would be a while before these new believers understood that the "anyone" included Gentiles. God had to work in a special way to make Peter understand that the message was meant for the whole world, not just the Jews (see Acts 10).

ANYONE IS ELIGIBLE
Quoting the prophet Joel, Peter announced that "anyone who calls on the name of the Lord will be saved." According to this verse (quoted also in Romans 10:13), the issue in salvation isn't who a person is or what he or she has done; the issue is simple trust and humility. *Anyone* who looks to the Lord for forgiveness will find it. That person *will* be saved. What a fantastic promise! Who in your life needs the saving touch of God? Ask the Father to work in their lives, to draw them to the Son (John 6:44), and to bring them to salvation.

2:22 **"People of Israel, listen! God publicly endorsed Jesus of Nazareth by doing wonderful miracles, wonders, and signs through him, as you well know."**NLT The coming of the Messiah, the miracles, and the events described by Joel were all well-established concepts to these *people of Israel* (the Jews). Now all that remained was for Peter to connect those events to *Jesus of Nazareth*—the teacher many of them had heard and seen, the teacher who had been crucified. The term "Messiah" (Christ) occurs often in this speech (2:31, 36, 38) as Peter made the clear connection between Jesus and the one David spoke of prophetically. "Jesus of Nazareth is the long-awaited Messiah" is the theme of this sermon (2:14-36) and the basis for the ensuing call to faith.

Peter began this sermon by stating that God himself had *publicly endorsed* Jesus by *doing wonderful miracles, wonders, and signs through him.* Certainly many of the gathered crowd had seen or heard of the famous ministry of Jesus. For several years he had been speaking to huge crowds and performing incredible miracles, often in the full view of thousands of people (the miraculous "feedings," for example). Thus, when Peter said *as you well know,* he was reminding his audience that many of them were familiar with Jesus and his ministry.

2:23 **"But you followed God's prearranged plan. With the help of lawless Gentiles, you nailed him to the cross and murdered him."**NLT With little forewarning Peter suddenly accused his Jewish audience of an awful participation in the Messiah's death. This is a perfect presentation of God's sovereignty and people's responsibility—both in the same sentence. God's prearranged plan was his sovereign will to bring salvation to people through the death and resurrection of Christ. Though God's will is sovereign, he works through people and events of history (see 4:28). Even putting Jesus to death fulfilled God's plan. *God's prearranged plan* led to Christ's death, but people were culpable. The *lawless Gentiles* (the Romans) had been involved, but they had been merely "helping." Ultimately, the Jews had been responsible. Whether or not anyone in this audience had literally participated in the trials, accusations, and crucifixion (many in the crowd *could* have been involved) was not important. Peter was saying that they were at least culpable because, as Jews, they had missed their Messiah and had allowed their leaders to kill him. Thus, they were guilty by their relationship to the actual murderers. It was as if Peter were pointing his finger at the crowd and shouting, *"You nailed him to the cross and murdered him."*

> When I get to heaven, I shall see three wonders there: The first wonder will be to see many people there whom I did not expect to see.
>
> The second wonder will be to miss many people whom I did expect to see. The third and greatest wonder of all will be to find myself there.
>
> *John Newton*

ACCESSORIES TO MURDER
Peter boldly blamed Christ's murder on the Jews gathered for Pentecost. It is possible that some in Peter's audience *were* actually part of the mob that shouted to Pilate, "Crucify him!" (Luke 23:18-24). But others were probably not even in Jerusalem during those fateful events. Nevertheless, Peter identified them all ("people of Israel"—2:22 NLT) as accomplices in the execution of Christ: "You nailed him to the cross and murdered him" (2:23 NLT). There is a sense in which we all—Jews and "lawless Gentiles" alike—share the blame for Christ's death. Our sins sent him to Calvary. He was nailed to the cross for our crimes. He was punished in our place. When is the last time you thanked God for this stunning display of mercy and grace?

2:24 **"But God raised him up, having freed him from death, because it was impossible for him to be held in its power."**NRSV But the murdered Messiah had not stayed dead. *God raised him up,* and many people could testify to having seen the risen Christ. This was a powerful statement because many of the people listening to Peter's words had been in Jerusalem fifty days earlier at Passover and may have seen or heard about the crucifixion of this "great teacher." Jesus' resurrection was the ultimate sign that what he said about himself was true. Without the Resurrection, no one would have any reason to believe in Jesus (1 Corinthians 15:14).

Notice here that the Resurrection is attributed to God himself. The Resurrection is a foundational part of the preaching of Acts (see 2:32; 3:15, 26; 4:10; 5:30; 10:40; 13:30, 33-34, 37; 17:31; 26:23). The grave could not keep the author of life, the Creator (John 1:1-14; Colossians 1:15-17). Peter phrased it appropriately: *it was impossible* for the author of life to be *held* by the power of the grave!

2:25-28 **"David said about him: 'I saw the Lord always before me. Because he is at my right hand, I will not be shaken. Therefore my heart is glad and my tongue rejoices; my body also will live in hope, because you will not abandon me to the grave, nor will you let your Holy One see decay. You have made known to me the paths of life; you will fill me with joy in your presence.'"**NIV Peter continued his witness to Jesus' Messiahship by quoting from Psalm 16:8-11, written by David. He explained that David was not writing about himself because David had died and was buried (2:29); his audience would have walked right past his tomb many times in their pilgrimages to Jerusalem. This quote from Psalm 16 and the one from Psalm

110:1 (2:34-35) were both prophesying Jesus' resurrection (2:24). Peter's audience understood "decay" to mean the grave. The emphasis is that Jesus' body had not been left to decay but had been, in fact, resurrected and glorified. Peter wanted his audience to realize that David, though confident of his own resurrection, was predicting the resurrection of the Messiah in these psalms.

2:29-31 "Brothers, I can tell you confidently that the patriarch David died and was buried, and his tomb is here to this day. But he was a prophet and knew that God had promised him on oath that he would place one of his descendants on his throne. Seeing what was ahead, he spoke of the resurrection of the Christ, that he was not abandoned to the grave, nor did his body see decay."NIV The Old Testament makes a solid case for the resurrection of the Messiah—and this was very important for Peter's Jewish listeners to understand. Peter argued that the words of this psalm could not have been referring to David himself, for David *died and was buried.* The reference to *his tomb* may have been a site on the south side of Jerusalem, near the pool of Siloam.

THE EMPTY TOMB
Peter spoke forthrightly about the Resurrection. As Peter preached, the events of Christ's passion were still hot news, less than two months old. Christ's execution had been carried out in public before many witnesses. His empty tomb was available for inspection just a short distance away. If Christ had not truly died, Peter's message would have been laughed at or even ignored. If Christ had not been resurrected, authorities could have produced his body and put an end to this new faith. But Peter and the apostles had witnessed the risen Christ. Changed men, they announced the news with great passion and conviction. Our faith and our credibility also rest on the truth of the empty tomb.

If David was not speaking of himself, then he was speaking as a *prophet;* he was writing about one who would be resurrected from the dead. The *oath* looks back at Psalm 132:11 and 2 Samuel 7:15-16, recording the promises God made to David that *one of his descendants* would always sit *on the throne.* David did have children who ruled, but this promise was for someone to be on the throne for eternity. That king would be Jesus Christ. David, in writing this psalm, had been *seeing what was ahead* and therefore had written *of the resurrection of the Christ.* The Jewish listeners of Peter's day understood the words of this psalm, as well as others, as referring to the Messiah.

2:32 "This prophecy was speaking of Jesus, whom God raised from the dead, and we all are witnesses of this."[NLT] Having begun by tying these Old Testament references to Jesus of Nazareth, here Peter again made it clear that David's *prophecy was speaking of Jesus.*

The resurrection of Christ had taken place less than two months previously. The post-Resurrection appearances and instruction sessions of the forty days prior to Christ's ascension must have caused a stir around the city. Peter pointed out that he and the others with him—who had just experienced this Spirit's coming—had been *witnesses* to the predicted resurrection of Christ.

2:33 "Now he sits on the throne of highest honor in heaven, at God's right hand. And the Father, as he had promised, gave him the Holy Spirit to pour out upon us, just as you see and hear today."[NLT] Peter had one more major point to make: this crucified one, the resurrected one, is now the exalted one, who occupies the *throne of highest honor in heaven, at God's right hand* (see 5:30-31; Ephesians 1:20; Colossians 3:1; Hebrews 1:3; 8:1; 10:12; 12:2; 1 Peter 3:22). Not only is Christ the predicted one in the psalms; not only had he risen from the grave; he now sits in the most authoritative, sovereign position in the universe.

That is why Jesus had the authority to *pour out* the Spirit with results that the audience could *see and hear.*

2:34-35 "For David did not ascend to heaven, and yet he said, 'The Lord said to my Lord: "Sit at my right hand until I make your enemies a footstool for your feet."'"[NIV] In Psalm 110:1, again David was not speaking of himself but of Christ. This verse is the most frequently quoted Old Testament passage in the New Testament (thirteen times) and was the primary text used to explain the exaltation of Christ. The Jews believed that this psalm referred to their coming Messiah. All three synoptic gospels—Matthew 22:41-46; Mark 12:35-37; Luke 20:41-44—report that Jesus applied this verse to himself as the one having the highest authority because he would be instructed to *sit at my [God's] right hand.* The victory belongs to Christ and not to any created being. The greatest arch-angels stand before God (Luke 1:19; Revelation 8:2), but none are allowed to sit, for sitting next to God would indicate equality. Jesus' sitting also indicates the completion of his task, the successful accomplishment of his mission.

God promised to make Jesus' *enemies a footstool*—they would be under his feet. This pictures Christ as completely victorious over his enemies. God does not place Jesus' enemies under Jesus' feet because Jesus is not capable of doing it himself. Instead, this action shows that the Father approves of Jesus' work. The two work together for a common purpose. Jesus' honor cannot be superseded. Implicit in the quote of this psalm, Peter was warning his listeners that they should not want to be numbered any longer among the "enemies" of this one who was now high and lifted up.

2:36 "So let it be clearly known by everyone in Israel that God has made this Jesus whom you crucified to be both Lord and Messiah!"NLT Peter, ever the good "witness" that Jesus had said he would be, concluded his message with a solid review of his main point: *So let it be clearly known by everyone in Israel* that Jesus was the Messiah. In the prophesied plan of God, this Jesus of Nazareth had been *crucified* by the Jews, raised from the dead, and exalted to the throne of God.

> A Savior not quite God is like a bridge broken at the further end.
> *Bishop Moule*

Throughout his message, Peter consistently applied the messianic prophecies, the messianic psalms, and the miraculous Resurrection to Jesus of Nazareth (see 2:22-23, 32). His concluding remarks did so as well. With the proclamation of Jesus as *Lord and Messiah,* Peter reached the climax of his message. The reference to Jesus as "Lord" was likely, in this context, connecting Jesus to Yahweh. It was another clear affirmation of Christ's deity.

2:37 When the people heard this, they were cut to the heart and said to Peter and the other apostles, "Brothers, what shall we do?"NIV The term "cut to the heart" speaks of genuine pain. It means to "strike, prick violently, sting sharply, stun." The crowd was stunned! They asked the question that warms the heart of any messenger of the gospel: *"What shall we do?"* Peter was ready with the answer.

TRANSFORMING TRUTH

After Peter's powerful, Spirit-filled message, the people were deeply moved and asked, "What shall we do?" This is the basic question to ask. It is not enough to be sorry for our sins—we must let God forgive them; then we must live like forgiven people. Has God spoken to you through his Word or through the words of another believer? Remember: God didn't give his truth to merely provide more information; instead, he wants transformation. Like Peter's audience, ask God what you should do; then obey without delay.

2:38 Peter replied, "Each of you must turn from your sins and turn to God, and be baptized in the name of Jesus Christ for the forgiveness of your sins. Then you will receive the gift of

the Holy Spirit."[NLT] In answer to the people's question, Peter presented a fourfold challenge:

> Christianity tells people to repent and promises forgiveness. It therefore has nothing to say to people who do not know they have done anything to repent of, and who do not feel that they need any forgiveness. It is after you have realized that there is a real Moral Law, and a Power behind the law, and that you have broken that law and put yourself wrong with that Power—it is after all this, and not a moment sooner, that Christianity begins to talk. When you know you are sick, you will listen to the doctor.
>
> *C. S. Lewis*

1. *Turn from your sins*—In other words, "repent." The Greek word, *metanoesate,* means "change your outlook" or "change your mind." This is not just sorrow or even sorrow for sin but an actual change in the way a person thinks. It is a basic and wholehearted change of mind that results in a change of purpose, direction, and values. "Each of you" reminds the listener (and modern reader) that this message is for all. Everyone needs to make a decision about Christ. His offer is the only effective solution for the sin problem that plagues every descendant of Adam.
2. *Turn to God*—In addition to turning from sin, people must turn to God. It does no good to turn from sin without turning then to the one who can solve the sin problem.
3. *Be baptized in the name of Jesus Christ for the forgiveness of your sins*—Some believe that baptism was already being used for Jewish converts as a sign of their conversion to Judaism. John the Baptist had called for baptism as a sign of repentance and a changed heart—an external, nonverbal expression or cele bration of an inward reality. For believers, baptism is visible proof of repentance and commitment to follow Jesus, the Messiah.

   The idea of baptism "for the forgiveness of sins" does not mean that baptism results in forgiveness of sins but rather that forgiveness of sins as a result of accepting Jesus as Savior should result in a baptism—an outward display of an inner conviction. Repentance, not baptism, is what brings forgiveness.

> No matter how far you have gone on a wrong road, turn back.
>
> *Turkish proverb*

4. *Receive the gift of the Holy Spirit*—Only through the coming of the Holy Spirit into believers' hearts can they truly experience forgiveness of sin. The "gift of the Holy Spirit" (not multiple or varied gifts but rather a singular gift) is the Spirit himself.

The Holy Spirit is a gift from God. As Jesus had promised, he is the Comforter and the one who guides his people.

FOLLOWING CHRIST
Peter told those who had responded to his message to repent and be baptized. True followers of Christ recognize the necessity of repentance and the importance of baptism. To repent means literally to "change your mind"—about who God is (he is the Lord and Judge and Savior of all the earth) and about where to find life (not in living selfishly and rebelliously but in humble trust and obedience to God). Practically, it involves changing course. We stop running away from our holy God, and we turn to Christ, depending only on him for forgiveness, mercy, guidance, and purpose. In repentance we recognize that we cannot save ourselves—only God can save us. Baptism is that crucial step of obedience that identifies us with Christ and with the community of believers. It is one of the marks of a true disciple and a strong sign of faith. Have you repented of your sin and trusted in Jesus for salvation? Have you been baptized?

2:39-40 "The promise is for you and your children and for all who are far off—for all whom the Lord our God will call." With many other words he warned them; and he pleaded with them, "Save yourselves from this corrupt generation."NIV The truths presented in the previous verses here find their universal application. This *promise* of the work of the Spirit in the life of the believer has a personal application *(for you),* a generational application *(and your children),* and a global application (*for all who are far off,* perhaps foreshadowing those who were far away from this Jewish temple, that is, the Gentiles). Luke recorded no more of Peter's words to the gathered crowd except to say that Peter kept talking for a long time *(with many other words),* warning and pleading with the people to be saved.

2:41 Those who believed what Peter said were baptized and added to the church—about three thousand in all.NLT What a response! *Three thousand* people believed and took the step of faith in Christ. *Those who believed . . . were baptized*—they took that first step of obedience, publicly identifying themselves with Christ. And they were *added to the church;* that is, they immediately joined the fellowship of believers.

THE BELIEVERS MEET TOGETHER / 2:42-47

Books about church planting, church health, and church growth are popular. Seminars about the church abound, with pastors and church boards eager to copy the techniques of a successful pastor or a fast-growing congregation. The following paragraph is a snapshot of the church a few days old. At Pentecost, after the coming of the Holy Spirit, the gathering of 120 exploded! In one day three thousand people came to faith in Christ. Now what do they do? This handful of verses provides a concise summary of what the early church was about; it provides a model that can be applied to the modern church, as well.

2:42 **They joined with the other believers and devoted themselves to the apostles' teaching and fellowship, sharing in the Lord's Supper and in prayer.**[NLT] This first report of the newborn church describes early church worship in the first decade of the church. These key elements have been called the four pillars of worship.

The three thousand new believers *joined with the other believers.* That is, they gathered with others of like mind and faith. "Devoted themselves" implies that they were regularly, continually persisting in the activities that follow. These activities form a practical map for not only the day-old church but for any church of any age.

The Bible is alive, it speaks to me; it has feet, it runs after me; it has hands, it lays hold on me. *Martin Luther*

The *apostles' teaching* was central to the content of what was to be studied. This was one reason that the replacement of Judas was so important—the apostles, the eyewitnesses of all Jesus had done (and earwitnesses of all he had said) would be the ones whom the Holy Spirit would remind of the crucial truths by which the church would be directed for centuries to come (John 14:17, 25-26; 16:13). From the beginning the early church was devoted to hearing, studying, and learning what the apostles had to teach.

There is nothing more unchristian than a solitary Christian. *John Wesley*

The *fellowship (koinonia)* means association and close relationships. This was more than just getting together, certainly more than just a religious meeting. It involved sharing goods, having meals together, and praying together.

Sharing in the Lord's Supper is "the breaking of bread." It refers to communion services that were celebrated in remembrance of Jesus and patterned after the Last Supper, which Jesus had eaten with his disciples before his death (Matthew 26:26-29). It likely included a regular meal shared together (Acts 2:46; 20:7; 1 Corinthians 10:16; 11:23-25; Jude 1:12).

Prayer joins "sharing in the Lord's Supper" to explain the word "fellowship." These are at least two of the activities that were part of their regular meetings. Prayer has always been a mark of the believers' gatherings.

2:43 **A deep sense of awe came over them all, and the apostles performed many miraculous signs and wonders.**[NLT] The word "awe" is the Greek word *phobos,* literally translated "fear." This awe was partly caused by the *many miraculous signs and wonders* performed by the apostles. The "wonders" *(terata)* were fabulous miracles that evoked awe in those who saw them. The "miraculous signs" *(semeia)* were given to authenticate the message and the messenger, pointing observers toward a divine source of the miracle or a divine truth. Here these signs and wonders authenticated the apostles' message, identifying it as divine truth.

2:44-45 **All the believers were together and had everything in common. Selling their possessions and goods, they gave to anyone as he had need.**[NIV] A cognate word of "fellowship" appears here: "common" is the Greek word *koina,* from which comes the word *koinonia* (fellowship—2:42). Of the thousands of Jews who had made the pilgrimage to Jerusalem for Pentecost, many may have come as early as Passover (fifty days earlier). Now they were extending their stay in Jerusalem even longer to learn the basics of this newfound Christian faith. Many would likely need financial or physical help from those who lived in Jerusalem to be able to remain this long. When a need arose, believers would sell their possessions to help the needy person. This practice of having *everything in common* was likely a response to that specific need. After the incidents of 5:1-11 (Ananias and Sapphira), there is no further mention of this particular practice of sharing everything, at least to the extent that it was practiced in the first few weeks of the church's life.

Should we not see that lines of laughter about the eyes are just as much marks of faith as are the lines of care and seriousness? Is it only earnestness that is baptized? Is laughter pagan? We have already allowed too much that is good to be lost to the church and cast many pearls before the swine. A church is in a bad way when it banishes laughter from the sanctuary and leaves it to the cabaret, the nightclub and the toastmasters.

Helmut Thielecke

2:46-47 **Every day they continued to meet together in the temple courts. They broke bread in their homes and ate together with glad and sincere hearts, praising God and enjoying the**

JOY IN THE BOOK OF ACTS

Wherever the gospel message went, it brought joy to those who believed. Follow this theme through the book of Acts (verses are quoted from the NIV).

2:46	"Every day they continued to meet together in the temple courts. They broke bread in their homes and ate together with glad and sincere hearts."
5:41	"The apostles left the Sanhedrin, rejoicing because they had been counted worthy of suffering disgrace for the Name."
8:8	"So there was great joy in that city [Samaria]."
8:39	"When they came up out of the water, the Spirit of the Lord suddenly took Philip away, and the eunuch did not see him again, but went on his way rejoicing."
11:23	"When he [Barnabas] arrived and saw the evidence of the grace of God, he was glad and encouraged them all to remain true to the Lord with all their hearts."
12:14	"When she recognized Peter's voice, she was so overjoyed she ran back without opening it and exclaimed, 'Peter is at the door!'"
13:48	[In Iconium] "When the Gentiles heard this, they were glad and honored the word of the Lord; and all who were appointed for eternal life believed."
13:52	"And the disciples were filled with joy and with the Holy Spirit."
14:17	[Paul speaking in Lystra] "Yet he has not left himself without testimony: He has shown kindness by giving you rain from heaven and crops in their seasons; he provides you with plenty of food and fills your hearts with joy."
15:3	"The church sent them [Paul and Barnabas] on their way, and as they traveled through Phoenicia and Samaria, they told how the Gentiles had been converted. This news made all the brothers very glad."
15:31	"The people read it [the letter from Jerusalem] and were glad for its encouraging message."
16:34	"The [Philippian] jailer brought them into his house and set a meal before them; he was filled with joy because he had come to believe in God—he and his whole family."

---

favor of all the people. And the Lord added to their number daily those who were being saved.NIV With these words this marvelous chapter comes to a close. Luke pointed out the everyday nature of the church's meetings. Believers were gathering both *in the temple* (that is, in large groups, possibly for apostolic teaching) and *in their homes* (at least to celebrate the Lord's Supper and, presumably, for fellowship, the sharing of needs, and prayer).

A common misconception about the first Christians (who were Jews) was that they rejected the Jewish religion. But these believers saw Jesus' message and resurrection as the fulfillment of everything they knew and believed from the Old Testament. At first the Jewish believers did not separate from the rest of the Jewish community. They still went to the temple and synagogues for worship and instruction in the Scriptures. But their belief in Jesus created great friction with Jews who didn't believe that Jesus was the Messiah. Thus, believing Jews were forced to meet in private homes for communion, prayer, and teaching about Christ. By the end of the first century, many of these Jewish believers were excommunicated from their synagogues.

FAMILY MATTERS

Recognizing other believers as brothers and sisters in the family of God, the Christians in Jerusalem shared their possessions and money so that all could benefit from God's gifts. It is tempting—especially if we have accumulated wealth—to cut ourselves off from others, only taking care of our own interests. As part of God's spiritual family, however, it is our responsibility to help other believers, especially those who are suffering and who are poor, whenever possible. God's family works best when its members work together.

We also see here one of the repeated themes of the book of Acts: joy. These believers had *glad and sincere hearts, praising God.* The early church was marked by joy.

Two final statements reveal two significant results of the presence of this regularly meeting, money-sharing, miracle-working, Bible-studying, God-praising group:

1. The watching community was favorably impressed (the believers were *enjoying the favor of all the people*).
2. The watching community was coming to faith *(and the Lord added to their number daily those who were being saved).*

These are two measurable results of any church that is living like the early church. Note, too, that the credit for the salvation of souls is not given to Peter's preaching, the apostles' miracles, or the Spirit's manifestations—it was the Lord who was adding to their number daily.

ALIVE AND GROWING
The Jerusalem church experienced both qualitative and quantitative growth. Eager for this same result, many church leaders flock to church growth seminars. It would be wiser to concentrate on church health. Why? Because it is the nature of a healthy organism to grow. When a church body emphasizes strong worship and solid biblical teaching in an atmosphere of true fellowship mixed with consistent evangelism, it will be healthy. And a healthy Christian community will attract people to Christ. What are you doing to make your church a healthy place that will draw others to Christ?

Acts 3

PETER HEALS A CRIPPLED BEGGAR / 3:1-11

Commissioned by Christ to preach the gospel to all the earth (Matthew 28:18-20), the apostles had his authority. Miracles such as healing the sick (9:34; 19:11-12; 28:8), liberating the demon possessed (5:16; 8:7), even raising the dead (9:36-42; 20:7-12) highlighted their ministries. These supernatural signs authenticated the message being preached and drew people to the Savior. The first eleven verses record a miracle. Peter's ensuing sermon explains the point of the miracle, particularly for the Jewish audience who witnessed it.

3:1 **One day Peter and John were going up to the temple at the hour of prayer, at three o'clock in the afternoon.**[NRSV] The Jews observed three times of prayer—morning (9:00 A.M.), afternoon (3:00 P.M.), and evening (sunset). At these times devout Jews and Gentiles who believed in God often would go to the temple to pray. Peter and John were going to the temple at 3:00 P.M.

Note, too, that Peter and John were still living, for the most part, as obedient Jews, keeping the appointed times of prayer, though they now had a significantly different mission.

3:2-3 **As they approached the Temple, a man lame from birth was being carried in. Each day he was put beside the Temple gate, the one called the Beautiful Gate, so he could beg from the people going into the Temple. When he saw Peter and John about to enter, he asked them for some money.**[NLT] The apostles were in the habit of going to prayer at the temple at the set times (3:1); likewise, this lame beggar was in the habit of begging there at these times. Both verb tenses are imperfect, setting forth the idea of regular, habitual action—each day they "were going" up to pray; each day he "was being put" beside the Temple gate.

Beggars would often wait in places where they would have the most traffic—such as along the roads near cities or, as here, at the entrance to the temple. The *Beautiful Gate* was one of the favored entrances into the temple complex, and many people passed through it on their way to worship. Since giving money to beggars was considered praiseworthy in the Jewish religion, the

TIME TO PRAY

The Jews had set times of prayer, but the clear teaching (and example) of the New Testament is that believers are to be in a spirit of prayerfulness at all times. Our lives should be one long, running conversation with the Father. (Verses quoted from NLT.)

Scripture	*Command*
Romans 1:9-10	"Day and night I bring you and your needs in prayer to God."
Ephesians 6:18	"Pray at all times and on every occasion. . . . Be persistent in your prayers for all Christians everywhere."
Colossians 1:3	"We always pray for you."
1 Thessalonians 1:3	"We . . . pray for you constantly."
1 Thessalonians 2:13	"We will never stop thanking God."
1 Thessalonians 5:17	"Keep on praying."
2 Timothy 1:3	"Night and day I constantly remember you in my prayers."

lame man wisely had himself placed where he could catch the almsgivers headed both to and from religious gatherings. As *Peter and John* entered the temple area, the lame man called out to them and *asked them for some money.*

DIVINE APPOINTMENTS
Peter and John had made plans to attend a three o'clock prayer service. Perhaps they hoped to share their new faith with some old friends. Or maybe they wanted to make contact with one of the other apostles. As busy religious leaders on an important religious mission, they might have brushed off the lame beggar who accosted them at the temple gate for a handout. But Peter and John recognized the sovereign nature of this encounter. In the name of Christ (and by his power), they healed the beggar. This precipitated a series of evangelistic opportunities that no one—except God—could have predicted. Be careful that you don't get so preoccupied with doing God's work that you miss God's will right before your eyes.

Usually disabled in some way, beggars were unable to work for a living. Medical help was not available for their problems, and people tended to ignore their obligation to care for the needy (Leviticus 25:35-37). Thus, beggars had little hope of escaping their degrading way of life. For this lame man, begging was his only means of support.

The man's crippled condition is a picture of the hopeless condition of the sinner (see Romans 5:6; Ephesians 2:12). The healing that follows is a picture of what Christ, the Great Physician, can do in the face of hopelessness.

3:4-6 Peter looked straight at him, as did John. Then Peter said, "Look at us!" So the man gave them his attention, expecting to get something from them. Then Peter said, "Silver or gold I do not have, but what I have I give you. In the name of Jesus Christ of Nazareth, walk."NIV In this powerful scene, Peter and John *looked straight at* the beggar. The term for "looked straight" is *atenisas*—it speaks of intensity (see 1:10; 23:1). Peter demanded the man's attention, and the beggar *gave them his attention,* obviously anticipating a handout. What was offered, however, was not what the man was seeking *(silver or gold),* but rather something far more valuable. Peter, having no money to offer the man, nor the power in himself to heal him, commanded the beggar to *walk.* Note that the command was not by Peter's authority but rather in the *name of Jesus Christ of Nazareth.* In the Jewish mind-set, the name of an individual stood for all that a person was. A name was more than a label; instead, it represented that person's being and carried his or her authority. By calling on the "name of Jesus Christ," Peter was calling on Christ's power and authority. Therefore, to walk "in the name of Jesus Christ" meant to walk "by the authority of Jesus Christ." The apostles were doing this healing through the Holy Spirit's power given to them by Christ, not their own (see Luke 10:17).

> Do little things as if they were great, because of the majesty of the Lord Jesus Christ, who dwells in thee; and do great things as if they were little and easy, because of his omnipotence. *Pascal*

GOD'S BEST

The crippled man asked for money, but Peter gave him something much better—the use of his legs. We often ask God to solve a small problem, but he wants to give us a whole new life and help for all our problems. When we ask God for help, he may say, "I've got something even better for you." Ask God for what you want, but don't be surprised when he gives you what you really need.

3:7 **Then Peter took the lame man by the right hand and helped him up. And as he did, the man's feet and anklebones were healed and strengthened.**NLT To encourage the lame man to begin walking, Peter reached for him to help him up. The terms that follow here reflect Dr. Luke's medical orientation—*the man's feet and anklebones,* which to this point had never been able to support the man, *were healed and strengthened.* The description here pictures a complete healing (the word "strengthened" comes from a Greek medical term—*estereothesan*—used elsewhere in Greek literature in reference to sockets being reset).

3:8 **Jumping up, he stood and began to walk, and he entered the temple with them, walking and leaping and praising God.**NRSV It did not take the man long to realize that indeed he was healed. Not only could he stand, but he also immediately tried out his new legs at full throttle, moving quickly from standing, to beginning to walk, to ultimately *leaping.* This healed beggar was aware that the source of his healing was not Peter but God. In the midst of his excitement and this obviously emotional moment, he praised God, who had given him a new lease on life.

> God has two dwellings: one in heaven and the other in a thankful heart.
> *Isaak Walton*

THANKING PEOPLE, PRAISING GOD

In his excitement the formerly crippled man began to jump and walk around. Then he also began praising God! As he did, those who recognized him were awed by this obvious display of God's power. This scene is a good reminder of the importance of recognizing the true source of our blessings. God often uses people to be the vessels through whom he works; consequently, we should thank those who help us. But we should reserve our praise for the God who is behind every "good and perfect" gift (James 1:17).

3:9-10 **All the people saw him walking and praising God, and they recognized him as the one who used to sit and ask for alms at the Beautiful Gate of the temple; and they were filled with wonder and amazement at what had happened to him.**NRSV This must have been some scene. The beggar, known for years for his crippled condition *(they recognized him as the one)* danced into the temple area with words of praise to God. There could be no doubt about who he was or about what had happened. Nor could there be any doubt about whom the beggar thought should get the credit for the miracle. The people, quite appropriately, *were filled with wonder and amazement.*

CHANGED!
As they watched the beggar, the people could see an obvious change in his life. Before, he had been lame; now he was walking. The difference was amazing. Though we may not be the recipients of a physical miracle of healing, God can change us emotionally and psychologically. These kinds of internal changes are just as miraculous as external healings and can fill others with "wonder and amazement." In what ways has God changed you? Can others see the changes? Praise God for all he has done in your life.

3:11 **While the beggar held on to Peter and John, all the people were astonished and came running to them in the place called Solomon's Colonnade.**NIV The scene broadened as the beggar, almost like a young child, was pictured clinging to Peter and John. Even more people came running to *the place called Solomon's Colonnade,* a covered porch or entrance with columns that stood just east of the outer court of the temple. The reference to this site would remind the Jews of the golden days of Israel's history, making the healing here all the more poignant.

For the Jewish observers and readers, the sign here was too spectacular to overlook. Isaiah had written of such a time: "The lame will leap like a deer, and those who cannot speak will shout and sing!" (Isaiah 35:6 NLT). All this Jewish audience needed was a "witness" to explain the significance to them. Peter, ever the one to take advantage of such a situation, seized the moment to bring a pointed message to an *astonished* audience.

PETER PREACHES IN THE TEMPLE / 3:12-26

A good sermon introduction is supposed to capture attention, raise a need, and orient listeners to the subject at hand. Peter and John's healing of the lame man in the temple courts did all those in a powerful way. It drew a huge crowd of awed spectators. It prompted these onlookers to want to know how such a miracle was possible. It gave the apostles an open door to declare plainly that Jesus, crucified and resurrected, was the long-awaited Messiah who fulfilled all the predictions of the prophets.

Peter's sermon here is similar to the one he preached at Pentecost (2:14-40). He proclaimed the truth, enhanced richly with Old Testament Scripture (3:12-16), and then called for repentance (3:17-26). In this sermon, however, Peter more clearly developed the teaching of the person of Jesus—as God's servant, the holy and righteous one, the author of life, and a prophet like Moses. Its design was to once again witness to the nature of the one who had come to save, and to encourage listeners to come to faith. It's hard to believe this was the same Peter who had three times denied even *knowing* Jesus. Here he stood before a potentially hostile audience, powerfully claiming the name of Christ and pointedly accusing his listeners of their role in Christ's death.

TEACHABLE MOMENTS
Peter had an audience, and he capitalized on the opportunity to share Jesus Christ. He clearly presented his message by emphasizing Jesus' true identity, explaining how the Jews had rejected him and why their rejection was fatal, and telling what they needed to do to change the situation. Peter told the crowd that they still had a choice. God offered them the opportunity to believe and receive Jesus as their Messiah and Lord. Displays of God's mercy and grace, such as the healing of this crippled man, often create teachable moments. Pray to have courage like Peter to see these opportunities and to use them to speak up for Christ.

3:12 **Peter saw his opportunity and addressed the crowd. "People of Israel," he said, "what is so astounding about this? And why look at us as though we had made this man walk by our own power and godliness?"**NLT Peter took advantage of a gathered, attentive crowd, and he addressed them by making it clear that this miracle was not the product of his personal *power* or *godliness.* Rather, this miracle had been performed by God himself, for a very explicit purpose.

3:13 **"For it is the God of Abraham, the God of Isaac, the God of Jacob, the God of all our ancestors who has brought glory to his servant Jesus by doing this."**NLT Peter wanted to make it clear to this Jewish crowd that this miracle was the handiwork of the very God they claimed to follow, *the God of Abraham, the God of Isaac, the God of Jacob, the God of all our ancestors.* The miracle also had purpose: to bring *glory to his servant Jesus.* God the Father was exalting the Son through this miracle. The term "servant" called to mind the Servant of Yahweh in Isaiah 42:1; 49:6-7; 52:13; 53:11. Peter wanted Jesus identified with the Servant-Messiah of the Old Testament. Then, as his audience was thinking about this connection, he pressed home the brutal truth:

"This is the same Jesus whom you handed over and rejected before Pilate, despite Pilate's decision to release him."NLT Peter told them point-blank that they were responsible for Jesus' death. The Roman leader, *Pilate,* had decided to *release* Jesus, but the Jews had *rejected* Pilate's offer and had clamored to have Barabbas, a murderer, released instead (see Luke 23:13-25). When Peter said, *Jesus whom you handed over,* he meant it literally. Jesus' trial and death had occurred right there in Jerusalem only weeks earlier. It wasn't an event of the distant past—most of these people had heard about it. Some may have actually participated in the trials or witnessed the Crucifixion. At any rate, all Jews were there (and thus guilty) through their representative leadership. Remember, the people had pressured Pilate for Jesus' crucifixion and Barabbas's release. In light of that fact, note the number of times in the balance of the sermon Peter used the words "you" or "your." This was a pointed condemnation of those who stood before him: *You* handed him over. . . .*You* rejected. . . .*You* killed. . . . what *you* did to Jesus . . . Now turn from *your* sins.

The term "gave him up" occurs twice in the Greek text of Isaiah 53:12, the Servant-Messiah passage from the Old Testament. These are also the words used of the Father giving his Son to die for the sins of the world (Romans 8:32) and of the Son in giving himself (Galatians 2:20).

GOOD INTENTIONS

The Jews (especially the Pharisees) of Jesus' day are often portrayed as sinister and villainous. This is an unfortunate (and inaccurate) representation. They lived moral lives. They were diligent students and teachers of Scripture. They were highly respected in their culture. When a charismatic carpenter came on the scene with his revolutionary teachings and unorthodox practices, he threatened a whole culture. He made claims that were hard to swallow (given the Jews' religious traditions and presuppositions). Fearing a reprisal by the ruling Romans and also that the populace might be led astray by such a popular false teacher, the Jewish rulers felt they had no choice but to squelch this Jesus of Nazareth. They were only trying to preserve their way of life. Ironically, they killed the very one who had come to give them life! The book of Proverbs says it well: "There is a path before each person that seems right, but it ends in death" (16:25 NLT).

3:14 **"You rejected this holy, righteous one and instead demanded the release of a murderer."**NLT Peter called Jesus the *holy (hagios)* and *righteous (dikaios)* one. This clearly identified Jesus' equality with God. But the Jews had *rejected* him. The horrendous nature of their deed was made all the worse by the contrasting character of the *murderer* (Barabbas) whose release they had *demanded.*

3:15 **"You killed the author of life, but God raised him from the dead. We are witnesses of this."**NIV Not only had the Jews rejected him, but they had *killed* him. With a ring of irony, Peter stated that they had killed *the author of life,* the one who had written the book on life, the Creator (John 1:1-4; Colossians 1:16). The term "author" *(archegon)* means the "prince, leader, pioneer, originator," a champion who is victorious in behalf of those whom he represents. The sense of outrage here is heightened by the use of three strong contrasts in three straight verses: (1) 3:13—the Jews had delivered Jesus to be killed, though Pilate had decided to free him; (2) 3:14—they had rejected Jesus, and requested the release of a murderer; (3) 3:15—they had killed Jesus, though *God raised him from the dead.* The one the Jews had killed was presently alive, raised by God himself! Peter and hundreds of others were *witnesses of this* (see 1 Corinthians 15:5-8).

3:16 **"The name of Jesus has healed this man—and you know how lame he was before. Faith in Jesus' name has caused this healing before your very eyes."**NLT Peter referred to the miracle that had gotten everyone's attention. As before, he took no credit for himself or his companions but, instead, credited the *name of Jesus* with the healing. As in his earlier use of the "name," Peter was referring to the full identity of Jesus. Jesus was the Healer. The NIV translates the final phrase of this verse as "this complete healing"; this comes from the Greek term *holoklerian.* In context, it denotes the thoroughness of the restoration of the man's crippled legs.

THE REQUIREMENT OF REPENTANCE

John the Baptist prepared the way for Jesus by preaching repentance. The apostles' message of salvation also included the call to repentance—acknowledging personal sin and turning away from it. Many people want the benefits of being identified with Christ without admitting their own disobedience and turning from sin. The key to forgiveness is confessing sin and turning from it (see 2:38).

When we repent, God promises not only to wipe out our sins but to bring spiritual refreshment. At first repentance may seem painful because it is hard to give up certain sins. But God will give us a better way. As Hosea promised, "Let us acknowledge the LORD; let us press on to acknowledge him. As surely as the sun rises, he will appear; he will come to us like the winter rains, like the spring rains that water the earth" (Hosea 6:3 NIV). Do you feel a need to be refreshed?

3:17-18 **"And now, friends, I know that you acted in ignorance, as did also your rulers. In this way God fulfilled what he had foretold through all the prophets, that his Messiah would suffer."**NRSV The concluding ten verses record Peter's plea to his audience to make a change. Having begun his message with strong words of condemnation, Peter took a more appeasing tone, calling them *friends* (*adelphoi*—literally, "brothers"). He acknowledged that their actions were done *in ignorance,* as were the actions of their *rulers* (see also 17:30; Ephesians 4:18; 1 Peter 1:14).

The phrase "had foretold through all the prophets, that his Messiah would suffer" probably refers to such prophecies as Psalm 22, Isaiah 50:6, and Isaiah 53:1-12. The Jews had not expected a suffering Messiah; instead, they had anticipated a great ruler, a conquering king. When he arrived as a lowly carpenter and then died a criminal's death, they missed it. But Peter explained that it wasn't too late. They may have acted in ignorance, but now they could understand that Jesus was exactly what the Messiah had been prophesied to be.

3:19 **"Now turn from your sins and turn to God, so you can be cleansed of your sins."**NLT They had rejected, despised, and killed Jesus, but they could still *turn* from their sins, *turn to God,* and *be cleansed.* They could change their minds about Jesus. The words "turn from your sins" are the standard Greek term *(metanoeo)* for repentance. The verb means to turn away from a former way of life and toward a new way of life.

The term "cleansed" *(exaleiphthenai)* is often used in Greek as a figure of speech, meaning to erase, especially of writing. In this case the "eraser" was God, and the "writing" was a list of their sins—not just their sins of killing the author of life, but *all* their sins (see Psalm 103:12; Isaiah 1:18).

WHAT'S ON YOUR LIST?

What would God have in writing down your list of sins? That list, in the words of Peter here, can be totally wiped out, erased, cleansed. God doesn't save your list for some future time when he might want to resurface your failures. They are wiped out, separated from us as far as east is from west (Psalm 103:12), a scarlet list made white as snow (Isaiah 1:18). That's the power of the Cross. Every person who ever lived has such a list. To everyone is made the offer of divine "erasing." And to all we must, with Peter, make the offer: "Turn from your sins and turn to God." Forgiveness is available for all, at the foot of the cross.

3:20-21 **"Then wonderful times of refreshment will come from the presence of the Lord, and he will send Jesus your Messiah to you again. For he must remain in heaven until the time for the final restoration of all things, as God promised long ago through his prophets."**NLT The "turning" of 3:19 promises two results: (1) the coming of *wonderful times of refreshment,* and (2) the return of *Jesus your Messiah to you again.* In other words, the repentance of Peter's audience would have a part in bringing in the marvelous events of the end times. The expressions "times of refreshment" and "the time for the final restoration of all things" are unique to the New Testament. The word for "restoration" *(apokatastaseos)* means to return something to its original state. It is used of restorative healing (Matthew 12:13; Luke 6:10) and pictures the Messiah's work (Malachi 4:5-6; Mark 9:12; Matthew 17:11; Acts 1:6). Peter explained that a national restoration could happen if the Jews would turn from their sin and to God by accepting Jesus as their long-awaited Messiah.

While hotly debated among the scholars, this "final restoration" likely refers to the final era of salvation—the Second Coming, the promised coming kingdom of God, the Last Judgment, and the removal of sin from the world. It appears from Peter's words here that church history would have been quite different if Israel had recognized Jesus Christ as the Messiah.

3:22-23 "For Moses said, 'The Lord your God will raise up for you a prophet like me from among your own people; you must listen to everything he tells you. Anyone who does not listen to him will be completely cut off from among his people.'"NIV This quote from Moses in Deuteronomy 18:15 refers to Christ. The Messiah would come with deliverance, just as Moses had. Most Jews thought that Joshua was this prophet predicted by Moses. Peter explained that the *prophet . . . from among your own people* was Jesus Christ. Jesus had fulfilled this prophecy, for he was their long-awaited Messiah! Moses had warned the people that they should *listen to everything he [the Messiah]* would tell them. Those who refused to listen would be *completely cut off* from the true people of God—the believers.

HEARING VS. LISTENING

In ancient times Moses had spoken of the prophet (the Messiah) who would come one day. Moses urged the Jewish people to listen to this one sent from God. Both the Hebrew (Deuteronomy 18:15, 19) and the Greek words (Acts 3:22-23) translated "listen" mean more than just receiving auditory signals with one's ears. The words contain the additional idea of hearing with a view toward obeying. What is your posture when the Word of God is preached or presented? Do you hear it only? Does the message go "in one ear and out the other"? Or do you listen with the intention of being a doer of the Word (James 1:22)? Let the words of Christ lodge in your heart and change the way you live.

3:24 "Indeed, all the prophets from Samuel on, as many as have spoken, have foretold these days."NIV The prophet *Samuel* lived during the transition between the judges and the kings of Israel, and he was the first in a succession of prophets. Samuel had anointed David as king and had spoken clearly of the establishment of David's kingdom (1 Samuel 13:14; 15:28; 16:13; 28:17; see also 2 Samuel 7:12-16). Peter wanted his audience to come to grips with the fact that from the inception of the prophetic office down through the whole order of the prophets, *all* had spoken of *these days,* which had found their ultimate fulfillment in Jesus Christ.

3:25 **"You are the children of those prophets, and you are included in the covenant God promised to your ancestors. For God said to Abraham, 'Through your descendants all the families on earth will be blessed.'"**NLT The Jews to whom Peter was speaking were *the children of those prophets.* God had promised *Abraham* that he would bless the world through Abraham's descendants, the Jewish race (Genesis 12:3), from which the Messiah would come. They were *included in the covenant,* for God intended the Jewish nation to be a separate and holy nation that would teach the world about God, introduce the Messiah, and then carry on his work in the world. Through them, because of the Messiah coming from them, *all the families on earth* would be *blessed.* Israel had been given the promise of one who would come from the line of Abraham and sit forever on David's throne. Peter was saying as clearly as possible to his Jewish brothers: "The long-expected Messiah has already come. God promised him to Abraham. Moses reaffirmed the promise. Samuel, the first prophet, and every single prophet who followed him, spoke of this coming Messiah. Now he has come and you are in danger of missing him." The covenant with Abraham helped motivate the church to carry out the worldwide mission Christ had given to it.

3:26 **"When God raised up his servant, he sent him first to you people of Israel, to bless you by turning each of you back from your sinful ways."**NLT In Greek, the phrase "first to you" stands at the start of the sentence; it is placed there for emphasis. The message of salvation came first to the *people of Israel,* the descendants of Abraham, Moses, Samuel, and the prophets. They—of all people—should have known the prophecies and recognized him when he came. They were to have been the prime beneficiaries of the blessings of the covenant.

Notice that the primary nature of the blessing was to turn them *back from [their] sinful ways.* Christ's work, at its core, is to turn lives around, taking individuals on sinful paths and turning them from those paths to the path of blessing. Israel had every reason to turn to Jesus—history, heritage, bloodline, centuries of warning from prophetic messengers. And they had not recognized him.

GOODNESS
Peter concluded his message with the statement that God wants to turn people away from sin in order to "bless" them. This is exactly the opposite of what many believe. They consider God the ultimate party pooper, a kind of cosmic killjoy who wants to turn people from sin in order to make them miserable. Why do we tend to think like this? Because of the craftiness of our enemy. The consummate liar, he has—since the beginning of the human race—been successful in tempting us to doubt God's goodness. If God withholds something from us—fruit in a place called Eden, illicit sex, etc.—it must be because he is trying to deny us some secret blessing. That is how we reason if we doubt the goodness of God. But if we embrace the truth that God is good, then we acknowledge that God prohibits certain things in order to bless our lives "infinitely more than we would ever dare to ask or hope" (Ephesians 3:20 NLT). Don't let Satan cause you to doubt God's goodness.

Acts 4

PETER AND JOHN BEFORE THE COUNCIL / 4:1-22

While Acts is a record of powerful sermons, astounding miracles, and the rapid spread of the Christian church throughout the world, it is also a reminder of the truth of spiritual warfare. Whenever believers are seeking to impact their culture, whenever the gospel is preached in power, wherever the church is growing and making inroads, the enemy stirs up fierce opposition. Persecution is the proof that the gates of hell are being stormed and that spiritual captives are being set free.

In these verses the same authorities who had tried and killed a "dangerous" rabbi from Nazareth (named Jesus) now sought to intimidate and silence his followers.

4:1 **While Peter and John were speaking to the people, the leading priests, the captain of the Temple guard, and some of the Sadducees came over to them.**[NLT] Evidently a large crowd had gathered at Solomon's Colonnade (3:11) where *Peter and John were speaking to the people.* This crowd drew the attention of the religious leaders, so they, too, *came over* to see what was going on. The *leading priests* (also called "chief priests") were mostly *Sadducees.* The Sadducees were members of a small but powerful Jewish religious sect who believed that the Pentateuch alone (Genesis through Deuteronomy) was God's Word. Because they could find no evidence of resurrection in those writings, they refused to believe in resurrection of the dead. (However, Jesus had an answer for them—see Matthew 22:23-33.) Sadducees were, for the most part, descendants of the Hasmoneans, who were the ruling party from the time of the Maccabees to the rule of Herod (142–63 B.C.). They were the religious leaders who stressed cooperation with the Roman Empire. They also rejected the idea of a coming Messiah, believing that he was an ideal, not a person who would intervene in history. The Sadducees, the Pharisees, and the teachers of the law made up the three main Jewish religious leadership "parties." For a description of these groups, see the chart titled "Prominent Jewish Religious and Political Groups."

PROMINENT JEWISH RELIGIOUS & POLITICAL GROUPS

Name and Selected References	*Description*	*Agreement with Jesus*	*Disagreement with Jesus*
PHARISEES Matthew 5:20 Matthew 23:1-6 Luke 6:2 Luke 7:36-47	Strict group of religious Jews who advocated obedience to the most minute portions of the Jewish law and traditions. Very influential in the synagogues.	Respect for the law, belief in the resurrection of the dead, committed to obeying God's will.	Rejected Jesus' claim to be Messiah because he did not follow all their traditions and he associated with notoriously wicked people.
SADDUCEES Matthew 3:7 Matthew 16:11-12 Mark 12:18	Wealthy, upper-class, Jewish priestly party. Rejected the authority of the Bible beyond the five books of Moses. Profited from business in the temple. They, along with the Pharisees, were one of the two major parties of the Jewish High Council.	Showed great respect for the five books of Moses, as well as the sanctity of the temple.	Denied the resurrection of the dead. Thought the temple could also be used as a place to transact business.
TEACHERS OF RELIGIOUS LAW Matthew 7:29 Mark 2:6 Mark 2:16	Professional interpreters of the law—who especially emphasized the traditions. Many teachers of religious law were Pharisees.	Respect for the law, committed to obeying God.	Denied Jesus' authority to reinterpret the law. Rejected Jesus as Messiah because he did not obey all of their traditions.

The *captain of the Temple guard* was also a high-ranking Sadducee. He was the leader of the guards who ensured order in and around the temple. The captain was considered second in authority only to the high priest himself. The temple guard had arrested Jesus in the Garden of Gethsemane (see Luke 22:52-54).

4:2 They were greatly disturbed because the apostles were teaching the people and proclaiming in Jesus the resurrection of the dead.[NIV] Imagine these Sadducees, who did not believe in the resurrection of the dead, listening to Peter *proclaiming,* right there in the temple, *the resurrection of the dead.* No wonder *they were greatly disturbed!* "Disturbed" can also be translated "annoyed, irritated,

Name and Selected References	Description	Agreement with Jesus	Disagreement with Jesus
SUPPORTERS OF HEROD Matthew 22:16 Mark 3:6 Mark 12:13	A Jewish political party of King Herod's supporters.	Unknown. In the Gospels, they tried to trap Jesus with questions and plotted to kill him.	Afraid of Jesus causing political instability. They saw Jesus as a threat to their political future at a time when they were trying to regain from Rome some of their lost political power.
ZEALOTS Luke 6:15 Acts 1:14	A fiercely dedicated group of Jewish patriots determined to end Roman rule in Israel.	Concerned about the future of Israel. Believed in the Messiah but did not recognize Jesus as the one sent by God.	Believed that the Messiah must be a political leader who would deliver Israel from Roman occupation.

incensed." Peter and John were refuting one of the Sadducees' fundamental beliefs and thus threatening their authority as religious teachers. In addition, with their *teaching,* the apostles were upsetting the status quo and perhaps would bring the wrath of Rome (that had almost happened a few weeks earlier with Jesus—Luke 23). The religious leaders had thought this uprising would be finished with the death of its leader, so it disturbed them to find Jesus' followers teaching the people in the temple.

THE IMPORTANCE OF THE RESURRECTION
Whenever the early church talked about Jesus, they strongly emphasized his resurrection. Why? For a number of important reasons. According to the apostle Paul in 1 Corinthians 15, the resurrection of Christ means that he is the Son of God and that his word can be trusted. It means that his sacrifice for sin was acceptable to God, so we can be completely forgiven. It means that our Savior is alive and active, able to help us in times of need. It also means that one day we, too, will conquer death. The Christian faith rests on the basic fact of the empty tomb. Don't neglect this essential part of the gospel when you share your faith with others.

4:3 They arrested them and, since it was already evening, jailed them until morning.[NLT] Even though Israel was under Roman rule, the Sadducees had almost unlimited power over the temple grounds. Thus, they were able to arrest Peter and John for no reason other than teaching something that contradicted their beliefs.

Assuming that the healing of the crippled man occurred as Peter and John made their way to the 3:00 P.M. prayer time (3:1) and that Peter's sermon to the gathered masses followed this miracle, it would have been too late in the day *(already evening)* to gather the necessary religious leaders to hold an official inquiry. Perhaps the night in jail was intended to "sober them up," to give them time to reflect on their actions and to recant.

4:4 But many of the people who heard their message believed it, so that the number of believers totaled about five thousand men, not counting women and children.[NLT] The Jewish religious leaders were able to arrest (at least for one night) Christ's messengers; they could not, however, stop the spread of Christ's message. The miraculous healing of the crippled man in such a visible place, combined with the powerful preaching of the apostles, sent spiritual shock waves through Jerusalem. This brought the total number of believers to *about five thousand men, not counting women and children.* God was mightily using Peter, for at his first sermon, three thousand people had become believers (2:41)! Estimates of Jerusalem's population at this time range from twenty-five thousand to eighty-five thousand. Josephus recorded that there were a total of six thousand Pharisees in Palestine. Thus, a total of five thousand Jewish Christian men (not counting women and children) was a very high percentage of the population!

RISKS AND REWARDS
Peter and John shared the gospel and ended up in jail. That's not likely to happen to Western believers today. Still, there are risks in trying to win others to Christ—being misunderstood, rejected, ridiculed, ostracized, stared at, whispered about. We might be willing to face a night in jail if it would bring five thousand people to Christ, but shouldn't we also be willing to suffer for the sake of one lost soul? What do *you* risk in witnessing? Whatever the risks, realize that nothing done for God is ever wasted. And no matter how great the risk, the reward will certainly be greater.

4:5 The next day the council of all the rulers and elders and teachers of religious law met in Jerusalem.[NLT] The *rulers, elders,* and *teachers of religious law* made up the Sanhedrin, or Jewish *council*—the same Council that had condemned Jesus to death (Luke 22:66). This Council acted as the ruling government of Israel. They handled the local problems and religious questions but had to work under Rome's supervision. For crimes that carried capital punishment, they had to obtain Rome's approval. For instance, the Council had condemned Jesus to death, but it could not carry out the sentence; the Roman leader in the area alone had the authority to order an execution. That is why the religious leaders had taken Jesus to Pilate, the Roman leader in the Jerusalem area (Luke 23:1).

The Council had seventy members plus the current high priest, who presided over the group. The Sadducees held a majority in this ruling group. These were the wealthy, intellectual, and powerful men of Jerusalem. Jesus' followers stood before this Council, just as he had.

RELIGIOUS AND LOST
The men gathered to interrogate Peter and John were a "who's who" of the most powerful and prominent religious leaders of Israel. These men knew the Old Testament Scriptures in painstaking detail. They were completely immersed in a world of religious ritual. They could argue theology for hours on end. The only problem was, they were spiritually lost! God, in the person of Jesus Christ, had been in their very presence, and they had missed him. Worse than that, they had killed him! Now they were blindly trying to silence the messengers of Christ. Here is a powerful demonstration of the truth that knowing *about* God is not enough. We must know him in a personal way. Until we encounter God through Christ and humbly receive his forgiveness, all our religious acts count for nothing.

4:6 **Annas the high priest was there, along with Caiaphas, John, Alexander, and other relatives of the high priest.**[NLT] By listing these names, Luke was making the point that opposition to the early church came mostly from the ranks of the Sadducees. In this first trial of the apostles, the powerful Sadducees were well represented. *Annas* had been deposed as high priest by the Romans, who then had appointed *Caiaphas,* Annas's son-in-law, in his place. But because the Jews considered the office of high priest a lifetime position, they still called Annas by that title and gave him respect and authority within the Council. *John, Alexander, and other relatives of the high priest* were also there, supporting the power base of the high priest's office. (Eventually Annas would arrange for all five of his sons, his son-in-law, and one grandson to be appointed to the office of high priest.) Annas and Caiaphas had played significant roles in Jesus' trial (John 18:24, 28). It did not please them that the man whom they thought they had sacrificed for the good of the nation (John 11:49-51) had followers who were just as persistent and who promised to be just as troublesome as he had been.

4:7 **They had Peter and John brought before them and began to question them: "By what power or what name did you do this?"**NIV The Council asked Peter and John *by what power or what name* they had healed the man (see 3:6-7). "By what name" refers to exorcism practices. They wanted to know what formula Peter and John had used. Their concern was more about the apostles' teaching, but they began their questioning with the miracle, for the healed man was there as well (4:14). The actions and words of Peter and John threatened these religious leaders who, for the most part, were more interested in their reputations and positions than in the glory of God.

4:8-10 **Then Peter, filled with the Holy Spirit, said to them: "Rulers and elders of the people! If we are being called to account today for an act of kindness shown to a cripple and are asked how he was healed, then know this, you and all the people of Israel: It is by the name of Jesus Christ of Nazareth, whom you crucified but whom God raised from the dead, that this man stands before you healed."**NIV Jesus had told his disciples, "On my account you will be brought before governors and kings as witnesses to them and to the Gentiles. But when they arrest you, do not worry about what to say or how to say it. At that time you will be given what to say, for it will not be you speaking, but the Spirit of your Father speaking through you" (Matthew 10:18-20 NIV). Peter, the rough ex-fisherman, stood before a room of disapproving, scowling faces and, *filled with the Holy Spirit,* began to speak. There are two kinds of courage: reckless courage that is unaware of the dangers it faces, and the courage that knows the peril and yet is undaunted. Peter's boldness is of the latter variety.

Empowered with supernatural boldness by the Holy Spirit, Peter:

- demonstrated respect for his opponents *(rulers and elders of the people);*
- noted with irony his and John's imprisonment for merely having performed *an act of kindness;*
- called attention to the former *cripple* (he had been either imprisoned with the apostles or brought in to testify);
- attributed the man's healing to *the name of Jesus Christ of Nazareth, whom you crucified but whom God raised from the dead.*

In a few words and a matter of seconds, Peter deftly turned the tables and put the Council on trial!

The Greek word *sozo,* translated *healed* in 4:9 is translated "to be saved" in 4:12. Peter's broad use of the word demonstrated that just as Christ alone is able to restore health physically, so he also is the sole provider of spiritual salvation.

TALKING ABOUT JESUS

As you read through the book of Acts, you discover that the apostles spoke about Christ at every opportunity. It was as natural for them to talk about Jesus as it is for us to talk about a day at work or a vacation at the shore. Why? Because they had personal experience with him. That's the most fundamental truth about witnesses—they *communicate* what they have seen and heard. If Christ is real to us, if he's important to us, if he's first in our hearts and minds, we will be like those first-century believers. We won't be able to keep from talking about him. Does your conversation ever feature matter-of-fact references to what God means to you or what he is doing in your life? Jesus said it best: "Whatever is in your heart determines what you say" (Luke 6:45 NLT).

4:11 "This is the 'stone which was rejected by you builders, which has become the chief cornerstone.'"NKJV Peter quoted a familiar Old Testament passage—Psalm 118:22—and invested it with new meaning. Most Jews regarded their nation, Israel, as the stone chosen by God but rejected by the nations. Here Peter, remembering Christ's own teachings (see Mark 12:10-11; Luke 20:17), identified Jesus Christ of Nazareth as the chief cornerstone. These "stone" passages (see Romans 9:30-33 and 1 Peter 2:7) were important for establishing the supremacy of Christ in apostolic times. Jesus had referred to himself as the *stone which was rejected by* the *builders.* The cornerstone was the most important stone in a building, used as the standard to make sure that the other stones of the building were straight and level. Israel's leadership, like the builders looking for an appropriate cornerstone, would toss Jesus aside because he didn't seem to have the right qualifications. They wanted a political king, not a spiritual one. Yet God's plans will not be thwarted. One day the rejected stone will indeed become *the chief cornerstone,* with all the right qualifications, for Jesus will come as King to inaugurate an unending kingdom. He already had begun a spiritual kingdom as the cornerstone of a brand-new "building," the Christian church (see also 1 Peter 2:7). Jesus' life, teachings, death, and resurrection would be the church's foundation.

Peter made it clear that the "builders" were the Jewish religious leaders and that they had rejected the Messiah ("rejected by you builders"). As long as they scorned Christ, their religious efforts to build a nation would be in vain (see 1 Corinthians 3:11-15). They were missing the most important ingredient. Implied in Peter's words was this exhortation: stop rejecting this one who is both Savior and Messiah!

4:12 "There is salvation in no one else! There is no other name in all of heaven for people to call on to save them."NLT Peter's argument reached a climax. The resurrected Jesus had healed the crippled man physically. That same Jesus, the long-awaited Messiah, can heal all people spiritually. Peter did not compromise or soft-pedal his answer. Salvation does not come from being a descendant of Abraham (Luke 3:8) or by following the law of Moses (John 6:32-33). The clear gospel teaching is that *there is salvation in no one else* but Jesus (John 14:6; 1 Timothy 2:5). How, then, are people saved? By calling on the name of Jesus. It can't get much simpler than that.

ONLY ONE WAY

Many people react negatively to the claim that salvation is found in Christ alone ("There is salvation in no one else!"). "How narrow-minded, exclusive, and arrogant!" is the common charge leveled against Christianity. But two facts are worth remembering: First, this is not something the church arbitrarily decided; it is the specific teaching of Jesus himself (John 14:6). Second, rather than reacting to the phrase, "in no one else," people would be better served to focus on the wonderful promise, "There is salvation." *That* is the good news of the gospel! God has provided a way for sinners to be forgiven and granted entrance into eternal life! To be sure, it *is* a narrow way (Luke 13:24), but it is a way nonetheless. If your cruise ship is sinking, it is foolish to remain on deck criticizing the emergency evacuation plan. The wiser course of action is to take a seat in the nearest lifeboat!

4:13 The members of the council were amazed when they saw the boldness of Peter and John, for they could see that they were ordinary men who had had no special training. They also recognized them as men who had been with Jesus.NLT Christ had originally chosen the Twelve so that they "might be with him and that he might send them out to preach and to have authority" (Mark 3:14-15 NIV). Here that purpose reached fruition. Peter and John, fishermen by trade, had never received formal theological or rhetorical training in the rabbinical schools; they were *ordinary men who had had no special training.* Yet their testimony before *the members of the council* was astonishing. Peter and

John were bold, composed, confident, and undaunted in their defense. As the apostles stood there with the healed cripple, speaking with authority, the members of the Council *recognized them as men who had been with Jesus.* Their boldness was possible only because they were filled with the Holy Spirit (4:8; cf. 4:29, 31; 9:27-28; 13:46; 14:3; 18:26; 19:8; 26:26; 28:31).

THE DIFFERENCE
Knowing that Peter and John were unschooled, the Council was amazed at what being with Jesus had done for them. Only weeks before, they had been timid, wishy-washy bumblers. Now they were fearless, confident, articulate, and passionate spokesmen. A changed life convinces people of Christ's power. One of your greatest testimonies is the difference others see in your life and attitudes since you have believed in Christ. What are the most obvious changes Christ has brought about in your life?

4:14-15 But since the man who had been healed was standing right there among them, the council had nothing to say. So they sent Peter and John out of the council chamber and conferred among themselves.[NLT] In the same way that the words and works of Jesus had often left the Jewish leaders speechless (Mark 12:34), the Council had *nothing to say* in the face of this supernatural healing and preaching. The *council chamber* was cleared so that the leaders could decide on a course of action.

How Luke knew what went on in this closed discussion has been debated. Possibly a sympathizer among the Council "leaked" the information. Perhaps Gamaliel, a member of the Council, told his student Paul, who later told Luke (5:34; 22:3).

REJECTING REJECTION
Although the evidence was overwhelming and irrefutable (changed lives and a healed man), the religious leaders refused to believe in Christ and continued to try to suppress the truth. We shouldn't be surprised if some people reject us and our positive witness for Christ. When hearts are hard and minds are closed (blinded by Satan—see 2 Corinthians 4:4), even the clearest and most passionate presentation of the facts won't be heard. But this doesn't mean we should give up. We must pray fervently for those who are opposed to the truth.

4:16-17 "What should we do with these men?" they asked each other. "We can't deny they have done a miraculous sign, and everybody in Jerusalem knows about it. But perhaps we can stop them from spreading their propaganda. We'll warn them not

to speak to anyone in Jesus' name again."NLT The Council was in a quandary. The apostles had performed an undeniable, widely publicized *miraculous sign.* The masses were gravitating toward this new sect. How could the religious leaders save face (in light of the obviously healed man), discourage further teaching and healing in the name of Jesus, and preserve the status quo? Their solution was to order the apostles *not to speak to anyone in Jesus' name again.* It seems as though they thought that their power and position could convince these men to be silent. Unfortunately, they completely ignored the miraculous sign and what it meant, preferring instead to attempt to stop the apostles from doing any more such good deeds. There is a certain irony in the Council's forbidding the apostles to speak in Jesus' name, because it was in Jesus' name that the man had been healed.

> The trouble with so many people is that the voice of their neighbors sounds louder in their ears than the voice of God.
> *H. G. Wells*

4:18 **So they called them and ordered them not to speak or teach at all in the name of Jesus.**NRSV Because Peter and John had not broken any laws and were enjoying popular support among the people, the Jewish Council's best attempt at damage control was to summon the apostles and try to scare them into silence with vague warnings. They were simply *ordered . . . not to speak or teach at all in the name of Jesus.* Jewish law specified that at the first instance of wrong or illegal action, the guilty were to be warned and released. The second time they did wrong, they were to be beaten with rods (5:28, 40). With this official order, the Council would have legal grounds to impose more punishment in the future should the apostles choose to disobey.

FEAR IN WITNESSING

Sometimes believers can be afraid to share their faith in Christ, because people might feel uncomfortable and might reject them. In contrast, Peter and John's zeal for the Lord was so strong that they could not keep quiet, even when threatened. If your courage to witness for God has weakened, pray that your boldness may increase. Remember Jesus' promise, "If anyone acknowledges me publicly here on earth, I will openly acknowledge that person before my Father in heaven" (Matthew 10:32 NLT).

4:19-20 **But Peter and John replied, "Judge for yourselves whether it is right in God's sight to obey you rather than God. For we cannot help speaking about what we have seen and heard."**NIV Commanded by Christ to be witnesses (1:8) and utterly convinced of the truth of the gospel, *Peter and John* announced their rejection of any such ban on speaking in the name of Jesus. In effect, the apostles' response accused the Council of being at odds with the will of God. The apostles already knew the answer, so they asked the Council members to judge for themselves whether they should obey the Council's orders or God's. This principle of obeying God rather than people is a major Christian ethical principle (see commentary at 5:29).

These men had indeed "been with Jesus" (4:13), and he had completely transformed their lives. They had lived with him; they had witnessed his resurrection; they had experienced the infilling of the Holy Spirit. And so they said, *"We cannot help speaking about what we have seen and heard."* To have obeyed the Council's command would have been to disobey God.

CREDIBILITY
What if, when threatened by the Sanhedrin, the disciples had abruptly changed their story and curtailed their witness? How credible would the gospel have been after that? The fact that they stood strong in the face of severe persecution gave their message a lot more credibility. Likewise, when we make the daily decision to do what is right, when we stand up boldly for Christ against a hostile crowd, people take notice. They look closer at our lives and listen more carefully to our message.

4:21-22 **After further threats they let them go. They could not decide how to punish them, because all the people were praising God for what had happened. For the man who was miraculously healed was over forty years old.**[NIV] Stunned by the courage of Peter and John and fearful of their popularity among the masses, the religious leaders could do nothing more than give *further threats* and then *let them go.* One would think that these "religious" leaders would be thrilled that the people were *praising God for what had happened.* But that was not the case. Luke's parenthetical comment on the man's age heightens the significance of the miracle—the man had been healed of a forty-year-old condition.

THE BELIEVERS PRAY FOR BOLDNESS / 4:23-31

After being sternly threatened by the same group of men who had orchestrated the crucifixion of Jesus only six weeks earlier, the followers of Jesus gathered and prayed. Their prayers weren't for an end to persecution or for easy times. Rather, the believers asked God for the boldness necessary to continue proclaiming the good news about Jesus. God gave them what every church needs: a reminder of his power and a fresh infilling of the Holy Spirit.

4:23 As soon as they were freed, Peter and John found the other believers and told them what the leading priests and elders had said.[NLT] Upon their release, the apostles *found the other believers* and shared with them the details of their experience with *the leading priests and elders* who made up the Council.

4:24 When they heard this, they raised their voices together in prayer to God. "Sovereign Lord," they said, "you made the heaven and the earth and the sea, and everything in them."[NIV] In the face of this recent persecution, the believers spontaneously joined *together in prayer* to acknowledge God's sovereign control of all things (see Psalm 146:6; Isaiah 37:16). The Greek word *despota,* translated "Sovereign Lord," is the word from which we derive our English "despot." Used infrequently in the New Testament (Luke 2:29; 2 Peter 2:1; Jude 1:4; Revelation 6:10), this term calls to mind God's powerful and absolute control. The believers undoubtedly found comfort in remembering that the God they served had made *the heaven and the earth and the sea, and everything in them.* This appeal to the God of creation shows that God, who had power to create the universe, will have power over their enemies. Everything in heaven and earth is subject to God and his will.

> Pray for great things, expect great things, work for great things, but above all—*pray.* *R. A. Torrey*

PRAYING THROUGH PROBLEMS

Notice how the believers prayed. First they praised God; then they told God their specific problem and asked for his help. They did not ask God to remove the problem but to help them deal with it. This is a model for us to follow when we pray. We may ask God to remove our problems, and he may choose to do so. But we must recognize that often he chooses to leave our problems in place and then give us the strength and courage to deal with them.

4:25-26 "You spoke by the Holy Spirit through the mouth of your servant, our father David: 'Why do the nations rage and the peoples plot in vain? The kings of the earth take their stand and the rulers gather together against the Lord and against his Anointed One.'"[NIV] The group's prayer (probably voiced by a single individual) cited Psalm 2, a messianic hymn written by King David. Psalm 2 describes the rebellion of the nations and the coming of Christ to establish his eternal reign. David may have written these words during a conspiracy against Israel by leaders of some of the surrounding nations. Chosen and anointed by God, David knew that God would fulfill his promise to bring the Messiah into the world through his bloodline (2 Samuel 7:16; 1 Chronicles 17:11-12). This psalm is also cited in other places in the New Testament (see 13:33; Hebrews 1:5-6; 5:5; Revelation 2:26-27; 12:5; 19:15) because of its prophetic description of Jesus, the Messiah.

The believers saw the Jewish leaders' opposition to Jesus (and to them, his appointed representatives) as fulfilling this ancient prophecy. What irony that the Jewish rulers themselves took the place of the raging Gentile nations and became the object of the church's mission. Jesus is identified both here and again in 4:27 as the *Anointed One*—God's Messiah. The raging *nations* are paralleled with the Gentiles, the *peoples* with Israel. The *kings of the earth* compare to Herod, and the *rulers* are represented by Pontius Pilate, as noted in the following verse.

4:27 **"Indeed Herod and Pontius Pilate met together with the Gentiles and the people of Israel in this city to conspire against your holy servant Jesus, whom you anointed."**[NIV] In fulfillment of the prophecy in Psalm 2, "kings" and "rulers" had gathered against God's Anointed One. *Herod* was Herod Antipas, appointed by the Romans to rule over the territory of Galilee. *Pontius Pilate* was the Roman governor over Judea who had bowed to pressure from the mob of *Gentiles and the people of Israel* in Jerusalem. All of these had conspired against Jesus, God's *anointed.*

When Jesus was brought to trial, the Jewish Council had, without concern for justice or their own laws, found a way to sentence him to death. But they could not carry out capital punishment—the Romans had to do that. So the religious leaders had taken Jesus to Pilate in order to gain the death penalty and have it carried out. Pilate, at first, had not wanted to execute Jesus, because he could not find any crime that Jesus had committed. After Pilate had heard that Jesus was from Galilee, he had promptly sent him to be judged by Herod, tetrarch of Galilee, who was in Jerusalem for the Passover celebration. Herod, however, had only mocked Jesus and sent him back to Pilate. By this time mobs had formed calling for Jesus' death. (Read Matthew 26:57–27:26; Mark 14:53–15:15; Luke 22:66–23:24; John 18:12–19:16.) For more on Herod, see the chart "The Herod Family" on page 417 [25:21-22].

4:28 **"In fact, everything they did occurred according to your eternal will and plan."**[NLT] While it seemed that Satan had gotten the upper hand when the Son of God was crucified on the cross, in reality, *everything . . . occurred according to [God's] eternal will and plan.* The believers declared that God is the sovereign Lord of all events; he rules history to fulfill his purpose. What his will determines, his power carries out. No army, government, or council can stand in God's way.

4:29-30 "Now, Lord, consider their threats and enable your servants to speak your word with great boldness. Stretch out your hand to heal and perform miraculous signs and wonders through the name of your holy servant Jesus."NIV Common in the Old Testament are imprecatory prayers (requests for God to bring swift and harsh justice on the enemies of his people)—Psalms 7, 35, 40, 55, 58, 59, 69, 79, 109, 137, 139, 144. Here the apostles prayed not for divine vengeance but that God would *consider* the *threats* that had been leveled against them by the Jewish leadership. The believers did not pray that God would remove the threats, take away the possibility of persecution, or even protect them. Instead, they prayed that God would *enable* the believers, his *servants,* to continue to witness *with great boldness,* no matter what. They also asked for displays of power to confirm their message—*stretch out your hand to heal and perform miraculous signs and wonders.* These believers were not afraid to ask God for great power and wonders in order that his name would be glorified.

BIBLICAL BOLDNESS
Boldness is not reckless impulsiveness. Boldness requires courage to press on through our fears and do what we know is right. How can we be more bold? Like the disciples, we need to pray with others for that courage. To gain boldness, you can:
- pray for the power of the Holy Spirit to give you courage;
- look for opportunities in your family and neighborhood to talk about Christ;
- realize that rejection, social discomfort, and embarrassment are not necessarily persecution; and
- start where you are by being bolder in small ways.

4:31 After this prayer, the building where they were meeting shook, and they were all filled with the Holy Spirit. And they preached God's message with boldness.NLT God's answer of the apostles' prayer was both swift and powerful. When the building *shook,* the believers realized that God had not only heard their prayer, but he also was pleased with it. The believers received a fresh filling *with the Holy Spirit,* which renewed their courage to go out and preach *God's message with boldness,* just as they had requested (4:29).

THE BELIEVERS SHARED THEIR POSSESSIONS / 4:32-37

The final verses of chapter 4 provide a glimpse into the inner workings of the early church. The first-century Christians enjoyed a sense of closeness and unity that caused the world to sit up and take notice. "Behold how they love one another!" was the startled response, as those outside the church watched believers care for one another and share with one another in extravagant ways. It's one thing to talk of loving others; it's quite another to sell one's valuable possessions and give the proceeds to those less fortunate. Yet that kind of generosity was common in the early church. And that kind of selflessness is the essence of true fellowship. Fellowship in its purest form invites sharing.

4:32 **All the believers were of one heart and mind, and they felt that what they owned was not their own; they shared everything they had.**[NLT] In summarizing the daily activities of the early church, Luke noted the believers' unselfishness. Surely the church's spiritual unity *(all the believers were of one heart and mind)* prompted this material generosity. No one was required to contribute to the needs of others; this "communal purse" was voluntary. Yet the believers willingly *shared everything they had,* not holding tightly to possessions, for *they felt that what they owned was not their own.*

The early church considered itself to be the "righteous remnant" of Israel, spoken of so often in the prophets. Isaiah wrote, "Once more a remnant of the house of Judah will take root below and bear fruit above. For out of Jerusalem will come a remnant, and out of Mount Zion a band of survivors. The zeal of the LORD Almighty will accomplish this" (Isaiah 37:31-32 NIV). See also Jeremiah 6:9; 31:7; Micah 7:18. These people were Jewish Christians, so they had learned the Scriptures. They may have desired to follow God's law as recorded in Deuteronomy 15:4, "There should be no poor among you" (NLT).

Differences of opinion are inevitable among human personalities and can actually be helpful if handled well. But spiritual unity is essential—loyalty, commitment, and love for God and his Word. Without spiritual unity, the church could not survive. Paul wrote 1 Corinthians to urge the church in Corinth toward greater unity.

The early church was able to share possessions and property as a result of the unity brought by the Holy Spirit working in and through the believers' lives. This way of living is different from communism because the sharing was voluntary, didn't involve all private property but only as much as was needed, and was not a membership requirement in order to be a part of the church. The spiritual unity and generosity of these early believers attracted others to them. This organizational structure is not a biblical command, but it offers vital principles for us to follow.

FAMILY SHARING
Since none of these first-century believers felt that what they had was their own, they were able to give and share, eliminating poverty among them. Those with plenty helped those who were in need. How do you feel about your possessions? We should adopt the attitude that everything we have belongs to God (Psalm 24:1), comes from God (James 1:17), and is to be used for his glory.

4:33 **With great power the apostles continued to testify to the resurrection of the Lord Jesus, and much grace was upon them all.**[NIV] Ignoring the threats of the Jewish ruling Council (4:18), the apostles *continued to testify to the resurrection of the Lord Jesus.* As a result, the entire church experienced much "grace" (a word found frequently in the book of Acts—see 6:8; 11:23; 13:43; 14:3, 26; 15:11, 40; 18:27; 20:24, 32). Here the idea may be that they experienced God's grace together with the favor of the people. *Much grace was upon them all* refers to God's favor and blessing. God worked powerfully among them (see 6:8) to empower their witness and to meet their material needs. Jesus had told his disciples, "Your love for one another will prove to the world that you are my disciples" (John 13:35 NLT). As the outside world saw the believers' generosity with one another, their care for the needy, and their powerful witness, they were drawn to the Lord Jesus.

4:34-35 **There was no poverty among them, because people who owned land or houses sold them and brought the money to the apostles to give to others in need.**[NLT] So widespread was the generosity of the Jerusalem believers that *there was no poverty among them.* Lavish gifts from the sale of land or houses were brought to the apostles for distribution *to others in need.* Such gifts were exceptional expressions of social concern for those in need. These good times, however, would not last. A famine (see the prophecy of Agabus in 11:28) would eventually result in the Jerusalem church becoming dependent on the gifts of believers in Asia (see Romans 15:25-28; Galatians 2:10).

4:36-37 **For instance, there was Joseph, the one the apostles nicknamed Barnabas (which means "Son of Encouragement"). He was from the tribe of Levi and came from the island of Cyprus. He sold a field he owned and brought the money to the apostles for those in need.**[NLT] *Barnabas (Joseph)* is introduced here because he gave money from the sale of *a field he* *owned* to the apostles to give to those in need. Barnabas would prove to be a respected and important leader in the life of the early church. He was a Levite by birth (a member of the Jewish tribe that carried out temple duties) but a resident of Cyprus. This may explain why he was a landowner (Levites were forbidden to own land in Israel—see Numbers 18:20-24 and Deuteronomy 10:9; 18:1-2). Barnabas would later travel with Paul on Paul's first missionary journey (13:4). John Mark (author of the Gospel of Mark) was his cousin. "Barnabas" means *Son of Encouragement,* and it would prove, over and over, to be most appropriate.

Acts 5

ANANIAS AND SAPPHIRA / 5:1-11

Acts 5:1–8:3 tells of internal and external problems facing the early church. Inside, there were dishonesty (5:1-11) and administrative headaches (6:1-7); outside, the church was being pressured by persecution. While church leaders were careful and sensitive in dealing with the internal problems, there was not much they could do to prevent the external pressures. Through it all, the leaders kept their focus on what was most important—spreading the gospel of Jesus Christ.

The church has always attracted people with impure motives: hucksters who want to profit financially from religion, power mongers seeking control, the self-centered who want to be pampered and cared for, and glory seekers who want to be noticed and affirmed for their "holy" acts.

> God cannot stand unfaithfulness, and pretending to be holy is contemptible mockery.
> *John Calvin*

Ananias and Sapphira, a married couple in the Jerusalem church, fell into this last category. They concocted a plan whereby they hoped to give a little to God but get credit for a lot. Their scheme was dishonest, and God's judgment was swift and severe. As you ponder their story, ask yourself the question, What are my motives for serving and giving?

5:1-2 Now a man named Ananias, together with his wife Sapphira, also sold a piece of property. With his wife's full knowledge he kept back part of the money for himself, but brought the rest and put it at the apostles' feet.[NIV] The word "also" ties back to 4:36-37, where Barnabas was introduced as a man who had "sold a field . . . and brought the money to the apostles for those in need" (4:37 NLT). Chapters 4 and 5 have two examples of sharing. One is Barnabas, the positive example; the second is Ananias and Sapphira, the negative example. At the inception of the church, the practice of selling one's possession in order to give money to those in need showed the believers' willingness to help other believers. Not everyone was liquidating everything, nor was there pressure to do so (Mary, John's mother, still owned her home—12:12). This was a freewill offering, and it appears to have been practiced only here in the early Palestine church.

Barnabas had been introduced in the previous chapter because he would be a major player in the immediate future of the church and an example of a generous giver. Many believe that the positive response of the church to gifts from people like Barnabas became a source of envy for Ananias and Sapphira. Desiring that same esteem from others, *Ananias, together with his wife Sapphira, also sold a piece of property,* desiring to give money to the apostles for the needy. They could have given any amount of the selling price, but because they apparently desired the esteem that Barnabas had received, they pretended to give all the money they had received for the field. Instead, however, they *kept back part of the money.* That would have been their prerogative. The problem was that they were representing what they gave to the apostles as the total selling price. Their initial sin was lying—misrepresenting themselves to the apostles and the believers. They were hypocrites, boasting in a gift when they deceptively held back some for themselves. They also sinned in being selfish. They were serving themselves, not others, by their cover-up. Proverbs 15:8 says, "The LORD hates the sacrifice of the wicked" (NLT).

> Half of the misery in the world comes from trying to *look* instead of to *be* what one is not.
> *George MacDonald*

5:3-4 **Then Peter said, "Ananias, why has Satan filled your heart? You lied to the Holy Spirit, and you kept some of the money for yourself. The property was yours to sell or not sell, as you wished. And after selling it, the money was yours to give away. How could you do a thing like this? You weren't lying to us but to God."**NLT Given insight by the Holy Spirit, Peter saw through Ananias's lie. Apparently involved in the new church, Ananias and Sapphira had succumbed to temptation and allowed *Satan* into their hearts, so they had lied to Peter about the amount of money they were giving. They brought the money from the sale of their property, but *kept some of the money* for themselves. The word for "kept" is the same one used in the Septuagint of Achan who "kept" some of the spoils of Jericho, which ultimately caused a great defeat of Israel (Joshua 7:1-26).

The sin Ananias and Sapphira committed was not stinginess or holding back part of the money. Their sin was lying to God and God's people—saying they gave the whole amount but holding back some for themselves and trying to make themselves appear more generous than they really were. This act was judged severely because dishonesty, greed, and covetousness are destructive in a church. All lying is bad, but when people lie to try to deceive God and other believers about their relationship with him, they destroy their testimony.

BARNABAS DEEDS

Ananias and Sapphira were jealous of Barnabas. The proper response to a "Barnabas deed" is not to become jealous but to follow the example. When we see a Christian life lived correctly, a marriage done right, or children reared successfully, we must not become envious; instead, we should rejoice with them and be motivated to continue in our own task of growing into Christ's likeness.

Ananias and Sapphira had likely been at the worship service when Barnabas had laid his gift at the apostle's feet—a great gift, a great moment. The "wow" of the crowd, who probably knew what the gift was worth and what level of sacrifice it was, had followed. The "buzz" probably followed on the streets, in their small group meetings: "Can you believe Barnabas gave all that away? What a man of God!" Ananias and Sapphira wanted the same reputation, and they lied in order to get it.

In this passage the Holy Spirit is equated with God (one of the great passages in the New Testament on the deity of the Holy Spirit—see Matthew 28:19; 1 Corinthians 6:11; 2 Corinthians 13:13 for other passages that teach of the Spirit's deity).

PURE CHURCH AND HOLY GOD

Some read the account of Ananias and Sapphira being struck down and accuse God of being harsh. "I thought God was supposed to be loving and forgiving. I thought all that wrath stuff was for Old Testament times." With an emphasis on grace and mercy, it's easy to overlook the equally important truth of God's holiness. We must remember that God has not changed (Malachi 3:6). He still hates sin as much as he ever did. And he is especially offended when his own people cut moral corners and try to hide behind the cloak of forgiveness. Thus, sinning Christians were removed from fellowship in order to preserve the purity of the church.

5:5-6 Now when Ananias heard these words, he fell down and died. And great fear seized all who heard of it. The young men came and wrapped up his body, then carried him out and buried him.[NRSV] *When Ananias* realized that Peter knew all about his scheme, *he fell down and died.* The Greek word *ekpsucho* literally means "to breathe one's last, to die" and usually connotes death by divine judgment (see 5:10; 12:23; 1 Corinthians 10:6; 1 John 5:16).

Obviously *fear* would seize any who heard of this event! It is important to note that Peter didn't kill Ananias, nor did he ask the Holy Spirit to kill him. Peter condemned the lying, and the Spirit of God executed judgment. See also 13:11, where Elymas the sorcerer was struck blind at Paul's command.

5:7-8 **About three hours later his wife came in, not knowing what had happened. Peter asked her, "Tell me, is this the price you and Ananias got for the land?" "Yes," she said, "that is the price."**NIV Sapphira showed up *about three hours later . . . not knowing what had happened* to her husband. Peter's questions to Sapphira expose her complicity in the deed. Peter gave her the opportunity to tell the truth, but she told the same lie that her husband had told. In so doing she revealed a hardness of heart that had not been touched by the grace of God.

No man can for any considerable time wear one face to himself and another to the multitude without finally getting bewildered as to which is the true one.
Nathaniel Hawthorne

5:9 **And Peter said, "How could the two of you even think of doing a thing like this—conspiring together to test the Spirit of the Lord? Just outside that door are the young men who buried your husband, and they will carry you out, too."**NLT To *test* God is to see how much one can get away with before God will respond or act according to his Word (see Exodus 17:2; Deuteronomy 6:16; Matthew 4:7; Luke 4:12 for further passages on testing God). The entire direction of this lie by Ananias and Sapphira was wrongheaded, self-serving, church-destroying, and, to put it simply, sinful.

This is reminiscent of God's words to Samuel regarding outward appearances: "The LORD doesn't make decisions the way you do! People judge by outward appearance, but the LORD looks at a person's thoughts and intentions" (1 Samuel 16:7 NLT). Jesus rebuked the Pharisees for a similar sin: "You like to look good in public, but God knows your evil hearts. What this world honors

People who are displeased about God being excessively severe are too arrogant themselves. Rather, we should reflect how one day we will have to stand before God's judgment-seat. If we are trying to deceive God and not be punished for our misdeeds, we are despising his sacred power and majesty.
John Calvin

is an abomination in the sight of God" (Luke 16:15 NLT). Winning the approval of God, not people, should be the motivation for our actions.

Ananias and Sapphira had conspired together to mock God, to lie and think they could get away with it as if God would not know. They had tried to *test the Spirit of the Lord,* referring to the Holy Spirit in the body of believers—specifically the apostles before whom this lie was told (John 16:8).

5:10 **Immediately she fell down at his feet and died. When the young men came in they found her dead, so they carried her out and buried her beside her husband.**NRSV *Immediately* upon hearing Peter's words, Sapphira, *fell down at his feet and died.* As she and Ananias had been joined in their "testing" of God (5:9), so they were joined in death. This is more than just a historical record of events in the early church. This serves as a warning that no one should trifle with the Holy Spirit or take lightly the importance of telling the truth.

While the judgment on Ananias and Sapphira came because of their deceitfulness, the temptation to hoard money selfishly must not be overlooked. Greed corrupts Christians' lives. It can affect families, churches, and ministries of all kinds. We must be very careful in handling money.

We do not know the identities of these *young men;* all that we are told is that they had the grim duty of carrying the bodies out of the room. If nothing else, this would be a serious lesson for these (and other) future members and leaders of the church!

VALUE OF HONESTY
God knew that the church could not survive unless its people had high standards—including honesty. Believers should be honest in private as well as in public. It would be lying to leave something out of a story, tell a half-truth, twist the facts, or invent a falsehood. God warns us against deception. Lying to each other disrupts unity by creating conflicts and destroying trust. It tears down relationships and leads to open warfare in a church. Ephesians 4:25 says, "So put away all falsehood and 'tell your neighbor the truth' because we belong to each other" (NLT). Even though deception is a way of life for many people, God's people must not give in to it!

5:11 **Great fear gripped the entire church and all others who heard what had happened.**NLT This is the first appearance of the term "church" (*ekklesia,* meaning "assembly") in the book of Acts—and notice it is a moment of judgment! It will become the regular word for the universal church and the local church in the remainder of the book (7:38; 8:1; 9:31; 11:22; 13:1; 14:23; 15:22, 41; 16:5; 20:28).

God's judgment on Ananias and Sapphira produced *great fear* among the believers, making them realize how seriously God regards sin in the church. The repetition of the expression of great fear (*phobos megas*—see also in verse 5) emphasized the response of *the entire church* and the surrounding community *(all others who heard what had happened).*

THE FEAR OF GOD
Upon witnessing the holy wrath of God on sinning people, the church (as well as those outside the church) was gripped with great fear! We must be careful, in an age of marketing the church and trying to make the gospel user-friendly, that we do not skim over this truth: God is to be feared! It is true that he is a God rich in love and abounding in mercy. But it is also true that he hates and judges sin. Note the response of everyone in the Bible who ever caught a glimpse of God. The reaction was always one of dread (for example, Isaiah 6:1-6). The good news of the gospel is that because of what Christ has done on our behalf, we can come boldly into the very presence of God (Hebrews 4:16). But let us do so with "deep reverence and fear" (Philippians 2:12 NLT). God is holy!

THE APOSTLES HEAL MANY PEOPLE / 5:12-16

Even as word spread of the sudden deaths of Ananias and Sapphira, the apostles continued to preach boldly about Jesus right in the temple courts. Large crowds continued to gather. Miraculous healings and exorcisms gave credence to the message. Because of the power of God and the faithfulness of his people, the gospel was spreading, taking root, and bearing fruit in lives.

5:12 Meanwhile, the apostles were performing many miraculous signs and wonders among the people. And the believers were meeting regularly at the Temple in the area known as Solomon's Colonnade.NLT *Solomon's Colonnade* was part of the temple complex built by King Herod the Great in an attempt to strengthen his relationship with the Jews. A colonnade is an entrance or porch supported by columns. Jesus taught and performed miracles in the temple many times. When the believers met *regularly at the Temple,* they were undoubtedly in close proximity to the same religious leaders who had conspired to put Jesus to death.

In answer to the apostles' prayer, "Stretch out your hand to heal and perform miraculous signs and wonders" (4:30 NIV), God granted the apostles power to perform *miraculous signs (semeia)* and *wonders (terata).* The miracles were from God, but administered through the hands of the *apostles.* These healings were not random acts of kindness by a benevolent God, but rather sign-miracles intended to convince Jewish onlookers of the credibility of the Christian message and movement.

5:13 **No one else dared join them, even though they were highly regarded by the people.**[NIV] Although many people *highly regarded* the apostles and the other believers, few "outsiders" *dared join them* in the temple or in their faith. According to the Gospel of Luke, the people sided with Jesus until his crucifixion. In Acts, the people (the Jews in Jerusalem in this case) sided with the disciples until the Gentile mission began. The terminology of this verse seems to refer to association on intimate terms—the watching community respected these believers (2:47) but likely found God's direct and obvious work through them to be intimidating. Some may have been afraid to face the same kind of persecution the apostles had just faced (4:17), while others may have feared a fate similar to the one that fell on Ananias and Sapphira. This may simply be a reference to the fact that no more hypocrites or pretenders dared to join the group. Persecution has always had a tendency to separate the curious from the committed, the fakers from the followers, the make-believers from the true believers.

BEING COMMITTED
The early church was blessed by the very presence of God. Undeniable miracles were taking place. The apostles were teaching eternal, life-changing truths. But a large number of people hung back. They refused to join the fellowship, opting instead to watch from a distance. Beware of this reluctance to commit, a natural human tendency. Being part of what God is doing in this world may mean hard work, heavy responsibility, harsh criticism, and possibly even danger. Those who refuse to jump in, however, miss out on untold blessings. They miss the fulfillment they were created to enjoy and settle instead for a mediocre, mundane existence on the spiritual sidelines. When it comes to church, don't be a distant observer. Dive in! Commit! Be a part of something eternal.

5:14 **Yet more than ever believers were added to the Lord, great numbers of both men and women.**[NRSV] In what seems like a contradiction to 5:13, Luke explained that despite many unbelieving Jews hanging back, *more than ever believers were added to the Lord, great numbers of both men and women.* More of the responsive Jews than ever were coming to faith. The Spirit was working. Genuine seekers were still coming to faith in Christ. The thousands who joined the first day (2:41) were daily joined by more (see 2:47; 4:4; 6:1, 7; 9:31).

5:15-16 As a result of the apostles' work, sick people were brought out into the streets on beds and mats so that Peter's shadow might fall across some of them as he went by. Crowds came in from the villages around Jerusalem, bringing their sick and those possessed by evil spirits, and they were all healed.[NLT] The word was beginning to spread beyond Jerusalem, drawing people *from the villages around Jerusalem.* In the same way that healing had "flowed" from Christ during his ministry on earth (see Mark 5:25-34), here it was Peter—one of Jesus' "witnesses"—whose *shadow* simply had to *fall across* the *sick and those possessed by evil spirits,* and they would be healed. These miraculous signs confirmed the validity of the apostles' witness and connected their work to Christ's healing ministry (see Luke 4:33-37; 8:26-39).

> The way to spread Christianity is to be Christian. . . . Jesus sends us out not to argue men into Christianity, still less to threaten them into it, but to attract them into it; to live so that its fruits may be so wonderful that others will desire them for themselves.
>
> *William Barclay*

CHURCH GROWTH
What makes Christianity attractive? It is easy to be drawn to churches because of programs, good speakers, size, beautiful facilities, or fellowship. People were attracted to the early church by expressions of God's power at work; by the generosity, sincerity, honesty, and unity of the members; and by the character of the leaders. Have our standards slipped? God wants to add believers to his church, not just newer and better programs or larger and fancier facilities. Make the truth about God the center of your witness.

Evil (unclean) spirits, or demons, are ruled by Satan. They were not created by Satan, because only God can create. Evil spirits and demons are fallen angels who joined Satan in his rebellion and thus became perverted and evil. At times, these evil spirits enter people's bodies, take up residence, and control them. Though not all disease comes from Satan, sometimes demons can cause a person to become mute, deaf, blind, or insane. In every case recorded in Scripture where demons were confronted by the power of God, they lost their power. God limits what evil spirits can do.

What did these miraculous healings do for the early church?

They attracted new believers, confirmed the truth of the apostles' teaching, and demonstrated that the power of the Messiah, who had been crucified and had risen, was now with his followers.

THE APOSTLES MEET OPPOSITION / 5:17-42

On the night before he was arrested, Jesus had assured his followers: "Since they persecuted me, naturally they will persecute you. . . . The people of the world will hate you. . . . For you will be expelled from the synagogues" (John 15:20-21; 16:2 NLT). It's not a promise most believers eagerly claim, but its fulfillment was and is just as certain as any other divine guarantee.

Smarting from the apostles' refusal to heed their threats, and in light of the growing popularity of the Christian movement, the Jewish authorities clamped down. They arrested and jailed Peter and his colleagues. When God miraculously freed his spokesmen in the night, the apostles marched straight back to the temple and resumed their preaching!

Detained again and commanded to stop speaking about Jesus, the apostles vowed to continue their relentless proclamation of the gospel, vowing to obey God above any human authority.

Not even a severe beating at the hands of the Jewish Council could dampen the apostles' enthusiasm, lending credibility to Gamaliel's observation that perhaps he and his colleagues were fighting a losing battle "against God" (5:38-39).

> All I can say is I look for perpetual conflicts and struggles in this life, and I hope for no other peace, only a cross, while on this side of eternity.
> *George Whitefield*

5:17-18 **The high priest and his friends, who were Sadducees, reacted with violent jealousy. They arrested the apostles and put them in the jail.**NLT The religious leaders did not listen and learn the gospel message that focused on their own Messiah; instead, they reacted to the apostles with *violent jealousy.* The word "jealousy" translates the word *zelos,* which can also mean "zeal." The zeal of the religious leaders was to wipe out this new movement. Peter and the apostles were already commanding more respect than the religious leaders had ever received. In addition, the apostles could do the most amazing miracles, a power the *high priest* and his fellow *Sadducees* lacked. (For more on the Sadducees, see commentary on 4:1.) This event was occurring only weeks after Jesus' trial and crucifixion, so the high priest would still have been Caiaphas, who had condemned Jesus to death, and the other men on the Council (Sadducees and Pharisees) would also be the same.

The key difference between the religious leaders and the apostles was that the religious leaders demanded respect and reverence for themselves, while the apostles' goal was to bring respect and reverence to God. The apostles were respected not because they demanded it but because they deserved it. It was the jealousy of the Saddducees that drove the events of this chapter, the first being that the leaders *arrested the apostles and put them in the jail.*

DANGER! TROUBLE AHEAD!
The apostles experienced power to do miracles, great boldness in preaching, and God's presence in their lives, yet they were not free from hatred and persecution. They were arrested, put in jail, beaten, and slandered by community leaders. Faith in God does not make troubles disappear; it makes troubles appear less frightening because it puts them in the right perspective. Don't expect everyone to react favorably when you share something as dynamic as your faith in Christ. Some will be jealous, afraid, or threatened. Expect some negative reactions, and remember that you must be more concerned about serving God than about the reactions of people (see 5:29).

5:19-20 But during the night an angel of the Lord opened the doors of the jail and brought them out. "Go, stand in the temple courts," he said, "and tell the people the full message of this new life."NIV The jealous religious leaders thought they could silence the apostles by throwing them into jail. But God would not allow his servants to be silenced. In a startling moment, *an angel of the Lord opened the doors of the jail and brought them out!*

Angels are spiritual beings created by God to help carry out his work on earth. They bring God's messages (Luke 1:26), protect God's people (Daniel 6:22), offer encouragement (Genesis 16:7), give guidance (Exodus 14:19), carry out punishment (2 Samuel 24:16), patrol the earth (Zechariah 1:9-14), and fight the forces of evil (2 Kings 6:16-18; Revelation 20:1-2). There are both good and bad angels (Revelation 12:7). Because bad angels are allied with the devil, Satan, they have considerably less power and authority than good angels. Eventually, the main role of angels will be to offer continuous praise to God (Revelation 7:11-12).

The phrase "angel of the Lord" *(angelos kuriou)* denotes divine intervention. The *angel of the Lord* refers to God's presence (see also 8:26; 12:7, 23; Matthew 1:20, 24; 2:13, 19; 28:2; Luke 1:11; 2:9). What made this incident even more remarkable was that the Sadducees, who had sent the apostles to jail (5:18), did not believe in angels!

The angel of the Lord gave the apostles the necessary encouragement to continue in their task despite this latest opposition. The angel's charge to the apostles was to go back out to the *temple courts* and *tell the people the full message of this new life.* In other words, they were to tell everyone everything, the "full message." They should not leave out anything, or anyone. The nature of this message is life—"new life."

The apostles' experience (which would be repeated later for Peter in 12:6-10 and again for Paul in 16:26-27) beautifully pictures the work God can and will do for those who are his witnesses. God will come into any dungeon—there is none too dark or deep. He holds the keys to unlock any door—there is none too complicated or confusing for him.

5:21 **So the apostles entered the Temple about daybreak and immediately began teaching.**[NLT] *So the apostles entered the Temple.* Without a moment's hesitation, the apostles did just exactly as commanded by the angel of the Lord. They obeyed immediately, boldly, and courageously. The temple at *daybreak* was a busy place. Many people stopped there to pray and worship at sunrise. The apostles were already there, ready to tell them the good news of new life in Jesus Christ. It would only be a matter of time before their absence at the jail would be noticed and they would have a chance to witness in front of a much more hostile group than those worshipers at the temple. Their boldness serves as a model for us. We should courageously proclaim the message of Christ as the Spirit creates opportunities for us.

> Every great person has learned *how* to obey, *whom* to obey and *when* to obey. *William Ward*

COMMANDS THAT BRING CRISIS

The angel of the Lord gave the apostles a command that, when followed, would lead to a brutal flogging. If that strikes you as odd, it is probably because of the prevailing idea among many believers that obedience inevitably leads to blessing (defined as "a problem-free, blissful existence"). Serious students of the Bible know, however, that obeying God often results in pain and suffering. They also recognize that being persecuted for Christ is a deeper kind of blessing. What biblical commands, if obeyed, might result in discomfort for you today? Will you commit to live them out anyway?

When the high priest and his officials arrived, they convened the high council, along with all the elders of Israel. Then they sent for the apostles to be brought for trial.[NLT] With a great sense of how to tell a good story, Luke moved to another scene: "meanwhile back at the courthouse. . . ." The scene that follows with the *high council* (also called the Sanhedrin) is filled with irony. The *high priest, his officials,* and *all the elders of Israel* must have prepared for this meeting, during which they would reprimand their prisoners—these "Jesus followers." This "high council" included the entire group of seventy men plus the high priest, the same group that had assembled for Jesus' trial only weeks before (for more information, see the commentary on 4:5). This would be no small trial. The religious leaders would do anything to stop these apostles from challenging their authority, threatening their secure position, and exposing their hypocritical motives to the people. They had taken care of Jesus (or so they thought), and they would take care of his followers, as well.

After convening the entire Council, *they sent for the apostles to be brought for trial.* But the Council would be surprised.

AN UNSTOPPABLE WITNESS!
Suppose someone threatened to kill you if you didn't stop talking about God. You probably would be tempted to keep quiet. But consider the response of the apostles: after being threatened by powerful leaders, arrested, jailed, and miraculously released, they went right back to preaching. This was nothing less than God's power working in and through them (4:13)! When we are utterly convinced of the truth of Christ's resurrection, and when we know intimately the presence and power of his Holy Spirit, let us speak out for Christ.

5:22-23 **But when the Temple guards went to the jail, the men were gone. So they returned to the council and reported, "The jail was locked, with the guards standing outside, but when we opened the gates, no one was there!"**NLT The prisoners were being called for trial, so *the Temple guards went to the jail* to get them. These "temple guards" were stationed around the temple to ensure order in that very busy place. They were Jewish priests from the tribe of Levi, stern defenders of orthodoxy and temple order, who worked for the high priest. However, they returned rather dumbfounded, reporting that the door of the cell *was locked,* the *guards* were faithfully *standing outside* at their posts, but when they opened the cell door, *no one was there!* So complete was the miracle that no one could deny that God's power was behind it.

5:24 **Now when the captain of the temple and the chief priests heard these words, they were perplexed about them, wondering what might be going on.**NRSV The *captain of the temple* and the *chief priests* were *perplexed* (*dieporoun,* literally, "were at a loss to explain") about how these men had escaped from a locked cell. Professional guards do not lose twelve prisoners! The "captain" was a high-ranking official belonging to the priestly aristocracy (Sadducees), second in authority only to the high priest.

5:25-26 **Then someone came and said, "Look! The men you put in jail are standing in the temple courts teaching the people." At that, the captain went with his officers and brought the apostles. They did not use force, because they feared that the people would stone them.**NIV Picture the scene: the high council is convened and waiting while the temple guards are searching for prisoners who are no longer in custody. In the middle of their deliberations, they receive a report that the escaped prisoners are right back where they were first arrested, doing the very thing for which they had been arrested!

Note that the officers *did not use force,* because they *feared that the people would stone them.* The expanding reputation of the church and various "power" events associated with it—miraculous healings, the death of some members for lying to the church, this miraculous jailbreak—would certainly make the leaders careful. Jealousy over the apostles' popularity with the people had been one of the main motivating factors for their arrest in the first place (5:17-18). Yet that very popularity caused them to be careful during this arrest. They did not want a riot to break out. The same concern had been expressed with respect to arresting Jesus (Matthew 21:46).

5:27-28 **Having brought the apostles, they made them appear before the Sanhedrin to be questioned by the high priest. "We gave you strict orders not to teach in this name," he said. "Yet you have filled Jerusalem with your teaching and are determined to make us guilty of this man's blood."**NIV The temple was close to the complex where the high priest lived. The *apostles* went peaceably with the temple guard to *appear before the Sanhedrin* (the high Council) *to be questioned by the high priest.* In Caiaphas's remarks, note that he would not even mention the name of the one in whose authority the apostles were teaching; instead, he strictly ordered the apostles *not to teach in this name,* because the leaders did not want to be considered *guilty of this man's blood* (even though they were—see Matthew 27:25). See 4:10, where Peter blamed the Council for Jesus' death.

The high priest said "this name" and "this man's blood"—both times refusing even to speak the name of Jesus and, by his avoidance of it, proclaiming it all the louder. These leaders' jealousy, even their hatred of the name (that is, the character, the person) of Jesus, was made clearer than ever.

The angel of the Lord's command to preach the message (5:20) was being fully carried out, for the jealous Sanhedrin unwittingly confirmed that the apostles had *filled Jerusalem with [their] teaching.*

The Jewish leaders wanted the apostles to stop teaching in Christ's name and to stop accusing them of culpability in Christ's death. Both problems would surface again quite clearly in the words of Peter, recorded in the next four verses.

5:29 **But Peter and the apostles answered, "We must obey God rather than any human authority."**NRSV With this comment Peter stated the primary necessity of obeying God first and foremost. These words are almost identical to his earlier ones in 4:19-20 (see commentary there). The New Testament makes it clear that believers are to obey governmental authority (Romans 13:1-7 and 1 Peter 2:13-17), but not when the authority requires believers to sin. It would have been sinful for these apostles to obey the leaders' mandate not to speak when they had been clearly commanded by God himself to speak (5:20). God is the highest authority and rules in the highest court anywhere. Our first obedience is always to him. In that case, they had to *obey God rather than any human authority.*

OBEY HIM!
Declaring their intent to obey God, the apostles proclaimed their priorities. While believers should try to live at peace with everyone (Romans 12:18), conflict with the world and its authorities is sometimes inevitable (John 15:18). Situations will come where we cannot obey God and please those in charge. At those times, we must obey God and trust his Word. When you must make such a choice, remember Jesus' words in Luke 6:22: "God blesses you who are hated and excluded and mocked and cursed because you are identified with me, the Son of Man" (NLT).

5:30 **"The God of our ancestors raised Jesus from the dead after you killed him by crucifying him."**NLT When Peter, the Galilean fisherman-turned-preacher, spoke to this group of religious leaders, he identified their common heritage with the phrase *the God of our ancestors.* These words tied the miracles these leaders had been hearing about to the Old Testament miracles, with which they were thoroughly familiar. The God who had parted the Red Sea and had led the Israelites to the Promised Land had also *raised Jesus from the dead.* These words would have baffled the Sadducee party in the Sanhedrin, for Sadducees did not believe in any type of resurrection (see the chart, "Prominent Jewish Religious and Political Groups" on pages 56–57 [4:1]). All the leaders must have been angered by the time Peter repeated his accusation, *you killed him by crucifying him.* Jesus, whose name the high priest would not even speak (5:27-28), had been killed by the Jewish leaders, but he had been raised from the dead by God himself.

5:31 **"God exalted him to his own right hand as Prince and Savior that he might give repentance and forgiveness of sins to Israel."**NIV Not only had God raised Jesus, he also had *exalted him to his own right hand.* "Right hand" signified the place of highest honor and authority. In ancient royal courts, the right side of the king's throne was reserved for the person who could act in the king's place. God "exalted" Christ to this position—for Christ, who had been killed by humans, has been raised to the highest position of power with God.

The term "Prince" *(archegon)* means "originator, leader, pioneer," one who leads the way. Instead of demanding his rights as prince, however, Christ lowered himself to become the *Savior:* "Though he was God, he did not demand and cling to his rights as God. He made himself nothing; he took the humble position of a slave and appeared in human form. And in human form he obediently humbled himself even further by dying a criminal's death on a cross" (Philippians 2:6-8 NLT). Through that death, Christ "made peace with everything in heaven and on earth by means of his blood on the cross" (Colossians 1:20 NLT). Jesus is "Savior" because through his death he can offer *repentance and forgiveness of sins to Israel.* With these words Peter was offering salvation to the very people who had crucified the Savior. They, along with all the rest of Israel, could find forgiveness through the crucified and risen Christ. Peter mentioned only Israel here, for it was not until later (see chapter 10) that Peter would understand that Gentiles were to be included in this offer of repentance and forgiveness.

This is the heart of the gospel, repeated over and over in the book of Acts (see also 2:38; 3:16, 19; 4:12; 8:22; 17:30; 26:20), the "full message" that the apostles were called to proclaim (5:20 NIV). Reconciliation with God is impossible without the sacrifice of Christ and the repentance of people. "Repentance" means to turn away from sin. More than just feeling bad about one's sins, it means desiring to make a change in one's purpose and direction, along with a heartfelt desire not to sin (see also 2:38). Because of Jesus' sacrifice on the cross, taking sin's penalty upon himself, people can come to God in repentance and receive forgiveness for their sins.

5:32 "And we are witnesses to these things, and so is the Holy Spirit whom God has given to those who obey him."NRSV
Standing before the high Council, the apostles explained that they had been *witnesses to these things* of which they spoke. They had seen the risen Christ, and they had seen the exalted Christ as he had been taken into heaven. Peter's inclusion of the *Holy Spirit* as part of the witness points back to the Spirit's coming in power on the day of Pentecost, an event with which the present audience would have been familiar (at least by reputation). It also points back to Jesus' promise in John 15:26-27, "But I will send you the Counselor—the Spirit of truth. He will come to you from the Father and will tell you all about me. And you must also tell others about me because you have been with me from the beginning" (NLT). Peter wanted them to know that this same Holy Spirit was still at work among them because the Spirit was being *given* by God *to those who obey him.* This gift of the Holy Spirit, given to those who accept Christ as their Savior, was described by Paul as "God's guarantee that he will give us everything he promised and that he has purchased us to be his own people" (Ephesians 1:14 NLT).

We are not to preach sociology, but salvation; not economics, but evangelism; not reform, but redemption; not culture, but conversion; not progress, but pardon; not a social order, but a new birth; not revolution, but regeneration; not renovation, but revival; not resuscitation, but resurrection; not a new organization, but a new creation; not democracy, but the Gospel; not civilization, but Christ; we are ambassadors, not diplomats.
Hugh Thomsen Kerr

TELLING TRUTH
In both Luke and Acts, the Holy Spirit was clearly associated with witnessing. Almost every time the Spirit was mentioned, someone testified about God or proclaimed the good news of Christ. If we are filled with the Spirit (Ephesians 5:18), if we are letting him lead us (Galatians 5:16), we, too, will speak of Christ. Think back over your conversations from the previous week. If you realize that you rarely or never mentioned God to others, it is a good sign that you are "stifling the Holy Spirit" (1 Thessalonians 5:19).

5:33-34 When they heard this, they were furious and wanted to put them to death. But a Pharisee named Gamaliel, a teacher of the law, who was honored by all the people, stood up in the Sanhedrin and ordered that the men be put outside for a little

while.NIV The high Council listened to the apostles' words and became so *furious* that they *wanted to put them to death.* Except for one lone and wise voice from an unlikely source, this Council surely would have gotten rid of these followers just as they had gotten rid of their leader. The previous night God had used supernatural means to free the apostles from jail; here he used a less "flashy" but just as miraculous means—a *Pharisee* defending the church!

The Pharisees were the other major party in the high Council with the Sadducees (see the chart "Prominent Jewish Religious and Political Groups" on page 56–57 [4:1]). The Pharisees were the strict keepers of the law—not only God's law but hundreds of other rules they had added to God's law. They were careful about outward purity, but many had hearts full of impure motives. Jesus confronted the Pharisees often during his ministry on earth. They followed a similar pattern of jealousy, inquiry, and then hostility with the apostles as they had with Jesus. *Gamaliel* was an unexpected ally for the apostles, although he probably did not support their teachings. He was a distinguished member of the Council, *a teacher of the law,* and was *honored by all the people.* He was either the son or grandson of Hillel, the great Hebrew scholar who had been the head of a school for the training of Pharisees. Gamaliel *stood up* to speak to the assembly, but first he ordered that the apostles be taken from the room so that the situation could be discussed.

5:35-37 **Then he said to them, "Fellow Israelites, consider carefully what you propose to do to these men. For some time ago Theudas rose up, claiming to be somebody, and a number of men, about four hundred, joined him; but he was killed, and all who followed him were dispersed and disappeared. After him Judas the Galilean rose up at the time of the census and got people to follow him; he also perished, and all who followed him were scattered."**NRSV Gamaliel's point was that revolutions come and revolutions go. It would not be wise to get embroiled in this one too deeply, for if it was like the others, it would disappear of its own accord.

There is controversy over Gamaliel's references to *Theudas* and *Judas the Galilean* regarding the historical data. Josephus, the Jewish historian, mentions a Theudos who persuaded many to take their possessions and move with him to the Jordan River area. He posed as a second Moses who promised to lead the Jews out of Roman oppression. He was unsuccessful. The revolt to which Josephus alluded, however, was likely larger and later than the one mentioned by Gamaliel. Judas the Galilean likely had led a religious and nationalist revolt against Caesar that had been crushed by Rome. Some think his movement was continued by other insurrectionists. The Zealots were an active group at this time but did not come into full, organized force until A.D. 60–70. In both cases, when the leader was *killed,* his followers disbanded. If this Christ movement were like these others, with Jesus dead and gone (so they thought), his followers would soon disperse and disappear.

5:38-39 "Therefore, in the present case I advise you: Leave these men alone! Let them go! For if their purpose or activity is of human origin, it will fail. But if it is from God, you will not be able to stop these men; you will only find yourselves fighting against God."NIV Gamaliel offered sound advice. With the leader gone, this new movement would *fail* and fade away on its own if its *purpose or activity* was *of human origin.* If, however, this movement truly was *from God,* then even these religious leaders would be unwise to fight against it, because not only would they *not be able to stop these men* (the apostles), but they would end up *fighting against God.*

The concept of "fighting against God" would be frightening for a devout Jew, so Gamaliel's logic prevailed. Gamaliel spoke these words probably not because he was a church sympathizer nor a secret follower of Christ but rather because he had confidence in the sovereign operation of God in the affairs of people. In typical Pharisaic style, he urged extreme caution in areas of the administration of justice, and his counsel defused the situation. Gamaliel's speech turned out to be a prophecy unconsciously given, much like Caiaphas's speech in John 11:50-52.

FIGHTING AGAINST GOD?

Gamaliel presented some sound advice about reacting to religious movements. Unless disciples in these groups endorse obviously dangerous doctrines or practices, often it is wiser to be tolerant rather than repressive. Sometimes only time will tell if they are merely the work of humans or if God is trying to say something through them. The next time a group promotes differing religious ideas, consider Gamaliel's advice just in case you "find yourself fighting against God."

God used Gamaliel, a Pharisee and respected member of the Jewish community, to help free the apostles. This has always been a fascinating strategy of God. He often has used the most unlikely sources to help his people or to get his message across. For Joseph, he used Pharaoh; with Nehemiah, he used Artaxerxes; with Daniel, God used Nebuchadnezzar, Belshazzar, and

Darius; for the Jews to return to their homeland, he used Cyrus of Persia. Proverbs 21:1 says, "The king's heart is in the hand of the LORD; he directs it like a watercourse wherever he pleases" (NIV). Elsewhere, the Old Testament records God using rebels, adulterers, thieves, and even a donkey to get his message across.

5:40 The council accepted his advice. They called in the apostles and had them flogged. Then they ordered them never again to speak in the name of Jesus, and they let them go.[NLT] *The council accepted* Gamaliel's sound *advice* and decided not to put the apostles to death (5:33). Gamaliel's advice to the Council gave the apostles some breathing room to continue their work. The Council decided to wait, hoping that this would all fade away harmlessly. They couldn't have been more wrong. Ironically, Paul, later one of the greatest apostles, was one of Gamaliel's students (22:3). Gamaliel may have saved the apostles' lives, but his real intentions probably were to prevent a division in the Sanhedrin and to avoid arousing the Romans (or maybe even just to prevent the Sadducees from winning the point). The apostles were popular among the people, and killing them might have started a riot.

Yet the Council was not going to let the apostles off easily. After calling the apostles back into the room, the Council *had them flogged.* This was Jewish law (see 4:18, where they were warned). This was not a simple slap on the wrist. In a flogging, leather thongs made into whips were beaten against the bared upper body of the bound prisoner. The prisoner would be made to kneel, then the triple-strap whip would be beaten across both chest and back, with two beatings on the back for every one on the chest. This punishment would be given to people judged guilty of crimes: "If the guilty man deserves to be beaten, the judge shall make him lie down and have him flogged in his presence with the number of lashes his crime deserves, but he must not give him more than forty lashes. If he is flogged more than that, your brother will be degraded in your eyes" (Deuteronomy 25:2-3 NIV). Often the Jews would give only thirty-nine lashes to make sure that they did not miscount and give more than forty. The Council was probably careful to observe the correct number of lashes, while ignoring the fact that the men they had flogged had not been judged guilty of any crime. This flogging fulfilled Jesus' words to his followers in Mark 13:9, "You will be handed over to the local councils and flogged in the synagogues" (NIV).

Once again, the leaders gave the foolish order, which likely none of them even believed would be carried out, that the apostles *never again . . . speak in the name of Jesus* (see 4:18).

At least one of Luke's purposes for including this incident was probably to inform readers of the sad but consistent path the Jewish leadership had taken (and the nation with them) in the total rejection of Jesus as Messiah. Much more is included in the chapters that follow.

SUFFERING FOR CHRIST
Peter and John were warned repeatedly not to preach, but they continued despite the threats. Believers today should also live as Christ has asked, sharing the faith no matter what the cost. You may not be beaten or thrown in jail, but you may be ridiculed, ostracized, or slandered. To what extent are you willing to suffer for the sake of sharing the gospel with others?

5:41 **As they left the council, they rejoiced that they were considered worthy to suffer dishonor for the sake of the name.**[NRSV] These apostles had endured tremendous pain, yet they left the Council, rejoicing *that they were considered worthy to suffer dishonor for the sake of the name* of Jesus Christ—the name that the high priest would not even say (5:28), the name in which they had been forbidden to speak (5:40).

Notice the attitude of the early church toward difficulty: they were imprisoned, threatened, beaten. Their response was to rejoice—not because they had all these bad things happen but because they had been "considered worthy" of disgrace from their association with Christ.

PRAISE GOD FOR PERSECUTION
Have you ever thought of persecution as a blessing, as something worth rejoicing about? This beating suffered by Peter and John was the first time any of the apostles had been physically abused for their faith. These men knew how Jesus had suffered, and they praised God that he had allowed them to be persecuted like their Lord. If you are mocked or persecuted for your faith, it isn't because you're doing something wrong but because God has counted you "worthy to suffer dishonor for the sake of the name." So don't resent opposition, but regard it as a sign that you have been faithful to Christ.

5:42 **Day after day, in the temple courts and from house to house, they never stopped teaching and proclaiming the good news that Jesus is the Christ.**[NIV] Instead of making the apostles fearful, the suffering they had endured at the hands of the Jewish leaders only made them more courageous. *Day after day* they *never stopped teaching and proclaiming the good news that Jesus is the Christ.* These apostles wanted everyone to know that Jesus was the fulfillment of all the Old Testament prophecies—he was the promised Messiah! This was the message prohibited by the Jewish high Council. But the threat of prison, beatings, and even death would not deter this group of witnesses from their appointed task. The heat was on, but it was only spreading the fire!

This summary statement, much like the summary at the end of chapter 2, records a church doing the work of teaching and proclaiming the Good News in both large settings *(temple courts)* and small ones *(from house to house).* It is likely that the apostles taught in the larger groups, while the house-to-house meetings were more focused on fellowship, the breaking of bread, and prayer (see 2:46).

AN ANCIENT STRATEGY

The apostles taught from house to house. Home Bible studies are not new. As the believers needed to grow in their new faith, home Bible studies met their needs while introducing new people to the Christian faith. During later times of persecution, meeting in homes became the primary method of passing on Bible knowledge. Christians throughout the world still use this approach when under persecution. Meet regularly in a small group with other believers.

Acts 6

SEVEN MEN CHOSEN TO SERVE / 6:1-7

From arrests at the hands of the Jews to the attempted deception within the congregation, the early days of the church seemed difficult. Yet the growth was phenomenal! Chapter 6 returns to an internal problem—some apparent discrepancies in the distribution of goods to the needy widows in the congregation. The result: complaints from those who thought they were being discriminated against and a rising tide of anger. It was a potential disaster. But the Spirit-filled apostles wisely solved the young church's problem.

The rapid growth of the church meant more people. More people meant more programs and larger ministries. More programs meant administrative and logistical problems that threatened to consume all the apostles' time. Rather than neglect the spiritual disciplines of prayer and teaching, the apostles called and commissioned a group of men to attend to the pressing needs of the body. Finding qualified people who can and will help share the load of work is a mark of a healthy congregation.

6:1 **But as the believers rapidly multiplied, there were rumblings of discontent. Those who spoke Greek complained against those who spoke Hebrew, saying that their widows were being discriminated against in the daily distribution of food.**[NLT] The number of believers in Jerusalem made it necessary to organize the sharing of resources. People were being overlooked, and some were complaining. The believers *who spoke Hebrew* were the native Jewish Christians, "locals" who spoke Aramaic, a Semitic language. The believers *who spoke Greek* were the Grecian Jews from other lands who had been converted at Pentecost. They could not speak Aramaic, the native tongue of the Jews living in Israel. They were probably at least bilingual, speaking their native tongue and Greek but not Aramaic. There had developed a class distinction between the two groups, similar to racism. Though all were Christians, their backgrounds and outlooks were different.

The Greek-speaking Christians *complained* that *their widows were being discriminated against in the daily distribution of food.* There were many more widows than usual since many of the widows who came from other Greek-speaking countries had returned to Jerusalem to live out their years and be buried with their ancestors. Their money may have run out, and they needed help. Widows in general needed help since property was passed on from father to son, and the son was responsible to care for the mother. She had no wealth of her own. (It should be noted that early in church history, "widows" became a recognized group worthy of help from the church—see 9:41; 1 Timothy 5:3-16.) This "discrimination" against the Greek-speaking believers was more likely caused by the language and class barrier.

The early church took seriously the meeting of both the physical needs (distributing food and supplies) and the spiritual needs (teaching the Word) of the body of believers.

NO PERFECT CHURCH
When we read the descriptions of the early church—the miracles, the sharing and generosity, the fellowship—we may wish we could have been a part of this "perfect" church. In reality, the early church had problems just as we do today. No church has ever been or will ever be perfect until Christ returns. All churches have problems. If your church's shortcomings distress you, ask yourself: "Would a perfect church allow me to be a member?" Then do what you can to make your church better. A church does not have to be perfect to be a powerful and effective witness for Christ.

6:2 So the Twelve gathered all the disciples together and said, "It would not be right for us to neglect the ministry of the word of God in order to wait on tables."NIV Out of the conflict there arose a meeting. The *Twelve* (referring to the apostles) *gathered all the disciples* (referring to the rest of the believers) *together* and made a statement. They noted that it would *not be right* for them to *neglect the ministry of the word of God in order to wait on tables.* From both physical energy and time restraints, it would be impossible for them to do both. The Greek here translated "wait on tables" is literally "to serve tables" *(diakonein trapezais),* which could refer to the tables used for serving food or maybe even for passing out funds to those in need. The reason was not that the apostles thought that they were "above" waiting on

> Good character is more to be praised than outstanding talent. Most talents are, to some extent, a gift. Good character, by contrast, is not given to us. We have to build it piece by piece—by thought, choice, courage, and determination. *John Luther*

tables; rather, they knew that they had been called to preach and teach the Word of God, and that had to be their priority.

6:3-4 **"Therefore, friends, select from among yourselves seven men of good standing, full of the Spirit and of wisdom, whom we may appoint to this task, while we, for our part, will devote ourselves to prayer and to serving the word."**[NRSV] To correct the situation, the apostles said that the believers should choose respected Greek-speaking men and put them in charge of the food distribution program. Five requirements were clearly spelled out: the candidates had to be (1) *men* (*andras*—a specific Greek term for men); (2) believers *(from among yourselves);* (3) possessing good reputations *(good standing)*, known as men of integrity; (4) solid spiritually *(full of the Spirit);* (5) full of *wisdom*—demonstrating their ability to apply God's truth appropriately to life situations. *Seven* was the typical number of men used to handle public business in a Jewish town, the official council.

MATCHING GIFTS WITH NEEDS

As the early church increased in size, so did its needs. One great need was to organize the distribution of food to the poor. Since the apostles were called to focus on preaching and praying (6:4), they chose others to administer the food program. A prominent New Testament teaching is that each person has a vital part to play in the life of the church (see 1 Corinthians 12). If you are in a position of leadership and find yourself overwhelmed with responsibilities, prayerfully determine what your priorities should be, and then find others to respond to the other legitimate needs. If you are not in leadership, realize that you have gifts that can be used by God in various areas of the church's ministry. Serve him with these gifts.

"Fullness" of the Spirit means a Spirit-following lifestyle. To be "full of the Spirit" was not an elitist position; instead, it indicated a mature, healthy Christian life. These people had demonstrated that the Spirit was working in them.

The person who was full of wisdom *(sophias)* would have demonstrated the ability to get to the best ends by the best means; that is, someone who had common sense. People who carry heavy responsibilities and work closely with others should have these qualities. We must look for spiritually mature and wise men and women to lead our churches.

The apostles kept their priorities straight. They were successful in part because they realized that both tasks were important: the task of meeting the physical needs of the church body and the task of meeting the spiritual and educational needs of the body. They had to ask themselves the basic question: since we can only do *some* things, *which* of these many good things to do are the most important and the most appropriate for us? For the apostles, the answer was clearly praying and teaching the Word, as they had been commissioned to do.

EVERY MEMBER A MINISTER
The apostles' priorities were correct. The ministry of the Word should never be neglected because of administrative burdens. Pastors should not try, or be expected to try, to do everything. Instead, full-time ministers are called to "equip God's people to . . . build up the church" (Ephesians 4:12 NLT). That's the New Testament model: in every church each and every member is a minister! By getting believers involved in this way, churches are able to utilize and enjoy the gifts that have been given to each person, thus multiplying their impact.

6:5 **This proposal pleased the whole group. They chose Stephen, a man full of faith and of the Holy Spirit; also Philip, Procorus, Nicanor, Timon, Parmenas, and Nicolas from Antioch, a convert to Judaism.**[NIV] The *whole group* (meaning all the believers) was *pleased* with the solution, so seven men were chosen, though how this was done was not recorded. *Stephen* and *Philip* were likely placed first because they are the only two whose ministries will be explained later in Acts (chapters 7–8). All seven of these names are Greek, which means that the men were probably Hellenistic Jews. This would lay a good foundation for the future spread of the gospel to the Greek world. Nothing more is known about *Procorus, Nicanor, Timon, Parmenas,* or *Nicolas.*

CHOOSING THE BEST
When it came time for the church to assemble a team of servants, note what happened. First, they did not select just any candidates. They picked the godliest men they could find! Second, these highly qualified men did not grumble at the thought of serving food to the elderly! Rather they served gladly. Is this how things work in your church? Are ministry slots filled with "the best person" or with "just a warm body"? How about those unglamorous but necessary positions of service? Do members rush to fill them, or do they run from them? For a church to be effective, it needs an army of godly servants who are willing to do whatever is asked of them. Are you such a person?

6:6 **They had these men stand before the apostles, who prayed and laid their hands on them.**[NRSV] Spiritual leadership is serious business and must not be taken lightly by the church or its leaders. In the early church, those chosen to serve would be ordained or commissioned (set apart by prayer and laying on of hands) by the apostles. Laying hands on someone, an ancient Jewish practice, was a way to set a person apart for special service (see Numbers 27:23; Deuteronomy 34:9).

Were these men the church's first deacons? Some say these were not deacons, deacon-predecessors, or even elder-predecessors but rather temporary, nonofficial positions created to meet the need at hand. They are never called "deacons" but rather "the seven men who had been chosen to distribute food" (21:8 NLT). The word "serve" *(diakonein)* in 6:2 is used elsewhere in Acts to describe acts of service, not to signify an office of deacon (see 1:17, 25; 11:29; 12:25; 19:22; 20:24; 21:19). There is no denying, however, that the seven men performed the function of deacons as the office would later be defined.

That the apostles *laid their hands on them* was a common gesture used in the commissioning of individuals to a task or office. It was also a granting of some sort of authority (see 8:17-19; 13:3; 19:6; 1 Timothy 4:14; 5:22; Hebrews 6:2). The apostles were hereby identifying themselves with the seven men and granting them a portion of their authority, at least for the task at hand.

EFFECTIVE LIFE MANAGEMENT

Here are the ABCs of management from the apostles:

Assess your problem *accurately* (6:1-2)—Are you attacking the right problem?

Budget your time *strategically* (6:2, 4)—Are your priorities right?

Choose your leaders *wisely* (6:3)—Are you choosing and following biblically qualified leaders?

Distribute your load *widely* (6:3, 5-6)—Are you delegating the load? Are you doing your part?

6:7 God's message was preached in ever-widening circles. The number of believers greatly increased in Jerusalem, and many of the Jewish priests were converted, too.NLT Here Luke placed one of his common punctuation marks (see 9:31; 12:24; 16:5; 19:20; 28:31)—a report that the Word of God was spreading in *ever-widening circles.* Jesus had told the apostles that they were to witness first in Jerusalem (1:8). In a short time, their message had infiltrated the entire city and all levels of society. Even some *Jewish priests* were being converted (as many as eighteen thousand priests may have been living in Jerusalem at the time)!

The work increased, and the Word spread, at least in part because the apostles were dedicating more of their energies to that ministry. They could not have imagined, however, an explosion of the magnitude that lay just around the corner in the short but significant ministry of the church's first martyr.

THE SPREADING GOSPEL
The Word of God spread like ripples on a pond where, from a single center, each wave touches the next, spreading wider and farther. The gospel still spreads this way today. You don't have to change the world single-handedly; it is enough just to be part of the wave, touching those around you, who in turn will touch others until all have felt the movement. Your part, no matter how small, is significant and important.

STEPHEN IS ARRESTED / 6:8-15

Around the world, the gospel has most often taken root in places fertilized by the blood of martyrs. Before people can give their lives for the gospel, however, they must first live their lives for the gospel. One way that God trains his servants is to place them in insignificant positions. Their desire to serve Christ translates into the reality of serving others. Stephen was an effective administrator and messenger before becoming a martyr. For faithfully discharging his duties as a believer, Stephen was arrested.

QUALITIES OF AN EFFECTIVE CHRISTIAN WORKER
In Acts 6:3, 5, and 8, the description of Stephen provides a great model for us to develop in our own lives. He was said to be full of (controlled by) the following five elements: (1) the Holy Spirit, (2) wisdom, (3) faith, (4) grace, and (5) power. Ask God to fill you with these qualities.

6:8 Stephen, full of grace and power, did great wonders and signs among the people.[NRSV] *Stephen* was one of the managers of food distribution in the early church (6:5). The most important prerequisite for any kind of Christian service is to be filled with God's *grace* and the *power* of the Holy Spirit. By the Spirit's power, Stephen was a wise servant (6:3), miracle worker (6:8), and evangelist (6:10). His demonstration of *great wonders and signs among the people* tied his ministry (and the ministry of the seven men of 6:1-6) to the work of the apostles and, of course, to Christ. Stephen is the first non-apostle to whom miracles are ascribed, as well as the first non-apostle whose sermon is recorded, in the book of Acts.

It is unknown how long Stephen's ministry continued before the events of this chapter and the next occurred, but he obviously had a powerful, visible, and influential ministry.

6:9-10 Opposition arose, however, from members of the Synagogue of the Freedmen (as it was called)—Jews of Cyrene and Alexandria as well as the provinces of Cilicia and Asia. These men began to argue with Stephen, but they could not stand up against his wisdom or the Spirit by whom he spoke.[NIV] The *Freedmen* were probably a group of Jewish slaves and children of Jewish slaves who had been freed by Rome and had formed their own synagogue in Jerusalem. *Cyrene* was in northern Africa, as was *Alexandria* (in Egypt). *Cilicia* was Paul's home province, so he may be one of those mentioned here.

Besides being a man of high character as well as one who was used of God in doing great works of power (see 6:8), Stephen was also a skilled debater. His ministry was mainly to these Hellenistic Jews; the opposition came from that segment. Notice again the combination of Stephen's *wisdom* and the empowering work of *the Spirit by whom he spoke* (6:3-5).

Jesus had predicted such a capability on the part of those who would follow him. He said the Spirit would give the words to his representatives in those situations where they were brought before others because of their faith (Matthew 10:19-20; Luke 21:13-15). In the haunting words of Gamaliel (5:39), *these men* who *began to argue* with Stephen were, in fact, arguing with God!

6:11-12 So they persuaded some men to lie about Stephen, saying, "We heard him blaspheme Moses, and even God." Naturally, this roused the crowds, the elders, and the teachers of religious law. So they arrested Stephen and brought him before the high council.[NLT] Some men lied about Stephen, causing him to be arrested and brought *before the high council* (the Jewish Council, also called the Sanhedrin, before whom the apostles had just recently appeared—4:5-7; 5:26-27). This verse, as well as 6:15, when Stephen's face became bright like an angel's, parallels Jesus' life (see also 3:10). The group falsely accused Stephen of blaspheming Moses, partly because they knew that the Sadducees, who controlled the Council, believed only in Moses' laws. They thought they could make the charge of blasphemy stick with the power brokers if they could convince them that the accused had been attacking the laws of Moses. The Sadducees, the dominant party in the Council, accepted and studied only the writings of Moses (Genesis through Deuteronomy). In their view, to *blaspheme Moses* was a crime. But Stephen's speech (7:2-53) would prove that accusation false. In that speech Stephen's review of Israel's history is based on Moses' writings.

The entire Council is mentioned here as being *roused* against Stephen—*the elders, and the teachers of religious law* (also called "scribes"; see the chart "Prominent Jewish Religious and Political Groups" on pages 56–57 [4:1]). The *crowds* were riled up as well.

Having nothing legally against Stephen, the people from the Synagogue of the Freedmen (6:9) led the charge against Stephen by influencing others to begin making charges against him of blasphemy—first against Moses (a hero of these keepers of the Law), and then even against God himself. These were vague charges, hard to prove and even harder to refute, but they were quite inflammatory.

6:13-14 They produced false witnesses, who testified, "This fellow never stops speaking against this holy place and against the law. For we have heard him say that this Jesus of Nazareth will destroy this place and change the customs Moses handed down to us."[NIV] Similar to the way that Jesus had been handled, Stephen was the victim of a lying conspiracy. When Stephen was brought before the Jewish high Council, the accusation against him was the same that the religious leaders had used against Jesus (Matthew 26:59-61). As it was with Jesus and here with Stephen, this was not a wholesale fabrication but rather a subtle misrepresentation of Stephen's actual words. It is likely that Stephen had repeated Jesus' words from Mark 14:58, when Jesus was speaking of his death and resurrection (John 2:19-21)—words that were twisted at Jesus' trial to accuse him of saying that he wanted to destroy the temple (Matthew 26:61). (Jesus never said that he would destroy the temple; rather, he said that the Jews would destroy his temple—that is, his body.) Or, possibly, Stephen had repeated Jesus' prophetic words that the temple would indeed be destroyed (Mark 13:2). Certainly, the Council would have remembered this.

Stephen, following the lead and instruction of the apostles, had probably also taught some version of the Good News, that the "new temple" was the believer, in whom the Holy Spirit dwelled, and that the "new law" was the law of God implanted in every believer's heart. Such teaching could be turned into *speaking against* the temple *(holy place)* and *against the law.*

If your cause is right, be not afraid of criticism: Advocate it, expound it, and, if need be, fight for it. Critics always will be, but to the strong-minded they are a help rather than a hindrance. As the horse spurts forward when prodded with the spur, so the doers forge ahead under the lash of criticism. Take your part on life's stage and play your part to the end: Stand for that which is good: Be a doer, not a drone: Look the world in the face and let the critics criticize.

Thomas Jefferson

They even twisted his comments into making him say that *Jesus of Nazareth will destroy this place [the temple] and change the customs Moses handed down.* Christ changes more than "customs." He brings about a revolution of tremendous proportions—starting with the heart (John 3:3-18; 2 Corinthians 5:17; Galatians 2:20). Jesus did not nullify Moses' law, but rather he completely fulfilled it. The religious leaders did not see this, however, and only saw someone seeming to make changes to what Moses had spoken. To them, that was blasphemy.

COUNTENANCE
Apparently, as Stephen stood before the Jewish Council, his faced glowed with an undeniable supernatural glory. This is similar to what happened to Moses as a result of being with God on Mount Sinai (Exodus 34:29-35). It also brings to mind the time that Jesus was transfigured in the presence of Peter, James, and John (Matthew 17:1-9; Mark 9:2-10; Luke 9:28-36). Modern-day Christians may never glow in a literal sense of emitting supernatural light, but they should exude a brightness and warmth. Our faces should reflect the unearthly joy and peace that come from knowing Christ. Are you a walking advertisement for the glory of God? Can others look at your life and see something different . . . and attractive?

6:15 **At this point everyone in the council stared at Stephen because his face became as bright as an angel's.**[NLT] After the false witnesses had finished twisting Stephen's teaching, everyone turned to Stephen for his reaction. They found his face shining *as bright as an angel's* (see Judges 13:6; Luke 9:28-29). Stephen's "glowing face" would certainly call to mind the experience of Moses after being with God (Exodus 34:29, 35). The avid followers of Moses among his accusers (especially the Sadducees) would have made the connection.

Stephen's glowing face, like Moses', was likely a literal reflection of God's glory, a sign of having been in God's presence. Maybe Stephen had been given a glimpse of the vision that would be more evident at the moment of his death (7:55). Maybe his change in countenance was in part because of the fullness of the Spirit, a characteristic that had marked his life and ministry. Whatever it was, the moment was at hand for the first witness of Christ to lose his life for the faith.

With a Moses-like glow on his face, the books of Moses solidly in his head and heart, the courage of Moses before Pharaoh, and the fullness of the indwelling power of the Holy Spirit of God, Stephen courageously answered his accusers.

Acts 7

STEPHEN ADDRESSES THE COUNCIL / 7:1-60

This chapter records the first major speech of a non-apostle in the book—as well as the longest speech of anyone in Acts! It also records the first believer to die for his faith. Stephen—one of the seven men chosen to distribute food in the young church—was falsely accused by the Jewish religious leaders of commiting blasphemy and inciting rebellion against the temple. Then he was dragged before the Jewish authorities. In his speech to them, he spoke little in his own defense but said a great deal about Israel's historical tendency toward missing what God was doing. Stephen didn't seem nervous as he stood before the high priest and powerful Jewish Council. He gave a concise review of Jewish history and then abruptly called them "stubborn people . . . heathen at heart and deaf to the truth" (7:51 NLT). Having said that, he accused the Council of murdering the long-awaited Messiah (v. 52).

Their response to Stephen was typical of the Jews' response to every prophet throughout their history, down to and including Jesus himself: violence. This blunt and pointed sermon sent the Jewish leaders into a rage and resulted in the first martyrdom of the church.

Stephen died as his Master had died, asking God to forgive his tormentors. In describing this scene, Luke noted that among those present at Stephen's violent death by stoning was a young man named Saul (7:58), the soon-to-be convert to Christianity and missionary to the Gentile world.

Stephen didn't really defend himself. Instead, he took the offensive, seizing the opportunity to summarize his teaching about Jesus. Stephen was accusing these religious leaders of failing to obey God's laws—the laws they prided themselves in following so meticulously. This was the same accusation that Jesus had leveled against them. We can learn from Stephen's example. When we witness for Christ, we don't need to be on the defensive. Instead, we can simply share our faith.

7:1 Then the high priest asked Stephen, "Are these accusations true?"NLT This high priest was probably Caiaphas, the same man who had questioned and condemned Jesus (John 18:24) and had

MAJOR THEMES OF STEPHEN'S SPEECH

1. The Jews always reject God's leaders (7:39).
2. God doesn't dwell in temples made with hands (7:48).
3. God transcends the laws (7:50).
4. Israel's tendency toward apostasy (7:51).
5. Israel rejects God's messengers (7:52).

just recently interrogated the apostles (4:6-7; 5:26-28). He was high priest from A.D. 18–36. Annas, often named as the high priest, had been deposed by the Romans, who then had appointed Annas's son-in-law, Caiaphas, in his place. Because the Jews considered the office of high priest a lifetime position, they still called Annas by that title and gave him respect and authority within the Council. Either Annas or Caiaphas gave Stephen a chance to speak in his defense by asking him, *"Are these accusations true?"* just as Caiaphas had asked Jesus, "Aren't you going to answer these charges? What do you have to say for yourself?" (Matthew 26:62 NLT).

BEING PREPARED
Stephen stood before the hostile Jewish Council with the angry eyes of Israel's most influential and powerful religious leaders focused on him. What would he say? Would he water down his message so as not to antagonize his accusers? Stephen made the most of the moment, and he did so with uncommon boldness. Stephen was a faithful servant before he became a martyr. Thus, when this moment arrived, he was ready. What steps have you taken to defend your faith? Could you be as faithful as Stephen under such criticism and scrutiny?

7:2-3 **To this he replied: "Brothers and fathers, listen to me! The God of glory appeared to our father Abraham while he was still in Mesopotamia, before he lived in Haran. 'Leave your country and your people,' God said, 'and go to the land I will show you.'"**NIV Stephen launched into a speech about Israel's relationship with God. From Old Testament history, he showed that the Jews had constantly rejected God's message and his prophets and that the current Jewish leaders had rejected the Messiah, God's Son. He made three main points: (1) Israel's history is the history of God's acts in the world; (2) people worshiped God long before there was a temple because God does not live in a temple; and

(3) the Jewish leaders' rejection of Jesus was just one more example of Israel's rebellion against and rejection of God.

Before the Jewish Council, Stephen began his response to the accusations by reviewing the call of the Jewish patriarch *Abraham* from *Mesopotamia.* One of the themes of the speech is that God has been creatively and sovereignly directing his kingdom program through many different people and in many different places. God's revelation was not limited to the land or people of Israel.

STEPHEN'S SPEECH

This form of address is called by some "historical retrospect," a well-established form of address. Obviously Stephen knew his Old Testament Scriptures.

Stephen's speech began as a selective history of the Old Testament. He started his discourse with Abraham (7:2-8), moved to Joseph (7:9-16), then to Moses (7:17-43). The final section before his concluding condemnation (7:51-53) used the man-made tabernacle and temple of Solomon as examples for the fact that the temple was not God's dwelling place but rather a place of worship and approach to him (7:44-50). Each of the sections leading up to the discourse on the temple clearly demonstrates Israel's habitual, historical rejection of God's spokespeople. The climax of the speech is in 7:51-52, where the rejection of the Righteous One, the Messiah, Jesus Christ, was laid squarely upon the shoulders of Stephen's audience. Their response was a maddening, murderous stoning (7:54-60), adding yet another living example of the point of Stephen's speech.

When Stephen said *brothers and fathers,* he was calling attention to the legacy he shared with his audience—he was one of them. His mention of *the God of glory* refers to the glory of God that appeared on Mount Sinai, in the tabernacle, and later in the temple.

Stephen's point seems to be that the glory of God came to Abraham *while he was still in* Mesopotamia. These religious leaders were too Jerusalem focused, too temple obsessed. They had better get their eyes open, Stephen was saying, or they would miss what God was doing. It was happening, not in the temple recesses, in the Holy Place, or Holy of Holies, but rather in the temple courtyard and in the streets of Jerusalem. There the gospel of Jesus Christ was being preached and confirmed with powerful exhibitions of God's power working through the apostles.

> All I have seen teaches me to trust the Creator for all I have not seen.
> *Ralph Waldo Emerson*

7:4-5 "So Abraham left the land of the Chaldeans and lived in Haran until his father died. Then God brought him here to the land where you now live. But God gave him no

inheritance here, not even one square foot of land. God did promise, however, that eventually the whole country would belong to Abraham and his descendants—though he had no children yet."NLT

Faith is like radar that sees through the fog the reality of things at a distance that the human eye cannot see.
Corrie Ten Boom

The land of the Chaldeans is the same as Mesopotamia, mentioned in the previous verse. The first stop on Abraham's journey to the land of Canaan was at *Haran,* a large city in the upper Euphrates valley.

Even after settling in the Promised Land (curiously referred to as *the land where you now live*), Abraham owned no property. Only very late in his life, when he needed a place to bury Sarah, did he buy any property there (Genesis 23). Stephen referred to both the *land,* of which Abraham owned *not even one square foot,* and the promised *descendants*—none of whom had even been born yet, both crucial aspects of the covenant promise God had given Abraham.

The point so far seems to be that Abraham had to believe the unfulfilled promises of God. He had to look ahead in faith to what God was doing, not to what seemed best or most logical.

LESSONS IN FAITH

Stephen used his knowledge that all Jews were well acquainted with the story of Abraham to prod his listeners into going beneath the mere facts of the patriarch's existence. Stephen pointed to spiritual lessons from Abraham's life. Abraham trusted God in situations where common sense would have led most people to doubt. Similarly, human reason had convinced the Jewish leaders that a simple carpenter from Nazareth could not possibly be the promised Messiah. Using the life of Abraham, Stephen reminded his audience that God seldom acts in an expected manner. Don't let your familiarity with Bible stories blind you to God's working behind the scenes. Learn the lessons of faith that are gained from reflecting on the lives of biblical saints.

7:6-7 "God spoke to him in this way: 'Your descendants will be strangers in a country not their own, and they will be enslaved and mistreated four hundred years. But I will punish the nation they serve as slaves,' God said, 'and afterward they will come out of that country and worship me in this place.'"NIV Abraham's faith was tested further when he was told that his *descendants* would be *enslaved and mistreated four hundred years.* This mention of "four hundred years" is the first of a number of difficulties in this speech concerning historical numbers, sequences, and biblical quotations. For example, see the discrepancies between the numbers in Genesis 15:13, the numbers in Exodus 12:40, and Paul's reference in Galatians 3:17 as to the length of time of the Egyptian enslavement. In these issues and others, readers must remember that Stephen may have been referring to traditional reckonings by the scholars of the day (some of whom were listening to this speech) or perhaps even to popular writings of the day. Often Stephen appears not to be strictly quoting a particular passage of Scripture but alluding to the interpretations that were common to the thinking of the day.

Along with his references to Mesopotamia, Haran, and Abraham's lack of property, Stephen added the details of the trek to Egypt (7:14-15). The Hebrews did eventually *come out of that country* to *worship* God in Israel, but God had been with them in Egypt—still revealing himself to them, still guiding them, and still blessing them. The key was God, his will, and his guidance, not the *place* of the blessing.

THE PROBLEM WITH RITUAL

The Jewish rite of circumcision, like Israel's regular sacrifices and annual feasts, was intended to be a very meaningful event. As with all religious rituals, circumcision was designed to serve as an outer symbol of an inner reality. Those who participated thoughtfully would be reminded of profound spiritual truths. But we know from our own experiences of repeating the church creeds, saying the Lord's Prayer, or celebrating ordinances like baptism and the Lord's Supper that it is difficult to avoid merely going through the motions. We are often guilty of participating passively and mindlessly in religious exercises. Make it your goal to give God your full attention (body, soul, and spirit) the next time you pray, take Communion, or take part in a church ceremony.

7:8 **"Then he gave Abraham the covenant of circumcision. And Abraham became the father of Isaac and circumcised him eight days after his birth. Later Isaac became the father of Jacob, and Jacob became the father of the twelve patriarchs."**NIV *Circumcision* was a sign of the promise or *covenant* made between God, Abraham, and the entire nation of Israel (Genesis 17:9-13). Stephen pointed out that God always had kept his side of the promise, but Israel had failed, again and again, to keep its side. Although the Jews in Stephen's day still circumcised their baby boys, they failed to obey God. The people's hearts were far from him. Their lack of faith and lack of obedience meant that they had failed to keep their part of the covenant.

Isaac was Abraham's son, born to him in his old age (see

Genesis 20–28 for Isaac's story). *Jacob,* in turn, was one of Isaac's twin sons, born with Esau (see Genesis 25–35; 46–49 for Jacob's story). These three men formed the foundation of the nation of Israel; God is called "the God of Abraham, Isaac, and Jacob" (see Exodus 3:16). Jacob *became the father of the twelve patriarchs;* this means that Jacob's twelve sons became the ancestors of each of the twelve tribes of Israel (see Genesis 49).

7:9a "Because the patriarchs were jealous of Joseph, they sold him as a slave into Egypt."[NIV] Stephen's speech moved to a brief summary of the life of Joseph. The mention of *the patriarchs* and their jealousy of Joseph showed that, from the very start, Abraham's descendants had a tendency to be jealous.

The word "patriarchs" refers to Joseph's brothers who *were jealous of Joseph* for a number of reasons. Their father, Jacob, obviously favored his first son by his beloved wife, Rachel (Genesis 35:24; 37:3). Joseph alone received a valuable gift from his father, a beautiful robe. Joseph's brothers hated him. They couldn't say a kind word to him (Genesis 37:4). In addition, Joseph had dreams that seemed to place him as ruler over the family; then he would tell the brothers about those dreams (Genesis 37:5-11). This irritated them even more. When they had opportunity, the jealous brothers *sold [Joseph] as a slave into Egypt.* The story is recorded in Genesis 37:12-36.

7:9b-10 "But God was with him and delivered him from his anguish. And God gave him favor before Pharaoh, king of Egypt. God also gave Joseph unusual wisdom, so that Pharaoh appointed him governor over all of Egypt and put him in charge of all the affairs of the palace."[NLT] God was indeed *with* Joseph. Genesis 39–50 records Joseph's ups and downs in Egypt—yet he always remained faithful to God. In the end, *God gave him favor before Pharaoh* himself. Joseph had shown *unusual wisdom* in every place that he had served, *so that Pharaoh appointed him governor over all of Egypt and put him in charge of all the affairs of the palace.* As the following verses demonstrate, Joseph become the savior of his people.

Notice how often God is mentioned in this verse: God was with him; God gave Joseph favor; God gave Joseph unusual wisdom; God was working in an unusual way in an unusual place

> God moves in a
> mysterious way
> His wonders to perform;
> He plants his footsteps
> in the sea
> And rides upon the storm.
> Deep in unfathomable
> mines
> Of never-failing skill,
> He treasures up His
> bright designs
> And works His sovereign
> will. *William Cowper*

(outside of Israel). A wise student of history would expect God to intervene again.

7:11-13 "Then a famine struck all Egypt and Canaan, bringing great suffering, and our fathers could not find food. When Jacob heard that there was grain in Egypt, he sent our fathers on their first visit. On their second visit, Joseph told his brothers who he was, and Pharaoh learned about Joseph's family."[NIV] When a *famine struck all Egypt and Canaan,* the leaders in Egypt were not caught off guard, for Pharaoh had foreseen it in a dream from God, which God had given Joseph the ability to interpret. As a result Joseph had wisely suggested that during the good years before the famine, extra grain be collected and held so that when the famine years came, there would be food for everyone (Genesis 41). The famine reached all the way to Canaan, *bringing great suffering,* and *our fathers* (referring to Jacob and his twelve sons) *could not find food.* Word came *that there was grain in Egypt* (thanks to Joseph's wise planning), so people from all over the world traveled to Egypt to purchase grain. Jacob sent his sons *on their first visit* to Egypt to get food, and Joseph recognized them immediately. He did not reveal himself, however, for he wanted to find out first if their characters had improved since that day they had sold him as a slave.

It was on the brothers' *second visit* that Joseph revealed himself to them, having thoroughly tested them for changes in their attitudes. In what has to be one of the most emotional scenes in all of Scripture (Genesis 45), Joseph revealed himself to his brothers. On this second trip, Pharaoh *learned about Joseph's family;* this opened the door for moving the entire patriarchal band to Egypt. This was all part of God's sovereign plan to provide for Israel's needs in the famine and to move them to Egypt, as had been predicted to Abraham (Genesis 15:13).

7:14-15 "Then Joseph sent for his father, Jacob, and all his relatives to come to Egypt, seventy-five persons in all. So Jacob went to Egypt. He died there, as did all his sons."[NLT] After his reunion with his brothers, *Joseph sent for his father, Jacob, and all his relatives to come to Egypt.* Joseph had not forgotten his faith, his roots, or his beloved father, despite a change of fortune and culture! Stephen said that there were *seventy-five persons* who made the trek to Egypt. He must have been using the Septuagint when he made this quote or citing a Hebrew text different than the Masoretic Text, which reads "seventy" (see Genesis 46:27; Exodus 1:5). (One Dead Sea Scroll manuscript of Exodus 1:5 says "seventy-five" persons.)

OBSERVING THE CLUES
Stephen recognized the amazing way in which Joseph's life paralleled and pointed ahead to the life of Christ. The similarities are startling: both loved by their fathers, hated by their brothers, taken to Egypt, falsely accused, exalted after suffering, forgave the ones who wronged them, and saved their nation. Because God wants us to know him, he has left evidence of his existence, activity, and plan throughout the universe and in our lives. Are we like the religious leaders who listened to Stephen? Are we so caught up in our prideful presuppositions that we are missing the divine clues all around us? We must open our eyes and see God's divine plan at work in history.

7:16 "Their bodies were brought back to Shechem and placed in the tomb that Abraham had bought from the sons of Hamor at Shechem for a certain sum of money."NIV There is a problem with Stephen's apparent reference to the location of Abraham's tomb. Genesis states that *the tomb that Abraham had bought* was located in Hebron (Genesis 49:29–50:13). Evidently, *their bodies* that were *brought back to Shechem* refers to Joseph and his family and does not include Abraham, Isaac, and Jacob and their wives, who were buried in Hebron.

The section on Abraham now completed, Stephen moved to his longest segment—the life of Moses and the events immediately following.

7:17-19 "As the time drew near for God to fulfill his promise to Abraham, the number of our people in Egypt greatly increased. Then another king, who knew nothing about Joseph, became ruler of Egypt. He dealt treacherously with our people and oppressed our forefathers by forcing them to throw out their newborn babies so that they would die."NIV The four hundred years had almost passed, and so *the time drew near for God to fulfill his promise to Abraham* (Genesis 15:13-15). God had told Abraham that after his descendants had been in Egypt for four hundred years, he would "punish the nation they serve as slaves, and afterward they will come out with great possessions" (Genesis 15:14 NIV).

The nation of Israel was "born" in Egypt. The *number* of the *people in Egypt greatly increased* (from seventy-five to likely over 2 million—see Exodus 12:37), and they experienced great prosperity until Egyptian dynasties changed and *another king, who knew nothing about Joseph, became ruler of Egypt.* The reference to throwing *out their newborn babies* is a reminder of the events of Exodus 1:15-22; Pharaoh ordered the Hebrew midwives to kill every male newborn. The slaughter of the innocents by Herod at the birth of Jesus Christ a few short decades earlier should have been ringing a bell in the minds of Stephen's listeners.

THE GREATER REALITIES
Stephen's review of Jewish history presents a clear testimony of God's faithfulness and sovereignty. Despite the continued failures of his chosen people and swirling world events, God was working out his plan. When faced by a confusing array of circumstances, remember that: (1) God is in control—nothing surprises him; (2) this world is not all there is—it will pass away, but God is eternal; (3) God is just, and he will make things right, punishing the wicked and rewarding the faithful; (4) God wants to use you (like Joseph, Moses, and Stephen) to make a difference in the world.

7:20-22 "At that time Moses was born—a beautiful child in God's eyes. His parents cared for him at home for three months. When at last they had to abandon him, Pharaoh's daughter found him and raised him as her own son. Moses was taught all the wisdom of the Egyptians, and he became mighty in both speech and action."NLT During the days when the Hebrew midwives were under orders to kill Hebrew baby boys, *Moses was born.* God did not choose a convenient time for the child to be born; instead, he chose the worst of times. During this horrible time in Israel's history, the nation's first real "deliverer" was born. He was *a beautiful child in God's eyes.* Stephen dealt briefly with the early rearing of the child *at home,* the rescue by *Pharaoh's daughter* (by adoption), and the rearing of Moses in *all the wisdom of the Egyptians,* to the point that he became *mighty in both speech and action.* The story is told in Exodus 1–2.

NOTHING WASTED
Stephen's review of Moses' early life shows how God prepares his people for future service. Though Moses was cruelly taken from his family, his privileged Egyptian upbringing provided him with the practical training and cross-cultural insights he would need later in life when it came time to lead the Jews to the Promised Land. Because God is sovereign, nothing about our lives is ever accidental. Nothing is ever wasted. Trust God to take all your hard times, educational opportunities, and life experiences and weave them together to equip you to be effective for his kingdom.

Moses was a great figure of the nation of Israel, greater in the estimation of many than even the founding father, Abraham.

Moses was the vehicle God used for the salvation of the nation, for letting in so much of his light through the revelation on Mount Sinai, and for bringing the nation to the very edge of entrance into the Promised Land. Though Moses' estimation of himself was quite different than Stephen's statement here (see Exodus 4:10), history records him as truly a "mighty" man.

Again Stephen emphasized that God was working in the nation, but through some very odd circumstances (adoption by an Egyptian princess) and in a strange location (outside the borders of geographic Israel).

7:23-25 **"When Moses was forty years old, he decided to visit his fellow Israelites. He saw one of them being mistreated by an Egyptian, so he went to his defense and avenged him by killing the Egyptian. Moses thought that his own people would realize that God was using him to rescue them, but they did not."**NIV Moses' first attempt to lead his people came when he tried to save an Israelite who was *being mistreated by an Egyptian.* Moses, the prince, came to the *defense* of his fellow Israelite *and avenged him by killing the Egyptian.* Apparently, Moses knew his calling and *thought that his own people would realize that God was using him to rescue them.* Unfortunately, *they did not.*

This is the first of four direct references to the fact that Israel had totally missed the work of a "redeemer" sent by God (see 7:27, 35, 39). Such a pattern of behavior was replayed many times in Israel's history and was happening again in the first century, as the Jews were missing their Redeemer, Jesus.

GOD'S PLAN, IN GOD'S TIME

Why did Stephen relate the incident in which Moses killed a cruel Egyptian taskmaster? Perhaps to remind the Jewish leaders of the truth that "There is a path before each person that seems right, but it ends in death" (Proverbs 14:12 NLT). Weeks earlier, the religious leaders had convinced themselves and each other that Jesus was a dangerous threat. They thought he had to be eliminated. So they killed the very one sent to bring them life! In Moses' case, God *did* want to use him to deliver the Jews, but not at that time and not in that way. Don't run ahead of God. Don't take action without first spending much time in earnest prayer and without seeking wise and godly counsel.

7:26-28 **"The next day Moses came upon two Israelites who were fighting. He tried to reconcile them by saying, 'Men, you are brothers; why do you want to hurt each other?' But the man who was mistreating the other pushed Moses aside and said, 'Who made you ruler and judge over us? Do you want to kill**

me as you killed the Egyptian yesterday?'"[NIV] The incident with the *two Israelites who were fighting* presents an even more compelling case for the absurdity of Israel's initial rejection of Moses as deliverer. The two fighters questioned Moses as he interceded in their argument, *"Who made you ruler and judge over us?"* The Jewish Council showed the same belligerence concerning Stephen's speech, in effect saying, "What makes you think this Jesus of Nazareth should be ruler and judge over us?"

"Listen, Israel!" Stephen was saying, "Your Redeemer has come, but you have misunderstood his motive and his method." The parallels between the nation's rejection of Jesus and its early rejection of Moses should have been another wake-up call. But they weren't.

7:29-30 "When Moses heard that, he fled the country and lived as a foreigner in the land of Midian, where his two sons were born. Forty years later, in the desert near Mount Sinai, an angel appeared to Moses in the flame of a burning bush."[NLT] Rejected by his own people and fearing for his life because he had killed an Egyptian, Moses *fled the country and lived as a foreigner in the land of Midian* (northwest Arabia). For *forty* long *years,* he served his father-in-law as a shepherd. Eighty years of his life gone—it seemed that Moses had spent most of his life waiting. But the wait soon would be over. There in the *desert,* after what must have seemed an eternity, God spoke to him.

> I must be poor and want, before I can exercise the virtue of gratitude; miserable and in torment, before I can exercise the virtue of patience.
> *John Donne*

Stephen reminded his audience of the incredible moment when *an angel appeared to Moses in the flame of a burning bush* (see Exodus 3–4). God was working. God was speaking. God was about to deliver his people. There was no temple here, no tabernacle, and they were nowhere near Jerusalem. God had chosen to speak from a bush in the desert!

WAITING ON GOD

Stephen's message before the Jewish Council was filled with references to the passing of time, to the long years that God's people spent waiting on God to act and fulfill his promises. It seems that humans always hate to wait. We get impatient, doubt God's plan, and try to implement our own agendas. But taking matters into our own hands usually leads to heartache, if not outright disaster. How much better it is to wait on God, to let him reveal himself and his plan, and then to humbly trust and obey!

7:31-32 "When he saw this, he was amazed at the sight. As he went over to look more closely, he heard the Lord's voice: 'I am the God of your fathers, the God of Abraham, Isaac and Jacob.' Moses trembled with fear and did not dare to look."[NIV] Quite appropriately, Moses *was amazed at the sight.* As he approached the burning bush, *he heard the Lord's voice.* What a moment! God was speaking on Mount Sinai as he would on so many other occasions, revealing more and more of himself and his unfolding plan of redemption for his people and, beyond them, the world.

The mention of *Abraham, Isaac and Jacob* would connect this present revelation to all that had been said and done through the patriarchs. As God had spoken to Abraham in a foreign land, as he had led Jacob and his family to a foreign land, so now in the desert of Midian, God was speaking to Moses, preparing him to lead his people to the next stage of their salvation journey.

Stephen wanted his audience to remember how amazed Moses was and how unusual were the timing, place, and form of revelation that God used. It was entirely unexpected and without historical precedent in God's dealing with his people. Moses, as one would expect, *trembled with fear* and evidently hid his face from the direc-tion from which the voice was coming. Moses had moved *over to look more closely* and had listened to the voice of God. Why hadn't the Jewish religious leaders done the same?

We need never shout across the spaces to an absent God. He is nearer than our own soul. Closer than our most secret thoughts. *A. W. Tozer*

7:33-34 "Then the Lord said to him, 'Take off the sandals from your feet, for the place where you are standing is holy ground. I have surely seen the mistreatment of my people who are in Egypt and have heard their groaning, and I have come down to rescue them. Come now, I will send you to Egypt.'"[NRSV] The command to remove *the sandals* from his feet and God's designation of *the place* as *holy ground* was significant in Stephen's argument. It reminded his audience that God can speak from wherever he wishes and that any place becomes "holy ground" when God is there. God has worked in the past and will continue to work in the future outside of the boundaries of the Holy Land or any building called holy (such as a sanctuary).

God reminded Moses that though eighty years had passed in his life and though four hundred years had passed in Israel's life in Egypt, God had *surely seen the mistreatment* of his people and had *heard their groaning.* So he would intervene at this point in history and *come down to rescue them.*

But God would not be doing the rescue alone. He planned to use Moses: *"Come now, I will send you to Egypt"*—surely the last place that Moses wanted to go. God's method has always been people. He uses people from every walk of life to do his work. Moses would soon be one of them.

GOD SEES
God always sees the plight of his own. The same God who appeared to the exiled Hagar (Genesis 16:1-16) saw Israel's suffering in Egypt. He saw it and would do something about it, but on *his* timetable, in *his* way, and with *his* chosen rescuer. If you have come to a place in your life where you wonder if your troubles have been missed by God, overlooked, and pushed aside for some more urgent heavenly matter, take heart from Moses and the children of Israel. God *sees* it all. And he *will,* in his time, take action.

7:35 "This is the same Moses whom they had rejected with the words, 'Who made you ruler and judge?' He was sent to be their ruler and deliverer by God himself, through the angel who appeared to him in the bush."[NIV] This verse summarizes Stephen's talk and wraps up this review of Moses' life. The man sent back to Egypt as Israel's *ruler and deliverer* was *the same Moses whom they had rejected.* The sender was *God himself,* who, *through the angel who appeared* in the burning bush, revealed himself to Moses.

The word translated "deliverer" or "savior" is the Greek term *lutrotes.* It conveys the idea of redemption and is used only of Moses in the New Testament. In the succeeding verses, Stephen also notes that Moses was a prophet (7:37) and mediator (7:38). Stephen's point seems to be that even greater than Moses, the lawgiver who "saved" Israel from Egyptian bondage, was Jesus, the grace-giver who offered eternal freedom from the sin of slavery. If Moses was beloved and revered, Jesus should be to an infinitely greater degree.

7:36 "And by means of many miraculous signs and wonders, he led them out of Egypt, through the Red Sea, and back and forth through the wilderness for forty years."[NLT] The miracle of Israel's deliverance from Egyptian bondage, the saving of the firstborn through the blood spread upon the door frames (the Passover—Exodus 12), the direct leading of God, the destruction of the pursuing armies of Pharaoh, the feeding by God—all these displays of God's presence and power *(many miraculous signs and wonders),* as well as God's revelation at Mount Sinai, were monumental miracles in Israel's history. But this was not their only purpose. So much of what God had revealed, so many of the miracles God had performed, and much of what lay behind the intricate system of sacrifices (which he would show Moses), would help God's people recognize the coming Messiah. God wanted his people to be ready to recognize and receive the ultimate Deliverer (the one who would deliver people from their sins) when he came. A significant purpose for the design of the miracles and the ensuing feasts and sacrifices was to teach people about the holiness of their God and the necessity of the spilling of blood to remove the stain of sin. This would better enable them to recognize the "Lamb of God who takes away the sin of the world" (John 1:29 NLT) when he came.

The reminder of the journey *back and forth through the wilderness for forty years* was yet another example of Israel ignoring the command of God and rejecting his direction of them. For forty years they wandered through the wilderness, burying the entire older generation (with the exception of Moses, Joshua, and Caleb—see Numbers 14:21-45). It was Israel's stubborn, Holy Spirit-resisting (see 7:51) refusal to recognize the leading of God that got them excluded from experiencing his blessing in the land. Stephen's current generation would do well to remember their forefathers' propensity to miss what God was saying and doing.

7:37-38 "This is that Moses who told the Israelites, 'God will send you a prophet like me from your own people.' He was in the assembly in the desert, with the angel who spoke to him on Mount Sinai, and with our fathers; and he received living words to pass on to us."NIV The Jews originally thought this *prophet* was Joshua. But Moses had been prophesying about the coming Messiah (Deuteronomy 18:15). Peter also had quoted this verse as referring to the Messiah (3:22).

Stephen used the word *ekklesia* (translated *assembly*) to describe the congregation or people of God *in the desert.* This word means "called out ones" and was used by the first-century Christians to describe their own community or "assembly." Stephen's point was that the giving of the law through Moses to the Jews was the sign of the covenant. By obedience, then, would they continue to be God's covenant people. When they disobeyed (7:39), however, they broke the covenant and forfeited their right to be the chosen people—God's congregation.

From Galatians 3:19 and Hebrews 2:2, it appears that God had given the law to Moses through angels. Exodus 31:18 says God wrote the Ten Commandments himself (inscribed by the "finger of God"). Apparently, God used angelic messengers as mediators to deliver his law to Moses, who *received* those *living words to pass on to* the nation. This message is called "living words" or "life-giving words." These words point to life and give life to those who follow their instruction (Deuteronomy 30:19; 32:47; Romans 7:10).

7:39 **"But our ancestors rejected Moses and wanted to return to Egypt."**NLT Stephen again stated what had become an obvious theme, especially from the life of Moses. The Jewish ancestors of the audience and of the speaker *(our ancestors)* had *rejected Moses*—his message, his leadership, and his claim to be speaking for God. Incredibly, they *wanted to return to* the slavery and idolatry of *Egypt* (Numbers 14:1-4).

THE DEADLINESS OF UNBELIEF
Stephen's reference to Israel's failures in the wilderness should have caused an alarm to go off in the minds and hearts of the Jewish Council members. Imagine the suffering they could have avoided if the Jews in the wilderness had not instigated the incident with the golden calf. Imagine the consequences if God had granted their silly wish to return to Egyptian bondage. How unfortunate that the Jewish leaders did not realize through Stephen's words their own propensity for foolish unbelief. How tragic that they did not turn away from their sin and call on the mercy of God. We need to learn from their history that when we reject God's will and resist the leadership of his appointed servants, we consign ourselves to lives of misery.

7:40-41 **"They told Aaron, 'Make us gods who will go before us. As for this fellow Moses who led us out of Egypt—we don't know what has happened to him!' That was the time they made an idol in the form of a calf. They brought sacrifices to it and held a celebration in honor of what their hands had made."**NIV The Jews' ancestors had not only rejected Joseph and Moses, at one crucial point in their history they had also rejected God! While Moses was up on Mount Sinai receiving the Law, the children of Israel got tired of waiting. They forgot about God and decided that because they didn't *know what [had] happened to* Moses, they needed a new leader and a new god. They asked Aaron to construct a god *who [would] go before* them because the God who had done all the miracles in Egypt had apparently forgotten them! In one sorry, sinful deed, the children of Israel blatantly, publicly, and corporately defied God. This "invisible" God and "absent" Moses were too much to bear. They wanted something they could see, even if it was the product of their own hands. Stephen's wording highlights the idiocy of it all, as he pictured them bringing *sacrifices to* the calf and holding a *celebration in honor of what their hands had made.* The story is told in Exodus 32.

7:42-43 "But God turned away and gave them over to the worship of the heavenly bodies. This agrees with what is written in the book of the prophets: 'Did you bring me sacrifices and offerings forty years in the desert, O house of Israel? You have lifted up the shrine of Molech and the star of your god Rephan, the idols you made to worship. Therefore I will send you into exile beyond Babylon.'"NIV The Israelites' worship of the golden calf was the beginning of a downward spiral. At times they returned to God, but far more often they were running after the gods of the evil nations surrounding them. The reference to *heavenly bodies* refers to Israel's practice of worshiping deities associated with stars and planets (see Jeremiah 8:1-2). It was a form of godless worship that became more prevalent in the later years of the kingdom.

This quote from Amos (Amos 5:25-27) supports Stephen's accusation that Israel had a history of idol worship. *Molech* and *Rephan* were planetary divinities. Molech was an Ammonite deity associated with child sacrifice, while Rephan was a god "borrowed" from Egypt. Both became popular options for Israel's idolatry as her history progressed.

The ancestors of Stephen's current audience, the audience who stood in rejection of Jesus Christ, had a history of rejecting not only God's messengers but even of turning from God himself to their own handmade gods. The cost for their idolatry had been *exile beyond Babylon.* No one within the sound of Stephen's voice could have any doubt about the historical accuracy of that statement.

7:44 "Our ancestors carried the Tabernacle with them through the wilderness. It was constructed in exact accordance with the plan shown to Moses by God."NLT Suddenly, the subject switches to this intriguing section concerning the tabernacle. Having sufficiently denied the charge against him that he had blasphemed Moses (6:11), Stephen proceeded to address the charge that he had blasphemed God. The tabernacle was a movable worship center used by the Israelites prior to the construction of the temple by Solomon. The detailed instructions for constructing the tabernacle were spelled out for Moses and the people of Israel (see Exodus 25–31). The construction plans were *shown to Moses by God* himself. This large and mobile tent was suitable for the wilderness wanderings because it could be taken apart and moved easily from location to location. It was the place where, after the nation left Mount Sinai, Moses would meet with God (Exodus 29:42; 30:6, 36; Numbers 17:4).

LIVING TEMPLES
Stephen had been accused of speaking against the temple (6:13). Although he recognized the importance of the temple, he knew that it was not more important than God. God is not limited; he doesn't live only in a house of worship but wherever hearts of faith are open to receive him (Isaiah 66:1-2). Solomon knew this when he prayed at the dedication of the temple (2 Chronicles 6:18). Is your worship of God confined to church on Sunday? God wants to live in us at all times (1 Corinthians 6:19).

7:45 **"Years later, when Joshua led the battles against the Gentile nations that God drove out of this land, the Tabernacle was taken with them into their new territory. And it was used there until the time of King David."**NLT When the people finally moved into the land of Canaan under Joshua's leadership, *the Tabernacle was taken with them* and remained with them as they settled the land and had many *battles against the Gentile nations.* Stephen reminded his audience that *God drove* the Gentiles out of the Promised Land. This temporary and mobile tabernacle remained with the people *until the time of King David,* when Jerusalem was made the capital city and David began making plans for a temple.

7:46-47 **"David found favor with God and asked for the privilege of building a permanent Temple for the God of Jacob. But it was Solomon who actually built it."**NLT *King David found favor with God and asked* to build a permanent structure *for the God of Jacob.* He desired this so much that he wrote about it in a psalm: "How he swore to the Lord and vowed to the Mighty One of Jacob, 'I will not enter my house or get into my bed; I will not give sleep to my eyes or slumber to my eyelids, until I find a place for the LORD, a dwelling place for the Mighty One of Jacob'" (Psalm 132:2-5 NRSV).

Second Samuel 7:1-16 relates God's answer to David's request: "When you die, I will raise up one of your descendants, and I will make his kingdom strong. He is the one who will build a house—a temple—for my name" (2 Samuel 7:12-13 NLT). David's son Solomon, the next king of Israel, would oversee construction of a glorious temple to God in Jerusalem (1 Kings 5–8).

Only in Christ, however, would this vision of David and

promise of God ever be realized. The ultimate "temple" would be the new dwelling place of God—the hearts of men and women.

7:48-50 "However, the Most High doesn't live in temples made by human hands. As the prophet says, 'Heaven is my throne, and the earth is my footstool. Could you ever build me a temple as good as that?' asks the Lord. 'Could you build a dwelling place for me? Didn't I make everything in heaven and earth?'"[NLT] The tabernacle had been God's home on earth. He had filled it with his glory. Almost five hundred years later, Solomon built the temple, which replaced the tabernacle as the central place of worship. God also filled the temple with his glory (2 Chronicles 5:13-14). But when Israel turned from God, his glory and presence departed from the temple, and it was destroyed by invading armies (2 Kings 25). The temple was rebuilt in 516 B.C., and God's glory returned in even greater splendor nearly five centuries later when Jesus Christ, God's Son, entered it and taught. When Jesus was crucified, God's glory again left the temple. However, God no longer needed a physical building after Jesus rose from the dead. God's temple now is his church, the body of believers.

> When men stop worshipping God, they promptly start worshipping man, with disastrous results. *George Orwell*

God *(the Most High) doesn't live in temples made by human hands.* To support this, Stephen quoted from *the prophet* Isaiah: *"Heaven is my throne, and the earth is my footstool"* (Isaiah 66:1-2a). King Solomon, at the dedication ceremony of the new temple, expressed a similar sentiment: "Will God indeed dwell on the earth? Even heaven and the highest heaven cannot contain you, much less this house that I have built!" (1 Kings 8:27 NRSV).

Stephen wanted his audience to be reminded of the truth of Scripture that the temple was a building and *just* a building. It was an important one, but it did *not* contain God, nor was it deserving of the "temple-olatry" that prevailed among the Jewish religious leadership of the day. They had magnified the temple's importance far beyond God's intention, and were giving more attention to the building (and "sins" or "blasphemy" against it) than they were to the God for whose glory it had been constructed!

As it was with in Jesus' ministry, the religious leaders were more intent on scrupulously guarding the temple building and their traditions than they were in exhibiting the virtues of justice, mercy, and faithfulness (see Matthew 23:23-24).

Interestingly enough, Stephen made this exact point by what

he did *not* say in this verse. He stopped his quotation of Isaiah 66:1-2 right in the middle of the second verse, leaving off the balance of verse 2, which says, "But this is the one to whom I will look, to the humble and contrite in spirit, who trembles at my word" (NRSV). Surely every member of the scholarly Jewish Council would have known the second half of that verse, probably quoting it in their head as Stephen was saying it. They had let their priorities slip greatly.

WRONG PRIORITIES
Stephen's words about the tabernacle and later the temple were aimed at a people who had developed an unhealthy view of their place of worship. Through the years the Israelites had come to revere the actual structure and its contents more than God himself. Rather than being a place to meet with God, the temple had become for them a source of religious snobbery. Stephen's words convey the truth that God cannot be confined to a building and suggest that, despite the prideful presuppositions, the temple was *not* the holiest place on earth and had become a mere gathering place for infidels! Be careful not to become so caught up in human religious systems that you forget the God who lives now. Those who replace God or try to confine him are guilty of idolatry.

7:51 **"You stiff-necked people, with uncircumcised hearts and ears! You are just like your fathers: You always resist the Holy Spirit!"**[NIV] Stephen moved to the critical point of his speech. He had responded brilliantly to the accusations against him. All that remained was to drive the point of application home to his audience. If the sermon has a major idea or theme, this verse is it. Stephen accused his hearers of being a product of their parentage—they were *just like [their] fathers.* Those who stood before him had not broken the cycle of sin that had been passed down to them.

"Stiff-necked" is the very term God had used of Israel at Mount Sinai (Exodus 33:3) and refers to their unbending stubbornness in their unjust and unholy causes and their absolute refusal to turn back to God.

Stephen's reference to *uncircumcised hearts and ears* pointed out the fact that though his audience had been circumcised in the literal sense and, thus, bore upon their bodies the sign of the Abrahamic covenant, their hearts were untouched, unbroken, and unavailable to the voice of God as spoken by his *Holy Spirit.* They were resisting the Holy Spirit. This means that they were willfully thwarting his leading by disobedience or rebellion. (For more information, see *Life Application Commentary: Ephesians* on Ephesians 4:30, and *Life Application Commentary: 1 and 2 Thessalonians* on 1 Thessalonians 5:19.)

UNCIRCUMCISED HEARTS:
The "uncircumcised heart" pictures religious activity (circumcision being the sign of the covenant with Abraham) with no corresponding internal spiritual reality. Today many religious activities can lull us to sleep. Many will boast of their church attendance, baptism, confirmation, grand building, or large ministry—and yet their hearts have not been "circumcised," that is, touched, changed, *converted* by God himself. Make sure your heart is devoted to God and that your activities reflect that reality.

7:52-53 "Which of the prophets did your ancestors not persecute? They killed those who foretold the coming of the Righteous One, and now you have become his betrayers and murderers. You are the ones that received the law as ordained by angels, and yet you have not kept it."[NRSV] Indeed, many of their *prophets* had been persecuted or killed: Uriah (Jeremiah 26:20-23), Jeremiah (Jeremiah 38:1-6), Isaiah (tradition says he was killed by King Manasseh; see 2 Kings 21:16), Amos (Amos 7:10-13), Zechariah (not the author of the Bible book, but the son of Jehoiada the priest, 2 Chronicles 24:20-22), and Elijah (1 Kings 19:1-2). Jesus had made the same charges against the Jews (Matthew 23:37; Luke 11:47-48). Jesus had also told a parable about how the Jews had constantly rejected God's messages and had persecuted his messengers (Luke 20:9-19). See Hebrews 11:35-38 on the killing of the prophets.

Not only had the Jews killed the prophets who had *foretold the coming of the Righteous One* (the Messiah, Jesus Christ), but they had *become his betrayers and murderers.* It is almost inconceivable. How could they not see their forefathers' tendency to miss what God was doing right in their midst? The world had yawned while Abraham had packed his belongings and had left the civilized world to go to who knows where. The brothers of Joseph (the literal sons of Israel) had jealously sold their future savior into slavery. The children of Israel had rejected their deliverer, Moses, from the start to the finish of his ministry. How could they be the very ones who had *received the law as ordained by angels* and yet all along the way had *not kept it?* God himself had been rejected in their ancestors' constant forays into idolatry. God's Messiah, the Righteous One, the Savior of the world, was the latest victim of their rebellion. They were about to kill another—Stephen himself.

LAWBREAKERS
Stephen concluded his sermon to this group, who prided themselves on knowing and keeping the commandments of God, by making the accusation that they had deliberately disobeyed God's law. Their ancestors had been guilty of murdering the prophets (7:51-52) and testifying falsely against Christ (violations of Deuteronomy 5:17, 20). They had ignored Moses' clear command to listen to the great prophet who would be sent by God (Deuteronomy 18:15). They were surrounded by truth, but that truth never pierced their hearts. Instead of convicting them and changing their lives, the law became something they used to condemn others and to justify themselves. The only way we can avoid a similar fate is to humble ourselves before God's Word. Rather than using the Bible to condemn others, apply it first to your life, and make the required changes.

7:54 **When they heard this, they were furious and gnashed their teeth at him.**[NIV] These strong and sudden accusations (stronger even than Peter's in 3:13-15) must have suddenly incited the crowd. These final words so enraged his hearers that they *were furious and gnashed their teeth at him.* "Gnashing their teeth" meant clenching their teeth or grinding them as a sign of anger. Their rage could no longer be restrained.

> We can easily forgive a child who is afraid of the dark; the real tragedy of life is when men are afraid of the light. *Plato*

THE DEATH SENTENCE
Stephen's defense before the Council stung his listeners. As he preached his bold defense, Stephen must have known that he was speaking his own death sentence. Members of the Council would not tolerate having their evil motives exposed. But Stephen was not speaking out of spite. His manner was not one of cold indifference or harsh judgment. While being stoned to death, Stephen lovingly prayed for the forgiveness of his enemies! This is a powerful reminder of the truth that when we confront others with the fact of their sin, we must be motivated solely by a compassionate desire to see them right with God.

7:55-56 **But Stephen, full of the Holy Spirit, gazed steadily upward into heaven and saw the glory of God, and he saw Jesus standing in the place of honor at God's right hand. "Look, I see the heavens opened and the Son of Man standing in the place of honor at God's right hand!"**[NLT] In contrast to their rage, Stephen was still in control, *full of the Holy Spirit,* the ultimate source of strength and courage (see also 6:3, 5, 8, 15). The text tells us that as the maddened crowd drew nearer, Stephen kept his gaze *steadily upward.* In the process he *saw the glory of God, and he saw Jesus standing in the place of honor at God's right hand.*

This is the first record of the appearance of the resurrected Christ since his ascension in Acts 1. The posture of the Savior is of no small importance. Scripture makes it clear that Christ's normal posture upon completion of his work of redemption was to "sit" at the right hand of the Father (verses quoted from NIV, italics ours):

> Stephen has been confessing Christ before men, and now he sees Christ confessing his servant before God. The proper posture for a witness is the standing posture. Stephen, condemned by an earthly court, appeals for vindication to a heavenly court, and his vindicator in that supreme court is Jesus, who stands at God's right hand as Stephen's advocate.
>
> *F. F. Bruce*

- Psalm 110:1, "The LORD says to my Lord: '*Sit* at my right hand until I make your enemies a footstool for your feet.'"
- Mark 14:62, "'I am [the Messiah],' said Jesus. 'And you will see the Son of Man *sitting* at the right hand of the Mighty One and coming on the clouds of heaven.'"
- Colossians 3:1, "Since, then, you have been raised with Christ, set your hearts on things above, where Christ is *seated* at the right hand of God."
- Hebrews 1:3, "After he [Christ] had provided purification for sins, he *sat* down at the right hand of the Majesty in heaven."
- Hebrews 1:13, "To which of the angels did God ever say, '*Sit* at my right hand until I make your enemies a footstool for your feet?'"
- Hebrews 8:1, "The point of what we are saying is this: We do have such a high priest, who *sat* down at the right hand of the throne of the Majesty in heaven."
- Hebrews 10:12, "But when this priest had offered for all time one sacrifice for sins, he *sat* down at the right hand of God."
- Hebrews 12:2, "Let us fix our eyes on Jesus, the author and perfecter of our faith, who for the joy set before him endured the cross, scorning its shame, and *sat* down at the right hand of the throne of God."

Just before his death, however, Stephen saw Christ standing. Luke 12:8 records Jesus saying: "If anyone acknowledges me publicly here on earth, I, the Son of Man, will openly acknowledge that person in the presence of God's angels" (NLT). In this scene, as the church experienced the first (of many) to die for faith in Christ, Luke wanted his readers to know martyrs do not die alone—as if out of the gaze of their Savior. Christ was not only present at the right hand of the Father, but he also was (at least in Stephen's case) standing to receive his faithful servant home. There can be no greater nor more honorable reception than to have the Son of Man standing at one's entrance into his presence.

Stephen saw *the heavens opened.* This is a very important term for the presence of God and a sign of his revelation. The heavens opened at the baptism of Jesus (Luke 3:21-22) as a sign of affirmation of Jesus' deity. It was accompanied by the voice of God and the descending of the Spirit.

Stephen's reference to Jesus as *the Son of Man* is a rare use of that title for Christ outside of the Gospels. Jesus exclusively referred to himself as the Son of Man (Luke 9:22; 12:8). At Jesus' trial before the Jewish Council, Jesus promised the revelation of the Son of Man (Matthew 26:64) and then was tried for blasphemy. Luke was making the connection between Stephen and Jesus, which would have reassured those readers who feared persecution for their faith.

SPEAKING THE TRUTH

Stephen spoke bluntly about the Jewish leaders' guilt. Hard-hearted and blinded by sin, they would not tolerate Stephen's words, so they dragged him out and killed him. People may not kill us for witnessing about Christ, but they will let us know that they don't want to hear the truth and will often try to silence us. Keep honoring God in your conduct and words; though many may turn against you and your message, some will follow Christ. Remember, Stephen's death made a profound impact on Paul, who later became the world's greatest missionary. Even those who oppose you now may later turn to Christ.

7:57-58 But they covered their ears, and with a loud shout all rushed together against him. Then they dragged him out of the city and began to stone him; and the witnesses laid their coats at the feet of a young man named Saul.NRSV This pictures a violent mob taking the law into their own hands. The wording of this scene—covering *their ears,* shouting loudly, rushing together, and dragging Stephen out of the city—leads one to the conclusion that this was a sudden, impassioned, violent (and probably illegal) action.

With dramatic style Luke gave what would seem to be a

passing piece of information about the one who kept the *coats* while the stoning occurred: *a young man named Saul.* Saul, of course, is Paul (see 13:9), the great missionary who wrote many of the letters in the New Testament. Saul was his Hebrew name; Paul, the Greek equivalent, was used as he began his ministry to the Gentiles.

Paul hated and persecuted Jesus' followers. This is a great contrast to the Paul about whom Luke would write for most of the rest of the book of Acts—a devoted follower of Christ and a gifted gospel preacher. Paul was uniquely qualified to talk to the Jews about Jesus because he had once persecuted those who believed in Jesus, and he understood how the opposition felt. Paul is a powerful example of how no one is impossible for God to reach and change. Surely his close proximity to this emotional scene was a major part of tearing down the walls he had built between himself and God.

UNSEEN IMPACT

To our way of thinking, Stephen died prematurely. So gifted, so much to offer—yet his life was snuffed out after preaching one short sermon. A waste? Not really. A young man named Saul stood in the crowd. Saul not only was exposed to the supernatural quality of Stephen's life, but he was also one of the "targets" of Stephen's dying prayer for the salvation of his accusers. In short, Stephen may not have had a long ministry, but he had a strategic one. He played a vital part in the conversion of Saul, who became the great apostle who shook the world for Christ. Don't minimize the kind of impact you can have. We never know how God will use our seemingly small and insignificant actions to bring glory to himself.

CLOSING YOUR EARS:

The leaders covered their ears at Stephen's words (7:57). This is not very different from how the world has responded—how *we* have responded—to God's revealed truth through the years. How many times have you rejected the truth that was sent your way, relying on your practice of religion (with all its temple vestiges) to save you—a baptism, a confirmation, a membership, or a walked aisle? How often have you resisted Christ's overtures to you or even reacted in rage at God and what he has said? Are we so different from this mob, with hands over our ears like a two-year-old yelling at nothing in particular, trying to shut out the truth that is coming in? God wants us to turn back, to bow the knee, to stop before someone gets hurt—before *we* get hurt.

THE EFFECTS OF STEPHEN'S DEATH

Stephen's death was not in vain. Below are some of the events that were by-products, either directly or indirectly, of the persecution that began with Stephen's martyrdom.

1. Philip's evangelistic tour (8:4-40)
2. Paul's (Saul's) conversion (9:1-30)
3. Peter's missionary tour (9:32–11:18)
4. The founding of the church in Antioch of Syria (11:19-26)

7:59-60 **While they were stoning him, Stephen prayed, "Lord Jesus, receive my spirit." Then he fell on his knees and cried out, "Lord, do not hold this sin against them." When he had said this, he fell asleep.**[NIV] As they were in the process of stoning Stephen, he made two fascinating statements, both reminiscent of Christ's words on the cross. The first, *"Lord Jesus, receive my spirit,"* is similar to Christ's final words in Luke 23:46 (in some manuscripts). The second is a word of forgiveness: *"Lord, do not hold this sin against them."* Stephen had obviously learned from his Master some important lessons about how to live and how to die.

The final words of this chapter record the beautiful euphemistic reference for the death of one who belongs to Christ—*he fell asleep* (see also 1 Corinthians 11:30; 15:6, 18, 20; 1 Thessalonians 4:13-15).

FORGIVING ENEMIES
As Stephen died, he spoke words very similar to Jesus' words on the cross (Luke 23:34). The early believers were glad to suffer as Jesus had suffered because that meant they were counted worthy (5:41). Stephen was ready to suffer like Jesus, even to the point of asking forgiveness for his murderers. Such a forgiving response comes only from the Holy Spirit. The Spirit can also help us respond as Stephen did—with love for our enemies (Luke 6:27). We must show Christ's forgiveness even when we are criticized and maligned for our faith.

Acts 8

PERSECUTION SCATTERS THE BELIEVERS / 8:1-3

After the martyrdom of Stephen, the Jews stepped up their persecution of the followers of Christ. The man introduced as Saul (8:1) proved to be a major leader in this widespread campaign of intolerance and terror. From a human perspective, this was a dreadful turn of events; from a divine perspective, it produced a far greater good. The Christians who had been comfortable and perhaps a bit too complacent in Jerusalem were now forced to migrate to the surrounding regions of Judea and Samaria. Chapters 8–11 could be called "steps to the Gentile mission." The believers had not begun to fulfill the great commission, because they didn't understand it. In line with the Old Testament, they expected the Gentiles to come to them. So the Spirit forced them to go to the Gentiles, beginning with the persecution that drove them out of Jerusalem. Acts 1:8, going to Judea, was the first step. During these times of terrible persecution, the church grew!

This chapter gives us a look at the early stages of ministry by another of the "seven"—Philip (6:5). In contrast to Stephen, Philip lived to old age, evangelizing and pastoring throughout the region (see 21:8). A comparison of Stephen and Philip provides a beautiful reminder that God uses his servants *how* and *how long* he sees fit. Both were solid, spiritual men. Both were effective evangelists. Both were mightily used of God in the spread of the gospel message. Yet Stephen was killed as the church's first martyr, while Philip was left to serve faithfully for decades. This should be an encouragement to all believers to continue working where God has planted us, for as long as he leaves us, and to stop worrying about what he chooses to do with others (see John 21:20-22). It is *his* message and *his* church.

8:1 And Saul was there, giving approval to his death.[NIV] In the final words of Luke's record of Stephen's martyrdom, Saul was introduced subtly into the text as a young man in charge of keeping the coats of those who were stoning Stephen (7:58). The opening verse of this chapter adds the information about Saul's current attitude: he was not just there by accident or just passing by. He *was there,* *giving approval to his [Stephen's] death.* Evidently, Saul was in total agreement with the action taken against this "heretic," a fact he acknowledged later in his report of the incident (22:20).

Saul was a native of Tarsus, a city in Cilicia (modern-day south-central Turkey), and may have entered into the controversy with Stephen at the synagogue in Jerusalem where Stephen had been debating (6:9-10). Luke mentioned him only in passing here, before recording the details of his conversion in chapter 9. When we get to chapter 13, Paul's ministry will be the entire focus of the book *and* the main instrument for the church's outreach to the Gentile world.

THE OFFENSIVENESS OF THE GOSPEL

For telling others the good news of Jesus' death, burial, and resurrection, the members of the early church were persecuted. Sometimes, as in the case of Stephen, they were even put to death. Christ had promised his followers that living for him would lead to trouble (see Luke 21:12-19). This is still true. If we boldly live out our faith, the light of our lives will expose the sinfulness of others. Our words of truth will pierce their souls. Some will be convicted and yield to the leading of the Spirit. Others will become angry and hardened in their hatred of the truth. As Jesus said, "The people of the world will hate you because you belong to me" (John 15:21 NLT). We shouldn't be surprised or abandon our faith when we are persecuted.

On that day a great persecution broke out against the church at Jerusalem, and all except the apostles were scattered throughout Judea and Samaria.[NIV] The terminology "on that day" implies that Stephen's martyrdom was the impetus for an immediate increase of persecution against those who followed Christ. Such a public exhibition would encourage other groups, who may have been holding back until this point, to proceed with *persecution . . . against the church at Jerusalem.* The persecution forced the Christians out of Jerusalem and into Judea and Samaria—thus fulfilling the second part of Jesus' command (see 1:8). Evidently, they had become somewhat comfortable sticking close to Jerusalem. All of that was instantly changed with Stephen's death and the resultant persecution.

Virtually *all* the Christians *except the apostles were scattered throughout Judea and Samaria.* The Greek word for "scattered" *(diesparesan)* is related to the Greek word for "seed," thus carrying the rich picture of God spreading his Word to bear fruit in an ever widening circle from Jerusalem (see 6:7). Not every Christian left Jerusalem, for a church remained there for the balance of the New Testament era. Why the apostles stayed in Jerusalem instead of scattering with the others is a matter of speculation. Leadership of the Christian movement continued from the Jerusalem church for quite some time (see chapter 15). Eventually, the major missionary center moved north to Antioch (chapter 13 and following). Paul would regularly return to Jerusalem to report and to bring monetary support to the suffering Jerusalem saints from the Asian and European churches (16:4; 21:15-20).

8:2 **Godly men buried Stephen and mourned deeply for him.**[NIV] What a contrast between this verse and the next one! *Godly men buried Stephen and mourned deeply for him,* while Saul was "ravaging the church." The expression "godly men" was used by Luke for the Jews who had been open to the Christian message at Pentecost (2:5). He had used the adjective "godly" to describe Simeon (Luke 2:25) and would use it later for Ananias (22:12). Thus, these "godly men" probably were some Jewish Christians.

Obviously the loss of a person so important, respected, and needed in the church would be a huge blow. Likely, many were forced to rethink their understanding of the sovereign God who had been blessing his church. Meanwhile, an intense Pharisee by the name of Saul began attacking the church.

8:3 **But Saul was ravaging the church by entering house after house; dragging off both men and women, he committed them to prison.**[NRSV] Evidently spurred on by the Jewish Council's murder of Stephen, Saul zealously went on the attack. The word translated "ravaging" *(elumaineto)* appears in the Old Testament Greek translation (the Septuagint) to describe wild boars destroying a vineyard (Psalm 80:13). Saul passionately tried to protect the Jewish faith (see 9:1, 13). He later described these activities thoroughly in his testimony before King Agrippa (26:9-11).

Saul was *dragging off both men and women* and putting them in *prison.* Evidently, Saul had been given legal authority to carry out this persecution (see comments on 9:1-2).

BEHIND THE SCENES
Luke portrayed Saul as a man totally determined to crush this new entity called the church. As we read about Saul's systematic, relentless, and brutal assault on Christians, it's difficult to realize that he was just days away from becoming a devout follower of Christ. This is a good reminder that God is working behind the scenes where least expected. Perhaps the vehement opponent of the gospel in your community will be the next convert. Trust God that opponents to Christianity can actually be converted. Don't give up on anyone.

MISSIONARIES OF THE NEW TESTAMENT AND THEIR JOURNEYS

Name	*Journey's Purpose*	*Scripture in Acts*
Philip	One of the first to preach the gospel outside Jerusalem	8:4-40
Peter and John	Visited new Samaritan believers to encourage them	8:14-25
Paul (Saul) (journey to Damascus)	Set out to capture Christians but was captured by Christ	9:1-25
Peter	Led by God to one of the first Gentile families to become Christians—Cornelius's family	9:32–10:48
Barnabas	Went to Antioch as an encourager; traveled on to Troas to bring Paul back to Jerusalem from Antioch	11:25-30
Barnabas, Paul, John Mark	Left Antioch for Cyprus, Pamphylia, and Galatia on the first missionary journey	13:1–14:28
Barnabas and John Mark	After a break with Paul, they left Antioch for Cyprus	15:36-41
Paul, Silas, Timothy, Luke	Left Antioch to revisit churches in Galatia, then traveled on to Asia, Macedonia, and Achaia on a second missionary journey	15:36–18:22
Apollos	Left Alexandria for Ephesus; learned the complete gospel story from Priscilla and Aquila; preached in Athens and Corinth	18:24-28
Paul, Timothy, Erastus	Third missionary journey, revisiting churches in Galatia, Asia, Macedonia, and Achaia	18:23; 19:12–1:14

PHILIP PREACHES IN SAMARIA / 8:4-25

This is the second step of the Gentile mission in Acts 1:8—"to Samaria." Philip's trip into Samaria and his ministry there reveal the marvelous truth that Jesus, the promised Jewish Messiah, was also the king and Savior of Gentiles. The message of Christ is a worldwide gospel. All nations and languages are invited and included (see Isaiah 56:3; Daniel 7:14) in the kingdom of God.

BEHIND THE PAIN
Persecution forced the believers out of their homes in Jerusalem, but with them went the gospel. Sometimes we have to become uncomfortable before we'll move. We may not want to experience it, but discomfort may be the best thing for us because God may be working through our pain. When you are tempted to complain about uncomfortable or painful circumstances, stop and ask if God might be preparing you for a special task.

Opposition to the gospel from Simon the sorcerer failed to halt Philip. Filled with the Holy Spirit, he performed miraculous signs to validate his message. The underlying truth is clear: nothing can stop God's powerful and eternal plan to fill heaven with worshipers from "every nation and tribe and people and language" (Revelation 7:9 NLT).

8:4 **But the believers who had fled Jerusalem went everywhere preaching the Good News about Jesus.**[NLT] The persecution caused the *believers who had fled Jerusalem* to scatter into other nations. As they went, they were *preaching the Good News about Jesus.* The gospel message was spreading like wildfire! The good news about Jesus spread everywhere. Satan had attempted to defeat the young church, but all he did was encourage the spread of the gospel.

8:5 **Philip went down to the city of Samaria and proclaimed the Messiah to them.**[NRSV] Israel had been divided into three main regions—Galilee in the north, Samaria in the middle, and Judea in the south. The city of Samaria (in the region of Samaria) had been the capital of the northern kingdom of Israel in the days of the divided kingdom, before it was conquered by Sargon of Assyria in 722 B.C. During that war, Sargon had taken many captives, leaving only the poorest

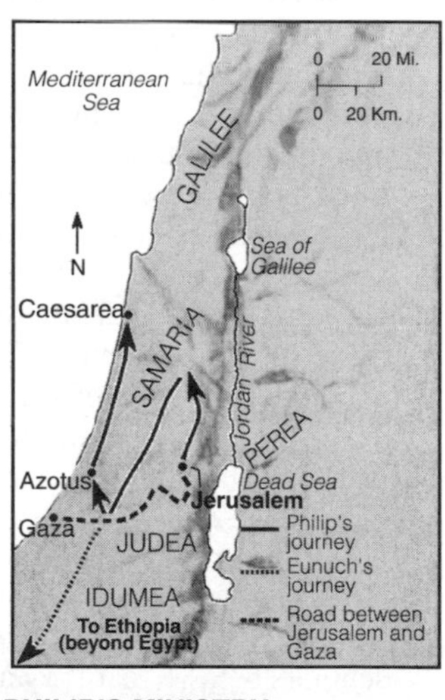

PHILIP'S MINISTRY
To escape persecution in Jerusalem, Philip fled to Samaria, where he continued preaching the gospel. While he was there, an angel commanded him to meet an Ethiopian official on the road between Jerusalem and Gaza. The man became a believer before continuing on to Ethiopia. Philip then went from Azotus to Caesarea.

people in the land and resettling it with foreigners. These foreigners had intermarried with the Jews who were left, and the mixed race became known as Samaritans. The Samaritans opposed the rebuilding of Jerusalem in the sixth century B.C. (Nehemiah 2:10–6:14). During the time of Alexander the Great, the Samaritans built their own temple on Mount Gerazim. The Samaritans were considered half-breeds and religious apostates by the "pure" Jews in the southern kingdom of Judah, and the two groups hated each other. But Jesus went into Samaria (John 4), and he commanded his followers to spread the gospel there (1:8).

Philip is not the apostle Philip (John 1:43-44) but a Greek-speaking Jew; he was one of the seven men who had been chosen to help distribute food in the Jerusalem church (6:5). Philip went directly to *the city of Samaria and proclaimed the Messiah to them.* The Samaritans responded in large numbers.

8:6-8 When the crowds heard Philip and saw the miraculous signs he did, they all paid close attention to what he said. With shrieks, evil spirits came out of many, and many paralytics and cripples were healed. So there was great joy in that city.[NIV] The effectiveness of Philip's ministry is highlighted here as *crowds* gathered and saw Philip perform *miraculous signs.* These miracles authenticated the message and the messenger and got the attention of onlookers. Thus, the gathered crowds paid *close attention* to all he said. *With shrieks, evil spirits* were cast out of people. The "shrieks" of these spirits revealed their rage at encountering a power greater than their own. Demons are never pleased to be told to leave their human dwellings, but they have no choice but to submit to the higher authority (see Mark 9:25-26).

> One filled with joy preaches without preaching. *Mother Teresa*

Philip's miraculous acts were reminiscent of Jesus' ministry. He also encountered and drove out many demons during his ministry on earth. Demons, or evil spirits, are ruled by Satan. Most scholars believe that they are fallen angels who joined Satan in his rebellion against God and who, in some cases, may cause a person to be mute, deaf, blind, or insane. Demons also tempt people to sin. Although demons can be powerful, they are not omnipotent or omniscient and cannot be everywhere at once. Demons are real and active, but Jesus has authority over them, and he gave this same authority to his followers. Although Satan is allowed to work in the world, God is in complete control. God can drive demons out and end their destructive work in people's lives. Eventually, Satan and his demons will be thrown into the lake of fire, forever ending their evil work in the world (Revelation 20:10).

In addition to freeing people from demon possession, Philip also healed *many paralytics and cripples.* As a result of the healings and the message he brought, *there was great joy in that city.* Joy is a recurring theme of the book of Acts and should be an ingredient of any legitimate Christian ministry (see the chart "Joy in Acts" on page 40 [2:46]).

8:9-11 Now for some time a man named Simon had practiced sorcery in the city and amazed all the people of Samaria. He boasted that he was someone great, and all the people, both high and low, gave him their attention and exclaimed, "This man is the divine power known as the Great Power." They followed him because he had amazed them for a long time with his magic.[NIV] The balance of this chapter reports two significant experiences of Philip as he faithfully spread the gospel. The first incident involved a sorcerer named *Simon.* Evidently, Simon had quite a following in the region and was using his sorcery to draw crowds of his own (he had *amazed all the people of Samaria . . . for a long time with his magic*). Simon's magic was not for entertainment or to trick people. He was a charlatan whose goal was to get money. Later, there was a legendary figure called Simon Magus who may have been this Simon. Justin Martyr, who was a Samaritan Christian, said Simon lived in Samaria and later moved to Rome. In Samaria, Antiochus Epiphanes built a temple to Zeus on Mount Gerazim, so there was pagan worship in Samaria. Later a sect of Gnostic Christians claimed Simon as a founder.

Simon's "magic" was the practice of his *sorcery.* In the days of the early church, sorcerers and magicians were numerous and influential. They worked wonders, performed healings and exorcisms, and practiced astrology. The "wonders" included magic tricks, but the sorcerers utilized the power of Satan or other evil spirits (Matthew 24:24; 2 Thessalonians 2:9). Simon had done so many wonders that some even thought that he was *the divine power known as the Great Power* (in other words, the Messiah); however, his powers did not come from God (see 8:18-24). Evidently, Simon's ego played a large part in promoting his popularity, as he *boasted that he was someone great.*

8:12-13 But now the people believed Philip's message of Good News concerning the Kingdom of God and the name of Jesus Christ. As a result, many men and women were baptized. Then Simon himself believed and was baptized. He began following Philip wherever he went, and he was amazed by the great miracles and signs Philip performed.[NLT] In sharp contrast to Simon and his magic is Philip and the *message of Good News concerning the Kingdom of God* (both the present kingdom in the hearts of believers and the coming kingdom reign of Christ on earth—see commentary at 1:3).

Both *men and women* came to believe in Jesus Christ and *were baptized.* Even the sorcerer himself appeared to believe and was baptized. So now the man who had previously had a large and diverse following was *following Philip wherever he went,* himself being *amazed by the great miracles and signs* that Philip, in the power of Christ, was performing. The wording of these verses makes it sound as though Simon's belief focused on the miraculous power (which he desired) more than on Christ. Jesus had faced people like Simon: "Because of the miraculous signs he did in Jerusalem at the Passover celebration, many people were convinced that he was indeed the Messiah. But Jesus didn't trust them, because he knew what people were really like" (John 2:23-24 NLT). Jesus was well aware of the truth of Jeremiah 17:9, which states, "The heart is deceitful above all things and beyond cure. Who can understand it?" (NIV). Jesus knew that the faith of some followers was superficial. Some of the same people claiming to believe in Jesus at that time would later yell, "Crucify him!"

Simon may have found it easy to believe when it was exciting and everyone else was caught up in the excitement. There is some question, however, about the sincerity of his profession of faith and the genuineness of his conversion. In his conversation with Peter (see 8:18-24), the description of Simon does not have the sound of one who truly had come to faith.

AMAZING GRACE

The people of Samaria were amazed by Simon's magic tricks. Then Simon saw God working powerfully in and through Philip, and *he* was amazed. This is a good reminder to us that no human ability or demonic power is as astonishing as the gospel of Jesus Christ. When we are filled with the presence of God and we allow his power and love to first transform us and then touch others, those around us are dumbfounded. They may not embrace God's amazing grace, but they cannot deny the supernatural presence that pervades our lives.

8:14 Now when the apostles at Jerusalem heard that Samaria had accepted the word of God, they sent Peter and John to them.[NRSV] *Peter and John* were sent to Samaria as apostolic representatives to find out whether or not the Samaritans were truly becoming believers. The Jewish Christians, even the apostles, were still unsure whether Gentiles (non-Jews) and Samaritans (half-Jews) could receive the Holy Spirit. For more about the strained relations between Jews and Samaritans, see commentary on 8:5. It wasn't until Peter's experience with Cornelius (chapter 10) that the apostles became fully convinced that the Holy Spirit was for all people. It had been John who had asked Jesus if they should call fire down from heaven to burn up a Samaritan village that refused to welcome them (Luke 9:51-55). Ironically, John and Peter were the ones sent to *Samaria.*

8:15-16 When they arrived, they prayed for them that they might receive the Holy Spirit, because the Holy Spirit had not yet come upon any of them; they had simply been baptized into the name of the Lord Jesus.[NIV] This was a crucial moment for the spread of the gospel and for the growth of the church. Peter and John had to go to Samaria to help keep this new group of believers from becoming separated from other believers. There was deep-seated hostility between Jews and Samaritans that went back centuries. The Jews looked down on the Samaritans for not being pure Jews; the Samaritans resented the Jews for their arrogance. However, Samaritans were coming to faith in Christ through Philip's preaching, and there could be no denying that they should be included among the believers. So *they had . . . been baptized into the name of the Lord Jesus,* but this baptism was not yet connected with the church in Jerusalem.

> Never let us think evil of men who do not see as we do. From the bottom of our hearts let us pity them, and let us take them by the hand and spend time and thought over them, and try to lead them to the true light.
> *Henry Drummond*

When Peter and John saw the Lord working in these people, they were assured that the Holy Spirit worked through all believers—Gentiles as well as Jews. So *they prayed for them that they might receive the Holy Spirit.* It may seem odd that *the Holy Spirit had not yet come upon any of them.* Some have interpreted this event to point out that the Samaritans' faith was inadequate or that the filling of the Holy Spirit is a second work of grace after regeneration. But such conclusions are not necessary. There is a simpler solution.

Many scholars believe that God chose to have a dramatic filling of his Spirit as a sign at this special moment in history—a "Samaritan Pentecost" paralleling the Pentecost that the apostles had experienced in chapter 2. Normally, the Holy Spirit enters a person's life at conversion; it is then that the Spirit baptizes, seals, and indwells that person. But this was a special event. The pouring out of the Spirit would happen again with Cornelius and his family (10:44-47), a sign that the uncircumcised Gentiles could receive the gospel.

With the verification by Peter and John that the Samaritans' faith was genuine, these new believers were incorporated into the church. When the Samaritans were converted, they received the Spirit, as was essential for regeneration, but their participation in the church was needed for the full expression of the gifts of the Spirit.

GOD'S CHANGES

Look at the growth John had demonstrated in just a few years. As Christ's disciple, John had asked Jesus if the disciples could call down fire from heaven to burn up an unwelcoming Samaritan village (Luke 9:51-55). Here (8:14-16), after the Resurrection and the coming of the Holy Spirit at Pentecost, that transformed disciple was in Samaria laying hands on the believers there for them to receive the Holy Spirit, a "fire" of a different sort. This is a beautiful example of what changes Christ can make in a life. Don't discount how Christ can change your attitudes about people. Let his love transform your mind.

8:17 Then Peter and John laid their hands upon these believers, and they received the Holy Spirit.[NLT] These Samaritan believers *received the Holy Spirit* through the laying on of the apostles' hands. This event has been called the "Samaritan Pentecost" because of its parallels to Pentecost in chapter 2. Receiving the Spirit would both confirm Philip's evangelistic work among the Samaritans and tie the Samaritan church spiritually to the church in Jerusalem. There have been various theological interpretations of this event. Catholics emphasize the sacrament of confirmation as separate from baptism. Charismatics have used it to justify the doctrine of baptism in the Spirit as a second work of grace. But in the New Testament and specifically in Acts, there doesn't seem to be any set pattern or formula.

One of the likely reasons for the delay between water baptism and the baptism of the Spirit was to keep the Samaritan church united with the Jewish church. Because of the historical conflict between these two groups, it would be crucial to have an apostolic presence for this significant event. The presence of apostles, especially two with such a high profile—Peter and John—would give unquestionable credibility to the Samaritan spiritual movement. These two apostles, through whom the Samaritans first received the Holy Spirit, would confirm to the rest of the Jerusalem church that indeed God was doing the same thing among the Gentiles that he was doing among the Jews. This Samaritan Pentecost also demonstrated to the Jerusalem church God's expansion plans for the Gentiles and the ever-widening scope of the gospel ministry. Chapters 7–12 are a careful record of that first critical move of Christianity out of the confines of Jerusalem—and, more importantly, beyond the confines of the Jewish faith.

SIMONY

The term "simony," the buying or selling of a church office or other things considered religious or sacred, comes from this incident, where Simon sought to buy the power of the Spirit from the apostles.

"Everything has a price" seems to be true in this world of bribes, wealth, and materialism. Simon thought he could buy the Holy Spirit's power, but Peter harshly rebuked him. The only way to receive God's power is to do what Peter told Simon to do—turn from sin, ask God for forgiveness, and be filled with his Spirit. No amount of money can buy salvation, forgiveness of sin, or God's power. These are gained only by repentance and belief in Christ as Savior.

The book of Acts records a time of great transition. The old order of things—pre-Messiah, pre-Cross, pre-Resurrection, pre-Pentecost—was being replaced by the new order (the New Testament). Acts reports much of that transition—all that God was doing around the coming of his one and only Son to earth (John 1:17), his death, his resurrection, and the coming of the one whom Christ had promised to send after his return to the Father.

One of the most significant changes in God's relationship to people was the nature of the Spirit's work in the life of a person of faith. Rather than a temporary visitor to individuals, the Spirit became a permanent resident of the community of believers (see the comments in 2:4-10). Some had believed in God but had not heard of Christ or of the coming of the Holy Spirit. Others had been baptized with John's baptism but had not heard the rest of the story about the one who followed John (for example, Apollos in 18:24-26). Still others (like these Samaritans) had heard of Christ and had been baptized with water but had not yet received the Holy Spirit.

> Money is an instrument that can buy you everything but happiness and can pay your fare to every place but heaven.
> *Unknown*

8:18-19 **Now when Simon saw that the Spirit was given through the laying on of the apostles' hands, he offered them money, saying, "Give me also this power so that anyone on whom I lay my hands may receive the Holy Spirit."**[NRSV] Evidently there were some visible manifestations of the *power* of the Holy Spirit that accompanied this laying on of hands, possibly similar to those present at Pentecost in chapter 2 (such as the violent wind and the tongues of fire). *Simon* was the sorcerer from 8:9-13 who had supposedly believed and been baptized. But he was more interested in miracles than in Christ. So *when Simon saw that the Spirit was given through the laying on of the apostles' hands,* he wanted to have that power as well. Simon foolishly believed that Peter and John were in the same business as he had been (sorcery and magic), so he *offered them money* for the power to give the Holy Spirit through his hands to *anyone.*

8:20-23 **But Peter replied, "May your money perish with you for thinking God's gift can be bought! You can have no part in this, for your heart is not right before God. Turn from your wickedness and pray to the Lord. Perhaps he will forgive your evil thoughts, for I can see that you are full of bitterness and held captive by sin."**[NLT] Peter's stern answer was a stinging rebuke. Simon's errant *thinking* had led him to believe that *God's gift* could *be bought.* Note the terminology Peter used in rebuking Simon: his *heart* was *not right before God;* his behavior was called *wickedness;* his thinking was called *evil;* he was said to be *full of bitterness;* and, in the most sweeping of condemnations, Peter said that Simon was still, despite his supposed conversion, *held captive by sin.* The implication was that Simon had not genuinely come to Christ ("perish" is a very strong word!). It appears that Simon still had an internal spiritual problem that had not been corrected; he was still held captive by sin, rather than being freed from it (John 8:31-32, 36; Galatians 5:1). He was at least having serious trouble with spiritual perception. We see here God's attitude about the absolutely free nature of grace and salvation!

> I cannot, by direct moral effort, give myself new motives. After the first few steps in the Christian life, we realize that everything which really needs to be done in our souls can be done only by God.
>
> *C. S. Lewis*

MOTIVES AND GIFTS
Simon went to the apostles and asked to purchase the ability to bestow the Holy Spirit on people. Why? Apparently (based on Peter's response) for selfish reasons: to have power, to make money, or to gain prestige. God doesn't give us abilities to enhance our own lives. He grants us gifts so that we may bring him glory by building up others. When you find yourself wishing for an ability that would put you into the limelight or somehow enrich you personally, check your motives. And instead of sitting around wishing for talents you don't have, spend your time serving God and others with the gifts you *do* possess.

8:24 "Pray to the Lord for me," Simon exclaimed, "that these terrible things won't happen to me!"NLT Simon was apparently terrified. He seemed to respond well to the rebuke, asking Peter to *pray to the Lord* for him. It is hard to tell whether his outcry was simply a fear of *terrible* consequences for having insulted these powerful visitors or a genuine change in heart toward God. It may well be that Simon was a typical pseudoconvert, a make-believer, rather than a genuine one (notice that he didn't pray himself but asked Peter to pray). If so, he is a biblical example of the many who play around the fringe of religion but never come totally in, who see religion as useful only for the avoidance of bad consequences rather than the initiation of a life-changing relationship with God.

8:25 After testifying and preaching the word of the Lord in Samaria, Peter and John returned to Jerusalem. And they stopped in many Samaritan villages along the way to preach the Good News to them, too.NLT The witnessing work of the apostles, as predicted by Christ, was spreading beyond Jerusalem to Samaria, the second stop on the gospel's march to the world: ". . . Judea and Samaria, and to the ends of the earth" (1:8). Likely encouraged by what they had just experienced in Samaria, Peter and John made their way back to Jerusalem *testifying and preaching the word of the Lord,* the *Good News,* in *many Samaritan villages.* As Peter and John continued to learn God's strategy for reaching the world, the rest of the apostles would also be enlightened, and through them, so would the church back in Jerusalem.

EVERYDAY EVANGELISM

Peter and John eagerly shared Christ everywhere they went. They did not see evangelism as an event to do only at scheduled times and only in carefully designated places. For them evangelism was a way of life—because for them, Jesus was life! Convinced of the Resurrection, changed by their relationship with Jesus, and filled with the Holy Spirit, they looked for opportunities at every turn to talk about the reality of the eternal. Do we think in these terms and act in like manner? If not, what does that say about us?

PHILIP AND THE ETHIOPIAN EUNUCH / 8:26-40

This passage is set carefully and strategically *after* the initial work in Jerusalem and *before* the conversion of Paul, the apostle to the Gentiles (chapter 9). This is the third step of expansion to the uttermost parts of the world (1:8). The gospel of Christ was leaving a purely Jewish audience and beginning to be spread to the world. In the story of Philip and the Ethiopian eunuch, we have a wonderful picture of God's global love and his surprising plan to get the good news of Christ to those who have never heard. Philip was instructed by God to suddenly leave Samaria to go south into the desert. There he met a prominent official from the court of Candace, queen of Ethiopia. The official, called a "eunuch," was reading (but not understanding) the writings of the prophet Isaiah.

After the man invited Philip into his carriage, Philip was able to "tell him the Good News about Jesus" (8:35 NLT). The man embraced the gospel, was baptized into the faith, and returned to Ethiopia rejoicing (and, one can only presume, sharing what he had learned). Meanwhile, Philip was instantly transported more than twenty miles away to the city of Azotus! Obviously, God had also prepared the hearts of people there to respond to the truth.

8:26-28 Then an angel of the Lord said to Philip, "Get up and go toward the south to the road that goes down from Jerusalem to Gaza." (This is a wilderness road.) So he got up and went. Now there was an Ethiopian eunuch, a court official of the Candace, queen of the Ethiopians, in charge of her entire treasury. He had come to Jerusalem to worship and was returning home; seated in his chariot, he was reading the prophet Isaiah.[NRSV] The *angel of the Lord* appeared at various times in Scripture giving directions to people: an angel spoke to Hagar (Genesis 16:9); Abraham (Genesis 22:11-15); Moses (Exodus 3:2); Balaam (Numbers 22:22-35); the nation of Israel (Judges 2:1, 4); Gideon (Judges 6:12, 21-22); Samson's parents (Judges 13:3-21); Elijah (1 Kings 19:7; 2 Kings 1:3, 15); Joseph (Matthew 1:20; 2:13, 19); Zechariah (Luke 1:11); shepherds (Luke 2:9); Peter in jail (Acts 5:19; 12:7). In this instance, an angel of the Lord directed *Philip* to go south. Philip, without one single question being asked (or at least recorded by Luke), *got up and went.* God handled the details—set up the appointment, timed the arrival of the Ethiopian, and told Philip which chariot and what to do. After this encounter Philip would be whisked to his next assignment.

In the sovereign strategy of God, Philip was sent to the side of the road, where he met *an Ethiopian eunuch* traveling home from a pilgrimage to Jerusalem. Ethiopia is located in Africa, south of Egypt. The eunuch was obviously dedicated to God, because he had traveled such a long distance to worship in Jerusalem. The

Jews had contact with Ethiopia (known as Cush) in ancient days (Psalm 68:31; Jeremiah 38:7), so this man may have been a Gentile convert to Judaism. That he had a copy of Isaiah's prophecy points to that probability.

"Candace" was a title for the monarch of Ethiopia, somewhat the way "Pharaoh" was used in Egypt and "Caesar" in Rome. The fact that this *court official* was *in charge of her entire treasury* shows that he was an extremely high-placed and well-trusted member of the government.

The law prohibited a eunuch from entering "the assembly of the LORD" (Deuteronomy 23:1), but Isaiah 56:3-5 speaks of eunuchs being accepted by God. In Greek writings, however, "eunuch" may have been simply a governmental title as opposed to the usual meaning—a man who has been emasculated. The distance of Ethiopia from Israel underscores the tremendous commitment of this individual to *come to Jerusalem to worship.* And how this trip of this faithful worshiper was rewarded! The fact that the official was *seated in his chariot* and *reading the prophet Isaiah* are clues to his importance and wealth. Because the eunuch was seated, he must have had a hired driver. To own a scroll of the Scriptures (handwritten and thus rare) likewise indicated wealth.

MYSTERIOUS WAYS

Philip was having a successful preaching ministry to great crowds in Samaria (8:5-8), but he obediently left that ministry to travel on a desert road. Because Philip went where God sent him, Ethiopia was opened up to the gospel. Follow God's leading, even if it seems like a demotion. At first you may not understand his plans, but the results will prove that God's way is right.

8:29-30 The Holy Spirit said to Philip, "Go over and walk along beside the carriage." Philip ran over and heard the man reading from the prophet Isaiah; so he asked, "Do you understand what you are reading?"NLT The *Holy Spirit* himself directed Philip at this point to go *over and walk along beside the carriage.* Again, Philip immediately complied.

There were plenty of differences between Philip and the eunuch that a less resolute person than Philip may have used as excuses not to engage in conversation. There were racial differences (Greek/Ethiopian), religious differences (Jew/Gentile), vocational differences (evangelist/government worker), socioeconomic differences (poor/rich), physical differences (Philip possibly hot and dirty from walking/the Ethiopian likely cool and clean in his chariot). Philip could have backed down because of those differences and because he could have been thought a robber, a beggar, or a fool. But he didn't. Philip went. All Christians would do well to ask themselves as they study Philip, "Do I follow God this simply and completely? Do I share Christ as boldly across social, racial, economic, and ethnic boundaries?"

As Philip *ran over,* he *heard the man reading from the prophet Isaiah.* After observing for a moment, Philip asked a brilliant question: *"Do you understand what you are reading?"* In so doing, Philip exhibited two of the most important characteristics of an effective evangelist: The first is patience. He waited to find out where the man was in his understanding before diving in with the gospel. A second characteristic is the power of observation. Philip looked for an opportunity to engage the man at a meaningful level.

8:31 **"How can I," he said, "unless someone explains it to me?" So he invited Philip to come up and sit with him.**[NIV] The court official expressed the frustration that every Bible student throughout the ages has felt from time to time: *"How can I* understand this passage *unless someone explains it to me?"* This perfect lead-in to the gospel was made even better considering the passage he was reading. First-century Jews debated the meaning of the "suffering Servant." They were unsure if it meant Isaiah, the nation of the Jews as a whole, or the Messiah. It took Jesus to reveal the true meaning.

OLD AND NEW

Some think that the Old Testament is not relevant today, but Philip led this man to faith in Jesus Christ by using the Old Testament. Jesus Christ is found in the pages of both the Old and New Testaments. God's entire Word is applicable to all people in all ages. If the Old Testament in your Bible looks new and unused compared to the New Testament, you are missing out on a major portion of God's revelation of himself and the record of his dealings with his people.

8:32-34 **The eunuch was reading this passage of Scripture: "He was led like a sheep to the slaughter, and as a lamb before the shearer is silent, so he did not open his mouth. In his humiliation he was deprived of justice. Who can speak of his descendants? For his life was taken from the earth." The eunuch asked Philip, "Tell me, please, who is the prophet talking about, himself or someone else?"**[NIV] As Philip was invited to join the eunuch in the chariot, he discovered which *passage of*

Scripture the eunuch was reading—Isaiah 53. Here God continued his sovereign work. There is no better place to be reading in the Old Testament for a picture of Jesus Christ than Isaiah 53. The passage is Isaiah's prophecy about the great suffering Servant—his rejection, his silence before his accusers, his death with wicked men, the substitutionary nature of his suffering, his burial in a rich man's grave, and his ultimate resurrection.

The eunuch asked about the identity of the individual presented in the passage, the one who was silent *before the shearer . . . deprived of justice . . . his life taken.* In an almost pleading tone, he said, *"Tell me, please, who is the prophet talking about?"* What an opening!

PERSONALIZING THE GOSPEL

Philip found the Ethiopian man reading Scripture. Taking advantage of this opportunity to explain the gospel, Philip asked the man if he understood what he was reading. Philip (1) followed the Spirit's leading, (2) began the discussion from where the man was (immersed in the prophecies of Isaiah), and (3) explained how Jesus Christ fulfilled Isaiah's prophecies. When you share the gospel, start where the other person's concerns are focused. Then you can bring the gospel to bear on those concerns.

8:35 **So Philip began with this same Scripture and then used many others to tell him the Good News about Jesus.**[NLT] Philip *began with this same Scripture,* added to it *many others,* and told the eunuch *the Good News about Jesus.* It is important to note that Philip began where the man was; only then did he directly and clearly take him to where he needed to go. This means he listened, thought, adapted the message to his audience, and then explained the Good News.

At least one of the lessons from Philip's style of evangelism is his willingness to listen and adapt his message to the needs of his audience. Are you waiting for others to adapt to *you?* to learn *your* lingo? to come to *your* meeting? to enter *your* safe, Christian culture? Or are you ready to go out into the world outside your Christian environment, find those who need Christ, listen to them, love them, and lead them to your King? The failure to spread the Good News is often not for lack of courage but for lack of willingness to be inconvenienced, to spend the time necessary for getting into another person's world and problems. In this day of the "busy Christian," perhaps one of the hindrances to the spread of the gospel is our unwillingness to commit ourselves to the hard and time-intensive task of listening, adapting, and loving others into a relationship with Christ.

WHAT ARE YOU HEARING?

- At the *office* when you hear: "I'm worried about my job, my future, my marriage, my child. I'm scared of dying." It could be your passing chariot, an open door for the good news of the gospel.
- At *school* when you hear: "I don't like myself. Nobody likes me. Should I be involved in this or that? What does God have to do with all this?" It could be your passing chariot, an open door for the good news of the gospel.
- *Anywhere you are in life* (neighborhood, gym, club) when you hear: "My boyfriend asked me to marry him. I'm having a baby. My cancer is back. My wife is leaving." It could be your passing chariot, an open door for the good news of the gospel.

Be ready to ask and answer those all-important questions about this life and the life to come.

8:36 As they were going along the road, they came to some water; and the eunuch said, "Look, here is water! What is to prevent me from being baptized?"NRSV Whatever Philip said to the court official, it is obvious that he came to faith. Evidently included in what Philip had taught was the fact that baptism was the next step of obedience in this newfound faith. The official seemed to be exhibiting some of the eager characteristics of a new believer: *"Look, here is water! What is to prevent me from being baptized?"*

Philip began where the Ethiopian was, but he did not stay there. Philip gave the Ethiopian the rest of the story—maybe the rest of Isaiah 53—including the coming of Christ, his substitutionary death, his resurrection, and his offer of eternal life.

8:37 Then Philip said, "If you believe with all your heart, you may." And he answered and said, "I believe that Jesus Christ is the Son of God."NKJV Most of the earlier Greek manuscripts do not include this verse, so it is likely an intrusion into the text. It is a full and complete statement of belief: *". . . believe with all your heart . . . believe that Jesus Christ is the Son of God."* It may have come from the church's early baptismal liturgy and been put in because there is no mention of the eunuch's conversion prior to baptism. It is easiest to assume that the official's conversion was clearly verbalized to Philip, whether in the above words or not. Otherwise, the baptism never would have taken place.

8:38 He commanded the chariot to stop, and both of them, Philip and the eunuch, went down into the water, and Philip baptized him.NRSV After commanding *the chariot to stop,* the official and Philip *went down into the water.* There *Philip baptized him.* The witnesses to the baptism included at least Philip and the chariot driver, though a man of such high position may have been traveling with a sizable entourage.

Commanded by Christ (Matthew 28:18-20), water baptism was an outward, visible sign of one's identification with Christ and with the Christian community. This was one of the first acts of new converts in the early church. In submitting to baptism, this official was proclaiming his faith in Christ publicly. Deeply symbolic and meaningful, baptism sends a powerful message to onlookers about one's obedience to Christ.

8:39-40 When they came up out of the water, the Spirit of the Lord snatched Philip away; the eunuch saw him no more, and went on his way rejoicing. But Philip found himself at Azotus, and as he was passing through the region, he proclaimed the good news to all the towns until he came to Caesarea.[NRSV] Philip was suddenly transported by *the Spirit of the Lord* to a different city (likely his next job site). *Azotus* is Ashdod, one of the ancient Philistine capitals, about twenty miles north of Gaza. This miraculous sign may be here to show the urgency of spreading the message to the Gentiles. Philip continued his single focus: proclaiming *the good news to all the towns.* Philip disappears from the Acts story at this point, but ultimately he ended up in Caesarea. The only other mention of Philip is in 21:8-9. Twenty years later, Philip was still at Caesarea with four daughters, all of whom were prophetesses.

Nothing else is recorded about the newly converted eunuch, other than this wonderful report that he *went on his way rejoicing*—clear evidence of the Spirit's work in this new believer's life (Galatians 5:22).

PRINCIPLES OF EFFECTIVE EVANGELISM LEARNED FROM PHILIP:

- Be *where* God wants you (8:26-30, 39).
  God set up the appointment, timed the arrival of the Ethiopian, and told Philip which chariot and what to do.
- Be *watching* the people around you (8:27, 32, 34).
  God will help you to perceive who will be receptive.
- Be *ready* to adapt yourself to where others are (8:35-36).
  Philip began where the man was, then directly and clearly took him to where he needed to go. This means listening first, then meeting the person at his or her point of need or understanding.
- Be *bold* in telling those you meet about Christ (8:35-36).

Acts 9

SAUL'S CONVERSION / 9:1-19A

Acts 1:8 seems to be a concise outline for the entire book. Chapters 1–7 describe the gospel being preached in Jerusalem. Chapter 8 shows believers, under threat of persecution, taking the good news of Jesus to Judea and Samaria.

Chapter 9 records a monumental event in the history of the church—the conversion of Saul of Tarsus. Saul (later known as Paul) would be God's apostle to the Gentiles (Galatians 2:8; Ephesians 3:8). He would lead the church in spreading Christianity "to the ends of the earth" (1:8). Therefore Paul, more than any other person, figures prominently in chapters 10–28.

No one was better suited to the task than Paul: a "real Jew if there ever was one" (Philippians 3:5 NLT; see also Galatians 1:14); a native of Tarsus thoroughly acquainted with Greek culture (17:22-31); a citizen of Rome (16:37); trained in a trade so that he could support himself (18:3) as he traveled and ministered.

Before Christ could use this highly gifted man, however, he first had to transform him. Little did Saul know what lay ahead for him on the road to Damascus!

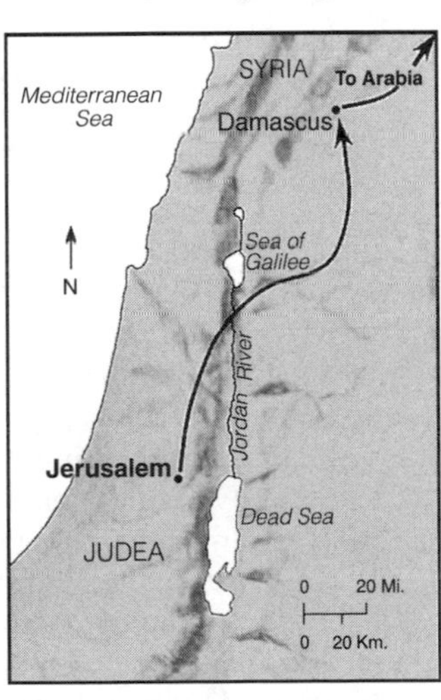

SAUL TRAVELS TO DAMASCUS
Many Christians fled Jerusalem when persecution began after Stephen's death, seeking refuge in other cities and countries. Saul tracked them down, even traveling 150 miles to Damascus in Syria to bring Christians back in chains to Jerusalem. But as he neared the ancient city, he discovered that God had other plans for him.

9:1-2 **Meanwhile, Saul was uttering threats with every breath. He was eager to destroy the Lord's followers, so he went to the high priest. He requested letters addressed to the synagogues in Damascus, asking their cooperation in the arrest**

of any followers of the Way he found there. He wanted to bring them—both men and women—back to Jerusalem in chains.NLT *Saul* (later called Paul, the equivalent of "Saul" in Greek), first mentioned as a participant in the stoning of Stephen (see 7:58; 8:1), was so zealous for his Jewish beliefs that he began a persecution campaign against all who believed in Christ, all who were *followers of the Way* (see Paul's testimony in Philippians 3:6). This name implied "the way of the Lord" or "the way of salvation." Christ had earlier claimed to be "the way" (John 14:6). This designation is found a number of times in Acts (19:9, 23; 22:4; 24:14, 22; see also 16:17; 18:25-26).

GOD'S WAY

As Saul traveled to Damascus, pursuing Christians, he was confronted by the risen Christ and brought face-to-face with the truth of the gospel. Sometimes God breaks into a life in a spectacular manner, and sometimes conversion is a quiet experience. Beware of people who insist that you must have a particular type of conversion experience. The right way to come to faith in Jesus is whatever way God brings *you*.

Why would the Jews in Jerusalem want to persecute Christians as far away as Damascus? There are several possibilities: (1) to seize the Christians who had fled; (2) to prevent the spread of Christianity to other major cities; and (3) to keep the Christians from causing any trouble with Rome.

The *letters* requested by Saul would not only introduce him, but they would provide him with the high priest's authorization to seize followers of Christ and bring them *back to Jerusalem.* Most synagogues in Syria probably recognized this right of extradition. Not only was Saul going to pursue them, he also was going to arrest *both men and women* and bring them back *in chains.*

9:3 **As he journeyed he came near Damascus, and suddenly a light shone around him from heaven.**NKJV Damascus, a key commercial city, was located about 175 miles northeast of Jerusalem in the Roman province of Syria. Several trade routes linked Damascus to other cities throughout the Roman world. Damascus was one of the ten cities known as the Decapolis (see Mark 5:20; 7:31). Saul may have thought that by stamping out Christianity in Damascus, he could prevent its spread to other areas.

Nearing his destination, at about noon, when the sun was at its full height (see 22:6; 26:13), Saul suddenly found himself awash in a brilliant heavenly *light.* Though the text does not overtly state that Saul saw Christ, that fact is implied, since seeing the resurrected Lord was a requirement of New Testament apostleship (see 1 Corinthians 9:1; 15:8). Also, the testimonies of Ananias (9:17) and Barnabas (9:27) confirm an eyewitness encounter.

9:4-5 **He fell to the ground and heard a voice saying to him, "Saul, Saul, why do you persecute me?" He asked, "Who are you, Lord?" The reply came, "I am Jesus, whom you are persecuting."**[NRSV] Not only did Saul witness the brilliant glory of the Lord, but he also *heard* the voice of Jesus Christ. (For the rest of what Jesus said, see 22:8, 10, 17, 21; 26:15-18.) Saul thought he was pursuing heretics, but according to the voice, his actions were tantamount to attacking Jesus himself—*I am Jesus, whom you are persecuting*. Anyone who persecutes believers today is also guilty of persecuting Jesus (see Matthew 25:40, 45) because believers are the body of Christ on earth. This is a powerful statement about the union that exists between Christ and his church.

> Whoever sees Christ as a mirror of the Father's heart, actually walks through the world with new eyes. *Martin Luther*

As he lay there in the dust, Saul must have been reeling from the realization that Jesus, the crucified founder of this detested sect, had been resurrected by God and exalted in divine glory. Saul was not serving God, as he had thought, but opposing him!

RELIGION VS. RELATIONSHIP

Paul referred to his encounter on the road to Damascus as the start of his new life in Christ (1 Corinthians 9:1; 15:8; Galatians 1:15-16). At the center of this wonderful experience was Jesus Christ. Paul did not see a vision; he saw the risen Christ himself (9:17). Paul did not "get religion" (he was already a very religious man!); he found a relationship with Jesus. Paul acknowledged Jesus as Lord, confessed his own sin, surrendered his life to Christ, and resolved to obey him. True conversion comes from a personal encounter with Jesus Christ and leads to a new life in relationship with him.

9:6 **"Now get up and go into the city, and you will be told what you are to do."**[NLT] According to Paul's own testimony in 26:16-18, Christ gave him, at this moment, a brief preview of his future as an apostle to the Gentiles. Further details would come once he made his way into the city of Damascus.

9:7 **The men with Saul stood speechless with surprise, for they heard the sound of someone's voice, but they saw no one!**[NLT] Those accompanying Saul heard *the sound of someone's voice* and saw some kind of light (see 22:9), but they didn't understand the full significance of this encounter. *They saw no one,* nor had they heard the specific words spoken to Saul (26:14).

9:8-9 **As Saul picked himself up off the ground, he found that he was blind. So his companions led him by the hand to Damascus. He remained there blind for three days. And all that time he went without food and water.**[NLT] Saul was temporarily blinded by this revelation (an event with Old Testament precedence—see Genesis 19:11; 2 Kings 6:17-20), *so his companions led him by the hand to Damascus.* Saul's subsequent fast (going *without food and water*) was most likely motivated by shock as he tried to ponder the full significance of his experience. Typically, fasting indicated a period of mourning or repentance.

> If you have to be reasoned into Christianity, some wise fellow can reason you out of it. But if you come to Christ by a flash of the Holy Ghost . . . no one can ever reason you out of it.
> *A. W. Tozer*

A CHANGED LIFE

Saul's conversion was undeniable:

- He went storming out of Jerusalem in a huff; he came stumbling into Damascus in humility (9:8-9).
- He went to arrest Christians; he ended up being arrested by Christ (9:1-5).
- He began the trip determined to wipe out the message of Christ; he ended the trip devoted to the cause of taking that message to the ends of the earth (9:19-22).
- He went from being a persecutor to being a persecuted one (9:23-25).

In short, Saul's whole mind-set and belief system were turned upside down. He realized that Christ was not dead, but alive. Christ was not merely a Nazarene rabble-rouser; he was the Messiah, the Son of God.

Saul certainly had a lot to think about during those *three days.* He realized that despite his zeal for God, his recent activity of arresting Christians had been in direct opposition to God—otherwise, he would not have received this rebuke. The voice from heaven had told him that in persecuting the Christians, he was persecuting this one named Jesus, who, Saul realized, was associated with God, because of the heavenly light and glory he had seen. Saul then would have been forced to realize that Jesus was indeed the Messiah for whom the Jews were still waiting—the Messiah who had come and gone, murdered by Saul's own contemporaries. Saul probably would have begun to think about the many prophecies that he had studied in his training as a Pharisee, prophecies that spoke of the coming Messiah. He would have been forced to conclude that Jesus had indeed met the requirements and fulfilled the prophecies. These Christians, whom Saul had been chasing, believed that Jesus had risen from the dead—and Saul had just seen the risen Christ in his glory. Suddenly, all that Saul had believed was being torn down and replaced with a new truth—the very truth that he had been seeking to extinguish. As Saul was thinking about all this, he was also praying (9:11).

9:10 Now there was a disciple in Damascus named Ananias. The Lord said to him in a vision, "Ananias." He answered, "Here I am, Lord."[NRSV] As Saul waited for further directions, the Lord began speaking to *Ananias,* "a godly man in his devotion to the law [who] was well thought of by all the Jews of Damascus" (22:12 NLT). Ananias, a Jew, had become a believer in Christ—*disciple.* Ananias responded to the call of God with the same words of submission uttered by his forefathers, Abraham (Genesis 22:1), Jacob (Genesis 31:11), Moses (Exodus 3:10), and Samuel (1 Samuel 3:10): *"Here I am, Lord."*

GOD'S CHOSEN PEOPLE

Given Saul's selection as a key person in the vast program of God, we might think that Peter or one of the other apostles should have been chosen to minister to this important new convert. Not so. God called an unknown disciple named Ananias for this task. This has been true throughout church history. Consider this list of "nobodies":

- John Staupitz: The man who helped lead Martin Luther to Christ.
- John Egglen: Instrumental in the conversion of C. H. Spurgeon.
- Edward Kimball: Just a shoe salesman . . . who happened to be D. L. Moody's spiritual mentor.
- Mordecai Ham: A little-known evangelist who preached the night that Billy Graham yielded his life to Christ.

We never know how God might use us to touch a life that will, in turn, touch millions. Yield yourself to the purposes of God, and be faithful when he calls.

9:11-12 The Lord said, "Go over to Straight Street, to the house of Judas. When you arrive, ask for Saul of Tarsus. He is praying to me right now. I have shown him a vision of a man named Ananias coming in and laying his hands on him so that he can see again."[NLT] The meeting

> Prayer is the autograph of the Holy Ghost upon the renewed heart.
> *Charles H. Spurgeon*

between Saul and Ananias was divinely arranged. The Lord gave specific instructions to Ananias about where to go and for whom to look; in a separate vision, he told Saul to expect Ananias's arrival. Such divine revelation with separate individuals having similar visions would be repeated again in 10:1-23.

Straight Street was and still is one of the main thoroughfares of Damascus. Ananias was directed to the street and *to the house of Judas.* Somehow God had led those in Paul's entourage to take him to this particular house; then God prepared his other servant to meet Saul. Ananias had been chosen to be the instrument of healing and help to the new convert.

9:13-14 **"But Lord," exclaimed Ananias, "I've heard about the terrible things this man has done to the believers in Jerusalem! And we hear that he is authorized by the leading priests to arrest every believer in Damascus."**[NLT] Ananias was understandably shaken by the Lord's command to go and find Saul of Tarsus. Christians wanted to stay far away from Saul. His reputation as an enemy of the church was well documented, and the intent of this particular mission to Damascus was widely known. Ananias knew that Saul had been *authorized by the leading priests to arrest every believer in Damascus.* Fearful of what might happen, Ananias began to protest, *"But Lord . . . I've heard about the terrible things this man has done to the believers in Jerusalem!"* The ultimate measure of faith is how believers respond to commands that seem illogical (see Exodus 14:16; 1 Kings 17:3-14; 2 Kings 5:10; John 9:1-11). Despite his protests, however, Ananias was up to the task.

MISSION "IMPOSSIBLE"
"Not him, Lord; that's impossible. Saul would *never* become a Christian!" In essence, that's what Ananias said when God told him of Saul's conversion. After all, Saul was persecuting believers to their deaths. Despite these understandable feelings, Ananias obeyed God and ministered to Saul. We must not limit God—he can do anything. Nothing is too hard for him (Genesis 18:14). We must obey and follow God's leading, even when he leads us to difficult people and places.

9:15-16 **But the Lord said to Ananias, "Go! This man is my chosen instrument to carry my name before the Gentiles and their kings and before the people of Israel. I will show him how much he must suffer for my name."**[NIV] Ananias's protest was met with a divine statement that Saul was God's *chosen instrument.* What irony that the most zealous Jew and most anti-Gentile would be the chosen witness to the Gentiles. The literal translation of the Greek word *skeuos* is "vessel, jar, or dish." It pictures an object that can contain, carry, and convey something else. In short, the Christian-hater from Tarsus had been handpicked by God to *carry* the *name* and message of Christ *before the Gentiles and their kings and before the people of Israel.* For the rest of his life, Saul marveled that he would be the recipient of such mercy and grace, as well as be the appointee for such a noble task. Saul, who had caused horrible suffering for so many Christians, would find that he, too, *must suffer.* The remainder of the book of Acts and the many letters that Saul wrote that are included in the New Testament chronicle the words of this verse: Saul would find himself witnessing for Christ in front of Gentile audiences, Jewish audiences, and even kings. He also would suffer severely for his faith.

THE SNOWFLAKE PRINCIPLE

Saul was perfect for the task given him by God: thoroughly versed in Jewish theology, language, and culture; a native of Tarsus and, thus, equally at home in Greek culture; a citizen of the Roman Empire; trained in the secular trade of tentmaking, thus able to support himself financially. This is a great example of the truth that God has a tailor-made ministry for each Christian. It's the snowflake principle. We're all different. No one else would have been suited to do what Paul did. And no one else can do what you can do. No one else has your circle of friends, your abilities, your situations. In a sense, each believer has an apostolic call. God wants to send you out, to commission you to do something significant. You may not play a prominent or highly visible role, but God has a fulfilling plan for you that will bring him glory by building his church.

9:17 **So Ananias went and entered the house. He laid his hands on Saul and said, "Brother Saul, the Lord Jesus, who appeared to you on your way here, has sent me so that you may regain your sight and be filled with the Holy Spirit."**NRSV Ananias's actions fulfilled at least two purposes. First, he functioned almost in a prophetic role, serving as God's confirming mouthpiece in the commissioning of the great apostle—*the Lord Jesus, who appeared to you . . . has sent me.* Second, his visit served as a ministry of personal encouragement. Saul must have been encouraged when he heard Ananias greet him as *Brother.* God had told Ananias to go to Saul and lay his hands on him "so that he can see again" (9:12 NLT). So when Ananias arrived, he told Saul that Jesus had sent him so that Saul could *regain* his *sight and be filled with the Holy Spirit.* Although there is no mention of a special and dramatic filling of the Holy Spirit for Saul (such as occurred for the twelve apostles), his changed life and subsequent accomplishments bear strong witness to the Holy Spirit's presence and power in his life. Evidently, the Holy Spirit filled Saul when he received his sight and was baptized.

TAKING RISKS

Ananias found Saul, as he had been instructed, and greeted him as "Brother Saul." Ananias feared this meeting because he knew that Saul had come to Damascus to capture believers and take them as prisoners to Jerusalem (9:2, 14). In obedience to the Holy Spirit, however, Ananias greeted Saul with love. It is not always easy to show acceptance to others, especially when we are afraid of them or doubt their motives. Nevertheless, we must follow Jesus' command (John 13:34) and Ananias's example, demonstrating genuine warmth and kindness to other believers.

9:18-19a Instantly something like scales fell from Saul's eyes, and he regained his sight. Then he got up and was baptized. Afterward he ate some food and was strengthened.NLT Upon the conclusion of this experience *something like scales fell from Saul's eyes, and he regained his sight.* Saul was *baptized,* presumably by Ananias, and he ended his three-day fast (9:9). Following this encounter, nothing more is known about Ananias. Because this faithful man was willing to go where God sent him, he was used by God to prepare a man who would evangelize most of the known world and write a significant portion of the New Testament.

SAUL IN DAMASCUS AND JERUSALEM / 9:19B-31

The change in Saul was instantaneous. In less than one week, he went from being eager to destroy the Lord's followers (9:1) to preaching about Jesus in the synagogues (9:20). The believers were understandably suspicious, but Saul's powerful and persistent preaching, coupled with efforts by the Jewish leaders to kill him (9:23), finally convinced the apostles that his conversion was genuine. According to Galatians 1:17-18, Saul spent three years in Arabia between the time of his conversion (9:3-6) and his journey to Jerusalem (9:26).

According to Luke, following Saul's acceptance by the apostles, the church enjoyed another growth spurt and a time of peace.

9:19b-20 Saul spent several days with the disciples in Damascus. At once he began to preach in the synagogues that Jesus is the Son of God.NIV Saul obeyed his new calling immediately, for *at once he began to preach.* As would become his lifelong pattern, Saul went first to the *synagogues* so that he might preach the truth about Jesus to his Jewish kinsmen. His message, in summary, was *that Jesus is the Son of God.* This is the only time the phrase "Son of God" is used in the book of Acts (Acts 8:37 is not part of the original text of Acts). Describing Jesus as the "Son of God" had three implications: (1) it spoke of Jesus' intimate and unique relationship with God the Father; (2) it placed Jesus in the kingly line of David; (3) it identified Jesus as the long-awaited Messiah of Israel (Matthew 26:63; Mark 14:61; Luke 22:67-70). Saul could do this so soon after his conversion because his experience on the road to Damascus had been unmistakable. Saul knew that Jesus was alive, that Jesus was God's Son, and that Jesus was the Messiah.

TELLING YOUR STORY
Immediately after receiving his sight and spending some time with the believers in Damascus, Saul went to the synagogue to tell the Jews about Christ. Some Christians counsel new believers to wait until they are thoroughly grounded in their faith before attempting to share the gospel. Notice that Saul took time alone to learn about Jesus before beginning his worldwide ministry, but he did not wait to witness. Although we should not rush into a ministry unprepared, we do not need to wait before telling others the story of our encounter with Christ.

9:21 All who heard him were amazed and said, "Is not this the man who made havoc in Jerusalem among those who invoked this name? And has he not come here for the purpose of bringing them bound before the chief priests?"NRSV
The change in Saul caused his hearers to be *amazed.* They had expected Saul to show up and begin arresting followers of Jesus, for that was how he had *made havoc in Jerusalem* among the Christians. They also knew why he had come to Damascus in the first place—to bring Christians back to Jerusalem *bound before the chief priests.* Yet here was this enemy of Christianity preaching the Christian message! Surely these Jews made this information known to their leaders back in Jerusalem (9:23).

THE BEST ARGUMENT
Saul's arguments for Christ were powerful because he was a brilliant scholar. But what made his gospel presentation even more convincing was his transformed life. People knew that what Saul taught was real because they could see the evidence in the way he lived. It is important to know what the Bible teaches and how to defend the faith, but be sure your words are backed up with your new life.

9:22 Yet Saul grew more and more powerful and baffled the Jews living in Damascus by proving that Jesus is the Christ.[NIV] The Jews were *baffled* (literally, "thrown into consternation, confounded") by Saul's *powerful* preaching. His words were filled with power as he continued *proving that Jesus is the Christ.* The verb "prove" as used here means "to put together." Essentially, what Saul was doing was taking Old Testament prophecies of the Messiah and putting them together with the facts of Jesus' life, thus proving to *the Jews living in Damascus* that Jesus was the one to whom the Scriptures pointed.

9:23-25 After a while the Jewish leaders decided to kill him. But Saul was told about their plot, and that they were watching for him day and night at the city gate so they could murder him. So during the night, some of the other believers let him down in a large basket through an opening in the city wall.[NLT] According to Galatians 1:17-18, Saul left Damascus and traveled to Arabia, the desert region just southeast of Damascus, where he lived for three years. It is unclear whether his three-year stay occurred between verses 22 and 23 or between verses 25 and 26. Some commentators say that "several days" could mean a long period of time. They suggest that when Saul returned to Damascus, the governor under Aretas ordered his arrest (2 Corinthians 11:32) in an effort to keep peace with influential Jews.

> A real fire brand is distressing to the devil and when a wide-awake believer comes along, taking the Gospel seriously, we can expect sinister maneuvering for his downfall.
> *Vance Havner*

The other possibility is that Saul's night escape occurred during his first stay in Damascus, just after his conversion, when the Pharisees were especially upset over his defection from their ranks. He would have fled to Arabia to spend time alone with God and to let the Jewish religious leaders cool down.

Regardless of which theory is correct, there was a period of at least three years between Saul's conversion (9:3-6) and his trip to Jerusalem (9:26). What is clear is that Saul's preaching had made such headlines that *the Jewish leaders decided to kill him.* But God had plans for Saul, and so he protected him. *The other believers,* too, convinced of Saul's transformed life, were willing to help him escape the city. They *let him down in a large basket through an opening in the city wall* so that he could bypass the *city gate,* where people were watching for him in order to *murder him.* In some of the ancient walled cities, houses were built right on the city walls (see Joshua 2:15). It would not have been too

GREAT ESCAPES IN THE BIBLE

Who escaped	*Reference*	*What happened*	*What the escape accomplished*
Jacob	Genesis 31:1-55	Left his father-in-law, Laban, after almost 20 years of service	Allowed Jacob to return home for Isaac's death and for reconciliation with Esau, his brother
Moses	Exodus 2:11-15	Fled Egypt after killing an Egyptian in defense of a fellow Israelite	Saved his own life and began another part of God's training
Israelites	Exodus 12:28-42	Escaped Egypt after 430 years, most of that time in slavery	Confirmed God's choice of Abraham's descendants
Spies	Joshua 2:1-24	Escaped searchers in Jericho by hiding in Rahab's house	Prepared the destruction of Jericho and preserved Rahab, who would become one of David's ancestors—as well as an ancestor of Jesus
Ehud	Judges 3:15-30	Assassinated the Moabite King Eglon but escaped undetected	Broke the control of Moab over Israel and began 80 years of peace
Samson	Judges 16:1-3	Escaped a locked city by ripping the gates from their hinges	Postponed Samson's self-destruction because of his lack of self-control
Elijah	1 Kings 19:1-18	Fled into the desert out of fear of Queen Jezebel	Preserved Elijah's life but also displayed his human weakness
Saul (Paul)	Acts 9:23-25	Lowered over the wall in a basket to get out of Damascus	Saved this new Christian for great service to God
Peter	Acts 12:1-11	Freed from prison by an angel	Saved Peter for God's further plans for his life
Paul and Silas	Acts 16:22-40	Chains loosened and doors opened by an earthquake, but they chose not to leave the prison	Pointed out the powerlessness of humans before God

difficult, therefore, for one of the believers who lived in such a house to use a window in his home for Saul's escape.

9:26 **When Saul arrived in Jerusalem, he tried to meet with the believers, but they were all afraid of him. They thought he was only pretending to be a believer!**[NLT] After his three-year sojourn in Arabia, *Saul arrived in Jerusalem* only to find himself in a delicate situation. Word had come from Damascus about Saul's shocking conversion, for the Jewish leaders had already tried to kill him (9:23). But when Saul *tried to meet with the believers . . . they were all afraid of him.* This shows how terrible Saul's persecution had been. The Jerusalem church viewed Saul's behavior with suspicion. Where had he been for three years? If Saul had become a follower of Christ, why had he not reported to the apostles in Jerusalem? Clearly, the believers viewed this unexpected turn of events as part of a plot to infiltrate the church and do more harm.

9:27 **But Barnabas took him and brought him to the apostles. He told them how Saul on his journey had seen the Lord and that the Lord had spoken to him, and how in Damascus he had preached fearlessly in the name of Jesus.**[NIV] *Barnabas,* in keeping with his nickname ("Son of Encouragement"—see 4:36), encouraged Saul by acting as his "sponsor." He vouched for the genuine transformation of Saul's life. Galatians 1:18-19 explains that Saul stayed in Jerusalem only fifteen days and that he met only with Peter and James (the brother of Jesus). Barnabas told these two apostles about Saul's experience on the Damascus road (*how Saul . . . had seen the Lord and that the Lord had spoken to him),* as well as about his work in Damascus *(he had preached fearlessly in the name of Jesus).* These facts seem to have convinced the apostles of the genuineness of their former enemy's conversion.

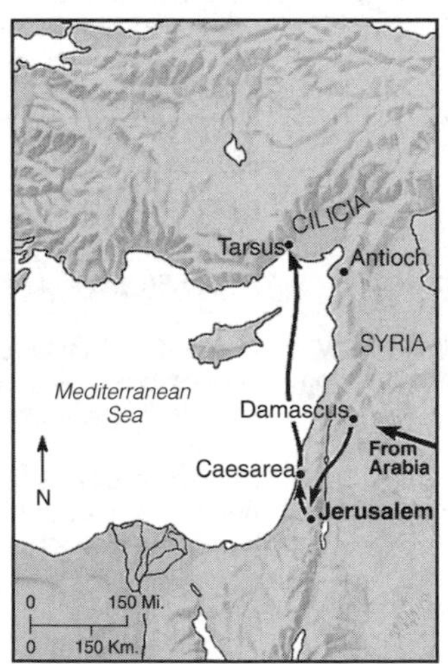

SAUL'S RETURN TO TARSUS
At least three years elapsed between Acts 9:22 and 9:26. After time alone in Arabia (see Galatians 1:16-18), Saul (Paul) returned to Damascus and then to Jerusalem. The apostles were reluctant to believe that this former persecutor could have become one of them. He escaped to Caesarea, where he caught a ship and returned to Tarsus.

9:28 So Saul stayed with them and moved about freely in Jerusalem, speaking boldly in the name of the Lord.NIV Satisfied with the character reference supplied by Barnabas, the apostles received Saul into their fellowship. He *stayed with them* (for fifteen days according to Galatians 1:18) and promptly began *speaking boldly in the name of the Lord.*

REVAMPED REPUTATION

It is difficult to change one's reputation, and Saul had a *terrible* reputation with the Christians. But Barnabas, a Jewish convert (mentioned in 4:36), became the bridge between Saul and the apostles. New Christians (especially those with tarnished reputations) need sponsors, people who will come alongside to encourage them, teach them, and introduce them to other believers. By guiding and mentoring those who are young in the faith, we help them establish a new identity as followers of Christ. Find a new believer in your church who needs practical help and encouragement in growing. Become a Barnabas to that person.

9:29-30 He debated with some Greek-speaking Jews, but they plotted to murder him. When the believers heard about it, however, they took him to Caesarea and sent him on to his hometown of Tarsus.NLT While in Jerusalem, Saul felt led to witness to the very same audience that had masterminded the stoning of Stephen—*some Greek-speaking Jews* (6:9-10). As might be expected, he encountered furious opposition. Saul was, in their eyes, a turncoat and a traitor, so they immediately began to devise a way to give him the same treatment they had given Stephen—*they plotted to murder him.* In these short sentences, we can see two characteristics of Saul, even as a new believer in Christ: he was bold, and he stirred up controversy. These would characterize Saul's ministry for the rest of his life.Here we must insert the added details provided by 22:17-21. God reminded Saul of his calling to go to the Gentiles. With the help of *the believers* (literally, "brothers," meaning fellow Christians, members of God's family), Saul escaped to *Caesarea,* where he then made his way *to his hometown of Tarsus.* Saul's departure helped quiet conflicts with the Jews. Galatians 1:21-24 probably refers to Saul's continued ministry both in Caesarea and Tarsus.

9:31 Then the church throughout Judea, Galilee and Samaria enjoyed a time of peace. It was strengthened; and encouraged by the Holy Spirit, it grew in numbers, living in the fear of the Lord.NIV After Saul, the most zealous persecutor, was converted, the church enjoyed a brief *time of peace.* Here is one of Luke's familiar summary statements or church progress reports (see also 2:46-47; 4:4, 32; 5:12-14; 6:7; 12:24; 16:5; 19:20; 28:30-31). After every crisis the power of God was present, and the church grew. The gospel was spreading, and the church was growing in *Judea, Galilee and Samaria.* It was now time for the message of Christ to be taken to the "ends of the earth" (1:8).

Saul now disappears from the record until Acts 11:25, several years later. In the interim, Paul had some experiences that are not recorded in Acts but are refered to in 2 Corinthians 11.

POISED FOR GROWTH
Was the church growing because it was enjoying a time of peace? No. The key to the church's growth here is found in the last part of this verse. The believers were "encouraged by the Holy Spirit." As long as Christians live and worship in the Spirit, demonstrating changed, supernatural lives (Galatians 5:22-23), the church will always attract unbelievers.

PETER HEALS AENEAS AND RAISES DORCAS / 9:32-43

After describing Saul's astounding conversion, Luke focused again on the ministry of Peter, specifically on the miraculous signs that accompanied his preaching. As a medical doctor (Colossians 4:14), Luke recognized that only supernatural power could instantly heal a paralyzed man like Aeneas (9:33-34). Even more amazing was the resurrection of Dorcas, a believer with a long history of doing good deeds for others. Her restoration to physical life caused many in Joppa to believe in Christ.

The final verse of chapter 9 mentions Peter's lodging with Simon, a leatherworker (also called a "tanner"). This is significant because under Jewish law, leatherworkers (people who made leather out of animal hides) were considered "unclean." Like a trickle of water through a dike, this single sentence foreshadows the great and imminent flood of God's mercy to the Gentiles.

9:32 Peter traveled from place to place to visit the believers, and in his travels he came to the Lord's people in the town of Lydda.[NLT] *Peter,* the leader of the apostles, was last mentioned in 8:25 returning from Samaria to Jerusalem with John. Capitalizing on the newfound climate of religious tolerance (the result of Saul's conversion and departure to Tarsus), Peter began an itinerant ministry intended to strengthen and encourage believers scattered throughout Israel. He came to *Lydda,* a predominantly

Gentile community about twenty-five miles west of Jerusalem. Lydda was a fairly large town and commercial center at the intersection of highways connecting Egypt to Syria and Joppa (on the Mediterranean coast) to Jerusalem.

When Peter arrived in Lydda, *he came to the Lord's people.* The gospel likely came to Lydda as a direct result of the mass conversion at Pentecost (chapter 2) or from those who had fled the Jerusalem persecution (8:1).

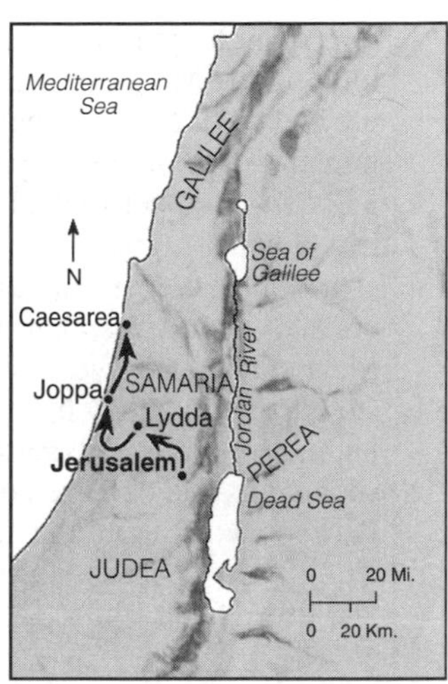

PETER'S MINISTRY
Peter traveled to the ancient crossroads town of Lydda, where he healed crippled Aeneas. The believers in Joppa, an old port city, sent for him after a wonderful woman died. Peter went and brought her back to life. While in Joppa, Peter had a vision that led him to take the gospel to Cornelius, a Gentile in Caesarea.

9:33-34 **There he found a man named Aeneas, a paralytic who had been bedridden for eight years. "Aeneas," Peter said to him, "Jesus Christ heals you. Get up and take care of your mat." Immediately Aeneas got up.**[NIV] Nothing more is known about Aeneas other than this fact of his miraculous healing from an eight-year crippling illness. It could be assumed that the word "there" refers to the community of believers, and that one of these believers was this *paralytic.* The healing was done by *Jesus Christ,* and it was immediate. No longer an invalid, Aeneas would have no further need to sit on his *mat.* He could *get up* and take it home.

9:35 **Then the whole population of Lydda and Sharon turned to the Lord when they saw Aeneas walking around.**[NLT] This miracle was not an end in itself but a confirming sign of the truth of the gospel. The phrase "the whole population" was probably not meant to be taken literally; rather, it was Luke's way of reporting that a vast number of people *turned to the Lord* and were saved, including not only those in Lydda but in the whole area of Sharon, a coastal plain about ten miles wide and fifty miles long stretching north from Lydda toward Carmel.

9:36-37 **In Joppa there was a disciple named Tabitha (which, when translated, is Dorcas), who was always doing good and helping the poor. About that time she became sick and died, and her body was washed and placed in an upstairs room.**[NIV] The important harbor city of *Joppa* sits 125 feet above sea level, overlooking the Mediterranean Sea. Joppa was the town into which the cedars of Lebanon had been floated to be shipped to Jerusalem and used in the temple construction (2 Chronicles 2:16; Ezra 3:7). The prophet Jonah had left the port of Joppa on his ill-fated trip (Jonah 1:3).

It was customary to bury corpses before sundown. The believers had only *washed* her body (without yet giving it the customary anointing), however, and had laid it *in an upstairs room,* suggesting that they believed that she could be raised. The church had not previously experienced miracles of this nature, though such signs had occurred during the life and ministry of Christ. Perhaps word about the healing of Aeneas had reached Joppa from Lydda, because the believers dispatched two men to find and bring Peter (9:38).

A POWERFUL IMPACT
Dorcas made an enormous difference in her community by "always doing good and helping the poor." Specifically, she was known for making robes and other clothing (9:39). When she died, the room was filled with mourners, very likely many of the people she had helped. And when she was brought back to life, the news raced through the town. God uses great preachers like Peter and Paul, but he also uses those who have gifts of kindness, like Dorcas. Rather than wishing you had other gifts, make good use of the gifts God has given you.

9:38-39 **Since Lydda was near Joppa, the disciples, who heard that Peter was there, sent two men to him with the request, "Please come to us without delay." So Peter got up and went with them; and when he arrived, they took him to the room upstairs. All the widows stood beside him, weeping and showing tunics and other clothing that Dorcas had made while she was with them.**[NRSV] Joppa was only about ten miles northwest of Lydda. To go and find Peter and bring him back would have taken these *two men* six to eight hours. Once located and presented with the need in Joppa, Peter *got up and went with them.* The text indicates the haste with which all this was accomplished. Arriving, Peter was immediately ushered to *the room upstairs* (probably an atticlike structure atop the flat roof of the home). There he met a group of mourning widows. In all probability, these weeping women were wearing the various articles of clothing that Dorcas had so lovingly made for them. Clearly, this woman's death was a major blow to the church in Joppa.

9:40-41 But Peter asked them all to leave the room; then he knelt and prayed. Turning to the body he said, "Get up, Tabitha." And she opened her eyes! When she saw Peter, she sat up! He gave her his hand and helped her up. Then he called in the widows and all the believers, and he showed them that she was alive.[NLT] This scene bears striking resemblance to Jesus' raising of the daughter of Jairus (Mark 5:35-43). Peter had been an eyewitness to that miracle. Like Christ, he first *asked them all to leave the room.* Then, after getting down on his knees to pray, Peter uttered a command that was almost identical to the one spoken by Jesus. Whereas Jesus had said in Aramaic, *"Talitha, cumi"* (translation: "Little girl, arise!"), Peter said, *"Tabitha, cumi"* ("Tabitha, arise!")—a difference of only one letter. Perhaps Peter even smiled at the replication of the whole situation.

> Behind every work of God you will always find some kneeling form.
> *D. L. Moody*

Tabitha (Dorcas was her name in Greek) *opened her eyes* and *sat up.* Only then did Peter touch the woman (probably in keeping with the Jewish ceremonial laws against touching corpses—see Leviticus 21:1; Numbers 5:2; 9:6-10; 19:11), helping her to her feet. Then he presented this back-from-the-dead saint to her overjoyed friends.

9:42-43 The news raced through the whole town, and many believed in the Lord. And Peter stayed a long time in Joppa, living with Simon, a leatherworker.[NLT] As a result of this startling miracle, *many* citizens of Joppa *believed in the Lord. Peter stayed a long time in Joppa,* at the home of *Simon,* probably in order to teach the people more thoroughly the full implications of the gospel. Perhaps Peter recognized the truth that a faith built solely on miraculous experiences tends to be rather shaky.

It is significant that Peter stayed with a man who was, by vocation, a *leatherworker* (also translated "tanner"). A leatherworker made animal hides into leather. Hence, this occupation involved contact with dead animals, and Jewish law considered it an "unclean" job. Peter was already beginning to break down his prejudice against people who were not of his kind and customs that did not adhere to Jewish religious traditions. This would set the stage for what is reported in the next chapter.

Acts 10

CORNELIUS CALLS FOR PETER / 10:1-8

In his earthly ministry, Jesus had said that the Spirit of God was like a wind blowing unpredictably through human lives (John 3:8), convicting individuals of their sin and drawing them to himself (John 16:8, 13). In the history of the early church recorded in the first nine chapters of Acts, this saving work of God's Spirit was mostly confined to the Jews. Suddenly, Acts 10 describes the Spirit's sovereign activity in a Gentile army officer stationed on the Mediterranean coast.

An angel of the Lord visited the Roman officer, Cornelius, in a vision. He told Cornelius to summon Peter the apostle. This is a turning point in the history of the church. The one true God—the God of the Hebrews—was about to unveil his eternal plan, hidden through the ages: "There is no longer Jew or Gentile . . . you are all Christians . . . one in Christ Jesus" (Galatians 3:28 NLT).

The book of Acts continues with its steady, singular message: God is directing the expansion of his church, founded on the crucified and resurrected Christ. The conversion of Cornelius, the first Gentile convert recorded in Acts, portrays a significant step in the process of expansion. The Word was spreading and the church was on the threshold of a whole new phase of Jesus' promised progress (1:8).

10:1 In Caesarea there lived a Roman army officer named Cornelius, who was a captain of the Italian Regiment.[NLT] This *Caesarea,* sometimes called Palestinian Caesarea, was located on the coast of the Mediterranean Sea, thirty-two miles north of Joppa. The largest and most important port city on the Mediterranean in Palestine, Caesarea was the capital of the Roman province of Judea. This was the first city to have Gentile Christians and a non-Jewish church.

This *Roman army officer* was a "centurion," a commander of one hundred soldiers. A centurion was similar to a noncommissioned officer in the military today. The *Italian Regiment* could have included up to six hundred soldiers. Although stationed in Caesarea, *Cornelius* would probably have had to return soon to

Rome. Thus his conversion may have helped to spread the gospel to the empire's capital city.

At no time in the New Testament does Jesus rebuke a military person for being in the military. God wants Christians to reach others in many walks of life, including those in military service (see Jesus' dealings with his first Gentile contact in Luke 7:2-9; see also Matthew 8:5-11; 27:54; Mark 15:44-45; Acts 22:25-26; 23:17-18; 27:6, 43).

Because of frequent outbreaks of violence, Roman soldiers had to be stationed to keep peace throughout Israel. But most Romans, hated as conquerors, did not get along well in the nation. As an army officer, Cornelius was in a difficult position. He represented Rome, but he lived in Caesarea. During Cornelius's years in Israel, he had been conquered by the God of Israel. With a reputation as a godly man who put his faith into action, Cornelius was respected by the Jews (10:2).

GOD SEEKS

Cornelius's story demonstrates God's willingness to use extraordinary means to reach those who desire to know him. God does not play favorites and does not hide from those who want to find him. God sent his Son "to seek and save those . . . who are lost" (Luke 19:10 NLT) because he loves the whole world—and that includes Peter, Cornelius, and you. Even at this very moment, the Father is drawing men and women, boys, and girls to himself (John 6:44). Watch for signs today of God at work in the heart of someone who is spiritually hungry.

10:2 **He and all his family were devout and God-fearing; he gave generously to those in need and prayed to God regularly.**NIV
Four significant aspects of Cornelius's character are noted: (1) He was *devout;* (2) he was *God-fearing;* (3) he was a generous giver; and (4) he was consistent in prayer.

Cornelius's sincere search for God is evident in this description of him. The term for "devout" *(eusebes)* is used only here and in 10:7 to describe one of his soldiers. The term "God-fearing" is a technical term for a Gentile who attended the synagogue and followed the Jewish laws but had not been circumcised. This is different from a "proselyte," who was more thoroughly committed to Judaism and, thus, often harder to reach for Christ.

The reference to Cornelius's being devout is supported by his activity of giving to those in need and praying regularly. Cornelius's faith had hands—he was regularly involved in activities that displayed his interest in serving others.

THOSE WHO HAVE NEVER HEARD

"What will happen to the heathen who have never heard about Christ?" This question is often asked when considering God's justice. Cornelius wasn't a follower of Christ, but he was seeking God and was reverent and generous. Therefore God sent Peter to tell Cornelius about Christ. Cornelius is an example that God "rewards those who sincerely seek him" (Hebrews 11:6 NLT). Those who earnestly seek God will find him! God made Cornelius's knowledge complete.

10:3 **One afternoon at about three o'clock he had a vision in which he clearly saw an angel of God coming in and saying to him, "Cornelius."**NRSV The time—*about three o'clock*—was likely one of Cornelius's regular times of prayer. This was one of the hours of prayer at the temple. Cornelius may have prayed faithfully for many years before this day when *an angel of God* came to speak to him. Later, Cornelius would describe this angel as "a man in dazzling clothes" (10:30).

> All happenings, great and small, are parables whereby God speaks. . . . The art of life is to get the message.
>
> *Malcolm Muggeridge*

GETTING OUR ATTENTION

Cornelius had a vision featuring a heavenly messenger. God spoke to other Bible characters through a variety of means—the burning bush of Moses (Exodus 3:1-4); the talking donkey of Balaam (Numbers 22:21-30); the gentle whisper heard by Elijah (1 Kings 19:11-14); the strange object lessons of Jeremiah (Jeremiah 13:1-11). Simply put, God speaks to his people in remarkably different ways—through the written Scriptures, through the words of others, through circumstances and events. It is up to us to listen, to be perceptive, to be alert. What is God trying to say to you today?

10:4 **Cornelius stared at him in fear. "What is it, Lord?" he asked. The angel answered, "Your prayers and gifts to the poor have come up as a memorial offering before God."**NIV Even this veteran soldier showed fear before the angel of the Lord. God saw Cornelius's sincere faith. His prayers and generous giving had been a *memorial offering before God,* a sacrificial offering to the Lord. The "memorial offering" conveys that Cornelius's faithful prayers had been noticed by God (Leviticus 2:2; Philippians 4:18). God answers the sincere prayers of those who seek him by sending the right person or the right information at the right time.

Luke had already mentioned the habit of Cornelius to care for those in need (10:2), and the angelic messenger did so as well. Believers must never forget God's love for the poor (James 2:5) and the importance of caring for them (Exodus 22:22-27; Leviticus 25:35-37; Proverbs 14:31; Luke 6:21; Galatians 2:10; 1 Timothy 5:3-5). Jesus could not have been clearer on the importance of the subject (Matthew 25:44-45).

The angel painted Cornelius's actions as offerings to God. That is a beautiful picture of what our properly motivated acts of faith are like—they ascend to God like the smoke of the sacrifice. This is the language of the Levitical sacrifice (see Leviticus 2:2), commonly applied to our prayers and good deeds done in Christ's name (see Philippians 4:18; Hebrews 13:15-16).

A GIFT TO GOD

Cornelius was generous in helping the poor. Here are eight common excuses for not helping the poor and needy:

(1) They don't deserve help. They got themselves into poverty; let them get themselves out.

(2) God's call to help the poor applies to another time.

(3) I don't know any people like this.

(4) I have my own needs.

(5) Any money I give will be wasted, stolen, or spent. The poor will never see it.

(6) I may become a victim myself.

(7) I don't know where to start, and I don't have time.

(8) My little bit won't make any difference.

Instead of making excuses, ask what can be done to help. Does your church have programs to help the needy? Could you volunteer to work with a community group that fights poverty? As one individual, you may not be able to accomplish much, but join up with similarly motivated people, and watch mountains begin to move.

10:5-6 "Now send some men down to Joppa to find a man named Simon Peter. He is staying with Simon, a leatherworker who lives near the shore. Ask him to come and visit you."[NLT] God told Cornelius to send for *a man named Simon Peter* because Peter would give him more knowledge about the God he was already seeking to please. Cornelius was directed to *Joppa* (thirty-two miles south of Caesarea) to find Peter, who was still *staying with Simon, a leatherworker* (see 9:43). Cornelius was instructed to invite Peter *to come and visit.*

10:7-8 As soon as the angel was gone, Cornelius called two of his household servants and a devout soldier, one of his personal attendants. He told them what had happened and sent them

off to Joppa.[NLT] Cornelius responded without delay (reminiscent of the centurion in Jesus' dealings in Luke 7:8) because he understood the nature of giving and receiving orders. He obeyed the message of the angel and sent his most trusted aides to get Peter. Three men were sent—two *household servants* and *a devout soldier,* the latter of whom is described as *one of his personal attendants.* Obviously, the godly character of Cornelius had made an impact on those closest to him.

The word used to describe Cornelius's description of *what had happened* is the word from which we get the term "exegesis" (exegesamenos), meaning to "explain" clearly and in detail.

THE GREAT CONDUCTOR
The picture in Acts 10 (and really the whole Bible) is of God orchestrating big events and individual lives to bring about his eternal purposes. God has a vast, cosmic plan that he is bringing to pass, and he is using willing, obedient servants to make it happen. Are you in a place and of such a mind to be used by the Great Conductor? Get ready! God may send someone across your path today who needs the benefit of your wisdom or gifts.

PETER VISITS CORNELIUS / 10:9-33

Even as Cornelius's messengers were on their way to get Peter, the apostle was having a divine vision of his own. In this vision, three times Peter was commanded to kill and eat a number of unclean animals. Of Jewish descent, Peter was both horrified and confused by this strange dream.

The meaning of the vision slowly became clear, however, when the messengers arrived and told their story (10:17-23). Peter recognized God working in and through all these unusual events. Freed from his Jewish prejudices (see 10:28), Peter accompanied the men back to Caesarea.

10:9-10 **About noon the next day, as they were on their journey and approaching the city, Peter went up on the roof to pray. He became hungry and wanted something to eat; and while it was being prepared, he fell into a trance.**[NRSV] Like Cornelius, Peter prayed daily. Morning and evening were the common times to pray, and evidently Peter made it a habit to pray in the middle of the day as well (see Nehemiah 1:4-11; Psalm 55:17; Daniel 6:10). This significant opening of the door to the Gentiles was God-directed, but note that the two men were devout, God-dependent, regular seekers of God through prayer. It is no coincidence that Peter and Cornelius were both found praying when God revealed more of himself to them.

Peter *went up on the roof to pray.* Houses in Bible times usually had flat roofs accessed by an outside staircase. The roof would have given Peter privacy. As he prayed, he *became hungry* and evidently *fell into a trance* while he was waiting for lunch to be prepared. During this trance God spoke to him.

WITHOUT CEASING

Many Jews prayed legalistically—going through the motions of prayer at certain times of the day so as to fulfill their religious duty. Peter, however, had learned from his Master, Jesus, that prayer is more than ritual; it is communion with the Father, an expression of love and trust. When believers understand that prayer is the vital link to the living God, and when they begin to see prayer not as a luxury but as a moment-by-moment necessity in the Christian life, then, and only then, will they have intimacy with God and experience his power and presence. Make prayer a priority.

10:11-13 He saw heaven opened and something like a large sheet being let down to earth by its four corners. It contained all kinds of four-footed animals, as well as reptiles of the earth and birds of the air. Then a voice told him, "Get up, Peter. Kill and eat."[NIV] Peter saw *something like* a sheet being let down to earth from *heaven.* The *voice,* obviously that of someone in authority (probably God himself), told Peter that he was free to *"Get up. . . . Kill and eat"* the animals, including *reptiles* and *birds.* According to Jewish law, these particular foods were forbidden (see Leviticus 11). These food laws made it difficult for Jews to eat with Gentiles without risking defilement. The point of this vision, as was about to be made clear, was that God was working outside of Israel, beyond Israel, and if Peter was to be a part of what God was doing, he needed to understand that nothing was unclean.

10:14 "Surely not, Lord!" Peter replied. "I have never eaten anything impure or unclean."[NIV] Peter, always ready to voice his opinion, expressed directly to the *Lord* the courage of his conviction not to eat anything *impure or unclean.* Once again, Peter was questioning God about something with which he disagreed (see Matthew 16:23; John 13:8; 21:20-21). It is unclear whether the sheet included both clean and unclean animals or just unclean. Whatever the case, Peter would not "get up, kill, and eat," because these animals had been prohibited by God's law (Leviticus 11). Peter had *never eaten* of such food and was not about to start.

10:15-16 The voice spoke to him a second time, "Do not call anything impure that God has made clean." This happened three times, and immediately the sheet was taken back to heaven.[NIV] This educating of Peter, as with the educating of most believers, took a little repetition. God was revealing something that would be startling to Peter's Jewish mind; God was basically nullifying the Jewish dietary laws and, by analogy, God was preparing Peter to meet an unclean Gentile. This, in essence, was what Jesus had taught (Mark 7:14-23; see also 1 Timothy 4:4). The repetition of this truth *three times* is a testimony in part to the seriousness of the message and possibly to Peter's difficulty in recognizing this as God's genuine revelation to him. The repetition was meant to drive home the message about reaching "unclean" people groups. Some link this with Peter's threefold denial of Christ (John 18:17, 25-27) and his threefold restoration by Christ (John 21:15-17).

AGREEING WITH GOD
Steeped in Jewish tradition and filled with certain biases, Peter was convinced his views on the Gentiles were correct. It took a three-part heavenly vision for God to change Peter's mind. One of the most basic and practical lessons from this encounter is that when God speaks, we must not challenge what he says. Doubting God is the rebellion of Eden. When God says something is so, we must not debate with him. The right response is humble submission to his revealed truth. Are you trying to argue with God over some point that he has already made clear?

10:17-18 Peter was very perplexed. What could the vision mean? Just then the men sent by Cornelius found the house and stood outside at the gate. They asked if this was the place where Simon Peter was staying.[NLT] *Peter was very perplexed,* and his confusion is understandable. For centuries the dietary restrictions had been in place for devout Jews. As Peter reflected over what *the vision* could mean, his God-sent visitors arrived to provide an opportunity for Peter to apply what the voice from heaven had said. God's timing is always impeccable, and his sovereign hand over the spread of the gospel is an ever present part of Luke's record.

10:19-20 While Peter was still thinking about the vision, the Spirit said to him, "Simon, three men are looking for you. So get up and go downstairs. Do not hesitate to go with them, for I have sent them."[NIV] Peter's perplexity was set aside as *the Spirit* spoke to him. In order to help Peter more quickly get the point of this difficult new arrangement, God told him to *get up and go downstairs.*

There he would meet the men whom God had sent *(I have sent them).* These men would take Peter to see the real meaning behind the vision of the sheet and the animals. In this event, an angel of God spoke to Cornelius, a voice from heaven spoke to Peter, and here the Holy Spirit spoke directly to Peter. We must not be too narrow in our interpretation of how God speaks to people today.

10:21-22 Peter went down and said to the men, "I'm the one you're looking for. Why have you come?" The men replied, "We have come from Cornelius the centurion. He is a righteous and God-fearing man, who is respected by all the Jewish people. A holy angel told him to have you come to his house so that he could hear what you have to say."NIV Peter had experienced denying Christ three times (Luke 22:54-62), being restored three times by Christ (John 21:15-17), and seeing the same vision three times (Acts 10:16). Peter was greeted by three men at the door (10:19-20) who introduced the one they represented *(Cornelius)* as *a righteous and God-fearing man* and added that he was *respected by all the Jewish people.* Cornelius's godly character had obviously built him a good reputation. Peter was informed of the heavenly message that Cornelius had received, and he recognized it as being somehow related to his own.

The openness of Cornelius to whatever Peter would have to say *(so that he could hear what you have to say)* was a beautiful foreshadowing of the coming Gentile openness to the message of the Cross.

THE INADEQUACY OF SINCERITY

Cornelius was religious, devoted, generous, respected, and sincere (10:1-2). However, he was still spiritually separated from God. Because he needed to understand the gospel, God sent Peter to present to him the truth about salvation. Be careful not to equate earnestness with righteousness before God. We are brought into right standing with God by faith alone in Christ alone. Have you trusted in Jesus? Are you sharing with others—even those who are religious—the truth that Christ is the only way to God?

10:23-24 Then Peter invited the men into the house to be his guests. The next day Peter started out with them, and some of the brothers from Joppa went along. The following day he arrived in Caesarea. Cornelius was expecting them and had called together his relatives and close friends.NIV Peter had been staying at the house of Simon the leather-

> The desire for safety stands against every great and noble enterprise. *Tacitus*

worker. Peter continued to remove barriers: not only was he staying in a place that his prejudices would have previously prohibited (see commentary on 9:42-43), he went a further step by inviting Gentiles into that home to be his guests. This kind of fellowship would have been unacceptable to a strict Jew. A sheet had been let down from heaven, and Peter's eyes were being opened.

> The primary change agents in the spread of faith . . . were the men and women who earned their livelihood in some purely secular manner, and spoke of their faith to those whom they met in this natural fashion.
> *Kenneth Scott Latourette*

Peter was wise to take with him *some of the brothers from Joppa* (six believers, according to 11:12). Some things, particularly changes as radical as Peter suspected were on the horizon, were better observed firsthand rather than explained secondhand. Possibly Peter knew that it was easier for him to accept this new Gentile openness to the gospel because he had been present at the "Samaritan Pentecost" (8:15-17). If God were truly doing something new, it would be best that other believers could see it as well.

The eagerness and expectation of Cornelius was obvious, for he *called together his relatives and close friends,* probably many, considering Cornelius's reputation for kindness and piety. Note, too, his confidence that Peter would come.

THE EVANGELIST

We must not miss Cornelius's example as an evangelist. He anticipated a message from Peter and invited his family and friends to hear the message that he himself had not yet heard! There's an example of someone who had great confidence in what God was going to do and who was willing to take the relational and reputational risks to expose those he loved to the gospel. Are you willing to do the same?

10:25-27 As Peter entered his home, Cornelius fell to the floor before him in worship. But Peter pulled him up and said, "Stand up! I'm a human being like you!" So Cornelius got up, and they talked together and went inside where the others were assembled.[NLT] The reaction of Cornelius to Peter's arrival was that of one who felt he was in the presence of a messenger of God. The text says he *fell to the floor . . . in worship (prosekunesen),* an action entirely unacceptable for Cornelius to give a mortal messenger. Peter ordered Cornelius to stand. In the Jewish faith, worship given to a human being would be blasphemy.

Peter's statement *"I am a human being like you"* was profound. Certainly these words would be spread throughout the Gentile world, that the great apostle had equated himself with a Roman centurion.

Evidently the two men were outside the house and alone; they *talked together* awhile before going *inside where the others were assembled.* Again, Peter's prejudices had to be put aside in order for him to enter this Gentile home to fellowship with those gathered there. Word would spread. Tongues would wag, and they did (see 11:2-3). But God was behind this opportunity. Peter knew this and obeyed.

HANDLING PRAISE

This act of worship on the part of a grateful Cornelius could have caused Peter to become arrogant. After all, this powerful man was bowing before him. Instead of succumbing to the temptation, Peter pointed Cornelius to Christ. We, too, should remember our humanity, our mortality, our frailty whenever we are flattered, praised, or honored. Use these opportunities to give glory to God. Be like John the Baptist, who said, "He must become greater and greater, and I must become less and less" (John 3:30 NLT).

10:28-29 Peter told them, "You know it is against the Jewish laws for me to come into a Gentile home like this. But God has shown me that I should never think of anyone as impure. So I came as soon as I was sent for. Now tell me why you sent for me."NLT Peter acknowledged his breaking of *Jewish laws* to enter this *Gentile home,* but he continued and gave the gathered audience the benefit of God's vision of the sheet from heaven. Peter had gotten the message. The vision was not primarily about food; the dietary issues were secondary to the human ones. (The Jews were not prohibited from fellowshipping with Gentiles, but the Gentile dietary practices made them "ceremonially" risky to associate with.) The vision was from *God* and was about people, specifically those people whom the Jews (and, as a carryover, the Jewish Christians) still considered "unclean." Without reserve, Peter stated that God had shown him that he *should never think of anyone as impure.*

10:30 Cornelius replied, "Four days ago at this very hour, at three o'clock, I was praying in my house when suddenly a man in dazzling clothes stood before me."NRSV Cornelius re counted his experience for the sake of Peter and his gathered guests. Luke recorded it because it is a very important vision, and in each retelling, more details were added or emphasized. This will be repeated again by Peter in the next chapter (11:4-14). Here

Cornelius added to his description of the angelic messenger, saying that he had been wearing *dazzling clothes.*

10:31-32 "He told me, 'Cornelius, your prayers have been heard, and your gifts to the poor have been noticed by God! Now send some men to Joppa and summon Simon Peter. He is staying in the home of Simon, a leatherworker who lives near the shore.'"NLT Cornelius recounted to Peter what the angel had told him to do. Surely the specifics that had been given to Cornelius about Peter's whereabouts showed how God was behind this meeting.

> It is always God who takes the first step. When the human mind begins to seek and the human heart begins to long, God comes to meet us far more than half way. . . . When we go to God we do not go to one who hides himself and keeps us at a distance; we go to one who stands waiting for us, and who even takes the initiative by coming to meet us on the road. *William Barclay*

10:33 "Therefore I sent for you immediately, and you have been kind enough to come. So now all of us are here in the presence of God to listen to all that the Lord has commanded you to say."NRSV Cornelius commended Peter for being *kind enough to come* (literally, "you have done well"). He then stated the obvious and important fact that those present *(all of us)* were in a holy convocation—*in the presence of God*— and that their sole purpose was *to listen to all that the Lord has commanded you* [Peter] *to say.* Cornelius had sure, solid confidence that God was about to speak to them through Peter, and on behalf of all those gathered there, he expressed eagerness to hear what God had to say. If ever there was an ideal audience for a preacher or teacher, this was it.

THE GENTILES HEAR THE GOOD NEWS / 10:34-43

Having been sovereignly (even miraculously) guided to the home of Cornelius and having been impressed by the truth that God doesn't show partiality (10:34), Peter took the keys of the kingdom of heaven given him by Christ (Matthew 16:19) and, in a epoch-changing moment, opened the door of salvation to the Gentiles.

Peter's message was simple and brief: Christ lived, died, and rose again, and "everyone who believes in him will have their sins forgiven through his name" (10:43 NLT).

10:34-35 Then Peter began to speak to them: "I truly understand that God shows no partiality, but in every nation anyone who fears him and does what is right is acceptable to him."NRSV

NAMES AND TITLES FOR JESUS IN ACTS

Reference	*Name/Title*
1:6	Lord
1:21	Lord Jesus
2:22	Jesus of Nazareth
2:27	Holy One
2:30-31, 36	Messiah
2:38	Jesus Christ
3:13	his [God's] servant Jesus
3:15	the author of life
3:20	Jesus your Messiah
5:31	Prince and Savior
7:52	the Righteous One
7:56	the Son of Man
9:20	the Son of God
10:36	Lord of all
10:42	the judge of all—the living and the dead
10:43	the one all the prophets testified about
13:23	God's promised Savior of Israel
16:7	the Spirit of Jesus
17:7	king
24:24	Christ Jesus
28:20	the hope of Israel

Peter's words marked a great change in the life of the church—the door of the gospel was swinging wide open to the Gentiles. Look at Peter's wording: *no partiality, every nation, anyone.* These terms express Peter's clear understanding of the universal application of Christ's work on the cross and the subsequent universal offer of the gospel. For more on God's acceptance of all kinds of people, see Ephesians 6:9; Colossians 3:25; James 2:1, 9; 1 Peter 1:17. Because God doesn't discriminate on the basis of race, economics, or sex, neither should any believers.

A HUNGER FOR GOD
Cornelius demonstrated an amazing eagerness to know and obey God. He responded "immediately" to the vision given to him by God and expressed gratefulness to Peter for coming to tell him about God. He sensed God's presence in the moment and demonstrated a receptive, teachable heart. Are you eager to hear from God and to do his will? Ask the Spirit of God to give you a thirst for himself. He must implant these holy desires within you. You cannot produce them in your own efforts or strength.

10:36 **"I'm sure you have heard about the Good News for the people of Israel—that there is peace with God through Jesus Christ, who is Lord of all."**NLT Assuming that his audience had already *heard* much of the information about the coming of Christ and the birth of the church, Peter proceeded to tell the story of Christ's life and death in detail. This is a beautiful summary of the teaching of the apostles, and it perfectly parallels the Gospel of Mark (who probably received much of his information from Peter). This verse expresses the clear purpose of the gospel—to provide an opportunity for people to experience *peace with God.* The means by which that happens is *through Jesus Christ,* to whom Peter referred here by the powerful title, *Lord of all.*

Many writers point to the structure of this speech and the nature of the wording and believe that Peter was probably preaching in Aramaic, perhaps through an interpreter.

10:37-38 **"You know what has happened throughout Judea, beginning in Galilee after the baptism that John preached—how God anointed Jesus of Nazareth with the Holy Spirit and power, and how he went around doing good and healing all who were under the power of the devil, because God was with him."**NIV Peter started where Mark's Gospel does—with the *baptism that John preached.* He moved on to mention Christ's ministry from *Galilee and throughout Judea,* including the good works and miracles Jesus had done. Peter's audience would likely have been familiar with most of these events. The miracles and the healings were a demonstration of Jesus' power over *the devil,* as well as the fact that *God was with him* and in fact had *anointed* him *with the Holy Spirit and power* (Isaiah 61:1-3; Luke 4:16-21). The anointing of which Peter was speaking had occurred at Jesus' baptism, when the Holy Spirit, in the form of a dove, had descended upon him (Mark 1:9-11; Luke 3:21-22).

NO "WINDY" WITNESSES!
Peter's brief and powerful sermon contains a concise statement of the gospel: Jesus' perfect life of servanthood, his death on the cross, his resurrection—personally witnessed and experienced by Peter—his fulfillment of the Scriptures, and the necessity of personal faith in him. A sermon or witness for Christ does not need to be long to be effective. It should be Spirit-led and should center simply on Christ as the way, the truth, and the life.

10:39-41 "We are witnesses to all that he did both in Judea and in Jerusalem. They put him to death by hanging him on a tree; but God raised him on the third day and allowed him to appear, not to all the people but to us who were chosen by God as witnesses, and who ate and drank with him after he rose from the dead."NRSV In short order Peter stated the fact that he and others *(we)* had been *witnesses* to the ministry of Jesus, including his crucifixion and his resurrection. They had been *chosen* by God as witnesses (the word "witness" occurring twice), in that Christ had appeared to them (Peter, the apostles, and hundreds of others—1 Corinthians 15:5-7) and even *ate and drank* with them after his resurrection. Peter acknowledged that there was no general appearance of Christ to the public but rather to those who had been chosen by God. In no way should that diminish the magnitude of the miracle or the credibility of the testimony of the witnesses. The fact that they had eaten and had drunk with him should squelch any rumor that Jesus had appeared in some "phantom" form.

This was solid, decisive proof of Christ's resurrection and was confirmed by one who had been there, had seen it, and had participated fully in it. What more would they need to hear? There were dozens of other readily available eyewitnesses, if anyone cared to confirm it.

10:42 "He commanded us to preach to the people and to testify that he is the one whom God appointed as judge of the living and the dead."NIV Christ came to judge (see 2 Timothy 4:1; 1 Peter 4:5). The command of the resurrected Christ was for these witnesses *to preach to the people and to testify* that Christ was the appointed *judge of the living and the dead.* He is the one before whom ultimately all people (Jew and Gentile alike) will stand and give account. For Christ's commands to the disciples, see Acts 1:8, also Matthew 28:18-20; Mark 16:15-18; Luke 24:47-48.

10:43 **"He is the one all the prophets testified about, saying that everyone who believes in him will have their sins forgiven through his name."**[NLT] Christ came to forgive sin. In contrast to the preceding verse, Peter turned to the prophets' testimony for the flip side of judgment—salvation. Jesus Christ was the long-awaited Savior who would offer forgiveness of sins to *everyone who believes in him* (John 3:16). Two examples of prophets testifying about Jesus and his forgiveness of sins are Isaiah (see Isaiah 52:13–53:12) and Ezekiel (see Ezekiel 36:25-26).

Note again that Peter made it clear that this message is for everyone, not just the Jews. Everyone sins. Everyone needs to be saved. Everyone needs forgiveness. All that is needed is faith.

> Not long before she died in 1988, in a moment of surprising candor on television, Marghanita Laski, one of our best-known secular novelists, said: "What I envy most about you Christians is your forgiveness; I have nobody to forgive me."
> *John Stott*

THE GENTILES RECEIVE THE HOLY SPIRIT / 10:44-48

To confirm the Gentiles' acceptance by God and their full inclusion in his kingdom as heirs of grace, Luke recorded these new converts' experience of the Holy Spirit. Exactly as had happened with the Jewish believers at Pentecost (chapter 2), these Gentile converts began speaking in unlearned foreign languages. The Jewish believers who had accompanied Peter from Joppa (10:23) were amazed (10:45). But there could be no doubt about what they had just witnessed.

10:44 **Even as Peter was saying these things, the Holy Spirit fell upon all who had heard the message.**[NLT] Peter's sermon was interrupted *(even as Peter was saying these things)* by *the Holy Spirit,* who *fell upon all who had heard the message.* Luke recorded the original Pentecost in chapter 2. Chapter 8 told of the "Samaritan Pentecost." This event could be called the "Gentile Pentecost." The Spirit came upon all those in attendance.

Unlike the Samaritan believers who had waited between belief and the baptism of the Spirit, which had come by the laying on of apostolic hands (see 8:17-18), the Spirit *fell* on these Gentile believers, just as he had at the first Pentecost—no laying on of hands, no praying for the Spirit to fall; God just did it!

WORDS OF POWER
Peter's words—heartfelt, accurate, urgent—would have been powerless without the Holy Spirit, who was working in the lives of these assembled Gentiles. This is a good reminder that successful preaching or witnessing does not depend on flashy rhetoric, biblical expertise, or heart-tugging stories. Those can be helpful, but it is the Spirit who does the real convicting and convincing. It is *his* power that changes minds, hearts, and wills. We are merely tools. Use your gifts, but trust in the power of the Spirit.

10:45-46a **The circumcised believers who had come with Peter were astonished that the gift of the Holy Spirit had been poured out even on the Gentiles. For they heard them speaking in tongues and praising God.**[NIV] The *circumcised believers* could be translated "the Jewish believers" (see also 11:2). These were the men who had accompanied Peter (10:23). They *were astonished* (*exestesan*—literally, "beside themselves") that the same phenomena of Pentecost were being demonstrated *even on the Gentiles.* As at Pentecost, reported in chapter 2, these Gentiles experienced *speaking in tongues and praising God.* It is likely that without these accompanying signs, the skeptical Jewish contingency of the church would not have believed that these Gentiles were genuinely converted and Spirit-indwelled. With these visible signs, there could be no doubt.

God will not give us the Holy Spirit to enable us to gain celebrity or to procure a name or to live an easy, self-controlled life. The spirit's passion is the glory of the Lord Jesus, and [the Spirit] can make His abode [only] with those who are willing to be at one with Him in this. *F. B. Meyer*

This was a powerful testimony to Peter and his Jewish contingency of the necessity of fully accepting Gentile believers into the body of Christ. Whatever lingering questions Peter may have had about his vision of a sheet and animals or about Cornelius's visit by an angelic messenger would have been put aside in light of this event. The apostles had not invited these Gentiles into the kingdom—God had. Like so many other amazing salvation scenes in the book of Acts, the apostles realized that their role was not as operatives (that's the Spirit's work) but rather as witnesses (those who watch and report what they see).

10:46b-47 **Then Peter asked, "Can anyone object to their being baptized, now that they have received the Holy Spirit just as we did?"**[NLT] In this case the believers were *baptized* after they received the Holy Spirit, publicly declaring their allegiance to Christ and identification with the Christian community. Peter's words *(received the Holy Spirit just as we did)* reveal the impressiveness of what they had just seen. It was undeniable, irrefutable evidence that God had come to the Gentiles. They were now full-fledged, Spirit-indwelled members of the body of Christ. No human opinion, apostolic or otherwise, could change that.

THE MOSAIC OF GOD
Cornelius and Peter were very different. Cornelius was wealthy, a Gentile, and a military man. Peter was a Jewish fisherman-turned-preacher. But God's plan included both of them. In Cornelius's house that day, a new chapter in Christian history was written, as a Jewish Christian leader and a Gentile Christian convert each discovered something significant about God at work in the other person. Cornelius needed Peter and his preaching of the gospel to find the way to salvation. Peter needed Cornelius and his salvation experience to know that Gentiles were included in God's plan. You and another believer may also need each other to understand how God works!

10:48 **So he gave orders for them to be baptized in the name of Jesus Christ. Afterward Cornelius asked him to stay with them for several days.**[NLT] These new Spirit-baptized believers were then *baptized* with water *in the name of Jesus Christ,* and Peter was invited by his new Christian brother to *stay with them for several days,* presumably for further instruction on what had just happened and what was next in this new life in Christ.

HUNGERING FOR GROWTH
Cornelius wanted Peter to stay with him for several days. As a new believer, he realized his need for teaching and fellowship. Are you as eager to learn more about Christ? Do you look for ways to grow deeper and stronger in your spiritual walk? Recognize your need to be with more mature Christians, and strive to learn from them.

Acts 11

PETER EXPLAINS HIS ACTIONS / 11:1-18

Word of Peter's eating with Gentiles caused a negative reaction among the Jewish believers back in Jerusalem. The incident violated Hebrew customs and presuppositions. Following a detailed explanation of events by a persuasive and changed Peter, however, the others became convinced that God had ordered these surprising circumstances. The Jerusalem church began to accept the Gentile mission.

11:1-3 Soon the news reached the apostles and other believers in Judea that the Gentiles had received the word of God. But when Peter arrived back in Jerusalem, some of the Jewish believers criticized him. "You entered the home of Gentiles and even ate with them!" they said.[NLT] *Gentiles* are people who are not Jews; the *Jewish believers* are sometimes referred to as "the circumcised believers." Some have suggested that the term "circumcised believers" does not refer to all Jewish believers but to those who were more zealous for retaining much of the law in the worship and ethics of the young church. Most Jewish believers thought that God offered salvation only to the Jews because God had given his law to them (Exodus 19–20). A group in Jerusalem believed that Gentiles could be saved, but only if they followed all the Jewish laws and traditions—in essence, if they became Jews before they became Christians (this would be the topic of discussion at the Jerusalem council—chapter 15). Both groups were mistaken. God chose the Jews and taught them his laws so they could bring the message of salvation to the whole world (see Genesis 12:3; Psalm 22:27; Isaiah 42:4; 49:6; 56:3-7; 60:1-3; Jeremiah 16:19-21; Zechariah 2:11; Malachi 1:11; Romans 15:9-12).

> A lie can travel halfway around the world while the truth is putting on its shoes. *Mark Twain*

Note that the *apostles* were still in Jerusalem; they had not scattered with those who had fled the persecution following Stephen's martyrdom (see commentary at 8:1).

Peter was criticized for entering a Gentile home and then eating a meal with Gentiles. Both practices were terribly offensive to devout Jews who feared accidentally breaking one of their strict dietary regulations.

As is often the case, the critics criticized first and gathered their information later. Before Peter even *arrived back in Jerusalem,* the *news reached the apostles and other believers in Judea that the Gentiles had received the word of God.* Instead of rejoicing, however, *some of the Jewish believers criticized him.* The criticism of Peter was not that he had gone to Caesarea or that he had preached to Gentiles but rather that he had eaten with them. Some Jews were so obsessed with the Jewish dietary restrictions that they rushed to "strain out a gnat" while "swallowing a camel" (Matthew 23:24). This was also the attitude of the Jewish leaders in Jesus' day. Peter, however, was in good company, for this was an accusation commonly leveled at Jesus (see Mark 2:16; Luke 15:2). Eating with Gentiles would also later become a source of conflict between Paul and Peter, when Peter had begun to change his position (Galatians 2:12) and then incurred the rebuke of Paul for walking away from grace in his practice.

The word of God being received by the Gentiles was big news in Jerusalem. A Samaritan or two did not seem to be controversial. A solitary Ethiopian official, likewise, was easy to understand and rejoice over. But an entire gathering of influential Gentiles in a Gentile city in a Gentile setting? (Not to mention that they received the Holy Spirit in the same fashion that the newborn church had at Pentecost!) That was a frightening shift of emphasis for this still very Jewish church. The potential for a division within the church between Jews and Gentiles and the problems that would erupt at the "fellowships" (which invariably involved food—2:42, 46) could cause grave problems. The result could easily have been two entirely separate churches instead of one—had not the apostles handled it wisely.

SUSPENDING JUDGMENT

When Peter brought the news of Cornelius's conversion back to Jerusalem, the believers were shocked that Peter had eaten with Gentiles. After they heard the whole story, however, they praised God (11:18). Their reactions demonstrate how to handle disagreements with other Christians. Before judging the behavior of fellow believers, it is important to hear them out. The Holy Spirit may have something important to teach us through them.

11:4-7 Then Peter began to explain it to them, step by step, saying, "I was in the city of Joppa praying, and in a trance I saw a vision. There was something like a large sheet coming down

> If words are to enter men's hearts and bear fruit, they must be the right words shaped cunningly to pass men's defenses and explode silently and effectually within their minds.
> *J. B. Phillips*

from heaven, being lowered by its four corners; and it came close to me. As I looked at it closely I saw four-footed animals, beasts of prey, reptiles, and birds of the air. I also heard a voice saying to me, 'Get up, Peter; kill and eat.'"[NRSV] Peter repeated the events in great detail—*step by step* (see comments at 10:30). Evidently he thought the best defense against his critics would be simply to tell the story as it happened. The material from this point to 11:15 leaves out the nonessential details from the original accounts of Peter's vision and of the angelic messenger who spoke to Cornelius (10:1-23 and 10:30-48—see the commentary in those sections for a more detailed discussion).

Peter wanted this potentially hostile (already critical) audience to know that he had been *praying* at the time that he saw the vision. Peter told them that the sheet *came close* to him and that he *looked at it closely*. This account also mentions the more detailed presence of animals that would have been prohibited by the levitical restrictions, adding *beasts of prey* to the list described in 10:12.

CAREFUL COMMUNICATION

A surprising turn of events. A volatile issue. Confused people. Here were all the ingredients for a major misunderstanding—possibly leading to a giant rift in the church. Notice what Peter did: he explained what had happened to him "step by step." This detailed recounting required effort, energy, and time. He might have said, "Look, I know what happened to me. I know what God said. I don't have to explain myself to *you.*" But Peter worked hard to keep the peace and promote understanding. Often, good communication and peacemaking takes time. When peacemaking is needed, don't rush or skip essential conversations with others (even when it's hard or inconvenient).

11:8-10 "I replied, 'Surely not, Lord! Nothing impure or unclean has ever entered my mouth.' The voice spoke from heaven a second time, 'Do not call anything impure that God has made clean.' This happened three times, and then it was all pulled up to heaven again."[NIV] Peter repeated for his audience his refusal to "kill and eat" (11:7) these animals as instructed by the Lord. He quoted the response of the *voice . . . from heaven,* instructing him *not* to *call anything impure that God has made* clean. Finally, he noted the threefold repetition of this dialogue between himself and the Lord, and the pulling of the sheet back *up to heaven again.* This event and all the effects of it in Cornelius's life became a primary argument for the Gentile mission in the early church.

THE WHOLE COUNSEL OF GOD
Throughout Scripture, God had promised that he would reach the nations. This began with his general promise to Abraham (Genesis 12:3; 18:18) and became very specific in Malachi's statement: "My name will be great among the nations, from the rising to the setting of the sun" (Malachi 1:11 NIV). But this was an extremely difficult truth for Jews—even Jewish believers in Christ—to accept. The Jewish believers understood how certain prophecies were fulfilled in Christ, but they overlooked other Old Testament teachings. Too often we are inclined to accept only the parts of God's Word that appeal to us and support our own agendas, ignoring the teachings we don't like. We must accept all of God's Word as absolute truth.

11:11-12 **"Just then three men who had been sent from Caesarea arrived at the house where I was staying. The Holy Spirit told me to go with them and not to worry about their being Gentiles. These six brothers here accompanied me, and we soon arrived at the home of the man who had sent for us."**NLT Peter added to this recounting the exact timing of the whole event—*just then*—as he spoke of the arrival of the *three men . . . from Caesarea.* Upon the command of no one less that the *Holy Spirit,* Peter had accompanied them, citing the Spirit's command *not to worry about their being Gentiles.*

He had taken *six brothers* (fellow believers, who were still present) with him to Caesarea to witness what was to happen and help recall it accurately. Peter understood that God was at work and deduced that something controversial (or potentially divisive) might take place. The potential for misunderstanding was evidently great enough for these men to have also accompanied Peter back to Jerusalem to report to the apostles. Jewish law only required two witnesses. Peter's having six witnesses reveals the gravity of the issue and the significance of the event.

11:13-14 **"He told us how an angel had appeared to him in his home and had told him, 'Send messengers to Joppa to find Simon Peter. He will tell you how you and all your household will be saved!'"**NLT In two sentences Peter summarized the experience of Cornelius, which has already been recorded twice (see 10:1-7 and 10:30-32). It would be important to the Jewish audience to hear that an angelic messenger had also appeared to the principle Gentile figure in the drama.

Peter added a significant statement that had been excluded from the other accounts of Cornelius's experience: the angel had told Cornelius that he and all his *household will be saved.* In other words, God's intent from the start was to bring this Gentile soldier, along with his friends and family, to Christ. Perhaps Cornelius had told this to Peter when they first met (10:27).

11:15-17 **"As I began to speak, the Holy Spirit came on them as he had come on us at the beginning. Then I remembered what the Lord had said: 'John baptized with water, but you will be baptized with the Holy Spirit.' So if God gave them the same gift as he gave us, who believed in the Lord Jesus Christ, who was I to think that I could oppose God?"**NIV Peter described that crucial moment in recounting his meeting with the Gentiles when *the Holy Spirit came on them as he had come on [the Jewish believers] at the beginning.* The "beginning" refers to Pentecost (chapter 2).

There was no missing Peter's intentional and overt word choice here: the Holy Spirit of God had come on these Gentile believers just as he had come on the Jewish believers. There was no difference between the two "Pentecosts" other than that the Jews' experience had come first. These subsequent events, parallel to Pentecost, proved to the Jerusalem church that they must accept each new group of converts (the Samaritans, the Gentiles) because God had put his guarantee on them by repeating Pentecost.

NO FAVORITES WITH GOD

The gift of the Spirit on the Gentiles was a stunning revelation to Peter. It was positive proof that God does not play favorites (10:34; Romans 2:11). This marvelous truth—that the Creator is a God who invites all people into a relationship with himself—should reveal the great evil of sins like prejudice and racism. Heaven will be filled with individuals from "every nation and tribe and people and language" (Revelation 7:9 NLT).

Peter added what he had been thinking when the event had occurred, for he *remembered* something the risen Christ had said right before his ascension: *"John baptized with water, but you will be baptized with the Holy Spirit"* (1:5). Up until the event in Cornelius's house, Peter (along with the rest of the Jewish believers) must have thought that the baptism of the Holy Spirit was reserved exclusively for Jewish believers. Having witnessed the baptism of the Holy Spirit on Gentile believers, Peter realized that Jesus' words had a much broader application.

In fact, Jesus had also demonstrated clearly that he and his message were for all types of people. He had preached in Samaria (John 4:1-42), in the region of the Gerasenes, populated by Greeks (Mark 5:1-20), and he had even reached out to Romans (Luke 7:1-10). The apostles shouldn't have been surprised that they were called to do the same.

11:18 When the others heard this, all their objections were answered and they began praising God. They said, "God has also given the Gentiles the privilege of turning from sin and receiving eternal life."NLT The theological discussion stopped with the report that God had given the Holy Spirit to the Gentiles. This was a turning point for the early church. They had to accept those whom God had chosen, even Gentiles.

The response was one of *praising God* as the congregation remarked on the fact that *God has also given the Gentiles the privilege of turning from sin and receiving eternal life.* This is a remarkable example of the spiritual health of this young church. Though steeped in centuries of Jewish rules and regulations, they had seen enough of God's wonders over the past few months to know that God was moving in some new ways. Even though they had the words and example of Christ pointing them toward the Gentile world (Matthew 28:19; Acts 1:8), they had to overcome enormous inertia. The fact that they were so open to what God was doing and so responsive to Peter's leadership speaks well of the work of the Spirit in their lives.

CELEBRATING FOR THE RIGHT REASONS

Once the Jewish believers heard the full story from Peter about the salvation of the Gentiles, they immediately praised God. This is a godly response. Sadly, it is the opposite of what so often happens: Someone who is different experiences blessing, and we secretly mourn their good fortune. A person not in our circle finds trouble, and we take a curious delight in their plight. We need to embrace the biblical mandate that says "When others are happy, be happy with them. If they are sad, share their sorrow" (Romans 12:15 NLT). When God blesses someone else, do you celebrate or complain?

THE CHURCH IN ANTIOCH OF SYRIA / 11:19-30

To show that Peter's evangelistic encounter with the Gentile Cornelius was not an exception, Luke mentioned the widespread outreach that had begun taking place in Antioch. This effort by believers from Cyprus and Cyrene to preach to non-Jews had both the power and the blessing of God on it, so that "large numbers of these Gentiles believed and turned to the Lord" (11:21 NLT).

It was just a matter of time until Antioch became the church's base of operations. From there the disciples of Christ (or "Christians" as they were coming to be known—11:26) would carry on a sovereignly directed, full-scale Gentile mission.

The closing verses of chapter 9 and the record in chapter 10 describe Peter's preparation for the universal dissemination of the gospel; and the opening verses of chapter 11 describe the apostles' preparation for the universal nature of the gospel, then these final verses of chapter 11 describe the preparation of the church at Antioch for the same thing. The focus of the church is shifting to the north, to this incredible missionary church in Antioch of Syria. The balance of this chapter gives a close-up view of a church that can be used mightily of God to change an entire empire and, beyond it, the world.

11:19 Meanwhile, the believers who had fled from Jerusalem during the persecution after Stephen's death traveled as far as Phoenicia, Cyprus, and Antioch of Syria. They preached the Good News, but only to Jews.NLT As Peter was dealing with this new issue of Gentiles entering the church, God was at work elsewhere. *Meanwhile,* the seeds of missionary work were being sown after Stephen's death, for many believing Jews were persecuted and scattered, settling in faraway cities and spreading the gospel. The *Good News* was being preached, but *only to Jews.* The believers who had scattered had not yet received the news that the gospel message was meant for Gentiles, as well, but all that was about to change. When the church accepted Peter's testimony that the gospel was also for Gentiles, Christianity expanded into Gentile areas, and large numbers of Gentiles became believers.

At this point, the Jerusalem church was no longer the "sending center," partly because of the anti-Christian sentiment in Jerusalem and partly because of the new Gentile thrust of the outreach. Antioch became the new sending center—three hundred miles north of Jerusalem. An important commercial center and the third largest city in the Roman Empire (population 500,000), the city of Antioch was located fifteen miles inland from the Mediterranean Sea on the Orontes River. The city had been founded in 300 B.C. by the Seleucids and had been the western capital of their empire. Under the Roman Empire, Antioch became the capital of the province of Syria. The city was beautified by Caesars Augustus and Tiberius, with the help of Herod the Great. The city enjoyed a beautiful location and abundant water supply.

There was also a large Jewish population in Antioch. When

persecution against Christians broke out in Jerusalem after the death of Stephen, many Christians fled to Antioch in Syria. Antioch was a horribly corrupt city and was the center of worship for several pagan cults that promoted sexual immorality and other forms of evil common to pagan religions. This city would be home to the church that would be the sovereignly chosen group to fund and direct the next decade of church expansion under a new missionary, Paul.

11:20-21 But among them were some men of Cyprus and Cyrene who, on coming to Antioch, spoke to the Hellenists also, proclaiming the Lord Jesus. The hand of the Lord was with them, and a great number became believers and turned to the Lord.[NRSV] Cyprus is an island off the Mediterranean coast from Antioch, and Cyrene was a city in northern Africa. Fortunately, *some men of Cyprus and Cyrene* had the courage to spread the gospel of *the Lord Jesus* outside of the confines of Judaism. The word "Hellenists" refers to Greeks. It is unknown whether these Hellenists were Greek proselytes to Judaism or unconverted Gentiles. When these believers spoke, however, *the hand of the Lord was with them, and a great number became believers and turned to the Lord.*

> Some like to dwell
> Within the sound of
> Church and chapel bell.
> But I want to run a rescue shop
> Within a yard of Hell.
> *C. T. Studd*

AN AWESOME TASK

Antioch (of Syria) was a huge city—cosmopolitan, commercialized, and corrupt. With over half a million people (and most of them pagan in their beliefs), this godless metropolis might have intimidated the followers of Christ who had fled there. Not so! The believers arrived in Antioch with the Good News on their lips. They permeated the entire city, so much so that they earned the nickname "Christians" (Christ's ones). And the church that God raised up there became the church that commissioned and supported Paul in his worldwide missionary work. Wherever we live, we should trust God for that same kind of boldness and that same impact. Our eyes must be ever outward to the world in need of the message.

Evidently this small beginning turned Antioch into a place where the believers aggressively preached to the Gentiles. Philip had preached in Samaria (8:5), but the Samaritans were part Jewish. Peter had preached to Cornelius, but he already worshiped God (10:2). Believers who were scattered after the outbreak of persecution in Jerusalem spread the gospel to other Jews in the lands where they had fled (11:19). Finally, the believers began actively sharing the Good News with Gentiles, with great results.

11:22-23 **When the church at Jerusalem heard what had happened, they sent Barnabas to Antioch. When he arrived and saw this proof of God's favor, he was filled with joy, and he encouraged the believers to stay true to the Lord.**NLT The Hellenist "revival" (11:20-21) prompted the leaders of the Jerusalem church to send someone to investigate. *Barnabas* was the emissary. He was a wise choice for a number of reasons. From Cyprus, he would have had a natural national connection with the "evangelists" who had started the movement in Antioch. Barnabas was a generous man, having participated in the offering for the needs of the early Jerusalem church (4:36-37). His most redeeming quality, however, was wrapped up in the meaning of his name—"son of encouragement." Barnabas had been the one willing to stick his neck out when everyone else was afraid of Saul of Tarsus and suspected Saul's conversion to have been a trap for Christians (9:27). Barnabas began living up to his name by encouraging the believers. The Greek term here for encouraging is *parekalei* and can carry the idea of "encouragement," "comfort," "help," or even "strong urging" and "counsel." This was the verb form of the word Jesus used for the Holy Spirit, the coming "Counselor" (John 14:16; 15:26).

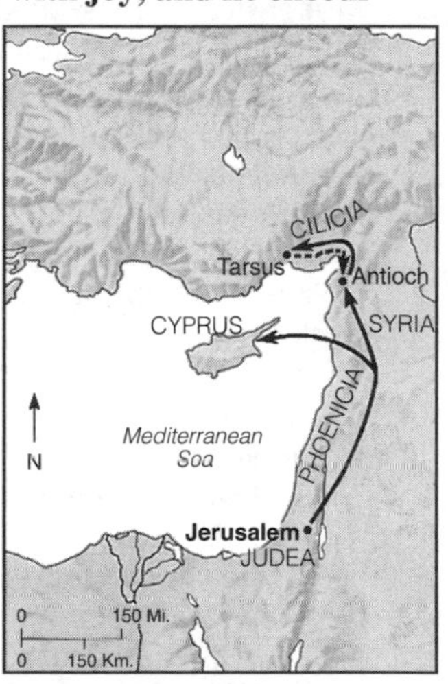

BARNABAS AND SAUL IN ANTIOCH

Persecution scattered the believers into Phoenicia, Cyprus, and Antioch, and the gospel went with them. Most spoke only to Jews, but in Antioch, some Gentiles were converted. The church sent Barnabas to investigate, and he was pleased with what he found. Barnabas went to Tarsus to bring Saul (Paul) back to Antioch.

11:24 **He was a good man, full of the Holy Spirit and faith, and a great number of people were brought to the Lord.**NIV Barnabas is described by three modifiers here: (1) *a good man;* (2) *full of the Holy Spirit* (reminiscent of the qualifications of the "seven" in 6:1-6); (3) *[full of] faith.* These latter two characteristics were specifically used to describe Stephen in 6:5. The ministry of the gospel was thriving—*a great number of people were brought to the Lord.*

11:25-26 **Then Barnabas went to Tarsus to look for Saul, and when he had found him, he brought him to Antioch. So it was that for an entire year they met with the church and taught a great many people, and it was in Antioch that the disciples were first called "Christians."**[NRSV] *Saul* had been sent to his home in Tarsus for protection after his conversion caused an uproar among the Jewish religious leaders in Jerusalem (9:26-30). He stayed there for several years before Barnabas brought him to help the church at *Antioch.* Evidently, the work at Antioch had grown so that it was too much for Barnabas to handle alone.

Barnabas and Paul's ministry in Antioch was marked by their teaching *(for an entire year they met with the church and taught a great many people).* Those who became believers were consistently and systematically instructed by these two teachers in the basics of their newfound faith.

> One of the highest of human duties is the duty of encouragement. . . . It is easy to laugh at men's ideals; it is easy to pour cold water on their enthusiasm; it is easy to discourage others. The world is full of discouragers. We have a Christian duty to encourage one another. Many a time a word of praise or thanks or appreciation or cheer has kept a man on his feet. Blessed is the man who speaks such a word.
>
> *William Barclay*

The young church at Antioch was a curious mixture of Jews (who spoke Greek or Aramaic) and Gentiles. It is significant that this was the first place where the believers were called *Christians* ("Christ's ones"—the ending "-ian" means "belonging to the party of"). There has been a great deal of debate about who gave them the name "Christians." It is not likely that the believers themselves invented the name, because they had other terms for themselves like "disciples" or "saints" or "brothers." Certainly, the Jews would never want their term "Messiah" *(christos)* associated with this new movement. It is likely, therefore, that the term "Christian" was invented by the non-Christian culture of Antioch. One of the earliest extrabiblical occurrences of the term comes from a remark made by Emperor Nero. Whatever the case, the believers in Christ were becoming an identifiable group, distinct from Judaism and, at least in Antioch, primarily Gentile in composition.

11:27-28 **During this time some prophets came down from Jerusalem to Antioch. One of them, named Agabus, stood up and through the Spirit predicted that a severe famine would spread over the entire Roman world. (This happened during**

TITLES IN ACTS FOR THE REDEEMED PEOPLE OF GOD

Believers (1:15; 2:44; 4:32; 5:12; 9:41; 10:45; 15:2, 23; 16:1, 15; 21:25)

The church (5:11; 8:1, 3; 9:31; 11:22; 12:1, 5; 13:1; 14:23; 15:2-4, 41; 16:5; 18:22; 20:17)

Disciples (6:1-2, 7; 9:1, 10, 19, 26, 36; 11:29; 13:52; 14:20-22; 18:23; 19:9; 21:4-5, 16)

Brothers (6:3; 9:17, 30; 10:23; 11:1 29; 12:17; 14:2; 15:3, 22, 32-33, 36; 16:2, 40; 17:6, 10; 18:18, 27; 21:7, 17; 28:14-15)

The Way (9:2; 19:9, 23; 24:22)

The Lord's people (9:32)

Christians (11:26; 26:28)

Followers (17:34; 22:4, 24:14)

The flock (20:28-29)

---

the reign of Claudius.)[NIV] *Prophets* were not limited to Old Testament times (see 13:1; 15:32; 21:9). God appointed certain people to be prophets to the church, and Paul ranked "prophets" second only to apostles in his list of those gifted by the Holy Spirit (1 Corinthians 12:28). The Jews believed that prophecy had ceased during the time of the Exile but would resurface as a sign of the Messiah's coming. Peter had quoted the prophet Joel in his sermon at Pentecost: "Your sons and daughters will prophesy" (2:17). Prophets had special gifts in ministering God's messages to his people. At times, they would foretell the future (as Agabus did here), but the gift of prophecy was also valued for its role in exhorting, encouraging, and strengthening God's people (1 Corinthians 14:31). God spoke through prophets, inspiring them with specific messages for particular times and places.

SIX CHARACTERISTICS OF A *USABLE* CHRISTIAN

1. ***U*nstained by our Culture** (11:19-20, 22, 26)
At Antioch the believers were first called Christians, the "Christ-ones." There are some distinctions of a church that must be kept intact. We bear the name of our Savior.

2. ***S*tretched to our Limits** (11:19; 12:1-3)
From a close look at the early church, we see clearly that struggle, rejection, criticism, and even death for believers was the norm.

3. ***A*dhering to the Savior** (11:21, 23, 26)
Barnabas encouraged the believers to make a serious, solid attachment to Christ and Christ alone.

4. ***B*old in our Witness** (11:19-21, 24)
This church spoke, told, and preached the Good News. People believed and turned to the Lord.

5. ***L*iberal in our Giving** (11:22, 22, 27-30)
The Antioch church gave. They were unselfish, others-centered, and giving-oriented, even to a culturally and racially different congregation.

6. ***E*quipped in the Scriptures** (11:23, 26)
This church was taught. The picture here is of classrooms, courses, study memorization . . . work. Before Antioch became a sending place, it was a studying place. We have the picture of an equipping church and an equipped people. No wonder they changed the world.

In the early church, these prophets seem to have traveled from place to place. *Agabus* was part of a group of prophets who *came down from Jerusalem to Antioch. Through the Spirit,* Agabus *predicted that a severe famine would spread over the entire Roman world.* Agabus later would predict Paul's arrest in Jerusalem (see 21:10-11). What happened was actually a series of famines during the *reign of* Emperor *Claudius* (A.D. 41–54). This enigmatic pair of verses seems to introduce the reason for the Antioch church's support of the "mother" church in Jerusalem, mentioned in 11:29-30.

HELPING NEW BELIEVERS
Barnabas gives us a wonderful example of how to help new Christians. Filled with the Spirit (11:24), he demonstrated strong faith, ministered joyfully with kindness and encouragement, and taught new believers about God (see 9:26-30). Remember Barnabas when you see new believers, and think of ways to help them grow in their faith.

11:29-30 So the believers in Antioch decided to send relief to the brothers and sisters in Judea, everyone giving as much as they could. This they did, entrusting their gifts to Barnabas and

Saul to take to the elders of the church in Jerusalem.NLT Because there were serious food shortages during this time due to the famine, *the believers in Antioch* assisted the church in Jerusalem. Luke phrases it: *everyone giving as much as they could* (see 1 Corinthians 16:2; 2 Corinthians 9:7). The daughter church had grown enough to be able to help the mother church. The language implies sacrificial giving on the part of the believers in Antioch. The solid reputation for the spiritual integrity of *Barnabas and Saul* is affirmed by the fact that they were the ones entrusted with the money to be taken *to the elders of the church in Jerusalem.* This visit was most likely the second visit of Paul to Jerusalem, occurring in about A.D. 46. This visit corresponds to Galatians 2:1-10. His first visit was in Acts 9:26-29, and that correlates with Galatians 1:18-20.

MAKING DISCIPLES

Barnabas and Saul stayed at Antioch for a full year, teaching the new believers. They saw the importance of follow-through and training. Have you helped someone to believe in Christ? Spend time teaching and encouraging that person. Spiritual birth is only the beginning; spiritual growth must follow. Are you a new believer? Remember, you are just beginning your Christian life. Your faith needs to grow and mature through consistent Bible study and teaching.

This is the first mention of "elders" in the New Testament (see 15:4, 6; 16:4; 21:18). By the time of the establishment of the church at Antioch, elders were appointed to manage the affairs of the congregation. Not much is known about their role in those days, but clearly, at least part of their responsibilities included managing the church's financial affairs. See 1 Timothy 3:1-7 and Titus 1:5-9 for a later listing of their qualifications; see 1 Peter 5:1-4 and Acts 20:28-32 for some clues as to their responsibilities.

The chapter ends with a very healthy picture of this burgeoning, young, and mostly Gentile church. They had two high-quality teachers, Barnabas and Saul. They had a solid contingency of giving saints—donating enough money to tend to the local needs of the congregation *and* send something to the "mother church" at Jerusalem. The idea of a Gentile-Christian congregation sending help to a Jewish-Christian church highlights the quality of its spiritual character.

The church at Antioch would be used mightily by God in the next phase of the spread of the gospel. After a few more events, the first real "missionary team" would be sent out from this congregation. With a generous hand reaching back to help those who had planted this church and an aggressive vision looking forward to what God would do through it, this church would be a major force over the next decade in reaching a lost world for Christ.

GENEROUS GIVING

The people of Antioch were motivated to give generously because they cared about the needs of others. This is the "cheerful" giving that the Bible commends (2 Corinthians 9:7). Reluctant giving reflects a lack of concern for people and a worldly focus (Matthew 6:19-21). When you remember how much God has done for you and when you focus your concern on the needy, you will be motivated to give.

Acts 12

JAMES IS KILLED AND PETER IS IMPRISONED / 12:1-5

The rapid growth of the church in Jerusalem (6:1) brought fierce opposition (8:1). Persecution often accompanies progress. Unable to stop the masses from embracing this new faith, the Jews launched a direct attack upon the Christian leaders. Beyond mere threats and warnings (see 4:18-21; 5:40), this time Herod had James executed and Peter arrested.

These were tense and traumatic times, but the church began to pray "very earnestly" (12:5 NLT). It is important to remember that God was not finished with the church at Jerusalem nor the Jewish element of Christianity just because the emphasis would soon shift to Paul and the Gentile outreach. God was still using Jewish believers for his work.

12:1 **About that time King Herod Agrippa began to persecute some believers in the church.**[NLT] The church was growing dramatically, but the king was increasing the persecution. This was *King Herod Agrippa* I, the son of Aristobulus and grandson of Herod the Great. His sister was Herodias, who had been responsible for the death of John the Baptist (see Mark 6:17-28). Herod Agrippa I was partly Jewish. The Romans had appointed him to rule over most of Palestine, including the territories of Galilee, Perea, Judea, and Samaria. He persecuted the Christians in order to please the Jewish leaders who opposed them, hoping to solidify his position. Agrippa is mentioned in the Bible only in this chapter. He died suddenly in A.D. 44 (see 12:20-23), a fact also recorded by the historian Josephus.

Agrippa related fairly well to his Jewish subjects. Because he had a Jewish grandmother of royal blood (Mariamne), he was grudgingly accepted by the people. In his youth he was temporarily imprisoned by the emperor Tiberias; in due course he was trusted by Rome and got along well with the emperors Caligula and Claudius.

The Christian movement created an unexpected opportunity for Herod to gain new favor with the Jews. Gentiles began to be accepted into the church in large numbers. Many Jews had been tolerating this new movement as a sect within Judaism, but its rapid growth alarmed them. Persecution of Christians was revived, and even the apostles were not spared. Agrippa orchestrated the first execution of an apostle, James, followed by the imprisonment of Peter.

FAMILY TIES
Four generations of the Herod family are mentioned in the Bible. Unfortunately, each of the Herods left behind an evil legacy: Herod the Great murdered Bethlehem's children; Herod Antipas was involved in Jesus' trial and John the Baptist's execution; Herod Agrippa I murdered the apostle James; Herod Agrippa II was one of Paul's judges. This is a prime example that for good or evil, parents have a lasting and powerful influence on their offspring. Traits and qualities are passed on to the next generation, and often the mistakes and sins of the parents are repeated by the children. What example are you setting for your children? It is not what we say that counts, but how we live. They will copy our actions more than they will listen to our lectures.

12:2 **He had James, the brother of John, killed with the sword.**[NRSV] *James* and *John* were two of the original twelve disciples who followed Jesus. They had asked Jesus for special recognition in his kingdom (Mark 10:35-40). Jesus said that to be a part of his kingdom would mean suffering with him ("drinking from the same cup"—Mark 10:38-39). James and John did indeed suffer—Herod executed James, and later John was exiled (see Revelation 1:9). These two brothers were the first and the last apostles to die. Their lives and ministries somewhat parallel two of the "seven" from 6:1-6—Stephen and Philip. In the sovereign plan of God, one was taken early, and the other was left to minister for many years. These are reminders again that believers have a "General" in charge of the troops, who will send, move, protect, and then bring home his soldiers as he sees fit. See also John 21:20-22, where Peter inquires about how he and John might die. Christ's answer was, "What is that to you? You follow me" (NLT). This illustrates the devoted service that Jesus' disciples should render to him.

There is a great deal to be learned here from what did not happen to James and what did happen to Peter later in this chapter. Imagine being a part of both prayer meetings. The church surely had prayed as fervently for James as they did for Peter. The church may have been praying at the same location, involving most of the same people, perhaps even the same servant girl

THE FATE OF THE APOSTLES

Name	*Fate*
Simon Peter	Crucified
James, son of Zebedee	Martyred by Herod Agrippa (Acts 12:1-2)
John, son of Zebedee	Exiled to Patmos; later died of old age (one legend is that Domitian had John thrown into a pot of boiling oil, but he was unharmed)
Andrew	According to tradition was crucified (on a cross in the form of an X) at Pagrae a city of Achaia, because he rebuked Aegeas, the proconsul for idolatry
Philip	According to tradition, died as a martyr at Hierapolis
Bartholomew/ Nathanael	Said to have preached the gospel in India, or perhaps Armenia, where conflicting reports have him flayed alive or crucified upside down
Matthew/Levi	According to legend, preached in unspecified foreign nations
Thomas	According to tradition, preached in Parthia and Persia and died as a martyr by being speared with a lance
James, son of Alphaeus	Not known
Thaddaeus/ Judas, son of James	Not known
Simon the Zealot	Not known
Matthias	According to tradition, went to minister in Ethiopia, where he was eventually martyred
Saul/Paul	According to tradition, was beheaded at Nero's command along the Appian Way

(Rhoda—see 12:1-3). Peter was miraculously set free. James, however, was *killed with the sword* (referring to beheading).

Was there something wrong with the way the believers prayed for James as opposed to Peter? The wrong words? Scriptures?

posture? Was there not enough faith? Did God love Peter more than James? The answer to all these questions is, of course, no, but they are the kinds of questions Christians invariably ask when faced with such a clear example of the contrasting will of God for two lives. The sovereign choices of God in the lives of these two apostles—equally loved by God, needed by the church, and missed by their friends and family—should teach believers to trust God more.

THE RANDOMNESS OF EVIL AND PAIN
Why did God allow James to die and yet miraculously save Peter? Life is full of difficult questions like this. Why is one child physically disabled and another child athletically gifted? Why do people die before realizing their potential? These are questions we cannot possibly answer in this life, because we do not see all that God sees. He has chosen to allow evil in this world for a time. In the meantime we can hope in God's promise to destroy all evil eventually. And we can trust in God to use our suffering to build our character and glorify himself.

12:3-4 **When Herod saw how much this pleased the Jewish leaders, he arrested Peter during the Passover celebration and imprisoned him, placing him under the guard of four squads of four soldiers each. Herod's intention was to bring Peter out for public trial after the Passover.**[NLT] Herod, in the self-serving spirit of the previous Herods of the New Testament (see the chart "The Herod Family" on page 417 [25:21-22]), took special delight in the positive political benefits he received from executing James. *Herod* Agrippa's uncle was Herod Antipas, who had participated in the execution of Christ (Luke 3:1; 23:6-12), and his grandfather was Herod the Great—the paranoid murderer of Bethlehem babies as he attempted to kill the newborn Christ (Matthew 2:1-17). Since James's execution *pleased the Jewish leaders,* Herod Agrippa then *arrested Peter* during the Feast of Unleavened Bread, the week-long festival directly following *Passover.* This was a strategic move since more Jews were in the city than usual, and Herod could impress the most Jews by imprisoning the most visible of the church leaders.

Peter was well guarded by *four squads of four soldiers each*—each squad would have guarded Peter for one-fourth of a day! Evidently, Herod knew of Peter's previous escape (5:19-24) and wanted to be sure that such would not happen this time. Luke stressed this detail to set the scene for the mighty power of God. No one could escape under human power alone. Herod planned to give Peter a *public trial after the Passover.*

12:5 **While Peter was kept in prison, the church prayed fervently to God for him.**[NRSV] Herod undoubtedly was planning to execute Peter, but the believers were praying *fervently* for Peter's safety. The earnest prayer of the church significantly affected the outcome of these events. The Greek structure of this sentence emphasizes the contrast here between the imprisoned apostle and the prayers of the saints. On the one hand, *Peter* was *kept.* On the other, prayers were sent. Something was bound to happen. The believers are here called *the church,* a clearly identified entity in Jerusalem.

> The great tragedy of life is not unanswered prayer, but unoffered prayer.
> *F. B. Meyer*

PETER'S MIRACULOUS ESCAPE FROM PRISON / 12:6-19

James was already dead. Peter was in prison. From a human perspective, the situation appeared terribly grim, but from a heavenly perspective, this was just another opportunity to display the infinite power of God—"the rulers plot together against the LORD. . . . but the one who rules in heaven laughs. The LORD scoffs at them" (Psalm 2:2, 4 NLT).

When an angel of the Lord miraculously delivered Peter from prison, Herod left for Caesarea (12:19). The plan and purposes of God cannot be thwarted. Jesus assured his followers, "I will build my church" (Matthew 16:18).

> Have courage for the great sorrows of life and patience for the small ones; and when you have laboriously accomplished your daily task, go to sleep in peace. God is awake.
> *Victor Hugo*

This section of Acts is one of the most exciting and most humorous scenes in the whole book: exciting, because Peter was in jail and was prayed out by a faithful, fervent, praying church; humorous, because this praying church didn't really believe God had answered their prayer even when they had their answer in the flesh at the front door of their prayer meeting. This chapter teaches a great deal about prayers, answers, and the God who is behind them all.

12:6 **The night before Herod was to bring him to trial, Peter was sleeping between two soldiers, bound with two chains, and sentries stood guard at the entrance.**[NIV] Peter, a few years later, would write these words in one of his letters: "When they hurled their insults at him, he did not retaliate; when he suffered, he made no threats. Instead, he entrusted himself to him who judges justly" (1 Peter 2:23 NIV).

Luke carefully recorded the location of the soldiers (12:4) in charge of making sure this reputed jail-breaking apostle (5:19-24) did not slip away again and leave Herod with a serious public-relations problem. *Two soldiers* were chained to Peter, one on either side, and *sentries stood guard at the entrance.* Luke again stressed the power of God over earthly rulers. Herod was doing his best to prevent another escape. But it would not be enough.

12:7-8 Suddenly an angel of the Lord appeared and a light shone in the cell. He tapped Peter on the side and woke him, saying, "Get up quickly." And the chains fell off his wrists. The angel said to him, "Fasten your belt and put on your sandals." He did so. Then he said to him, "Wrap your cloak around you and follow me."NRSV This same type of jailbreak had happened to the apostles before, as recorded in 5:19-24, but more detail is given here. From his sleep, Peter was roused by an angel tapping him *on the side* and was told, *"Get up quickly."* The command was accompanied by his *chains* falling *off his wrists.* The term for "falling off" comes from the Greek word *ekpipto,* meaning to "drop away." Evidently, neither the angel nor Peter touched the chains—they came off because God was setting Peter free.

> I fear John Knox's prayers more than an army of ten thousand men. I had rather stand against the cannons of the wicked than against the prayers of the righteous.
> *Mary, Queen of Scotland*

ANGELS

God sent an angel to rescue Peter. Angels are God's messengers. They are divinely created beings with supernatural powers. In the Bible they are depicted as occasionally taking on human appearance in order to talk to people. Although angels are heavenly beings, they should not be worshiped because they are not divine (Colossians 2:18; Hebrews 1:13-14). Angels are God's servants, just as we are. Worship Jesus! That's what the angels do (Luke 2:13-14; Hebrews 1:6). As the writer of Hebrews notes, "God's Son is far greater than the angels" (Hebrews 1:4 NLT).

One can picture the groggy Peter, thinking that he was dreaming (12:9), needing the instruction of his angelic liberator to help him get his clothes on. Peter complied with the angel's directions, but he had to be reminded to put on his coat (*"Wrap your cloak around you"*). Then he followed the angel out of the cell.

Nothing is written about the whereabouts of the guards, who were likely not the only prison guards around. A couple of them would have been posted at every gate, every door, and at any possible escape route from the prison. The soldiers may have been dazed, asleep, or blinded from the whole event. In the end, it would be a deadly miracle for them (12:19).

12:9-10 **Peter followed him out of the prison, but he had no idea that what the angel was doing was really happening; he thought he was seeing a vision. They passed the first and second guards and came to the iron gate leading to the city. It opened for them by itself, and they went through it. When they had walked the length of one street, suddenly the angel left him.**[NIV] Peter seemed dazed as he followed the angel's instructions because *he thought he was seeing a vision.* Peter thought this was similar to his experience with the sheet let down from heaven, recorded in chapter 10 (the same word is used here for "vision" that was used for his vision at Joppa in 10:17). Though Peter was following the angel as they made their way *out of the prison,* he was not really aware of what *was really happening.*

They passed two sets of *guards* before arriving at *the iron gate* which led *to the city.* With dramatic effect, the gate mysteriously, miraculously *opened for them by itself* (the Greek is *automate*—"automatically"), and they passed through it into the city. The angel stayed with Peter a little longer, then *suddenly* left Peter alone.

12:11 **Then Peter came to himself and said, "Now I am sure that the Lord has sent his angel and rescued me from the hands of Herod and from all that the Jewish people were expecting."**[NRSV] Whether Peter just took a while to wake up or there was something about the angel's work that had him dazed, and the night air brought him to, is unknown. The text just says *Peter came to himself* and, speaking to himself, verbalized his confidence that *the Lord has sent his angel and rescued me.* The term translated "rescued" means to "deliver or save" and implies a daring rescue, just in the nick of time.

Peter also verbalized his awareness of Herod's motives and Herod's plans to use Peter's incarceration (and possible execution) as another way to ingratiate himself to the Jews *(all that the Jewish people were expecting).* Peter's awareness of his life-threatening situation, particularly in light of the recent execution of James (see 12:2), made his peaceful sleep in the prison cell all the more marvelous. Peter had seen enough to trust that the Father was in control of his life.

12:12 When this had dawned on him, he went to the house of Mary the mother of John, also called Mark, where many people had gathered and were praying.[NIV] Once he realized that he was not dreaming, Peter went directly to *the house of Mary the mother of John, also called Mark.* John Mark, mentioned here in passing, was the author of the Gospel of Mark and became an important character on the first journey of Paul (see 13:5, 13; 15:37-39).

> When I pray coincidences happen, and when I do not they don't.
>
> *William Temple*

Mary's house was large enough to accommodate a meeting of many believers. An upstairs room in her house may have been the location of Jesus' last supper with his disciples (Luke 22:8) and/or the place where the 120 earliest believers met for prayer (1:15; 2:1). Evidently Mary's home was a common place of meeting for the Jerusalem church (or part of it), at least for prayer. This particular night, with their beloved Peter in prison and the apostle James recently martyred, a large group had *gathered and [was] praying.*

ANSWERS

The prayers of the group of believers were answered even as they prayed. But when the answer arrived at the door, they didn't believe it. Only Rhoda, the servant girl, believed what had happened. We should be people of faith who, like Rhoda, are confident that God answers the prayers of those who seek his will. When you pray, trust that you'll get an answer. And when the answer comes, don't be surprised. Instead, be thankful!

12:13-15 Peter knocked at the outer entrance, and a servant girl named Rhoda came to answer the door. When she recognized Peter's voice, she was so overjoyed she ran back without opening it and exclaimed, "Peter is at the door!" "You're out of your mind," they told her. When she kept insisting that it was so, they said, "It must be his angel."[NIV] This is a comical scene. Peter *knocked at the outer entrance. Rhoda,* the *servant girl,* answered the door. Mary's house must have had a vestibule or hallway to the street with an outer door at the street and an inner door opening into the house. Rhoda was so excited to hear *Peter's voice* that she forgot to open the door! Meanwhile, the sober, serious saints, hard at the work of praying for Peter's release, failed to realize that the answer to their prayer was standing *at the door,* trying to get in! They even went so far as to accuse the poor girl of being crazy *(out of your mind).* At her insistence, they speculated that maybe Peter's *angel* was at the door, indicating they thought that he must have been executed already! Luke records their reaction but doesn't comment on it. Evidently, Jewish superstition believed that guardian angels could appear and look like the person they guarded. No one went to open the door!

12:16 **Meanwhile, Peter continued knocking. When they finally went out and opened the door, they were amazed.**[NLT] One wonders what was going through this usually impatient apostle's mind at this point. Certainly, his absence from prison would be noticed soon. The guards would likely know exactly where to look for him. The servant girl had recognized Peter's voice, but the others, so busy praying for Peter's release, wouldn't come to the door to let the freed apostle into the house! If ever people should stop praying and do something, that was the time!

As *Peter continued knocking,* someone *finally* went to the outer door and *opened* it. Everyone was *amazed* (in Greek, *exestesan*—the word is used in 10:45 to describe the reaction of the Jewish believers who had witnessed the Holy Spirit coming to the Gentiles in the house of Cornelius).

12:17 **Peter motioned with his hand for them to be quiet and described how the Lord had brought him out of prison. "Tell James and the brothers about this," he said, and then he left for another place.**[NIV] The pandemonium was so loud that Peter had to quiet the crowd by motioning *with his hand.* He recounted the story of his escape (though an angel had been used, it was *the Lord* who had *brought him out of prison*).

Peter instructed that the information about this miracle be passed on to *James and the brothers.* This James was Jesus' brother, who became a leader in the Jerusalem church (15:13; Galatians 1:19). The James who had been killed earlier (12:2) was John's brother and one of the original twelve disciples. Peter's instruction to inform James indicates that James may have already been recognized as one of the leaders (if not *the* leader) of the Jerusalem church. Perhaps through this very series of events and this statement before the gathered church, Peter was officially moving out of direct leadership of the Jerusalem believers. Possibly he sensed that this latest brush with Herod was God's sovereign shifting of him to plow another field.

In short order, likely because of his certainty that Herod's soldiers would be after him, Peter *left for another place.* It is unknown exactly where he went.

12:18-19 **At dawn, there was a great commotion among the soldiers about what had happened to Peter. Herod Agrippa ordered a thorough search for him. When he couldn't be found, Herod**

interrogated the guards and sentenced them to death. Afterward Herod left Judea to stay in Caesarea for a while.[NLT] Meanwhile, back at the prison, *there was a great commotion.* Under Roman law, guards who allowed a prisoner to escape were subject to the same punishment the prisoner was to receive. Their lives were on the line, so a commotion was in order! After a *thorough search* for Peter, these sixteen guards were *sentenced . . . to death.*

Herod's departure to *Caesarea* sets up the next scene. The Jews considered Jerusalem their capital, but the Romans made Caesarea their headquarters in Palestine. That was where Herod lived. (For more on Caesarea, see commentary on 10:1.)

THE DEATH OF HEROD AGRIPPA / 12:20-25

Herod Agrippa's fate should not surprise us. The Scriptures proclaim that pride goes before a fall. "Your sin will find you out" (Numbers 32:23 NLT); "Pride goes before destruction." (Proverbs 16:18 NLT); "You will always reap what you sow!" (Galatians 6:7 NLT). By foolishly setting himself against God and refusing to give him glory, Herod guaranteed his own disastrous demise: he was "consumed with worms" (12:23 NLT).

12:20 He had been quarreling with the people of Tyre and Sidon; they now joined together and sought an audience with him. Having secured the support of Blastus, a trusted personal servant of the king, they asked for peace, because they depended on the king's country for their food supply.[NIV] *Tyre and Sidon,* coastal cities on the Mediterranean, were free and self-governing but economically dependent on Judea. It is unknown why Herod *had been quarreling* with them, but representatives from those cities were trying to appease him by *having secured the support of Blastus, a trusted personal servant of the king.* They probably "secured" this support through a bribe. Presumably, through him, they *asked for peace,* needing the benefit of the Galilean market for their *food supply.*

12:21-22 On an appointed day Herod put on his royal robes, took his seat on the platform, and delivered a public address to them. The people kept shouting, "The voice of a god, and not of a mortal!"[NRSV] *Herod,* bedecked in his *royal robes,* was seated *on the platform* to address the people of Tyre and Sidon, who were trying to get a trade agreement out of him. Herod used a festival for Caesar as the *appointed day.* This was A.D. 44 and may have been just before Passover,

> None are so empty as those who are full of themselves.
> *Benjamin Whichcote*

approximately one year after Peter's escape from prison. The people had already bribed Herod's personal assistant, but here they also resorted to ridiculous flattery—*shouting* out to the ego-driven Herod that his voice was *the voice of a god, and not of a mortal.* The Greek historian Josephus also recorded this event in his *Antiquities of the Jews* (19.334).

12:23 **Instantly, an angel of the Lord struck Herod with a sickness, because he accepted the people's worship instead of giving the glory to God. So he was consumed with worms and died.**[NLT] While neither account (Luke's or Josephus's) described Herod Agrippa's response to the crowd, Luke explained that *God* acted, and he did so *instantly. An angel of the Lord* was God's vehicle to strike Herod with a horrible illness, described in gory detail: *So he was consumed with worms and died.* Some scholars suggest that the worms were intestinal roundworms, which grow ten to sixteen inches long and rob the body of nutrients while causing intense pain.

> O what a constant companion, what a tyrannical commander, what a sly, subtle and insinuating enemy is this sin of pride!
>
> *Richard Baxter*

The reason for this judgment was that Herod *accepted the people's worship instead of giving the glory to God.* God knew what was going on in Herod's heart and refused to share his glory with any earthly potentate. Herod died a horrible death accompanied by intense pain; he was literally eaten alive, from the inside out, by worms. To be eaten by worms was considered to be one of the most disgraceful ways to die. Pride is a serious sin. God chose to punish Herod's pride immediately. God does not immediately punish all sin, but he will bring all to judgment (Hebrews 9:27). Those who set themselves against God are doomed to ultimate failure.

PRIDE BEFORE THE FALL

For political advantage, Herod Agrippa I had killed James, imprisoned Peter, and persecuted the Christians (12:1-4). Because religion was important to Herod only as an aspect of politics, he had no reverence for God and no qualms about receiving praise that only God should have. God hates arrogance and pride (see 1 Samuel 15:23; Proverbs 8:13; Isaiah 13:11). This event demonstrates that judgment belongs to God; he will judge those who defy him. Don't let your position or accomplishments make you proud. Pride can shut you off from the truth and lead you away from God.

12:24 **But God's Good News was spreading rapidly, and there were many new believers.**[NLT] In great contrast with the verse above, Luke described quite a different scenario for the church. *God's Good News was spreading rapidly.* The death of James, the imprisonment of Peter, and other persecutions had not slowed the steady expansion of the church.

This sovereignly directed, expanding influence of Christianity is the theme of Luke's book (see 1:1-8). Verses like this one form transition points for the book, as Luke wrapped up one section and moved on to the next one (see 2:47; 6:7; 9:31; 12:24; 16:5; 19:20; and 28:30-31). With this verse, the middle section of the book comes to a close. The gospel message has made its way from Jerusalem to Judea to Samaria.

Along the way, a Jewish zealot named Saul had been converted (chapter 9). Saul (later called Paul), along with his various traveling companions (some of whom have been introduced already in passing), will become the focal point of Luke's record for the remainder of the book.

UNSTOPPABLE

Try as they might to stop the spread of the gospel, the enemies of God could only sit by and watch more and more people put their faith in Christ. The church was a juggernaut, guided and energized by almighty God. The same is true today. Nothing—no government, no law, no evil leader, no amount of persecution—can stop God from adding to his church.

12:25 **When Barnabas and Saul had finished their mission in Jerusalem, they returned to Antioch, taking John Mark with them.**[NLT] This verse picks up from the story in 11:27-30, where *Barnabas and Saul* had been sent with the famine relief funds from the church at Antioch for the believers in Jerusalem. That had been *their mission.* Barnabas and Saul were probably not in Jerusalem for the events of this chapter; instead, they made the trip some time after Herod's death. Luke, in his arrangement of his materials, chose to put the events of Peter and Herod at this point in the story.

Upon the completion of their mission, Barnabas and Saul *returned to Antioch,* having picked up *John Mark* in the process. John Mark was also Barnabas's cousin (Colossians 4:10). His mother, Mary, often would open her home to the church (12:12), so John Mark would have been exposed to most of the great teachers and teachings of the early church. He had become a believer and had the great opportunity to travel with these two men of God. It would be the education of a lifetime, but not in the way he expected.

Acts 13

BARNABAS AND PAUL ARE SENT OUT / 13:1-3

Luke's history of the church changes focus to the Gentile ministry and the subsequent spread of the church around the world. Beginning in chapter 13 with the Spirit's selection of Paul and Barnabas to become special missionaries, Paul replaces Peter as the central figure in the book of Acts as the church continued its Spirit-led penetration farther out into the world beyond Jerusalem.

13:1 **Now in the church at Antioch there were prophets and teachers: Barnabas, Simeon who was called Niger, Lucius of Cyrene, Manaen a member of the court of Herod the ruler, and Saul.**[NRSV] The *church at Antioch* became the sending center of the mission to reach the world (the last part of Jesus' commission in 1:8). This first verse gives us an idea of its truly international makeup and of the broad spectrum of people who were being reached by the gospel.

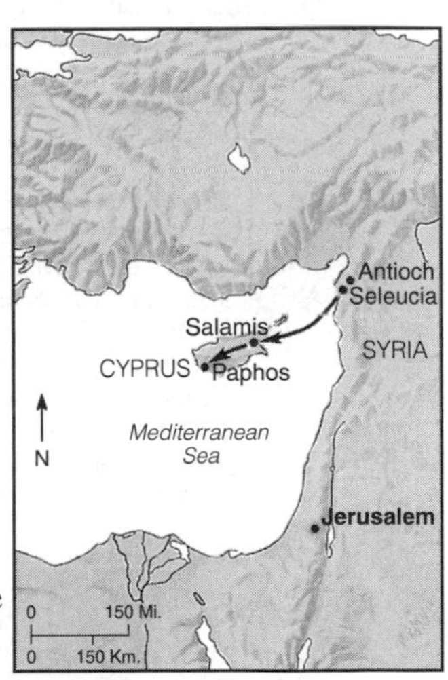

MINISTRY IN CYPRUS
The leaders of the church in Antioch chose Paul and Barnabas to take the gospel westward. Along with John Mark, they boarded ship at Seleucia and set out across the Mediterranean for Cyprus. They preached in Salamis, the largest city, and went across the island to Paphos.

Until this point it appeared that Barnabas and Paul had been the principle teachers in the church of Antioch (11:26). This list shows, at least, these three others who were said to have had the gifts of being *prophets and teachers.* It is unclear as to whether these men had one or the other or both of these gifts. *Barnabas* appears first on the list because he was likely the leader of the group. *Simeon* had a Latin nickname, *Niger*—which means "black-skinned"—probably because of his dark complexion.

There is some speculation that this was the same Simon of Cyrene who carried the cross of Christ (Mark 15:21), but that is unknown. The next name on the list is a man from *Cyrene* by the name of *Lucius.* Cyrene was in North Africa. Lucius was probably among the Cyprian and Cyrenian men who first preached the gospel to Gentiles in Antioch (see 11:20-21). The fourth individual was *Manaen* (whose name means "comforter"). He was involved at the highest levels of government, as he was *a member of the court of Herod the ruler.* How ironic that one of the church leaders was a member of Herod's court!

Saul was a highly trained rabbinic Jew and a Roman citizen. His name closes the list of this very diverse group. He may have been listed last because he was the newest believer or possibly because he was, at this point, the second most important person on the list (in Greek, sometimes the two most important words of a sentence are placed at the first and last positions in a sentence). Whatever the case, Saul would not be in the background much longer.

The social, geographic, and racial variety of these people shows that the Spirit of God had been moving rapidly and over a broad geographic area. Not only had the Good News spread to these areas, but the Spirit of God used cosmopolitan Antioch to put together a diverse team for the next "phase" of kingdom expansion.

A HUMAN PATCHWORK

Barnabas, Simeon, Lucius, Manaen, Saul—what variety is found in God's church! These five men were from different cultural and, likely, racial backgrounds. It's reasonable to assume that they had different skills, ages, appearances, personalities, likes, and dislikes. The common thread among them was their deep faith in Christ. We must never exclude anyone whom Christ has called to follow him. One sign that we are in God's will is when our churches are filled with a patchwork of radically different people who are united by the love of Christ.

13:2-3 While they were worshiping the Lord and fasting, the Holy Spirit said, "Set apart for me Barnabas and Saul for the work to which I have called them." So after they had fasted and prayed, they placed their hands on them and sent them off.NIV
The believers *were worshiping the Lord and fasting* when God sent them a special message. Just as both Peter and Cornelius received messages while praying (chapter 10), so God spoke to these believers as they were seeking him. "Fasting" means going without food for a specified period of time in order to focus on the Lord. People who are fasting can set aside the time of preparing and eating meals and use it to worship and pray. Also, their

hunger pangs will remind them of their complete dependence upon God (see also 2 Chronicles 20:3; Ezra 8:23; Esther 4:16; Matthew 6:16-18).

The Spirit spoke—possibly through one of the members of this group (there were prophets among them—13:1). The Spirit told them to *set apart . . . Barnabas and Saul.* The word for "set apart" is *aphorizo.* It is used to describe three important events in Paul's life: (1) his birth (Galatians 1:15); (2) his conversion (Romans 1:1); and (3) here, his sending to the Gentile mission field. Because God *called them* to *the work,* they had his blessing from the start.

The laying on of hands was a symbolic act that indicated public recognition of calling and ability as well as the association of a particular congregation with a ministry. The roots of the practice are found in the Old Testament, where it was used to set someone aside for an office (Numbers 27:23), bless someone (Genesis 48:14), or dedicate something to God (Leviticus 1:4). The church at Antioch was identifying itself with these two men and with their mission.

Even after the Spirit had spoken and the choice had been made, there was more prayer and fasting before the congregation endorsed these two to the task at hand. With that, they *sent them off.*

PAUL'S FIRST MISSIONARY JOURNEY / 13:4-12

Having been chosen by God to embark on what came to be called the "first missionary journey," Paul and his entourage (Barnabas and John Mark, at the very least) set sail. The target of this evangelistic thrust was the Gentile population of Asia Minor. The mission stopped first on the island of Cyprus, where they confronted a false prophet named Bar-Jesus. Twice in this short narrative, the Holy Spirit is mentioned so as to demonstrate the truth that the spread of the gospel is God's idea and can only be done in and by the Spirit's power.

Why did Paul and Barnabas go where they did? The Holy Spirit led them. They followed the communication routes of the Roman Empire—this made travel easier. They first visited Barnabas's home country. Then they visited key population and cultural centers to reach as many people as possible.

13:4 Sent out by the Holy Spirit, Saul and Barnabas went down to the seaport of Seleucia and then sailed for the island of Cyprus.NLT The *Holy Spirit* was the central force in sending *Saul and Barnabas* (along with John Mark—13:5) on their journey. For more on the theology of the Holy Spirit in Acts, see commentary in chapters 1 and 2. *Seleucia* was a seaport of Antioch, a few miles north of the city at the mouth of the Orontes River. *Cyprus,* an important island in the Mediterranean, was about one hundred miles to the southwest.

BEING A MISSIONARY AT HOME
Saul, Barnabas, and John Mark sailed to Cyprus (13:4). Located in the Mediterranean Sea, the island of Cyprus (with a large Jewish population) was Barnabas's home. Perhaps the Spirit of God led the missionaries to familiar territory to underline the truth that if a person's Christianity isn't believable at home, then there's no sense taking it on the road. This was also the pattern established by Christ in Acts 1:8. We must share Christ first where we are, with those who know us best. Credibility and effectiveness at home are prerequisites to more elaborate outreach endeavors. As one wise old saint noted, it takes more than a trip to some faraway locale to make someone into a missionary.

13:5 **There, in the town of Salamis, they went to the Jewish synagogues and preached the word of God. (John Mark went with them as their assistant.)**[NLT] *Salamis,* the leading city on Cyprus, was their first stop. It was located on the east coast of the island and was the seat of government. As would become his custom for years, Saul began his witness in *the Jewish synagogues* (Romans 1:16). Saul's credentials as a highly trained Pharisee—a former student of Gamaliel (22:3)—would have been more than enough to prompt an invitation to speak, at least until his reputation for bringing such a radical message began to precede him.

John Mark was on the trip *as their assistant.* The nature of Mark's job is not spelled out, though the word used here *(hupereten)* has led to speculation that he instructed the new converts and also was in charge of practical needs. His premature departure from the journey would become a source of friction between Saul and Barnabas (15:37-39).

BEING A HELPER
Luke records that John Mark accompanied Saul and Barnabas, acting as their "assistant." This is a good reminder that sharing the gospel is a team effort. Some serve in highly visible, up-front capacities; others attend to crucial details behind the scenes. Which role is more important? Neither. Both are necessary to accomplish the task. Perhaps God wants you to assist someone else this week in the work of building his church. Or maybe he wants you to find someone who's sitting by idly, so he or she can assist you in helping fulfill God's plan.

13:6-7 They traveled through the whole island until they came to Paphos. There they met a Jewish sorcerer and false prophet named Bar-Jesus, who was an attendant of the proconsul, Sergius Paulus. The proconsul, an intelligent man, sent for Barnabas and Saul because he wanted to hear the word of God.[NIV] The missionary team *traveled* the length of the island from east to west (about one hundred miles), arriving at the town of *Paphos,* a regional center of government. There they *met a Jewish sorcerer* (Greek: *magos*—which means "magician"). *Bar-Jesus* is further described as a *false prophet* who was an *attendant of the proconsul, Sergius Paulus.*

A "proconsul" was a high Roman official. Also described as *an intelligent man,* this proconsul functioned as the governor of the island of Cyprus. He may have been the same Sergius Paulus who was a high official in Rome under Emperor Claudius. Such leaders often kept private sorcerers. As governor, Sergius Paulus was conducting an official investigation. He had received news of these traveling Jewish evangelists and was concerned about disruptions in the Jewish communities. For Paul and Barnabas, presenting the gospel to the proconsul was a great opportunity (see 13:12).

13:8 But Elymas, the sorcerer (as his name means in Greek), interfered and urged the governor to pay no attention to what Saul and Barnabas said. He was trying to turn the governor away from the Christian faith.[NLT] Trouble was brewing, however, because Bar-Jesus realized that if Sergius Paulus believed in Christ, he would no longer need a sorcerer. Apparently Bar-Jesus' Greek name was *Elymas* (meaning "sorcerer" or "magician"), and he was going to do his best to stop any influence Barnabas and Saul might have on the governor.

13:9-10 Then Saul, who was also called Paul, filled with the Holy Spirit, looked straight at Elymas and said, "You are a child of the devil and an enemy of everything that is right! You are full of all kinds of deceit and trickery. Will you never stop perverting the right ways of the Lord?"[NIV] At this point Luke noted that *Saul* was also known as *Paul.* The implication is that he already had both names but began to go by the latter, preferring to use his Roman name for the balance of his Gentile-oriented mission. No person, apart from Jesus himself, shaped the history of Christianity like the apostle Paul. After this, Paul is always called by his Roman name in Luke's record.

Paul was *filled with the Holy Spirit,* a phrase reminiscent of the way the apostles were used earlier in Acts (see 2:4; 4:8, 31; 7:55), as well as one of the requirements for the choosing of the "seven" in chapter 6. For the first time, Paul took center stage. Evidently this was a big turning point in Paul's leadership of the mission.

Not intimidated by his spiritual rival, Paul boldly *looked straight at Elymas* and exposed the source of his sorcery. In Aramaic the name Bar-Jesus means "son of Jesus," so Paul played on that name to confront him (in the presence of the listening Sergius Paulus) with the accusation that Bar-Jesus was actually a *child* (literally, "son") *of the devil* (Greek *diabolos*) and *an enemy of everything that is right* (literally, "righteousness"). This is the first recorded presentation of the word of God to the Roman world, and it would be crucial that a clear distinction be made between Christianity and the perverted spiritualism so prevalent in the Empire. Paul further characterized Elymas's sorcery as *full of all kinds of deceit and trickery.* Evidently Paul had seen enough of what Elymas did to know what he was up to, and he was not going to allow this intelligent Roman governor to be fooled anymore.

13:11 "Now the hand of the Lord is against you. You are going to be blind, and for a time you will be unable to see the light of the sun." Immediately mist and darkness came over him, and he groped about, seeking someone to lead him by the hand.NIV Paul's rhetorical questioning of the sorcerer turned to an announcement of judgment, telling him that the Lord's *hand* was against him.

13:12 When the proconsul saw what had happened, he believed, for he was astonished at the teaching about the Lord.NRSV This miracle was all it took to convince Sergius Paulus. *He believed.* Notice also that his astonishment was not at the powerful act he had just witnessed but rather *at the teaching about the Lord.* Sergius Paulus is the highest ranking converted official recorded in the New Testament.

PAUL PREACHES IN ANTIOCH OF PISIDIA / 13:13-43

Leaving the city of Paphos on the island of Cyprus, Paul and his companions sailed north, arriving at Perga. For an unknown reason, John Mark abruptly left the venture at that time and returned to Jerusalem. Paul and Barnabas continued inland to Antioch of Pisidia.

As would be his custom throughout his ministry, Paul went first to the Jews. In the synagogue he reviewed God's historic dealings with the Jews and then argued that Jesus was "God's promised Savior" (13:23 NLT), the fulfillment of every ancient messianic prophecy. The initial reaction to Paul's preaching was favorable.

13:13 Now Paul and those with him left Paphos by ship for Pamphylia, landing at the port town of Perga.[NLT] Having traveled Barnabas's homeland (Cyprus) from coast to coast, the party boarded a ship for the mainland. They arrived at the province of *Pamphylia,* landing in the *port town of Perga.*

There John Mark left them and returned to Jerusalem.[NLT] Why *John Mark left them* is never explained. Perhaps:

- he was homesick;
- he resented the change in leadership from Barnabas (his cousin) to Paul;
- he became ill (an illness that may have affected all of them—see Galatians 4:13);
- he was unable to withstand the rigors and dangers of the missionary journey;
- he may have planned to go only that far but had not communicated this to Paul and Barnabas.

MINISTRY IN PAMPHYLIA AND GALATIA
Paul, Barnabas, and John Mark left Paphos and landed at Perga in the humid region of Pamphylia, a narrow strip of land between the sea and the Taurus Mountains. John Mark left them in Perga, but Paul and Barnabas traveled up the steep road into the higher elevation of Pisidia in Galatia. When the Jews rejected his message, Paul preached to Gentiles, and the Jews drove Paul and Barnabas out of the Pisidian city of Antioch.

Paul implicitly accused John Mark of lacking commitment, and, therefore, Paul refused to take Mark along on another journey (see 15:37-38).

John Mark's story does not end here, though. It is clear from Paul's later letters that Paul grew to respect Mark (Colossians 4:10) and that he needed him in his work (2 Timothy 4:11). Somewhere along the way, after what must have been a miserable season in his life, John Mark got back on track. He became one of four privileged writers of a New Testament Gospel. He was restored completely to usefulness even in the ministry of Paul; he is a great inspiration for believers of moving beyond failures to faithfulness.

13:14 But Barnabas and Paul traveled inland to Antioch of Pisidia. On the Sabbath they went to the synagogue for the services.[NLT] This is *Antioch of Pisidia,* not Antioch of Syria, home of the sending church where the ministry was flourishing (11:26).

This Antioch, in the region of Pisidia, was a hub of good roads and trade and had a large Jewish population. It had been founded in 281 B.C. by Seleucius I, and he had named it after his father, Antiocus. It had been declared a Roman colony city and became the most important city of southern Galatia. It had a mix of Romans, Greeks, Orientals, and Phrygians.

When they went to a new city to witness for Christ, Paul and Barnabas *went* first *to the synagogue.* They would go *on the Sabbath,* taking advantage of the Jewish custom of inviting itinerant teachers to speak (Jesus also did this—see, for example, Luke 4:16). Sometimes the Jews who were there believed in God and diligently studied the Scriptures. Tragically, however, many could not accept Jesus as the promised Messiah, because they had the wrong idea of what kind of Messiah he would be. He was not, as they desired, a military king who would overthrow Rome's control, but he was a servant king who would defeat sin in people's hearts. Paul and Barnabas did not separate themselves from the synagogues but tried to show clearly that the very Scriptures the Jews studied pointed to Jesus.

THE BACK DOOR TO SUCCESS

John Mark deserted Paul and Barnabas (13:13). John Mark's failure early on in ministry did not ruin him. He later on became quite useful to the church, possibly to Peter (see 1 Peter 5:13), and certainly to Paul (Colossians 4:10; 2 Timothy 4:11). His life is an illustration that, in the words of baseball sage Yogi Berra, "It ain't over till it's over." John Mark could have easily called it quits. He had the reputation of a loser, a quitter—at least in the eyes of Paul, the new leader of the missionary movement of the whole church! But he didn't quit. He made the long journey back and became an effective worker for God. And he even was given the privilege of composing one of the four Gospels. How about you? Have you failed someone or somewhere? What you do from this point on will determine whether that failure becomes the story of your life, or whether your return from it brings glory to God.

13:15 After the reading from the Law and the Prophets, the synagogue rulers sent word to them, saying, "Brothers, if you have a message of encouragement for the people, please speak."[NIV] In a synagogue service, first the "Shema" would be recited (this is Deuteronomy 6:4, which Jews would repeat several times daily). Then certain prayers would be spoken, followed by a reading from the *Law* (Genesis through Deuteronomy), a reading from the *Prophets* (intended to illustrate the law), and a sermon.

The *synagogue rulers* would decide who was to lead the service and give the sermon. A different person would be chosen to lead each week. Since it was customary for the synagogue leader to invite visiting rabbis to speak, Paul and Barnabas usually would have an open door when they went go to a synagogue. But as soon as they spoke about Jesus as Messiah, the door would often slam shut. Usually they would not be invited back by the religious leaders, and sometimes they would be thrown out of town!

The invitation from the synagogue rulers was to speak *a message of encouragement.* What an open invitation for the gospel! There can be no more encouraging word than the fact that God has come to earth and opened a door to heaven, providing an atonement for sin and offering new life in Jesus Christ! Such an invitation was all Paul needed.

ENCOURAGEMENT

The synagogue rulers in Antioch invited Paul and Barnabas to share a "message of encouragement" (13:15 NIV). The word "encouragement" derives from a Greek verb that literally means "to call alongside." The idea is providing exhortation or consolation. Thus, encouragement is that process whereby we enter the lives of others and give them what they most need—a kind word of challenge or a compassionate word of hope. Who in your life needs a reminder to "keep doing right" or to "hang in there"? Perhaps someone needs to be consoled with the truth that God is in control and that he is faithful. If you have a message of encouragement, "please speak"!

13:16 So Paul stood, lifted his hand to quiet them, and started speaking. "People of Israel," he said, "and you devout Gentiles who fear the God of Israel, listen to me."[NLT] Paul's sermon, which continues from here to 13:41, probably was included as a typical example of what Paul would say to a synagogue gathering. It shows how Paul first preached the gospel to a Jewish congregation.

The opening address to the *people of Israel* and to the *devout Gentiles who fear the God of Israel* covered both groups of possible worshipers—Jews by birth and Gentile God-fearers (see remarks about Cornelius at 10:2).

13:17-18 "The God of this people Israel chose our ancestors and made the people great during their stay in the land of Egypt, and with uplifted arm he led them out of it. For about forty years he put up with them in the wilderness."[NRSV] Paul began his message by emphasizing God's covenant with Israel *(God . . .*

chose our ancestors). This was a point of agreement because all Jews were proud to be God's chosen people. Paul would go on to explain how the gospel fulfills the covenant. His review of Israel's history is like Stephen's lengthy review of the same in his sermon to a Jewish crowd in Jerusalem (chapter 7). This was a common form of address known as an "historical retrospect"—a sketch of the course of God's work in the nation's history. Paul would move quickly from Abraham to Moses, Samuel, and David and eventually come to Jesus (13:23).

The sermon has three major parts, with each section marked by Paul's direct address to the audience: (1) the preliminary historical figures leading up to the coming of Messiah in 13:16-25; (2) the rejection, crucifixion, and resurrection of Christ (13:26-37); and (3) the appeal to believe (13:38-39).

After the implied mention of Abraham ("chose our ancestors"), Paul moved to the *stay in the land of Egypt.* Moses' name is not mentioned, but rather, God is pictured *with uplifted arm* leading Israel out to *the wilderness* (see Exodus 6:1, 6 and Psalm 136:11-12 for the Old Testament picture of God's "uplifted arm").

13:19-20 **"Then he destroyed seven nations in Canaan and gave their land to Israel as an inheritance. All this took about 450 years. After that, judges ruled until the time of Samuel the prophet."**[NLT] Paul passed over any reference to the giving of the law, though he would later speak about its inability to save people (13:39). He did not name the *seven nations in Canaan* whose land had been given *to Israel as an inheritance*—these were well known to Paul's audience (see Deuteronomy 7:1 for the list).

HISTORY LESSONS

Many of the sermons in Acts look back over Israel's history. This is because the first-century believers understood that God has a sovereign plan for the human race that spans all time. History truly is "his story." Events were not seen as random acts but as the outworkings of a perfect and exciting eternal purpose, all moving toward a certain goal. Likewise, a knowledge of history (biblical history, church history, one's own spiritual background, etc.) can provide us with a framework for understanding the present and the future. Make it your goal to learn more about your rich spiritual heritage. Clues for how God will work in the future are found in how he has worked in the past.

The *450 years* was an inclusive figure for all the events that had occurred so far in Paul's survey—from the move to Egypt (four hundred years), the wandering in the wilderness (forty years), through the distribution of the land under Joshua (ten years).

Paul summarized the period of the judges with two words, "judges ruled," leading up to the time of the prophets, beginning with *Samuel,* who was considered the first prophet.

13:21 "Then they asked for a king; and God gave them Saul son of Kish, a man of the tribe of Benjamin, who reigned for forty years."NRSV Israel's kingdom period began with *Saul son of Kish* (1 Samuel 9:1-2), who was the first king.

13:22 "After removing Saul, he made David their king. He testified concerning him: 'I have found David son of Jesse a man after my own heart; he will do everything I want him to do.'"NIV Saul, of course, had been removed from the throne because of his disobedience (or "partial" obedience—see 1 Samuel 13:1-14 and 15:1-25). Then *David son of Jesse* had become the new king, replacing the rejected Saul, who did not possess the same *heart* for God, nor was he one who would *do everything* God wanted *him to do* (1 Samuel 13:14).

13:23 "And it is one of King David's descendants, Jesus, who is God's promised Savior of Israel!"NLT A large jump over Old Testament history occurred here, as Paul went from King David directly to one of his *descendants, Jesus.* Paul described Jesus as *God's promised Savior of Israel.* This is the only place recorded in Acts where Paul called Jesus "Savior." Peter used the same term in 5:31.

TAILORING THE MESSAGE

Paul began where his listeners were and then introduced them to Christ. Because Paul was speaking to devout Jews, he began with the covenant, Abraham, David, and other familiar themes (13:17-22). Later, when speaking to the Greek philosophers in Athens (17:22-32), he would begin by talking about what he had observed in their city. In both cases, however, Paul centered the sermon around Christ and emphasized the Resurrection. When you share the Good News, begin where your audience is—then tell them about Christ.

13:24-25 "Before the coming of Jesus, John preached repentance and baptism to all the people of Israel. As John was completing his work, he said: 'Who do you think I am? I am not that one. No, but he is coming after me, whose sandals I am not worthy to untie.'"NIV This reference to *John* refers to John the Baptist. John was the last of the prophets, the one who would prepare the way for the coming of Messiah. Yet even this great prophet had not considered himself *worthy to untie* the sandals of the Messiah, who would come after him. John's whole thrust was to try to turn Israel to the Savior by preaching *repentance and baptism.* "Repentance" means turning away from sin and to God—an about-face from a sinful life to a life lived for God. Baptism with water was a way of publicly showing one's commitment to turn away from sin and toward God.

> I have dwelt forty years practically alone in Africa. I have been thirty-nine times stricken with the fever, three times attacked by lions, and several times by rhinoceri; but let me say to you, I would gladly go through the whole thing again, if I could have the joy of again bringing that word "Savior" and flashing it into the darkness that envelops another tribe in Central Africa.
>
> *Willard Hotchkiss, pioneer missionary in Africa*

13:26 **"Brothers—you sons of Abraham, and also all of you devout Gentiles who fear the God of Israel—this salvation is for us!"**[NLT] With this direct address to his Jewish *brothers,* Paul appealed for them to come to faith in Jesus Christ—the one to whom all the prophecies of their Scriptures pointed. The *salvation* that Christ offers is for both Jews *(sons of Abraham)* and *devout Gentiles* (fearers of God who aligned themselves to worship in the Jewish community).

The two main streams of thought that will follow are: (1) Jesus' death and resurrection fulfilled Old Testament Scripture; and (2) through that death, the offer of forgiveness of sins is made to all people. To his Jewish brothers, Paul made a potent declaration: *"This salvation is for us!"*

13:27 **"The people in Jerusalem and their leaders fulfilled prophecy by condemning Jesus to death. They didn't recognize him or realize that he is the one the prophets had written about, though they hear the prophets' words read every Sabbath."**[NLT] Paul joined Peter and Stephen in blaming the Jews who rejected Christ *(the people in Jerusalem and their leaders)* for killing Jesus. Yet that had *fulfilled prophecy* (see Psalm 118:22; Isaiah 53:3). The failure of the Jews to *recognize him or realize that he* was *the one the prophets had written about* was made all the worse by the fact that they had sat *every Sabbath* and had heard the *prophets' words read.* They had been exposed to the prophecies but had missed the fulfillment of those prophecies (see Luke 24:46; Acts 3:18).

13:28 **"Even though they found no cause for a sentence of death, they asked Pilate to have him killed."**[NRSV] Although the Jewish leaders *found no cause for a sentence of death* during Jesus' trial, they still *asked Pilate to have him killed.* Because of the Roman occupation of the land of Israel, the Jewish leaders could not carry out the execution. So, after the Jews had condemned Jesus, they had to get permission from the Roman ruler of their province—and that was Pilate. Pilate had even pointed out to the Jewish accusers the fact that they had no grounds for execution, but he gave in to their demands (Luke 23:4, 14-15, 22).

DEAF TO THE TRUTH
Paul reminded his audience of a sobering fact: It is possible to read the truth, hear the truth preached "every Sabbath," even see the truth—and still miss it. This is what happened to the Jews in A.D. 29 who had been waiting for the Messiah. He came—right into their midst—and they not only "didn't recognize him," but they condemned him to death! Jesus warned of this tendency to be spiritually deaf (Matthew 13:14-15). Ask yourself: Is my heart *really* open to the truth? Do I let God's Word penetrate deep into my soul and change the way I think and live? Ask God to help you take out any spiritual earplugs you might be wearing so that you will have "ears to hear" (Matthew 13:43 NKJV).

13:29 "When they had fulfilled all the prophecies concerning his death, they took him down from the cross and placed him in a tomb."NLT Jesus' death *had fulfilled all the prophecies.* Oddly enough, the very Jews who had killed Jesus were the ones who would have been the most well versed in all those prophecies. In their blindness they killed Jesus because they had refused to believe that he was their Messiah—all the while fulfilling the Scriptures about the death of their Messiah! After Jesus had been crucified on *the cross,* he had been *placed . . . in a tomb* (Luke 23:44-56).

13:30 "But God raised Him from the dead."NKJV But the tomb was not the end of the story. In this note of triumph, Paul reported what most would think impossible—*God raised Him from the dead* (Luke 24). Without the Resurrection, there would be no gospel, no salvation, no Good News to spread. But Paul, though he had not been among the apostles to witness the Resurrection, had seen the risen Christ and, thus, could testify to the truth of this statement (9:1-6).

13:31 "And he appeared over a period of many days to those who had gone with him from Galilee to Jerusalem—these are his witnesses to the people of Israel."NLT The credibility of the Resurrection had been affirmed by *witnesses*—his followers, *those* *who had gone with him from Galilee to Jerusalem.* They had seen the resurrected Christ *over a period of many days.* (See the chart, "Jesus' Appearances after His Resurrection" on page 3 [1:3].)

13:32-33 **"And now Barnabas and I are here to bring you this Good News. God's promise to our ancestors has come true in our own time, in that God raised Jesus. This is what the second psalm is talking about when it says concerning Jesus, 'You are my Son. Today I have become your Father.'"**[NLT] The structure of these last few verses follows a four-part Christian confession much like the one in 1 Corinthians 15:3-5: Jesus was crucified, placed in a tomb, raised from the dead, and seen by many in the days that followed.

Paul tied together all of the events that he had been recounting to that moment when he and Barnabas were standing before them as the bearers of *this Good News.* The *promise* God had made to their common *ancestors* had *come true in [their] own time.* After centuries of waiting, watching, and wanting, the Messiah had come. His name is Jesus.

To support this statement, Paul quoted from three Old Testament texts already considered by most Jews to have been referring to the Messiah—Psalm 2:7; Isaiah 55:3; and Psalm 16:10.

In these verses, Psalm 2:7 pictures God the *Father* as speaking to his *Son.* This moment had been publicly recognized (although it already was a reality) in Christ's life on the day of his baptism (Luke 3:22; 9:35; commentary at Acts 10:38).

13:34 **"The fact that God raised him from the dead, never to decay, is stated in these words: 'I will give you the holy and sure blessings promised to David.'"**[NIV] A more direct proof for the Resurrection came from Isaiah 55:3, which promised *holy and sure blessings.* This prophecy by Isaiah was a reference back to the covenant first promised to David by Nathan the prophet in 2 Samuel 7:6-16. The eternal throne did not find fulfillment in David. But in Jesus Christ, who rose from the dead, there is an eternal King who will reign forever.

13:35 **"So it is stated elsewhere: 'You will not let your Holy One see decay.'"**[NIV] Psalm 16:10 also offers proof of the promised Resurrection. This argument was the same one Peter had used on the day of Pentecost (see comments at 2:27) and was a strong promise of resurrection for the *Holy One* of God. Judging from the popularity of its use, this psalm must have been one of the strongest cases to the Jewish audience for the necessity of the resurrection of the Messiah.

13:36-37 **"Now this is not a reference to David, for after David had served his generation according to the will of God, he died**

and was buried, and his body decayed. No, it was a reference to someone else—someone whom God raised and whose body did not decay."[NLT] The words of Psalm 16:10 could not have referred *to David,* because David *died and was buried,* and his body did, in fact, suffer decay—many in Paul's audience had likely been to the site of David's tomb in Jerusalem. Therefore, Paul was saying that David must have been writing prophetically of one who would come after he had died, *someone whom God raised and whose body did not decay.* That person was Jesus of Nazareth.

A LIVING SAVIOR

Paul's message to those gathered at the synagogue in Antioch of Pisidia was a clear announcement of the truth that Christ had been raised from the dead. He did *not* remain in the tomb. He was resurrected, and he lives forevermore. Unlike many modern-day believers who seem to have a "ho-hum" attitude concerning the doctrine of Christ's resurrection, the apostles were utterly transformed by this truth. It was central to their faith, and it dominated their preaching. When was the last time you pondered deeply the fact of the empty tomb? The implications of this historical reality are life changing!

13:38-39 "Therefore, my brothers, I want you to know that through Jesus the forgiveness of sins is proclaimed to you. Through him everyone who believes is justified from everything you could not be justified from by the law of Moses."[NIV] With his scriptural support for the Resurrection stated, Paul explained the spiritual significance of what Christ had done; then he called his audience to believe. With Christ's substitutionary death and the approval of God as demonstrated in the Resurrection (Romans 1:4; 4:25), *through Jesus* (his sacrifice) *the forgiveness of sins* has been made available. This proclamation included the necessity of "belief" and the promise of "justification." These rich theological terms, the cornerstones of Paul's theology, are spelled out in his letters to the Galatians and the Romans.

Note that this justification is *from everything you could not be justified*

> If we or the world could be saved through human kindness or clear thinking, Jesus either would have formed a sensitivity group and urged us to share our feelings or would have founded a school and asked us to have discussions. But knowing the ways of God, the way of the world, and the persistence of human sin, he took up the cross, called disciples, gathered the church, and bade us follow him down a different path of freedom.
>
> *William H. Willimon*

from by the law of Moses. The law could not give them justification. Instead, being "justified" could occur only through the sacrificial death of Christ on the cross (Romans 5:9). Because God is holy, he cannot accept people by simply disregarding or ignoring their sins. Nor can he accept his own people, the Jews, merely on the basis of their relationship to Abraham or by their trying to follow the law of Moses, for the sinful human nature had to be dealt with. And God did this through the sacrificial death of his Son. This justification is God's approval, given to people only on the basis of what Christ did. It is an acquittal that sets free all those who are otherwise hopeless prisoners of sin. Because of Christ's shed blood on the cross, people no longer have to bear the penalty for their sin—death (Romans 6:23). Jesus paid it all.

THE PURE AND SIMPLE GOSPEL
This is the good news of the gospel: that forgiveness of sins and freedom from guilt are available through faith in Christ to all who believe—including you (13:37-39). Justification is the act whereby God declares people "not guilty!" (because of what Christ has done) the moment they put their faith in him. Have you received this forgiveness? Are you refreshed by it each day?

13:40-41 "Take care that what the prophets have said does not happen to you: 'Look, you scoffers, wonder and perish, for I am going to do something in your days that you would never believe, even if someone told you.'"[NIV] Paul's final words were words of warning. He drew from a common theme sounded by many of the prophets—"Be careful that you don't miss what God is doing right before your very eyes." Paul cited Habakkuk 1:5 as a representative passage in which the prophet warned Judah of its impending judgment—the exile to Babylon. In the same way that their ancestors had failed to recognize what God was doing among them, Paul's audience was about to miss what God was doing in its day.

13:42 As Paul and Barnabas were leaving the synagogue, the people invited them to speak further about these things on the next Sabbath.[NIV] After the sermon the reception must have been positive, for *Paul and Barnabas* were invited back to *speak further . . . on the next Sabbath.* But this warm welcome would not last long.

13:43 Many Jews and godly converts to Judaism who worshiped at the synagogue followed Paul and Barnabas, and the two men urged them, "By God's grace, remain faithful."[NLT] The two groups addressed twice by Paul—*Jews and godly converts* (see remarks at 13:16, 26)—followed them out of the synagogue. These were probably the ones who were ready to respond to the gospel message or perhaps even already had. The simple message from these two missionaries was to urge them, *"By God's grace, remain faithful"* (literally to "continue in the grace of God"). That is, they should continue in the direction they were headed.

PAUL TURNS TO THE GENTILES / 13:44-52

Declaring boldly the death and resurrection of Christ and the forgiveness that is possible only through him (see 13:38-39), Paul and Barnabas drew huge crowds on their second Sabbath in Antioch of Pisidia. Among those gathered were a number of jealous Jewish leaders (13:45). Despite efforts by these leaders to discredit Paul and his message, the assembled Gentiles eagerly embraced the gospel. This further enraged the Jewish leaders, who were eventually able to stir up a mob that ran Paul and Barnabas out of town.

These events serve as a kind of microcosm of the entire ministry of Paul: stiff opposition from most Jews and joyous acceptance of the gospel message by many Gentiles.

13:44-45 On the next Sabbath almost the whole city gathered to hear the word of the Lord. When the Jews saw the crowds, they were filled with jealousy and talked abusively against what Paul was saying.[NIV] In one short week, the news had spread through the city of Antioch so that *on the next Sabbath almost the whole city gathered to hear* what Paul and Barnabas had to say. This huge and unusual turnout was likely due to a Gentile influx rather than a Jewish one, since the Jewish attendance at the synagogue probably was fairly constant.

> Envy is that consuming desire to have everybody else as unsuccessful as you are.
> *Frederick Buechner*

The Jews in attendance *were filled with jealousy.* Jealousy is obviously a dangerous and deadly emotion! The jealousy of the Jews led them to talk *abusively* against Paul's message, although it must have been difficult taking on this brilliant rabbi in a debate. The Greek term *blasphemountes* (from which comes the word "blasphemy") describes the Jews' abusive arguing.

13:46-47 Then both Paul and Barnabas spoke out boldly, saying, "It was necessary that the word of God should be spoken first to you. Since you reject it and judge yourselves to be unworthy of eternal life, we are now turning to the Gentiles. For so the Lord has commanded us, saying, 'I have set you to be a light

for the Gentiles, so that you may bring salvation to the ends of the earth.'"NRSV In answer to this jealous and abusive response from the Jews, Paul and Barnabas *spoke out boldly,* stating the necessity of their going to the Jews first *(it was necessary that the word of God should be spoken first to you).* Why was it necessary for the gospel to go first to the Jews? God planned that through the Jewish nation, all the world would come to know him (Genesis 12:3). Also, the message of Jesus is basically a Jewish one, steeped in Old Testament prophecy and promises directly made to the Jews. They, of all people, should have been the most ready for the fulfillment that had come in Christ.

BEWARE OF JEALOUSY
The Jewish leaders attacked Paul and Barnabas on "theological grounds," but Luke wrote that the real reason for their hostility was that "they were filled with jealousy" (13:14). When we see others succeeding where we haven't or receiving the affirmation we crave, it is hard to rejoice with them. In fact, jealousy is a more common reaction. But how tragic it is when our own jealous feelings cause us to try to stop God's work. If a work is God's work, and lives are being impacted for Christ, rejoice—no matter who is in the spotlight.

In addition, Paul, a Jew himself, loved his people (Romans 9:1-5) and wanted to give them every opportunity to find the truth and then join him in proclaiming God's salvation. Unfortunately, many Jews did not recognize Jesus as the Messiah and did not understand that God was offering salvation to anyone, Jew or Gentile, who comes to him through faith in Christ. They should have been the ones evangelizing their Gentile neighbors; instead, someone else would have to do it. Paul quoted Isaiah 49:6. God had *set* the Jew to *be a light for the Gentiles.* He wanted them to be the privileged announcers of *salvation to the ends of the earth.* But it was not to be. Their jealous hatred of the good news of Christ was but a foreshadowing of the anger that surfaces against those spreading his good news. In rejecting their Messiah, the Jews had, in essence, judged themselves *unworthy of eternal life.*

The evangelistic thrust was thus turned *to the Gentiles.* God had planned for Israel to be the light (Isaiah 49:6). But Israel had forsaken that task, so it was given to the church to carry out. Through Israel came Jesus, the light of the nations (Luke 2:32). This light would spread out and enlighten the Gentiles; Israel had been disobedient, unresponsive, and blind.

13:48 When the Gentiles heard this, they were very glad and thanked the Lord for his message; and all who were appointed to eternal life became believers.[NLT] Contrast this Gentile response to that of the Jews· *They were very glad and thanked the Lord for his message.* In a strong statement about the sovereign hand of God, Luke wrote: *and all who were appointed to eternal life became believers.* The Greek verb for "appointed" is *tetagmenoi* from *tasso,* a military word meaning to "arrange" or "assign." Various people were "assigned" to eternal life by him (the unmentioned "Appointer"). The significance, of course, is the fact that these "appointed" were Gentiles.

Thus was set the pattern that would surface again and again—the Jews reject, the Gentiles respond in great numbers, and, in turn, the Jews become belligerent and often physically violent against the Christians.

13:49-50 Thus the word of the Lord spread throughout the region. But the Jews incited the devout women of high standing and the leading men of the city, and stirred up persecution against Paul and Barnabas, and drove them out of their region.[NRSV] Again, Luke noted the *spread* of the *word of the Lord* despite the Jews who *stirred up persecution against Paul and Barnabas.* The Jews used their contacts in high places—*women of high standing* and *leading men*—to drive Paul and Barnabas out of their part of the country. The "women of high standing" were probably Gentile women from the upper class who were proselytes and attended the synagogue. The "leading men" were city magistrates. Christianity was not an official religion like Judaism, and these women and men may have feared that Paul would disturb their fragile relationship with the Roman government.

WHEN THE TRUTH HURTS

Instead of accepting the truth, the Jewish leaders stirred up opposition and ran Paul and Barnabas out of town (13:50). When confronted by a disturbing truth, people often turn away and refuse to listen. When God's Spirit points out needed changes in our lives, however, we must listen to him, even though to do so is painful. Otherwise, we may be pushing away our only hope for healing, growth, joy, and peace.

Evidently, these jealous Jews would stop at nothing to get the missionaries out of their city. Using every type of pressure available—political, economic, social—they worked hard at ridding themselves of this perceived threat to their way of life. This was a sad moment: those so desperately in need of salvation driving from their city the bearers of the Good News—news of forgiveness, of justification before God. And they drove it *out of their region.*

13:51 **So they shook the dust off their feet in protest against them, and went to Iconium.**NRSV Often, Jews would shake the dust off their feet when leaving a Gentile town, on the way back to their own land. For Paul and Barnabas to do this to Jews demonstrated that Jews who reject the gospel are not truly part of Israel and are no better than pagans. It was a gesture of utter scorn and disassociation. Jesus had told his disciples to shake from their feet the dust of any town that would not accept or listen to them (Mark 6:11). This symbolized cleansing themselves from the contamination of people who did not worship God. The disciples were not to blame if the gospel was rejected, as long as they had faithfully presented it.

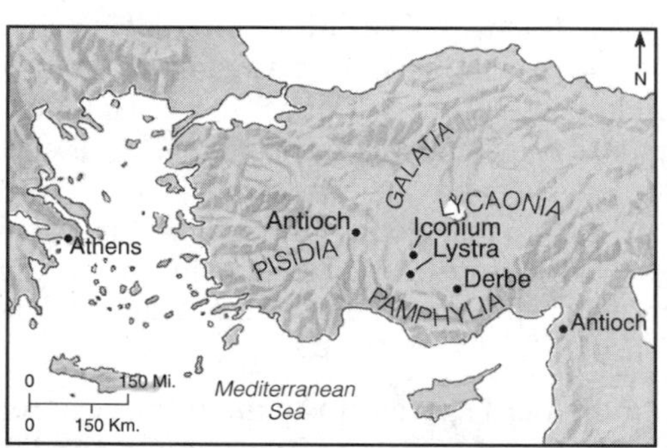

CONTINUED MINISTRY IN GALATIA
Paul and Barnabas, thrown out of Antioch in Pisidia, descended the mountains, going east into Lycaonia. They went first to Iconium, a commercial center on the road between Asia and Syria. After preaching there, they had to flee to Lystra, twenty-five miles south. Paul was stoned in Lystra, but he and Barnabas traveled the fifty miles to Derbe, a border town. The pair then boldly retraced their steps.

13:52 **And the believers were filled with joy and with the Holy Spirit.**NLT In contrast with the paranoid, politicking Jews, working hard to rid themselves of the gospel messengers, the *believers,* most of whom were Gentiles, *were filled with joy and with the Holy Spirit.* Like the coming of the Holy Spirit in Jerusalem at Pentecost (2:3-4), in Samaria at the laying on of the apostles' hands (8:17), and in Caesarea during Peter's preaching (10:44-46), the believers here were "filled with joy"—the kind of inexplicable and overflowing joy of one freshly filled with the loving, forgiving Spirit of God.

Acts 14

PAUL AND BARNABAS IN ICONIUM / 14:1-7

Chased out of Antioch of Pisidia (13:50), Paul and Barnabas journeyed southeast to the region of Galatia, stopping first in the city of Iconium. Again the missionaries went straight to the synagogues, where they preached the gospel with great power and saw many believe in Christ. Alarmed by the success of this message, the Jews in Iconium immediately launched an attack against the messengers who had brought it (14:2). Ignoring the miraculous signs that confirmed the divine nature of the gospel, the Jews (together with some unbelieving Gentiles) made plans to stone Paul and Barnabas. Learning of this plot, the missionaries fled, taking their message to the cities of Lystra and Derbe and the surrounding area.

14:1 **In Iconium, Paul and Barnabas went together to the synagogue and preached with such power that a great number of both Jews and Gentiles believed.**[NLT] *Iconium* was located about sixty miles east and a bit south of Antioch of Pisidia. What happened there confirmed the fact that the mighty movement of God in Antioch was no fluke—God was working *with such power that a great number of both Jews and Gentiles* were coming to faith. As in Antioch, Paul and Barnabas began in *the synagogue,* presumably preaching upon the invitation of the leaders there (see comments at 13:5).

TEAMING UP

The Gospels and Acts record a great number of ministry endeavors in which followers of Christ were sent out in teams of at least two (Mark 6:7; Luke 10:1; Acts 3:1; 4:1; 13:2; cf. Ecclesiastes 4:9-12). By ministering together with another committed believer, we are less likely to yield to temptation, get discouraged, or stop serving God. We can make up for one another's weaknesses as well as combine our gifts. With whom are you teaming up to make a difference? Who is your ministry partner?

14:2 **But the Jews who spurned God's message stirred up distrust among the Gentiles against Paul and Barnabas, saying all**

sorts of evil things about them.NLT As in Antioch, the *Jews* in Iconium opposed the gospel. They *spurned God's message,* rousing the Gentiles and stirring up *distrust* against Paul and Barnabas.

These tactics, similar to what had been used in Antioch of Pisidia, appear to have riled up the entire population. Again, the jealous Jews incited a smear campaign, as they likely ascribed motives and methods to the missionaries that were the product of their own imaginations.

14:3 So Paul and Barnabas spent considerable time there, speaking boldly for the Lord, who confirmed the message of his grace by enabling them to do miraculous signs and wonders.NIV The persecution seems to have partially been the reason that *Paul and Barnabas spent considerable time* in Iconium (the word "so" is the Greek *oun,* meaning "therefore"). The powerful preaching of 14:1 is further qualified as *speaking boldly for the Lord* (see 4:13; 13:46).

As had been the case everywhere they had gone, God *confirmed the message of his grace by enabling* Paul and Barnabas *to do miraculous signs and wonders*—probably healing the sick and casting out demons. These kinds of miracles had also been present in the ministry of the apostles (3:1-11; 5:12-16). Paul would later refer back to the miracles that God did on this mission as validation of God's working among them (Galatians 3:5; see also 2 Corinthians 12:12; Hebrews 2:3-4).

In Acts, signs and wonders are key to revealing the work of salvation in Christ and to proclaiming the gospel. They authenticated the apostles' authority and the authority of those associated with them (Barnabas in 14:2-3; Stephen in 6:8; Philip in 8:5-6). A "sign" *(semeion)* is a miracle whereby God shows himself to be almighty. A "wonder" *(teras)* is an amazing miracle that causes astonishment. In the Old Testament, the word "wonder" referred to God's redemptive activity when Moses led the Hebrews from Egypt (Deuter-onomy 26:5-11). In the early church, these great miracles, empowered by the Spirit, showed God's new redemptive work in Christ. Following are some of the verses in Acts where signs, wonders, and miracles are mentioned (quoted from NLT):

- 2:19—"I will cause wonders in the heavens above."
- 2:22—"God publicly endorsed Jesus of Nazareth by doing wonderful miracles, wonders, and signs through him."
- 2:43—"The apostles performed many miraculous signs and wonders."
- 4:30—"May miraculous signs and wonders be done."

- 5:12—"The apostles were performing many miraculous signs and wonders."
- 6:8—"Stephen . . . performed amazing miracles and signs."
- 7:36—"By means of many miraculous signs and wonders, he led them out of Egypt."
- 8:6—"Crowds listened intently to what he had to say because of the miracles he did."
- 8:13—"He was amazed by the great miracles and signs Philip performed."
- 14:3—"The Lord proved their message was true by giving them power to do miraculous signs and wonders."
- 15:12—"Everyone listened as Barnabas and Paul told about the miraculous signs and wonders God had done through them among the Gentiles."

14:4 But the residents of the city were divided; some sided with the Jews, and some with the apostles.[NRSV] In Iconium, a rift developed among the *residents.* Some believed the rumors and *sided* with the Jews, while others sided *with the apostles.*

UNCONVINCED
We may wish we could perform a miraculous act that would convince everyone once and for all that Jesus is the Lord. But we see here that even if we could perform miracles, it wouldn't convince everyone. God gave Paul and Barnabas power to do great wonders to confirm that their message was true, but people were still divided. Don't spend your time and energy wishing for miracles. Sow your seeds of Good News on the best ground you can find in the best way you can, and leave the convincing to the Holy Spirit.

14:5-7 A mob of Gentiles and Jews, along with their leaders, decided to attack and stone them. When the apostles learned of it, they fled for their lives. They went to the region of Lycaonia, to the cities of Lystra and Derbe and the surrounding area, and they preached the Good News there.[NLT] A *mob,* stimulated by *their* mind-poisoning *leaders,* became much more brutal than had been the case at any point in the apostles' ministry. Apparently a coalition had formed between the Gentile and the Jewish leaders in opposition to the apostles. They decided to *attack* the apostles *and stone them.* Fortunately, the apostles heard of the plan and *fled for their lives.* The opposition did not stop their message. Paul and Barnabas *went to the region of Lycaonia.* The next stop was *Lystra,* a smaller city about twenty miles south of Iconium. Paul may have picked this smaller place in order to let the storm of opposition quiet down a bit. The events that occurred in *Derbe* are recorded in 14:21.

PAUL AND BARNABAS IN LYSTRA AND DERBE / 14:8-20

At Lystra, the missionaries healed a man crippled from birth. The pagan Gentiles of the area saw this miracle and concluded that Paul and Barnabas must be Greek "gods in human bodies" (14:11 NLT). Despite an immediate rejection of this foolish notion and loud explanations to the contrary, the apostles "could scarcely restrain the people from sacrificing to them" (14:18 NLT)!

Suddenly, the fickle mob turned murderous, prodded by some angry Jews from nearby Antioch and Iconium. Together they stoned Paul, dragged him out of Lystra, and left him for dead. Then, in one of most amazing moments of New Testament history, the bloody apostle got up and went back into the city. His joyful perseverance in the face of extreme persecution is testimony to the power of the Holy Spirit in a believer's life.

14:8 In Lystra there was a man sitting who could not use his feet and had never walked, for he had been crippled from birth.[NRSV] In contrast to what had been mostly a preaching ministry so far (although there is a reference to signs and wonders in Iconium—14:3), the major event of Lystra involved a man who *had been crippled from birth.* This verse has the identical wording used in Luke's description of the lame man healed by Peter in 3:2. The fact of his being "crippled from birth" assures that the healing was real. The people of the area would *know* beyond a shadow of a doubt that this person had a lifelong physical ailment that could not be cured.

Other similarities between this miracle and the healing recorded in chapter 3 include the steady gaze of the apostle (compare 14:9 to 3:4) and the exuberant response of the healed man (compare 14:10 to 3:8). To the early readers of this book, the miracle confirmed Paul's status as an agent of God, comparable to Peter.

14:9-10 He listened to Paul as he was speaking. Paul looked directly at him, saw that he had faith to be healed and called out, "Stand up on your feet!" At that, the man jumped up and began to walk.[NIV] Paul recognized the fact that this man *had faith to be healed,* so he addressed the man with authority. *"Stand up on your feet!"* the apostle commanded, and the man *jumped up and began to walk* for the first time ever.

This is a wonderful example of how God changes lives. When Paul was sensitive to the moment, when he made himself available to be used by God, and when the crippled man put his faith in the power of God, then God worked a miracle! God wants to do big things in and through his people, but they need to live with a sense of eager expectancy. To see changes in their lives, believers must trust fully in God (Matthew 13:58).

14:11-12 When the listening crowd saw what Paul had done, they shouted in their local dialect, "These men are gods in human bodies!" They decided that Barnabas was the Greek god Zeus and that Paul, because he was the chief speaker, was Hermes.[NLT] Evidently, the crowd that witnessed this miracle was large. The response was immediate and emotional. Concluding that these men were *gods in human bodies,* they went so far as to decide that Paul was *Hermes* and Barnabas, *Zeus.* They called Barnabas "Zeus," the father of the gods, perhaps due to Barnabas's seniority or appearance. Paul, as the *chief speaker,* was seen as Hermes (the messenger of the gods).

According to Greek and Roman mythology, Zeus and Hermes (the Roman names were Jupiter and Mercury) were two gods. People from Lystra claimed that these gods had once visited their city and, according to the legend, no one offered them hospitality except an old couple. So Zeus and Hermes killed the rest of the people and rewarded the old couple.

When the citizens of Lystra saw the miracles of Paul and Barnabas, they assumed that the gods were revisiting them. Remembering the story of what had happened to the previous citizens, they immediately honored Paul and Barnabas, showering them with gifts. The fact that they shouted *in their local dialect* shows why Paul had let the crowd go so far. He knew neither the language nor the local myth.

14:13 The priest of Zeus, whose temple was just outside the city, brought oxen and garlands to the gates; he and the crowds wanted to offer sacrifice.[NRSV] The matter quickly got out of hand. The *priest of Zeus* was in the process of bringing *oxen* for a *sacrifice.* He would not want to be caught up short with such noble visitors in town! Both *he and the crowds* were ready to offer sacrifices to these two who must be gods. There was plenty of religion in Lystra; it was just misguided.

> When people stop believing in God, they do not believe in nothing. They believe in anything.
> *G. K. Chesterton*

14:14-15 When the apostles Barnabas and Paul heard of it, they tore their clothes and rushed out into the crowd, shouting,

"Friends, why are you doing this? We are mortals just like you, and we bring you good news, that you should turn from these worthless things to the living God, who made the heaven and the earth and the sea and all that is in them."NRSV Barnabas and Paul were horrified by news of an impending sacrifice on their behalf, so they *tore their clothes,* a common Jewish gesture of horror or sorrow. Can you imagine being a servant of the Most High God and having someone try to worship you?

Paul and Barnabas affirmed the fact that they were not visiting gods but mere *mortals* just like the residents of Lystra. They immediately took advantage of the startled, gathered, and attentive crowd to preach the *good news.* What a perfect platform! These sincere, excited believers in Zeus had been ready to spend the time, money, and effort to worship a god that didn't exist. So Paul directed them to *the living God, who made the heaven and the earth.* The residents of Lystra needed to redirect their affection and attention from *these worthless things* (referring to their pantheon of gods) to the one true God.

EVIDENCE OF GOD

Responding to the people of Lystra, Paul and Barnabas reminded them that God never leaves himself "without a witness" (14:17). Rain and crops, for example, are evidence of God's goodness. Later, Paul wrote that this evidence in nature leaves people without an excuse for unbelief (Romans 1:20). When in doubt about God, look around, and you will see abundant evidence that he not only exists but that he also is at work in your world.

14:16-17 **"In past generations he allowed all the nations to follow their own ways; yet he has not left himself without a witness in doing good—giving you rains from heaven and fruitful seasons, and filling you with food and your hearts with joy."**NRSV Contrast this sermon to a crowd of idol-worshiping pagans with Paul's sermon in chapter 13 to the Scripture-literate Jews. This message was perfectly designed for a crowd accustomed to superstitious worship built around the various gods of nature. This is one of two speeches to Gentiles recorded in Acts (see also 17:22-31) and differs from Jewish sermons in its absence of Old Testament references. This shows creative adaptability.

God had been trying to get the people's attention. The first *witness* these people should have noticed was the *good* things that God had made and had given abundantly to all—the *rains,* the *fruitful seasons, food,* and even *joy.* This general revelation was in place to encourage all observers to seek God.

God had *allowed* them *to follow their own ways,* not as a concession to their sinfulness, but as a gracious, patient Creator, waiting for them to see what was in plain view.

14:18 Even with these words, they had difficulty keeping the crowd from sacrificing to them.NIV The impact of the miracle of the healed man was almost too strong to counter. The worshipers of Zeus refused to be deterred from worshiping these two "miracle workers." In spite of the message of the apostles, *they had difficulty* stopping what appeared to be a sacrificial ceremony. It is further testimony to the character of Paul and Barnabas that such was not allowed to happen.

14:19 But Jews came there from Antioch and Iconium and won over the crowds. Then they stoned Paul and dragged him out of the city, supposing that he was dead.NRSV A small Jewish contingent in Lystra may have informed Jews from *Antioch and Iconium* of the presence of these "troublemakers." The healing miracle would only have deepened the jealousy and heightened the resolve to take drastic action to rid themselves of them.

> Sometimes a majority simply means that all the fools are on the same side. *Claude McDonald*

The *Jews* were effective in wooing a manipulable crowd, winning them *over* to their view that the apostles and their movement should be fought. Paul was *stoned* and *dragged* out of the city, left for *dead.* According to Scripture records, this is the only time Paul was stoned (2 Corinthians 11:25). Nothing is said about what they did to Barnabas.

14:20 But as the believers stood around him, he got up and went back into the city. The next day he left with Barnabas for Derbe.NLT This is one of the most powerful moments in the whole book. Paul, surely bloody and bruised from the stoning he had just endured, surrounded by *believers* (maybe some who had just come to faith through his ministry), *got up and went back into the city.* Some writers believe that Luke's presentation of this scene sounds and feels like a miracle, but there is nothing in the text that dictates such. Certainly Paul experienced miracles in his life because he was filled with the Holy Spirit. This courageous messenger, who had faith-

> Perhaps to be able to explain suffering is the clearest indication of never having suffered. Sin, suffering, and sanctification are not problems of the mind, but facts of life— mysteries that awaken all other mysteries until the heart rests in God. *Oswald Chambers*

fully preached the Good News and had been hounded for it at every turn, got up, dusted himself off, and went back to work. Others would have quit, but not Paul. *The next day he left* for the next stop on his missionary journey—the town of *Derbe.*

Most of the grand truths of God have to be learned by trouble; they must be burned into us with the hot iron of affliction, otherwise we shall not truly receive them. No man is competent to judge in matters of the kingdom, until first he has been tried; since there are many things to be learned in the depths which we can never know in the heights.
Charles H. Spurgeon

PAUL AND BARNABAS RETURN TO ANTIOCH OF SYRIA / 14:21-28

Following a successful evangelistic campaign in Derbe, the missionaries backtracked through all the cities visited on their missionary journey. The goal was to strengthen the believers and to appoint elders in the churches.

Having done this, Paul and Barnabas returned to their home base in Antioch of Syria and reported to the church there.

This brief passage not only demonstrates God's grace and faithfulness, it also sets the stage for the coming controversy over the presence of newly converted Gentiles in a previously all-Jewish church.

HUMAN NATURE

The people in Lystra had thought that Paul and Barnabas were gods, and they wanted to offer sacrifices to them. Suddenly their adoration turned to anger, and they stoned Paul and left him for dead. That's human nature. Jesus understood how fickle crowds can be (John 2:24-25). When many people approve of us, we feel good, but that should never cloud our thinking or affect our decisions. We should not live to please the crowd—especially in our spiritual lives. Be like Jesus. Know the nature of the crowd, and don't put your trust in it. Put your trust in God alone.

14:21-22 After preaching the Good News in Derbe and making many disciples, Paul and Barnabas returned again to Lystra, Iconium, and Antioch of Pisidia, where they strengthened the believers. They encouraged them to continue in the faith, reminding them that they must enter into the Kingdom of God through many tribulations.[NLT] Paul and Barnabas once again preached *the Good News,* this time *in Derbe.* The phrase "making many disciples" shows that there was more than just an

ELDERS

Near the end of their first missionary journey Paul and Barnabas went back through the cities where they had ministered and "appointed elders in every church . . . turning them over to the care of the Lord" (14:23). What does the New Testament teach about the office of elder?

Meaning of term	The Greek term is *presbuteros,* meaning "older person"
Function/ role	To rule the church (Titus 1:7; 1Peter 5:2-3); to watch over/shepherd God's flock (Acts 20:28; 1 Peter 5:2; Hebrews 13:17); to teach the truths of God (1 Timothy 3:3; Titus 1:9) to the people of God
Qualifications	To be one "whose life cannot be spoken against. He must be faithful to his wife. He must exhibit self-control, live wisely, and have a good reputation. He must enjoy having guests in his home and must be able to teach. He must not be a heavy drinker or be violent. He must be gentle, peace loving, and not one who loves money. He must manage his own family well, with children who respect and obey him. For if a man cannot manage his own household, how can he take care of God's church? . . . not a new Christian, because he might be proud of being chosen so soon, and the Devil will use that pride to make him fall. Also, people outside the church must speak well of him so that he will not fall into the Devil's trap and be disgraced" (1 Timothy 3:2-7, NLT; see similar list in Titus 1:6-9)
Number of elders	A plurality of elders is described, if not prescribed in the New Testament (Acts 14:23; Philippians 1:1; Titus 1:5). Nowhere is a certain number mandated, however.
Length of term	The New Testament does not specifiy a precise term of eldership.
How elected	Those meeting the qualifications seem to be appointed or chosen by those already functioning as elders (Acts 14:23; Titus 1:5). Ordination to the office involved a ceremony that included laying on of hands, prayer, and fasting (Acts 14:23).
Proper response to	Obedience and submission (Hebrews 13:17; 1 Corinthians 16:16); respect (1 Thessalonians 5:12).
Discipline of elders	Accusations or criticisms against an elder should be received according to 1 Timothy 5:19-21. If the elder is guilty of an offense, he is to be counseled by fellow elders with a view toward restoration (Galatians 6:1-2).

evangelistic campaign in progress. There is no mention of opposition in Derbe. Perhaps that is why they were able to get to the discipleship phase of ministry.

Having reached the easternmost part of this first journey, as incredible as it must seem, Paul and Barnabas retraced their footsteps, returning *to Lystra, Iconium, and Antioch of Pisidia,* even to places where they had experienced rejection of the most violent sort! What a courageous pair! They went home the hard way!

The purpose of this return trip was mainly to strengthen *the believers* and encourage *them to continue in the faith.* Apparently, the believers left behind in these cities were facing persecution from the sources that had attacked Paul and Barnabas, for Paul had to tell them that *they must enter into the Kingdom of God through many tribulations.*

14:23 Paul and Barnabas appointed elders for them in each church and, with prayer and fasting, committed them to the Lord, in whom they had put their trust.[NIV] To evangelism and discipleship was added organization. The apostles established healthy churches in the areas where people responded to the gospel. They *appointed elders* (Greek *presbuterous*—the first reference to such in church history) *in each church.* The further explanation, *with prayer and fasting,* recalls the way this missionary team had been commissioned (13:3) and the meticulous spiritual process by which they proceeded through every major decision. The commissioning *(committed them to the Lord)* probably involved laying on of hands.

FACING RESPONSIBILITIES

Paul and Barnabas returned to visit the believers in all the cities where they had recently been threatened and physically attacked. These men knew the dangers they faced, yet they believed that they had a responsibility to encourage the new believers. No matter how inconvenient or uncomfortable the task may seem, we must always support new believers who need our help and encouragement. Whenever we do evangelism, we should have a clear strategy for follow-through care for new believers.

14:24-25 After going through Pisidia, they came into Pamphylia, and when they had preached the word in Perga, they went down to Attalia.[NIV] Paul and Barnabas had faced stoning in Lystra (14:19), a violent mob of Gentiles and Jews in Iconium (14:5), and a jealous, manipulating coalition of influential Jews in Antioch of Pisidia (13:50). Yet they retraced their footsteps exactly, returning to each place they had been. Their preaching *in Perga* most likely included the same prayerful selection and commissioning of elders mentioned in 14:23, as well as the strengthening of the believers and encouragement to continue in the faith mentioned in 14:22. Paul and Barnabas were thorough, loving, and faithful church planters and pastors (see 1 Thessalonians 1:8; 2:11-12).

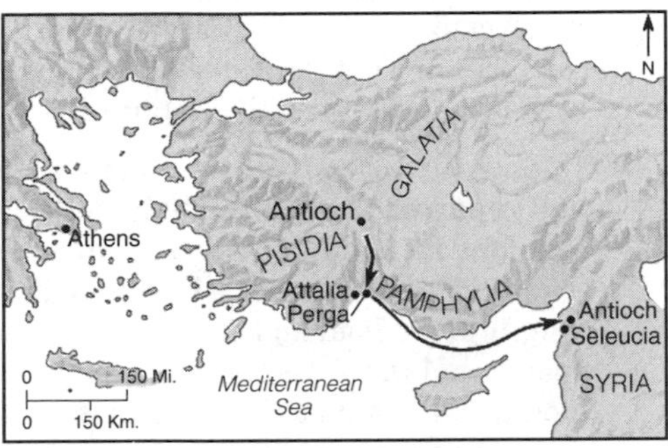

THE END OF THE FIRST JOURNEY
From Antioch in Pisidia, Paul and Barnabas went down the mountains back to Pamphylia on the coast. Stopping first in Perga, where they had landed, they went west to Attalia, the main port that sent goods from Asia to Syria and Egypt. There they found a ship bound for Seleucia, the port of Antioch in Syria. This ended their first missionary journey.

It seems that they had not preached in Perga on the outward leg of the journey. The record states only that John Mark had left them there (13:13). They may have left that region quickly and gone into higher ground because of sickness that had affected them. (This may have been the cause of John Mark's departure.) On the way back, however, they did minister in Perga.

LEADERSHIP
Part of the reason that Paul and Barnabas risked their lives to return to these cities was to organize the churches' leadership. They were not just following up on a loosely knit group; they were helping the believers get organized with spiritual leaders who could help them grow. Churches grow under Spirit-led leaders, both laypersons and pastors. Pray for your church leaders, and support them. And if God puts his finger on you, humbly accept the responsibility of a leadership role in your church.

14:26 Finally, they returned by ship to Antioch of Syria, where their journey had begun and where they had been committed to the grace of God for the work they had now completed.[NLT] *Finally,* from the port city of Attalia, they sailed back to *Antioch of Syria,* the point of their commissioning *to the grace of God* (see 13:1-3). The road-weary travelers had completed *the work* for which they had been sent.

And what a *journey* it had been! There were two more journeys yet to come in the book of Acts, plus a trip to Rome, and even these do not finish the story of Paul's ministry. All that had been *completed* was this first trip out.

14:27-28 Upon arriving in Antioch, they called the church together and reported about their trip, telling all that God had done and how he had opened the door of faith to the Gentiles, too. And they stayed there with the believers in Antioch for a long time.[NLT] Paul and Barnabas returned to their sending church in *Antioch* and *called the church together* to report about their trip. Even though Paul and Barnabas had been the active subjects of the story, they made it clear that the real work had been done by God. *God* was the one who *had opened the door of faith to the Gentiles.* Paul and Barnabas had witnessed it with their own eyes.

Imagine the rapt attention the two missionaries received at those meetings. They recounted the stories that Luke recorded—ships and sorcerers; Roman government officials coming to faith and powerful political enemies mounting a smear campaign; mob scenes; hurried getaways; one deadly time where Paul, at least, did not escape; the names and the faces. Surely Paul and Barnabas would speak at length about the new faces of those brand-new brothers and sisters in Christ and that privileged moment, repeated hundreds of times, when the spark of faith ignited into a roaring flame. Yes, there had been horrible difficulties, but none bad enough to erase the thrill of seeing that fire or frightening enough to diminish the resolve of finding more faces.

There were now churches needing prayer, elders to encourage, conflicts to manage, and heresies to challenge. God himself was beginning something great among the Gentiles, and this bloody but unbeaten team, sent by this praying church in Antioch, was determined to be a part of it!

They (Paul and Barnabas) *stayed there with the believers in Antioch for a long time.* This journey had probably taken the better part of a year and had aroused the interest of the Jerusalem church, who would want the apostles' report as well (see the next chapter).

Paul probably wrote his letter to the Galatians while he was staying in Antioch (A.D. 48 or 49) after completing his first missionary journey. There are several theories as to what part of Galatia Paul was addressing, but most agree that Iconium,

Lystra, and Derbe were part of that region for whom the letter was intended. Galatians was probably written before the Jerusalem council (chapter 15) because, in the letter, the question of whether Gentile believers should be required to follow Jewish law was not yet resolved. The council would meet to solve that problem, as recorded in the next chapter.

Acts 15

THE COUNCIL AT JERUSALEM / 15:1-21

As many Gentile believers came into the church, legalistic Jews demanded that these new converts be circumcised. Fierce arguing about this issue resulted in the first church council. At Jerusalem, the apostles and elders convened to consider the relationship between Jewish Christians and Gentile Christians, between Moses' law and the gospel of grace.

The council concluded, based on the Old Testament book of Amos (as expounded by James, leader of the proceedings), and in light of the experiences of both Peter and Paul, that Gentiles were accepted. Further, the council ruled that salvation depended solely on simple belief in Jesus, not on keeping the law of Moses.

15:1 **Some men came down from Judea to Antioch and were teaching the brothers: "Unless you are circumcised, according to the custom taught by Moses, you cannot be saved."**[NIV] These *men* were of a group called the Judaizers (see comments on 15:5). They came *from Judea* (perhaps from Jerusalem) *to Antioch;* they held the opinion that Gentiles could not be saved unless they were *circumcised.*

God had made the covenant of circumcision with Abraham (Genesis 17). This covenant was a sign of Abraham's and his descendants' obedience to God in all matters, and it signified the Jews as God's covenant people. Once circumcised, there was no turning back. The circumcised man would be identified as a Jew forever. More than any other practice, circumcision separated God's people from their pagan neighbors. The phrase "custom taught by Moses" refers to circumcision as part of the law (Moses wrote Genesis through Deuteronomy), but it had been originally given to Abraham through the covenant. Jesus said, "Because Moses gave you circumcision (though actually it did not come from Moses, but from the patriarchs), you circumcise a child on the Sabbath" (John 7:22 NIV).

The problem described in this verse involves the terms under which Gentiles could be admitted into the church. These Jews from Judea were not disputing that Gentiles could be saved. They were insisting, however, that Gentiles must adhere to the laws of Moses, including the physical rite of circumcision. In effect, this was tantamount to saying that Gentiles must first become Jews before they could become Christians.

These so-called Judaizers were not evil; unlike their hard-hearted and hateful Hebrew brothers who rejected Jesus, these legalists were sympathetic to the teachings of Jesus. In some way they had associated with the fledgling church. Although moral and God-fearing, Paul called them "false brothers," for their beliefs were far from the true gospel (Galatians 2:1-10).

To understand the Judaizers' actions, we need to understand their mind-set. They were steeped in the long and proud history of the Jews. Certainly the Hebrews were God's chosen people. God had given the Jews numerous advantages, blessings, and responsibilities. He had been faithful to them, even during their rebellious periods. And Jesus, their long-awaited Messiah, had come. Then they had experienced the bewildering and exciting events of Pentecost.

In the early days, all of the believers were Jews. In fact, the early church was viewed as a sect within Judaism. But soon Gentiles began putting their faith in Christ. Furthermore, Paul and his colleagues were intentionally seeking to bring Gentiles into the community of faith. To the strict Jews among them, this was acceptable, except that they believed Paul's message to be dangerously incomplete. Paul wasn't asking these Gentile converts to follow the old ways! He wasn't saying anything to these ex-pagans about circumcision and keeping the law! So the Judaizers set about to correct the problem. They believed that they had Scripture on their side (Genesis 17:14; Exodus 12:48-49). Even Jesus had said, "I did not come to abolish the law of Moses or the writings of the prophets. No, I came to fulfill them" (Matthew 5:17 NLT). Given all these presuppositions, the Judaizers concluded that Christianity was not intended to *bypass* Judaism but to *build* on it. Judaism, with its centuries of history and tradition, was the prerequisite. They saw Jesus (and his message) as the final step in the long process.

The Judaizers were afraid that soon there would be more Gentile than Jewish Christians. Also, they were afraid that moral standards among believers would be weakened if they did not follow Jewish laws. Paul, Barnabas, and the other church leaders believed that the Old Testament law was very important but that it was not a prerequisite to salvation. Their message was that the law cannot bring salvation; only by grace through faith in Jesus Christ can a person be saved.

JUDAIZERS VERSUS PAUL

As the debate raged between the Gentile Christians and the Judaizers, Paul found it necessary to write to the churches in Galatia. The Judaizers were trying to undermine Paul's authority. The debate over Jewish laws and Gentile Christians was officially resolved at the Jerusalem council.

What the Judaizers said about Paul	*Paul's defense*
They said he was perverting the truth.	He had received his message from Christ himself (Acts 9:15; Galatians 1:11-12).
They said he was a traitor to the Jewish faith.	He was one of the most dedicated Jews of his time. Yet in the midst of one of his most zealous acts, God had transformed him through a revelation of the Good News about Jesus (Acts 9:1-30; Galatians 1:13-16).
They said he compromised and diluted his message for the Gentiles.	The other apostles declared that the message Paul was preaching was the true gospel (Acts 9:28; Galatians 2:1-10).
They said he was disregarding the law of Moses.	Far from degrading the law, Paul put the law in its proper place. He wrote that it shows people where they have sinned and points them to Christ (Galatians 3:19-29).

15:2 Paul and Barnabas, disagreeing with them, argued forcefully and at length. Finally, Paul and Barnabas were sent to Jerusalem, accompanied by some local believers, to talk to the apostles and elders about this question.[NLT] This was no small difference of opinion. The Greek words for *disagreeing* and *argued forcefully* convey the idea of great strife, discord, disunion. They are translated elsewhere in the New Testament as "riot" or "insurrection"! This debate over circumcision and keeping the law was a major dispute, a serious theological and ecclesiastical crisis. The atmosphere was supercharged. If not handled wisely, the debate could have split the church. So *Paul and Barnabas were sent to Jerusalem* along with *some local believers.* They would meet with the *apostles and elders* in Jerusalem *about this question.*

Understanding the reason for Paul and Barnabas's going to Jerusalem to talk with the leaders requires knowledge of the events leading up to this theological and ecclesiastical crisis. By correlating and synthesizing the New Testament records, here is a likely chronology:

- Saul (Paul) was converted on the road to Damascus (9:1-19).
- Paul made his first postconversion visit to Jerusalem after he left Damascus (9:26-30).
- About three years later (after spending time in Arabia—see Galatians 1:17), Paul made a second visit to Jerusalem with Barnabas to bring relief to the Christians who were suffering because of the famine taking place there (11:27-30).
- It is likely that Paul met during this visit with the leaders of the Jerusalem church (Peter, James, and John) to consult with them about the message he was preaching. (This meeting is described in Galatians 2:1-10.)
- Paul and Barnabas then went on the first missionary journey (13:1-3).
- Paul and Barnabas returned to report to the church in Antioch (14:21-28).
- When Peter came to Antioch from Jerusalem, Paul confronted him about his refusal to eat with Gentiles when Jews were present (see Galatians 2:11-14).
- While in Antioch, Paul apparently had heard about the Judaizers (who were infiltrating the churches planted on the first journey), and then he met them (15:1-2). With that in mind (and perhaps also the recent behavior of Peter), Paul wrote the epistle to the Galatians (around A.D. 49).
- Paul then left with Barnabas for Jerusalem (to discuss this issue with the elders and apostles of the church). The meeting is recorded in this chapter.

FREEDOM IN CHRIST

The council at Jerusalem was convened to resolve the question of whether the Gentile believers should obey the law of Moses to be saved (15:1-2). This was a crucial question. The controversy intensified with the success of the new Gentile churches. The Judaizers in the Jerusalem church were led by converted Pharisees (15:5) who preferred a legalistic religion to one based on faith alone. If the Judaizers had won, the Gentiles would have been required to be circumcised and, in effect, converted to Judaism. This would have confined Christianity to simply being another sect within Judaism.

There is something of a "Pharisee" in each one of us. We may unwittingly mistake upholding tradition, structure, and legal requirements for obeying God. Make sure the gospel brings freedom and life, not rules and ceremonies, to those you are trying to reach.

15:3 The church sent the delegates to Jerusalem, and they stopped along the way in Phoenicia and Samaria to visit the believers. They told them—much to everyone's joy—that the Gentiles, too, were being converted.[NLT] On their journey to Jerusalem (a trip of about three hundred miles), Paul and Barnabas paid visits to several congregations. The church in Phoenicia was founded by believers who had fled from Jerusalem (11:19); Samaria had been evangelized by Philip (8:5). Rather than being alarmed at the news of the conversion of Gentiles, these believers expressed *much* (we get our English term "mega" from this Greek adjective *megalon*) *joy.*

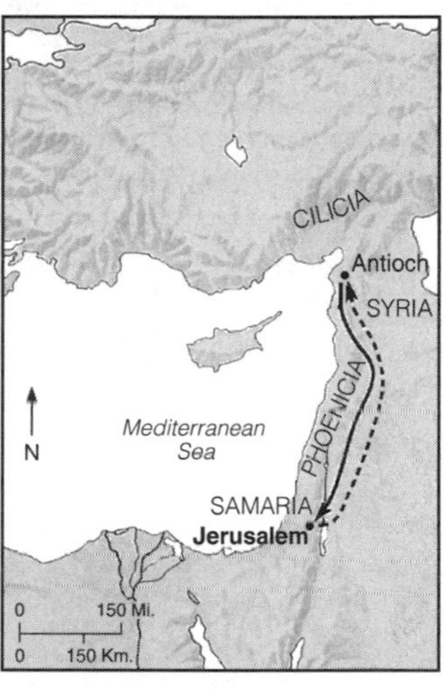

THE JERUSALEM COUNCIL
A dispute arose when some Judeans taught that Gentile believers had to be circumcised to be saved. Paul and Barnabas went to Jerusalem to discuss this situation with the leaders there. After the Jerusalem council made its decision, Paul and Barnabas returned to Antioch with the news.

15:4 When they arrived in Jerusalem, Paul and Barnabas were welcomed by the whole church, including the apostles and elders. They reported on what God had been doing through their ministry.[NLT] The language of the text suggests a public meeting. This group received Paul and Barnabas—they even welcomed them—although there were some in the group who still held a view far different than Paul's. Paul and Barnabas *reported* to the church that the events in question were things *God had been doing through their ministry.* The implication is that divine activity must indicate divine will. God surely would not be drawing the Gentiles to himself if he did not want them in his church or if they still had to fulfill other requirements before they could be saved.

15:5 Then some of the believers who belonged to the party of the Pharisees stood up and said, "The Gentiles must be circumcised and required to obey the law of Moses."[NIV] Called here *believers,* these Judaizers belonged *to the party of the Pharisees* and elsewhere are referred to as "false brothers" (Galatians 2:1-10). These Christians had been Pharisees before they converted (like Paul). They found themselves having compatible views with

THE FIRST CHURCH CONFERENCE

As long as most of the first Christians were Jewish, there was little difficulty in welcoming new believers; however, Gentiles (non-Jews) began to accept Jesus' offer of salvation. The evidence in their lives and the presence of God's Spirit in them showed that God was accepting them. Some of the early Christians believed that non-Jewish Christians needed to meet certain conditions before they could be worthy to accept Christ. The issue could have destroyed the church, so a conference was called in Jerusalem and the issue was formally settled there, although it continued to be a problem for many years following. Below is an outline of the three points of view at the conference.

Group	*Position*	*Reasons*
Judaizers (some Jewish Christians)	Gentiles must become Jewish first to be eligible for salvation.	1. They were devout, practicing Jews who found it difficult to set aside a tradition of gaining merit with God by keeping the law.
		2. They thought grace was too easy for the Gentiles.
		3. They were afraid of seeming too non-Jewish in the practice of their new faith—which could lead to persecution.
		4. The demands on the Gentiles were a way of maintaining control and authority in the movement.
Gentile Christians	Faith in Christ as Savior is the only requirement for salvation.	1. To submit to Jewish demands would be to doubt what God had already done for them by grace alone.
		2. They resisted exchanging a system of Jewish rituals for their pagan rituals, neither of which had power to save.
		3. They sought to obey Christ by baptism (rather than by circumcision) as a sign of their new faith.
Peter and James	Faith is the only requirement but there must be evidence of change by rejecting the old lifestyle.	1. They tried to distinguish between what was true from God's Word and what was just human tradition.
		2. They had Christ's command to preach to all the world.
		3. They wanted to preserve unity.
		4. They saw that Christianity could never survive as just a sect within Judaism.

Christianity because Pharisees believed in resurrection and in a Messiah, but many were reluctant to accept anyone who did not adhere to the oral tradition of law in addition to the Scriptures (Torah). Since only God knows the human heart, it is impossible to make a blanket statement regarding the eternal "destination" of this group. Probably some were sincere believers in the resurrection of Christ and his claim to be the Messiah (though obviously confused about the relationship between law and grace). Others likely were blindly trusting in their own moralistic efforts to make them acceptable to God. Still others may have been infiltrators with evil motives.

Whatever the "believers'" individual status before God, the common concern of all in the Judaizer camp was that all Gentile converts be *required to obey the law of Moses,* especially regarding circumcision.

15:6 **So the apostles and church elders got together to decide this question.**[NLT] The exact makeup of this council is unknown. Other apostles (besides Peter, Paul, and James) may have been summoned and present. Verses 12 and 22 indicate that this discussion took place in the presence of the entire congregation. But the clear implication is that the church leaders· *the apostles and church elders* (and not the whole assembly), deliberated and decided this volatile issue.

15:7 **After much discussion, Peter got up and addressed them: "Brothers, you know that some time ago God made a choice among you that the Gentiles might hear from my lips the message of the gospel and believe."**[NIV] The Gentile question prompted *much discussion.* Literally, the wording suggests that the delegates inquired, debated, questioned, and perhaps even argued. After lengthy interaction, *Peter* shared his experience of how God had used him to bring the *gospel* to the *Gentiles.* Specifically, he was referring to the incident described in chapter 10, where God had sovereignly led him to share the gospel with the Gentile Cornelius. If the Jerusalem council took place in about A.D. 50, then Peter was referring to an event that had occurred about ten years earlier.

15:8-9 **"God, who knows the heart, showed that he accepted them by giving the Holy Spirit to them, just as he did to us. He made no distinction between us and them, for he purified their hearts by faith."**[NIV] Jews considered Gentiles impure and required them to undergo proselyte baptism in order to convert to Judaism. Peter made it clear that God had purified Cornelius and his family as a result of faith alone. God had *made no distinction* between them as Gentiles and the Jewish believers (see 10:34-48). All kinds of people have access to forgiveness and eternal life through their faith in Christ.

Peter bolstered his argument by noting God's outpouring of the Spirit. The Gentiles had received the *Holy Spirit* when they believed *(by faith),* not because they had done any works of the law (see 10:44-46; Galatians 3:2). The presence of the Spirit in them was the clearest evidence of their acceptance by God (Romans 8:9).

HANDLING CONFLICT

It is helpful to see how the churches in Antioch and Jerusalem resolved their conflict:

- the church in Antioch sent a delegation to help seek a solution;
- the delegates met with the church leaders to give their reports and set another date to continue the discussion;
- Paul and Barnabas gave their report;
- James summarized the reports and drew up the decision;
- everyone agreed to abide by the decision;
- the council sent a letter with delegates back to Antioch to report the decision.

This is a wise way to handle conflicts within the church. Problems must be confronted, and all sides of the argument must be given a fair hearing. The discussion should be held in the presence of leaders who are spiritually mature and trustworthy to make wise decisions. Everyone should then abide by the decisions.

15:10-11 "Now therefore why are you putting God to the test by placing on the neck of the disciples a yoke that neither our ancestors nor we have been able to bear? On the contrary, we believe that we will be saved through the grace of the Lord Jesus, just as they will."NRSV Peter warned that by making strict adherence to the law a prerequisite for salvation, the church would be guilty of *putting God to the test* (that is, doubting his wisdom and plan and thus arrogantly pursuing a different course of action). Furthermore, the Jewish believers would be putting an unbearable *yoke* on the Gentiles. The word "yoke" was a common figurative term for religious "obligations." It was the heavy wooden harness used by oxen to pull carts or plows. Here it suggests less of a religious duty and more of an onerous burden (see Matthew 23:4; 11:28-30).

If the law was a yoke that *neither* the Jews of that day nor their *ancestors* had *been able to bear,* however, how did having the law help them throughout their history? Paul wrote that the law had been a guide that had pointed out their sins so they could repent and return to God and right living (see Galatians 3:24-25).

It was, and still is, impossible to obey the law completely. That would be a burden too hard for any human being.

In effect, Peter urged the council not to advocate a double standard. Salvation—whether for Jew or Gentile—is *through the grace of the Lord Jesus* (see Ephesians 2:8-9). What the law could never do, God did through Jesus Christ (Romans 8:1-4). "Grace" is God's kindness to us. People can do nothing to earn grace; it is simply given by God voluntarily to those he saves. No one deserves to be saved, and no religious, intellectual, or moral effort can earn salvation because it comes only from God's mercy and love. Without God's grace, no person can be saved. To receive God's salvation, people must acknowledge that they cannot save themselves and that only God can save them. Then they must trust in Christ.

15:12 **There was no further discussion, and everyone listened as Barnabas and Paul told about the miraculous signs and wonders God had done through them among the Gentiles.**[NLT] In much the same manner as Peter, Paul and Barnabas related their recent experiences in ministry among the Gentiles. What gave their presentation added authority was the report of *miraculous signs and wonders God had done through them among the Gentiles.* The missionaries gave full credit to God for these miracles. The Greek word for "signs" *(semeia)* suggests "miracles that point to a divine truth." "Wonders" *(teras)* are divine acts that produce awe. The clear implication is that these supernatural events signified God's endorsement and blessing of their ministry to non-Jews (see commentary on 14:3).

15:13-14 **When they had finished, James stood and said, "Brothers, listen to me. Peter has told you about the time God first visited the Gentiles to take from them a people for himself."**[NLT] ***James*** was Jesus' half brother and the writer of the Epistle of James (perhaps already written and distributed prior to this council). Very little is known about the relationship between James and Jesus when they lived in Joseph and Mary's home in Nazareth. It is known, however, that the townsfolk who saw Jesus as a boy and young man were amazed at his wisdom and miraculous power but rejected his adult claim to be the Messiah (Matthew 13:53-58). These skeptics included Jesus' own family. At one point in Jesus' ministry, his earthly family tried to stop him and restrain him (Mark 3:21); presumably James was one of the family members who claimed that Jesus was out of his mind. The apostle John reported, "Even His brothers did not believe in Him" (John 7:5 NKJV).

Yet just a few years after that incident, James became the leader of the church in Jerusalem (12:17). We don't know how

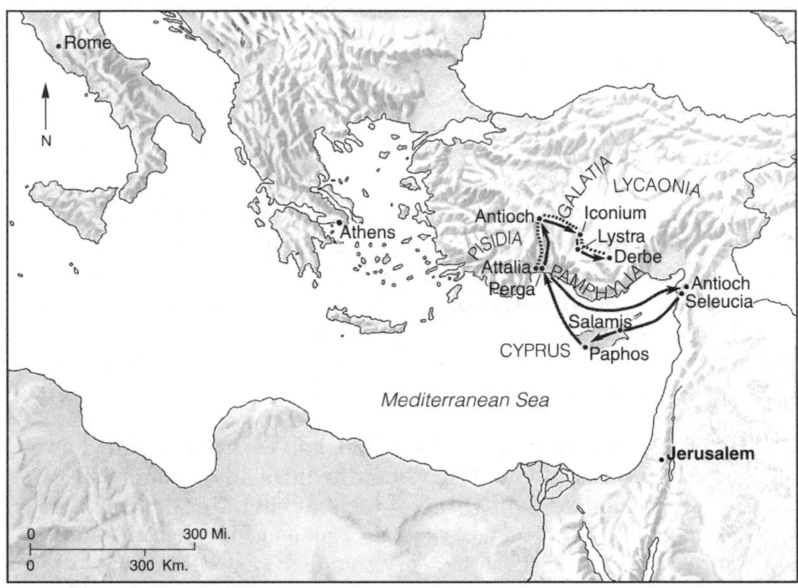

PAUL'S FIRST MISSIONARY JOURNEY (ACTS 13:1—14:28)

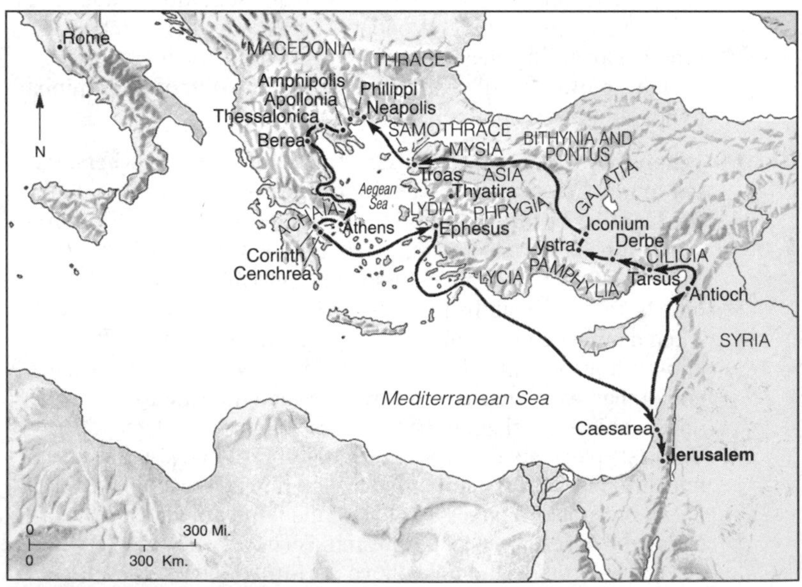

PAUL'S SECOND MISSIONARY JOURNEY (ACTS 15:36—18:22)

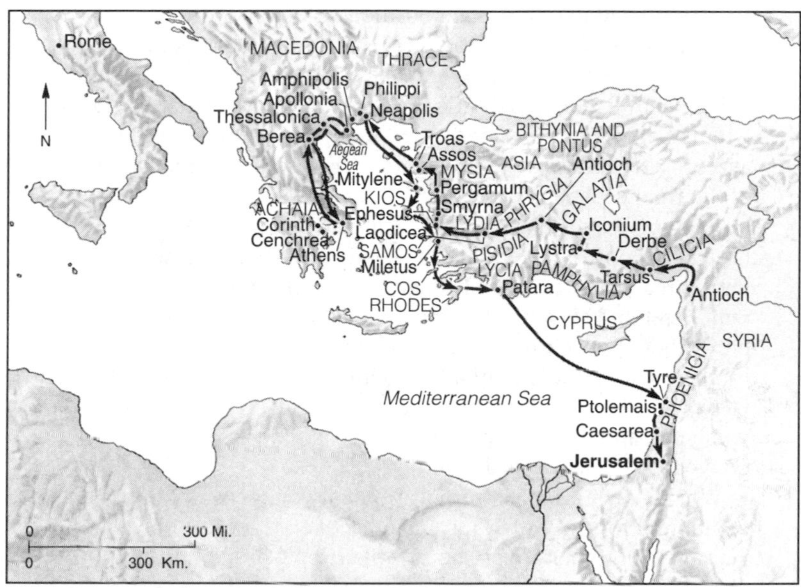

PAUL'S THIRD MISSIONARY JOURNEY (ACTS 18:23—21:16)

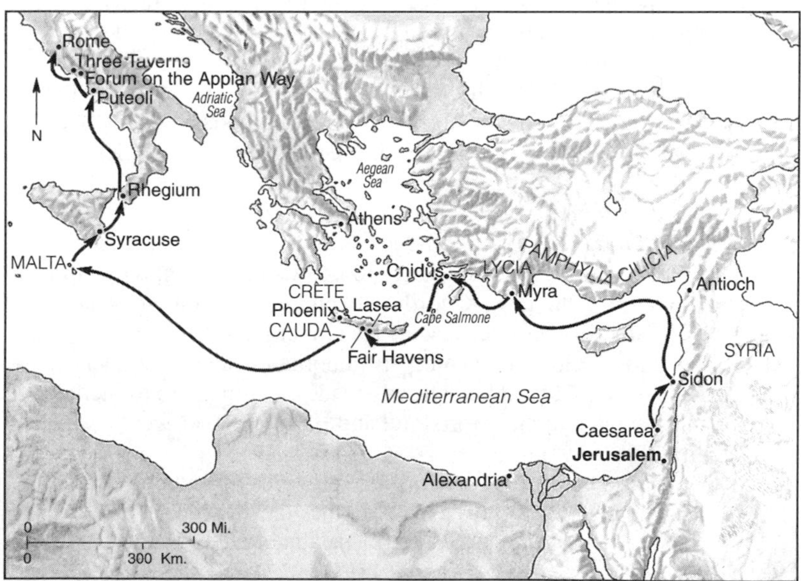

PAUL'S JOURNEY TO ROME (ACTS 21:17—28:31)

James attained that important position (Clement of Alexandria wrote that he was chosen for the office by Peter and John), but clearly he was the leader. When this controversy over Gentile believers threatened to divide the church, Barnabas and Paul met with the elders and apostles in Jerusalem and submitted to their authority to James as the moderator, spokesman, and announcer of the final decision.

That *this* James is the James mentioned earlier as Jesus' brother is confirmed by Paul in Galatians 1:18-19, "It was not until three years later that I finally went to Jerusalem for a visit with Peter and stayed there with him for fifteen days. And the only other apostle I met at that time was James, our Lord's brother" (NLT). Later Paul adds, "James, Peter, and John, who were known as pillars of the church, recognized the gift God had given me, and they accepted Barnabas and me as their co-workers" (Galatians 2:9 NLT).

What changed James from a skeptical younger brother to a committed follower of Jesus and outspoken leader of the church? He saw his brother alive—he saw the risen Christ! Writing to the Corinthians, Paul listed the eyewitnesses to the Resurrection: "I passed on to you what was most important and what had also been passed on to me—that Christ died for our sins, just as the Scriptures said. He was buried, and he was raised from the dead on the third day. . . . He was seen by Peter and then by the twelve apostles. After that, he was seen by more than five hundred of his followers at one time, most of whom are still alive, though some have died by now. Then he was seen by James and later by all the apostles. Last of all, I saw him, too" (1 Corinthians 15:3-8 NLT).

Then, after the Ascension, we find James with the apostles, Mary, and others, praying continually and waiting for the Holy Spirit as Jesus had told him to do (1:4-14). The description of events here suggests that, as the leader of the church in Jerusalem, James was highly respected and known for his righteous life and devotion to the law. According to church tradition, he was called "Camel Knees" because of his prayer habits.

The phrase "God first visited" is important because it underlines the truth that God had already made clear his plan to include Gentiles in the church before Paul and Barnabas ever went on the first missionary venture.

The phrase "a people for himself" (previously used only of the Jews as the people of God) here describes the Gentiles. This would have been heard as a remarkable statement by James.

15:15-18 "This agrees with the words of the prophets, as it is written, 'After this I will return, and I will rebuild the dwelling of

David, which has fallen; from its ruins I will rebuild it, and I will set it up, so that all other peoples may seek the Lord—even all the Gentiles over whom my name has been called. Thus says the Lord, who has been making these things known from long ago.'"NRSV Recognizing the need to base any forthcoming decision on something more substantial than mere experience, James went to the Scriptures. He demonstrated how all the events in question corresponded with the witness of the Old Testament prophets. This was the ultimate test.

Scholars have long wondered about this passage of Acts and the Old Testament quote it contains. James's quote includes a text different from the Hebrew text and different even from the Septuagint (an ancient Greek translation of the Old Testament). It is not clear why James did this, but it is obvious how he understood and applied this passage to the crisis facing the early church.

THE TEST OF TRUTH

Despite the compelling experiences of Peter, Barnabas, and Paul, James turned to God's Word as the ultimate test of truth (15:15-18). This should be the way we evaluate events. We all have beliefs (some of them fervent). We all have experiences. And the tendency is for us to want to measure others by our yardstick. It is common for believers to think that their experience, their conviction, is true and should be the norm. Different ideas are thought to be inferior or invalid. Ultimately, however, what matters is what God's Word says. The more we know God's Word, the more we read it and study it and memorize it and meditate on it, the better we will be able to discern what is right and best in times of controversy or doctrinal disagreement.

Without going so far as to explicitly say that this prophecy found in Amos 9:11-12 was being "fulfilled" in these events, James did say that what was happening in the church (God's obvious acceptance of the Gentiles and their genuine conversion and their inclusion in this new entity called the church) "agreed" completely with *the words of the prophets* that had been written long before in the Old Testament. In God's judgment *the dwelling of David* was reduced to *ruins.* God's covenant with David stated that one of David's descendants would always sit on his throne (2 Samuel 7:12-16). The exile of the Jews made this promise seem impossible. But *after this* God would *rebuild* and restore the kingdom to its promised glory. This was a promise to both Israel and Judah, not to be fulfilled by an earthly, political ruler but by the Messiah, who would renew the spiritual kingdom and rule forever. James quoted these verses, finding this promise fulfilled in Christ's resurrection and in the presence of both Jews and Gentiles in the church. *All other peoples may seek . . . even all the Gentiles* envisions the messianic kingdom, which will be universal and include the Gentile nations. When God bring in the Gentiles, he is restoring the ruins. After the Gentiles are called together, God will renew and restore the fortunes of the new Israel. All the land that was once under David's rule will again be part of God's nation.

DIVERSITY VERSUS UNITY
The early church experienced the difficulty of bringing together diverse peoples. Jews and Gentiles had so little in common! Different histories, traditions, practices, customs, cultures, languages. How do you possibly take such dissimilar groups and make them one? One solution is to say, "You don't." Instead, you rewrite the rules. You segregate, isolate, and study each other with suspicion and from a distance. This response profoundly affects both our effectiveness and attractiveness. When there is snobbery or a judgmental atmosphere, the church betrays the teachings of Christ and loses all appeal. The other solution is to submit our prejudices and presuppositions to the greater purposes of God. When we imitate him (Ephesians 5:1), we become tolerant, understanding, and accepting. However, such tolerance is not meant to include sinful lifestyles. James mentioned a few laws that the Gentile believers should keep, with an understanding that basic morality and living for God would cover the rest. When believers of different races, ethnic backgrounds, and social strata come together in love and worship of the Savior, nothing gives greater glory to God or provides a more compelling witness.

Even though James quoted just one prophet, Amos, he said "prophets" (plural), perhaps alluding to other written Scriptures, like Isaiah 2:2; 11:10; 25:8-9; and Zechariah 8:23. His main point was that Gentile salvation apart from the law does not in any way contradict the Old Testament Scriptures.

15:19-21 **"It is my judgment, therefore, that we should not make it difficult for the Gentiles who are turning to God. Instead we should write to them, telling them to abstain from food polluted by idols, from sexual immorality, from the meat of strangled animals and from blood. For Moses has been preached in every city from the earliest times and is read in the synagogues on every Sabbath."**NIV Without explicitly mentioning circumcision, James echoed Peter's argument by ruling that *we* (referring to the leaders in the church who were Jewish) *should not make it difficult* (literally, "annoy") *for the Gentiles* to become Christians and join the church. This was, in effect, a rejection of the circumcision requirement.

This judgment also included the stipulation that the Gentile converts should *abstain from food polluted by idols.* This was a problem in the New Testament churches whereby meat was first sacrificed to idols and then sold in butcher shops (see 1 Corinthians 8:1-13; 10:18-33). They were also to abstain *from sexual immorality,* which was often a part of idol worship, although this probably referred to the common Gentile violation of Levitical matrimonial laws against marrying close relatives. The prohibition here was probably meant regarding prohibited marriage relationships like incest and homosexuality (see Leviticus 18:6-20). Finally, they were not to eat the *meat of strangled animals* or to consume *blood.* This reflected the biblical teaching that life is in the blood. Strangling an animal would keep the blood in the circulatory system and not drained away, thus causing blood to be eaten with the meat (see Genesis 9:4; Leviticus 17:10-14).

THE SOURCE OF DIVISION

Like the early church, if believers today do their part to reach out to all who are lost, church congregations will eventually be comprised of people from different racial and cultural backgrounds. When this happens, we most often see our propensity to label and categorize. We are most comfortable with those who are just like us. Clearly, at the root of these tendencies is the ugly sin of prejudice. The more we understand the gospel and embrace God's version of the body of Christ, however, the more we will begin to transcend these differences. More than merely getting along, we will be able to honestly and authentically say from our hearts that we love each other.

If Gentile Christians would abstain from these practices, they would please God and get along better with their Jewish brothers and sisters in Christ. Of course, there were other actions inappropriate for believers, but the Jews were especially concerned about these four. This ruling reflected the law of love (described by Paul in 1 Corinthians 8–10). There was a sense in which the Jews needed to be patient with these new Gentile believers who were not familiar with all the Old Testament laws and rituals. And there was a sense in which the Gentiles needed to be sensitive to the Jews who were there first—being careful not to offend their weaker consciences.

THE LETTER FOR GENTILE BELIEVERS / 15:22-35

The Jerusalem council summarized in a letter its decision regarding Gentile circumcision. This letter was carried to Antioch of Syria by Judas and Silas. Paul and Barnabas accompanied these specially chosen messengers.

Essentially, the letter instructed the Gentile converts to strictly avoid idolatry, immorality, and eating the meat of strangled animals—activities, common among the Gentiles, that were especially offensive to Jewish sensibilities.

This directive brought joy to the believers at Antioch. The Jerusalem entourage stayed for a while, strengthening the believers and teaching the word of the Lord.

15:22 **Then the apostles and elders and the whole church in Jerusalem chose delegates, and they sent them to Antioch of Syria with Paul and Barnabas to report on this decision. The men chosen were two of the church leaders—Judas (also called Barsabbas) and Silas.**[NLT] The *apostles* did not hold a church office but a position and function based on specific gifts (see 1 Corinthians 12:28). *Elders* were appointed to lead and manage the local church. In this meeting, the apostles submitted to the judgment of an elder—James, Jesus' half brother.

> It is human to err, it is devilish to remain willfully in error. *Augustine*

A representative from the Jewish believers and one from the Gentile believers were appointed as *delegates* to go with Paul and Barnabas to deliver the council's decision to *Antioch of Syria* and the surrounding churches. *Judas* was a Jew; *Silas* was a Greek. They *were two of the church leaders* and are called "prophets" (see 15:32). Their presence together would give credence to the council's ruling. Later, Silas would accompany Paul on the second missionary journey in place of Barnabas, who would visit different cities with John Mark. Peter referred to Silas as the coauthor of 1 Peter (1 Peter 5:12), but it is not known when he joined Peter.

15:23 **With them they sent the following letter: The apostles and elders, your brothers, To the Gentile believers in Antioch, Syria and Cilicia: Greetings.**[NIV] This letter concisely summarized the findings of the Jerusalem council. It would serve to validate the verbal report that Paul, Barnabas, Judas, and Silas would be delivering *to the Gentile believers in Antioch, Syria and Cilicia.*

15:24-27 **Since we have heard that certain persons who have gone out from us, though with no instructions from us, have said things to disturb you and have unsettled your minds, we have decided unanimously to choose representatives and send**

them to you, along with our beloved Barnabas and Paul, who have risked their lives for the sake of our Lord Jesus Christ. We have therefore sent Judas and Silas, who themselves will tell you the same things by word of mouth.NRSV In this letter, the Jerusalem church disassociated itself from those *certain persons* who had been pressing for the circumcision of Gentile converts. Although the Judaizers had *gone out from* among the believers in Jerusalem, they had received *no instructions* from the apostles and had been acting without their approval. They were not to be regarded as spokesmen for the church. Rather, the men bringing the letter (Paul, Barnabas, Judas, and Silas) had been chosen as *representatives* of the church, with authority to speak on behalf of the elders and apostles.

DIFFERING CONVICTIONS

The early church faced a crisis because of its great diversity—people with wildly different backgrounds, beliefs, and behavior. The modern church also faces an ongoing crisis of diversity. Our congregations are filled with people who have wildly different convictions with regard to all kinds of behavior. Consider these often divisive issues (about which the Bible does not give black-and-white commands): drinking; going to movies; political party affiliation; home schooling; gambling; working on Sunday; TV viewing habits; credit card use; money borrowing; child-rearing practices; the recognition/celebration of certain holidays; stay-at-home moms vs. working moms; dating; preferences in music. We can let those differences divide us, but they don't have to. The New Testament reminds us of our freedom in Christ and our obligation to show love. Resist the urge to judge others. Do not be dogmatic where the Bible is not. Demonstrate grace.

The letter conveyed the unanimity of the leaders of the church in Jerusalem in these matters, as well as the great warmth and respect that the Jerusalem elders felt for Paul and Barnabas, who had *risked their lives for the sake of* the *Lord Jesus Christ.* The letter introduced *Judas and Silas* (see 15:22) who would also give their account of the decision made by the church leaders.

15:28-29 **For it seemed good to the Holy Spirit and to us to lay no greater burden on you than these requirements: You must abstain from eating food offered to idols, from consuming blood or eating the meat of strangled animals, and from sexual immorality. If you do this, you will do well. Farewell.**NLT The letter implies a clear leading of God in the decision rendered *(it seemed good to the Holy Spirit).* Two of the council's requirements involved issues of morality (avoiding idolatry and sexual immorality), and two involved issues of food. The dietary restrictions were because the early church often shared common meals (similar to modern-day church potluck dinners). Sometimes called "love feasts" and held in conjunction with the Lord's Supper (see 1 Corinthians 11:17-34), these meals would bring Jews and Gentiles together. In such settings, a Gentile might horrify the Jewish Christians by eating meat that was not kosher. In this compromise agreement, legalistic Jews no longer insisted that the Gentiles had to be circumcised to be saved, and the Gentiles accepted a change in their eating habits. These decisions should not be regarded as divine ordinances but rather as stipulations for fellowship between the two parties. Their concerns were not so much theological as practical. For more discussion on these four stipulations, see comments at 15:19-20.

False doctrine does not necessarily make a man a heretic, but an evil heart can make any doctrine heretical.
Samuel Taylor Coleridge

RESPONDING TO AUTHORITY
The decision by the Jerusalem council had great potential for trouble. The Jews could have balked—"That's *it?!* Only four requirements? No circumcision?" The Gentiles could have squawked—"What do you mean, give up our favorite foods? That's ridiculous! You elders caved in to the legalists! We thought Christianity was supposed to be based on liberty and freedom!" How believers responded to this decision would demonstrate to the world the real character of the church. Defiance would likely cause a split and give malcontents the courage to push their agendas. Submission by everyone would result in a close-knit, harmonious body that had a sense of order and stability.

15:30-31 **The four messengers went at once to Antioch, where they called a general meeting of the Christians and delivered the letter. And there was great joy throughout the church that day as they read this encouraging message.**[NLT] Luke painted a picture of a teachable, eager church in Antioch. Whereas the false teaching of the legalists had been burdensome and a source of great confusion, the divine wisdom behind the ruling of James and the elders resulted in a joyful, encouraged congregation. The law obligates; the gospel liberates.

The end result of the potential crisis was *great joy.* It's easy to see why. First, a wise and careful approach to conflict resolution

CHURCH CRISES: DANGEROUS OPPORTUNITIES!

The Chinese word for "crisis" consists of two letters: one means *danger* and the other means *opportunity*. Indeed, every church crisis involves a dangerous opportunity to bring either great glory or great shame to the name of Christ. Acts 15 is a good example of this truth.

Dangerous Opportunity?	*How Seen in Acts 15?*	*The Root of the Danger?*	*How to Avoid the Danger and Seize the Opportunity?*	*How the Situation Can Glorify God If Properly Handled?*
Disputes over doctrine	Judaizers wanted Gentile converts to be circumcised and to keep Mosaic law.	Presuppositions	Submit to the Word of God (rather than our own opinions).	Purity
Diversity in membership	Those from Jewish backgrounds (tending toward legalism) were in the same body with those from pagan backgrounds (tending toward license).	Prejudice	Submit to one another in love (rather than segregate from one another in suspicion).	Unity
Decisions by authority	Some Judaizers did not submit to the decision of the Jerusalem council; they defiantly continued their divisive campaign of deception and distortion (as seen in later epistles, such as Titus 1:10).	Pride	Submit to God-appointed leadership (rather than demanding and advancing our own agenda).	Humility

had been followed. Second, the leaders had ruled only after lengthy discussion and leading by the Spirit. Third, the members of the church had submitted to their God-appointed leadership. Churches today would be much happier and more peaceful if they followed these principles when handling conflict.

15:32-33 **Judas and Silas, who were themselves prophets, said much to encourage and strengthen the believers. After they had been there for some time, they were sent off in peace by the believers**

to those who had sent them.[NRSV] *Judas and Silas* remained in Antioch *for some time* and used their prophetic gifts (see commentary on 11:27-28) *to encourage and strengthen* the believers there. They then *were sent off in peace by the believers* and returned to Jerusalem.

I am quite sure that the best way to promote union is to promote truth. It will not do for us to be all united together by yielding to one another's mistakes.
C. H. Spurgeon

15:34 However, it seemed good to Silas to remain there.[NKJV] Several of the more reliable, ancient manuscripts do not contain this verse. It was most likely added by a later scribe attempting to solve the seeming discrepancy between Silas's departure (15:33) and his presence in Antioch (15:40). But in the process of trying to solve one problem, the anonymous scribe created another. Verse 34 contradicts verse 33. It must be assumed that Luke did not tell us that Silas returned to Jerusalem and then, later, was summoned to Antioch—probably by Paul.

WHY SUBMIT?
From the New Testament record, it appears that most of the church humbly submitted to the Jerusalem council's decision. Why is submission so hard? Why is it so important? It's difficult because we're not predisposed to accept authority. It grates on us to have to abide by others' decisions. But it's also *important* because God has designed the church to be guided by human leaders. Notice that the New Testament has high standards for who would be eligible to serve as elders (1 Timothy 3; Titus 1). Governing a church through appointed leaders does not always guarantee a perfect system— because it involves people—but it's a good system because if you have a number of individuals who are honestly trying to walk with God, listen to God, and do what God says, then the odds are good that the church will be led in a God-honoring fashion. Hebrews 13:17 says, "Obey your spiritual leaders and do what they say. Their work is to watch over your souls, and they know they are accountable to God. Give them reason to do this joyfully and not with sorrow. That would certainly not be for your benefit" (NLT). God has pledged to hold leaders accountable for their decisions. We will also give an account for how well we submit to their authority.

15:35 Paul and Barnabas stayed in Antioch to assist many others who were teaching and preaching the word of the Lord there.[NLT] The length of Paul and Barnabas's stay in Antioch is not known—"some days" (15:36) could indicate a period lasting as long as several months. The fact, however, that *many others* were ministering in Antioch opened up the opportunity for Paul to attempt another missionary endeavor.

PAUL AND BARNABAS SEPARATE / 15:36-41

When the time came for a second missionary journey, Barnabas and Paul had a sharp disagreement concerning John Mark. Barnabas wanted to take this young man, his nephew, but Paul refused, citing John Mark's desertion during the first evangelistic endeavor.

This incident demonstrates the sovereignty of God as two missionary teams were formed: Paul and Silas, and Barnabas and Mark. Even though no further word is given regarding the results of Barnabas and Mark's evangelistic efforts, we see kingdom messengers departing Antioch in two directions.

15:36 **After some days Paul said to Barnabas, "Come, let us return and visit the believers in every city where we proclaimed the word of the Lord and see how they are doing."**NRSV Paul wanted to take another trip, primarily to revisit the churches that had been established on the first missionary journey. Evangelism would prove to be a major component of Paul's mission, but establishing and equipping the *believers in every city* seem to have been his primary objectives (see Ephesians 4:11-12).

MINISTRY PRIORITIES

Paul never lost his great burden to preach the gospel (Romans 1:15; 15:20; 1 Corinthians 1:17; 9:16; Galatians 2:2). At the same time, however, he maintained a pastor's concern for the growth of his converts. Ministry is not *either* evangelism *or* edification; it is *both.* Christians have a dual role—to be both spiritual obstetricians and spiritual pediatricians. We help others become "born again" (John 3:3), and we aid them in growing up spiritually (1 Peter 2:2). We may have strengths in one area or the other, but like Paul, we should keep both goals in view.

15:37-38 **Barnabas agreed and wanted to take along John Mark. But Paul disagreed strongly, since John Mark had deserted them in Pamphylia and had not shared in their work.**NLT The grand plan of Paul and Barnabas to launch a follow-up campaign quickly unraveled when the topic of *John Mark* came up. The men disagreed over the inclusion of this young believer on another missionary trip. Paul adamantly did not want to take him along. Because he had *deserted* them on the first journey (13:13), Paul felt that he would be an unreliable person to have along. The debate between the old colleagues became heated—they *disagreed strongly.*

Why John Mark deserted has been a subject of great debate. He may have simply been homesick. He may have become afraid due to the opposition of certain parties to the gospel message. He may have intended to accompany Paul and Barnabas only as far as Pamphylia and had simply failed to communicate this fact.

Nevertheless, despite Mark's previous behavior, Barnabas saw great potential in this young man. Barnabas, the "encourager," as his name means, used that gift in developing this young man into someone who eventually would serve the church well, writing the Gospel of Mark as well as becoming a valuable help to Paul himself (see Colossians 4:10; 2 Timothy 4:11).

15:39 **Their disagreement over this was so sharp that they separated. Barnabas took John Mark with him and sailed for Cyprus.**[NLT] Barnabas and Paul's *disagreement* was *so sharp* that they ended up separating. Each formed his own missionary team. *Barnabas took John Mark* and sailed west to *Cyprus.* These two are not mentioned again in the book of Acts.

It is important to note that the disagreement was not about theology. Both men would continue to teach the true gospel message. Through this disagreement God doubled the missionary effort.

AGREEING TO DISAGREE
The disagreement over John Mark caused Paul and Barnabas to form separate ministry teams, opening up two missionary endeavors instead of one. Paul and Barnabas did not break fellowship or become bitter over this issue—Paul would later speak highly of Barnabas (1 Corinthians 9:6) and eventually be fully reconciled with Mark (Colossians 4:10). Here is a good reminder that God is able to work through our conflicts and disagreements. We will not always agree with our Christian brothers and sisters, but problems can sometimes be solved by working out agreements and letting God work.

15:40-41 **Paul chose Silas, and the believers sent them off, entrusting them to the Lord's grace. So they traveled throughout Syria and Cilicia to strengthen the churches there.**[NLT] Paul's second missionary journey, this time with *Silas* as his partner, began approximately three years after his first one ended. The two visited many of the cities covered on Paul's first journey, plus others. This journey would lay the groundwork for the church in Greece.

Silas had been involved in the Jerusalem council; he was one of the two men chosen to represent the Jerusalem church by taking the letter and decision back to Antioch (15:22). Paul, from the Antioch church, chose Silas, from the Jerusalem church, and they traveled together to many cities to spread the Good News. This teamwork demonstrated the church's unity after the decision at the Jerusalem council.

Acts 16

PAUL'S SECOND MISSIONARY JOURNEY / 16:1-5

The apostle Paul, concerned about the spiritual well-being of his Gentile children in the faith, took Silas and returned to the churches of Asia Minor. At Lystra, Paul met Timothy, who proved to be a beloved and dependable colleague. Together these men set about "from town to town" (16:4) to communicate the decision of the Jerusalem council and to strengthen the churches.

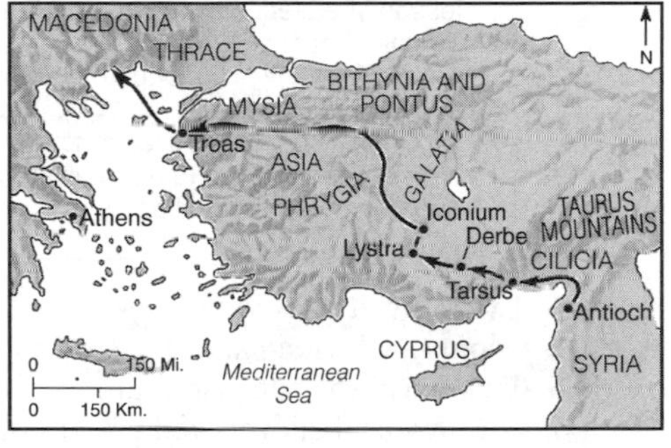

THE SECOND JOURNEY BEGINS
Paul and Silas set out on a second missionary journey to visit the cities Paul had preached in earlier. This time they set out by land rather than sea, traveling the Roman road through Cilicia and the Cilician Gates—a gorge through the Taurus Mountains—then northwest toward Derbe, Lystra, and Iconium. The Spirit told them not to go into Asia, so they turned northward toward Bithynia. Again the Spirit said no, so they turned west though Mysia to the harbor city of Troas.

Acts 16 records Paul and Silas embarking on what is called the second missionary journey. A few verses describe a quick trek over the cities of the first journey and a series of divine prohibitions about going in certain directions. Then Paul had a vision of a man in Macedonia calling out for help, and God's door swung wide open.

16:1 He came to Derbe and then to Lystra, where a disciple named Timothy lived, whose mother was a Jewess and a believer, but whose father was a Greek.[NIV] Acts 14:6-21 describes the rough treatment Paul and Barnabas had received during their last visit to the city of *Lystra.* That was where Paul had been stoned (likely the only stoning of his ministry), dragged out of the city, and left for dead. Paul had already gone back to that city once (14:21), and on this second journey, he returned again. If anyone ever doubted Paul's courage or tenacity, this verse ought to change that opinion! So concerned was Paul for the believers in these cities that he risked his life to make sure they were growing in the faith.

LEARNING FROM THE PAST
Shortly after his disappointing experience with John Mark, Paul recruited another eager young man, Timothy, to be his assistant. Some scholars speculate that Paul's intense personality was too much for John Mark to handle. If so, that quirk could easily have created the same problem in Paul's relationship with Timothy. But Paul seems to have learned a lesson in patience from his old friend Barnabas. As a result, Timothy became a "son" to Paul (see 1 Corinthians 4:17; 1 Timothy 1:2)—a lifelong colleague and friend. God speaks to us primarily through his Word but also in the midst of life's circumstances. He has lessons he wants us to learn about himself, about life, and about relating to others. Learn from prior experiences, and adjust your relational habits.

In Lystra lived *a disciple named Timothy.* Timothy probably had become a Christian after Paul's first visit to Lystra. Timothy had already had solid Jewish training in the Scriptures from his mother (a Jewish believer) and grandmother (see 2 Timothy 1:5; 3:15). When Paul arrived on this second journey, Timothy had grown into a respected disciple of Jesus.

Both this verse and the next one mention that Timothy's *father was a Greek.* The reason for mentioning this is explained in the following verse.

SPIRITUAL REPRODUCTION
Paul met Timothy at Derbe (16:1). Timothy is the first second-generation Christian mentioned in the New Testament. His mother, Eunice, and grandmother, Lois (2 Timothy 1:5; 3:15), had become believers and had faithfully influenced him for the Lord. Although Timothy's father apparently was not a Christian, the faithfulness of his mother and grandmother prevailed. Never underestimate the far-reaching consequences of raising one small child to love the Lord. Treat each child in your family or in your care as a potential Timothy.

16:2-3 Timothy was well thought of by the believers in Lystra and Iconium, so Paul wanted him to join them on their journey. In deference to the Jews of the area, he arranged for Timothy to be circumcised before they left, for everyone knew

that his father was a Greek.NLT Timothy's excellent reputation in the church *(well thought of by the believers)* and, evidently, Paul's need for an assistant like John Mark (see commentary at 13:5) compelled Paul to invite Timothy to *join them on their journey.*

Apparently, Timothy wanted to go, for he submitted to being *circumcised before they left*—clearly a mark of his commitment. Timothy was the son of a Jewish mother and Greek father. Under Jewish rabbinic law, since his mother was Jewish, Timothy was Jewish and needed to fulfill the covenant. So Paul asked Timothy to be circumcised in order to remove some of the stigma that might have hindered his effectiveness in ministering to Jewish believers. Timothy's mixed Greek/Jewish background could have created problems on their missionary journeys because many of their audiences would contain Jews who were concerned about keeping this tradition. Timothy's submission to the rite of circumcision helped to avoid that potential problem.

THE EXTRA STEP

As a Christian, Timothy was not required to be circumcised (the Jerusalem council had decided that—see chapter 15). Nevertheless, he voluntarily submitted himself to this to overcome any barriers to his witness for Christ. Sometimes we need to go beyond the minimum requirements in order to help our audience receive our testimony. What personal sacrifices would you be willing to make for the sake of the gospel?

Paul may appear to be inconsistent here with his teaching in Galatians 2:3-5, where he refused to let Titus be circumcised. This is easily resolved when considering the difference in the circumstances of the two situations. In Galatia, circumcision was being proclaimed (heretically!) as a method of justification. Paul wanted to clarify that it was not, so he intentionally left Titus uncircumcised to make his point. Here in Lystra, early on in his evangelistic endeavors, Paul was more intent on avoiding any potential offense that might hinder the spread of the gospel (see Romans 9:32-33; 1 Peter 2:8; 1 Corinthians 1:23; 9:19-23). Although the Jerusalem council had just ruled that circumcision was not necessary for Gentiles, Paul apparently thought that Timothy's mixed religious background might hinder his effectiveness. So, because Timothy was partly Jewish, he was circumcised. This was merely for effectiveness in spreading the gospel, not as a prerequisite for salvation.

16:4-5 Then they went from town to town, explaining the decision regarding the commandments that were to be obeyed, as decided by the apostles and elders in Jerusalem. So the churches were strengthened in their faith and grew daily in numbers.[NLT] At least one of the new items on the agenda of this trip was *explaining* the *decisions* (the Greek is plural—there were several issues ruled upon) *regarding the commandments that were to be obeyed,* as had been *decided by the apostles and elders* at the Jerusalem council (Acts 15). The Jewish/Gentile issues that had been decided at the council would likely arise again in the largely Gentile areas where Paul was traveling. Luke did not record which cities were visited, just that *they went from town to town.* The brevity of this report may have been in order to get on to the adventures of the new expansion of the gospel that would occur on this journey.

> Men make history and not the other way around. In periods where there is no leadership, society stinks still. *Harry Truman*

If Paul's letter to the Galatians was written between the first and second journeys (and before the Jerusalem council had met), Paul's instruction concerning the decisions of the council would further bolster the case he had made to these churches in that letter.

Another progress report indicates the completion of one section and the beginning of another (see commentary at 12:24). The term "strengthened" is the Greek word *estereounto,* which means "to be made solid or firm." Stability and growth *(grew daily in numbers)* were the marks of this healthy church, flourishing here as the church has done elsewhere through this book (2:47; 6:7; 9:31; 12:24). Rapid growth was important to this first part of the "Gentile" thrust of the gospel. Critics of Paul's Gentile-oriented ministry (especially the Jewish element) would be waiting greedily for an opening with which to shut Paul down or at least diminish his influence. Yet here, in the first real penetration of the gospel into the Gentile world, the church thrived in exactly the same way the mostly Jewish church had in its early days.

A CALL FROM MACEDONIA / 16:6-10

Forbidden by the Holy Spirit to go into the provinces of Asia and Bithynia, Paul and his companions were directed instead past Mysia to the city of Troas. There Paul had a divine vision instructing him to go to Macedonia. These supernatural events served to underline the sovereign guidance of God in Paul's evangelistic efforts. Sometime during the events described in this passage,

HOW GOD SOVEREIGNLY GUIDED HIS PEOPLE IN ACTS

Through direct revelation (1:4-5, 11; 8:29; 10:19; 13:2; 16:6-7; 20:23)

Through Scripture (1:20)

Through the casting of lots (1:23-26)

Through unexpected, supernatural acts (2:1-41)

Through the apostles' teaching (2:42)

Through judgment (5:1-11)

Through church "growing pains" (6:1-7)

Through persecution and evil opposition (7:54-8:1; 14:5-7; 20:3)

Through angelic messengers (8:26; 10:3-8; 27:22-26)

Through miraculous relocation (8:39)

Through direct, life-altering encounters with the risen Lord (9:39)

Through visions (9:10; 19:3-8, 9-16; 11:6; 16:9-10; 18:9-11; 23:11)

Through human messengers (9:17-19, 27-28)

Through times of intense prayer (10:9; 13:2)

Through bringing to their minds the words of the Lord (11:16)

Through prophetic utterances (11:28; 21:4; 10-12)

Through Spirit-led discussions among church leaders (15:1-31)

Through promptings by the Spirit (15:28; 19:21; 20:22)

Through closed doors (16:6-7)

Through favorable circumstances (19:8-11)

Through having them take advantage of civil rights (25:10-12)

Luke became part of Paul's entourage (see the pronoun "we" in 16:10).

16:6 **Next Paul and Silas traveled through the area of Phrygia and Galatia, because the Holy Spirit had told them not to go into the province of Asia at that time.**[NLT] The regions of *Phrygia and*

Galatia included much of modern-day Turkey, yet God, for reasons known only to him, did not allow the missionaries to go *into the province of Asia at that time.* "Asia" referred not to the continent but rather to the Roman province of that day by that name. In Paul's day Asia was the western part of what is today called Asia Minor. Ephesus probably would have been the leading city in this region. The gospel did soon make it to Ephesus (and the rest of Asia), but only in God's timing.

> He who cannot obey, must not command.
> *Ben Franklin*

The spread of the gospel was and always will be God's advancing program, not Paul's nor the apostles'. *The Holy Spirit* made the agenda and the travel itinerary, and *Paul and Silas* listened. We are told simply that the Holy Spirit *told them not to go* to the "province of Asia at that time." Eventually, these regions would be reached (see Acts 18:19–19:41; 1 Peter 1:1), but only in God's timing.

THE LEADING OF GOD

We don't know how the Holy Spirit told Paul that he and his companions should not go into Asia (16:6). It may have been through a prophet, a vision, an inner conviction, or some other circumstance. To know God's will does not mean we must hear an audible voice. He leads in different ways. When seeking God's will, (1) make sure your plan is in harmony with God's Word; (2) ask mature Christians for their advice; (3) check your own motives—are you seeking to do what you want, or what you think God wants?—and (4) pray for God to open and close the doors as he desires.

16:7-8 **When they came to the border of Mysia, they tried to enter Bithynia, but the Spirit of Jesus would not allow them to. So they passed by Mysia and went down to Troas.**[NIV] The travelers moved on *to the border of Mysia* and *tried to enter Bithynia,* a province just to the northeast of Asia, but again they were prohibited by God himself. The *Spirit of Jesus* is another name for the Holy Spirit (see Romans 8:9; Galatians 4:6; Philippians 1:19). The Holy Spirit had closed the door twice for Paul, so Paul must have wondered which geographical direction God wanted him to take in spreading the gospel. God's sovereign will over-

> Lord, day after day I thanked You for saying yes. But when have I genuinely thanked You for saying no? Yet I shudder to think of possible smears, the cumulative blots on my life had you not been sufficiently wise to say an unalterable, "NO."
> *Ruth Harms Caulkins*

ruled in this situation (see the chart, "How God Sovereignly Guided His People in Acts," page 275).

This group of missionaries was not sitting around waiting for some light to come on or some voice to speak before they began their work. Evidently, they were plowing until God told them to stop.

Like the obedient soldiers they were, Paul and Silas avoided Mysia and *went down to Troas.* There, at last, God opened the door.

DOING RIGHT/NOT DOING WRONG

As Paul and Silas learned by experience, the Holy Spirit guides Christians to the right places, and he also guides them away from the wrong places (6:6-8). As we seek God's will, it is important to know what God wants us to do and where he wants us to go, but it is equally important to know what God does not want us to do and where he does not want us to go. Someone has said that 90 percent of God's will for our lives is already revealed in the Bible. Are you aware of (and faithfully following) the instructions and prohibitions found in the pages of Scripture?

16:9-10 During the night Paul had a vision of a man of Macedonia standing and begging him, "Come over to Macedonia and help us." After Paul had seen the vision, we got ready at once to leave for Macedonia, concluding that God had called us to preach the gospel to them.[NIV] Finally God spoke. During the night, *Paul had a vision* in which he saw a *man of Macedonia* who was *standing and begging him* to *"Come over . . . and help us."* (See 9:10, 12; 10:3, 17; 18:9; 22:17 for other references of God communicating through visions.) Macedonia had been a Roman province since 146 B.C. and was located in what is today northern Greece.

> Alexander [the Great] had moved from west to east to conquer brilliantly and infuse [the world] . . . with everything Greek. Now a converted Jew was moving in the opposite direction, from Asia to Europe, to conquer for Christ. *Everett Harrison*

In the first of many sections where this occurs, Luke unobtrusively introduced his presence on this part of the journey by the simple use of the plural pronouns "we" and "us." The traveling group consisted at least of Paul, Silas, Timothy, and Luke. Clearly, Luke had experienced what he wrote.

This verse includes another overt reference to the sovereign direction of God for this Macedonian project. The whole Godhead is present in three verses: 16:6—"the Holy Spirit had told them" (NLT); 16:7—"the Spirit of Jesus would not allow"(NIV); and 16:10—"God had called us."

This anxious crew *got ready at once,* having drawn the obvious conclusion that God was behind the vision and that Macedonia had been prepared by God to respond to *the gospel.* Such would indeed be the case.

ADVENTURE HIGHLIGHTS FROM TIMOTHY'S LIFE
By God's grace, Paul saw great potential in Timothy. Paul demonstrated his confidence in Timothy by later entrusting him with important responsibilities:

- When Paul escaped to Athens from upheaval in Berea, Silas and Timothy remained behind, undoubtedly to continue to teach (Acts 17:10-15). Silas and Timothy later rejoined Paul in Corinth (Acts 18:1, 5).
- Paul remained in Ephesus but sent Timothy and Erastus (another assistant) on ahead into Macedonia (Acts 19:22).
- Timothy was in Corinth with Paul when Paul wrote his letter to the Romans (Romans 16:21).
- Paul sent Timothy to Thessalonica (1 Thessalonians 3:2); Timothy was also with Paul when Paul wrote to that church in response to the good news that Timothy had brought regarding the Thessalonians' faith (1 Thessalonians 1:1; 3:5).
- Timothy was with Paul when Paul wrote to the church in Philippi, and Timothy went as Paul's emissary to that church (Philippians 1:1; 2:19).
- Timothy was with Paul when Paul wrote his letters to the Colossians and to Philemon (Colossians 1:1; Philemon 1:1).

LYDIA OF PHILIPPI BELIEVES IN JESUS / 16:11-15

In response to the Macedonian call, Paul and his associates immediately boarded a ship at Troas and sailed across the Aegean Sea, landing at Neapolis, the port city for Philippi (in what is now northern Greece). Shortly after their arrival, the missionaries somehow learned of a group of God-fearing women who would meet each Sabbath on a riverbank to pray. After they spoke to these women, Lydia, a wealthy cloth merchant, embraced the gospel. She became the first European convert, and she hosted Paul and his entourage in her home during their ministry in Philippi.

Acts 16 highlights the stories of three individuals who became believers through Paul's ministry in Philippi: Lydia, the influential businesswoman (16:14), the demon-possessed slave girl (16:16-18), and the jailer (16:27-30). The gospel was affecting all strata of society, just as it does today.

16:11-12 We set sail from Troas and took a straight course to Samothrace, the following day to Neapolis, and from there to

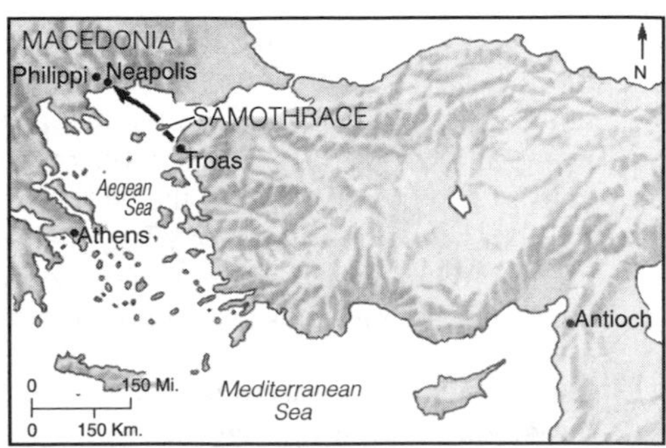

PAUL TRAVELS TO MACEDONIA
At Troas, Paul received the Macedonian call and he, Silas, Timothy, and Luke boarded a ship. They sailed to the island of Samothrace, then on to Neapolis, the port for the city of Philippi. Philippi sat on the Egnatian Way, a main transportation artery connecting the eastern provinces with Italy.

Philippi, which is a leading city of the district of Macedonia and a Roman colony. We remained in this city for some days.NRSV The travelers made their way across the upper portion of the Aegean Sea from *Troas* to *Samothrace* (a small island in the Aegean), then on to *Neapolis,* the port city for *Philippi.* From Neapolis, Philippi was a ten-mile journey inland.

Philippi was the *leading city of the* region of *Macedonia* (northern Greece today), although it was not the capital city. With mountains on every side and its port city of Neapolis on the Aegean Sea, Philippi had originally been a strategic site in the Greek Empire. Gold had been discovered at Mount Pangaeum to the west, tempting settlers from the Aegean island of Thasos to seize the area. They founded a city near the site of Philippi, naming it Krenides (meaning "spring") for the spring-fed marshlands in the valley.

When Philip II of Macedon (the father of Alexander the Great) ascended the throne of the Greek Empire, he captured the city (in about 357 B.C.), enlarged and strengthened it, and gave it his name. Philip used the yield of the gold mines to outfit his army.

In 168 B.C., the Romans conquered Macedonia. The mountain's gold was exhausted, and the city declined. But in 42 B.C., the city became a Roman colony. On the plains surrounding the city, Augustus defeated Brutus and Cassius (assassinators of Julius Caesar). He then gave the city the status of a *Roman colony* to celebrate his victory. A colony was considered a part of Rome itself. Its people were Roman citizens (a standing that carried high privilege), had the right to vote, were governed by their own senate, and had Roman laws and the Latin language. Later, the city received the right to the Law of Italy, giving it many privileges and immunities—most significantly, immunity from taxation. Philippi was also a garrison city with a Roman garrison stationed there to keep it secure. The Philippians were proud of their Roman heritage and standing. Philippi also boasted a fine school of medicine. Luke may have attended medical school in Philippi. Later, Paul would write a letter to the church he started in this city—the book of Philippians (probably from prison in Rome around A.D. 61). The letter is personal and tender, showing Paul's deep friendship with the believers there. The ministry in Philippi would be significant. The positive response to the gospel in this city, as described in the next few verses, was likely the reason for the missions team remaining there *for some days.*

16:13 **On the Sabbath we went a little way outside the city to a riverbank, where we supposed that some people met for prayer, and we sat down to speak with some women who had come together.**NLT Inscribed on the arches outside the city of Philippi was a prohibition against bringing an unrecognized religion into the city; this may have been the reason for the prayer meeting being held outside the city, on *a riverbank.* Ten Jewish males were necessary in a location to establish a synagogue. It appears there was no synagogue in Philippi, forcing Paul and his companions to search for the seekers of God elsewhere. They *supposed that some people met for prayer* at a location by the river (the Gangites River was a mile or so west of the city), and they did find and *speak with some women* there who had gathered for prayer. Jews typically gathered by rivers for prayer when a local synagogue was not available.

Paul's first evangelistic contact in Macedonia was with a small group of women. Paul never allowed gender or cultural differences to keep him from preaching the gospel. He presented the gospel to these women, and Lydia, an influential merchant, believed. This opened the way for ministry in that region. In the early church, God often worked in and through women.

THE ROLE OF WOMEN

The Bible is filled with examples of women who were greatly used by God—Deborah, Ruth, Hannah, Esther, Mary, Priscilla, and Lydia (to name just a few). In contrast to cultural standards where women were often treated as property or at least as second-class citizens, the Judeo-Christian ethic elevated women to a previously unheard-of status. Nowhere is this better seen than in Paul's shocking declaration in Galatians 3:28: "There is no longer Jew or Gentile, slave or free, male or female. For you are all Christians—you are one in Christ Jesus" (NLT). If the church is to become what God intends, women must be allowed to utilize their God-given gifts in keeping with the teaching of the New Testament.

16:14 **One of those listening was a woman named Lydia, a dealer in purple cloth from the city of Thyatira, who was a worshiper**

of God. The Lord opened her heart to respond to Paul's message.[NIV] *Lydia* was *a dealer in purple cloth,* a valuable and expensive material often worn as a sign of nobility or royalty. Lydia may have been a wealthy businesswoman. She was obviously a person of means, since she had guest rooms (16:15) and servants. Greek women of Lydia's day held elevated status and were able to conduct business and hold honorary public titles. *Thyatira* was a city known for its commerce, so Lydia may have brought her business to Philippi from there.

Lydia was *a worshiper of God.* This is similar to the almost technical description of Gentiles who were not official proselytes to Judaism but who did worship the God of Abraham (see the commentary on Cornelius at 10:2). Lydia was sincerely seeking the Lord, and the Lord was about to meet her. God was at work, for he *opened her heart to respond.*

THE MINISTRY OF HOSPITALITY
Lydia practically begged for the opportunity to host Paul and Silas in her home (16:15). Rather than seeing the apostles as a burden and their presence as a disruption of her family's routine, Lydia laid out the welcome mat. The notion of hospitality is related to the words "hospital" and "hospice." In other words, we practice hospitality when we generously and cordially throw open the doors of our homes to care for others. In hospitality, we nurture and strengthen and serve. And the result is that others find physical, spiritual, and emotional help. When they leave us, they are healthier and more whole than when they came. Is this your practice? Is your home a "hospital" for hurting or needy souls?

16:15 She was baptized along with other members of her household, and she asked us to be her guests. "If you agree that I am faithful to the Lord," she said, "come and stay at my home." And she urged us until we did.[NLT] After Lydia's conversion, *she was baptized along with other members of her household.* These same words are used to describe other conversions in Acts—Cornelius in 10:24, 44; the Philippian jailer in 16:31; and Crispus in 18:8 (see also Romans 16:10-11; 1 Corinthians 1:16). The other members of Lydia's household may have included servants as well as children. It is assumed, of course, that only those who truly had come to believe in Christ were baptized. As is commonly the case, however, the Lord may have reached whole families through the salvation of one of the members who shared the Good News with the other family members.

Baptism was a public sign of identification with Christ and the

Christian community. Although all members of Lydia's household may not have chosen to follow Christ, it had become a Christian home. One of the clues for thinking that Lydia was wealthy is the reference to "other members of her household" and the fact that she could easily accommodate at least four guests in her home at a moment's notice. Lydia's sincerity and the genuineness of her conversion appear in her invitation to the missionaries to use her house as their home base while in Philippi. Lydia convinced the travelers to stay at her home. She *urged* them until they gave in.

PAUL AND SILAS IN PRISON / 16:16-40

While in Philippi, Paul's missionary team encountered a demon-possessed slave girl who continually attempted to disrupt their ministry. When an exasperated Paul commanded the evil spirit to come out of her, the girl lost her fortune-telling ability. This infuriated her masters, who had Paul and Silas dragged before the city authorities and thrown in prison.

God used an earthquake to free his servants and bring about the salvation of the Philippian jailer and his family. The next day, after the city officials learned that they had unlawfully beaten and jailed two Roman citizens, they apologized and begged Paul and Silas to leave the city. They did so after a final visit with Lydia and the believers at her home. Despite opposition, the gospel continued to spread powerfully to all the strata of society

16:16 **One day as we were going down to the place of prayer, we met a demon-possessed slave girl. She was a fortune-teller who earned a lot of money for her masters.**[NLT] Luke continued his firsthand account of the events in Philippi *(we were going, we met).* Evidently, the *place of prayer* by the river continued as the spot where Paul and his companions would meet on a regular basis. There were likely many contacts, but Luke chose to describe only two others.

The next recorded contact by Paul came from a significantly different level of society. This verse describes the missionaries meeting a *slave girl.* Worse still, she was *demon-possessed* (see commentary on 5:15-16 for more on demon possession). Fortune-telling was common in Greek and Roman culture. People used many superstitious

> Their property held them in chains which shackled their courage and choked their faith and hampered their judgment and throttled their souls. If they had stored up their treasure in heaven, they would not be enslaved as they are to their own property. They are not the master of their money, but its slaves. *Bishop Cypria*

methods for trying to see the future—from interpreting omens in nature to communicating with the spirits of the dead. This young slave girl had an evil spirit, and she made her masters rich by interpreting signs and by fortune-telling. *Her masters* were exploiting her unfortunate condition for personal gain.

16:17 **This girl followed Paul and the rest of us, shouting, "These men are servants of the Most High God, who are telling you the way to be saved."**NIV What the slave girl said was true, although the source of her knowledge was a demon. Paul and his companions indeed were *servants of the Most High God* and, in fact, were telling others *the way to be saved.* Why did a demon announce the truth about Paul, and why did this annoy Paul? If Paul accepted the demon's words, he would appear to be linking the gospel with demon-related activities, not to mention the prophecy-for-profit approach that this girl's owners had taken. Such association would damage the message of Christ.

16:18 **She kept this up for many days. Finally Paul became so troubled that he turned around and said to the spirit, "In the name of Jesus Christ I command you to come out of her!" At that moment the spirit left her.**NIV Evidently, the young girl followed them every day as they made their way from Lydia's home to the place of prayer down by the river (or wherever else they went). *Finally Paul became so troubled* that he directly rebuked *the spirit* that was abusing the girl. Using the powerful *name of Jesus Christ,* Paul commanded the demon to depart. And *at that moment the spirit left her* (compare this with similar successes over demonic powers recorded in 8:9-24; 19:13-20).

HANDLING IRRITATIONS

The servant girl was annoying Paul and Silas, disrupting their ministry. Filled with frustration, Paul nevertheless responded in a Christlike fashion. He resisted the urge to react. Instead, he relied on the power of Christ to do something that would both glorify God and help the poor woman. This is a good reminder of how we should respond in troubling and vexing situations. Though we are tempted to lose our temper, we need to wait on God for a clear sense of his leading. When we let him guide, the end result is always better for all parties.

16:19 **But when her owners saw that their hope of making money was gone, they seized Paul and Silas and dragged them into the marketplace before the authorities.**NRSV The *owners* were angry with Paul. They had been using the servant girl and her demonic powers solely for *making money.* With cold heartlessness, they were not arguing about the young girl's cure but were infuriated that their business venture had been ruined. So they *dragged* Paul and Silas into *the marketplace before the authorities,* where they would seek their own brand of justice.

HIT IN THE WALLET

Faced with the loss of their slave girl's fortune-telling ability, the Philippian entrepreneurs were furious (16:19). Never mind that Paul and Silas were speaking eternal truths, never mind that the poor slave girl had been delivered from an awful existence; these men could only bemoan their economic loss! The gospel would also later hurt Ephesian idol makers financially (chapter 19), resulting in a citywide riot. When people care more about their own economic well-being than the glory of God and the salvation of lost souls, it is a clear sign of idolatry, greed, and worldliness.

16:20-21 They brought them before the magistrates and said, "These men are Jews, and are throwing our city into an uproar by advocating customs unlawful for us Romans to accept or practice."NIV These *magistrates* were obviously the "authorities" of 16:19. Each Roman colony had two of these "governors" over them. Paul and Silas were brought before them for some form of a trial.

The charge was not that they had performed an exorcism on a slave girl, but rather that these men were *Jews* and were *throwing* the *city into an uproar.* The mention of the men's Jewish roots was likely to arouse some of the anti-Semitic prejudice that was present in this Roman colony and may explain why Luke and Timothy (both at least part Gentile) were not accused.

The disruption of the city is said to be because of Paul and Silas's *advocating customs unlawful* for Romans. These two government officials would be interested in keeping the peace (an important aspect of their job in a Roman colony) as well as enforcing the laws against foreign religions proselytizing Romans in a Roman colony. They were interpreting the law to say that the exorcism was proselytizing Judaism. Thus, the accusations were effective.

16:22 A mob quickly formed against Paul and Silas, and the city officials ordered them stripped and beaten with wooden rods.NLT The twisting of the truth by these accusers was effective enough to motivate *a mob* to assemble *quickly.* This only gave credence to the accusation that Paul and Silas were "throwing the city into an uproar" (16:20).

Wanting to keep the peace, the *city officials ordered* Paul and

Silas to be *stripped and beaten with wooden rods.* Rods were wooden poles bound together and carried by these magistrates. The rods were used to beat offenders. This was not the only time that such had happened (or would happen) to Paul. He wrote in 2 Corinthians 11:25 that it happened three times—at least three up until the writing of that letter to Corinth.

16:23-24 **After they had given them a severe flogging, they threw them into prison and ordered the jailer to keep them securely. Following these instructions, he put them in the innermost cell and fastened their feet in the stocks.**NRSV After the *severe flogging,* Paul and Silas were thrown in prison, and Luke subtly introduced the next unsuspecting convert to Christianity—*the jailer*—who was ordered to *keep them securely.* Perhaps the stories of Christians mysteriously escaping from jail (12:3-17) or even of guards losing their lives (12:18-19) had made it as far as Philippi. Whatever the case, the jailer imposed his version of maximum security—taking them to the heart of his prison *(the innermost cell)* and there fastening *their feet in the stocks.*

"Stocks" were made of two boards joined with iron clamps, leaving holes just big enough for the ankles. The prisoner's legs were placed across the lower board, and then the upper board was closed over them. Sometimes both wrists and ankles were placed in stocks. Paul and Silas, who had committed no crime and were peaceful men, were put in stocks designed for holding the most dangerous prisoners in absolute security.

16:25 **Around midnight, Paul and Silas were praying and singing hymns to God, and the other prisoners were listening.**NLT What an incredible scene this must have been! *Paul and Silas* were barely into their first stop on what promised to be a wildly effective Macedonian evangelistic campaign—God had verbally called them there (16:9-10). In short order, however, they found themselves the victims of false and prejudicial charges, locked up in the depths of a Roman jail, in stocks! So what did they do? Moan? Whine? Blame God? Give up? No, their jail term was marked by only two activities: *praying and singing hymns to God.*

> The legs feel nothing in the stocks when the heart is in heaven. *Tertullian*

The other prisoners were listening as Paul and Silas sang and prayed. The Greek word for "listening" *(epekroonto)* is a strong word implying that the prisoners were listening intently. It is a reminder to all believers that the world is watching when they suffer. There is intrigue, interest, and even openness to believers' "answers" when they respond so unnaturally—so supernaturally—to difficulties. How believers respond to their troubles can play a major role in how others will respond to the Savior.

CHOOSING TO WORSHIP
Paul and Silas were stripped, beaten, and placed in stocks in the inner cell. Despite this dismal situation, they praised God, praying and singing as the other prisoners listened (16:22-25). Did they "feel" like worshiping? Probably not. They were likely aching, tired, and scared. But they were determined to give glory to God, who they trusted was in control of their situation. They clung to the hard-to-understand truth previously announced by Jesus: "Blessed are you when people insult you, persecute you and falsely say all kinds of evil against you because of me" (Matthew 5:11 NIV). The radical response to worship was a decision of their will. No matter what our circumstances, we can choose to praise God. Others may even come to Christ because of our example.

16:26 **Suddenly, there was a great earthquake, and the prison was shaken to its foundations. All the doors flew open, and the chains of every prisoner fell off!**NLT The answer to the prayers of Paul and Silas came with suddenness and authority in the form of a *great earthquake* (Greek *seismos megas*), shaking the *foundations* of the prison, bursting open doors, and breaking loose the *chains of every prisoner* in the place. Sometimes it pays just to be standing near when God pours his grace from heaven. There's always so much that it spills over on everybody who is even close by (see Ephesians 1:7; Romans 5:17; 1 Timothy 1:14).

16:27-28 **The jailer woke up to see the prison doors wide open. He assumed the prisoners had escaped, so he drew his sword to kill himself. But Paul shouted to him, "Don't do it! We are all here!"**NLT Guards were responsible for their prisoners and would be held accountable for their escape. The punishment was usually the same sentence that would have been the prisoner's. Sometimes the guards were even executed (see 12:19). Possibly in order to avoid a Roman execution or perhaps to avoid having to live with the shame of his career failure, the *jailer . . . drew his sword to kill himself.*

Paul intervened, shouting, *"We are all here!"* Paul was not speaking of just himself and Silas but of all the prisoners. All the prisoners were still there, sitting in a wide open jail, without chains. Why would the other prisoners not have fled the moment the doors were open? Perhaps they wanted to stay and learn more about this God who could shake a prison to its foundations. Most likely, God kept them there. The other prisoners had listened intently to all that had been prayed and sung (16:25). They knew that the earthquake surely had something to do with the praying and singing of the two prisoners.

These freshly liberated prisoners were now held captive by something stronger than chains—they wanted to know more about this God who could shake the world. They would not have to wait for long.

16:29-30 **Then he called for a light, ran in, and fell down trembling before Paul and Silas. And he brought them out and said, "Sirs, what must I do to be saved?"**NKJV The jailer *called for a light.* A torch was needed to see into the unlit prison. Once inside, the jailer *fell down trembling before Paul and Silas.* Then he *brought them out,* evidently from the inner recesses where the stocks were located. He asked the question, the most profound and important question in life, *"What must I do to be saved?"*

SALVATION, PURE AND SIMPLE

Stunned by the unearthly behavior of Paul and Silas, and terrified by the earthquake and the possible consequences of escaping prisoners, the jailer despaired of his life. Then, realizing his own true condition and need, he risked every- thing to find the answer. The problem was he thought he could "do" something to find deliverance. The Christian good news of salvation was simply expressed by Paul and Silas: "Believe on the Lord Jesus Christ, and you will be saved" (see Romans 10:9; 1 Corinthians 12:3; Ephesians 2:8-9; Philippians 2:11). When we recognize Jesus as Lord and trust in him with our entire lives, salvation is assured. There is nothing we can do to make it happen. We must simply accept what Jesus has done.

16:31-32 **So they said, "Believe on the Lord Jesus Christ, and you will be saved, you and your household." Then they spoke the word of the Lord to him and to all who were in his house.**NKJV This is the profound and important answer to the most profound and important question of the previous verse. The answer to the jailer's query is *"Believe."* This is not just faith for faith's sake; it is faith with a very serious object. It is belief *on the Lord Jesus Christ.* The result is that *you will be saved.*

The application of such a message was broader than just the jailer. It was relevant to his whole *household.* It was also relevant to the whole group of unfettered prisoners who were surely listening with rapt attention. It was relevant to their households as well (though we are never told whether they were rechained or not). Luke included the interesting phrase *they spoke the word of the Lord to him* to summarize the rest of what Paul and Silas said to the jailer.

Paul and Silas spoke also to the jailer's family *(all who were in his house).* Behind this whole scene echoes the promise of the Savior in 1:8: "You will be my witnesses." Surely no one who heard Jesus that day would have ever believed that one of those places of witness would be a Philippian prison stockade freshly opened by a heaven-sent earthquake.

16:33-34 **That same hour the jailer washed their wounds, and he and everyone in his household were immediately baptized. Then he brought them into his house and set a meal before them. He and his entire household rejoiced because they all believed in God.**NLT The jailer's conversion, like Lydia's, was followed by clear, demonstrated deeds reflecting the reality of the life-change that had occurred internally.

The terms "that same hour" and "immediately" show that the new convert did not waste any time about changing his life or about making his public profession of allegiance to Jesus Christ through baptism. Those in his *household* who became believers were baptized as well.

Afterward, the *entire household rejoiced because they all believed in God.* Who in that household could ever have dreamed that one of their father's prisoners, bound in chains, would one day bring a message that would set them all free from their sin?

A FAMILY AFFAIR

Paul and Silas took the family unit seriously. So the offer of salvation was made to the jailer's entire household—family and servants (16:32). Yet it was not the jailer's faith that saved them. Each person needed to come to Jesus in faith and believe in him in the same way the jailer had. Yet his entire family did believe, and all were saved. Ask God to use you to introduce Jesus to your family so that they may come to believe in him.

16:35-36 **The next morning the city officials sent the police to tell the jailer, "Let those men go!" So the jailer told Paul, "You and Silas are free to leave. Go in peace."**NLT What brought the *city officials* to the decision of freeing the prisoners is not stated. Maybe it was the way the officials had let the mob determine their actions. Perhaps it was the brutal nature of the punishment of two with so little evidence against them. Maybe it was the earthquake that shook some sense into the governing authorities. Whatever the case, Paul and Silas were told by the jailer, who had become a brother in Christ: *"You and Silas are free to leave."*

16:37 **But Paul said to the officers: "They beat us publicly without a trial, even though we are Roman citizens, and threw us into prison. And now do they want to get rid of us quietly? No! Let them come themselves and escort us out."**NIV That would not be the last word, however. Paul had often been unfairly treated, beaten, and stoned—all illegally in light of his Roman citizenship. Yet here he chose to speak up. He may have wanted to give the new young church in Philippi some breathing room from the local authorities. A public *escort* out of the prison by the Roman magistrates would certainly buy the church some precious time to grow and strengthen rather than being preoccupied with possible arrests and trials of the members. The word would spread that Paul and Silas had been found innocent and freed by the leaders, expressing the truth that believers should not be persecuted—especially if they were Roman citizens.

Wisdom is learning what to overlook. *William James*

DON'T BE A DOORMAT!

Paul refused to take his freedom and run (16:37). He wanted to teach the rulers in Philippi a lesson and to protect the other believers from the treatment that he and Silas had received. It is true that believers should "turn the other cheek" (Matthew 5:39) and endure hardship and persecution for Christ, but in some situations, believers should stand up for their rights. Ask God for the wisdom to be able to discern when you would best represent him by submitting and when the gospel would require you to hold others accountable for their actions.

16:38-39 **The officers reported this to the magistrates, and when they heard that Paul and Silas were Roman citizens, they were alarmed. They came to appease them and escorted them from the prison, requesting them to leave the city.**NIV Roman citizenship had certain privileges. These Philippian authorities were alarmed because it was illegal to have a Roman citizen flogged. In addition, every citizen had the right to a fair trial—which Paul and Silas had not been given. Roman citizens were allowed to travel throughout the Empire under Rome's protection. They were not subject to local legislation or local legislators! Even Roman governors had no authority to beat, imprison, or torture a Roman citizen without direct permission from Rome. No wonder the *magistrates* were *alarmed* when they heard that Paul and

Silas both were Roman citizens. The magistrates' jobs (and lives) were in jeopardy, in the very hands of the ones they had treated so unfairly.

The magistrates personally, politely, contritely came *to appease,* escort, and request that Paul and Silas *leave the city.* What a far cry this was from the harsh treatment of the day before. And what a sad day for them. They were asking the bearers of God's light to leave their city; they were sending away the ones who had the words of eternal life. Once again, the theme is repeated: the light shines—some believe, some refuse, and many—far too many—just simply miss it.

In Philippi, one wealthy business owner had caught it, as had a pitiful little slave girl with huge problems. So, too, a prison official. As diverse as they were, they had all found a Savior. Their paths to Christ had been different, but the result was the same. How sad that these leaders of the community would send away the ones who had the answers they all so desperately needed.

16:40 **Paul and Silas then returned to the home of Lydia, where they met with the believers and encouraged them once more before leaving town.**[NLT] ***Paul and Silas*** left the prison and *returned* to Lydia's home. As had been their custom everywhere they had been, they spent time meeting with the new believers *and encouraged them* for a while longer before they took their message to the next city.

Note that Luke returned to the third person "they" in this verse, as the first "we" section of Acts ends. This may indicate that Luke stayed behind in Philippi to continue the work while Paul and Silas moved on toward Athens. The next "we" section begins at 20:5.

The book of Philippians stands as a testimony to the health of this first church in Europe. Lydia's generosity and the jailer's kindnesses exemplified the solid, spiritual character of the early days of the Philippian church. Who could have known what their influence would be? A few years hence, when Paul was sitting out a trial in Rome, he would write them a note and, in it, commend them for supporting him (see Philippians 1:5, 7; 4:16-19).

Acts 17

PAUL PREACHES IN THESSALONICA / 17:1-9

Leaving Luke in Philippi, Paul, Silas, and Timothy journeyed in a southwesterly direction along the Grecian coast, eventually arriving at Thessalonica. There Paul repeated his usual procedure: go first to the synagogue and preach to the Jews and God fearing Greeks there. The response was typical—a revival among the Greeks, a riot at the hands of the Jewish leaders! Here the mob accused the Christians of turning "the world upside down" (17:6).

MINISTRY IN MACEDONIA
Luke stayed in Philippi while Paul, Silas, and Timothy continued on the Egnatian Way to Amphipolis, Apollonia, and Thessalonica. But trouble arose in Thessalonica, and they fled to Berea. When their enemies from Thessalonica pursued them, Paul set out by sea to Athens, leaving Silas and Timothy to encourage the believers.

17:1 **Now Paul and Silas traveled through the towns of Amphipolis and Apollonia and came to Thessalonica, where there was a Jewish synagogue.**[NLT] *Thessalonica* was about one hundred miles from Philippi, along the Egnatian Way toward Athens. *Amphipolis* was about thirty miles from Philippi, and *Apollonia,* an additional thirty miles. No record is given of any ministry occurring in these towns, though surely the missionaries would have taken every opportunity to speak about Christ.

Thessalonica was one of the wealthiest and most influential cities in Macedonia, with a population of over 200,000. This is the first city where Paul's teachings attracted a large group of socially prominent citizens. The most important Roman highway (the Egnatian Way)—extending from Rome all the way to the Orient—went through Thessalonica. This highway, along with the city's thriving seaport, made Thessalonica one of the wealthiest and most flourishing trade centers in the Roman Empire. Recognized as a free city, Thessalonica was allowed self-rule and was exempted from most of the restrictions placed by Rome on other cities in the Empire. With its international flavor, however, came many pagan religions and cultural influences that challenged the faith of the young Christians there.

After his ministry in Thessalonica, Paul would write two letters to the Thessalonian believers (1 and 2 Thessalonians), encouraging them to remain faithful and to refuse to listen to false teachers who tried to refute their beliefs.

17:2-3 And Paul went in, as was his custom, and on three sabbath days argued with them from the scriptures, explaining and proving that it was necessary for the Messiah to suffer and to rise from the dead, and saying, "This is the Messiah, Jesus whom I am proclaiming to you."NRSV A synagogue (a group of Jews who would gather for teaching and prayer) could be established wherever there were ten Jewish males. Paul's regular practice was to preach in synagogues as long as the Jews would allow it. See 13:46-47 on why Paul went to Jews first. Often those who weren't Jews would come to these services and hear Paul's preaching. For a description of a synagogue service, see the commentary at 13:15.

Paul spent *three sabbath days* ministering to the Jews, and Luke used three different words to describe his ministry:

- "argued" is the Greek word *dialexato,* which means "discussed" or "conversed"—contrast this with 17:17 where Paul debated *(dialego);*
- "explaining" is the Greek word *dianoigon,* which literally means "opening"; it is used of Jesus' instruction of the two on the road to Emmaus in Luke 24:32;
- "proving" is the Greek word *paratithemenos,* which carries the idea of "bringing something forward as a way of proof;" here Paul brought the appropriate Old Testament *scriptures* before his audience, particularly those that taught the suffering, death, and resurrection of *the Messiah, Jesus.*

The fact that Paul spent three Sabbaths in the synagogue does not mean he spent only three weeks in Thessalonica. Paul probably was there for much longer (a time period that occurred between 17:4 and 17:5). He had to have been there long enough to do everything mentioned in his letter to the Thessalonians, such as work at his trade (1 Thessalonians 2:7-9), win converts, instruct new believers in the Christian life (1 Thessalonians 4:1-2), and form a strong bond of love with these believers (1 Thessalonians

2:17-20). Paul's letter to the Philippians indicates that he was in Thessalonica long enough to receive from the Philippians financial help "more than once" (Philippians 4:16 NLT).

WISE WITNESSING
When Paul spoke in the synagogues, he wisely began by talking about Old Testament writings and explaining how the Messiah fulfilled them, moving from the known to the unknown (17:2-3). This was a good strategy. When we witness for Christ, we should begin where people are, affirming the truth they do know, and ultimately move toward presenting Christ, the one who is truth.

17:4 **Some of the Jews were persuaded and joined Paul and Silas, as did a large number of God-fearing Greeks and not a few prominent women.**[NIV] The response at Thessalonica was typical of the response Paul had experienced from the beginning days of his missionary travels. *Some of the Jews were persuaded and joined* them. In addition, a *large number of God-fearing Greeks* also joined (see commentary on Cornelius at 10:2). The gospel continued to reach more Gentiles than Jews ("a large number" of Greeks as opposed to "some" Jews).

In Thessalonica, however, a third group responded—*not a few prominent women* (the Greek word for "prominent," *proton,* means "first," "chief," or "most important"). These were influential women in the upper class (see 16:14; 17:12). "Joining" Paul and Silas means that they had come to faith, had been baptized, and were actively participating in whatever aspects of discipleship and instruction were available.

17:5 **But the Jews were jealous; so they rounded up some bad characters from the marketplace, formed a mob and started a riot in the city. They rushed to Jason's house in search of Paul and Silas in order to bring them out to the crowd.**[NIV] So far Paul's ministry was following its usual course. The gospel was preached in the synagogues with meager response from the Jews. The Gentiles, however, were responding in great numbers (both worshipers in the synagogues and others). Then, as had been the custom, the nonresponding Jews became *jealous* and set their sights on running these "heretics" out of town or worse.

The Jewish leaders didn't refute the theology of Paul and Silas, but they were jealous of the popularity of these itinerant preachers. Their motive for causing the riot was rooted in personal jealousy, not doctrinal purity. They *rounded up some bad characters off the streets, formed a mob,* and *started a riot in the city.*

The leaders of the mob knew where to find Paul and Silas—

at *Jason's house.* Jason was an early Thessalonian convert who, like Lydia, had convinced the travelers to stay in his home.

The term "crowd" may be an allusion only to the gathered mob. More likely, however, it is a technical reference for the governing body of Thessalonica—the "Assembly."

IN THE LINE OF FIRE

Jason was persecuted because of his association with Paul and Silas (17:6-7). We don't know much about Jason except that he evidently was the local host and sponsor of Paul and Silas. Jason is just one of many unsung heroes who faithfully played their part to help spread the gospel. Because of Jason's courage, Paul and Silas were able to minister more effectively. As you serve Christ, you may not receive much attention (in fact you may receive only grief). But God wants to use you. Lives will be changed if you demonstrate courage and faithfulness.

17:6-7 **Not finding them there, they dragged out Jason and some of the other believers instead and took them before the city council. "Paul and Silas have turned the rest of the world upside down, and now they are here disturbing our city," they shouted. "And Jason has let them into his home. They are all guilty of treason against Caesar, for they profess allegiance to another king, Jesus."**NLT The mob had not found Paul and Silas at Jason's house. Perhaps Paul and Silas had been informed and had hurried away from the dangerous crowd. So the mob grabbed *Jason and some of the other believers* and brought them before the *city council.* They shouted out their accusations, presumably because of the noise of the gathered mob.

Their accusations, like all good lies, bore some resemblance to the truth but were presented in their worst light. Paul and Silas were not *guilty of treason against Caesar* just because they declared allegiance to the King of kings, for Christ's kingdom is of an entirely different sort than Caesar's was.

The Jewish leaders had difficulty manufacturing an accusation that would be heard by the city government. The Romans did not care about theological disagreements between the Jews and these preachers. Treason, however, was a serious offense in the Roman Empire. Although Paul and Silas were not advocating rebellion against Roman law, their loyalty to *another king* sounded suspicious.

17:8-9 **The people of the city, as well as the city officials, were thrown into turmoil by these reports. But the officials released Jason and the other believers after they had posted bail.**NLT The story told by the leaders of the riot had its desired result. The whole lot of them—from the *city officials* to the *people of the city—were thrown into turmoil* by these manipulative accusations.

Because there was no substantive case, however, and because *Jason and the other believers* had done little more than house the accused, they were *released.* Jason *posted bail*—putting up cash for freedom. This probably was not "bail" as we know it, insuring his presence at a future trial—there was really nothing to "try." More likely it was a pledge of sorts, assuring the authorities that Paul and Silas would leave town and not return. In Paul's first letter to this church, his statement about Satan blocking a future trip (1 Thessalonians 2:18) may refer to the events described here.

PAUL AND SILAS IN BEREA / 17:10-15

God continued to use persecution and opposition to spread the good news of forgiveness and eternal life through Jesus Christ. The uproar in Thessalonica forced Paul and Silas to journey to Berea, where they found a very teachable and receptive Greek audience. In a short time, however, hostile Jews came from Thessalonica to attack Paul's work in Berea. But this succeeded only in getting the great evangelist to Athens!

A SPIRITUAL REVOLUTION

Paul and Silas were accused of turning the world upside down. What a reputation the early Christians had! The power of the gospel revolutionized lives, broke down social barriers, threw open prison doors, caused people to care deeply for one another, and stirred them to worship God. Our world needs similarly to be turned upside down. At its core, the gospel is not about establishing new programs or encouraging good conduct; it is about dynamically transforming lives. Ask God for the courage and the wisdom to know how you can help spread his Good News all over your world.

17:10 As soon as it was night, the brothers sent Paul and Silas away to Berea. On arriving there, they went to the Jewish synagogue.[NIV] Waiting for the protection of darkness, *the brothers,* who had obviously been hiding Paul and Silas from the riot in Thessalonica, sent them on their way *to Berea.* There they would begin again in *the Jewish synagogue.*

Even though in every city the missionaries faced angry crowds, it is important not to miss what was *really* happening along the way. The term "brothers" describes men and women of both Jewish and Greek descent, who just a few weeks earlier (maybe just a few days) had been lost in their sins and living in darkness. God, working through two faithful messengers, had brought them the light. They had come to Christ, had received forgiveness of sins, and had begun walking in that light (Ephesians 5:8-10). Even though they were terribly young in the faith, they had put their lives, their jobs, their reputations, and their friendships on the line for the sake of the gospel and these gospel messengers (see 1 Thessalonians 1:7-10; 2:14-16).

17:11 And the people of Berea were more open-minded than those in Thessalonica, and they listened eagerly to Paul's message. They searched the Scriptures day after day to check up on Paul and Silas, to see if they were really teaching the truth.[NLT]

Berea was about forty-five miles south of Thessalonica. The people of Berea *were more open-minded than those in Thessalonica.* The Greek word for "open-minded" is *eugenesteroi,* meaning "noble" or "generous—free from prejudice." Instead of hurling attacks, *they listened eagerly to Paul's message.* Instead of forming a mob to run the missionaries out of town, they *searched the Scriptures day after day* to confirm whether or not Paul and Silas were *teaching the truth.*

> I want to know one thing: the way to heaven. . . . God himself has condescended to teach the way. For this very end he came from heaven. He hath written it down in a book. O give me that book! At any price, give me the book of God!
>
> *John Wesley*

What an ideal audience! They exhibited the characteristics that every teacher of the Word would love to find in a listener:

- "Open-minded"—they were teachable.
- "Eager listeners"—they were open to hear the truth.
- "Scripture searchers"—they did not take everything and everyone at its word. They did their homework.
- "Truth seekers"—they were looking for truth—absolute truth.

BEING A "BEREAN" BELIEVER

How do you evaluate sermons, books, and teachings? The people in Berea opened the Scriptures for themselves and searched for truths to verify or disprove the teaching they heard (17:11). Always compare what you hear or read with what the Bible says. A preacher or teacher who gives God's true message will never contradict or explain away anything that is found in God's Word. But serious Bible study will be needed to verify what we read and hear.

17:12 Many of the Jews believed, as did also a number of prominent Greek women and many Greek men.NIV Here, in contrast to so many cities before, *many of the Jews believed,* as well as many Greeks—described as *prominent* men and women. See 17:4 for comparison with prominent people in Thessalonica. God honored the fact that these leading men and women of the city were searching for the truth.

17:13 When the Jews in Thessalonica learned that Paul was preaching the word of God at Berea, they went there too, agitating the crowds and stirring them up.NIV What began as a wonderful situation did not last, however. Though there appeared to be no trouble at all from the Berean Jews, trouble followed Paul from *Thessalonica.* When the Jews there heard of Paul's ministry *at Berea,* they *went there too* in order to agitate the crowds.

BLIND JEALOUSY

The jealous Jews in Thessalonica followed Paul to Berea to cause trouble (17:13). How ugly and all-consuming is the sin of jealousy! Do you know people who follow this pattern with their lives—even with their so-called ministry? They spend their days in well-concealed envy, operating under some very well-articulated, pious-sounding principles. While they never really build anything positive themselves, they do a great job of destroying or blocking that which they envy in the work of others. If this has been a pattern of yours in the past, do learn from these envy-blinded, violent Jews. They, like so many of their kindred before them, were attacking the very spokesman of God himself.

17:14-15 Then the believers immediately sent Paul away to the coast, but Silas and Timothy remained behind. Those who conducted Paul brought him as far as Athens; and after receiving instructions to have Silas and Timothy join him as soon as possible, they left him.NRSV Again, *the believers* rushed to protect Paul, sending him *away to the coast.* Fortunately, the gospel message was so identified with Paul that it caused most of the Jewish anger to be directed at him, leaving his traveling companions more freedom to build up the churches. Thus, *Silas and Timothy* were allowed to stay behind in Berea.

Those who were escorting Paul took him *as far as Athens.* They *left him* there only after he instructed them *to have Silas and Timothy join him as soon as possible.*

PAUL PREACHES IN ATHENS / 17:16-34

Paul's brief stay in Athens is a remarkable case study in the universality of the gospel. The Athenians were cosmopolitan, philosophical people, given to all sorts of idolatrous beliefs. At Mars Hill, Paul demonstrated his ability to be all things to all people (1 Corinthians 9:22), preaching the gospel of the resurrected Christ with concepts and terms that the Athenian philosophers could easily grasp. Some scoffed at his message, but others indicated an interest in hearing more.

This chapter deals with the early stages of Paul's second missionary journey. He and his fellow travelers worked their way down the peninsula of modern-day Greece. Luke recorded Paul's message to the idol-worshiping academicians at Athens at length. That message revealed Paul's God-led wisdom for dealing with those who knew very little about the true God but who felt very secure in their intellectual abilities.

TORMENTED BY TRANSGRESSION

As Paul walked about the city of Athens, he saw a marketplace lined with idols. This fact "deeply troubled" him (17:16). The Greek word is *paroksuno,* from which we get our word "paroxysm." It means "sudden, violent emotion." Paul was filled with a combination of anger and grief. Seeing people spiritually lost, blinded by Satan, and trapped in a pagan culture caused Paul to be in a state of emotional upheaval. Though highly educated, the Athenians were ignorant of the one true God. It's interesting to note that Paul turned his internal turmoil into positive action: he looked for opportunities to share the truth about Jesus. Does the lostness of people move us to action? And if so, what action? Do we shun unbelievers and talk ill of them? Or do we seek opportunities to speak the gospel?

17:16 **While Paul was waiting for them in Athens, he was deeply troubled by all the idols he saw everywhere in the city.**NLT
What can be viewed today in Athens as wonderful works of art and architecture were, in their day, the worshipful expression of a culture steeped in godless idolatry. Athens was named after the goddess Athena, and there were temples in Athens for all the gods in the Greek pantheon. Paul was *deeply troubled* by all the idolatry he saw *everywhere in the city.* "Deeply troubled" is literally "greatly upset in his spirit." This representative of God could not help but be infuriated that such a great city and such a great culture would be so deeply involved in worshiping anything or anyone other than the living God. Paul would not be able to keep very silent for very long.

Athens, with its magnificent buildings and many gods, was a center for Greek culture, philosophy, and education. Philosophers and educated people were always ready to hear something new—thus their openness to hear Paul speak at their meeting in the

Areopagus (17:18-19). Athens had been the political, educational, and philosophical center of the world in its prime, the home of men such as Plato, Socrates, Aristotle, Epicurus, Zeno. But that was four hundred years before Paul's visit. When Paul arrived, it was a small town (ten thousand or so residents) reliving the glory days and filled with intellectuals spending their days philosophizing.

> Good philosophy must exist if for no other reason because bad philosophy needs to be answered. The cool intellect must work not only against cool intellect on the other side but against the muddy heathen mysticisms which deny intellect altogether. . . . The learned life is for some, a duty.
>
> *C. S. Lewis*

17:17 **He went to the synagogue to debate with the Jews and the God-fearing Gentiles, and he spoke daily in the public square to all who happened to be there.**[NLT] Paul had a balanced and adaptive approach to his ministry in Athens. In *the synagogue,* he debated with the Jews and worshiping Gentiles, likely using the arguments recorded at other places in the book of Acts (for example, 13:16-41), seeking to prove to them that Jesus was the long-awaited Messiah.

Between his Sabbath debates with the worshipers in the synagogues, however, Paul *spoke daily in the public square* (the agora, which was the central marketplace) to whomever would listen.

DEBATING WITHOUT BERATING

Luke wrote that Paul went to the synagogue to "debate" with those who were there (17:17). He was discussing, listening carefully, and yet gently and firmly stating his convictions. Effective witnessing doesn't include yelling, belittling, or attempting to ram beliefs down someone's throat. This caricature of evangelism probably explains why so many believers are so reluctant to engage their unbelieving friends and neighbors in spiritual conversations. The good news about the Good News is that we can share it in an inoffensive manner! Ask God for an opportunity to engage in dialogue about your faith.

17:18 **A group of Epicurean and Stoic philosophers began to dispute with him. Some of them asked, "What is this babbler trying to say?" Others remarked, "He seems to be advocating foreign gods." They said this because Paul was preaching the good news about Jesus and the resurrection.**[NIV] The Epicureans and Stoics were the dominant philosophers in Greek culture. The Epicurians, followers of Epicurus (341–270 B.C.), believed that the chief purpose for living was pleasure and happiness. If God existed, he didn't interfere in human affairs. Epicurians are similar to modern-day materialists and hedonists.

The Stoics were followers of Zeno (320–263 B.C.), who taught on a porch or patio called a "stoa," hence the name "Stoics." The Stoics were pantheistic and felt that a great "purpose" was directing history. Humans' responsibility was to align themselves with that purpose through duty and self-discipline. This, quite logically, led to pride and self-sufficiency ("I am the master of my fate!"). The Stoics are similar to modern-day New Age followers and pantheists.

These philosophers *began to dispute* with Paul. The word for "dispute" in this context connotes the batting around of ideas. Some of these philosophers characterized Paul's arguments as "babbling" (literally, "seed picker"—a picture that calls to mind a bird fluttering around and picking up any shred of food with no thought of order or consistency; this was not a compliment!). In the same way that a bird collects seeds, or a junk collector gathers trash, Paul was accused of collecting little pieces of knowledge that wouldn't take him anywhere. They were saying that his ideas were not as well thought through or as valid as theirs.

Others of these philosophers recognized in Paul's teaching *about Jesus and the resurrection* the fact that he was *advocating foreign gods.*

17:19-20 Then they took him and brought him to a meeting of the Areopagus, where they said to him, "May we know what this new teaching is that you are presenting? You are bringing some strange ideas to our ears, and we want to know what they mean."NIV Paul's dialogue in the marketplace led to an invitation to address the *Areopagus,* which had been the judicial and legislative seat of government of Athens—a council or court. By Paul's time, however, their responsibilities involved little more than overseeing certain areas of religion and education.

The Areopagus often met on a low hill in Athens near the Acropolis. As Paul stood there and spoke about the one true God, his audience could look down on the city and see the many idols representing gods that Paul knew were worthless.

These intellectuals, ever interested in hearing new ideas, wanted to hear *this new teaching* that Paul was presenting. The word "know" will surface a good deal in the verses that follow. Here the descendants of the most influential thinkers in Western civilization, who had been on a centuries-long quest for knowledge, were given an opportunity to receive the ultimate knowledge—God entering the human race to redeem fallen humanity and put them in a position to know not philosophy but rather a person, the person of Jesus Christ.

17:21 **(It should be explained that all the Athenians as well as the foreigners in Athens seemed to spend all their time discussing the latest ideas.)**NLT Luke, in somewhat of an aside, explained this predisposition of the *Athenians* and many who were residing there *(foreigners)* to spend days at a time *discussing the latest ideas.* Evidently, these were somewhat highbrow intellectuals, who loved to hear and discuss the latest fads in philosophy and theology. The picture is that they rarely actually did anything they discussed; they just enjoyed tossing around ideas.

17:22-23 **Paul then stood up in the meeting of the Areopagus and said: "Men of Athens! I see that in every way you are very religious. For as I walked around and looked carefully at your objects of worship, I even found an altar with this inscription: to an unknown god. Now what you worship as something unknown I am going to proclaim to you."**NIV Paul was well prepared to speak to this group. He came from Tarsus, an educational center, and had the training and knowledge to present his beliefs clearly and persuasively. Paul was a rabbi, taught by the finest scholar of his day, Gamaliel, and he had spent much of his life thinking and reasoning through the Scriptures.

> Before you can convince a man of anything, you must first convince him that you are his true friend. *Abraham Lincoln*

Luke recorded this sermon in more detail than many of the others, likely as a sample of how Paul addressed the typical lost, intellectual Greek. Rather than arguing the Scriptures as he would with a Jewish audience, he adapted his message and backed up a step or two to speak of a Creator; then he moved toward speaking about a Savior and Judge. The speech had three major movements: (1) the introduction in 17:22-23; (2) the section on the unknown god in 17:24-29; and (3) the section explaining the revelation of God in 17:30-31.

Paul began his address by affirming the "religious" nature of his audience: *"I see . . . you are very religious."* Some suggest that Paul's statement was derogatory rather than complimentary, but the latter is most likely the case. He chose a starting point, a place where they could agree, rather than starting with their differences. The term translated "very religious," however, is a combination of the Greek words *deido* (to fear or revere) and *daimon* (evil spirits), which may contain a subtle rebuke concerning the spiritual realities behind their religion.

Paul next explained what he had seen in their city. Note that Paul did not come in and blast their religion without seeking to understand it first. Nor did he fail to do some appropriate observation of their culture, art, and architecture before addressing the fallacies. We would do well to learn from his example. The Athenians had built an idol to the *unknown god* for fear of missing blessings or receiving punishment. The Athenian philosophers were either polytheistic (worshiped many gods) or pantheistic (believed all nature was god), so it would be natural for them to build an altar, superstitious that they might have overlooked a god. Archaeological finds have shown many such altars with the inscription, "to the unknown god(s)." Paul's opening statement to the men of Athens was about their "unknown god." Paul was not endorsing this god but using the inscription as a point of entry for his witness to the one true God.

TAILORING THE MESSAGE

Paul began his address to the Athenians by highlighting their religious interests (17:22). This address is a good example of how to communicate the gospel. Paul did not begin by reciting Jewish history as he usually would do when addressing Jews, for that would have been meaningless to his Greek audience. He began by building a case for the one true God, using examples the philosophers understood (17:22-23). Then he established common ground by emphasizing what they agreed on about God (17:24-29). Finally, he moved his message to the person of Christ, centering on the Resurrection (17:30-31). When you witness to others, you can use Paul's approach: use examples, establish common ground, and then move people toward a decision about Jesus Christ.

The final statement in Paul's opening section is an adept piece of rhetoric. He promised that in the balance of his speech he would *proclaim to* them the answer that the inscription "to an unknown god" was seeking. If the purpose of a good introduction is to strike a point of need as well as stimulate interest, Paul had begun eloquently. He would give these seekers the information that they and their ancestors had sought for centuries. Surely he had their undivided attention at this point.

MAKING THE VAGUE SPECIFIC

Paul explained the one true God to these educated men of Athens (17:24-25); although these men were, in general, very religious, they did not know God. Today we have a "Christian" society, but to most people God is still unknown. We need to proclaim who he is and make it clear what he did for all mankind through his Son, Jesus Christ. We cannot assume that even religious people around us truly know Jesus or understand the importance of faith in him.

17:24-25 **"The God who made the world and everything in it, he who is Lord of heaven and earth, does not live in shrines made by human hands, nor is he served by human hands, as though he needed anything, since he himself gives to all mortals life and breath and all things."**[NRSV] The central body of Paul's speech is a presentation of God as the Creator, the one *who made the world and everything in it.* In words reminiscent of Stephen's (7:48-50), Paul explained that this Creator *does not live in shrines* built by humans, even spectacular wonder-of-the-world Greek structures like the one a few hundred yards up the hill from where they sat (the Acropolis). God does not need anything from *mortals* since he himself is the source of *life and breath and all things.* This was likely a subtle shot at the Greek notion of the gods' needing human services; it would appeal to the Epicureans in the group, who believed the gods were above human events. Paul's remark about God as the source of "all life and breath" may have appealed to the Stoics in the crowd, who were trying to align themselves with the cosmic "purpose."

> We need to accept the non-Christian as he is, go for the cure, and then help him pick his way through the things that are destroying him. Whenever we get this sequence turned around, we become reformers rather than offerers of true healing.
>
> *Jim Peterson*

Certainly Paul understood the philosophical positions of his audience and was willing and able to dialogue with them in *their* frame of reference before leading them to *his.* Paul had no difficulty in speaking authoritatively concerning the Athenians' belief systems and pointing out their strong points and, soon, their flaws.

EQUIPPED TO WITNESS

When it comes to witnessing, passion alone is not enough. Like Paul, we must be equipped with a knowledge of Scripture. The more we know about the Bible, what it means, and how to apply it to our lives, the more convincing our words will be. This does not mean that we should avoid presenting the gospel until we feel adequately prepared. We should work with what we know, but we must make it a priority to keep learning. Our goal should be to reach more people by being prepared to answer their questions and arguments more effectively.

17:26-27 **"From one ancestor he made all nations to inhabit the whole earth, and he allotted the times of their existence and the boundaries of the places where they would live, so that they would search for God and perhaps grope for him and find**

SECULAR WRITERS

On four occasions at least, the apostle Paul quoted literary works. While these references do not prove that Paul attended plays or read many secular writers, they do indicate that he was familiar enough with certain works to include their sayings as illustrations in his sermons and letters.

Name	*When lived*	*Quote*	*From what source?*	*Quoted where in Scripture?*
Epimenides (a Cretan poet)	600 B.C.	"For in him we live and move and exist."	*Cretica*	Acts 17:28
Aratus (a Cilician poet)	315-240 B.C.	"We are his offspring."	*Phaenomena 5*	Acts 17:28
Menander (a Greek poet)	342-292 B.C.	"Bad company corrupts good character."	*Thais*	1 Corinthians 15:33
Epimenides	600 B.C.	"The people of Crete are all liars; they are cruel animals and lazy gluttons."	*De Oraculis*	Titus 1:12

---

him—though indeed he is not far from each one of us."NRSV From general characteristics of the Creator God, Paul moved to the more specific Judeo-Christian claims that God created all life and all nations *from one ancestor.* This would likely rub proud Greeks the wrong way, since they believed themselves to be racially superior to all other nations (whom they called "barbarians").

This Creator God not only created the nations, but he also *allotted the times of their existence* as well as the *boundaries* of their borders. The purpose of all this was so that people *would search for God . . . and find him.* The word "grope" is a vivid picture of the way a person in darkness (without the help of the light of God's revelation) searches for God (see Ecclesiastes 3:11). Paul was affirming the validity of the Athenians' search, though he painted the picture as "groping" rather than what they would likely prefer to call "intelligent, philosophical, and logical reasoning."

This "unknown god" is not only knowable, *indeed he is not far from anyone!* This contrasted to the Greek gods, which lived in seclusion and could not be approached. The need that motivated the construction of an altar "to an unknown god" (17:23) could be realized in Christ, for he was very near and available—to be known!

17:28 "For 'In him we live and move and have our being'; as even some of your own poets have said, 'For we too are his offspring.'"NRSV To illustrate and support his point, Paul quoted first from Epimenides, a Cretan poet from 600 B.C. (whom he also quoted in Titus 1:12): *In him we live and move and have our being.* The next quote is from Aratus (a Stoic poet from Cilicia, 315–240 B.C.) in a line from his work *Phainomena: For we too are his offspring.* Both of these statements from well-known and accepted literary sources of the day served Paul's purpose well in arguing for the fact that the creation and sustaining of life was in the hands of the one God whom they did not know but who was very near and very knowable. The sense of humanity being God's "offspring" means that all receive life and breath from him.

There are many seeking and finding words in 17:27-28: "search," "grope," "find," "not far," "in him," "we are his." These words and phrases would have been heard by those in the audience who were seeking for the truth. Paul was exposing three false Greek ideas: (1) God was unknowable; (2) God lived in man-made temples; (3) God was not involved in human affairs.

17:29-30 "And since this is true, we shouldn't think of God as an idol designed by craftsmen from gold or silver or stone. God overlooked people's former ignorance about these things, but now he commands everyone everywhere to turn away from idols and turn to him."NLT Paul began to wrap up his message, building this statement on all that he had presented thus far and gently correcting where the Greeks had been incorrect: *And since this is true,* they needed to make some changes. Their thinking had been incorrect. They should not *think of God as an idol* who could be constructed by human hands. God is profoundly bigger than any idol.

Also, the Athenians had to understand that although God had *overlooked people's former ignorance* (not in the sense that he condoned it but rather that he had not yet judged it—see Acts 14:16; Romans 3:25), he now commanded *everyone everywhere* to turn from idolatry and *turn to him.*

This was a serious and somber word to the gathered Athenians. They would do well to hear it and respond. Whatever the nature and consequences of their former failure to respond to God, it was nothing compared to ignoring what was being offered in the finished work of Christ.

17:31 "For he has set a day for judging the world with justice by the man he has appointed, and he proved to everyone who this is by raising him from the dead."[NLT] Paul confronted his listeners with Jesus' resurrection and its meaning to all people—either blessing or punishment. The Greeks had no concept of judgment. Most of them preferred worshiping many gods instead of just one. And though their gods became angry from time to time, there was no real accountability in the way that Paul was presenting.

God *has set a day for judging the world,* however, and the judge had been selected—*the man he has appointed.* "He was given authority, honor, and royal power over all the nations of the world, so that people of every race and nation and language would obey him. His rule is eternal—it will never end. His kingdom will never be destroyed" (Daniel 7:14 NLT). All judgment had been given to the one who was raised *from the dead*—Jesus Christ (see John 5:22)—the one Paul had been proclaiming in Athens since the day he had arrived (see 17:18).

To the Greek mind, the concept of resurrection was unbelievable and offensive, but on this issue the whole gospel hinged (1 Corinthians 15:13-14). Although Paul knew it would offend their precious philosophies, he did not hold back the truth. Paul often would change his approach to fit his audience, as he did with this one, but he never would change his basic message.

17:32 When they heard Paul speak of the resurrection of a person who had been dead, some laughed, but others said, "We want to hear more about this later."[NLT] The mention of *the resurrection* would, of course, draw an immediate reaction from this group of intellects. How absurd! *Some laughed,* yet there were others who seemed intrigued and asked if they could *hear more about this later.* The latter group may simply have been patronizing this fellow scholar and visiting lecturer. Paul's speech was not in vain, however, as the next verse shows.

17:33-34 That ended Paul's discussion with them, but some joined him and became believers. Among them were Dionysius, a member of the Council, a woman named Damaris, and others.[NLT] Though the discussion had ended with a few sneers and a polite invitation to return, Paul's time had not been wasted. *Some joined him and became believers,* one of them even a *Council* member named *Dionysius.* The Council was the Areopagus, or Council of Ares (see 17:19-20). It was the court of Athens that met on the Hill of Ares, or Mars Hill. It was like the Senate or city council (in Greece today, the Supreme Court is called the Areopagus).

SOME EFFECTIVE WAYS TO APPROACH A KNOW-IT-ALL WORLD

From Paul's approach to the Athenians, we find some great pointers on how to preach the gospel:

• Watch for ways to find common ground (Acts 17:22-23).
Paul went where people were physically and began where they were intellectually.

• Correct errant views of God (Acts 17:24-26).
Paul gently but firmly exposed the errant views of the Athenians. There *is* a knowable God. On that front they were wrong and needed correction.

• Nurture that part of each person that wants to know God (Acts 17:27).
Paul knew that there is a God-built part of every person that wants to know God. When we talk to those who don't know God, we need to assume this and nurture it.

• Offer the proof of Christianity—the Resurrection (Acts 17:31).
Paul spoke of the Resurrection. Christ's resurrection is the focal point of the faith, proving the central theme of Christianity. Without that fact we have nothing to stand on (1 Corinthians 15:13-14).

• Make clear every person's accountability for his or her life (Acts 17:30-31). Paul didn't mince words. There comes a time when folks need to be told of the final judgment.

• Expect a variety of responses (Acts 17:5-9, 13, 18-20, 32-33).
Paul received varied responses. Some will be jealous. Others will misrepresent what we are doing, accusing *us* of being troublemakers, agitating those we're trying to reach. But some will believe. And they are worth it!

Only one other convert is named, a *woman named Damaris,* though we are told there were *others.*

Although there is no record of a church being founded in Athens and Paul soon moved on to Corinth (chapter 18), his visit to Athens was not a failure. The responsibility of the messenger is to present the message, and Paul certainly did that (and did so brilliantly). The fruit was God's responsibility.

THE OUTCOME OF EVANGELISM
Paul's Mars Hill speech is often regarded as a brilliant, textbook example of evangelistic witness. Even so, it received a mixed reaction: some sneered, some kept searching for more information, and a few believed (17:33-34). We should expect similar results. Don't hesitate to tell others about Christ because you fear that some will not believe you. Don't expect a unanimously positive response to your witnessing. Even if only a few believe, it's worth the effort.

Acts 18

PAUL MEETS PRISCILLA AND AQUILA IN CORINTH / 18:1-17

The spread of the gospel requires a team effort by individuals with different gifts. In Corinth, Paul met Priscilla and Aquila, a married couple (and fellow tentmakers) who proved to be faithful partners in the gospel (see Romans 16:3; 1 Corinthians 16:19; 2 Timothy 4:19).

Paul's ministry in this decadent city was long and fruitful (18:11). Not even a concerted effort by the Jews could stop him from teaching the Word. When brought into court in Achaia, Paul was quickly released by Gallio, the proconsul, who adamantly

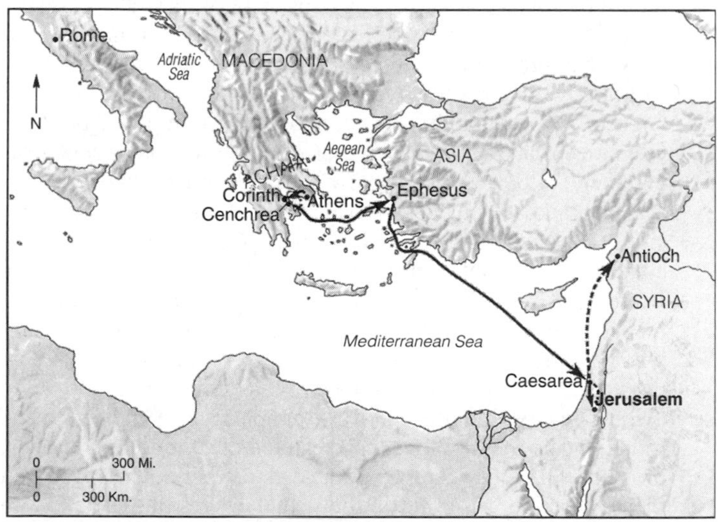

MINISTRY IN CORINTH AND EPHESUS

Paul left Athens and traveled on to Corinth, one of the greatest commercial centers of the Empire, located on a narrow neck of land offering direct passage between the Aegean and Adriatic seas. When Paul left from the port of Corinth at Cenchrea, he visited Ephesus. He then traveled to Caesarea, from where he went on to Jerusalem to report on his trip before returning to Antioch.

refused to intervene in their disagreement over "words and names and . . . Jewish laws" (18:15 NLT). This favorable decision enabled the gospel to continue to spread throughout the Roman Empire.

BURNED OUT?
After encountering the philosophers in Athens, Paul went to Corinth (18:1). Paul probably arrived emotionally and spiritually down. In 1 Corinthians 2, he wrote that he was in a state of weakness, "timid and trembling" (1 Corinthians 2:3 NLT). Why the low time? For one thing, his ministry in Athens had not achieved great results. For another, he was apparently traveling alone. Acts 18 reveals some of the wise steps Paul took to not only survive but to thrive during a difficult time. He found some Christian friends and got busy making tents as he continued the ministry. Eventually Paul felt reassured of God's presence and power in his life. At those tough spots and dry places in the Christian life, lean on God, lean on other Christians, and keep doing what God has called you to do.

18:1 Then Paul left Athens and went to Corinth.NLT Ancient Corinth had been destroyed by the Romans in 146 B.C., but it had been rebuilt by Julius Caesar in 46 B.C. because of its strategic seaport. By Paul's day (A.D. 50), the Romans had made Corinth the capital of Achaia (present-day Greece). Only fifty miles from Athens, Corinth by this time was regarded as the most influential city of Greece. The population was about 650,000, comprised of 250,000 free citizens and 400,000 slaves. Corinth was a major center of commerce. Located on a narrow strip of land near two bustling seaports, and at a busy crossroads for land travelers and traders, the city was wealthy and very materialistic. Corinth was a center of culture. Though not a university town like Athens, there was great interest in Greek philosophy and wisdom. Aristides claimed that on every street in Corinth one could meet a so-called wise man who had his own solutions to the world's problems. The city was permeated with religion—at least twelve temples were located there. The most infamous of these temples was dedicated to Aphrodite, the goddess of love, and featured one thousand "sacred" prostitutes. Another temple, dedicated to Apollo, employed young men whose job was to fulfill the sexual desires of male and female worshipers. Largely due to this fact, the city was notorious for its immorality. So brazen was the unbridled licentiousness that a new Greek verb was eventually coined: to "Corinthianize" meant to practice sexual immorality. When Plato referred to a prostitute, he used the expression "Corinthian girl."

From a human point of view, Corinth was not the type of place where one would expect to launch a thriving ministry, but Paul didn't view things from an earthly perspective. He saw Corinth as both a challenge and a great ministry opportunity. Later he would write a series of letters to the Corinthians dealing in large part with the problems of immorality. First and Second Corinthians are two of those letters.

18:2-3 There he found a Jew named Aquila, a native of Pontus, who had recently come from Italy with his wife Priscilla, because Claudius had ordered all Jews to leave Rome. Paul went to see them, and, because he was of the same trade, he stayed with them, and they worked together—by trade they were tentmakers.NRSV *Priscilla* and *Aquila* had just been expelled from Rome by Emperor Claudius's decree against Jews. A remark by the secular historian Suetonius hints at the reason for this dispersion. In *Life of Claudius,* Suetonius wrote of Jewish riots instigated by Chrestus, which may be a reference to religious upheavals between strict Jews and followers of Christ. Rather than taking the time to sort through this sectarian controversy, Claudius simply had *ordered all Jews to leave Rome.*

> Let temporal things serve your use, but the eternal be the object of your desire. *Thomas à Kempis*

Trained in the art of tentmaking, Aquila and Priscilla had packed up the tools of their trade and had made their way to Corinth. There they met Paul, who joined them in the business of tentmaking. Where had Paul learned tentmaking? Jewish boys were expected to learn trades from which they could earn their living. Apparently, Paul and Aquila had been trained from an early age to cut and sew leather into tents. Tents were much in demand because they were used throughout the Empire to house soldiers. Tentmakers also made canopies and other leather goods. It is highly likely, therefore, that the Roman army was a major purchaser of Paul's tents. As a tentmaker, Paul had a transportable livelihood that he could carry with him wherever God led him. Since ancient craftsmen did not compete as merchants do today but rather formed cooperative trade guilds and often lived in close proximity, it is not surprising that Paul and Aquila worked together. Because many of the trade guilds had adopted pagan practices, two God-fearing artisans would have been delighted to work together.

Paul chose to work to support himself during his stay in Corinth. The presence of so many religious promoters in Corinth may have added an incentive for Paul to earn his own living. Paul wanted to disassociate himself from those teachers who taught only for money. As Paul lived with Priscilla and Aquila, he must have shared with them his wealth of spiritual wisdom. They likely were already believers (or else Luke, it seems, would have mentioned their conversion). Perhaps they had embraced the gospel through the ministry of the Roman natives who had been in Jerusalem at Pentecost (see 2:10). They may even have been founding members of the church of Rome.

TEAMWORK
Some couples know how to make the most of life. They complement each other, capitalize on each other's strengths, and form an effective team. Their united efforts have a profound effect on those around them. Aquila and Priscilla were such a couple. The Bible never mentions them separately. In marriage and ministry, they were together. Working in concert, they made an eternal difference in countless lives. Consider your marriage. Do you and your spouse enjoy an intimacy that overflows into ministry? If not, what prevents you from being a dynamic duo for the Lord?

18:4 **Each Sabbath found Paul at the synagogue, trying to convince the Jews and Greeks alike.**[NLT] Paul never veered from this ministry philosophy. Because of his great burden for his lost Jewish brothers (see Romans 9:2-3), Paul would go *each Sabbath* to the *synagogue* (9:20; 13:5, 14; 14:1; 17:2, 10, 17; 18:19; 19:8). There he would speak to both *Jews and Greeks* (Gentiles who had converted to Judaism).

HOW TO ENCOURAGE YOUR PASTOR
Silas and Timothy provided a major boost to Paul's sagging spiritual state (18:5). Their mere presence was a great encouragement. The financial gift they brought was a major vote of confidence. Their report of Macedonian believers growing, serving, and persevering warmed his pastoral heart. Contrary to the wide misconception, pastors don't just have to work "one morning a week." They carry a heavy emotional and spiritual burden. If you, as a church member, are faithful—to grow, to attend, to give, to express appreciation—you can help your church leaders be more fruitful.

18:5 **When Silas and Timothy came from Macedonia, Paul devoted himself exclusively to preaching, testifying to the Jews that Jesus was the Christ.**[NIV] Upon the arrival of his colleagues, Paul was able to set aside his tentmaking and devote himself *exclusively to preaching.* Silas and Timothy must have brought with them a financial gift from the believers in Macedonia (see Philippians 4:15). They also brought a good word about the perseverance of the believers in Thessalonica

(1 Thessalonians 3:6-8). Paul must have been encouraged by all these factors. With newfound strength, he solemnly declared to the Jews that the Messiah was Jesus.

18:6 **But when the Jews opposed Paul and became abusive, he shook out his clothes in protest and said to them, "Your blood be on your own heads! I am clear of my responsibility. From now on I will go to the Gentiles."**NIV The hardcore *Jews* in Paul's audience *became abusive* and began to blaspheme and slander the apostle and his message. "Shaking his garments" (see 13:51) was a dramatic gesture that depicted Paul's desire to separate himself entirely from even the dust found in such a rebellious synagogue. His pointed statement *"Your blood be on your own heads!"* is a reference to the Jews' own responsibility for their eventual spiritual destruction and brings to mind the sobering warning of Ezekiel: "Then if those who hear the alarm refuse to take action—well, it is their own fault if they die" (Ezekiel 33:4 NLT). Because Paul had given his countrymen a clear opportunity to be saved, he would later be able to say, "I have been faithful. No one's damnation can be blamed on me" (20:26 NLT). In essence, Paul was telling the Jews that he had done all he could for them. Because they continued to reject Jesus as their Messiah, he would turn his attention to the *Gentiles,* who would prove to be more receptive.

> The enemy gets angry when we invade his territory and liberate his slaves. *Warren Wiersbe*

18:7-8 **Then Paul left the synagogue and went next door to the house of Titius Justus, a worshiper of God. Crispus, the synagogue ruler, and his entire household believed in the Lord; and many of the Corinthians who heard him believed and were baptized.**NIV *Titius Justus,* called *a worshiper of God,* was probably a Gentile. Some have speculated that this was Gaius (see Romans 16:23; 1 Corinthians 1:14). His house became Paul's base of operations, and its proximity to the synagogue gave the apostle convenient and ongoing contact with both Jews and God-fearing Greeks.

As the *synagogue ruler, Crispus* would have been responsible for maintenance of the synagogue complex and the services held there. Such a position would have made him a prominent and well-to-do person in the community. Thus, his conversion (and that of his household) was a significant breakthrough for the church.

18:9-11 **One night the Lord said to Paul in a vision, "Do not be afraid, but speak and do not be silent; for I am with you, and no one will lay a hand on you to harm you, for there are many in this**

city who are my people." He stayed there a year and six months, teaching the word of God among them.[NRSV] Apparently, the conversions of Crispus and other Corinthians (18:7-8), together with the formation of a growing "house church" right next door to the synagogue, must have provoked great controversy and opposition. Otherwise, the words of the Lord *("Do not be afraid")* in Paul's vision would make no sense. In contrast to his treatment elsewhere (see 17:5, 13), *no one* would *lay a hand on* Paul—he would not endure bodily harm during this time in Corinth.

The phrase "There are many in this city who are my people" likely refers to the group of believers already in Corinth together with the large number of people there who had been "appointed for eternal life" (Acts 13:48 NIV). Others who became Christians in Corinth were Phoebe (Romans 16:1—Cenchrea was the port city of Corinth), Tertius (Romans 16:22), Erastus (Romans 16:23), Quartus (Romans 16:23), Chloe (1 Corinthians 1:11), Gaius (1 Corinthians 1:14), Stephanas and his household (1 Corinthians 16:15), Fortunatus (1 Corinthians 16:17), and Achaicus (1 Corinthians 16:17).

As a result of this divine word of assurance, Paul spent eighteen months in Corinth preaching and teaching. During that year and a half, Paul established a church and wrote two letters to the believers in Thessalonica (1 and 2 Thessalonians).

COMFORT IN COMMUNITY

In what had to be a most encouraging vision, Christ told Paul that he had many people in Corinth (18:9-10). Sometimes we can feel alone or isolated, especially when we see wickedness all around us and when we are persecuted for our faith. Usually, however, there are others in the neighborhood or community who also follow Christ. Ask God to lead you to them or to those who are on the verge of faith.

18:12-13 While Gallio was proconsul of Achaia, the Jews made a united attack on Paul and brought him into court. "This man," they charged, "is persuading the people to worship God in ways contrary to the law."[NIV] God's promise was that Paul would not be personally harmed (18:9); this guarantee did not preclude an attack on his ministry. In time, the Jews would successfully manage to have Paul charged with promoting a religion not approved by Roman law. Such behavior amounted to treason. But Paul was not encouraging obedience to a human king other than Caesar (see 17:7), nor was he speaking against the Roman Empire. Instead, he was speaking about Christ's eternal kingdom.

This sequence of events took place when *Gallio,* the brother of Seneca the philosopher, was *proconsul of Achaia* (modern Greece). He had come to power in A.D. 51–52, and he enjoyed a good reputation among his people as a pleasant man.

18:14-15 But just as Paul started to make his defense, Gallio turned to Paul's accusers and said, "Listen, you Jews, if this were a case involving some wrongdoing or a serious crime, I would be obliged to listen to you. But since it is merely a question of words and names and your Jewish laws, you take care of it. I refuse to judge such matters."NLT This was an important judicial decision for the spread of the gospel in the Roman Empire. Judaism was a recognized religion under Roman law. As long as Christians were seen as a sect within Judaism, the court refused to hear cases brought against them. If they had claimed to be a new and separate religion, they could easily have been outlawed by the government. In effect, Gallio was saying, "I don't understand all your terminology and finer points of theology (and I don't wish to). Handle the matter yourself, and don't bother me."

Gallio's decision proved to be extremely beneficial for the emerging Christian church for the next ten years. His ruling became a legal precedent used in Paul's trial in Rome. If Gallio had found Paul guilty, every governor in every province where Paul or other missionaries traveled could arrest the Christians. By not ruling against Paul, the Romans were including Christianity (as a sect of Judaism) as one of the legal religions *(religio licita)* of the Roman Empire. Gallio, in effect, helped spread the gospel throughout the Empire.

18:16-17 And he drove them out of the courtroom. The mob had grabbed Sosthenes, the leader of the synagogue, and had beaten him right there in the courtroom. But Gallio paid no attention.NLT The fact that Gallio had Paul's Jewish accusers driven from the courtroom, rather than merely sent away, reveals his irritation with what he evidently felt were petty, trumped-up charges. Many prominent Romans viewed the Jews with disdain; they considered them uncultured, given to strange beliefs, and prone to troublemaking.

The official proceedings having been concluded, the gathered crowd became unruly and erupted in violence. This *mob* may have been Greeks venting their feelings against the Jews for causing turmoil, or it may have included some Jews. If the latter is true, *Sosthenes,* the newly designated leader of the synagogue (after the conversion of Crispus, see 18:8) became the focal point of the mob's anger and frustration probably because he was seen as the one responsible for losing the case against Paul and leaving the synagogue worse off than before. A man named Sosthenes is mentioned in 1 Corinthians 1:1, and this may be the same man. If so, he would later become a convert and a companion of Paul.

Whether the mob consisted of Greeks beating up a Jew or the Jews turning against one of their own in frustration, Gallio was unconcerned and *paid no attention.*

PAUL RETURNS TO ANTIOCH OF SYRIA / 18:18-23

Leaving Corinth, Paul set sail for Syria with Priscilla and Aquila. He made a brief stop in Ephesus, leaving his faithful colleagues there, and vowing—"God willing" (18:21)—to return later.

From there he continued in a southeastward direction to Caesarea, where he visited the church at Jerusalem to report on his activity. Then he traveled north to Antioch. This marked the end of Paul's second missionary journey.

THE TOGETHER TEAM

Priscilla and Aquila were marriage and ministry partners (18:18). Four timeless qualities enabled Priscilla and Aquila to have a marriage that resulted in major ministry:

1. They were steeped in the **T**ruth of God's Word. (Remember that Priscilla and Aquila spent a great deal of time with Paul making tents together. Obviously, they had heard him teach and preach many, many times. This explains the reason they were able to pull Apollos aside and explain the gospel to him. They were competent in handling the Scriptures.)

2. They had an eye on **E**ternity. (Though they were tentmakers by trade, they were focused on something far more significant. They were investing in people and seeking first and foremost to build Christ's church!)

3. They had an attitude of **A**vailability. (Always their home was open; always they were willing to pull up stakes and go where they were needed.)

4. They were radically committed to **M**inistry. (Everywhere they went, lives were touched. Because they were active, sensitive, faithful, and steady, they ended up having an impact on three of the most influential Christian leaders of their day—Paul, Apollos, and Timothy!)

How much ministry takes place in your marriage?

18:18 Paul stayed in Corinth for some time after that and then said good-bye to the brothers and sisters and sailed for the coast of Syria, taking Priscilla and Aquila with him. (Earlier, at Cenchrea, Paul had shaved his head according to Jewish custom, for he had taken a vow.)[NLT] Following the failure of the Jewish plot against him, Paul continued ministering in Corinth.

MARRIAGE WITH A MISSION

One of the more interesting couples in the New Testament is Priscilla and Aquila. Colleagues of the apostle Paul, this husband and wife team left a legacy of tireless Christian labor. Always willing to serve wherever needed, they are a wonderful role model for modern-day couples who want to use their marriages to make an eternal difference in this world.

Reference	*Location*	*Date*	*Event*
Acts 18:2	Rome	A.D. 49	Ordered by Claudius to leave Rome (with all the other Jews)
Acts 18:2-3	Corinth	A.D. 50–51	Made tents and ministered with the apostle Paul
Acts 18:18-19	Ephesus	A.D. 52	Left by Paul in Ephesus, where among other things, they helped Apollos sharpen his message
1 Corinthians 16:19	Ephesus	A.D. 55–56	Hosted a church in their home in Ephesus, and they sent greetings via Paul to Christian friends in Corinth
Romans 16:3-5	Rome	A.D. 56–57	Ministered back in Rome and hosted a house-church
2 Timothy 4:19	Ephesus	A.D. 67	In Ephesus once again, probably assisted young Timothy as he pastored there

(If Gallio's judgment came in the summer or fall of A.D. 51, it probably means that Paul stayed through the winter in Corinth before departing for the coast of Syria.)

The *vow* Paul took at *Cenchrea* (the seaport for the city of Corinth) may have been a temporary Nazirite vow, which would end with shaving the head and offering the hair as a sacrifice (Numbers 6:18). Or it could have been a personal vow of thanksgiving, offered in light of God's providential protection while in Corinth.

18:19-21 **They arrived at Ephesus, where Paul left Priscilla and Aquila. He himself went into the synagogue and reasoned with the Jews. When they asked him to spend more time with them, he declined. But as he left, he promised, "I will come back if it is God's will." Then he set sail from Ephesus.**[NIV] From Corinth, Paul sailed east with his coworkers Priscilla and Aquila. No reason is given for their relocation from Corinth. Perhaps, at Paul's request, they had agreed to champion the cause of Christ in Asia

Minor. Arriving at Ephesus at the mouth of the Cayster River, the missionary team disembarked. 18:23-28 reveals that Priscilla and Aquila settled in Ephesus; Paul merely used this layover to pay a quick visit to the Jewish synagogue.

Though the Jews were receptive to Paul's message, he apparently felt a more pressing need to return to Antioch. A few ancient manuscripts imply that Paul was also eager to arrive in Jerusalem in time to celebrate the Feast of the Passover. If this is accurate, Paul probably wanted to take advantage of the evangelistic opportunities presented by such a gathering of devout Jews. He promised to return to them *"if it is God's will"* (see James 4:15).

IT'S TIME

Heading for home after a two-year missionary adventure, Paul could have felt satisfied, tired, and perhaps even ready for some rest. During a scheduled stop in Ephesus, however, he left the ship to pay a brief evangelistic visit to the Jews at the local synagogue. The great apostle possessed a sense of urgency, a focus, and an unending compassion to see others meet the Christ he knew so well. Paul tried to make every moment count for eternity. The clock is ticking. Time, the substance of our lives, is slipping by. Are we making the most of the days God has allotted for us?

18:22 When he had landed at Caesarea, he went up to Jerusalem and greeted the church, and then went down to Antioch.[NRSV] With the five-hundred-mile voyage from Ephesus completed, Paul went *up to Jerusalem,* then *down to Antioch*—the prepositions indicate the geographical elevation of the ancient city. Having been away from Antioch of Syria for some two years, Paul had much good news to report to his fellow believers.

This verse marks the end of Paul's second missionary journey.

18:23 After spending some time in Antioch, Paul went back to Galatia and Phrygia, visiting all the believers, encouraging them and helping them to grow in the Lord.[NLT] Verse 23 marks the beginning of Paul's third missionary journey, which lasted from A.D. 53 to 57. Leaving the church at *Antioch,* Paul headed toward Ephesus, but along the way he revisited the churches in *Galatia and Phrygia.* The heart of this trip was a lengthy stay (two to three years) in Ephesus. Before returning to Jerusalem, Paul also visited believers in Macedonia and Greece.

As Paul set out, one of his priorities was *helping* the believers *to grow.* This verb *(episterizo)* is only used twice in the New Testament and conveys the idea of establishing or making strong; it connotes edification mixed with encouragement. Such was Paul's regular practice—to keep checking up on those he had led to Christ and the churches he had founded.

BUILDING UP PEOPLE
Paul seemed to view everyone as either a lost soul in need of being evangelized or a Christian in need of being edified and encouraged. His perspective was "I am here to serve others." His every encounter with another individual was a chance to do so in one way or the other. Imagine if your church members made it their daily goal to do this. Because life is often so discouraging, we need others who will come alongside us and help make us stronger and provide the motivation we need to press on. Be someone who builds others up—through acts of kindness, by passing on lessons learned, by admitting failures, by being real.

APOLLOS INSTRUCTED AT EPHESUS / 18:24-28

Left in Ephesus by Paul, Priscilla and Aquila met a gifted speaker named Apollos, who had great passion for Christ but an incomplete knowledge of the gospel. Equipping him with a more accurate message, they sent him on to Achaia, where he was used powerfully by God. This small investment in one life by the faithful Priscilla and Aquila resulted in enormous eternal dividends!

ON FIRE FOR GOD
Apollos taught with great fervor (18:25). How can we capture and maintain Apollos's zeal? The key is conviction. When beliefs move from our heads down into our hearts, when we are overpowered by truth and we become convinced in our souls that a thing is true and that it matters, then we become passionate. This is not a plea for us to try to conjure up feelings or attempt to live on an emotional high. But it *is* a warning for us to monitor our spiritual temperature. We must do the things that will increase our passion for God and avoid things that tend to sap us of our spiritual enthusiasm. If we don't worship or witness, if we don't experience God or spend time with new believers who are joyful and exuberant about their newfound relationship with God, we can very easily become stagnant and cold.

18:24 Meanwhile a Jew named Apollos, a native of Alexandria, came to Ephesus. He was a learned man, with a thorough knowledge of the Scriptures.NIV From *Alexandria,* the second most influential city in the Roman Empire, came a *Jew named Apollos* (the name is a possible contraction of "Apollonius"). Growing up in that Egyptian city's university atmosphere, Apollos was highly cultured and trained in philosophy and rhetoric.

As a Jew, he also possessed a wonderful grasp of the Old Testament. It is not stated what prompted him to move to Ephesus.

18:25 He had been instructed in the way of the Lord, and he spoke with great fervor and taught about Jesus accurately, though he knew only the baptism of John.[NIV] Apollos was an eloquent and powerful speaker. He had an accurate though incomplete message. While he had "thorough knowledge" (18:24 NIV) of the Old Testament, he was familiar with *only the baptism of John* (referring to John the Baptist).

In all likelihood, Apollos's preaching was a more polished version of John's message: "Turn from your sins and turn to God" (Matthew 3:2 NLT). John had focused on repentance from sin and on water baptism as an outward sign of commitment to and preparation for the Messiah's kingdom. Apollos was probably urging people in a more eloquent fashion to do the same.

Apollos was "fervent in spirit" (NASV). Acts 19:8 describes Paul's preaching and teaching in Ephesus as forceful and convincing. Clearly these were enthusiastic men. Our English word "enthusiasm" comes from an extrabiblical Greek word, *enthousiasmos,* meaning to be inspired, to be "in" *(en)* "God" *(theos).* The idea is one of strong excitement or feeling. An enthusiastic person inspires others because of his or her zeal or fervor. The ministries of Apollos and Paul were excellent, at least in part, because these men were filled with passion. Apollos needed to get the entire picture, and then he would be a powerful witness for Christ.

TOO PROUD TO LEARN?
Although his natural abilities could have made him proud, Apollos proved himself willing to learn (18:26). God used Priscilla and Aquila, fresh from months of traveling with and learning from Paul, to give Apollos the complete gospel. Because Apollos did not hesitate to be a student, he became an even better teacher. How much does your willingness to learn affect God's efforts to help you become all he wants you to be? Be humble enough to let others teach you truths and skills that can make you a more effective Christian witness.

18:26 When Priscilla and Aquila heard him preaching boldly in the synagogue, they took him aside and explained the way of God more accurately.[NLT] The eloquent, fiery young man who was so ably interpreting and applying the Old Testament messianic Scriptures in the synagogue was quickly noticed by *Priscilla and Aquila.* Upon hearing Apollos preach, they immediately recognized the deficiencies in his message. Consequently, they *took him* *aside* (probably to their home) and *explained the way of God more accurately,* telling him about the life of Jesus, his death and resurrection, and the coming of the Holy Spirit. As Aquila and Priscilla set forth the historical facts of the gospel, Apollos must have seen many Old Testament prophecies become clear. The reports of his subsequent ministry suggest that he was filled with new energy and boldness after he received the complete gospel message.

THE POWER OF HOSPITALITY
Priscilla and Aquila took Apollos aside and taught him (18:26). In an age when the focus is mostly on what happens *between* husband and wife, Aquila and Priscilla are an example of what can happen *through* husband and wife. Their effectiveness together speaks about their relationship with each other. Their hospitality opened the doorway of salvation to many. All their lives they used their home as a warm place for training and worship. Back in Rome years later, they hosted one of the house churches that developed (Romans 16:3-5). The Christian home is still one of the best tools for spreading the gospel. Do guests see Christ (and meet him) in your home?

18:27 **Apollos had been thinking about going to Achaia, and the brothers and sisters in Ephesus encouraged him in this. They wrote to the believers in Achaia, asking them to welcome him. When he arrived there, he proved to be of great benefit to those who, by God's grace, had believed.**[NLT] With his more complete theology, Apollos, who *had been thinking about going to Achaia,* was encouraged to do so by *the Christians in Ephesus.* They sent along a glowing letter of introduction, asking the *believers in Achaia* to *welcome him.* He quickly became the verbal champion of the Christians in Achaia (probably Corinth), debating the opponents of the gospel in public. Read what Paul says of Apollos's impact in 1 Corinthians 4:1, 6.

THE DANGER OF GIFTS
As often happens, Apollos's abilities eventually created a problem. Some of the Corinthians became more enamored with Apollos than with his message. An Apollos fan club developed. There is no evidence to suggest that Apollos encouraged this behavior. And Paul never blamed Apollos for this development. Still, Paul eventually had to confront the Corinthians about their divisiveness (see 1 Corinthians 1:12-13). Be glad for God's gifts, but always remember that they are given to bring honor to him. *He* is the point! *His* glory is the issue! Any ability or talent that calls undue attention to itself is sinful. Appreciate the gift, but more than that, praise the Giver of the gifts.

18:28 For he vigorously refuted the Jews in public debate, proving from the Scriptures that Jesus was the Christ.NIV Apollos proved to be a master debater. His arguments for the messiahship of Jesus were so powerful and logical that the Jews could not oppose him. His reputation spread far and wide (1 Corinthians 1:12; 3:4-6; 4:6), and Paul came to view him as a trustworthy co-worker in the gospel (1 Corinthians 16:12; Titus 3:13).

THE ROLE OF REASON

Apollos was from Alexandria in Egypt, the home of a great university and massive library. A scholar, orator, and debater, Apollos was used greatly by God to strengthen and encourage the church. A finely trained mind is a powerful tool when used for the glory of God. Apollos used the gift of reason to convince many in Greece of the truth of the gospel. You don't have to turn off your mind when you turn to Christ. If you have an ability in logic or debate, use it to bring others to God.

Acts 19

PAUL'S THIRD MISSIONARY JOURNEY / 19:1-7

Evidence from Paul's epistles suggests the great apostle launched out on his third missionary trip in an attempt to undo the damage caused among the churches by numerous opponents of the gospel. Beginning at Antioch, Paul journeyed in a northwesterly direction through Galatia and Phrygia (18:23), eventually coming to Ephesus on the west coast of Asia Minor. There he met some believers who, like Apollos, knew only John's baptism and had only a sketchy understanding of the gospel. Their reception of the Spirit confirmed Paul's authority as an apostle and gave them equal standing in the church.

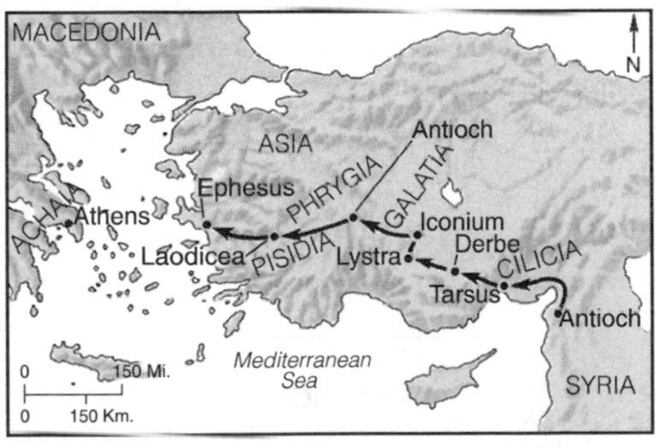

PAUL TAKES A THIRD JOURNEY
What prompted Paul's third journey may have been the need to correct any misunderstandings in the churches Paul had planted. So he hurried north, then west, returning to many of the cities he had previously visited. This time, however, he stayed on a more direct westward route toward Ephesus.

19:1 While Apollos was in Corinth, Paul traveled through the interior provinces. Finally, he came to Ephesus, where he found several believers.[NLT] After the parenthetical story of Apollos, Luke continued his record of Paul's third missionary journey, begun in 18:23. Paul traveled an interior road across Asia Minor, though no reason is given. It may have been the shortest (though least traveled and most dangerous) route to Ephesus, and the apostle may have simply been eager to arrive at the capital and leading business center of the Roman province of Asia (part of present-day Turkey). Or perhaps there were congregations along this path that

Paul wanted to visit. He arrived in Ephesus, a hub of sea and land transportation, ranking with Antioch in Syria and Alexandria in Egypt as one of the great cities on the Mediterranean Sea. The population of Ephesus during the first century may have reached 250,000. The temple to the Greek goddess Artemis (Diana is her Roman equivalent) was located there. The worship of Artemis was also a great financial boon to the area because it brought tourists, festivals, and trade.

Paul would stay in Ephesus for about three years. Ephesus had great wealth and power as a center for trade. It was a strategic location from which to influence all of Asia. From Ephesus he would write his first letter to the Corinthians to counter several problems that the church in Corinth was facing. Later, while imprisoned in Rome, Paul would write a letter to the Ephesian church (the book of Ephesians).

Upon his arrival, he promptly found a group of *several believers* (the Greek says "disciples"). Based on 19:3-5, these men probably were students of John the Baptist. They had embraced his ministry and teachings. One first-century sect of Jews actually believed that John the Baptist was the Messiah. There is evidence into the fourth century that some groups claimed John as their founder. As in the case of Apollos, these individuals were sincere but were hampered by an incomplete knowledge of the gospel.

THE MISSION

Paul and the rest of the early church were on a mission from God. They did not exist solely to have meetings or programs. They had Good News, and good news is for telling. It was so good that it was even worth going elsewhere to spread. It was worth telling even in the face of opposition (19:9). Does your church have that same sense of mission? Mediocrity says, "Let's just content ourselves with where and what we are. Let's just gather in our small groups and in our church building on Sunday mornings and have church. We'll care for each other and sponsor a few assorted programs." Be careful that you don't get so involved and absorbed in lots of *good* church activities that you forget about the *best* task of all—reaching out with the life-changing news of Christ.

19:2 He said to them, "Did you receive the Holy Spirit when you became believers?" They replied, "No, we have not even heard that there is a Holy Spirit."[NRSV] Paul's question to this group of Ephesian men underlines the truth that apart from the *Holy Spirit,* there is no salvation (Romans 8:9, 16; 1 Corinthians 12:13; Ephesians 1:13). The Spirit is the one who imparts life (John 3:5).

The reply of these men is difficult to interpret. John the Baptist had talked plainly about the coming of the Holy Spirit (Matthew 3:11; Mark 1:8; Luke 3:16; John 1:32-33). Perhaps this answer implies that they were unaware that the time of the Spirit's outpouring had come at last. Whatever the case, like Apollos (18:24-26), these men needed further instruction on the message and ministry of Jesus Christ. They believed in Jesus as the Messiah, but they did not understand the significance of his death and resurrection or the role of the Holy Spirit in the birth and life of the church. Since becoming a Christian involves turning from sin (repentance) and turning to Christ (faith), these "believers" were incomplete. They had repented but had not yet trusted in Christ. In truth, they were believers only in the sense that they were seeking to believe.

19:3 So Paul asked, "Then what baptism did you receive?" "John's baptism," they replied.[NIV] John's baptism was a sign of repentance from sin only (Matthew 3:2, 6, 8, 11; Mark 1:4-5; Luke 3:8), not a sign of new life in Christ. John's ministry had been preparatory. His baptism had anticipated something greater, pointing forward, toward Christ, the fulfillment of all things. Christian baptism, on the other hand, looked back on the finished work of Christ. These Ephesian men had experienced the former, not the latter.

19:4-5 Paul said, "John's baptism was a baptism of repentance. He told the people to believe in the one coming after him, that is, in Jesus." On hearing this, they were baptized into the name of the Lord Jesus.[NIV] After adequate explanation, these men *were baptized into the name of the Lord Jesus.* Given Paul's remarks in 1 Corinthians 1:14-17, it may be that an unnamed associate of Paul actually performed this ceremony. This is the only place in the New Testament where we find an instance of rebaptism.

19:6-7 Then when Paul laid his hands on them, the Holy Spirit came on them, and they spoke in other tongues and prophesied. There were about twelve men in all.[NLT] When Paul laid his hands on these twelve disciples (either to greet them as brothers or as a final part of the baptism rite), *the Holy Spirit came on them* in a similar fashion as at Pentecost. Pentecost was the formal outpouring of the Holy Spirit on the then mostly Jewish church, and it included outward, visible signs of the Holy Spirit's presence. Similar supernatural manifestations had occurred when the Holy Spirit first had come on Gentiles (see 10:45-47). The other outpourings in the book of Acts were God's way of uniting other (mostly Gentile) believers to the church. The mark of the true church is not merely right doctrine but right actions, the true evidence of the Holy Spirit's work.

In Acts, believers received the Holy Spirit in a variety of ways.

PARALLELS BETWEEN THE MINISTRIES OF PETER AND PAUL IN ACTS

Similarity	*Peter*	*Paul*
Healing crippled men	3:2-8	14:8-10
Healing via extraordinary means	5:15 (his shadow!)	19:12 (handkerchiefs!)
Casting out demons	5:16	16:18
Being flogged or beaten	5:40	16:23
Defeating sorcerers	8:18-24	13:6-11
Raising the dead	9:36-41	20:9-12
Escaping from prison	12:7-11	16:25-26

Usually the Holy Spirit would fill a person as soon as he or she professed faith in Christ. Here that filling happened later because these believers had not fully trusted in Christ as Savior. God was confirming to these believers, who did not initially know about the Holy Spirit, that they were a part of the church. The Holy Spirit's supernatural filling endorsed them as believers and showed the other members of the group that Christ was the only way.

What was the significance of the speaking in *tongues* among these Ephesian men? Perhaps to show that Paul had the same apostolic authority as did Peter to bestow the Spirit (see chapters 2 and 8). In any event, this is the final recorded instance of speaking in tongues in the book of Acts.

In order to interpret (and apply) the work of the Holy Spirit in Acts, believers must remember several truths. First, Acts is a book of transitions—documenting the end of the "old covenant" age of Israel and the law and the beginning of the "new covenant" age of the church and grace. Second, Acts is a history book that describes what did happen, not necessarily a doctrinal manual intended to prescribe what is supposed to happen. Third, there really is no set pattern for the reception of the Spirit in Acts. Sometimes people received the Spirit at baptism (2:38; 8:38), sometimes after baptism (8:15), and sometimes before baptism (10:47). The instances of tongues-speaking in Acts are erratic, not the general rule (see 2:4; 10:44-46; cf. 8:39; 13:52; 16:34). In Acts, Luke was primarily describing the spread of the gospel and its inclusiveness. In the epistles, the apostolic witnesses presented a more comprehensive doctrine of the Holy Spirit.

EVANGELISM OR EXPERIENCE?
Much has been made of the passages in Acts that depict believers speaking in tongues. Some have uncomfortably downplayed or dismissed these historical events. Others have tried to duplicate them. Few issues have prompted more argument and confusion or split more churches. We should remember that tongues-speaking is not the central theme of the book of Acts. The point of Luke's history is the faithful communication of the gospel to the ends of the earth. If we want to be doers of the Word (James 1:22), we will faithfully be involved in the same process of evangelism. Seek to share your faith in the power of the Holy Spirit (1:8), and leave it up to God to give you whatever experiences he thinks you need.

PAUL MINISTERS IN EPHESUS / 19:8-20

Paul's ministry in Ephesus lasted more than two years and was marked by an obvious movement of God's Spirit. Luke wrote that "the name of the Lord Jesus was held in high honor" (19:17 NIV) through bold preaching, supernatural healings, and transformed lives.

19:8 **Then Paul went to the synagogue and preached boldly for the next three months, arguing persuasively about the Kingdom of God.**[NLT] Paul was making good on a promise. He had paid an earlier visit to this same synagogue at the end of his second missionary journey, while on his way back to Antioch and Jerusalem (18:19-21). Though his visit had been brief, he had found a receptive group of Jews and had pledged to return at the first opportunity.

Given Paul's volatile history with the Jews (and his rather blunt preaching about Jesus as Messiah), it is surprising that he was able to minister at the synagogue for three full months before encountering stiff enough opposition requiring him to relocate.

KEEPING PROMISES
Paul had earlier told the Jews in Ephesus, "I will return again to you, God willing" (18:21 NKJV). About a year later, God gave Paul an opportunity to revisit the city, and Paul jumped at the chance to keep his word (19:8). For our words to be more than well-meaning sentiments and fuzzy intentions, we must keep track of the promises we make. Then we should follow through to keep those promises. How reliable are your words? Do you follow through on the vows you make?

19:9 But some of them became obstinate; they refused to believe and publicly maligned the Way. So Paul left them. He took the disciples with him and had discussions daily in the lecture hall of Tyrannus.[NIV] In time, Paul's teaching at the synagogue became too pointed, and the Jews *became obstinate.* In other words, a spiritual "hardness of heart" set in (see Hebrews 3:7-15), and they *refused to believe* the gospel. In their rebellion, they *publicly maligned* (spoke evil of, reviled, insulted) *the Way* (a common name for early Christianity—see 9:2; 19:23; 24:14).

Consequently, Paul moved his ministry to a nearby *lecture hall* (school). *Tyrannus* may have been a philosopher or merely the owner of the building. Such halls were used in the morning for teaching philosophy, but they were empty during the hot part of the day (about 11:00 A.M. to 4:00 P.M.). Because many people did not work during those hours, they would come to hear Paul's preaching.

Today, the meetings at the school of Tyrannus would be considered evangelistic "seeker meetings." The regular gatherings occurring in homes (2:46; 12:12; 16:40; 18:7; 20:20) would parallel small-group church gatherings.

THE COST

Some of the people refused to believe, and they maligned Paul (19:9). One of the obvious lessons from Acts is that excellent ministry always meets exceptional opposition. Believers who are serious in the quest to live faithfully for Jesus and proclaim the good news of the gospel will encounter stiff resistance, possibly even severe persecution (2 Timothy 3:12). No wonder Jesus told his followers to count the cost (Luke 14:25-33). There is a heavy price to be paid for faithfulness. But the cost is nothing compared to the glory that awaits those who determine to trust and obey the Lord. Following Christ is expensive (in terms of time, effort, energy, or material resources). Have you counted the cost? More importantly, will you pay the price?

19:10 This went on for the next two years, so that people throughout the province of Asia—both Jews and Greeks—heard the Lord's message.[NLT] Paul faithfully labored in Ephesus. His lectures were "daily" (19:9) and continued *for the next two years.* These were two of the most fruitful years for the expanding church. *The province of Asia* refers to Asia Minor or modern-day Turkey. During this time, spiritually hungry Asians must have traveled to Ephesus to hear Paul speak. "Throughout Asia" would include the area in which were the seven churches listed in Revelation 2 and 3 and the church in Colosse as well. Also Paul may have taken occasional breaks from teaching to go on short-term training missions to nearby cities.

PLODDING AWAY
"*Daily* meetings, Paul? For two *years?* Is this really necessary? Why don't we just meet every other week?" We don't know if anyone ever said this to Paul or if some believers at least had this thought, but the fact is, Paul took advantage of an open door and a receptive audience. He was a plodder. He did what he could with what he had. And in time all those days of faithful ministry added up. The eventual tally? "People throughout the province of Asia—both Jews and Greeks—heard the Lord's message" (19:10 NLT). Don't be discouraged by the seeming insignificance of one day's labor. Keep working faithfully, and the cumulative effect may one day astound you!

19:11-12 **God did extraordinary miracles through Paul, so that even handkerchiefs and aprons that had touched him were taken to the sick, and their illnesses were cured and the evil spirits left them.**[NIV] Paul's ministry in Ephesus was accompanied by *extraordinary miracles*—long-distance healings (involving the apostle's sweat cloths and workers' aprons) as well as exorcisms. The miracles had a threefold purpose: (1) to demonstrate God's ultimate power and authority (in a city where Satan had a stronghold; see 19:18-19); (2) to authenticate Paul as an apostle and a spokesman for the one true God (Mark 16:20; Romans 15:18-19; 2 Corinthians 2:12; Hebrews 2:1-4); and (3) most obviously, to demonstrate compassion and mercy to those in great need. Some scholars see in this passage an overt effort by Luke to show Paul as being equal with Peter (whose shadow healed people) and even with Jesus (whose robe healed people). See Mark 5:27-34; 6:56; Luke 8:44; Acts 5:15; and the chart, "Parallels between the Ministries of Peter and Paul in Acts" on page 326. Because of modern abuses of these kinds of displays by charlatans who would make money out of healing cloths "blessed" by a minister, we should take note. Only Jesus, Peter, and Paul were given this power. This power came from God, and the healing was granted to those who had faith.

19:13-14 **A team of Jews who were traveling from town to town casting out evil spirits tried to use the name of the Lord Jesus. The incantation they used was this: "I command you by Jesus, whom Paul preaches, to come out!" Seven sons of Sceva, a leading priest, were doing this.**[NLT] This *team of Jews* was traveling *from town to town* making a living by claiming to heal and drive out demons. This was a common occurrence in Israel (see

Luke 11:19). Often such people would recite a list of names in their incantation to be sure of including the right deity. Here they were trying to use Jesus' name in an effort to match Paul's power.

Many Ephesians engaged in exorcism and occult practices for profit (see 19:18-19). The *sons of Sceva* were impressed by Paul's work, obviously more powerful than their own. The Jewish historian, Josephus, recorded the names of all the priests until the time of the destruction of the temple in Jerusalem. There is no record of Sceva. He could have been posing as a priest, or somehow he was in the "priestly circle." His sons mentioned here failed to see that Paul's power to drive out demons came from God's Holy Spirit, not from incantations and magic formulas. They eventually discovered, with pain (see 19:15-16), that no one can control or duplicate God's power. These men were calling on the name of Jesus without knowing him personally.

UNCONTROLLABLE

The seven sons of Sceva thought they could manipulate God for selfish ends. If they just had the incantations right, the techniques down, and the process perfected—so they thought—they could "use" God for their own purposes. They failed to realize, however, that Christ's power cannot be accessed by reciting his name like a magic charm. God works his power only through those he chooses and only at times he determines. Beware of thinking that you can control God by your clever prayers or by precisely following man-made schemes. God is free to do as he likes.

19:15-16 One day the evil spirit answered them, "Jesus I know, and I know about Paul, but who are you?" Then the man who had the evil spirit jumped on them and overpowered them all. He gave them such a beating that they ran out of the house naked and bleeding.[NIV] The self-proclaimed exorcists, out for easy money, invoking the name of Jesus superstitiously, almost as one might rub a rabbit's foot, ended up so overpowered by one *evil spirit* in a man that they all received a *beating!* Eventually, they fled for their lives, feeling fortunate that they had lost only their clothes. Here is a clear incident that demonstrates the truth that knowing about Jesus is not the same as knowing him. The surprising knowledge and great strength of a demon-possessed person is recorded in other places (Luke 4:33; 8:28).

19:17 When this became known to the Jews and Greeks living in Ephesus, they were all seized with fear, and the name of the Lord Jesus was held in high honor.[NIV] The report of the encounter between the sons of Sceva and the evil spirit spread quickly throughout the area. The self-appointed exorcists were humbled and discredited. The *name of the Lord Jesus* came to be viewed as the most powerful name and not one to be taken lightly.

19:18-19 Many who became believers confessed their sinful practices. A number of them who had been practicing magic brought their incantation books and burned them at a public bonfire. The value of the books was several million dollars.NLT Ephesus was a center for black magic and other occult practices. The people would create magical formulas to give them wealth, happiness, and success in marriage. Superstition and sorcery were commonplace. Many of the Ephesian converts had been involved in these dark arts. However, the demonstrated power of the name of Jesus over evil spirits (19:11-17) became the impetus for a spiritual spring cleaning in the lives of many of the new believers in Ephesus. Specifically, they renounced their fascination with all occult practices (perhaps, as the original text suggests, even divulging their secret spells). Then, taking the remnants of their pagan pasts, they *burned them at a public bonfire.* Making a clean break with sin was costly—the magic books alone were worth *several million dollars* (literally, fifty thousand drachmas). A drachma was a silver coin equal to a worker's pay for one day.

> If you want to make enemies, try to change something.
> *Woodrow Wilson*

DENOUNCING THE DEMONIC

As the Ephesian believers realized, one cannot be a believer in Jesus and hold on to the occult, black magic, or sorcery. Once a person begins to dabble in these areas, it is extremely easy to become obsessed by them because Satan is very powerful. But God's power is even greater (1 John 4:4; Revelation 20:10). If you are mixed up in the occult, learn a lesson from the Ephesians, and get rid of anything that could keep you trapped in such practices.

19:20 In this way the word of the Lord spread widely and grew in power.NIV Here is another of Luke's "progress reports." As the events in Ephesus powerfully demonstrated, the gospel was spreading—touching hearts and changing lives. Christ was building his church, "and all the powers of hell will not conquer it" (Matthew 16:18 NLT). But that doesn't mean the powers of hell would surrender easily.

THE RIOT IN EPHESUS / 19:21-41

In the great cosmic conflict for the souls of men, every intrusion of good is met by the fierce resistance of evil. Such was the case in Ephesus. A silversmith named Demetrius, who manufactured small idols of the Greek goddess Artemis, became alarmed by the mass conversion of Ephesians to Christianity. Gathering his fellow tradesmen, he convinced them that Paul and his message were a serious threat to their livelihood. A riot at the city's amphitheater ensued, and it took a soothing plea from the mayor to rescue Gaius and Aristarchus, Paul's traveling companions.

19:21 **After all this had happened, Paul decided to go to Jerusalem, passing through Macedonia and Achaia. "After I have been there," he said, "I must visit Rome also."**[NIV] Why did Paul say, *"I must visit Rome"* ("must" meaning the sense of an inner, divinely guided compulsion)? Wherever Paul went, he could see Rome's influence. Paul wanted to take the message of Christ to the world's center of influence and power. His desire to preach the eternal truths of God in the so-called "eternal" city (see Romans 1:15) comprises the balance of the book of Acts.

ENGAGEMENT IN MINISTRY

Paul felt compelled to go to Rome. He was engaged in an ongoing, lifelong ministry to people. He—and the rest of the early church as well—took seriously the command to go and make disciples. At this point in history, the church was at least twenty years old. Those who had been with it from the beginning had seen some explosive growth—and lots of hard times. They might have been tempted to ease up, to say, "Let's take a few years to consolidate, assess, and regroup." They didn't. Paul, probably in his midfifties, had already been on two fruitful but difficult journeys. But he gave no thought to retiring. Off he went again, his passion being to get the message of Christ to the most people in the shortest time.

The lessons are clear. We cannot sit back. We must be the aggressors; we must go out into the world. That is the example we have in Christ. God engaged us. He initiated. We can't just put signs in our yards or on our church marquees and expect these to draw unbelievers to God! Get out of your comfort zone and move toward others.

19:22 **He sent his two assistants, Timothy and Erastus, on ahead to Macedonia while he stayed awhile longer in the province of Asia.**[NLT] Paul had already decided to depart from Ephesus before the trouble recorded in 19:23-41 broke out. But he *stayed awhile longer,* apparently to tie up some loose ends. He sent two of his young protégés—*Timothy and Erastus*—ahead to do advance work in the region (Macedonia) he intended to visit. It was a common practice for leaders to have assistants. Moses had Joshua. Elijah was served by Elisha. Even secular philosophers had disciples who assisted them.

Timothy did quite a bit of traveling for Paul (see the box, "Adventure Highlights from Timothy's Life" in 16:2-3). Timothy would eventually become an overseer/pastor in the church at Ephesus. Romans 16:23 refers to an Erastus who was the *oikonomos,* "city treasurer," or city manager of public works of Corinth. This may have been the same individual.

19:23-24 **But about that time, serious trouble developed in Ephesus concerning the Way. It began with Demetrius, a silversmith who had a large business manufacturing silver shrines of the Greek goddess Artemis. He kept many craftsmen busy.**NLT
Artemis was a goddess of fertility. She was represented by a carved female figure with many breasts. A large statue of Artemis (see 19:35) was in the great temple at Ephesus. That temple was one of the wonders of the ancient world. Supported by 127 pillars each six stories tall, the edifice was about four times larger than the Parthenon in Athens. The festival of Artemis involved wild orgies and carousing. Obviously, the religious and commercial life of Ephesus reflected the city's worship of this pagan deity.

After a period of relative peace and steady growth for the Ephesian church, the gospel became offensive and intolerable to the city's *craftsmen* because of the way it was undermining their ability to sell silver idols of Artemis. Converts to Christianity were no longer buying these products. Consequently, for economic and religious reasons, *the Way* (a reference to those who followed Christ) came under scrutiny, suspicion, and eventually attack. *Demetrius,* a leader and prominent member of the silversmiths' guild, was the instigator of this trouble.

AGAINST THE FLOW

The gospel was pretty much ignored in Ephesus until it began to affect the cash flow of the pagan merchants (19:23-24). Then things got wild! This is always the case. There is a ripple effect as the message of Christ is preached, hearts are touched, and attitudes are changed. Eventually, the gospel results in lifestyle changes. Followers of Christ no longer find within themselves a desire for worldly things. And if enough people turn to Christ, the repercussions can be felt all across a society. If we are ignored by our culture, it may be because we are not having an impact. Ask God to use you and your church to change lives on a wide scale.

19:25-26 He called the craftsmen together, along with others employed in related trades, and addressed them as follows: "Gentlemen, you know that our wealth comes from this business. As you have seen and heard, this man Paul has persuaded many people that handmade gods aren't gods at all. And this is happening not only here in Ephesus but throughout the entire province!"[NLT] In the first century, craftsmen united with one another to form professional trade guilds. Similar to modern-day unions, these groups adhered to self-prescribed standards and practices. In this instance, Demetrius, perhaps the leader of this powerful guild, gathered not only the silversmiths who produced the miniature images of Artemis for sale at the temple but also *others employed in related trades.* (Archaeologists have also located images of the goddess made out of terra-cotta and gold.)

During the months that Paul had preached in Ephesus, Demetrius and his fellow craftsmen had not quarreled with his doctrine. They only became concerned when his preaching threatened their profits. Because they derived major income from making and selling silver statues of the Ephesian goddess Artemis, the craftsmen knew their livelihood would suffer if people started believing in Jesus and discarding the idols.

19:27 "There is danger not only that our trade will lose its good name, but also that the temple of the great goddess Artemis will be discredited, and the goddess herself, who is worshiped throughout the province of Asia and the world, will be robbed of her divine majesty."[NIV] Demetrius's strategy for stirring up a riot was to appeal to his fellow workmen's love of money and then to encourage them to hide their greed behind the mask of patriotism and religious loyalty. It would be difficult to get Ephesian citizens worked up about the slumping sales of a group of idol makers. However, it would be easy to rally the masses behind a noble campaign to defend the honor and reputation of the goddess and her magnificent shrine. It seemed to be a perfect plan—the craftsmen would be able to guard their economic interests, and the Artemis-worshiping citizens of Ephesus would see themselves as heroes for the sake of their land and beliefs. Religious fervor, nationalism, and materialism make a volatile combination.

19:28-29 When they heard this, they were enraged and shouted, "Great is Artemis of the Ephesians!" The city was filled with the confusion; and people rushed together to the theater, dragging with them Gaius and Aristarchus, Macedonians who were Paul's travel companions.[NRSV] The ploy of Demetrius worked perfectly. In short order, the gathered crowd was *enraged* (literally, filled with wrath) at the Christians in their city and the subversive message of the gospel. They began to cry out, *"Great is Artemis of the Ephesians!"* This was a standard formula for pagan worshipers—to cry out "Great is ________" (inserting the name of their deity of choice).

Spilling out into the street, this group moved through the city, infecting other citizens with their passionate resentment. As the gathering became an unruly mob, they made their way *to the theater,* apparently to stage a large demonstration. Archaeologists have determined that this open-air auditorium, cut into the western slope of Mount Pion, could seat nearly twenty-five thousand people.

As the crowd rushed along, fueled by their fury, they managed to seize two of Paul's known *travel companions—Gaius and Aristarchus.* (Aristarchus, a native of Thessalonica, would later accompany Paul on other journeys—see 20:3-4; 27:1-2; Gaius is probably not the same Gaius mentioned in Romans 16:23 or 1 Corinthians 1:14.)

19:30-31 Paul wanted to appevar before the crowd, but the disciples would not let him. Even some of the officials of the province, friends of Paul, sent him a message begging him not to venture into the theater.[NIV] Paul *wanted* to go to the theater, most likely to speak up and defend his companions but also to have the opportunity to preach to such a large crowd. But the other believers, fearing for his safety, wouldn't let Paul go.

These *officials of the province* were the most prominent men of the province of Asia, responsible for the religious and political order of the region. Clearly, Paul's message had reached all levels of society, crossing all social barriers and giving Paul *friends* in high places. Out of a dual concern for both public order and the well-being of their Jewish Christian friend, these powerful authorities begged Paul *not to venture into the theater.*

19:32 Inside, the people were all shouting, some one thing and some another. Everything was in confusion. In fact, most of them didn't even know why they were there.[NLT] Luke's observations about many in the rioting crowd not even knowing *why they were there* would have brought a chuckle to his original readers, for Greek playwrights and authors commonly mocked human foibles. Irony and parody were common elements in Greek comedy.

The scene in the theater was one of total *confusion* and uninhibited expression. The word translated "confusion" literally means "to pour together" and conveys the idea of being stirred up, agitated, in an uproar.

MOB MENTALITY

Most of the crowd in the open-air theater did not know why they were shouting and rioting (19:32). This is a true picture of the phenomenon known as "mob mentality." People suspend their better judgment and stop thinking logically. They fall in with the group and feed off of a collective sense of power or rage. Such emotions, while making individuals feel wonderfully alive, are capable of sparking great destruction. It is for good reason that Moses warned the children of Israel in Exodus 23:2: "You shall not follow a crowd to do evil" (NKJV). When feelings are running high, take a step back, and examine your own heart. Engage your mind, and determine to obey God.

19:33-34 **Alexander was thrust forward by some of the Jews, who encouraged him to explain the situation. He motioned for silence and tried to speak in defense. But when the crowd realized he was a Jew, they started shouting again and kept it up for two hours: "Great is Artemis of the Ephesians! Great is Artemis of the Ephesians!"**NLT This *Alexander* may have been pushed forward by the Jews as a spokesperson to explain that the Jews were distinct from the new religion that was causing economic problems for the silversmiths. An uninformed mob might vent their anger on the Jews since they were well known for their monotheistic refusal to believe in pagan deities like Artemis. Long after Paul and his missionary friends left Ephesus, the Jews would still have to live and work there. So it seemed obvious to them that they needed to distance themselves from the Christians.

The attempt was futile. The gathering had become anti-Jewish as well as anti-Christian. Reasoning with a hysterical mob that has whipped itself into a frenzy is impossible. They shouted down Alexander by chanting, *"Great is Artemis of the Ephesians"* and keeping it up *for two hours!*

19:35-36 **But when the town clerk had quieted the crowd, he said, "Citizens of Ephesus, who is there that does not know that the city of the Ephesians is the temple keeper of the great Artemis and of the statue that fell from heaven? Since these things cannot be denied, you ought to be quiet and do nothing rash."**NRSV Into the chaos stepped the *town clerk* of Ephesus. This individual was the highest ranking civic official—something akin to our modern-day office of mayor. Such a person typically presided over citizen assemblies and was the city's representative at the provincial headquarters of Rome, located in Ephesus.

Perhaps fearing Roman reprisal—specifically the suspension of Ephesus's privileges as a "free" city with its own elected assembly—this respected leader somehow managed to get the attention of the angry mob. Then, using the same rhetorical tools of persuasion that Demetrius had employed to whip the crowd into a frenzy—appealing to their civic pride and religious devotion—he managed to bring about calm and order.

The mention of *the statue that fell from heaven* was likely a reference to a meteorite that was regarded as divine and placed in the Ephesian temple for the purposes of veneration. The presence of this mysterious object (perhaps it was even shaped like a woman) from above was considered proof that Artemis was a great and powerful goddess. In short, the clerk's argument was that the citizenry need not (for religious reasons) fear the intrusion of Christianity and should not (for political purposes) degenerate into incivility and disorder. Law and order, he was suggesting, should prevail in this instance.

19:37-39 "You have brought these men here, but they have stolen nothing from the temple and have not spoken against our goddess. If Demetrius and the craftsmen have a case against them, the courts are in session and the judges can take the case at once. Let them go through legal channels. And if there are complaints about other matters, they can be settled in a legal assembly."NLT With the crowd quiet and under some semblance of emotional control, the town clerk briefly reiterated the facts of the case involving the Christians. First, they were not "temple robbers," a term that can broadly refer to sacrilege. Nor had they uttered public denunciations of Artemis; instead, they simply were proclaiming the greatness of Jesus Christ. So, clearly, this was not a religious issue. Given that, if this was a conflict involving economic matters, Ephesus had an adequate legal system through which personal grievances could be addressed. Consequently, the clerk urged Demetrius and the members of the silversmiths' guild to pursue their dispute with the Christians through *legal channels.*

> Sometimes we assume we are thinking, when all we are really doing is rearranging our prejudices.
> *Author unknown*

Each province had a judge or proconsul who presided over a citizens' assembly, which looked into disputes and settled lawsuits. Since these forums were held at regular intervals, the plaintiffs could soon pursue justice through the proper legal channels, order could be preserved, and Rome would not end up taking disciplinary measures against the populace of Ephesus.

19:40-41 "For we are in danger of being charged with rioting today, since there is no cause that we can give to justify this commotion." When he had said this, he dismissed the assembly.NRSV

The city of Ephesus was under the domination of the Roman Empire. The main responsibility of the local city leaders was simply to maintain peace and order. If they failed to control the people, Rome would remove the appointed officials from office. The entire town could also be put under martial law, taking away many civic freedoms.

The clerk's straightforward reminder must have had a sobering effect on the Ephesian populace. The contrast is remarkable—a screaming mob rushing to fill the theater became an orderly group *dismissed* by the town clerk.

The riot in Ephesus convinced Paul that it was time to move on. But it also showed that the law still provided some protection for Christians as they challenged the worship of the goddess Artemis in the most idolatrous religion in Asia.

BARRIERS TO TRUTH

As the Ephesians filed out of the local amphitheater and back to their normal routines, how many reflected deeply on all the events they had just witnessed? Almost all of them probably knew about Paul, and perhaps most had even heard the gospel. But the majority refused to even consider the truth about Jesus because of their blind devotion to Artemis. Others were far too concerned with their present economic well-being to give any thought to eternal realities. This sad sequence of events reminds us that if we're not careful, we can allow our religious presuppositions or our worldly concerns to drown out the voice of truth. Ask God for ears to hear and for the courage to go against the flow in living out the truth.

Acts 20

This chapter records the conclusion of Paul's third missionary journey. Paul was heading for Jerusalem, intending to arrive before the Feast of Pentecost. On the way, he took time in Troas to encourage the believers, then he had a tearful farewell with the elders of the church in Ephesus. These events reveal the heart of the apostle. His speeches and actions offer a model for ministry.

PAUL GOES TO MACEDONIA AND GREECE / 20:1-6

Venturing down through Macedonia and into Achaia, Paul expressed a fatherly concern for the communities of believers that he had been instrumental in founding.

THROUGH MACEDONIA AND ACHAIA

A riot in Ephesus sent Paul to Troas, then through Macedonia to the region of Achaia. In Achaia he went to Corinth to deal with problems there. Paul had planned to sail from Corinth straight to Antioch of Syria, but a plot against his life was discovered. So he retraced his steps through Macedonia.

20:1 After the uproar had ceased, Paul sent for the disciples; and after encouraging them and saying farewell, he left for Macedonia.NRSV This *uproar* was the riot in Ephesus, described at the end of chapter 19. Paul then *sent for the disciples,* presumably those he had been teaching in Ephesus for two years.

The key word in this verse describing Paul's ministry is "encouraging." The Greek term is *paraklesis*—the same word used by Jesus for the coming Holy Spirit (John 14:16; 15:26). It literally means "called alongside," and possible meanings run the spectrum from "counsel" to "encourage" to "correct." The term carries with it two general ideas: (1) communication—the teaching of truth; and (2) compassion—the exhortation or encouragement that comes from a caring, concerned "Counselor." The word will show up again in 20:2 and 20:12 where, after the events in Troas, the people were "greatly comforted." Encouragement is a major theme in Acts; it is offered by Barnabas (4:36; 11:23) and by Paul (13:15; 16:40; 20:1-2; 27:35-36). See also 13:43; 14:22; 15:31-32; 18:27; 28:15.

After saying his *farewell,* Paul *left for Macedonia,* to continue his ministry of encouragement.

20:2-3 **Along the way, he encouraged the believers in all the towns he passed through. Then he traveled down to Greece, where he stayed for three months.**NLT Second Corinthians 2:12-13 and 7:5-7 give a few more details about this journey. Second Corinthians was written somewhere during this part of the journey. Paul had written 1 Corinthians while still in Ephesus. On this trip Paul likely retraced many of his steps, revisiting many of the churches he had established on his second journey (see 16–18) and arriving ultimately in *Greece* (specifically Corinth), *where he stayed for three months.*

> Our main business is not to see what lies dimly at a distance, but to do what lies clearly at hand.
> *Thomas Carlyle*

From Corinth Paul wrote the letter to the Romans. Although he had not yet been to Rome, believers had already started a church there (2:10; 18:2). Paul wrote to tell the Roman believers that he planned to visit them. The letter to the Romans is a theological essay on the meaning of faith and salvation, an explanation of the relationship between Jews and Gentiles in Christ, and a list of practical guidelines for the church.

WHEN GOD SAYS NO!

A reading of the first few verses of Romans (especially Romans 1:13) relates Paul's ardent desire to visit Rome and the sovereign hand of God that had prevented him from getting there up to this point. The combination of these two factors—Paul's impassioned desire to go to Rome and God's sovereign "no"—resulted in his sitting down to write the letter to the Romans—the undisputed "Magna Carta" of the Christian faith. Perhaps there are some "no's" in our lives that God is planning to use greatly, if we would just faithfully do what lies directly ahead of us instead of worrying about why we didn't get our way.

He was preparing to sail back to Syria when he discovered a plot by some Jews against his life, so he decided to return through Macedonia.NLT Paul's three-month stay was brought to a close in typical fashion, as a Jewish *plot* was *discovered* against the apostle, causing him to decide to *return through Macedonia.* Paul had been treated roughly in most of these locations—Philippi, Thessalonica, and Berea (16:11–17:14). But, like his difficult first journey through Phrygia and Galatia, to which he returned several times (see commentary at 14:21-22), Paul returned again to the places he had visited on his previous tours (see 19:21).

20:4-5 He was accompanied by Sopater son of Pyrrhus from Berea, Aristarchus and Secundus from Thessalonica, Gaius from Derbe, Timothy also, and Tychicus and Trophimus from the province of Asia. These men went on ahead and waited for us at Troas.NIV This is an unusually complete listing of those who *accompanied* Paul on this section of the journey. The company provided accountability. Paul was carrying the offering from the Asian churches for the suffering church at Jerusalem (see 2 Corinthians 8–9). Paul would not want the Jerusalem church to think he handled the money by himself, without others to account for it.

These men who were traveling with Paul also represented churches that Paul had started in Asia: (1) Galatia—*Gaius* and *Timothy;* (2) Asia—*Tychicus* and *Trophimus;* (3) Macedonia—*Sopater, Aristarchus,* and *Secundus.*

Having the men deliver the gifts to Jerusalem gave the gifts a personal touch and strengthened the unity of the universal church. This was also an effective way to teach the church about giving, because the men were able to report back to their churches the ways in which God was working through their giving. Paul discussed this gift in one of his letters to the Corinthian church (see 2 Corinthians 8:1-21).

20:6 But we sailed from Philippi after the Feast of Unleavened Bread, and five days later joined the others at Troas, where we stayed seven days.NIV Jews celebrated the Passover (which was immediately followed by the *Feast of Unleavened Bread*) according to Moses' instructions (see Exodus 12:43-51), even if they couldn't be at Jerusalem for the occasion. But Luke's reference to the feast does not necessarily mean that he, Paul, and the others celebrated it—an unlikely occurrence in this totally Gentile setting. It was simply a calendar marker, telling when all these things occurred. The use of "we" here shows that Luke again had joined the group. The last "we" section was 16:10-40.

PAUL'S FINAL VISIT TO TROAS / 20:7-12

In Troas, the believers gathered on Sunday, and Paul preached a lengthy, late-night sermon. A young man by the name of

Eutychus fell asleep and fell to his death out of the third-floor window in which he was sitting! Paul calmly restored Eutychus to life, and the church resumed its worship service.

20:7-8 On the first day of the week we came together to break bread. Paul spoke to the people and, because he intended to leave the next day, kept on talking until midnight. There were many lamps in the upstairs room where we were meeting.[NIV] The gathering of this group was *on the first day of the week.* This is one of the clearest New Testament references to the church meeting on Sunday rather than on Saturday, the Sabbath. The breaking of *bread* most likely refers to the Lord's Supper.

Evidently, the meeting began in the evening, presumably because the church members were not available to come during the day due to work. Because Paul and his companions *intended to leave the next day,* Paul had an extended teaching time and most likely recounted the news from all the other churches. He *kept on talking until midnight!* Paul did not want to leave Troas until he had made the most of every minute he had with the believers.

> The reason some people don't recognize opportunity is because it often comes disguised as hard work. *Anonymous*

The *many lamps* were candles in lanterns. The combination of the heat from the candles and the gathered number of people in an upstairs room probably made the room very warm. This no doubt helped Eutychus fall asleep.

20:9-10 As Paul spoke on and on, a young man named Eutychus, sitting on the windowsill, became very drowsy. Finally, he sank into a deep sleep and fell three stories to his death below. Paul went down, bent over him, and took him into his arms. "Don't worry," he said, "he's alive!"[NLT] Paul *spoke on and on,* and *Eutychus,* likely sitting in the window because of the crowd in the room, *sank into a deep sleep.* He *fell* out of the window, *three stories,* to *his death.*

Luke, the physician, confirmed the fact that Eutychus was dead. Paul went to the boy and took him into his arms (literally, the text says "he fell on" or "threw himself on" the boy). Paul

> The evangelistic harvest is always urgent. The destiny of men and of nations is always being decided. Every generation is strategic. We are not responsible for the past generation, and we cannot bear the full responsibility for the next one; but we do have our generation. God will hold us responsible as to how well we fulfill our responsibilities to this age and take advantage of our opportunities. *Billy Graham*

addressed the concerned flock. *"Don't worry,"* he said. Then, with those powerful Resurrection-reminiscent words, he added: *"He's alive!"* Can you imagine the impact that moment would have had on the watching congregation? on Eutychus's family? on Eutychus? The believers at Troas surely must have retold that story for years to come.

The raising of Eutychus would have reminded everyone of Peter's similar miracle with Dorcas (9:36-42). It also would have identified Paul's actions with Elijah and Elisha of the Old Testament (see 1 Kings 17:21; 2 Kings 4:32-35).

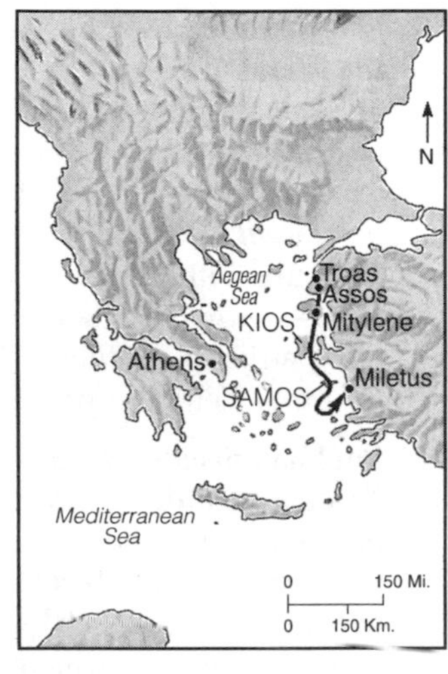

PAUL TRAVELS FROM TROAS TO MILETUS

From Troas, Paul traveled overland to Assos, then boarded a ship to Mitylene and Samos on its way to Miletus. He summoned the elders of the Ephesian church to say farewell to them, because he knew he would probably not see them again.

20:11-12 **Then he went upstairs again and broke bread and ate. After talking until daylight, he left. The people took the young man home alive and were greatly comforted.**[NIV] Following this amazing miracle, the meeting was resumed *upstairs* where they *broke bread* (most likely, they ate a meal, then celebrated the Lord's Supper), followed by Paul's continuing to teach *until daylight!* The believers were *greatly comforted* (literally, "encouraged")—a repeated feature of Paul's ministry.

PAUL MEETS THE EPHESIAN ELDERS / 20:13-38

Traveling south to Miletus, Paul summoned the elders of the Ephesian church in order to bid them farewell. In his charge to them, Paul reviewed his ministry among them, described the Spirit's leading him to Jerusalem, and challenged them to shepherd the church in their care. This discourse reveals Paul's pastoral heart (20:18-20, 31, 36-37), reiterates Paul's preoccupation with preaching the kingdom of God (20:24-25), and records the presence of a well-trained group of disciples who would be able to carry the message of Christ throughout Asia.

20:13-15 **Paul went by land to Assos, where he had arranged for us to join him, and we went on ahead by ship. He joined us there**

and we sailed together to Mitylene. The next day we passed the island of Kios. The following day, we crossed to the island of Samos. And a day later we arrived at Miletus.[NLT] Paul traveled ahead *by land to Assos,* which was about twenty miles away, a much shorter distance than a ship had to travel. The rest of the party *went on ahead by ship.* At Assos, the party was reunited, and Luke faithfully recorded the inland passage trek of their ship—*to Mitylene,* then past *the island of Kios* and *Samos,* eventually arriving *at Miletus.* Miletus was situated at the mouth of the Maeander River on the Aegean Sea (in modern-day Turkey).

20:16 **Paul had decided against stopping at Ephesus this time because he didn't want to spend further time in the province of Asia. He was hurrying to get to Jerusalem, if possible, for the Festival of Pentecost.**[NLT] Paul had missed attending the Passover in Jerusalem, so he was especially interested in arriving on time for Pentecost, which is fifty days after Passover. He was carrying gifts for the Jerusalem believers from churches in Asia and Greece (see Romans 15:25-26; 1 Corinthians 16:1-4; 2 Corinthians 8:1–9:15). The Jerusalem church had been experiencing difficult times.

HELPING THE HURTING

As Paul's involvement in the near tragedy with Eutychus demonstrates, the ministry is full of opportunities to help the hurting. It doesn't matter whether you are clergy or laity; being a Christian means helping those who need comfort. We need to be willing to go anywhere—from living rooms to intensive care units and funeral homes—to offer hugs, tears, or prayers for those who are suffering and grieving. Ask God to make you a source of comfort to some anguished soul today.

20:17 **From Miletus he sent a message to Ephesus, asking the elders of the church to meet him.**[NRSV] Paul wanted to meet with the *elders of the church* at *Ephesus,* so he sent word for them to come meet him at *Miletus.* Paul's message to the elders is an example of a typical address of Paul to the spiritual leaders of the churches he had begun.

In the same way that Luke included (more at length) a message of Paul to the Jews in the synagogues (13:16-41), a message to the Gentiles in the streets (14:15-17), and a message among the intellectuals in the "classroom" (17:22-31), here he recorded a sermon that reflects Paul's encouragement to those he had left in charge of the local churches. What a rich message it is for both church leaders *and* followers!

20:18-19 When they arrived he declared, "You know that from the day I set foot in the province of Asia until now I have done the Lord's work humbly—yes, and with tears. I have endured the trials that came to me from the plots of the Jews."[NLT] Paul's meeting with the Ephesian elders has three parts: (1) a review of Paul's past ministry in Ephesus (20:18-21); (2) an explanation of the present situation of Paul and the church (20:22-27); and (3) an instruction for these shepherds of God's flock to help them faithfully carry out their responsibilities in the future (20:28-35).

Paul described his ministry among the Ephesians, reminding the elders that they had observed his character *(You know).* The first mark of Paul's ministry was humility—he did the *Lord's work humbly.* As wildly successful as Paul's ministry was—the miracles, decisions, baptisms, and successfully discipled believers and planted churches—he did not boast. Under his ministry there, the word of the Lord had spread widely (19:20). The glory, however, was consistently given back to the one directing it all—it was the Lord's work, not Paul's.

> Only by desertion can we be defeated. With Christ and for Christ victory is certain. We can lose the victory by flight but not by death. Happy are you if you die in battle, for after death you will be crowned. But woe to you if by forsaking the battle you forfeit at once both the victory and the crown
>
> *Bernard of Clairvaux*

ENDURANCE

The way of the believer is not easy; being a Christian does not solve or remove all problems. Paul served humbly and "with tears," but he never quit, never gave up. The message of salvation was so important that Paul never missed an opportunity to share it. Although Paul preached his message in different ways to fit different audiences, the message remained the same—turning away from sin and turning to Christ by faith. The Christian life will have its rough times, tears, and sorrows, as well as joys, but we should always be ready to tell others what good things God has done for us.

Another characteristic of Paul's ministry to the Ephesians was the presence of *tears.* In other words, his work was done with passion and compassion. It was not a coldhearted teaching ministry or a distant discipleship ministry—there was warmth and cooperation, sympathy and empathy (see also Romans 9:2; 2 Corinthians 2:4; Philippians 3:18).

Paul's ministry also showed endurance. He spoke of the *trials* that had to be endured due to the *plots of the Jews.* The uproar at the end of Paul's ministry in Ephesus was from the Gentiles. Though Luke did not detail any of these plots from the Jews, surely they had caused trouble for Paul. That had marked his ministry from the beginning.

20:20-21 "Yet I never shrank from telling you the truth, either publicly or in your homes. I have had one message for Jews and Gentiles alike—the necessity of turning from sin and turning to God, and of faith in our Lord Jesus."NLT Paul's ministry in Ephesus exuded boldness in *telling . . . the truth,* whether in a public or private setting *(in your homes).* The mention of "homes" may refer to house churches. A good spiritual leader has the courage to tell the truth no matter what the consequences. Paul had one message for all. Both Jews and Gentiles alike were included in his mission, and both needed the central message of repentance and faith (see Acts 26:20-23; Romans 10:9-10; 2 Corinthians 5:20–6:2).

> If an offense comes out of the truth, it is better that the offense come than that the truth be concealed. *Jerome*

SPEAKING THE TRUTH

The gospel is a blunt package of raw truth (about how people are rebellious, lost sinners separated from a holy God) wrapped with exquisite cords of love (about how God offers forgiveness, acceptance, and eternal life to those who turn from sin to Christ in simple faith). Paul forcefully and passionately spoke that truth to those with whom he came in contact and essentially said: "You have eternal decisions to make. You are responsible for what you do with this information."

As you share the faith, don't shade the truth or try to soften the hardness of the gospel. Before people will ever see the goodness of the gospel, they must first realize the awfulness of their lost condition.

Paul's message to the Ephesians had been simple and single-minded—he had *one message for Jews and Gentiles alike*—the need for *faith* in Christ that follows a *turning from sin and turning to God.* What a great summary of the gospel: turn from sin, turn to God, and believe in the Lord Jesus Christ!

In this day of growing complexity, the church often falls prey to the temptation to become sophisticated and complicated, to fit into the culture. Believers must never let the message get lost in the trappings of the ministry (buildings, programs, schedules, calendars) or the ever-present busyness of church activities. The message must not be prejudiced—it's applicable to Jews and

Gentiles alike. It is not optional, and it must not be overly complicated. It is just one message: turn from sin, turn to God, and believe in Jesus Christ.

SIGNS OF HEALTH
Humility, compassion, endurance, boldness, simplicity—not a bad set of characteristics upon which to build a ministry, a marriage, or a family. Paul said those were the marks of his work in Ephesus (20:18-20). As he challenged the elders of the church at Ephesus to carry on the work, he was challenging spiritual leaders of every generation. How does your ministry measure up? How about your marriage? your home? your business?

20:22-23 **"And now I am going to Jerusalem, drawn there irresistibly by the Holy Spirit, not knowing what awaits me, except that the Holy Spirit has told me in city after city that jail and suffering lie ahead."**[NLT] Paul's message to the Ephesian elders shifted from a description of his past work among them to a description of the present and immediate future for him.

That future would begin in *Jerusalem,* where Paul said he was being *drawn . . . irresistibly by the Holy Spirit.* The word "holy" is not in the original Greek, leading to broad speculation as to whether this was God's Spirit or Paul's at work here. The best arguments lean toward this being God's leading of Paul. The word "drawn" in Greek is *dedemenos,* literally meaning "bound" (compare this with similar examples of the Holy Spirit's leading in Luke 2:27; 4:1; Acts 8:29; 10:19; 11:12; 16:6-7).

LIVING LIFE TO THE FULLEST
We often feel that life is a failure unless we're getting a lot out of it: recognition, fun, money, success. But Paul considered life worth "nothing" unless he used it for God's work (20:24). What he put into life was far more important than what he got out. Do you serve only those people who benefit you? Are your volunteer activities limited to people who give a lot in return? Consider your service to others as a gift back to Christ. Don't always look for what you can get out of it.

The Holy Spirit *told* Paul that he would be imprisoned and experience suffering. Paul anticipated this, as reflected in some of his letters: "Pray that I may be rescued from the unbelievers in Judea and that my service in Jerusalem may be acceptable to the saints there" (Romans 15:31 NIV). Even knowing this, Paul did not shrink from fulfilling his mission. His strong character was a good example to the Ephesian elders—as well as to all Christians, many of whom would suffer for Christ.

20:24 "However, I consider my life worth nothing to me, if only I may finish the race and complete the task the Lord Jesus has given me—the task of testifying to the gospel of God's grace."NIV Paul's statement of his priorities and values is a great perspective for any believer of any age. Self-preservation must be subservient to the faithful completion of *the task the Lord Jesus has given.* Paul used one of his favorite athletic pictures to illustrate what he meant—his life was a *race* that had to be finished (see 1 Corinthians 9:24-27; Philippians 2:16; 2 Timothy 4:7). Life or death was irrelevant to Paul. His sold-out, single-minded desire was to finish the race well. As he would tell the Philippians in a letter not too many months hence: "I eagerly expect and hope that I will in no way be ashamed, but will have sufficient courage so that now as always Christ will be exalted in my body, whether by life or by death" (Philippians 1:20 NIV). Paul was a single-minded person, and the most important goal of his life was to tell others about Christ (Philippians 3:7-13). No wonder Paul was the greatest missionary who ever lived.

> Leadership is not magnetic personality that can just as well be a glib tongue. It is not "making friends and influencing people that is flattery. Leadership is lifting a person's vision to higher sights, raising a person's performance to a higher standard, building a personality beyond its normal limitations.
>
> *Peter Drucker*

Paul further clarified what he meant by the "task" when he said that it was *testifying to the gospel of God's grace.* The gospel is a message of forgiveness, freedom, and a future. Note that it was not teaching skill or preaching skill nor any other gift or skill to which Paul alluded as his task—just simple testifying.

20:25 "And now I know that none of you to whom I have preached the Kingdom will ever see me again."NLT Paul may have been convinced that he would never see any of these men again. It is unknown if he ever did, but at this somber moment, Paul was saying good-bye to a group, most of whom were led to Christ by him and probably all of whom had been taught by him.

20:26-27 "Let me say plainly that I have been faithful. No one's damnation can be blamed on me, for I didn't shrink from declaring all that God wants for you."NLT In a solemn declaration, Paul claimed his innocence of anyone's damnation. He was likely referring to the people of Ephesus before whom he had boldly and thoroughly proclaimed what they needed to know to be saved and to grow in Christ. All of God's purpose that had been revealed to Paul, he had taught to them.

NO SHRINKING VIOLETS
Paul could look the Ephesian believers in the eyes and say, "I have not hesitated to proclaim to you the whole will of God" (20:27 NIV). Daily, for two years, he had faithfully preached and taught at the lecture hall of Tyrannus (see 19:9-10)! Why? Because he understood that there can be no growth in Christ without the transmission of truth. Are you fulfilling your God-given responsibility to declare God's truth to those he has sovereignly placed in your life—a spouse, a neighbor, a child? Or are you hesitating and shrinking back from such a task? The only way to have a clear conscience is to trust God and boldly speak out when opportunities present themselves. Ask God for such a situation today.

20:28 **"Keep watch over yourselves and all the flock of which the Holy Spirit has made you overseers. Be shepherds of the church of God, which he bought with his own blood."**NIV This begins the final section of Paul's message to the elders of Ephesus. The verbs have changed from the declarative (I did, we did) to the imperative (Go do!). There are basically three charges: (1) *"Keep watch"; (2) "Be shepherds";* and (3) "Be on your guard" (20:31 NIV). In this verse, Paul outlines the philosophy of the ministry that pastors and church leaders should follow.

The first charge was to "keep watch"—first over themselves and then over *all the flock of which the Holy Spirit has made you overseers.* Although Paul had likely chosen and trained most of them, the operative force behind everything had been the Holy Spirit. The flock was *the church of God,* an entity that God had *bought* (literally, "acquired, obtained") *with his own blood,* shed by Christ on the cross.

Those who lead God's people must keep a careful watch over themselves and the flock. This was important. The leadership (elders, pastors, deacons) would be the first line of attack from the enemy (the "wolves" mentioned in the next verse). Before the flock could be protected, the shepherds must protect themselves!

These leaders were to "be shepherds." They were to guide, direct, protect, feed, and help the flock to grow into its full potential (see Psalm 23; Ephesians 4:11; 1 Peter 5:1-4). In the early years of the church, there was no real distinction between the three terms for pastor: elder *(presbuteros),* a bishop or overseer *(episkopos),* or a shepherd or pastor *(poimen)*—the distinctions occurred later in church history. These leaders of the Ephesian church are described in this one passage as elders (20:17; see also 14:23), bishops (20:28), and shepherds (that is, pastors—20:28).

And from what did these elders need to guard themselves and the flock? The following verses explain.

20:29-30 **"I know full well that false teachers, like vicious wolves, will come in among you after I leave, not sparing the flock. Even some of you will distort the truth in order to draw a following."**[NLT] With a vivid, colorful shepherding image, Paul forewarned the Ephesian elders of the coming attack on the *flock* by *vicious wolves.* Some would attack from outside the church. These *false teachers* would invade the church after the departure of Paul and, like wolves, ruthlessly attack the flock. They would bring with them their fine-sounding words, *not sparing* a soul who would believe and follow them.

Other attacks would come from inside the church *(even some of you).* Paul warned that some of their own members, in order to build a *following,* would *distort the truth* and lead away a portion of the flock to their own doom. False teachers did, in fact, hound the church at Ephesus. This is confirmed in the later books of the New Testament (1 Timothy 1:6-7, 9-20; 4:1-3; 2 Timothy 1:15; 2:17-18; 3:1-9; Revelation 2:1-7; see also the chart "Beware of False Teachers!" in the *Life Application Bible Commentary: 1 & 2 Timothy, Titus* at 1 Timothy 4:1).

WOLF ATTACK

The damage that false teachers cause is not limited to the cults, nor to past days in church history. Some of the characteristics of false teachers show up in churches and ministries professing to be faithful to the true gospel. Many leaders and authorities today demand allegiance; some would even have us turn from Christ to follow them. Because they seem to know the Bible, their influence can be dangerously subtle. How can you recognize false teaching?

- It promotes controversies instead of helping people come to Jesus (1 Timothy 1:4).
- It is often initiated by those whose motivation is to make a name for themselves (1 Timothy 1:7).
- It will be contrary to the true teaching of the Scriptures (1 Timothy 1:6-7; 4:1-3).

To protect yourself from the deception of false teachers, you should learn what the Bible teaches and remain steadfast in your faith in Christ alone. Doctrine is right and true only to the extent that it agrees with God's Word.

20:31 "Watch out! Remember the three years I was with you—my constant watch and care over you night and day, and my many tears for you."[NLT] Paul's final warning is simply, *"Watch out!"* (literally, "keep awake"). The leaders needed to *remember* Paul's example of wakefulness, his *constant watch and care* over them *night and day.* Since the vicious enemy is always around (both inside and outside the church) and always looking for victims, the shepherd must never let down his guard.

The major role of elders is to guard the flock. They are to watch, make decisions, and protect the church from everything that comes against it: sin, laziness, deception, distraction, disaster. One of the major benefits of believers putting themselves under the leadership of a church elder is that they receive not just instruction or correction but protection as well.

Paul pointed to his own three-year shepherding of the Ephesian church as an example. The few incidents recorded in chapter 19 serve as examples of how constant and vicious the attacks could be. Remember them, Paul said, and stay awake! This is a good word for every church leader and person who seeks to live for Christ.

FLOCK WATCHING

Paul reminded the Ephesian elders that one of their major roles was to guard the flock (20:28). Churches are susceptible to all kinds of dangers—false teaching, satanic attack, spiritual disease, sin, laziness, apathy, deception, distraction, and divisiveness. Leaders have a holy obligation to keep the sheep from every teaching, attitude, and action that would turn them away from full devotion to Christ. Are you under the protection of someone (or some body of leaders) who is older, wiser, and more discerning? Are you looking out for those whom God has placed in *your* care?

20:32 "And now I commend you to God and to the message of his grace, a message that is able to build you up and to give you the inheritance among all who are sanctified."[NRSV] Paul pronounced a benediction of sorts to this group into whom he had poured so much of his life; he committed them to God and to *the message of his grace.* This was evidently a common parting phrase, as it occurs elsewhere in the book (14:23, 25; 15:40).

The "message" Paul was commending them to had two essential characteristics: (1) it was *able to build* them *up* ("edify"); and (2) it was able to *give*

> The task of pastoral ministry is, above all else, to arrange the contingencies for an encounter with the Divine.
> *Dietrich Bonhoeffer*

them *the inheritance among all who are sanctified* (26:18; Ephesians 1:18; Colossians 1:12; 1 Peter 1:4). This message is the Word of God, by which the believers would be built up in the faith.

20:33-34 **"I coveted no one's silver or gold or clothing. You know for yourselves that I worked with my own hands to support myself and my companions."**NRSV Returning to remarks similar to those with which he opened (20:18-20), Paul reminded the elders of three more characteristics of his ministry: (1) contentment and self-restraint—he had not *coveted* anyone's *silver or gold or clothing;* (2) diligence—he had worked hard with his *own hands to support* himself and his *companions;* and (3) selflessness (20:35)—he had sought to "help the weak," following Jesus' words concerning the advantage of giving over receiving.

Paul was a tentmaker; he supported himself with this trade. Paul worked not in order to become rich but to be free from being dependent on anyone. He supported himself and those who traveled with him (see Philippians 4:11-13; 1 Thessalonians 2:9).

MINISTERING WITH INTEGRITY

Paul didn't use his position as an apostle to profit financially (20:33), boost his ego, build a name for himself, win a following, or accumulate "spiritual" power. His motives were pure—he desired simply to see lives changed, the church built, and God glorified. He was satisfied with whatever he had, wherever he was, as long as he could do God's work.

Why do you teach, serve, or give? What are your real motives? If you find yourself getting something out of serving more than just the joy and fulfillment that comes from obeying Christ, then it may be time to reexamine your priorities. Look at the three areas that Paul addressed in these closing verses of chapter 20:

(1) *Contentment* (Am I happy, at peace with what I have?)

(2) *Diligence* (Am I doing my best at my job to provide for myself, my family, and my church?)

(3) *Selflessness* (Am I a giver or a taker in my relationships with my family? friends? children? parents?)

20:35 **"In all this I have given you an example that by such work we must support the weak, remembering the words of the Lord Jesus, for he himself said, 'It is more blessed to give than to receive.'"**NRSV Paul's hard work at tentmaking also enabled him to *support the weak,* those who were struggling physically, spiritually, emotionally, and maybe even financially, thus setting an example for the Ephesians to follow.

These words of Jesus—*"It is more blessed to give than to*

receive"—are not recorded in the Gospels. Obviously, since not all of Jesus' words were written down (see John 21:25), this saying must have been passed on orally through the apostles. Certainly the theology of this statement is found abundantly in Christ's teachings.

POINTING TO CHRIST
Paul's genuine humility is evident in his encounter with the Ephesians. He was not impressed with himself, nor did he call attention to his credentials or impressive résumé. Rather, he kept pointing to Christ. Strive to imitate this pattern of living, best expressed in the words of John the Baptist: "He [Christ] must become greater and greater, and I must become less and less" (John 3:30 NLT).

20:36-38 When he had said this, he knelt down with all of them and prayed. They all wept as they embraced him and kissed him. What grieved them most was his statement that they would never see his face again. Then they accompanied him to the ship.[NIV] Paul's relationship with these believers is a beautiful example of genuine Christian fellowship. He had cared for them and loved them, even *wept* with them in their needs. They responded with love and care for him and sorrow over his leaving. They *prayed* together and comforted one another. What a sorrowful scene this was. Yet how wonderful it must have been to be so thoroughly, completely, and healthily bound to others, not through the earthly cords of family or marriage, but with ties that are even closer—those of a shared Savior, a shared salvation, a shared solution to the deepest problems of the soul. These believers possessed in Christ the kind of depth and integrity in relating to one another that the world longs for but so rarely finds.

Like Paul, all believers can build strong relationships with other believers by sharing, caring, sorrowing, rejoicing, and praying with them. And—like Paul—the best way to gather others around is by giving oneself away to them and to the gospel. It is not surprising that these men *accompanied him to the ship.* They may have stood, wept, and prayed until the mast of their beloved shepherd's ship disappeared over the Aegean horizon, and only then returned to Ephesus, determined more than ever to shepherd their flock with the passion of the one who had so lovingly shown them the way.

Acts 21:1–22:29

PAUL'S JOURNEY TO JERUSALEM / 21:1-17

Upon making his way to Tyre, Paul was urged by the believers not to go to Jerusalem. Nevertheless, the apostle pressed on. At Caesarea further prophecies were given, warning Paul of certain imprisonment if he journeyed to Jerusalem. Unmoved, Paul adamantly determined to complete his mission even if it meant dying "for the sake of the Lord Jesus" (21:13 NLT). God's sovereignty is the underlying theme. This truth becomes more apparent upon viewing how this Jerusalem visit ultimately paved the way for Paul's trip to Rome!

This chapter looks more like a travelogue than a record of the Acts of the Apostles. Yet, all believers can learn a great deal

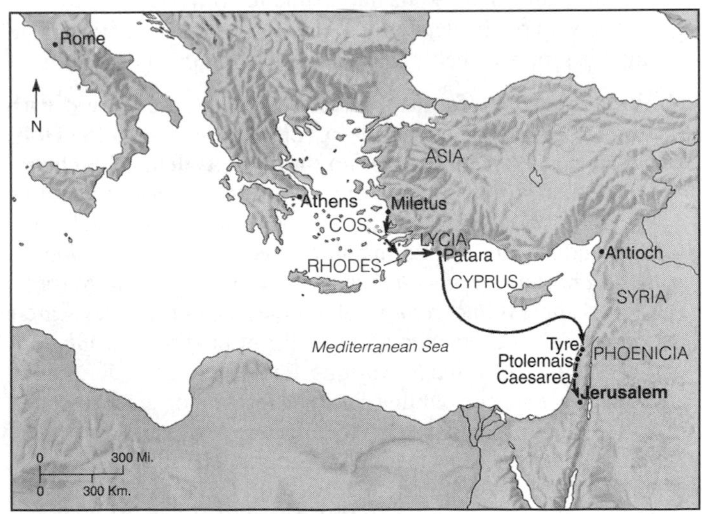

PAUL RETURNS TO JERUSALEM
The ship sailed from Miletus to Cos, Rhodes, and Patara. Paul and his companions then boarded a cargo ship bound for Phoenicia. They passed Cyprus and landed at Tyre, then Ptolemais, and finally Caesarea, where Paul disembarked and returned by land to Jerusalem.

about the benefits of being involved in the work of the gospel in people's lives. The challenge to us, of course, is to get involved in people's lives and introduce them to the Savior.

21:1-3 After saying farewell to the Ephesian elders, we sailed straight to the island of Cos. The next day we reached Rhodes and then went to Patara. There we boarded a ship sailing for the Syrian province of Phoenicia. We sighted the island of Cyprus, passed it on our left, and landed at the harbor of Tyre, in Syria, where the ship was to unload.[NLT] Having said *farewell to the Ephesian elders* at Miletus, Paul continued his journey to Jerusalem. At its most basic level, the Greek verb *apospao* (translated "saying farewell") carries the idea of "tearing away," picturing Paul "tearing himself away" from the embraces of his emotional friends.

The stops along the way—*Cos, Rhodes,* and *Patara*—were a normal day's run for the smaller ship they were on. At Patara they boarded a different ship, possibly a larger vessel that could make the longer, open-sea trip to *Phoenicia.* Luke recorded the sighting of *Cyprus* in their transit of the Mediterranean—surely sparking memories for Paul of his first journey with Barnabas. How many miles and memories had passed since then, not to mention how many souls had found the Savior!

The ship put in at *Tyre in Syria,* its destination, giving Paul and his group a week's rest before they shipped out again.

21:4 We went ashore, found the local believers, and stayed with them a week. These disciples prophesied through the Holy Spirit that Paul should not go on to Jerusalem.[NLT] A church had been founded in Tyre, probably soon after the dispersion of believers from Jerusalem following Stephen's martyrdom (8:1; 11:19). Paul and his traveling companions (see 20:4) *found the local believers* and *stayed with them a week.* The Greek word for "found" here is *aneurontes,* which means "to find after searching."

Certain believers who had the gift of prophecy *prophesied through the Holy Spirit,* warning Paul *not* to go to Jerusalem. Some have speculated that Paul was wrong or disobedient to go to Jerusalem against the advice of these believers, particularly ones such as these who spoke through the Holy Spirit.

Was Paul disobeying the Holy Spirit by continuing his journey to Jerusalem? It is very doubtful. More likely, the Holy Spirit warned these believers about the suffering that Paul would face in Jerusalem. They drew the conclusion that he should not go there because of that danger. This is supported by 21:12-14, where the local believers, after hearing that Paul would be turned over to the Romans, begged him to turn back. Acts 20:22 and 21:14 show that

Paul determined that it was God's will for him to go to Rome, as does the fact that God directly told him that he was supposed to go to Rome (23:11). Paul said that he was "irresistably drawn" by the Holy Spirit to go to Jerusalem (20:22). Paul believed that God wanted him to go to Rome in chains. The phrase "through the Holy Spirit" simply means that the Spirit had revealed Paul's suffering in Jerusalem and beyond. His importance to the church organizationally, and their love for him personally, compelled them to persuade him to stay safe. But, like his Savior before him, Paul "resolutely set out for Jerusalem" (Luke 9:51 NLT).

HELP FOR THE HARD TIMES

The last chapters of Acts contain a litany of Paul's troubles and struggles. Accused, attacked, and arrested, Paul could have been swallowed up in discouragement if not for the constant help he received from fellow believers. Specifically, he had friends who:

Hugged him (21:1, 13, 17)—Notice how many people seemed to genuinely and warmly love the apostle Paul.

Escorted him through life (21:1-5, 7-8, 15-16)—At every turn in these chapters, Paul is met with support—Ephesian elders who had to tear themselves away, disciples and their families who prayed with him, warm receptions, weeping good-byes.

Looked out for him (21:4, 11-14)—Paul always had a place to stay and caring people who looked out for his best interests, even trying to dissuade him from his trip to Jerusalem.

Prayed for him (21:5)—Don't miss the praying friends who, though they could not stop his progress toward Jerusalem, *did* bathe it in prayer and likely had a part in changing its outcome.

The obvious but often overlooked lesson from Paul's life is that he found this help as (and because) he was involved in the work of Christ. If Paul had been an independent, isolated individual, he would not have experienced help to this degree. Are you finding the help you need to endure? If not, could it be because you are not serving Christ alongside other believers?

21:5-6 When our days there were ended, we left and proceeded on our journey; and all of them, with wives and children, escorted us outside the city. There we knelt down on the beach and prayed and said farewell to one another. Then we went on board the ship, and they returned home.[NRSV] After the week was over, the *journey* continued. They were *escorted . . . outside the city* by *all* of the disciples of Tyre with whom Paul had been ministering. All of them came, along *with wives and children,* to say *farewell* to their friend.

As at Miletus (20:36-38), the farewell from Tyre was a tender time of prayer *on the beach.* Whenever someone says that Paul was cold or harsh (based on the stinging rebukes he passed out to churches like those in Galatia and Corinth or to individuals like Barnabas and even Peter), lead the person to passages such as these. Whether it was from the elders at Ephesus or the believers at Tyre, there was a warm, loving response to his ministry virtually everywhere he went.

BEING PRAYED FOR

Whole families turned out to say farewell to Paul and to pray for him (21:5-6). What a wonderful gift! What a blessing! To have the people of God lifting your name and reciting your needs before the throne of heaven. To be prayed for is to receive eternal help as well as temporal encouragement. If no one is praying for you, you probably have only yourself to blame. Though Christ is omniscient, his children are not! No one can read your mind. To be prayed for, you must be in a setting where people can get to know you and your struggles. As you reach out to others and minister to their needs, you will find others tending to treat you the same way.

21:7 The next stop after leaving Tyre was Ptolemais, where we greeted the brothers and sisters but stayed only one day.[NLT] *Ptolemais* was the only stop between Tyre and Caesarea, and there the stay was much shorter—*only one day.* Still, Paul and his companions *greeted the believers.* As with Tyre, there is no record of how or by whom the church had been planted in the area.

21:8-9 Then we went on to Caesarea and stayed at the home of Philip the Evangelist, one of the seven men who had been chosen to distribute food. He had four unmarried daughters who had the gift of prophecy.[NLT] In *Caesarea* lived *Philip,* called here *the Evangelist.* The last record of his activities is found in 8:26-40. Philip had been *one of the seven men . . . chosen* to serve the tables in the early days of the church at Jerusalem (6:5). In contrast to Stephen, one of the "seven" who was martyred very early on, Philip had ministered for many years, ending up in Caesarea (see the introductory remarks to chapter 8).

Philip *had four unmarried daughters* (Greek *parthenoi,* literally, "virgins"), and they all *had the gift of prophecy.* From this text we learn that the gift of prophecy was given to both men and women. Women actively participated in God's work (2:17; Philippians 4:3). Other women who are recorded in the Bible as prophesying include Miriam (Exodus 15:20), Deborah (Judges 4:4), Huldah (2 Kings 22:14), Noadiah (Nehemiah 6:14), Isaiah's wife (Isaiah 8:3), and Anna (Luke 2:36-38). It is a little surprising here that, in view of all the other prophecies concerning Paul's journey to Jerusalem and Rome, these four prophets made no mention of it.

SINGLES IN THE CHURCH
Philip's four unmarried daughters served the church with their God-given ability to prophesy (21:9). Today in our culture many local churches either ignore the ministry potential of single adults, or they tend to relegate them to the church sidelines. We ought to welcome single adult Christians into our ministries with open arms. They have spiritual gifts needed by the body of Christ, as well as the time to serve (see 1 Corinthians 7).

21:10-11 **After we had been there a number of days, a prophet named Agabus came down from Judea. Coming over to us, he took Paul's belt, tied his own hands and feet with it and said, "The Holy Spirit says, 'In this way the Jews of Jerusalem will bind the owner of this belt and will hand him over to the Gentiles.'"**NIV Fifteen years earlier, *Agabus* had predicted the famine in Jerusalem (11:27-29). He arrived at Philip's home *from Judea* and gave a graphic display of what lay ahead for Paul, giving more detail as to what the previous prophecies had been warning. Agabus gave the information of Paul's impending arrest—naming *the Jews of Jerusalem* as the culpable cause—and of his being handed *over to the Gentiles*—foreshadowing his long journey ultimately to a courtroom in Rome.

THE LIMITS OF TRUTH TELLING
Agabus could only share the revelation he had received from God (21:10-11). He could not force Paul to respond in a certain way. This is one of the most difficult aspects of working with people. Whether you are a pastor, small-group leader, parent, or friend, all you can do is speak truthfully and lovingly. You can urge a certain course of action as well as warn of possible consequences, but you cannot control others; nor should you try. Each person must make his or her own decisions. Beware of a demanding or manipulative spirit when you share personal concerns with another person.

21:12-14 **When we heard this, we and the people there urged him not to go up to Jerusalem. Then Paul answered, "What are you doing, weeping and breaking my heart? For I am ready not only to be bound but even to die in Jerusalem for the name of the Lord Jesus." Since he would not be persuaded, we remained silent except to say, "The Lord's will be done."**NRSV Spurred along by the graphic and forboding prophecy of Agabus, the

Christianity has not been tried and found wanting. It has been found difficult and not tried.
G. K. Chesterton

believers in Caesarea urged Paul *not to go up to Jerusalem.* Even Paul's traveling companions *(we)* added their voices to the crowd. Evidently, they had heard enough from the Holy Spirit on the subject and had decided that Paul should pursue another course. Paul was an invaluable and—to them—irreplaceable asset to the church. In addition, he had not always walked into a fight; instead, he had escaped many, fleeing some cities to save his life. Paul had avoided confrontation in Ephesus and had appealed to his Roman citizenship in Philippi. Why must he go to certain imprisonment in Jerusalem?

The answer, pure and simple, was that Paul knew God wanted him to go. Paul had faced rejection and persecution from the beginning. Doors had closed on the second journey (16:6-8) and then had swung wide open to Macedonia (16:9-10). God had led Paul, coming to him during difficult times to spur him on (18:10). Paul knew that he would be imprisoned in Jerusalem.

Although his friends pleaded with him to not go, Paul knew that he had to go because God wanted him to. No one enjoys pain, but a faithful disciple wants above all else to please God. Paul was not ignoring the warnings. He was not suicidal. Paul simply disagreed with his brothers and sisters in Christ as to whether the prophesied difficulties outweighed the potential progress that could be made for the gospel. And the ultimate issue—the will of God—was the one to which Paul's friends finally resigned themselves: *"The Lord's will be done."*

21:15-17 After this, we got ready and went up to Jerusalem. Some of the disciples from Caesarea accompanied us and brought us to the home of Mnason, where we were to stay. He was a man from Cyprus and one of the early disciples. When we arrived at Jerusalem, the brothers received us warmly.[NIV] The trip from *Caesarea* to *Jerusalem* was about sixty-five miles—a two-day journey on horseback. Notice that the entourage had been joined by a few more courageous *disciples from Caesarea* who were not afraid to join Paul.

The home of Mnason may have been in Jerusalem or at some point along the journey there. Mnason was *from Cyprus* and was *one of the early disciples.* He may have been converted during Paul and Barnabas's first missionary journey (13:4-12), or he may have been a convert from even earlier than that—perhaps one of the original Jerusalem disciples from the few weeks following that miraculous Pentecost (chapter 2).

Upon their arrival in Jerusalem, Paul and his friends were *received warmly,* a testimony to the growing reputation of the apostle and gratitude for the generous gift he was bringing from the churches (see 24:17; Romans 15:25-27; 1 Corinthians 16:1-4; 2 Corinthians 8:13-14; 9:12-13). Paul had not forgotten the charge of the Jerusalem church from years ago to remember the poor (Galatians 2:10). The Jerusalem elders had never thought that they would be the beneficiaries of Paul's obedience to their charge; much less had they imagined that the support would come from predominantly Gentile churches. How that must have bonded the Jewish and Gentile segments of the church!

PAUL ARRIVES AT JERUSALEM / 21:18-25

At long last, Paul reached his destination—Jerusalem. He was warmly welcomed by the believers there. A "detailed account of the things God had accomplished among the Gentiles through his ministry" (21:19 NLT) gave the leaders of the church reason to praise God.

Aware, however, of the strong Jewish animosity toward Paul, James and the elders encouraged the apostle to participate in a public Jewish ceremony of purification at the temple. Such an act, they felt, would quell the false rumors circulating about Paul—that he was actively undermining the Mosaic law.

21:18 The next day Paul went in with us to meet with James, and all the elders of the Jerusalem church were present.[NLT] *James,* Jesus' brother, was the leader of the Jerusalem church (15:13-21; Galatians 1:19; 2:9). He was called an apostle, even though he wasn't one of the original twelve who had followed Jesus. Of the inner circle of Peter, John, and James (John's brother, not the James of this chapter)—only Peter and John were still alive at this time. Both were actively involved in missionary endeavors elsewhere, leaving James, Jesus' brother, with the heavy responsibility of leading the mother church in Jerusalem. It was not only an influential church, but it had also been a horribly persecuted church (since Stephen's day), and at this particular time, it faced famine and poverty. This was obviously an important gathering, since *all the elders of the Jerusalem church were present.*

The "we" section ends here and will not appear again until 27:1. It is unclear whether Luke was no longer with them (an unlikely event) or whether he just changed his literary style.

21:19-20a Paul greeted them and reported in detail what God had done among the Gentiles through his ministry. When they heard this, they praised God.[NIV] The fact that Paul reported to this group shows his sincere humility and submission to these honored coworkers in spreading the gospel (Ephesians 5:21; Philippians 2:3-8). After a wildly successful missionary career at great cost to himself, he had plenty to boast about. He could easily have looked down at the "old guard," who were still ministering not far from the site of the great commissioning by Christ (1:8). But he didn't.

The Jerusalem elders responded well to Paul's report of *what God had done among the Gentiles.* They *praised God*—a testimony to their love for the spread of the gospel and their submission to the way God directed his movement. There was no envy, competition, or criticism from these leaders—only praise.

THOROUGH COMMUNICATION
Meeting with the leaders of the church at Jerusalem, Paul gave a detailed report of his ministry. Living in an era when monumental spiritual changes were taking place, accurate information was hard to come by, and rumors abounded. Paul took advantage of this occasion to sit down and provide his Christian colleagues with a thorough update. This is a model of good communication. It's hard for us to go wrong by talking to others and briefing them on our lives—what we're doing, what we're thinking and feeling, what our plans are. Usually it is when we don't "report in detail" what is taking place in our lives that distance creeps into our relationships. Who in your life deserves a detailed report today?

21:20b Then they said to Paul: "You see, brother, how many thousands of Jews have believed, and all of them are zealous for the law."NIV Everything was not going smoothly in the church at Jerusalem, however. The ancient Jewish historian Josephus described this time period (approximately A.D. 56 or 57) as being filled with political unrest and strong Jewish nationalism. There were several uprisings by Jews against their Roman leaders—all of which had been brutally put down by Felix, the Roman procurator. This caused even more anger from the Jews and intensified their hatred for Gentiles. Paul, missionary to the Gentiles, entered the city with news of vast Gentile conversions.

The elders informed Paul of the large contingency of Jews who had *believed.* The problem, however, was that *all of* those Jews were *zealous for the law* (15:5), meaning that they probably would not be rejoicing in the success of Paul's ministry among the Gentiles. This explains the wisdom of James and the elders to have a meeting alone with Paul rather than in an open forum. While they supported Paul and his ministry, he was somewhat of a hindrance to their continued ministry to the Jews. This was the reason behind their request that he join in the purification rites (21:22-24).

21:21 "They have been informed that you teach all the Jews who live among the Gentiles to turn away from Moses, telling them not to circumcise their children or live according to our customs."[NIV] The Jewish Christian "zealots" had *been informed,* through rumors, that Paul was teaching *all the Jews* he had contacted *who live among the Gentiles* to *turn away from Moses* ("turn away" is the Greek word *apostasian,* from which the word "apostasy" comes). Not only that, but they had heard that Paul was minimizing the rite of circumcision and allowing the Jews to stop living *according to* the Jewish *customs.*

The Jerusalem council (chapter 15) had settled the issue of circumcision of Gentile believers. Evidently, there was a rumor that Paul had gone far beyond the council's decision, even forbidding Jews to circumcise their children. It was true that Paul was downplaying the importance of circumcision and did not require keeping the Jewish customs, but that was for the Gentiles, not for the Jews. Paul had Timothy circumcised because his mother was Jewish (see commentary on 16:2-3). Paul taught both Jews and Gentiles that salvation did not depend on keeping the law (Galatians 3:24-29; 5:1; Colossians 2:11-17). He taught Gentiles not to get circumcised (1 Corinthians 7:18-19), but there is no evidence that he taught Jews to abandon the practice.

21:22-24 "What shall we do? They will certainly hear that you have come, so do what we tell you. There are four men with us who have made a vow. Take these men, join in their purification rites and pay their expenses, so that they can have their heads shaved. Then everybody will know there is no truth in these reports about you, but that you yourself are living in obedience to the law."[NIV] The rumors about Paul, of course, were not true, but Paul willingly submitted to this Jewish custom to show that he was not working against the council's decision and that he was still Jewish in his lifestyle. (Sometimes believers must submit to authorities to avoid offending others, especially when such offense would hinder God's work.)

The Jerusalem elders suggested that Paul join *four men* among their number who had made *a vow.* The details are unknown, but they seem to have taken the Nazirite vow (Numbers 6:13-21). Paul was to join and sponsor them *(pay their expenses)* for the final stages of *their purification rites.* Often a Jew who had been in Gentile territory for a lengthy time would undergo ritual purification upon returning to his homeland. The time period for this purification was seven days. This may have been what the elders were asking Paul to do. Evidently the other four participants were too poor to afford the expenses of the final sacrifices, so Paul's generous offer to pay these expenses and join them would refute the *reports* about him and show that he was *living in obedience to the law.*

There seems to have been a definite lack of resolve in this decision by the Jerusalem elders as they tried to appease the Jews who were so "zealous for the law" (21:20) that they were spreading the inaccurate "reports" about Paul. In reality, the zealots' zeal was misplaced. A far more appropriate response by the leaders would have been to say to these rumormongers: "The Jerusalem council made an authoritative decision (probably at least eight years ago by this time) and communicated it in written form at the time. Paul was here, agreed to abide by the ruling, and, to our knowledge, has announced and enforced the ruling everywhere he has gone. By all accounts he is a brave and godly soldier of the Cross who has been incredibly successful in announcing the Good News to the remotest parts of the Gentile world. Your rumors are untrue, so calm down." It seems absurd that this hardworking apostle, who had just brought to Jerusalem a generous offering from his Gentile ministry, should be asked for some of his hard-earned money to placate that group. But when asked, Paul graciously gave the money and went along with the leaders' suggestion.

The church seems to have always been susceptible to the legalist, the one who demands religious performance out of those who wish to be numbered among the faithful. These Jerusalem leaders seemed to have been intimidated by their Jewish Christian brothers and were riding a fence, placating the zealous at the price of grace.

There are two ways to think of the Jewish laws: Paul rejected one way and accepted the other: (1) Paul rejected the idea that the Old Testament laws could bring salvation to those who kept them. Salvation is freely given by God's gracious act and is received through faith. The laws are of no value for salvation except to point out sin. (2) Paul accepted the view that the Old Testament laws prepare for and teach about the coming of Jesus Christ. Christ fulfilled the law and released people from its burden of guilt. But the law still teaches many valuable principles and gives guidelines for living. Paul was not observing the laws in order to be saved. He was simply keeping the laws to avoid offending those he wished to reach with the gospel (see Romans 3:21-31; 7:4-6; 13:9-10; Galatians 3:23-29; 4:21-31; see also the chart "Three Distortions of Christianity," in the *Life Application Commentary—Galatians,* pages 142–3).

Those who think Paul was wrong for going along with this request by the elders forget one of the marks of Paul's ministry: "To the Jews I became like a Jew, to win the Jews. To those under the law I became like one under the law (though I myself am not under the law), so as to win those under the law" (1 Corinthians

9:20 NIV). This was one of those times when it was not worth offending the Jews, so Paul wisely chose to comply.

BENDING, NOT BREAKING

Evidently, these four men had made a religious vow. Paul participated with them, submitting to a purification ceremony before entering the temple (Numbers 6:9-20), and apparently even paying some of their required expenses. He engaged in this Jewish custom not because he had to but because he wanted to keep peace in the Jerusalem church. Although Paul was a man of strong convictions, he was willing to compromise on nonessential points, becoming all things to all people so that he might save some (1 Corinthians 9:19-23). Churches can split over disagreements about minor issues or traditions. Instead, like Paul, we should remain firm on Christian essentials but flexible on nonessentials. Of course, no one should violate his or her true convictions, but sometimes we need to exercise the gift of mutual submission for the sake of the gospel.

21:25 **"As for the Gentile believers, we have written to them our decision that they should abstain from food sacrificed to idols, from blood, from the meat of strangled animals and from sexual immorality."**NIV Here, quoting almost word for word, the elders stated the past ruling of the Jerusalem council: *the Gentile believers . . . should abstain from . . ."* (see 15:19-21). One wonders if any of these individuals had seen a copy of Paul's letter to the Romans or the Galatians. It is not clear who this restatement of the council ruling was for—themselves, Paul, or those among them who may have been wavering. Perhaps this statement is best understood as given to assure Paul that they were not changing the ruling or adding anything to what had been decided years earlier.

PAUL IS ARRESTED / 21:26-36

Paul's attempt to placate his enemies was an utter failure. A group of Jews from Asia spotted him in the temple and incited a crowd to seize him. Dead set in their determination to reject the message of salvation in Christ, these opponents of Paul refused to look objectively at the facts. Instead, they whipped the mob into a frenzy by making a series of false and highly inflammatory accusations against the apostle. Only the quick action of a detachment of Roman soldiers saved Paul from being beaten to death.

21:26 **So Paul agreed to their request, and the next day he went through the purification ritual with the men and went to the Temple. Then he publicly announced the date when**

their vows would end and sacrifices would be offered for each of them.[NLT] Paul's agreement *to their request* was a sign of his greatness. He had been a huge influence all over the world, yet he did not flaunt it. He had begun churches all over Asia and Europe—in such leading cities as Antioch, Philippi, Thessalonica, Corinth, and Ephesus. He had a huge following in Rome itself, although he had never been there. He had been the point of attack from both Jews and Gentiles. He had endured more blows, seen more converts, performed more miracles, trained more leaders, and made more of an impact than these elders could begin to know. He could have told them all that he had accomplished, but he didn't. In submission to their political sensitivity, he paid for a ceremony in order to appease the religious zealots. He began the *purification ritual* with the four others and proceeded to the temple area to be "a Jew to the Jew" (1 Corinthians 9:20) so that he might win some of them.

But Paul's gracious action appeased none of his detractors—at least not enough of them to stop those who were against him.

21:27-28 When the seven days were almost completed, the Jews from Asia, who had seen him in the temple, stirred up the whole crowd. They seized him, shouting, "Fellow Israelites, help! This is the man who is teaching everyone everywhere against our people, our law, and this place; more than that, he has actually brought Greeks into the temple and has defiled this holy place."[NRSV] The opposition to Paul appears to have come from unbelieving (that is, non-Christian) *Jews from Asia,* who recognized him *in the temple* during the time of his completion of the purification ritual. These Jews, present for the Feast of Pentecost, must have recognized Paul from his ministry in their area. Since they knew who Trophimus was (see next verse), they likely were from Ephesus and may have even been a part of the riot there (19:28-41).

They *stirred up the whole crowd, seized* Paul, and in moblike fashion (something with which Paul was very familiar) began to shout their biased case against Paul. Contrary to their emotional accusation, Paul had not been *everywhere,* nor had he taught *everyone,* nor had he been *against* the Jews, their laws, or their temple. The pinnacle of this argument the accusation that Paul had *actually brought Greeks into the temple,* thus defiling their *holy place.* The Greek to whom they were referring was Trophimus, the Ephesian who was traveling with Paul. Luke would clear up that accusation in the next verse.

THE RUMOR MILL
Some Asian Jews stirred up the people against Paul by spreading rumors about him. They knew how effective Paul's work had been. Their strategy was to discredit him so that his work would be weakened. Be alert when you hear accusations against God's workers. Be aware that bad reports often come from unbelievers who are merely trying to hinder the progress of Christianity by maligning Christians. Keep an open mind, and pray. Ask God to silence any rumormongers and to strengthen his servants.

21:29 **(For earlier that day they had seen him in the city with Trophimus, a Gentile from Ephesus, and they assumed Paul had taken him into the Temple.)**NLT Luke explained that the Jewish accusers *had seen* Paul *in the city with Trophimus,* whom they knew to be *a Gentile from Ephesus.* Then, without any investigation whatsoever, *they assumed Paul had taken [Trophimus] into the Temple* area. Gentiles were not permitted past the "Court of the Gentiles" under the direct threat of execution. No one would know that better than Paul. But they reported this event as though it had actually happened (21:28)!

TRUTH TWISTING
Paul had been seen in Jerusalem with Trophimus. Paul's enemies made a giant assumption and decided, without checking the facts, that Paul must have brought Greeks into the temple! False accusations are a common way that the enemy tries to make Christians look bad. We cannot keep people from distorting and twisting the facts or assuming the worst about us. Nor can we spend all our time trying to answer our critics. All we can do is live with integrity and let our true character dispel the rumors.

21:30-31 **The whole population of the city was rocked by these accusations, and a great riot followed. Paul was dragged out of the Temple, and immediately the gates were closed behind him. As they were trying to kill him, word reached the commander of the Roman regiment that all Jerusalem was in an uproar.**NLT The city was thrown into an uproar, *and a great riot followed.* In moblike fashion, Paul was *dragged out of the Temple,* and *the gates were closed behind him.* These were the gates between the inner court and the Court of the Gentiles. The temple guards (Levites) shut the gates to prevent the mob from coming inside. How ironic that the final scene at the temple in the book of Acts is the gates slamming shut to keep Paul out.

Evidently, the mob probably was going to try to beat him or stone him to death.

Because Jerusalem was under Roman control, an uproar in the city would quickly be investigated by Roman authorities. The *commander of the Roman regiment* at this time was Claudius Lysias (see 23:26). He was head of a cohort (a special group, part of a legion) of Roman soldiers, perhaps as many as a thousand men. Lysias was the senior Roman official in Jerusalem.

21:32-33 He immediately called out his soldiers and officers and ran down among the crowd. When the mob saw the commander and the troops coming, they stopped beating Paul. The commander arrested him and ordered him bound with two chains. Then he asked the crowd who he was and what he had done.NLT Lysias *called out his soldiers and officers* (centurions, who were in charge of one hundred men each). Since the word "officers" is plural, there must have been at least two hundred soldiers dispatched to the scene of the riot. The quick action of Lysias and the close proximity of the garrison (the Antonia Fortress was adjacent to the temple area) were all that saved Paul's life. The seizing of Paul by the crowd (in 21:30) was superseded by the seizing of Paul by the Roman soldiers.

Paul actually was fortunate to be *arrested* and *bound.* Luke, ever the one for details, wrote that Paul was bound with *two chains.* The chains handcuffed him to a Roman soldier on each side. This would be normal treatment for a criminal. After seizing Paul, the *commander* asked the crowd who the chained man was and what crime he had committed.

21:34-36 Some shouted one thing and some another. He couldn't find out the truth in all the uproar and confusion, so he ordered Paul to be taken to the fortress. As they reached the stairs, the mob grew so violent the soldiers had to lift Paul to their shoulders to protect him. And the crowd followed behind shouting, "Kill him, kill him!"NLT The commander could not get a direct answer to his question (21:33) because the crowd could not agree on what the issues were—of course, that had not stopped them in their murderous course a few moments earlier. Because the commander could not *find out the truth,* he *ordered Paul to be taken to the fortress,* probably the safest place for the apostle in all Jerusalem! This was the Fortress of Antonia, built by Herod the Great to defend the temple area. It was located northwest of the temple and connected by stairs to the Court of the Gentiles. The fortress housed nearly one thousand soldiers.

In the process of moving their prisoner, the mob, supposedly seeing the object of their anger being safely whisked away, *grew so violent* that Paul had to be carried by the soldiers! The murderous mob pursued, all the while shouting, *"Kill him, kill him!"* (literally, "Away with him"). These were almost identical to the words another murderous crowd had shouted to Pontius Pilate concerning Jesus of Nazareth just a few decades earlier (Luke 23:18; John 19:15).

PAUL SPEAKS TO THE CROWD / 21:37–22:23

Paul's defense before the Jewish mob in the temple courts is a textbook example of how to communicate to a hostile audience. He disarmed the Roman commander by speaking to him in Greek. Then he established common ground with the Jews gathered below him by speaking to them in their own language. Presenting his credentials as a devout Jew trained under the highly respected rabbi Gamaliel, Paul then described his unlikely encounter with the risen Christ on the Damascus Road.

The crowd listened attentively until Paul mentioned Christ's command to go "far away to the Gentiles" (22:21 NLT). At the very mention of that word, the mob erupted in anger. Although Paul knew his statement would cause controversy, he refused to dilute the truth.

21:37-38 As Paul was about to be taken inside, he said to the commander, "May I have a word with you?" "Do you know Greek?" the commander asked, surprised. "Aren't you the Egyptian who led a rebellion some time ago and took four thousand members of the Assassins out into the desert?"NLT By speaking in *Greek,* Paul showed that he was a cultured, educated man and not just a common rebel starting riots in the streets. The language grabbed the commander's attention and gave Paul protection and the opportunity to give his defense.

The historian Josephus wrote of an Egyptian who had led a revolt of thousands of Jews in Jerusalem in A.D. 54 (just three years previous). This self-proclaimed prophet had convinced his fanatical followers to accompany him to the nearby Mount of Olives. He said that, at his word, the walls of Jerusalem would collapse and this miraculous event would precipitate the destruction of the Roman Empire. Governor Felix had dispatched troops to deal with this insurrection. Hundreds of Jews were either killed or captured, and the Egyptian ringleader of this sect had disappeared into the desert. Lysias apparently assumed that Paul was this rebel, returning to make more trouble. Another assumption had been made (see 21:29), but this time Paul was able to clear up the confusion.

21:39-40 "No," Paul replied, "I am a Jew from Tarsus in Cilicia, which is an important city. Please, let me talk to these people." The commander agreed, so Paul stood on the stairs and motioned to the people to be quiet. Soon a deep silence enveloped the crowd, and he addressed them in their own language, Aramaic.NLT All these events took place outside the Fortress of Antonia, the Roman garrison that adjoined the temple area on the northwest side. From the headquarters of Claudius Lysias, two flights of stairs led down into the outer court of the temple. The staircase would prove to be an excellent platform from which to address a crowd gathered in the plazalike court below. And Paul was certainly up to the task.

The commander agreed to Paul's request. The text does not tell us why. Perhaps he was convinced that Paul was not some insurrectionist or rabble-rouser. He was a Jew and a proper citizen. The commander may have thought that Paul could explain to the crowd what had happened, and hopefully they would disperse peacefully. So he gave Paul permission to speak.

EFFECTIVE COMMUNICATION
Paul spoke Greek to the Roman officials and Aramaic to the Jews. He understood the principle that effective ministry requires that we speak the language of those we seek to impact. We may not actually know other languages besides our native tongue; nevertheless, we can stay abreast of popular terms and phrases (and we can avoid using Christian phrases and words that are meaningless to those outside the church). Effective communication requires that we expend the effort to build bridges of understanding to others.

Why did Paul try to further the cause of Christ in the middle of a near riot? First, the Jews had leveled some false charges against him (21:28), and it's likely that he wanted to set the record straight. Second, on a deeper level, Paul, the evangelist, felt great compassion for his confused, blinded countrymen. He verbalized this burden in Romans 9:1-4: "I speak the truth in Christ—I am not lying, my conscience confirms it in the Holy Spirit—I have great sorrow and unceasing anguish in my heart. For I could wish that I myself were cursed and cut off from Christ for the sake of my brothers, those of my own race, the people of Israel" (NIV)

Paul looked out on an enraged mob, and his heart broke. He ached for his people to understand the truth about Christ. He had been just like them—spiritually blind (until, ironically, Jesus had blinded him physically to "unblind" him spiritually). Paul wanted his Jewish brothers to experience this same salvation.

When Paul began speaking to the assembled crowd, he *addressed them in their own language, Aramaic,* the common language among Palestinian Jews. He spoke in Aramaic not only to communicate in the language of his listeners but also to show that he was a devout Jew and had respect for the Jewish laws and customs.

22:1-2 **"Brothers and esteemed fathers," Paul said, "listen to me as I offer my defense." When they heard him speaking in their own language, the silence was even greater.**[NLT] With this courteous salutation, Paul began the first of five defenses recorded by Luke in the book of Acts. He commanded the mob's attention by speaking Aramaic because many Jews of the Dispersion (that is, Hebrews who were born or reared outside of Palestine) could not speak Greek or Hebrew. The mob would have assumed that Paul, an outsider, could speak only Greek. Paul's ability to speak Aramaic gave his Jewish credentials even more weight and helped win him a hearing.

22:3 **"I am a Jew, born in Tarsus, a city in Cilicia, and I was brought up and educated here in Jerusalem under Gamaliel. At his feet I learned to follow our Jewish laws and customs very carefully. I became very zealous to honor God in everything I did, just as all of you are today."**[NLT] Paul began his defense with a brief personal history, almost a verbal résumé of his impressive Jewish credentials. In deliberate fashion, he answered the charges of his critics and tried to alleviate their suspicions by purposely highlighting all the personal facts that would build his credibility with them. He chose his words carefully, seeking to "find common ground with everyone" (1 Corinthians 9:22 NLT).

The statement "I am a Jew" declared Paul's brotherhood with the crowd. He was not hostile to Judaism. How could he be? He was a Jew by birth!

"I was brought up . . . in Jerusalem." Though born in *Tarsus,* Paul had been reared in the holy City of David. Not only that, but he had been *"educated . . . under Gamaliel,"* the most honored rabbi of that time. Gamaliel was well known and respected as an expert on religious law and as a voice for moderation (5:34). Who could say anything bad about a student of Israel's greatest scholar?

In our dealings with men, however unkind and hurting they are, we must exercise the same patience as God exercises with us. It is the simple truth that such patience is not the sign of weakness but the sign of strength; it is not defeatism, but rather the only way to victory.
William Barclay

At Gamaliel's feet, Paul had *"learned to follow our Jewish laws and customs very carefully."* The Pharisees were legendary for their rigorous keeping of the most minute details of the law (see Matthew 23). This statement by Paul was intended to refute the allegation in 21:28 that he had been telling everyone to disobey the Jewish laws.

In saying *"I became very zealous to honor God in everything I did, just as all of you are today,"* Paul was alluding to his former prominent role in the persecution of Christians. He recognized the sincere motives behind their desire to kill him and that a few years earlier, he had shared that same well-meaning but misguided passion.

AFFIRMING UNBELIEVERS
What was Paul thinking when he commended the zeal of the murderous mob in the temple court? He was looking for something in their behavior to affirm. He could have spoken bluntly: "You people are totally off spiritually! I used to be rash and violent like you." But such remarks would have inflamed the very people he was trying to win. Instead, he communicated this: "It's obvious that you have great zeal for God. I understand. I was the same way—only more so" (and then he detailed his prior hatred for the teaching known as the Way). When you witness for Christ, look for something to affirm. This is not to advocate flattery or manipulation—sooner or later people will see through such insincere techniques. It's just a reminder that people are much more likely to listen if they feel understood rather than attacked.

22:4-5 "I persecuted the followers of this Way to their death, arresting both men and women and throwing them into prison, as also the high priest and all the Council can testify. I even obtained letters from them to their brothers in Damascus, and went there to bring these people as prisoners to Jerusalem to be punished."NIV Having commended his Jewish audience for their zeal, Paul described how his passion for Judaism and against Christianity had been even more intense. Beyond merely accosting Christians on the temple grounds, Paul had sought *their death* (see 7:54-60; 26:10). Furthermore, with the official sanction of *the high priest and all the Council* (another compelling credential), Paul had actually traveled to far-off cities like *Damascus,* hunting and arresting the followers of Jesus. These were widely known, indisputable facts, making Paul's testimony extremely powerful.

22:6-9 "While I was on my way and approaching Damascus, about noon a great light from heaven suddenly shone about me. I

fell to the ground and heard a voice saying to me, 'Saul, Saul, why are you persecuting me?' I answered, 'Who are you, Lord?' Then he said to me, 'I am Jesus of Nazareth whom you are persecuting.' Now those who were with me saw the light but did not hear the voice of the one who was speaking to me."NRSV Paul's conversion is recorded in chapter 9. Here Paul told the story himself, as he later would to Felix and Agrippa (26:1-32). He made it clear that his conversion was not an issue of defection but a matter of divine intervention! Paul had been about his business, intent on his mission (rounding up the followers of Jesus)—and apparently very content and settled in his pro-Jewish, anti-Christian state of mind.

Suddenly, at *about noon* (at a real time) and *approaching Damascus* (at a real place), Paul had been blinded by *a great light from heaven,* so bright that it had knocked him to the ground. Even his companions had witnessed this flash. Next, Paul *heard a voice* addressing him by his former name *(Saul),* a voice claiming to be *Jesus of Nazareth.*

USING YOUR CREDENTIALS

Paul always tried to establish a common point of contact with those he wished to evangelize. With this crowd at the temple, he cited his Jewish credentials, mentioned certain connections, and won a hearing. Many Christians erroneously believe, "I don't have any credentials or connections with unbelievers! I could never be like Paul." Not true. You have children in school. Or a mortgage. Or classes. Or a marriage. Or a job. Or membership in a club. You have certain experiences. A certain background. Use *those* facts about yourself. Take your interests, passions, and skills, and use them as a springboard for the gospel.

This was nothing short of stunning. Paul's very own countrymen had condemned Jesus and had collaborated with Rome in his crucifixion. Paul himself, as everyone knew, had launched a personal campaign to persecute the followers of Jesus. And now here was Paul, "a real Jew if there ever was one . . . a member of the Pharisees" (Philippians 3:5 NLT), standing on the steps of the Antonia Fortress, claiming that he had reluctantly but undeniably encountered Jesus on the road to Damascus. For the audience in the temple court, this must have been a mind-numbing, heart-stopping moment. Without referring to a single Old Testament prophecy or launching into a theological discourse, Paul used his personal experience to press the points that Jesus was both alive and glorified.

WHAT'S YOUR TESTIMONY?

After gaining a hearing and establishing common ground with his audience, Paul gave his testimony. That is, he shared how he had come to faith in Christ. Sound reasoning, biblical arguments, and apologetics all have their place in evangelism, but it is most important to simply tell how we met Christ and what he has done in our lives. That's all a witness is and does. He or she relates what has been personally experienced. No matter how real our encounter with Christ was, no matter how compellingly we relate the story, not everyone will accept it. Still, we must faithfully and responsibly share our testimonies, then leave the results to God.

22:10-11 **"I said, 'What shall I do, Lord?' And the Lord told me, 'Get up and go into Damascus, and there you will be told all that you are to do.' I was blinded by the intense light and had to be led into Damascus by my companions."**[NLT] *Blinded,* confused, shocked, scared—Paul's mind must have been reeling as he lay in the dust. If this experience was true, Jesus had not been merely an itinerant Galilean rabbi with messianic ambitions. He was the resurrected and glorified Messiah, the Lord, from whom Paul would have to take all future marching orders. Paul must have realized in those moments that his way of thinking and his whole life would be forever altered. He had responded with a humble question, *"What shall I do, Lord?"*

Paul related to his audience the physical effects of this divine revelation. He had been unable to see and had to be led into Damascus by others. There Jesus had told him that he would receive further instructions. There is no record that his colleagues saw the vision or that any of them were converted.

TRUE SUBMISSION

Upon encountering Jesus, Paul recognized him as Lord of all, asked the only appropriate question, "What shall I do?" and then obeyed without reservation. This ought to be each believer's continual, daily response to God. Renewing the mind requires seeing Jesus as the one who controls all things and who alone deserves to direct our lives. Living the new life demands that we seek his will and then implement it. This is true submission. It explains why Paul was so fruitful for God. And it suggests how we can live effectively for Christ.

22:12-13 **"A man named Ananias lived there. He was a godly man in his devotion to the law, and he was well thought of by all the Jews of Damascus. He came to me and stood beside me and**

said, 'Brother Saul, receive your sight.' And that very hour I could see him!"NLT To give further credence to his testimony before such a zealous Jewish mob, Paul described the role *Ananias* had played in his conversion. Paul mentioned Ananias's stellar reputation among the Jewish community of Damascus as well as his utter *devotion to the law*—facts that Luke did not disclose in chapter 9.

Omitted here are the background details (revealed in chapter 9) about Ananias's faith in Christ, his charge from God to go and find Saul, and his understandable reluctance to seek out a known persecutor of the church. It is a streamlined version of events, but Paul did mention that it was Ananias who was instrumental in the restoration of his sight. Literally, Ananias had told Paul to "look up." The verb (*anablepson* as an imperative) also can convey the meaning of "see again."

22:14-15 **"Then he said, 'The God of our ancestors has chosen you to know his will, to see the Righteous One and to hear his own voice; for you will be his witness to all the world of what you have seen and heard.'"**NRSV Immediately following his undeniably miraculous healing (surely intended to signify that Ananias had divine authority), Paul reported that he had heard through the lips of this respected, devout Jew his unexpected, unsought commission. Ananias had made it clear that the supernatural events being experienced by Paul were the sovereign work of none other than *the God of our ancestors.* In zealously opposing Jesus and his followers, Paul had assumed that he had been serving and honoring the God of Abraham, Isaac, Jacob, and Moses. Through the announcement of Ananias, he had learned the truth. The God of the Hebrews—far from leading Paul to fight Christianity—was selecting him to become the leading spokesman for this new faith! Paul would be a *witness to all the world* (an implicit reference to the Gentiles) of the fact that Jesus of Nazareth, crucified by men, had been resurrected and exalted by God. In referring to Jesus as *the Righteous One,* the pious Ananias had employed a term previously used by Stephen (7:52) to designate Jesus as the Messiah.

22:16 **"'And now, why delay? Get up and be baptized, and have your sins washed away, calling on the name of the Lord.'"**NLT Baptism (see Matthew 28:18-20; Mark 1:4-8; Acts 2:41) indicates acceptance of and identification with a certain leader, group, or teaching (see notes on 2:38). Baptism in the name of Christ would be a powerful outward sign of Paul's inward cleansing from sin and his embracing of the gospel.

This verse does not teach, as some try to argue, that baptism saves—Paul was filled with the Spirit *before* his baptism with water (see 9:17-18)—nor does it teach that the ordinance of baptism literally washes away our sins. Faith alone, calling on the name of the Lord (Romans 10:9-13), saves, and baptism depicts that truth. A more literal rendering would be "get yourself baptized . . . having previously called upon his name." In other words, the text is saying: "Since you have called on the Lord's name, now get baptized."

UNBAPTIZED BELIEVERS?
The consistent record of Acts is that those who put their faith in Christ immediately sought to be baptized. In the early church, the notion of an unbaptized believer was unheard of. Sadly, many modern-day Christians mistakenly view baptism as optional—a matter of personal preference. By not obeying Christ's command to be baptized (Matthew 28:18-20), followers of Jesus end up not following him—at least not fully. For even he submitted to John's baptism. Furthermore, unbaptized believers miss out on a wonderful and meaningful event in their Christian life. Baptism (like the Lord's Supper) enables us to act out some of the rich spiritual blessings we have in Christ. Have you obeyed the command to be baptized?

22:17-18 **"One day after I returned to Jerusalem, I was praying in the Temple, and I fell into a trance. I saw a vision of Jesus saying to me, 'Hurry! Leave Jerusalem, for the people here won't believe you when you give them your testimony about me.'"**NLT Paul continued to answer the mob's accusations. He stated, in effect, that he was not antitemple (see 21:28). By praying and worshiping there, he demonstrated his continued respect for the temple—even as a follower of Jesus.

While he was *praying in the Temple,* Paul received a heavenly vision. The Greek word for "trance" is *ekstasei,* the same root used to describe Peter's dreamlike encounter on the rooftop in Joppa (10:10; 11:5). In this *vision,* Jesus appeared and warned Paul to promptly leave Jerusalem because the Jews would not accept his testimony.

In 9:29-30, Luke reported that Paul departed Jerusalem upon the advice of his Christian brothers. This apparent discrepancy is easily resolved by viewing Paul as led by both human counsel and divine revelation. The advice from worried believers probably came first, later being confirmed by that other, stronger, more irresistible voice (20:22).

22:19-20 **"And I said, 'Lord, they themselves know that in every synagogue I imprisoned and beat those who believed in you. And while the blood of your witness Stephen was shed, I myself**

was standing by, approving and keeping the coats of those who killed him.'"NRSV Never one to run from controversy or trouble, Paul protested mildly. He obviously felt convinced that his conversion from a notorious persecutor of Christians into an ardent evangelist for the Way would impress his Jewish accusers. Surely, they would marvel at the change in his life. He could not and would not have done such a complete about-face without compelling reasons.

Perhaps implicit in Paul's rejoinder was the thought that preaching to such a volatile audience might in some way make up for the damage he had done to the church—especially assisting in and approving of the killing of *Stephen.*

GOD'S GUIDANCE
God spoke to Paul through a vision and through his friends (9:29-30). He speaks to us in various ways—through his written Word, through circumstances and "coincidences," through Bible study, sermons, memories, nature, even art. The right question is not, "Is God speaking to me?" but "Am I listening for his voice?" Make it your goal to hear what God is saying. He wants to guide you and give you daily reminders of his power and presence in your life.

22:21 "But the Lord said to me, 'Leave Jerusalem, for I will send you far away to the Gentiles!'"NLT Paul's appeal to the Lord was unsuccessful. For Paul's own safety and for the fulfillment of God's eternal plan, Paul needed to *leave Jerusalem.* A plot on his life was in the works (see Acts 9:22-23).

Specifically, the Lord was commissioning Paul to take the message of salvation *to the Gentiles.* There are three confirmations of Paul's commission to the Gentiles: (1) God's words to Ananias (9:15); (2) Paul's record here; and (3) Paul's quote of Christ's words to him at his conversion (26:16-18). Given his own history, Paul surely must have realized that stating so explicitly this call would send the crowd below into a frenzy. But he did not minimize or avoid declaring the truth.

22:22-23 The crowd listened until Paul came to that word; then with one voice they shouted, "Away with such a fellow! Kill him! He isn't fit to live!" They yelled, threw off their coats, and tossed handfuls of dust into the air.NLT These people had *listened* intently to Paul, but the word "Gentiles" (22:21) brought out all their anger and exposed their pride. They were supposed to be a light to the Gentiles, telling them about the one true God, but they had renounced that mission by becoming separatist and exclusive.

Did the Jews hate the Gentiles? No. Continual efforts were made by the Jews to try to convert the Gentiles. The implications of Paul's testimony and Christian gospel were clear, however. He was suggesting that the Gentiles could be saved and made right with God without first subscribing to the law and submitting to Jewish circumcision. In effect, Paul was claiming divine approval for the idea that Jews and Gentiles could have equal standing before God. This message collided head-on with the blindness, pride, and prejudice of the Jews. The results were explosive.

But no matter how furious the mob or intense their opposition, God's plan would not be thwarted. The Gentiles were hearing the gospel through Jewish Christians such as Paul and Peter.

AUTHENTICITY
Paul demonstrated great candor and courage in sharing his conversion story. He could have hit lightly on controversial points or mumbled his way past them. But he didn't. Convinced of the truth of the message of grace that Christ had given, he spelled it out clearly. It is tempting in conversations with unbelieving friends or neighbors to gloss over our faith. And how wrong! Sometimes a simple sentence or two about "how God helped me during the grief process," "how prayer transformed my marriage," or "the comfort I found in a Bible promise" can be just the tool to open up a spiritual conversation. Ask God for opportunities this week to speak an honest word of testimony that he can use to bring forth new life.

PAUL REVEALS HIS ROMAN CITIZENSHIP / 22:24-29

Irritated at Paul for having created such a ruckus, and eager to force some sort of confession, the Roman commander ordered the apostle flogged. Paul barely escaped this sentence by mentioning his Roman citizenship. Here is yet another instance of God's sovereign control over lives and events. Who knows how the spread of the gospel might have been hindered had Paul not been a Roman citizen?

22:24-25 The commander brought Paul inside and ordered him lashed with whips to make him confess his crime. He wanted to find out why the crowd had become so furious. As they tied Paul down to lash him, Paul said to the officer standing there, "Is it legal for you to whip a Roman citizen who hasn't even been tried?"[NLT] The *commander,* who only minutes before had been impressed enough with Paul to give him the opportunity to speak to the crowd, suddenly became annoyed. Weary of the continual upheaval surrounding Paul, he ordered the apostle to be *lashed with whips.* He believed this examination by torture would force a confession by Paul or at least an explanation about what was really going on.

By his own testimony (see 16:22-23; 2 Corinthians 11:24-25), Paul had been beaten with rods and had even received, on several occasions, the Jewish "thirty-nine lashes." The scourging proposed here by commander Lysias was different. This was the same kind of flogging that Jesus had been subjected to just before his crucifixion. Using a short leather whip imbedded with bits of bone and metal, a Roman solider would rip away the flesh of his victim with each blow. If this punishment didn't kill or permanently maim the recipient, it took months or even years to recover.

Paul, ever the shrewd servant of the Lord, resorted to his civic privilege. By law, a Roman citizen could not be punished without first having a trial, nor could a Roman citizen be interrogated by beating or torture. The Roman law, *Lex Julia,* allowed citizens to appeal to Rome. The ancient Porcian and Valerian laws forbade such treatment. In dramatic fashion, just as the blows were about to begin falling, Paul asked, *"Is it legal for you to whip a Roman citizen who hasn't even been tried?"* Paul knew the law. He knew the answer to that question. It was most certainly not legal. There had been no trial, hearing, or formal charges presented.

USING COMMON SENSE

Why didn't Paul just submit to the beating? He, more than anyone, knew Jesus' teaching regarding the blessing of suffering for Christ, about turning the other cheek, about following the example of Christ. But none of those really fit in this instance. Paul utilized common sense. He realized that this beating would serve no purpose. It's one thing to be a martyr when you have no other recourse. But to submit to a brutal, avoidable beating would be masochism, pure and simple.

As Christians in a free society, we have tremendous civic privileges: first amendment freedoms (speech, press, religion), library privileges, voting rights, and the chance to run for public office, to write letters, march, and even protest! Are we making full use of these God-given opportunities?

22:26-28 The officer went to the commander and asked, "What are you doing? This man is a Roman citizen!" So the commander went over and asked Paul, "Tell me, are you a Roman citizen?" "Yes, I certainly am," Paul replied. "I am, too," the commander muttered, "and it cost me plenty!" "But I am a citizen by birth!"[NLT] Paul's question stunned and scared his captors. They had come dangerously close to violating strict Roman laws.

In quizzing Paul, the commander learned that Paul had been born a Roman citizen (apparently his father had somehow achieved this status). The commander admitted that he had been forced to purchase his citizenship. Buying one's citizenship (actually bribing the right people in power) was a common practice and a good source of income for the Roman government. Bought citizenship was considered inferior to citizenship by birth.

22:29 **Those who were about to question him withdrew immediately. The commander himself was alarmed when he realized that he had put Paul, a Roman citizen, in chains.**[NIV] Paul's revelation about himself effectively ended the proceedings. The text does not state so explicitly, but Roman laws (the *Lex Valeria* and *Lex Porcia*) prohibited even the fettering of Roman citizens. The commander realized how close he had come to breaking the law himself. Paul was likely freed from his chains immediately but still detained for the night at the Fortress of Antonia (for his own protection, given the volatile nature of the crowd).

Every experience of trial puts us to this test: "Do you trust God or don't you?" *Elizabeth Elliot*

Acts 22:30–23:35

PAUL APPEARS BEFORE THE SANHEDRIN / 22:30–23:11

Having been saved from the murderous mob at the temple the previous day, Paul was brought before the Jewish high Council. When he sensed the charged atmosphere (he was slapped after uttering the first sentence of his defense!), Paul decided to focus the Sanhedrin's attention on something even more controversial than himself—the theological debate concerning the resurrection of the dead. Immediately, the Pharisees and Sadducees began to argue, and Paul was led back to the safety of his cell. There the Lord appeared to him in a comforting vision, assuring him that he would preach the Good News in Rome. No amount of human opposition can thwart God's plan and purposes.

22:30 **The next day the commander freed Paul from his chains and ordered the leading priests into session with the Jewish high council. He had Paul brought in before them to try to find out what the trouble was all about.**[NLT] In an unusual move, the Roman *commander* ordered the *Jewish high council* (the Sanhedrin) *into session* in order to hear Paul's case (for more on the Jewish high Council, see commentary on 4:5). If Paul were found innocent there, the commander could release him. If found guilty by the Jewish court, however, then the commander would see that Paul, as a Roman citizen, would go before the Roman governor (and, if necessary, on to Rome).

> There is one thing alone that stands the brunt of life throughout its course: a quiet conscience.
>
> *Euripides*

Paul was *freed . . . from his chains* by the commander and brought in to state his case before the Council. Paul consistently used his times of persecution as opportunities for him to witness. His enemies were creating a platform for him to address the entire Council.

23:1 **Paul looked straight at the Sanhedrin and said, "My brothers, I have fulfilled my duty to God in all good conscience to this day."**[NIV] The Greek word for *looked straight at* is *atenisas,* meaning to "look fixedly" or "gaze." Its placement as the first word of the Greek sentence adds emphasis.

With clear, solid eye contact, the first words Paul said to the assembled Jewish religious leaders were, *"I have fulfilled my duty to God in all good conscience to this day."* Two times in Acts (here and in 24:16) and twenty-one times in his letters (see, for example, 1 Corinthians 4:4; 2 Corinthians 1:12; 1 Timothy 1:5; 2 Timothy 1:3), Paul referred to his clear conscience. He wanted his audience to know that he was committed to his spiritual and moral choices that had resulted in his trial before them. He was ready to stand before God and be accountable for his choices and actions. Inherent in Paul's statement, of course, was the challenge: were *they* ready?

The word for "fulfilled duty" is *pepoliteumai,* from which we get our word "politics"—doing one's duty as a citizen. Here, of course, Paul was referring to his duty as a citizen of the kingdom of God. In essence he was saying, "I am here today because I have been doing God's work!"

23:2-3 **Instantly Ananias the high priest commanded those close to Paul to slap him on the mouth. But Paul said to him, "God will slap you, you whitewashed wall! What kind of judge are you to break the law yourself by ordering me struck like that?"**[NLT] Almost as soon as Paul began speaking, he was slapped *on the mouth.* Obviously, Paul had already offended *Ananias the high priest,* his accuser! Ananias became high priest in A.D. 48, and he reigned through A.D. 58 or 59. Josephus, a respected first-century historian, described Ananias as profane, greedy, and hot-tempered. He was hated by many of his Jewish contemporaries because of his pro-Roman policies.

Paul's outburst came as a result of the illegal command that Ananias had given. Ananias had violated Jewish law by assuming that Paul was guilty without a trial and by ordering his punishment (see Deuteronomy 19:15). Maybe Paul had Leviticus 19:15 in mind in his accusation of Ananias's breaking the law himself: "You shall not render an unjust judgment; you shall not be par-

> As Christians, we are tempted to make unnecessary concessions to those outside the Faith. We give in too much. Now, I don't mean that we should run the risk of making a nuisance of ourselves by witnessing at improper times, but there comes a time when we must show that we disagree. We must show our Christian colours, if we are to be true to Jesus Christ. We cannot remain silent or concede everything away.
>
> *C. S. Lewis*

tial to the poor or defer to the great: with justice you shall judge your neighbor" (NRSV). Jesus also questioned the legality of his similar treatment during his mockery of a trial before this same Council (John 18:20-23). Paul had not yet been charged with a crime, much less tried or found guilty.

Paul's use of the term "whitewashed wall" also recalls Jesus' similar description of the Pharisees in Matthew 23:27. This amounted to calling Ananias a hypocrite. "Whitewashed wall" may refer to the practice of whitewashing gravestones. This created a clean and positive appearance for what contained death and corruption.

ADDRESSING WRONG
Paul was struck illegally—without accusation, trial, or verdict. He didn't care who had ordered the blow—he spoke out firmly and forcefully. How do you respond to wrong when you see it? Do you turn a blind eye or deaf ear to it? Do you follow the crowd? Or do you stand up and stand against sin? There are times when it may be appropriate to be silent before our accusers, but if we never speak out, we cannot be salt and light in a decaying and dark society.

23:4-5 Those standing nearby said, "Do you dare to insult God's high priest?" And Paul said, "I did not realize, brothers, that he was high priest; for it is written, 'You shall not speak evil of a leader of your people.'"NRSV When Paul was given the information that he did not know, that the one whom he had rebuked was the *high priest,* he apologized—not to the individual but to the office. It is clear that Paul was submitting to the Word as he quoted the appropriate passage from Exodus 22:28, a verse that prohibits speaking *evil of a leader of* the *people.* Paul's ministry and his life had been marked by his obedience to God. Here he exhibited again, even in a very difficult situation, that God's Word mattered.

Paul may not have recognized Ananias as the high priest because of poor eyesight. Or perhaps his words were ironic, expressing his amazement that one who would behave so badly (and illegally!) toward him could be the high priest. Most likely, Paul simply did not know who the high priest was or even that he was present at the trial. Because Paul had been in Jerusalem only sporadically for about twenty years, he may have never seen Ananias, maybe only knowing him by name or, more likely, by reputation. This meeting had been called by the Roman commander, not the Council members, so the members may not have been in their official robes, which would have identified the high priest (22:30).

SUBMITTING TO THE WORD
When Paul learned that the man he had rebuked sharply was none other than the high priest, he quickly apologized (23:4-5). Quoting Exodus 22:28, he made no attempt to rationalize, justify, blame, or complain. Rather, his whole attitude can be summed up by the word "submission." For Paul, the clear-cut Word (and will) of God was what mattered—not his own personal feelings or individual preference. How do you respond to God's Word? With obedience? rebellion? indifference? Paul's long-term effectiveness for Christ was due largely to his submission to God's Word.

23:6 **Paul realized that some members of the high council were Sadducees and some were Pharisees, so he shouted, "Brothers, I am a Pharisee, as were all my ancestors! And I am on trial because my hope is in the resurrection of the dead!"**NLT The *Sadducees* and *Pharisees* were two groups of religious leaders but with strikingly different beliefs. The Pharisees believed in a bodily resurrection, but the Sadducees did not. The Sadducees adhered only to Genesis through Deuteronomy, which contain no explicit teaching on resurrection. Paul's statement about his *hope* moved the debate away from himself and toward the religious leaders' festering controversy about *the resurrection of the dead.* (For more information, see the chart "Prominent Jewish Religious and Political Groups," in 4:1, pages 56–57.)

By identifying himself as a *Pharisee* and the descendant of Pharisees, Paul utilized three tactics: (1) he opened the door for inserting the gospel of the resurrected Christ, at least with the part of the Council who believed in resurrection; (2) he got some sympathy and support from a part of the Council; (3) he surfaced an ongoing controversy that would embroil the Council in hopeless debate.

Paul's sudden insight that the Council was a mixture of Sadducees and Pharisees is an example of the power that Jesus promised to believers (Mark 13:9-11). God will help his people when they are under fire for their faith. Like Paul, believers should always be ready to present their testimony. The Holy Spirit will give them power to speak boldly.

23:7-8 **This divided the council—the Pharisees against the Sadducees—for the Sadducees say there is no resurrection or angels or spirits, but the Pharisees believe in all of these.**NLT Paul's tactic worked. The Council was *divided* (Greek, *eschisthe,* from which we get our word "schism"). Their historic argument about the *resurrection, angels,* and *spirits* came to the surface. This was the same issue over which the Sadducees had tried to trap Christ (Matthew 22:23-33), but without success. (For more on Sadducees, see commentary on 4:1.) The Sadducees were a part of the Jews who believed the messianic age had begun with the Jewish revolt under Judas Maccabeus. They did not believe in any future heavenly reality.

It is not likely that Paul was simply causing a distraction, though that was the result. Rather, he was utilizing this opportunity, maybe his last with his Pharisee "brothers," to tell them the truth, to introduce them to his Savior. Reaching them was his main motive: "I know you believe in the resurrection, and I have a Resurrection you have to investigate!"

USING—NOT LOSING—OPPORTUNITIES
Some claim that Paul brought up the issue of the resurrection in order to distract the Council and get them into an argument with one another (23:7-8). More likely, Paul saw this occasion as probably his last opportunity to speak the truth to the leaders and opinion shapers of Israel. Paul had a deep passion for his countrymen (see Romans 10) and desperately wanted to reach them. This raises the question: How concerned are we for our friends, relatives, and neighbors? Do we have that kind of passion? Are we taking advantage of God-given opportunities to witness?

23:9 There was a great uproar, and some of the teachers of the law who were Pharisees stood up and argued vigorously. "We find nothing wrong with this man," they said. "What if a spirit or an angel has spoken to him?"NIV The dispute caused an immediate *great uproar.* As expected, the Pharisees came to the vigorous defense of one who spoke so positively about one of their valued positions—resurrection. Paul had, in fact, stated that the resurrection of the dead was the reason that he was on trial at all (23:6)! The Pharisees alluded to another area of their differences between them and the Sadducees by speculating on the fact that *a spirit or an angel* may have *spoken to him.* They may have drawn this conclusion based on some of Paul's remarks to the crowd at the temple court the day before (22:17-18). The Sadducees would have argued strongly that such communication was not possible because they didn't believe in the existence of spirits and angels.

23:10 The dispute became so violent that the commander was afraid Paul would be torn to pieces by them. He ordered the troops to go down and take him away from them by force and bring him into the barracks.NIV Finally the disagreement (literally, "standoff") became so heated that the Roman *commander* had to step in. Evidently, Paul was in the middle of it all and had to be removed by the Roman troops. From there he was safely removed to *the barracks* of the Antonia Fortress.

Just as had been Paul's experience for the last decade of ministry, he was once again attacked by the Jews and treated kindly by the Gentiles—locked in a Roman prison in order to protect him from the high court of the Jews!

A LASTING LEGACY

Like Paul, believers want to achieve long-term success in serving Christ. How can this happen? Acts 23:1-10 lists at least four ways to build a spiritual legacy that will last:

(1) *Live wisely as a citizen of heaven.* (23:1)—Paul's clear conscience was his platform from which to rebuke the Jewish Council. He took his citizenship in the kingdom of God seriously, and he lived in a way that he knew would be pleasing to the Sovereign.

(2) *Address wrong when you see it.* (23:2-3)—Paul took on the Sanhedrin, the high Council of the Jewish people. When he was struck illegally, he addressed the wrong that had been done to him.

(3) *Submit to the Word when you hear it.* (23:4-5)—When Paul was informed that his words were against the high priest, he backed down and apologized. His deep submission to the Word of God surfaced at this point.

(4) *Tell the Story when you get the opportunity.* (23:6-10)—Paul used his kinship with the Pharisees to promote the gospel. Their belief in the resurrection made them prime candidates for hearing the news of Christ's resurrection, and Paul used this platform to let them hear it.

23:11 That night the Lord appeared to Paul and said, "Be encouraged, Paul. Just as you have told the people about me here in Jerusalem, you must preach the Good News in Rome."[NLT] And when *night* came, *the Lord appeared to Paul* (literally, "stood by him"). The Lord had always been with Paul, but he knew that his faithful servant needed him closer that night.

> The bitterest cup with Christ is better than the sweetest cup without Him. *Ian MacPherson*

Look at the richness of the encouragement of the Lord here. Christ told Paul to *Be encouraged* and then gave him the substance of why he should be so. First, he gave Paul a word of praise for his faithfulness to the ministry—*just as you have told the people about me here.* Second, he gave Paul a word of promise—*you must preach the Good News in Rome.* God, in essence, promised Paul safe passage to another field of ministry.

"ENCOURAGEMENT" VISITS OF GOD TO PAUL

Passage	*Purpose*	*Result*
Acts 16:9	To send him on to Macedonia to preach.	Many converts and churches planted.
Acts 18:9-10	To get him to stay and preach boldly in Corinth.	Many converts, some new close co-workers, and a solid ministry begun.
Acts 22:17	To send him from Jerusalem for his safety.	Protection by the Roman military given.
Acts 23:11	To send him to preach the gospel in Rome.	Effective ministry in Rome and beyond continued.
Acts 27:22	To promise him protection and guidance through the shipwreck.	Safety for him and his companions provided.
2 Timothy 4:16-17	To encourage him in his trial in Rome.	Deliverance from the "lions" provided.

We might imagine that after this visit, another in a long line of God's encouragement appearances to Paul, the apostle rolled over and drifted off to the kind of restful sleep that only a child safe within his Father's strong arms can experience (Psalm 127:2).

THE PLAN TO KILL PAUL / 23:12-22

The morning after God had pledged to deliver Paul safely to Rome, a group of Jews gathered to plot the murder of the apostle. How futile! The Lord himself had declared through the prophet: "From eternity to eternity I am God. No one can oppose what I do. No one can reverse my actions" (Isaiah 43:13 NLT). Paul's nephew learned of the plot and revealed it to the Roman commander in Jerusalem.

> If sorrow makes us shed tears, faith in the promises of God makes us dry them. *Augustine*

23:12-13 The next morning a group of Jews got together and bound themselves with an oath to neither eat nor drink until they had killed Paul. There were more than forty of them.[NLT] The Lord himself had come to Paul in prison and essentially had promised him safe passage to Rome. Meanwhile, these zealous Jews *bound themselves with an oath to neither eat nor drink until they had killed Paul.* They put themselves under a solemn vow, like a curse, if they did not fulfill what they said. Paul had already been granted safe passage to Rome by God himself. Luke must have chuckled as he was writing these words, knowing that these sincere but misguided *Jews (more than forty of them)* would have to go without food for a long time. It would be ten years or so before Paul's death in Rome!

GOD'S PRESENCE
After two days of riots and mayhem, in which both the masses and the nation's leadership wanted to kill him, Paul must have been confused and concerned, if not downright discouraged. Graciously, Christ appeared to Paul and encouraged him (23:11). If you are feeling lonely or discouraged, be encouraged by the truth that you serve the same God who was with Paul in his darkest hour. God is with you. He is there. He is there in your darkest dungeon—it may be a scary hospital room, a quiet cemetery, or a lonely kitchen— wherever it is, if you're one of his, he's there, standing nearby. Look for signs of his presence. Lean on his tremendous promises.

23:14-15 They went to the leading priests and other leaders and told them what they had done. "We have bound ourselves under oath to neither eat nor drink until we have killed Paul. You and the high council should tell the commander to bring Paul back to the council again," they requested. "Pretend you want to examine his case more fully. We will kill him on the way."NLT This group of over forty men announced their oath to *the leading priests and other leaders.* Their plan was to get the *high council* to have Paul returned to a meeting with them under the guise of examining *his case more fully.* And, exposing their contemptible character, they planned to *kill him on the way.* The idiocy of the plan and the fanatic zeal of this crew is multiplied all the more when it is noted that they were willing to take on a number of hardened and armed Roman soldiers in order to attempt to kill Paul. Certainly, many of them would lose their lives in the process.

Evidently, the Jewish leaders thought this was a good idea and went along with it! To these leaders, politics and position had become more important than God. They were ready to plan another murder, just as they had done with Jesus. This also revealed the flimsiness of their case against Paul. They knew they had no case, but they so desperately wanted to get rid of him that they were willing to stoop to any means to do so. As always, however, God, not the Council, was in control.

GOD IS ENOUGH
A group of powerful and prominent movers and shakers pledged to kill Paul. This would have been a terrifying proposition except for the fact of God's promise to Paul: "You must preach the Good News in Rome" (23:11 NLT). From a human perspective, Paul made it safely to Rome because of imperial commanders and centurions and a detachment of almost five hundred soldiers. But the truth is that Paul eventually reached his divinely appointed destination because God is sovereign and because nothing can thwart his plans. As someone has said, we are utterly safe and invincible until God calls us home. Focus on God's presence, power, and promises, and watch your whole perspective change!

23:16-17 But Paul's nephew heard of their plan and went to the fortress and told Paul. Paul called one of the officers and said, "Take this young man to the commander. He has something important to tell him."NLT This is the only biblical reference to Paul's family. Some scholars believe that Paul's family disowned him when he became a Christian. Paul wrote of having suffered the loss of everything for Christ (Philippians 3:8). *Paul's nephew,* who is never named, was evidently able to visit Paul, even though Paul was in protective custody. Roman prisoners were often accessible to their relatives and friends who could bring them food and other amenities. How the nephew heard of the plan is not stated. There also is no mention of any others of Paul's relatives.

Once Paul received the information, he immediately sent his nephew to the *commander.* Although God had told Paul that he would go to Rome, God did not explain how he would be kept safe. There is a healthy balance here of Paul trusting in God's sovereignty and yet wisely utilizing the God-sent provisions that would come his way—his Roman citizenship, the Roman soldiers, the Roman prison, and now, a piece of important information from a relative. Paul trusted God, but he kept his eyes open to see just how the Father would deliver him.

CHILD'S PLAY
It is easy to overlook children or teenagers, assuming that they aren't old enough to do much for the Lord. But a young man (Paul's nephew) played an important human part in protecting the apostle's life. God can use anyone, of any age, who is willing to yield to him. Jesus made it clear that children are important (Matthew 18:2-6). Give children the importance God gives them.

23:18-19 So he took him to the commander. The centurion said, "Paul, the prisoner, sent for me and asked me to bring this young man to you because he has something to tell you." The commander took the young man by the hand, drew him aside and asked, "What is it you want to tell me?"NIV Paul's nephew was delivered to the *commander,* to whom the *centurion* dutifully reported the young man's purpose for being there. The commander, in a gentle motion, *took the young man by the hand* (giving the impression that the nephew was likely quite young) and pulled him out of the pressured limelight, probably in an attempt to get a correct story. He then asked, *"What is it you want to tell me?"*

The kindness with which the centurion and commander treated Paul and his nephew causes one to wonder what opinion they held of this whole situation. Their generous treatment may have been a result of their trying to correct their earlier failure to give Paul the protection a Roman citizen was due (and thus their jobs were in jeopardy—22:24-29), or perhaps Paul now was simply receiving the Roman citizen's correct treatment. It may be, however, that they recognized the drastic difference between the courageous, Christlike apostle and his paranoid, murderous rivals.

23:20-22 He said: "The Jews have agreed to ask you to bring Paul before the Sanhedrin tomorrow on the pretext of wanting more accurate information about him. Don't give in to them, because more than forty of them are waiting in ambush for him. They have taken an oath not to eat or drink until they have killed him. They are ready now, waiting for your consent to their request." The commander dismissed the young man and cautioned him, "Don't tell anyone that you have reported this to me."NIV Paul's nephew gave a detailed report of the plot (23:12-15). He boldly told this *commander,* whose military air and authority would likely be a little intimidating for a young lad, *"Don't give in to them . . . more than forty of them are waiting in ambush for him.*

The lad even knew about the oath. How he obtained the information is unknown, but there is no doubt about its accuracy. Evidently, the ambush was already in place, simply waiting for the commander's order to send the prisoner to the Council chambers.

The commander wisely told Paul's nephew to keep his silence on the report he had given. After this, the only member of Paul's family mentioned anywhere in the New Testament disappeared into the silence of unrecorded history.

PAUL IS SENT TO CAESAREA / 23:23-35

Guarded by an armed escort of almost five hundred Roman soldiers, Paul was transferred to Caesarea and the jurisdiction of Governor Felix. He would be safe there until it was time for him to leave for Rome. God's sovereignty is visible in both the actions of these secular authorities and in the resulting spread of the Good News.

23:23-24 **Then the commander called two of his officers and ordered, "Get two hundred soldiers ready to leave for Caesarea at nine o'clock tonight. Also take two hundred spearmen and seventy horsemen. Provide horses for Paul to ride, and get him safely to Governor Felix."**[NLT] There were 470 men dispatched to guard one prisoner—*two hundred soldiers, two hundred spearmen, and seventy horsemen.* The commander knew that the forty assassins would fight to the death, and he did not want to have to explain the assassination of a Roman citizen under his protection. The zealous desire to kill Paul on the part of the Jews in ambush was more than matched by the extent to which the Romans went to protect him.

On the other hand, after the visit by the Lord himself (23:11) and the sovereign exposure of the plot to his nephew (23:16), Paul was probably amused at all this commotion. With God on his side, he could have walked unarmed and unescorted to Caesarea and arrived without a scratch. Still, the Roman commander placed a contingent of soldiers around him. This commander probably would not be comfortable until he had this particular prisoner safely out of Jerusalem, where a group of murderous zealots were getting hungrier by the minute.

Instead of returning Paul to the Jewish Council, the commander sent him to Caesarea, sixty miles to the northwest. Jerusalem was the seat of Jewish government, but Caesarea was the Roman headquarters for the area. There

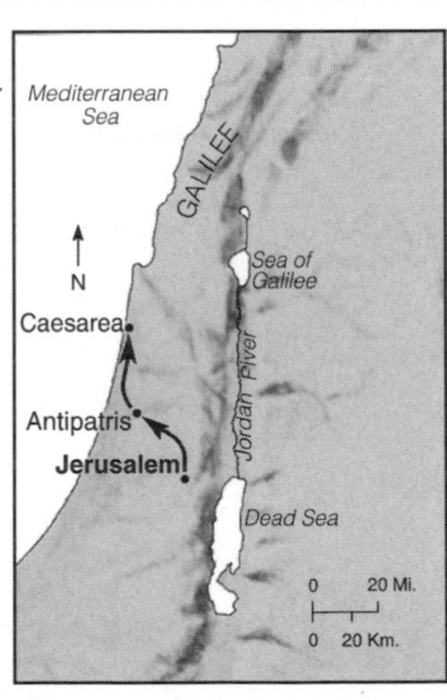

IMPRISONMENT IN CAESAREA
Paul brought news of his third journey to the elders of the Jerusalem church, who rejoiced at his ministry. But Paul's presence soon stirred up the Jews, who persuaded the Romans to arrest him. A plot to kill Paul was uncovered, so Paul was taken by night to Antipatris and then transferred to the provincial prison in Caesarea.

UNSUNG HEROES IN ACTS

When we think of the success of the early church, we often think of the work of the apostles. But the church could have died if it hadn't been for the unsung heroes, the men and women who through some small but committed act moved the church forward.

Hero	*Reference*	*Heroic action*
Crippled man	3:9-12	After his healing, he praised God. With the crowds gathering to see what happened, Peter used the opportunity to tell many about Jesus.
Five deacons	6:2-5	Everyone has heard of Stephen and many know of Philip, but five other men were also chosen to be deacons. They not only laid the foundation for service in the church, but their hard work also gave the apostles the time they needed to preach the gospel.
Ananias	9:10-19	He had the responsibility of being the first to demonstrate Christ's love to Saul (Paul) after his conversion.
Cornelius	10:30-35	His example showed Peter that the gospel was for all kinds of people—Jews and Gentiles.
Rhoda	12:13-15	Her persistence brought Peter inside Mary's home where he would be safe.
James	15:13-21	He took command of the Jerusalem council and had the courage and discernment to help form a decision that would affect literally millions of Christians over many generations.
Lydia	16:13-15	She opened her home to Paul, from which he led many to Christ and founded a church in Philippi.
Jason	17:5-9	He risked his life for the gospel by allowing Paul to stay in his home. He stood up for what was true and right, even though he faced persecution for it.
Paul's nephew	23:16-24	He saved Paul's life by telling officials of a murderous plot.
Julius	27:1, 43	He spared Paul when the other soldiers wanted to kill him.

the judicial process would be continued before the Roman court *(Governor Felix),* a process that was begun when Paul had exercised his rights as a Roman citizen (22:25).

GOD'S UNEXPECTED WAYS
God works in unexpected and amusing ways. God could have used any one of an infinite number of methods to get Paul to Caesarea, but he chose to use the Roman army (23:23-24). God's ways are not our ways. Ours are limited; his are not. Don't limit God by asking him to do things your way. When God intervenes, anything can happen, so much more and so much better than you could ever anticipate. Let God amaze you with his limitless power and his creative plans.

23:25-26 **He wrote a letter to this effect: "Claudius Lysias to his Excellency the governor Felix, greetings."**NRSV *Felix* was the Roman governor or procurator of Judea from A.D. 52 to 59. This was the same position that Pontius Pilate had held. While the Jews had been given much freedom to govern themselves, the governor ran the army, kept the peace, and gathered the taxes.

How did Luke know what was written in the letter from *Claudius Lysias?* In his concern for historical accuracy, Luke used many sources to make sure that his writings were correct (see Luke 1:1-4). This letter was probably read aloud in court when Paul came before Felix to answer the Jews' accusations. Also, because Paul was a Roman citizen, a copy may have been given to him as a courtesy.

The letter is technically called an *eloguim*—a formal letter that is a written statement of the case against the prisoner. Luke's words "to this effect" (the Greek is, literally, "after this form") imply that this is not a word-for-word record of the letter but simply an accurate report of its content.

The address "his Excellency" was a form of address reserved for important personages. The commander's full name is recorded here for the first time—*Claudius Lysias.* Lysias is a Greek name and is likely the one with which he was born. Claudius was probably added when he purchased his Roman citizenship, because it was the name of the emperor at the time (see 22:28).

23:27-30 **"This man was seized by the Jews and was about to be killed by them, but when I had learned that he was a Roman citizen, I came with the guard and rescued him. Since I wanted to know the charge for which they accused him, I had him brought to their council. I found that he was accused concerning questions of their law, but was charged with nothing deserving death or imprisonment. When I was informed that there would be a plot against the man, I sent him to you at once, ordering his accusers also to state before you what they have against him."**NRSV This letter has all the feel of a formal description of the events as well as the careful wording of a subordinate commander (Claudius Lysias) to his superior (Governor Felix). It must be noted that in his first sentence, the commander carefully rearranged the order of events, leaving out the fact that he had chained Paul and had been in the process of having him flogged when the information about his Roman citizenship was brought to light—a careful cover-up to protect himself (see 22:23-28). His phrase "I came with the guard and rescued him" was definitely a twisting of the story to present himself to the governor in the best possible light.

Notice, too, that Claudius is another prosecutor of the messengers of the gospel who completely exonerated Paul, a theme Luke wanted to bring out in his record. Gallo, the mayor of Ephesus, had done so (18:14-15); the Pharisees before Felix could not make the case against Paul (23:9); Festus and Agrippa in the chapters ahead would find Paul innocent as well (26:31-32). Here Claudius stated that Paul *was charged with nothing deserving death or imprisonment.* For the early readers of Acts, these would be encouraging precedents and may have helped them in their own struggles with the Jews or with Roman law.

Claudius's final sentence describes the plot and his choice to send Paul to Caesarea, where his safety could be more easily insured.

23:31-32 **So that night, as ordered, the soldiers took Paul as far as Antipatris. They returned to the fortress the next morning, while the horsemen took him on to Caesarea.**[NLT] Evidently, this a forced march *(that night, as ordered),* with the *soldiers* traveling by horseback *as far as Antipatris*—more than thirty-five miles. At that distance from Jerusalem (and at that speed), the prisoner would certainly be safe from pursuers, so the soldiers had been released to return to Jerusalem, leaving Paul with the seventy *horsemen* to accompany him the final twenty-five miles to Caesarea. The last few miles into Antipatris provided excellent terrain for an ambush, so that was likely part of the reason that the larger contingent went so far before turning back.

23:33-35 **When they arrived in Caesarea, they presented Paul and the letter to Governor Felix. He read it and then asked Paul what province he was from. "Cilicia," Paul answered. "I will hear your case myself when your accusers arrive," the governor told him. Then the governor ordered him kept in the prison at Herod's headquarters.**[NLT] And so Paul and his Roman escort *arrived in Caesarea* and were *presented* to Governor Felix. The governor ascertained Paul's province—*Cilicia*—and agreed to hear the case when his *accusers* arrived.

Felix was the governor (procurator) of Judea from about A.D. 52 to 59, holding the position that Pontius Pilate had held during Jesus' day. Felix had married Drusilla (24:24), a sister of Herod Agrippa II, the Agrippa mentioned in chapter 25. A man of low birth, Felix rose to power through the influence of his well-connected brother Pallas and his politically expedient marriages. He also married the granddaughter of Antony and Cleopatra. The historian Tacitus, however, described Felix's career with a stinging epigram: "He exercised the power of a king with the mind of a slave." He was regarded as a poor governor. He dispensed justice arbitrarily and served his own ends. Jewish revolts increased under his administration.

Thus, the platform was set for Paul to speak before the leading rulers of the area (recorded in the next three chapters). When God has a willing person, there will be no end to the places he or she can be used, with phenomenal opportunities for effective work.

The gospel was spreading by the sure, sovereign hand of God, through his trustworthy servant, the apostle Paul. Paul's testimony before these governors (chapters 24–26) was yet another step in God's getting the apostle to his long-awaited destination—Rome. And this journey was not at the expense of the church at Antioch, or Paul's tentmaking business, but rather the government of Rome!

GUARANTEES FOR THE GODLY

When we get involved in God's work, like Paul, we can expect some of the divine benefits Paul experienced:

- *God's Presence* (23:11)—God knows how much we can take and how deep we can sink; when we are doing his work, we can expect him to "stand near" us the way he did with Paul.
- *God's Protection* (23:12-32)—God preserves his children for the work at hand and keeps them safe until it is time to bring them home.
- *God's Platforms* (23:33-35)—God will open doors to new opportunities to share the gospel in strategic situations before many kinds of people.

Acts 24

PAUL APPEARS BEFORE FELIX / 24:1-27

The next three chapters provide a look at an interesting trio of politicians—Felix, Festus, and Agrippa. All three held significant offices in the Roman regime that dominated their world. All three came face-to-face with the gospel of Jesus Christ through the testimony of none other than the apostle Paul. As determined from the text, all three rejected Christ. The reasons were different, but the results were the same.

The first trial was before Felix, the Roman governor in Caesarea. Tertullus, a lawyer from Jerusalem, arrived with Ananias, the high priest, and presented the Jews' baseless case against Paul. Paul responded brilliantly, winning a reprieve from Felix. This legal postponement lasted about two years, during which time Paul had many opportunities to speak about Jesus Christ to Felix and his wife, Drusilla.

24:1 **Five days later Ananias, the high priest, arrived with some of the Jewish leaders and the lawyer Tertullus, to press charges against Paul.**[NLT] The accusers arrived—*Ananias, the high priest,* and *the lawyer Tertullus,* along with several Jewish leaders. They had traveled sixty miles to Caesarea, the Roman center of government, to bring their false accusations against Paul. Their murder plot had failed (23:12-15), but they were persisting in trying to kill him.

The term translated "lawyer" is the Greek word *rhetoros,* which literally means "public speaker." The word is only used here in the New Testament, but other Greek sources at the time used the term in courtroom settings, so it came to have the more specialized meaning of "attorney" or "advocate."

Tertullus had been hired by the Jewish Council to present its case before the Roman court. Because of the wealth and influence of his clients, he was likely one of the top lawyers available.

24:2-4 **When Paul was called in, Tertullus presented his case before Felix: "We have enjoyed a long period of peace under you, and your foresight has brought about reforms in this nation. Everywhere and in every way, most excellent Felix, we**

acknowledge this with profound gratitude. But in order not to weary you further, I would request that you be kind enough to hear us briefly."NIV *Tertullus* began the religious leaders' case against Paul before the Roman governor *Felix* (for the background material on Felix, see commentary at 23:33-35). The case, which surely is only summarized here, began with gushing flattery, which seems to have taken up almost as much time as the case itself! The flattery is even more sickening, given the historical record of Governor Felix, who is remembered as a violent and corrupt ruler and was hated by the Jews.

Tertullus the lawyer/orator spoke of *peace under* Felix, his *foresight,* and *reforms.* He said that the Jews had *profound gratitude* to him. In reality, there had not been "peace" but violence. Tacitus wrote: "[The Romans] create a desolation and call it peace." Felix's "foresight" was basically nothing more than his political maneuvering to enhance his position in Roman power politics. His "reforms" consisted of little more than lining his own pockets at the expense of his subjects. There was nothing *excellent* about the way he was ruling, nor had the Jews ever been grateful for anything he had done. Tertullus, the religious leaders' legal representation, was lying profusely.

FLATTERY

In his opening remarks, Tertullus made Felix sound like a wise and gentle ruler (24:2-4). Actually, Felix had a reputation for corruption, violence, and self-promotion. Given these facts, Tertullus was guilty of lying and flattery. Solomon had written, "To flatter people is to lay a trap for their feet" (Proverbs 29:5 NLT). It is appropriate to affirm others by truthfully acknowledging noble character traits or praiseworthy actions, but it is *never* right to exaggerate another's qualities for selfish motives. The next time you are prompted to praise people, ask yourself, "Why am I doing this? For them or for me?"

24:5-6 **"We have found this man to be a troublemaker, stirring up riots among the Jews all over the world. He is a ringleader of the Nazarene sect and even tried to desecrate the temple; so we seized him."**NIV Finally, Tertullus got to the case. He made three accusations against Paul: (1) he was a *troublemaker, stirring up riots among the Jews all over the world;* (2) he was the *ringleader* of an unrecognized *Nazarene sect,* which was against Roman law; (3) he had *tried to desecrate the temple.* The religious leaders hoped that these accusations would persuade Felix to execute Paul in order to keep the peace in Palestine.

While the charge that Paul was a "troublemaker" was insulting, it was too vague to be a substantial legal charge. The Greek word *loimon* means a "plague" or a "pestilent person." This charge was designed to persuade Felix that Paul was causing sedition against Rome, enough trouble to reflect poorly on the governor's responsibility of keeping peace in the Empire. Keeping peace was a major part of his job description and job security.

The second charge, that of Paul's leadership of a "Nazarene sect," of course, referred to the Christians—named here after Jesus' hometown of Nazareth. The Greek word translated "sect" is *haireseos*—literally, a "faction" or "party," from which comes the English word "heresy." Tertullus was attempting to distance Christianity from Judaism, since the latter religion was allowed by Rome. If Felix would not prosecute Paul on the basis of his disruption of the peace, maybe he would do so if Paul were seen as a leader of a religious sect or cult that was not sanctioned by the state. This designation of Christians as "Nazarenes" was probably used of Jewish Christians from the earliest days of the church, but it is unknown what Felix may have known about them or what opinion he may have had. Surely Tertullus was using the term to put the church in its most controversial light.

The third charge—desecration of the temple—was likely designed to push Felix toward allowing the Jews to put Paul to death. It was one of the few offenses for which the Jews could still exact the death penalty. There seems to be a slight modification of the charge against Paul in this area (see 21:28). Originally, Paul had been charged with actually bringing a Gentile (Trophimus) into the temple area, thus desecrating it. Here the charge was modified to read that Paul "tried" to desecrate the temple—an attempted desecration rather than an actual one. Evidently the accusers knew they had no proof of the actual desecration (and maybe they did have solid proof of the exact opposite), so they had to shift their strategy to say that they had *seized him* in order to prevent the desecration.

RELIGIOUS NAME-CALLING

Roman law permitted the Jews to practice their religion. Tertullus knew, however, that other "new religions" were prohibited. For this reason he spoke disparagingly of Christianity as a "Nazarene sect" (24:5-6). This had the effect of making the gospel appear to be cultish and strange. Such religious name-calling is still prevalent. Some secular people enjoy making fun of Christians' beliefs and behavior. We can't prevent them from doing this; all we can do is live with integrity. And as believers, we can certainly avoid branding other Christians with unflattering labels.

24:7 "But the commander Lysias came by and with great violence took him out of our hands."NKJV Most modern versions do not include this verse, because it is not found in the most ancient manuscripts. It was added to depict the Roman commander's arrest of Paul as an unwanted and inappropriate interference in an offense that the Jews had every right to prosecute.

24:8-9 "You can find out the truth of our accusations by examining him yourself." Then the other Jews chimed in, declaring that everything Tertullus said was true.NLT Tertullus's reference here is probably to Paul. Felix could learn the *truth* of the accusations by *examining him.* When Tertullus finished his remarks, *the other Jews chimed in,* affirming the truthfulness of their legal counsel's case.

THE TEST OF TRUTH

Tertullus's accusations seemed compelling; his case against Paul appeared to be airtight. And a parade of other prominent Jews corroborated his version of the events (24:8-9). Yet Tertullus was not being truthful. Paul had never disturbed the peace—though his enemies had, everywhere he went. And Paul had never even spoken ill of the temple, much less attempted to desecrate it! These false charges remind us not to believe everything we hear. People (even apparently believable and reputable people) often misrepresent facts and distort truth. Hear both sides of a story before you present your opinion.

24:10 Now it was Paul's turn. The governor motioned for him to rise and speak. Paul said, "I know, sir, that you have been a judge of Jewish affairs for many years, and this gives me confidence as I make my defense."NLT The *governor* gave the apostle permission to speak, so Paul began his defense. Tertullus and the religious leaders seemed to have made a strong argument against Paul, but Paul would refute their accusations point by point.

Paul's introductory remarks were much more cursory and to the point, in contrast to Tertullus's flowing flattery. Paul simply alluded to the fact that Felix had *been a judge of Jewish affairs for many years,* thus making him a good person before whom to make his *defense* (Greek *apologoumai,* from which comes the term "apologetics"). This is likely the only accomplishment on which Paul could compliment him—that he had been around long enough and had tried enough cases involving Jewish affairs to be familiar with the nature of what was before him.

While Paul's compliments weren't overflowing, his remarks

did show respect for the Roman government (see Romans 13:1-6) and *confidence* in the integrity of the due process of law.

24:11-13 "You can easily verify that no more than twelve days ago I went up to Jerusalem to worship. My accusers did not find me arguing with anyone at the temple, or stirring up a crowd in the synagogues or anywhere else in the city. And they cannot prove to you the charges they are now making against me."NIV Paul answered the first charge (stirring up riots) by stating the easily verifiable trip he had made to *Jerusalem . . . no more than twelve days* previously. The implication here was that he had not been in Jerusalem long enough to stir up trouble. Also, he stated that he had come to Jerusalem for the purpose of *worship* (he was there for the Feast of Pentecost) after an extended absence. He was not there to stir up trouble.

Paul's statement of easily provable or not provable evidence made a strong case. He said that the governor would not be able to find anyone who saw him *arguing with anyone* or *stirring up a crowd . . . in the city.* In good legal fashion, Paul explained that his accusers could not *prove . . . the charges.* He knew his accusers could not present a shred of evidence that he had desecrated the temple.

24:14 "But I admit that I follow the Way, which they call a sect. I worship the God of our ancestors, and I firmly believe the Jewish law and everything written in the books of prophecy."NLT In this verse, Paul began to answer the second accusation—that of being a ringleader of a Nazarene sect. His answer to this accusation continues through 24:16 and provides the opening for the gospel. Paul affirmed that he followed *the Way,* which his accusers called a *sect.* He obviously preferred the name "the Way" to the more disparaging term used by his accusers. The term "Nazarene" implied something sectarian and perhaps even militant. The term "the Way" was not only known to Felix (see 24:22), but it also reflected a more universal and positive nature of Christianity—it provided a "way" to the Father, a "way" to deal with sin, and a "way" to live (see 9:2; 19:9, 23; 22:4). "The Way" was the earliest name for the Christian church. It probably came from Isaiah 40:3, 10-11, referring to God's people led on God's way. It also had analogies to Matthew 7:14, "the way of salvation," and to John 14:6, where Jesus referred to himself as "the way."

Paul took this opportunity to tie the roots of the Christian movement to the God of the Jewish people—*the God of our ancestors*—and particularly to the Old Testament Scriptures. He affirmed before Felix his firm belief in *the Jewish law and everything writ-*

ten in the books of prophecy. It would be hard to make the "heretic" or "sectarian" label stick with an argument as strong as this one. Paul was still worshiping the same God and holding to the same moral code as his accusers. He would soon get more specific.

THE GENEALOGY OF CHRISTIANITY
Paul affirmed his Jewish roots and history (24:14). Paul and other members of the early church did not see themselves as ex-Jews but as completed Jews. They viewed the Old Testament Scriptures, law, and sacrificial system as pointing to Christ and finding their ultimate fulfillment in him. The Christian gospel, then, was not seen as an aberration or conflicting belief system. For Paul, it was simply the next step in God's unfolding plan for the world. Knowing and appreciating Christianity's Jewish heritage by studying the Old Testament can only give us a richer experience in Christ. Spend some time tracing your Jewish roots.

24:15-16 "I have hope in God, just as these men do, that he will raise both the righteous and the ungodly. Because of this, I always try to maintain a clear conscience before God and everyone else."[NLT] Paul moved on to some important specific parts of his beliefs, again presenting his case in the most general terms possible. Avoiding the controversial Messiah discussions, Paul went straight to the issue of resurrection and judgment. He stated, first of all, his *hope* of a resurrection of *both the righteous and the ungodly* (see Daniel 12:2). This is, of course, the proclamation he had made in his case before the Jewish Council that had won him support from the Pharisees and attack from the Sadducees (see 23:6-9).

Because of this resurrection of both the righteous and the wicked, Paul sought to *maintain a clear conscience before God and everyone else* (see comments at 23:1). Here is the strong personal testimony of one who expected to stand before his Maker and give account for his life. In stating it this way, Paul not only bore witness to the fact that he was ready to meet God but also—by implication—that all people must get ready for such a meeting of their own. In so doing, Paul aligned himself perfectly with the convicting work of the Holy Spirit, of whom Jesus said: "When he comes, he will prove the world wrong about sin and righteousness and judgment" (John 16:8 NRSV).

> Some say, dedicate the heart and the money will follow; but our Lord put it the other way around. Where your treasure is, there will your heart be also. If your treasure is dedicated, your heart will be dedicated. If it is not, it simply won't. It is as simple as that.
>
> *G. Timothy Johnson*

24:17 "After an absence of several years, I came to Jerusalem to bring my people gifts for the poor and to present offerings."NIV Paul finally moved to the last accusation, that he had tried to desecrate the temple. Paul stated the main purpose of his Jerusalem trip—*to bring my people gifts for the poor and to present offerings.* This is the only mention, at least in the book of Acts, of the collection for the saints in Jerusalem. Paul's letters refer to it several times (Romans 15:25-28; 1 Corinthians 16:1-4; 2 Corinthians 8:13-14; 9:12-13; Galatians 2:10), but, for the most part, it is left out of the Acts record. The gifts were important to Paul. This offering tied the Gentile church back to its theological and spiritual roots—the gift would build unity between the Jewish and Gentile factions of the church. It was also a tangible expression of the genuineness of the Gentiles' faith and the high level of their maturity in Christ.

Since Luke was likely compressing this whole court scene, Paul's words "to present offerings" were either a reference to the offerings he had agreed to fund at the prompting of the Jerusalem elders (21:24) or his own purification offerings for his past months of living among the "unclean" Gentiles.

HELPING THE POOR
This is the only reference in Acts of Paul's collection for the poor Jerusalem saints (24:17), though it is mentioned often in his letters. It forces us to remember that at the most basic level, the gospel is not about building big churches or launching worldwide evangelistic campaigns but about loving others. This is the essence of the law. When Christ rules in our hearts, we will have compassion for others—concern for both their spiritual and physical well-being. What is your church doing to assist those Christians who are struggling financially? What are *you* doing?

24:18-19 "I was ceremonially clean when they found me in the temple courts doing this. There was no crowd with me, nor was I involved in any disturbance. But there are some Jews from the province of Asia, who ought to be here before you and bring charges if they have anything against me."NIV As to the charge of desecration—Paul was *ceremonially clean* when he was discovered in the temple courts. As to the charge of causing an uproar, he stated, *"There was no crowd with me, nor was I involved in any disturbance."*

The problem came when *some Jews from the province of Asia* showed up. They, in fact, had caused the uproar, not Paul. In fact, said Paul, they should have been in the courtroom that day to *bring charges* against him if they had any. Their false accusations had caused the riot in Jerusalem (21:27). How could Paul be held culpable for what they did? This was a strong point in Paul's defense, one that his accusers simply could not refute.

24:20-21 "Ask these men here what wrongdoing the Jewish high council found in me, except for one thing I said when I shouted out, 'I am on trial before you today because I believe in the resurrection of the dead!'"NLT Paul suggested that Felix ask those members of the *Jewish high council* who were present what *wrongdoing* they found in him. Paul explained that he had made a controversial remark by claiming to believe *in the resurrection of the dead* (23:6). Paul knew it was unlikely that any of his accusers would attack that statement in Felix's presence, and they kept their silence.

This, of course, gave Paul a chance to present the Resurrection again, this time before Felix and his court, as well as to those Pharisees (accusers) who had been present at Paul's meeting with the Jewish Council in Jerusalem.

Thus the charges verbalized by Tertullus had been answered, and all that remained was for Felix to respond.

24:22-23 Felix, who was quite familiar with the Way, adjourned the hearing and said, "Wait until Lysias, the garrison commander, arrives. Then I will decide the case." He ordered an officer to keep Paul in custody but to give him some freedom and allow his friends to visit him and take care of his needs.NLT *Felix* had been governor for six years and would have known about the Christians (he was *quite familiar with the Way*). The Christian movement, which had involved thousands of people from the first day on (2:41, 47; 4:4), would have been a topic of conversation among the Roman leadership. Hopefully, too, the Christians' peaceful lifestyles had already proven to the Romans that Christians didn't go around starting riots. Some believe the language of this verse indicates that Felix had more than a little knowledge of Christianity. Maybe he had gotten his information through Drusilla, his wife, who was a member of the Herod family. Whatever the case, Felix's knowledge of and exoneration of the church seemed very important to Luke, and for good reason. Luke wanted the original readers of his book to have a solid record (and one of precedence) that found Christians innocent, even as they experienced ongoing persecution all over the Roman Empire. That is probably why Luke went to such lengths to record Roman court decisions from Gallio (18:14-15), Felix, Festus, and Agrippa (chapters 24–26).

Felix decided to delay the hearing until the commander,

Lysias, could get there to give his testimony as to what had transpired. It is not recorded whether Lysias came to Caesarea or not. Likely he did, but as the next few verses indicate, for various political and fiscal reasons, Felix did not want to complete Paul's trial. It appears that this postponement became indefinite.

Paul was kept *in custody,* but, evidently, he was given a great deal of *freedom* by Governor Felix, who allowed visits by *his friends* in order to *take care of his needs.* Paul had a number of Christian brothers and sisters in Caesarea who loved him dearly and would readily visit him and take care of him (21:8-14). Such freedom was likely the result of Paul's being a Roman citizen against whom no crime had yet been proven.

KNOWLEDGE ISN'T ENOUGH

Governor Felix was "quite familiar" with Christianity—its history and teachings. Knowing about something, however, is not the same as embracing it. It is possible to know what the Bible teaches and yet never do what it commands. It is possible to know about Christ without ever committing oneself to him. How sad to be so close to the truth yet never let it transform your heart and life. Be careful about complacency and laziness in your spiritual journey. You are responsible for every bit of revelation God gives. Luke had earlier recorded the sobering warning of Jesus: "Much is required from those to whom much is given" (Luke 12:48 NLT).

24:24 Some days later when Felix came with his wife Drusilla, who was Jewish, he sent for Paul and heard him speak concerning faith in Christ Jesus.[NRSV] After an unnamed period of time, Felix and *his wife Drusilla . . . sent for Paul and heard him speak concerning faith in Christ.* Drusilla was the daughter of Herod Agrippa I (see chapter 12) and the sister of Herod Agrippa II (see the chart "The Herod family" on page 417 [25:21-22]), making her part Jewish. At this time, she was likely only twenty years old. She had left a previous husband to marry Felix, which she did contrary to Jewish law, since Felix was a Gentile. Some sources say that Drusilla was the one most interested in what Paul had to say about Christ and Christianity. But it would be her husband who would come under conviction!

24:25-26 As Paul discoursed on righteousness, self-control and the judgment to come, Felix was afraid and said, "That's enough for now! You may leave. When I find it convenient, I will send for you." At the same time he was hoping that Paul would offer him a bribe, so he sent for him frequently and

talked with him.NIV Paul's discourse with Felix and Drusilla included an interesting trio of topics—*righteousness, self-control and the judgment to come.* Like Paul's remarks earlier in the trial (see 24:15-16), these three areas track with Jesus' description of the convicting work of the Holy Spirit (John 16:8) and would likewise be areas of great conviction for Felix. As stated earlier, Felix's career was marked by brutality and injustice; thus, the subject of righteousness and judgment would likely be more than a little uncomfortable. History also records that Drusilla was Felix's third wife, and he had to break up her previous marriage in order to free her for himself. Thus, a discourse on self-control would likely not have been something he would have enjoyed hearing.

What is the biggest obstacle facing the family right now? It is overcommitment; time pressure. There is nothing that will destroy family life more insidiously than hectic schedules and busy lives, where spouses are too exhausted to communicate, too worn out to have sex, too fatigued to talk to the kids. That frantic lifestyle is just as destructive as one involving outbroken sin. If Satan can't make you sin, he'll make you busy, and that's just about the same thing.
James Dobson

The content of Paul's message should also encourage believers. The Christian message is not abstract platitude or theology. It contains hard-hitting ethical and behavioral issues. Christianity was not a particularly comfortable message, and Felix responded like an individual under conviction: *That's enough for now! You may leave.* Felix was afraid. He surely did not like this shift from an enjoyable jousting about politics or religion into morality and responsibility. Like so many people today, Felix wanted to keep his religion contained, categorized, and irrelevant. Paul confronted Felix, forcing him to deal with its full convicting message. And Felix wanted no part of it. The trailing words of Felix's rejection of Paul's message are the most telling: *When I find it convenient, I will send for you.* What a pitiful statement for anyone to say. Translated: "I'm too involved, too busy with other things, to worry about God."

Notice, too, another example of Felix's poor character. He frequently sent for Paul, hoping the apostle would *offer him a bribe,* supposedly to buy his freedom. We are not told where the governor thought Paul would get the money. Maybe he had heard of the offering Paul had brought from the Asian and European churches. Perhaps he assumed that a leader of Paul's stature, influencing an institution of the church's stature, would have his hand in the church coffers (as Felix obviously did in Rome's).

He *sent . . . frequently* for Paul and, so, was regularly exposed to the truth. Felix seems to be a sorry example of one who "went to church" with regularity, listening to a personalized message from none other than the apostle Paul. Yet there is no record of Felix's ever coming to faith. How sad to be so regularly exposed to such profound truth and yet never take advantage of its life-changing, destiny-changing character.

PERSONALIZING THE GOSPEL
Paul's talk with Felix became so personal that Felix grew fearful (24:25). Felix, like Herod Antipas (Mark 6:17-18), had taken another man's wife. Paul's words were interesting until they focused on "righteousness, self-control and the judgment to come." Many people will be glad to discuss the gospel with you as long as it doesn't touch their lives too personally. When it does, some will resist or run. But this is what the gospel is all about—God's power to change lives. The gospel is not effective until it moves from principles and doctrine into a life-changing dynamic. When someone resists or runs from your witness, you have undoubtedly succeeded in making the gospel personal.

24:27 **Two years went by in this way; then Felix was succeeded by Porcius Festus. And because Felix wanted to gain favor with the Jewish leaders, he left Paul in prison.**NLT *Two years went by* this way—two full years while Felix toyed with the apostle Paul in the fashion described above. For two years this apostle to the Gentiles was out of commission, out of the pulpit, and serving as Felix's personal spiritual conversationalist.

On the other hand, one wonders what it was like for Paul. Were these rest and recuperation years? This hard-driving missionary must have been frustrated at the delay. Surely he must have thought about those who had gone before him who had suffered similar delays and disappointments—Joseph, Moses, Joshua, David, Jeremiah, Daniel, Nehemiah, and others.

By keeping Paul in prison, Felix could gain favor with the Jews. Eventually, *Porcius Festus* took over as governor of the region. He was a welcome successor. After Felix mishandled a political situation between the Jews and Greeks at Caesarea in A.D. 60, where he took unnecessarily harsh military action against the Jews, he was called back to Rome. Josephus wrote that things would have gone badly for him there, had not his brother, Pallas, interceded for him.

CONVENIENCE VS. CHRIST

Felix avoided making a decision about Christ with the age-old excuse, "It's not convenient." Literally, the Greek says, "when I find the time." Almost two thousand years later, people are still sidestepping the gospel, using the same line. "I'm too busy. I'm too involved in other things right now. Later on, when I find the time, I will think about these spiritual matters. I just can't right now." The truth is that knowing Christ and walking with him are the most important, most necessary issues in life. You will *always* be busy. There will *never* be a time when it is convenient. Those who are too busy to think about eternity now will have all of eternity to ponder their foolish indecision.

Festus is recorded in history as a more just ruler than Felix, although he was not on the scene very long. When Festus came into office, he inherited the imprisoned apostle and the Jewish leaders with a definite agenda.

Acts 25:1-22

PAUL APPEARS BEFORE FESTUS / 25:1-22

When Felix was replaced by Porcius Festus, the Jews once again made their case against Paul. During this trial before the new governor, Festus, Paul, using his rights as a Roman citizen, asked for and received the promise of a hearing before Caesar. This legal decision thwarted the final action of Paul's Jewish enemies.

25:1-2 Three days after Festus arrived in Caesarea to take over his new responsibilities, he left for Jerusalem, where the leading priests and other Jewish leaders met with him and made their accusations against Paul.[NLT] The new governor, *Festus,* wasted no time; after just *three days* on the job, he went to Jerusalem, where the leading power brokers of the nation resided—*the leading priests and other Jewish leaders.* Festus was procurator or governor of Judea A.D. 58–62. Little is known about Festus, though most of it is favorable, particularly in contrast with Felix, whom he succeeded. Luke's notation of the time is an indicator that Festus was ready to govern the region.

> It is not necessary for all people to be great in action. The greatest and sublimest power is often simple patience.
> *Harold Bushnell*

WAITING

Though God had promised that Paul would preach the gospel in Rome (23:11), the great apostle had to endure more than two years of Felix's refusal to decide his fate. In addition to this custody (24:27), Paul was subjected to other long stretches of time during which he could do little but trust God and wait for him to act. What do you do when it comes to the issue of waiting on God? Do you become anxious? angry? discouraged? Few things test our patience and faith like being forced to wait—which perhaps explains why our sovereign God often puts us in situations where we have no other choice.

One of the first items on his agenda was the prosecution of Paul. Three days into his governorship, the Jewish leaders *met with him and made their accusations against Paul.* God had allowed his most effective instrument for Gentile evangelism and church planting to sit in custody for two years, the apparent victim of Roman bureaucracy. But this was not God's perspective. The gospel would not be stopped simply by imprisoning Paul. Most likely, Paul was leading those around him to Christ, even in his chained condition.

25:3 They asked Festus as a favor to transfer Paul to Jerusalem. (Their plan was to waylay and kill him.)[NLT] Although two years had passed, the Jewish leaders still were looking for a way to kill Paul. The plot had expanded from the original forty-plus leaders (23:12-13) to all the Jewish leaders. They told *Festus* about Paul and tried to convince him to hold the trial in *Jerusalem* (so they could prepare an ambush). The ruthless Jews had obviously abandoned all hope of a conviction of Paul by the Romans, so they decided to take matters into their own hands. This request was likely a clever political move, and we can only imagine how these politically savvy Jewish leaders tried to explain how such a favor early on in Festus's administration would do wonders for their working relationship in the future.

> To carry a grudge is like being stung to death by one bee.
> *William H. Walton*

However, *their plan was* (as it had always been, here driven on by at least two years of failure) *to waylay and kill* Paul. Their passionate jealousy and hatred of Paul and the gospel were nothing short of astounding and, surely, were spurred by the devil.

DEADLY ANGER
The Jewish leaders planned to kill Paul (25:3). Two years earlier, the enraged Jewish leaders had managed to have Paul arrested and jailed. Though they had not been successful in their attempt to kill him, they had effectively put an end to his public preaching and teaching. Now, with a change of governors, their rage surfaced again. Remember, these were the respectable, prominent, "godly" leaders of Judaism—plotting an assassination! Here is a clear and powerful warning against the deadliness of uncontrolled anger. When we allow anger to turn into fury, when we do not submit our emotions to God, we risk becoming consumed by bitterness and blind rage. Do you have any unresolved anger in your life? Until it is dealt with, it will continue to surface.

25:4-5 But Festus replied that Paul was at Caesarea and he himself would be returning there soon. So he said, "Those of you in authority can return with me. If Paul has done anything

wrong, you can make your accusations."[NLT] By God's intervention, Festus decided to leave Paul in Caesarea. The trial would not be moved, so Festus informed the Jewish leadership that those *in authority* could *return with* him. In Caesarea, in his courtroom, they would be allowed to make their *accusations.*

25:6-7 **Eight or ten days later he returned to Caesarea, and on the following day Paul's trial began. On Paul's arrival in court, the Jewish leaders from Jerusalem gathered around and made many serious accusations they couldn't prove.**[NLT] After a few days, Festus *returned to Caesarea,* where on the very next day, the case of this Roman citizen, alleged troublemaker for the Jews, began again.

As before, the *Jewish leaders from Jerusalem* made *many serious accusations they couldn't prove*—probably all the same baseless accusations from two years before.

Luke's use of the words "gathered around" has led some to speculate that Paul was surrounded by his attackers. From their perimeter positions and their superior numbers, they hurled their vicious accusations at him. The apostle, standing in the middle alone, was left to answer their attacks.

FALSE ACCUSATIONS
Again, Paul had to sit and listen to his angry opponents hurl false accusations against him (25:7). This had been going on for years. There was nothing new in their argument. It was the same old litany of unsubstantiated charges. But even untrue words have power—power to damage reputations, wound the spirit, and keep feelings of ill will stirred up. Be careful not to imitate the behavior of these "religious" men. They were guilty of breaking the ninth commandment. Also, when others make untrue statements about you, do as Paul did: resist the urge to retaliate, simply speak the truth, and trust in a just God to make everything right.

25:8 **Then Paul made his defense: "I have done nothing wrong against the law of the Jews or against the temple or against Caesar."**[NIV] Paul succinctly denied all the charges that had just been blasted at him again: "I have done nothing wrong." He applied his denial to the three main areas of accusation: the *law,* the *temple,* and *Caesar.* These were the same charges brought by the Asian Jews (see 21:28; 24:5-6).

Paul's mention of Caesar was a new twist. This hints slightly at the direction he knew the trial was headed. Paul needed to keep the Roman law involved because the issues of the law and the temple were the Jews' jurisdiction and would lead to his immediate death.

25:9-11 Festus, wishing to do the Jews a favor, said to Paul, "Are you willing to go up to Jerusalem and stand trial before me there on these charges?" Paul answered: "I am now standing before Caesar's court, where I ought to be tried. I have not done any wrong to the Jews, as you yourself know very well. If, however, I am guilty of doing anything deserving death, I do not refuse to die. But if the charges brought against me by these Jews are not true, no one has the right to hand me over to them. I appeal to Caesar!"[NIV] Only about two weeks into this new procuratorship, Festus wanted to get off to a politically healthy start with the people he was governing. The Jews were known as a difficult people to govern, and many Roman political careers had been dashed at this Judean outpost (including that of Festus's immediate predecessor, Felix). It is not surprising that Festus would wish *to do the Jews a favor.* Catering to what he knew they desperately wanted, he asked Paul if he would be *willing to go up to Jerusalem* to stand trial before him (Festus) there. Festus knew that the Jews had no case against Paul, but either he wasn't willing to aggravate and enrage them further or he simply didn't know how to investigate such religious matters (see 25:20).

Whatever Festus's motive behind this offer to switch the location of the trial, it became irrelevant at Paul's next words. In short, Paul was saying: "I'm being tried where I belong—Caesar's court. I have done nothing wrong. I'm willing to die if guilty [for that was what the Jews wanted]. But if these charges are *not true,* you can't *hand me over to them."* Then Paul made a startling statement—*"I appeal to Caesar!"*

Every Roman citizen had the right to appeal to Caesar. This didn't mean that Caesar himself would hear the case but that the citizen's case would be tried by the highest courts in the Empire—it is much like appealing to the Supreme Court. This right of appeal to the emperor provided Roman citizens protection in capital offense trials carried out by local judges in the provinces. It was normal for a Roman judge to set up a group of advisors in a case. Festus might have proposed to have members of the Sanhedrin serve. Thus, there would be no fair trial in Jerusalem. Paul insisted on a court made up of a jury of all Roman citizens. He appealed to Emperor Nero, who in A.D. 60 had not yet started the persecution of Christians.

Festus saw Paul's appeal as a way to send him out of his jurisdiction and the country and, thus, pacify the Jews. Paul made this demand because he knew that he would not get a fair trial in Jerusalem, and so did Festus. If he were to be returned to Jerusalem, Paul knew that he probably would be killed in transit—Festus may have known this as well. Paul had been in custody for two years. He desperately wanted to go to Rome to preach the gospel (Romans 1:10). At this point he probably realized that this appeal to Caesar would provide the opportunity for him to safely get to Rome. To go to Rome as a prisoner was better than not to go there at all.

NO FEAR
Paul knew that he was innocent of the charges against him and that as a Roman citizen, he could appeal to Caesar's judgment. Because he had met his responsibilities as a Roman, he had the opportunity and right to claim Rome's protection. Likewise, when we walk with God, we enjoy the assurance and peace of knowing that we are guiltless before him and blameless in the sight of the world. Others may make accusations, but their charges will lack believability, and our own hearts will not condemn us.

25:12 **Festus conferred with his advisers and then replied, "Very well! You have appealed to Caesar, and to Caesar you shall go!"**[NLT] Festus probably felt enormous relief at having a way out of this difficult situation. Paul's request led Festus into a conference *with his advisers* (these were his legal experts and higher officials), giving what seems to be a quick reply: *"Very well! You have appealed . . . you shall go!"*

Humanly speaking, it is probably better that it happened this way. If Festus had ruled on the case, he likely would have set Paul free—free to make his own way (without an armed escort) back to Antioch or on to Rome. The bloodthirsty group of Jewish leaders would have done their best to make sure that Paul didn't live to see another day. Instead, Paul would have an armed guard all the way to his next preaching stop. Though he would have a few more audiences with whom to share the gospel between there and Rome, few were more prestigious than the one he was about to meet.

25:13-15 **A few days later King Agrippa and Bernice arrived at Caesarea to pay their respects to Festus. Since they were spending many days there, Festus discussed Paul's case with the king. He said: "There is a man here whom Felix left as a prisoner. When I went to Jerusalem, the chief priests and elders of the Jews brought charges against him and asked that he be condemned."**[NIV] *King Agrippa* was Herod Agrippa II, son of Herod Agrippa I, and a descendant of Herod the Great, the last of the Herod dynasty that ruled parts of Palestine from 40 B.C. to A.D. 100. Like great-grandfather, like grandfather, like father, like son—Agrippa inherited the effects of generations of powerful men with flawed personalities. Each son followed his father in weaknesses, mistakes, and missed opportunities. Each generation had a confrontation with God, and each failed to realize the importance of his decision.

At this time (A.D. 60) Agrippa II was a young man of about thirty-three. He ruled the territories northeast of Palestine, bearing the title of "king." With power over the temple, he controlled the temple treasury and could appoint and remove the high priest. *Bernice* was his sister. When she was thirteen (A.D. 41), she had married her uncle, Herod Chalcis, who died in A.D. 48. Then she became a mistress to her brother, Agrippa II. In A.D. 63, she married King Polemon of Cilicia, but in the early 70s, she became mistress to Emperor Vespasian's son, Titus. Here Agrippa and Bernice were making an official visit to Festus, *to pay their respects.* Agrippa, of Jewish descent, could help clarify Paul's case for the Roman governor.

ULTIMATE FAMILY DYSFUNCTION

Agrippa's family had a long history of encountering Christ. His great-grandfather, Herod the Great, the paranoid king, had tried to murder the baby Jesus. Agrippa's great uncle, Herod Antipas, actually met Jesus during his trial but failed to see him for who he was. Here Agrippa and his sister Bernice, carrying on an incestuous relationship, were confronted again by a gracious God with the truth of the gospel. As far as we know, they—like their ancestors—rejected the forgiveness and eternal life that is found only in Christ. We can learn a number of lessons from the Herods, but one of the most sobering is this: families tend to pass on both positive and negative traits to the next generation. What kind of spiritual example are you setting for your children? What will be your legacy?

Agrippa and Festus were anxious to cooperate in governing their neighboring territories. The relationship between the Herodian dynasty and the Roman governors had always been sticky (remember Herod Antipas and Pontius Pilate, for example, sending Jesus back and forth—Luke 23:1-12). Both rulers had certain authority—usually the governor over the military, and the Herodians over the temple and the priesthood. Both answered to Rome—though the governor did so more directly, since he was a direct appointee. Both walked a political tightrope over the difficult-to-rule Jews, who viewed both the Romans and the godless Herodians with pretty much equal skepticism. Though the Herods were partially Jewish, they used their "family" relationship with the Jews mostly to their personal political advantage.

This state visit was an extended one *(spending many days there),* giving Festus an opportunity to discuss *Paul's case with the king.* He began with a summary of the case his predecessor had left behind. Festus made it clear that the *chief priests and elders of the Jews* (with whom Agrippa would have had great influence because he was the one who appointed the high priest and controlled the temple treasury) had brought the charges and that they were asking to exercise their right to have Paul executed (see commentary at 24:5-6).

25:16-17 "Of course, I quickly pointed out to them that Roman law does not convict people without a trial. They are given an opportunity to defend themselves face to face with their accusers. When they came here for the trial, I called the case the very next day and ordered Paul brought in."NLT Festus described the details of the case with some embellishment. He included at the outset, for example, a statement about how he *quickly pointed out* to the Jewish leaders that *Roman law does not convict people without a trial* and how the accused *are given an opportunity to* face their accusers and *defend themselves.*

Festus was accurate, however, when he reported that he saw the case the very *next day* after the arrival of the Jewish leaders (the ones who would have Agrippa's interest).

25:18-20 "When his accusers got up to speak, they did not charge him with any of the crimes I had expected. Instead, they had some points of dispute with him about their own religion and about a dead man named Jesus who Paul claimed was alive. I was at a loss how to investigate such matters; so I asked if he would be willing to go to Jerusalem and stand trial there on these charges."NIV Quickly reviewing the facts, Festus explained that he had *expected* a different set of charges. He did not anticipate the *points of dispute* concerning *their own religion* and dispute over *a dead man named Jesus who Paul claimed was alive.*

Festus's retelling of the trial details to Agrippa reveals the fact that he *was at a loss how to investigate such matters.* Particularly confusing seems to have been the part about the "dead man" being allegedly alive. Festus may be remembered as an effective ruler because it is evident that he was willing to admit what he didn't know and to ask for help from someone else who possibly did.

In his review of the facts for Agrippa, Festus claimed that the reason for his desire to move the trial to Jerusalem was the religious nature of the case rather than the political pressure (or even the planned ambush) of the powerful Jewish leadership. This may or may not have been the case.

SECULAR MIND-SET
Festus's description of events is a vivid picture of the secular mind-set. He spoke of "a dead man named Jesus" and of being "at a loss how to investigate such matters." Festus's attitude is prevalent today. Unbelievers in this post-Christian culture do not understand Christian doctrine or terminology. Christian theology and presuppositions are completely foreign to them. Even the word "God" means something vastly different to a secular audience. If we are to communicate the gospel effectively, we can no longer assume anything. Take the time to understand the so-called "postmodern worldview," and ask the Spirit of God to help you learn how to take the old, old story to a new and rapidly changing culture.

FAMOUS GRAVES
The pyramids of Egypt are famous because they contained the mummified bodies of ancient Egyptian kings.
- Westminster Abbey in London is revered because in it rests the bodies of English nobles and notables.
- Mohammed's tomb is noted for the stone coffin and the bones it contains.
- Arlington Cemetery in Washington, D.C., is revered because it is the honored resting place of American soldiers.
- But the garden tomb of Jesus is famous because *it is empty.*

25:21-22 **"But Paul appealed to the emperor. So I ordered him back to jail until I could arrange to send him to Caesar." "I'd like to hear the man myself," Agrippa said. And Festus replied, "You shall—tomorrow!"**NLT Festus quickly concluded his review. Paul had *appealed to the emperor,* so he was kept in custody until arrangements could be made to get him to Rome.

Festus's quick review of the facts had its desired result: Agrippa wanted to *hear the man* himself. Agrippa no doubt knew a great deal about the Way, the story of Christ, the Resurrection, and all the uproar in Israel. Without having to ask for Agrippa's help, Festus was able to receive advice on the case. Little would be or could be changed in the disposition of the prisoner because he had already appealed to Caesar, but Festus was trying to learn about his new territory, and this would be an ideal opportunity.

Paul's audience with Agrippa was set for the following day. It would be a golden opportunity for all those present—Festus, Agrippa, Bernice, the royal entourage, the high-ranking officials (see 25:23)—to hear more from this ex-Pharisee about the "dead man named Jesus" who he claimed had come back to life!

THE HEROD FAMILY

Name	*Reference*	*Date of Rule*	*Description*
Herod the Great	Matthew 2:1-18; Luke 1:5	37–4 B.C.	Half-Jewish; eager to please the Roman authorities who decreed him king of the Jews; slaughtered the innocent baby boys of Bethlehem
Herod Philip I	Matthew 14:3b; Mark 6:17	4 B.C.–A.D. 34	Son of Herod the Great; married Herodias, his niece
Herod Antipas	Mark 6:14-29; Luke 3;1; 13:31-33, 23:7-12	4 B.C.–A.D. 39	Son of Herod the Great; tetrarch of Galilee and Perea; called a "fox" by Jesus; ordered the execution of John the Baptist; presided over the trial of Jesus
Herod Archelaus	Matthew 2:22	4 B.C.–A.D. 6	Son of Herod the Great; ethnarch of Judea, Samaria, and Idumea
Herod Phillip II	Luke 3:1	4 B.C.–A.D. 34	Son of Herod the Great; tetrarch of Iturea and Trachonitis; married Salome, the daughter of Herodias
Herod Agrippa I	Acts 12:1-11	A.D. 37–44	Grandson of Herod the Great; king over Palestine; had James the apostle killed and Peter imprisoned
Herodias	Matthew 14:3; Mark 6:17	———	Granddaughter of Herod the Great; sister of Agrippa I; married her uncle Herod Philip I, and later her uncle Herod Antipas
Herod Agrippa II	Acts 25:13-26; 32	A.D. 50–70	Son of Herod Agrippa I; tetrarch of Chalcis; presided over Paul's trial
Drusilla	Acts 23:25-24:27	———	Daughter of Herod Agrippa I; wife of Felix (procurator of Judea, A.D. 52–59)
Bernice	Acts 25:13; 26:30	———	Daughter of Herod Agrippa I; sister and mistress of Herod Agrippa II

Acts 25:23–26:32

PAUL SPEAKS TO AGRIPPA / 25:23–26:32

King Agrippa, in Caesarea with his sister Bernice for a political visit with the new governor, Festus, became embroiled in the controversy over Paul. Festus, mindful of Agrippa's familiarity with Jewish law and practice and needing to prepare some kind of legal paperwork for Caesar, arranged a special audience with Paul. Festus found Paul's testimony absurd; Agrippa found it pointed and a bit too personal. Nevertheless, Paul took advantage of this situation to tell about his encounter with Christ and his fervent belief in the truth of the gospel.

25:23 **So the next day Agrippa and Bernice arrived at the auditorium with great pomp, accompanied by military officers and prominent men of the city. Festus ordered that Paul be brought in.**[NLT] Into the room came the new governor, the king on a state visit, and a controversial prisoner. This description of the arrival of *Agrippa and Bernice* at the *auditorium with great pomp* is surely presented as irony. The Greek word for "pomp" is *phantasias,* meaning "pageantry" or "outward display." The English word "fantasy" comes from it, suggesting the imaginary and fleeting nature of this outward show. The real royalty in the room was the prisoner, the born-again child of the King of kings.

> All these Very Important People would have been greatly surprised and not a little scandalized had they been able to foresee the relative estimates that later generations would form of them and of the handcuffed Jew who stood before them to plead his cause.
>
> *F. F. Bruce*

Paul's audience included *military officers.* These were Roman cohorts—Greek *chiliarchois*—commanders of one thousand men each; five cohorts were stationed at Caesarea. Also present were *prominent men* of Caesarea. Paul probably had been given little or no advance notice of this interview and would have to depend on the Holy Spirit to tell him what to say. Jesus had predicted this kind of situation: "When you are brought before synagogues, rulers and authorities, do not worry about how you will defend yourselves or what you will say, for the Holy Spirit will teach you at that time what you should say" (Luke 12:11-12 NIV). Many "rulers and authorities" had gathered in that room; the Holy Spirit would give Paul the words to say.

CRISIS OR OPPORTUNITY?
Paul's status as a prisoner didn't stop him from telling others about Christ. Military officers and prominent city leaders met in the palace room with Agrippa to hear Paul's case. Paul saw this new audience as yet another opportunity to present the gospel. Rather than complain about your present circumstances, look for ways to use every situation to serve God and share him with others. Your problems may be opportunities in disguise.

25:24-25 **Then Festus said, "King Agrippa and all present, this is the man whose death is demanded both by the local Jews and by those in Jerusalem. But in my opinion he has done nothing worthy of death. However, he appealed his case to the emperor, and I decided to send him."**NLT Festus, as the Roman governor in charge of the court at Caesarea, opened the proceedings. Luke certainly wanted to include this concise exoneration of Christianity by an esteemed representative of the Roman Empire. Festus explained that the *local* Jewish leadership and *those in Jerusalem* were demanding Paul's death. In his judgment of the case, however, Paul had *done nothing worthy of death.* That would be a significant check to those who were chasing, imprisoning, and prosecuting Christians around the Roman world. Because Paul had *appealed his case to the emperor,* he would be sent to Rome.

25:26-27 **"But I have nothing definite to write to our sovereign about him. Therefore I have brought him before all of you, and especially before you, King Agrippa, so that, after we have examined him, I may have something to write—for it seems to me unreasonable to send a prisoner without indicating the charges against him."**NRSV Festus went on to explain how he was at a loss for what to *write* in his report to the emperor *(our sovereign).* He was required to prepare a legal brief, detailing the charges, that had to be sent along with the appeal to Emperor Nero. Explaining his reason for the gathering, Festus explained that he wanted Paul *examined. King Agrippa* could help Festus put into words *the charges against* Paul because Agrippa was "an expert on Jewish customs and controversies" (26:3 NLT).

AN EXEMPLARY LIFE
Festus, like Felix before him, examined Paul closely but could find nothing wrong in his life. That's because as a citizen of the Roman Empire, Paul lived with integrity. Since he had broken no civil laws, he had nothing to hide or fear. Paul's experience is reminiscent of the prophet Daniel who also was closely scrutinized by his enemies (see Daniel 6). How would you fare if your life were put under a microscope? Would your enemies be able to list various failures, illegalities, and inconsistencies in your life? Or would they conclude as Daniel's opponents did: "Our only chance of finding grounds for accusing ________ will be in connection with [his/her] religion" (Daniel 6:5 NLT).

26:1-3 **Then Agrippa said to Paul, "You may speak in your defense." So Paul, with a gesture of his hand, started his defense: "I am fortunate, King Agrippa, that you are the one hearing my defense against all these accusations made by the Jewish leaders, for I know you are an expert on Jewish customs and controversies. Now please listen to me patiently!"**NLT After hearing Festus's opening remarks, Agrippa ordered Paul to speak in his own defense. What follows is an excellent example of Paul's powerful oratory skills and the most complete statement of his *defense* (Greek, *apologeomai,* from which we get "apologetics" and "apology," meaning to "defend oneself" or "speak in one's own behalf").

Paul began with *a gesture of his hand,* likely a common oratorical practice of the day. The thoroughness of the record of this speech and details like this hand motion indicate that Luke must have been present.

The accusing Jewish leaders, however, were not present, so Paul would not be responding to specific charges. The absence of a strict prosecutorial air allowed the apostle to freely express his thoughts. Paul aimed his remarks most directly at Agrippa (26:1-28), though other very important people were in the audience. Agrippa's verdict, though not a formal judicial one in Paul's case, would be important for Paul and, thus, for all of Christianity. Agrippa not only was an *expert* on Jewish issues, he was also a very influential government figure for Israel.

This message flows in this fashion:

- Introductory remarks (26:1-3)
- Paul's early life (26:4-11)
- Paul's conversion and call by Christ (26:12-18)
- Paul's obedience to the vision and ministry (26:19-21)
- Paul's message (26:22-23)

The balance of this chapter contains Paul's exchange with Festus and then Agrippa and the conclusions of these two leaders concerning Paul.

While containing much of the same information about Paul's conversion recorded in chapter 9 and in his testimony before the Jewish crowd on the steps of the Antonia Fortress in chapter 22, there are a few subtle differences. One notable absence is the incident with Ananias, the devout Jew, and the restoration of Paul's sight (a large part of Paul's story in chapter 22). That part of Paul's testimony would not be as interesting to a Gentile crowd as it would have been for a Jewish one. The essence of Paul's message to this audience was that there was nothing in his life, calling, or ministry that promoted or deserved this legal and physical attack by the Jewish leaders. While it appears that Paul did not win Festus or Agrippa to Christ, he certainly won this case for his innocence (see 26:31-32).

Paul began with words of commendation for Agrippa; he seems to have felt genuinely *fortunate* (the Greek word is *makarion,* meaning "blessed" or even "happy") to get this opportunity to be evaluated by him. Paul alluded to Agrippa's knowledge of *Jewish customs and controversies.* The historian Josephus confirms the fact that Agrippa had a good understanding of Jewish history and theology.

Paul's plea to *please listen,* while directed singularly to Agrippa, would surely draw the whole crowd into what he was about to say.

26:4-5 **"All the Jews know my way of life from my youth, a life spent from the beginning among my own people and in Jerusalem. They have known for a long time, if they are willing to testify, that I have belonged to the strictest sect of our religion and lived as a Pharisee."**NRSV Paul began with his early life, which *from the beginning* had been spent among the Jews in Tarsus *and in Jerusalem* (where he had received much of his training and from where he had begun his persecution of the church). Paul's contemporaries, including some on the Jewish Council who were attacking him, knew of his solid Jewish heritage and the fact that he had *belonged to the strictest sect* of the Jews, the Pharisees. By saying this, Paul established that there could be no doubt about the thoroughness, seriousness, or excellence with which he pursued his Judaism. The Pharisees were renowned for their meticulous commitment to the knowledge of the Scriptures and to their hyper-scrupulous traditions. Being a Pharisee meant that

Paul was already committed to the importance of the resurrection from the dead—a major tenet of the Pharisees, one that prompted

their ongoing debate with the Sadducees, who did not believe in a resurrection (see 23:6-9). Of course, this issue would take on much more significance as Paul's message unfolded.

AN UNDENIABLE CHANGE
In his longest speech in the book of Acts, Paul reviewed his well-documented past (26:4-5). The power of his testimony lay in the abrupt changes that permeated his life. No one could deny the transformation in the tentmaker from Tarsus. While your conversion may not be as dramatic as Paul's, you should be able to cite some specific ways in which your life is no longer the same because of Christ. Attitudes, values, behaviors, interactions with others, healed relationships—what has changed in your life since you met the Savior?

26:6-7 **"Now I am on trial because I am looking forward to the fulfillment of God's promise made to our ancestors. In fact, that is why the twelve tribes of Israel worship God night and day, and they share the same hope I have. Yet, O king, they say it is wrong for me to have this hope!"**NLT Paul used the rich heritage of *God's promise* to his and Agrippa's common *ancestors* as a connection to Agrippa and to the Jews *(the twelve tribes of Israel).* They all shared *the same hope,* that God would keep the promise he had made to his people, a hope that was inextricably tied up with the resurrection of the dead (see 23:6; 24:15). If any Jew—from Abraham forward—had any hope for the fulfillment of any promise that God had made, it must be tied to a belief that he would be resurrected in some form at some time, or the whole concept of God's promises would be ludicrous. That was Paul's point. The absurdity was that Paul was being attacked for holding to *this hope* that was shared so adamantly by his Jewish brothers.

26:8 **"Why does it seem incredible to any of you that God can raise the dead?"**NLT While he was addressing the king singularly concerning their ancestral "hope" in 26:7, Paul addressed his question to the whole audience, which was mostly Gentile. He asked them why it was so *incredible* (literally, "unbelievable") to any of them *that God can raise the dead.*

Since so much of the Jewish hope was tied to a belief that God raises people to continued life beyond this one, why were the Jews arguing with Paul about resurrection? The reason, of course, was one well-documented case of a certain Resurrection that had been confirmed by hundreds of eyewitnesses. This had become the lifework of those who had been closest to the scene of this Resurrection. In addition, many had already given their very lives for the cause—a cause whose whole credibility rested on the veracity of the resurrection of this one whom Paul was about to name.

THE POWER OF GOD
In his defense, Paul affirmed the possibility of God raising the dead (26:8). Paul believed that the Resurrection was the doctrine upon which Christianity stood or fell (see 1 Corinthians 15). Many in his audience scoffed at such a notion, but to Paul it was a very credible proposition. Indeed, if we accept the existence of a God who created the world and every living thing out of nothing, and who "sustains the universe by the mighty sure this same Creator and Sustainer has the power to raise the dead. Miracles are not difficult to believe when we accept the premise of an infinite, all-powerful God.

26:9 "I too was convinced that I ought to do all that was possible to oppose the name of Jesus of Nazareth."[NIV] Paul named himself as one who theoretically believed in the resurrection of the dead as a solidly educated Pharisee but who vigorously opposed the movement that hung on the Resurrection of Jesus. He not only refused to believe that *Jesus of Nazareth* had been resurrected, he also *was convinced* that he should *do all that was possible* to kill the movement.

26:10-11 "Authorized by the leading priests, I caused many of the believers in Jerusalem to be sent to prison. And I cast my vote against them when they were condemned to death. Many times I had them whipped in the synagogues to try to get them to curse Christ. I was so violently opposed to them that I even hounded them in distant cities of foreign lands."[NLT] With the sanction of the *leading priests,* Paul began capturing *believers in Jerusalem* and sending them to *prison.* He even went so far as to *cast* his *vote against* Christians *when they were condemned to death.* Some believe this statement indicates that Paul was a member of the Jewish Council, but the expression is used metaphorically in other places and may be used in that sense here.

Much of Paul's work was done through *the synagogues,* where Paul found most of the Christians in the early days of the movement. This would remind Agrippa that the Christian movement had Jewish roots. In the synagogues Paul would have believers *whipped* in order to try to force them to *curse Christ* (literally, "to blaspheme"). Paul was so passionate, *so violently opposed* to those who knew Christ, that he *hounded them in distant cities of foreign lands.* He took his campaign of terror on the road, becoming a missionary for Judaism as he tried to protect the faith from these heretics who believed a man had been resurrected from the dead.

26:12 "On one of these journeys I was going to Damascus with the authority and commission of the chief priests."NIV Paul had been headed *to Damascus,* armed with the full *authority and commission of the chief priests.* He likely mentioned the priests again for the benefit of King Agrippa, the one who appointed, supervised, and funded the priesthood at Jerusalem. This was the same group that was attacking Paul. They were his former employers! The event that had moved Paul from his past position as a hunter *for* the priests to being hunted *by* the priests had been quite extraordinary.

26:13-14 "About noon, O king, as I was on the road, I saw a light from heaven, brighter than the sun, blazing around me and my companions. We all fell to the ground, and I heard a voice saying to me in Aramaic, 'Saul, Saul, why do you persecute me? It is hard for you to kick against the goads.'"NIV It is easy to imagine King Agrippa, in all his pomp, sitting on the edge of his seat as Paul told this part of his story. The event occurred *about noon,* when Paul saw *a light from heaven, brighter than the sun, blazing* around him and his traveling companions. The presence of this bright light from heaven is mentioned in all three accounts—in chapter 9 (the actual event), in chapter 22, and here.

The voice from heaven is also central to all three accounts. The revealed word of the risen Christ to the apostle Paul is the centerpiece of the story. *In Aramaic,* Paul had been addressed and asked, *"Why do you persecute me?"* Notice, as has been the case in every account, Jesus made it clear that Paul had not been persecuting heretics but, rather, Christ himself (see commentary at 9:1-2).

> The moment you wake up each morning, all your wishes and hopes for the day rush at you like wild animals. And the first job each morning consists in shoving it all back; in listening to that other voice, taking that other point of view, letting that other, larger, stronger, quieter life come flowing in. *C. S. Lewis*

One important addition to Christ's words here is not included in either chapter 9 or 22. Paul added that Christ had said, *"It is hard for you to kick against the goads."* Though this was a Greek proverbial statement, it was also familiar to Jews and all those who made their living in an agrarian culture. An oxgoad was a sharp stick used to prod cattle. It implies that Christ was already trying to "goad" (that is, "direct" or "steer") Paul in the right direction. His passion and his conviction were commendable, but he was not headed in the direction that God wanted him to go.

THE GREAT COMMUNICATOR
Paul mentioned here for the first time that the Lord had spoken to him on the Damascus road in Aramaic, his native tongue (26:14). This biblical evidence portrays a God who wants to reveal himself and his will to his creatures. He can and does speak through any and every possible means—burning bushes, stone tablets, enemies who shout curses and fling rocks, handwriting on walls, prophets, visions, dreams, nature itself, donkeys, still, small voices, even through an infant born in a run-down stable. God is always speaking. And he is doing that in a language that we can understand. The question is, are we listening?

26:15-16 "'Who are you, sir?' I asked. And the Lord replied, 'I am Jesus, the one you are persecuting. Now stand up! For I have appeared to you to appoint you as my servant and my witness. You are to tell the world about this experience and about other times I will appear to you.'"[NLT] Upon Paul's inquiry as to the identity of the speaker, the voice answered: *"I am Jesus, the one you are persecuting."* In that moment, in the flash of light, it all came together for Paul—the Resurrection, the pricks to his conscience (the "goads"), the deepening conviction that this movement called "the Way" held the truth.

The information to follow is also unique to this particular recounting of the Damascus road experience. From his prostrate position, Paul was commissioned by Christ himself. He was to be Christ's *servant* (1 Corinthians 4:1) and Christ's *witness* (the ongoing theme of Acts predicted in Christ's words in 1:8). Paul would *tell the world* about not only *this experience* at Damascus but also about the other times that Christ would come to him (see the record of some of those experiences in the chart called "'Encouragement' Visits of God to Paul" in chapter 23, page 387). Paul was to be the recipient of a great deal of God's "light" to both Jews and Gentiles.

26:17-18 "'I will rescue you from your own people and from the Gentiles. I am sending you to them to open their eyes and turn them from darkness to light, and from the power of Satan to God, so that they may receive forgiveness of sins and a place among those who are sanctified by faith in me.'"[NIV] Imagine this sobering word at the start of a ministry. When Jesus said, *"I will rescue you,"* inherent in this statement was the promise of danger from which Paul would need rescue. The two sources of the danger would be his *own people* (the Jews) and *the Gentiles,* in whose court he stood. At Paul's conversion, Jesus had promised Paul the kind of trouble that Paul had already been causing for the Christians. Despite the trouble, however, Christ promised him rescue.

Christ's words of commission to Paul sound like the work predicted of the Messiah in places like Isaiah 35:5; 42:7, 16; 61:1. Paul was to *turn* many people *from darkness to light,* which he did (see 2 Corinthians 4:4; Ephesians 4:18; 5:8; Colossians 1:12-13). Paul was to be God's instrument of turning both Jew and Gentile *from the power of Satan to God,* inviting them to *receive forgiveness of sins,* which he did (13:38; Ephesians 1:7; Colossians 1:14). Paul was also to offer both Jew and Gentile a full *place among those who are sanctified by faith,* which he did (Romans 8:17; Colossians 1:12). Paul took every opportunity to remind his audience that the Gentiles had an equal share in God's inheritance. This inheritance is the promise and blessing of the covenant that God made with Abraham (Ephesians 2:19; 1 Peter 1:3-4).

TRUE STATE

Paul gives us here a grim reminder of what it means to be lost. Apart from Christ, people are blinded and in spiritual darkness. They are under the sway of Satan and, because of their sins, unforgiven (under condemnation). Many times we forget these facts. Today when you look at people who are well dressed, polished, moral, and successful (at least in the world's eyes), do not automatically assume they have no needs. Until they put their total trust in Christ, they are in a terrible state. Let this way of thinking stir you to compassion (prayer) and action (evangelism).

26:19-20 "After that, King Agrippa, I was not disobedient to the heavenly vision, but declared first to those in Damascus, then in Jerusalem and throughout the countryside of Judea, and also to the Gentiles, that they should repent and turn to God and do deeds consistent with repentance."NRSV From that point, Paul had been obedient *to the heavenly vision* (1 Corinthians 9:1, 16). He had begun *in Damascus.* How shocking it must have been for the residents of Damascus (both unbelieving and believing Jews) to have seen the difference between the Paul they had heard of and the Paul who had arrived. Paul recorded his progress from Damascus to *Jerusalem,* to *Judea,* and beyond. Ultimately, his field of endeavor, under the sovereign leadership of God, was *the Gentiles.*

Though the locations changed and the nationalities changed, the message was the same at every stop: *"Repent . . . turn to God . . . do deeds consistent with repentance."* This message, of course, tied Paul to John the Baptist (Matthew 3:2, 8), Jesus

(Matthew 4:17), and Peter (Acts 2:38). They all called for personal conversion—a change of heart and mind that showed itself in a change of direction.

Paul had preached this message to both Jews and Gentiles in synagogues, streets, prisons, and courtrooms throughout the Empire. And many had decided to repent and believe.

THE "FESTUS EXCUSE"
Festus represents the individual who thinks he is too intelligent to listen to Christ. "I'm not convinced," say the Festuses of the world, "I'm too smart to believe that junk." No sensible Roman (or modern-day person) could believe in a resurrection. Festus is typical of many today—intelligent, logical, practical, and cynical. Yet Paul was saying to Festus that this message of Christ had been attested to for three decades. These events had happened. Jesus' death and resurrection were proven facts. In other words, Christianity makes sense. It gives real answers to real questions about real life, and life beyond, if you'll listen to it, read it, give it a chance. Most who reject Christ have never looked closely at Christ or his claims. Don't be afraid to show the "Festuses" in your world the risen Savior. There is plenty of convincing evidence for the cynics to see, if someone will just point them to it.

26:21-23 "Some Jews arrested me in the Temple for preaching this, and they tried to kill me. But God protected me so that I am still alive today to tell these facts to everyone, from the least to the greatest. I teach nothing except what the prophets and Moses said would happen—that the Messiah would suffer and be the first to rise from the dead as a light to Jews and Gentiles alike."NLT For his simple obedience to this incredibly powerful calling, for his faithful presentation of this gospel message, Paul had been *arrested . . . in the Temple.* Attempts had even been made on his life. But God had been true to his promise to rescue him (26:17). *God protected* him, leaving him *alive . . . to tell these facts to everyone,* including those before whom he was standing.

Then Paul summarized what he had said in front of every Jewish audience so far in his ministry: *I teach nothing except what the prophets and Moses said would happen* concerning the suffering Messiah and the promise of his resurrection (see 13:27-41 for a sample). This Resurrection, which followed the rejection and murder of the Messiah, would serve as a beacon, *a light to Jews and Gentiles alike.*

26:24 Suddenly, Festus shouted, "Paul, you are insane. Too much study has made you crazy!"NLT Festus could not stand it anymore, and he erupted (the Greek is *megale te phone,* literally, "with a great voice"). The message of this suffering Messiah was one thing, but to actually believe that he had been killed by his own people and then had been raised from the dead as a light to the world was too much for the humanistic mind of the Roman governor. He decided that Paul must be *insane*—that Paul had studied himself into insanity. All this talk about Moses and the Messiah, repentance and forgiveness—all of it confusing—compelled Festus to blurt out what he did.

26:25-27 **But Paul said, "I am not out of my mind, most excellent Festus, but I am speaking the sober truth. Indeed the king knows about these things, and to him I speak freely; for I am certain that none of these things has escaped his notice, for this was not done in a corner. King Agrippa, do you believe the prophets? I know that you believe."**NRSV Paul affirmed to the governor that he was *not out of* his *mind,* but was instead *speaking the sober truth* that had the most important of implications for all those within its hearing. Paul turned to Agrippa for confirmation of what he had just presented, stating his certainty that *none of these things* had *escaped his notice.* Agrippa's responsibilities for the temple activities at Jerusalem would surely have caused him to cross paths with the activities of the church. He would likely have been familiar with not only the Old Testament Scriptures but also the basics of Jesus' life and the start of the church in the wake of Jesus' crucifixion and claimed resurrection.

A REASONABLE FAITH

Paul was appealing to the facts—people were still alive who had heard Jesus and seen his miracles; the empty tomb could still be seen, and the Christian message was turning the world upside down (17:6). The history of Jesus' life and the early church are facts that are still open for us to examine. We still have eyewitness accounts of Jesus' life recorded in the Bible, as well as historical and archaeological records of the early church to study. Examine the events and facts as verified by many witnesses. Strengthen your faith with the truth of these accounts.

Paul's statement that *this was not done in a corner* is simply an idiomatic way of reminding his audience that Christianity had been a very public movement from the moment of the inception of the church on that first Pentecost, when three thousand people had been converted in the temple courts at Jerusalem in one day (chapter 2).

Next, Paul got very personal and direct with King Agrippa, asking and then answering his own question about Agrippa's knowledge of and belief in the prophets. Agrippa could provide, if he were so inclined, plenty of information to Festus on the subject of Judaism, the Messiah, Jesus, and the Way. He could corroborate what Paul had said so far and confirm that his message was not far removed from mainstream Judaistic theology. But Agrippa did not.

26:28 Then Agrippa said to Paul, "Do you think that in such a short time you can persuade me to be a Christian?"NIV Paul's direct question probably embarrassed Agrippa in front of this powerful crowd. His response, in what appears to be a condescending fashion, was to shoot back. It is difficult to tell whether Agrippa's tone of voice was harsh or joking, though the desired effect was to brush Paul off.

If Agrippa were to say that he did *not* believe the prophets, he would have lost influence with his Jewish constituency. If he were to say that he *did* believe the prophets, then he would have played into the hands of Paul the evangelist, who then would say that Agrippa would have no reason *not* to believe in Christ.

So Agrippa just retaliated quickly, reminding the apostle who was the prisoner and who was the potentate: *Do you think that in such a short time you can persuade me to be a Christian?* This translation is correct, though many are familiar with the King James Version, "almost thou persuadest me." The Greek phrase *en oligo* means "in a little while" or "briefly," not "almost," as the King James Version renders it. The question may have been a jab at Paul and his message, saying that he would not be as easily persuaded as Paul's other converts had been.

RESISTING THE TRUTH:
Agrippa heard the gospel from Paul but seems to have considered the message mild entertainment. Like so many before and after, Agrippa stopped within hearing distance of the kingdom of God. He left himself without excuse. He heard the gospel but decided it wasn't worth responding to personally. Unfortunately, his mistake isn't uncommon. Many who read his story also will not believe. Their problem, like his, is not really that the gospel isn't convincing or that they don't need to know God personally; it is that they choose not to respond. What has been your response to the gospel? Has it turned your life around and given you the hope of eternal life, or has it been a message to resist or reject? It may seem like too great a price to give God control of your life, but it is an even greater price by far to live eternally apart from him because you have chosen not to be his child.

26:29 Paul replied, "Short time or long—I pray God that not only you but all who are listening to me today may become what I am, except for these chains."NIV The passion of the apostle and the universal need of the gospel message comes through in Paul's response to Agrippa's brusque statement. Notice how Paul changed the tone of the exchange. This was not Paul the debater; this was Paul the evangelist with a tender heart for the lost souls in need of finding the Savior.

Paul explained that it didn't matter to him whether it took Agrippa a *short time* or a *long* time; he prayed that Agrippa, along with *all who* were *listening,* would become just like him, except for the chains. That is, Paul wanted them to find the Messiah who had found him that day on the road to Damascus. He wanted them to know that this Savior was needed by everyone—from the lowliest court janitor to the king and governor sitting in their seats of honor. He was saying, "Take it from the one who used to hunt Christians in the name of his religion; there isn't a soul that's too far away to be found by this Savior."

EXCUSES, EXCUSES

The Felix Excuse is: "I'm too *involved* in other pursuits to listen to Christ; it's not *convenient."*

The Festus Excuse is: "I'm too *intelligent* to listen to Christ; I'm not *convinced."*

The Agrippa Excuse is: "I'm too *important* to listen to Christ; it doesn't *concern me."*

Pride doomed the brightest of the angels; it will kill anyone who thinks himself above needing a Savior. Do you think you're too important for him? too powerful? You overestimate yourself. You underestimate your need. You underestimate him. What excuses do you use to avoid Christ? his Word? his work (the church)? The destiny of these three powerful rulers should warn us against pride and indifference to Christ.

26:30-31 Then the king, the governor, Bernice, and all the others stood and left. As they talked it over they agreed, "This man hasn't done anything worthy of death or imprisonment."[NLT] Agrippa may have been getting uncomfortable with the way the conversation had turned. Maybe he was moving toward conviction. Perhaps he had simply heard all he needed to hear to know what he thought of it all. In any case, Agrippa decided that the meeting was over.

Festus and Agrippa discussed the case and agreed that Paul was innocent. King Agrippa, a Jewish sympathizer and well versed in Jewish issues, added his legal vindication of the Christian movement. This word would be of great comfort and usefulness to believers around the Empire who were experiencing increasingly intense pressure from those who wanted to prosecute the Christian movement as being anti-Jewish and anti-Roman.

26:32 And Agrippa said to Festus, "He could be set free if he hadn't appealed to Caesar!"[NLT] Paul's appeal *to Caesar,* of course, had pretty much taken the matter out of the jurisdiction of Festus and Agrippa. Paul had to go to Rome. Though he could have been *set free,* Paul was instead free from the murderous Jews and setting out on an all-expense-paid trip to Rome.

Acts 27

PAUL SAILS FOR ROME / 27:1-12

At long last, Paul boarded a boat for Rome, probably in October (A.D. 59). He was accompanied, at the very least, by Luke (see the first-person plural pronoun "we" in this section) and Aristarchus. This was too late in the fall to be on the open seas. And, sure enough, bad weather made for rough sailing. Paul sensed real danger ahead and encouraged the crew to find safe harbor for the winter. Nevertheless, the leaders of the voyage pressed on.

27:1-2 **When the time came, we set sail for Italy. Paul and several other prisoners were placed in the custody of an army officer named Julius, a captain of the Imperial Regiment. And Aristarchus, a Macedonian from Thessalonica, was also with us. We left on a boat whose home port was Adramyttium; it was scheduled to make several stops at ports along the coast of the province of Asia.**[NLT] Some have wondered why Luke would devote such great emphasis to Paul's journey to Rome, since—the argument goes—the narrative doesn't really contribute to Luke's overall theological purpose. The answer partly lies in the literary conventions of the time. Stories of sea voyages and shipwrecks were popular fare. Typically, heroes survived these epic dramas, while evil people didn't. This story of Paul's journey also gives modern-day readers an eyewitness account of the details of ancient sea travel. It shows that God's sovereignty is at work in human history. Both in everyday occurences and in heroic narratives, God's work is being done.

> There are two things we cannot do alone; one is to be married. The other is to be a Christian.
> *Paul Tournier*

The first person plural pronoun "we" indicates that Luke had again joined Paul (for the first time since chapter 21). Perhaps Luke accompanied the apostle to Rome so as to serve as his personal physician. *Aristarchus* may have been acting as Paul's personal attendant or servant. Aristarchus was the man who had been dragged into the theater at the beginning of the riot in Ephesus (19:29; 20:4; Philemon 1:24). There is no evidence to suggest that Luke and Aristarchus had been arrested and would also be tried—they probably just wanted to support their friend and colleague in the gospel ministry. It is not stated whether the centurion *Julius* was a believer, but he took good care of Paul (see 27:3). Later, Julius would single-handedly protect Paul and the other prisoners from being executed during the shipwreck. He is one of several Roman centurions in the New Testament who are portrayed favorably (Luke 7:1-10; Luke 23:47; Acts 10:1-48).

A BUILT-IN NEED

Paul constantly received assistance from others as he traveled to Rome and during his imprisonment there. He had help from his colleagues Luke and Aristarchus (27:1-2). The centurion Julius took care of Paul, as did the Sidonian Christians (27:3). Following his shipwreck, the Maltese people demonstrated unusual kindness (28:2), and later they showered Paul and his friends with gifts, supplies, and articles of appreciation (28:10). Publius, the chief official of the island, gave Paul (and his entourage) a warm welcome and three days of hospitality (28:7). Then, upon arriving in Italy, Paul was met by two delegations of Roman Christians. This encouraged Paul and prompted him to thank God (28:15). The point is this: Everyone, even the great apostle Paul, needs others. Do you have people you can rely on for encouragement? for insight? for advice? Get involved with a fellowship of believers where you can both receive help and offer assistance.

27:3 **The next day when we docked at Sidon, Julius was very kind to Paul and let him go ashore to visit with friends so they could provide for his needs.**[NLT] *Sidon* was about seventy miles north of Caesarea, where this journey had begun. A brief stop in Sidon permitted the Christians there to provide food and supplies for Paul's needs. The Christian community there probably originated with the dispersion of believers from Jerusalem after the death of Stephen (see 11:19). The Roman officer named *Julius* showed kindness to Paul, who was a prisoner, allowing him to *go ashore to visit with friends.* Julius may have been advised by Festus to give preferential treatment to Paul.

27:4 **Putting out to sea from there, we encountered headwinds that made it difficult to keep the ship on course, so we sailed north of Cyprus between the island and the mainland.**[NLT] The most direct route from Sidon to Myra would have directed the ship south and west of Cyprus (the same route Paul had traveled when he had returned from his third missionary journey). The summer and early autumn winds, blowing from the west and northwest, however, required the ship to remain close to the coast, sailing *north of Cyprus between the island and the mainland.*

27:5-6 When we had sailed across the open sea off the coast of Cilicia and Pamphylia, we landed at Myra in Lycia. There the centurion found an Alexandrian ship sailing for Italy and put us on board.[NIV] Rounding the northeast peninsula of Cyprus, Paul's vessel would have once again faced the strong headwinds from the west and northwest. But by hugging the coastline and (most likely) taking advantage of the gentler night breezes, the ship was able to dock at *Myra.*

In this port city on the southern coast of Asia Minor (modern-day Turkey), Julius located an Egyptian *(Alexandrian)* ship *sailing for Italy.* This was a large grain ship (big enough to carry 276 passengers—see 27:37-38). Egyptian grain was a Roman staple at this time in history, and Myra was a key hub of the imperial grain service.

27:7-8 We had several days of rough sailing, and after great difficulty we finally neared Cnidus. But the wind was against us, so we sailed down to the leeward side of Crete, past the cape of Salmone. We struggled along the coast with great difficulty and finally arrived at Fair Havens, near the city of Lasea.[NLT] With the favorable travel period quickly coming to a close, the captain of the Alexandrian ship pushed westward in an attempt to reach Italy before winter. But the elements were already beginning to make sailing west difficult.

Cnidus, with its two harbors and ample accommodations, would have made an excellent stopping point from which to wait for favorable winds. But the weather conditions made it difficult to put in there. Thus the ship's captain chose to head south toward *Crete.*

Crete is the largest island in the Aegean Sea. In better weather, captains would sail to the north of Crete. With winter fast approaching, however, the northern route was suspect. The northern coast had few suitable harbors and left ships unprotected against the often dangerous winds; therefore, Paul's ship journeyed to the eastern tip of Crete and then west along the southern coast, where harbors were more available. Even this attempt to travel under the lee of the island (along the south coast) was a trial. The small harbor at *Fair Havens* (probably modern-day Limeonas Kalous) did not afford much protection. Nevertheless, since the coastline just beyond Fair Havens veers sharply northward and exposes vessels to the full force of the northwesterly winds, the ship put in there to wait for the wind to shift.

27:9-10 Much time had been lost, and sailing had already become dangerous because by now it was after the Fast. So Paul warned them, "Men, I can see that our voyage is going to be disastrous and bring great loss to ship and cargo, and to our own lives also."[NIV] Because of the reference to *the Fast* (the Jewish Day of Atonement, on the tenth day of the month Tishri), it is possible to set the date for this voyage as early October (A.D. 59). Waiting for favorable weather at Fair Havens, the ship's anxious commanders had a decision to make: Should they stay put and find winter quarters in Fair Havens (or nearby Lasea)? Or should they push on westward in an attempt to complete their journey to Italy before winter? A guiding principle of sailing was that it was *dangerous* from mid-September to mid-November and *disastrous* from mid-November to mid-February.

Luke did not record whether or not this decision was the subject of a public discussion. Nevertheless, Paul made his prediction known to the centurion and the ship's captain that to continue the trip would result in disaster. Paul's warning may have been stimulated by his own experience. Prior to this voyage, he had written, in 2 Corinthians 11:25, that he had already survived three shipwrecks. Paul probably was exhibiting common sense from the weather/sailing calendar. In ancient times ships had no compasses and navigated by the stars, so Paul understood that overcast skies and strong northwesterly winds made sailing west all but impossible and very dangerous. Later, Paul would be granted a further confirmation of the ship's (and its occupants') fate (see 27:21-26). Based on these verses, some conclude that Paul's warning here was prophetic.

27:11-12 But the officer in charge of the prisoners listened more to the ship's captain and the owner than to Paul. And since Fair Havens was an exposed harbor—a poor place to spend the winter—most of the crew wanted to go to Phoenix, farther up the coast of Crete, and spend the winter there. Phoenix was a good harbor with only a southwest and northwest exposure.[NLT] Apparently, by this time the worsening weather conditions had eliminated any remaining hopes of reaching Italy. Although the weather was not ideal for sailing, the pilot and the owner of the ship didn't want to spend the winter in an *exposed harbor* like *Fair Havens.* Because the ship had been contracted out for the official state transport of grain, the Roman officer could have overruled them. But he deferred to the captain's nautical expertise and decided to take a chance. The practical Roman regarded the advice of a seasoned sea captain as being more reliable than the religious intuitions of a Jewish tentmaker. The ship departed for *Phoenix,* only a few miles west along the southern *coast of Crete.*

THE STORM AT SEA / 27:13-26

Leaving the relative safety of Fair Havens, Paul's vessel encountered a violent "northeaster" (27:14) that "raged unabated for many days" (27:20 NLT). The crew tried valiantly to weather the storm but eventually gave up all hope of saving their lives, much less the battered ship. Paul gathered the ship's crew and encouraged them with two promises of God: (1) that he (Paul) had been guaranteed safe arrival in Rome; and (2) that everyone sailing with him would be protected from harm. One truth stands clear in the middle of this nerve-racking voyage: Life may get messy, complicated, or even frightening, but God's will cannot be thwarted!

27:13-15 **When a gentle south wind began to blow, they thought they had obtained what they wanted; so they weighed anchor and sailed along the shore of Crete. Before very long, a wind of hurricane force, called the "northeaster," swept down from the island. The ship was caught by the storm and could not head into the wind; so we gave way to it and were driven along.**[NIV] At this time of year, the winds in the Mediterranean made sea travel difficult. The winds were considered dangerous after September 15 and impossible between November 11 and March 10. But favorable winds and weather at that moment caused the captain to proceed with the journey. Had these conditions continued, the ship would have brought the passengers and crew to their destination within hours, certainly less than one day. But the air currents suddenly changed (a common occurrence in these waters), and the resulting north wind coming down off the mountains of southern Crete was deadly!

In describing this wind, Luke used the Greek word from which we get our English word "typhoon." The opposing currents of air created a whirling motion of both clouds and sea, but then the wind began to blow steadily in one direction.

Ancient ships lacked much ability to tack (i.e., follow a charted zigzag movement so as to make optimal use of unfavorable winds). When contrary winds arose, ships were mostly at their mercy and had to run away from land out into the open sea.

27:16-17 **We sailed behind a small island named Cauda, where with great difficulty we hoisted aboard the lifeboat that was being towed behind us. Then we banded the ship with ropes to strengthen the hull. The sailors were afraid of being driven**

across to the sandbars of Syrtis off the African coast, so they lowered the sea anchor and were thus driven before the wind.[NLT] The tiny island of *Cauda* (some twenty-three miles south) provided a temporary cover from the storm as the ship moved behind (south of) it. The sailors used this brief respite to tie everything down and prepare for the worst.

The *lifeboat* they managed to hoist aboard was an important tool in ancient sailing. It was typically used for landings and to maneuver the ship for primitive attempts at tacking. No doubt filled with water and on the verge of breaking loose or crashing into the mother ship, the lifeboat had to be brought on board. Anyone who has ever attempted to right an overturned canoe filled with water can appreciate the difficulty of such a task.

Another emergency measure was "banding" *the ship with ropes.* This involved passing ropes (or chains) under the ship to hold it together. Pulled tightly in a transverse fashion, such cables would hopefully help hold the timbers against the tremendous force of stormy waves.

Even though *Syrtis,* on the northern coast of Africa (Libya), was some four hundred miles away, the sailors began to fear the prospect of being driven there. The legendary quicksand and shoals in the southern Mediterranean were treacherous even in normal weather—so much so that Alexandrian ships would sail northward to Asia and then west to Italy to avoid this area. To combat this possible drift, the sailors *lowered the sea anchor.* This had the effect of giving the ship a dragging resistance to the wind and waves.

By putting the ship on a starboard tack (her right side to the wind) and by utilizing storm sails, the ship would have been able to drift slowly in a westerly direction.

27:18-19 We were being pounded by the storm so violently that on the next day they began to throw the cargo overboard, and on the third day with their own hands they threw the ship's tackle overboard.[NRSV] Despite all the emergency measures taken, the ship was being *pounded,* perhaps even beginning to take on water. Crew members began to jettison the *cargo* (the grain) to make the ship lighter. When this proved inadequate, the sailors eventually *threw the ship's tackle overboard.* This is likely a reference to nonessential gear—extra sails and yards (the stout poles used to support and spread the sails). Such actions indicate the crew's absolute desperation.

27:20 When neither sun nor stars appeared for many days and the storm continued raging, we finally gave up all hope of being saved.[NIV] The severity of the storm obscured the *sun* and *stars* (by which sailors navigated). The ship was being driven and tossed by the winds. It probably was leaking. A bleak sense of doom and despair permeated the passengers and crew.

27:21-22 **No one had eaten for a long time. Finally, Paul called the crew together and said, "Men, you should have listened to me in the first place and not left Fair Havens. You would have avoided all this injury and loss. But take courage! None of you will lose your lives, even though the ship will go down."**[NLT] The passengers and crew probably had not eaten due to fear, busyness, depression, or seasickness. They may have been fasting, or supplies may have been depleted (and were being rationed) due to the extra length of the journey.

> A crisis does not make a person; a crisis shows what a person is made of, and it tends to bring true leadership to the fore.
> *Warren Wiersbe*

Why would Paul talk to the crew this way? Perhaps this was merely his human side, which was not beyond the temptation to say, "I told you so." More likely, he was reminding the crew that, with God's guidance, he had prophesied this very problem (27:10). Because he had been right in the past, they should listen to him now and have hope. Paul told them, *"None of you will lose your lives."* For no one to die in a shipwreck would be considered a great miracle in the ancient world. In the future, they would listen to Paul (27:30-32), and their lives would be spared as a result.

Ancient pagans believed that a true philosopher would hold consistently and calmly to his teachings even in times of great calamity. False prophets would crack under pressure. Paul's demeanor gave him credence.

IN THE NICK OF TIME
At least three times (18:9-10; 23:11; 27:23-24), God gave Paul a timely word of encouragement. How gracious of God! Here he sends a divine messenger and dispatches him to the rocking, leaking, creaking ship—so as to soothe the troubled minds aboard. For us, encouragement may come in other, less dramatic, but equally meaningful ways: a phone call from a friend, a Bible verse, a needed hug, a note of encouragement, the meeting of a hidden need, the lyric of a song. If you're discouraged, ask God to give you some concrete reminder of his presence and promises. Then watch him act.

27:23-24 **"For last night there stood by me an angel of the God to whom I belong and whom I worship, and he said, 'Do not be**

afraid, Paul; you must stand before the emperor; and indeed, God has granted safety to all those who are sailing with you.'"[NRSV] Standing under dark skies on the deck of a ship that was bobbing like a cork, Paul stated the reason for his unlikely confidence. The previous night he had been visited by *an angel* of his God, the sum of whose message was, "Paul, relax! You're going to Rome. Nothing will prevent that. Everyone with you will be safe too." This was a reiteration of the assurance he had been given in 23:11.

27:25-26 **"So take courage! For I believe God. It will be just as he said. But we will be shipwrecked on an island."**[NLT] After relating this encouraging vision to his despairing shipmates, Paul admonished them (for the second time, see 27:22) to, literally, cheer up. Such a change in attitude was based not on some kind of false bravado. Paul felt cheered or encouraged because of his faith in God.

Having faith means taking God at his word. It means relying wholeheartedly on the clear-cut promises of God. The issue isn't whether a person has great faith but whether he or she has faith in a great God. This was true of Paul.

A shipwreck would not normally be considered good. Knowing about it in advance, however, would make the experience less terrifying for the passengers and crew.

THE SHIPWRECK / 27:27-44

God had revealed to Paul that a shipwreck was inevitable (27:26). Sure enough, the ship ran aground and began to break apart just off the coast of Malta. Though the experience proved to be harrowing, all 276 people on board were able to swim safely ashore. Repeatedly during this grim experience, Paul had proclaimed his faith in God. Now, during this end of Paul's two-week-long nightmare at sea, God demonstrated his faithfulness and mercy.

27:27-28 **On the fourteenth night we were still being driven across the Adriatic Sea, when about midnight the sailors sensed they were approaching land. They took soundings and found that the water was a hundred and twenty feet deep. A short time later they took soundings again and found it was ninety feet deep.**[NIV] In the two weeks that had passed since departing Fair Havens, the Alexandrian ship found itself adrift in the *Adriatic Sea* (here a reference to the central part of the Mediterranean Sea between Italy, Crete, and the northern coast of Africa).

Perhaps the sailors *sensed they were approaching land* because they heard the sound of breakers in the night. *Soundings* were made by throwing a weighted, marked line into the water. When the lead hit the bottom, sailors could tell the depth of the water from the marks on the rope.

Calculating a conservatively estimated rate of drift of some thirty-six miles per day (given the inclement weather conditions), a ship would, in two weeks' time, be very close to what is known as St. Paul's Bay at Malta. This calculation corresponds to the recorded soundings both cited by Luke and demonstrated by modern oceanographic research.

27:29 Fearing that we might run on the rocks, they let down four anchors from the stern and prayed for day to come.NRSV If breakers were being heard in the distance, to continue to push toward land in the dark would have been foolhardy. Anchors acted as a kind of primitive braking device; ships had many anchors (from five to fifteen). Therefore, the crew *let down four anchors* to keep the ship off the rocks and to keep the bow pointed toward the beach. They *prayed* for daylight so they could see where they were going.

GOD'S PART AND OUR PART

In the middle of a midnight squall, the passengers and crew (led by Paul) did all they could possibly do—they dropped some anchors to try to stop the runaway ship (27:29). Then Paul called on God to do what the pagan gods could not. This is a good reminder for us. We must never rely solely on our own wisdom or skills. But it is equally wrong to sit and do nothing when there are still actions we can take to overcome certain problems. Do all that you can to fix the problem. Then trust God to do his part.

27:30-32 In an attempt to escape from the ship, the sailors let the lifeboat down into the sea, pretending they were going to lower some anchors from the bow. Then Paul said to the centurion and the soldiers, "Unless these men stay with the ship, you cannot be saved." So the soldiers cut the ropes that held the lifeboat and let it fall away.NIV In the night, a group of sailors, not convinced by Paul's earlier assurances that all aboard would be saved, decided to *escape from the ship.* Under the guise of going out in the ship's dinghy to drop additional anchors and stabilize the vessel, the men intended to head for shore.

Somehow Paul discerned their real intentions. He may have been divinely warned or merely suspicious because of his own sailing experience. He alerted the *centurion,* Julius, and the Roman *soldiers* of the plot, implying that their own safety would be in jeopardy if these sailors were allowed to carry out their plan. Perhaps he felt that God's purposes in the imminent shipwreck included the presence of experienced seamen.

Unlike the situation at the beginning of the voyage, Paul had the centurion's ear and was functioning almost as the commander of the ship. Paul's words were followed completely, even when they went against common sense. The soldiers derailed the sailors' plan by cutting the lifeboat free. Without this smaller boat to ferry passengers to shore, everyone aboard was forced to depend on the Lord.

HANGING IN THERE

Apparently, a group of sailors concocted a plan to jump ship and leave everyone else to fend for themselves. The thought of remaining on a sinking ship seemed like sheer madness to them. But Paul learned of their plot and boldly spelled out the consequences. In essence, he told them exactly the opposite of what their senses told them: "You think you can find life by ignoring what God has said. Not true. You think you will experience death if you heed what God has said. Not true. No matter how desperate your situation seems, ultimate safety is found in remaining in God's will." This is a great lesson for us: It is far better to be with God in the midst of danger than to be without God in a place of apparent safety.

27:33-35 **As the darkness gave way to the early morning light, Paul begged everyone to eat. "You haven't touched food for two weeks," he said. "Please eat something now for your own good. For not a hair of your heads will perish." Then he took some bread, gave thanks to God before them all, and broke off a piece and ate it.**[NLT] With a voice-of-experience sense of the arduous task just ahead (making it to shore in cold, choppy waters), Paul encouraged his fellow travelers to gain strength and sustenance by eating. They had barely eaten for two weeks (due to a combination of fear, forced rationing, fasting, seasickness, and preoccupation with just surviving the storm). Again, Paul assured everyone of God's promise of safety. There, in the midst of dire circumstances, Paul presided over a traditional Jewish meal. Some believe that Luke's wording at this juncture indicates that Paul was actually celebrating communion. If so, it is likely that many of the recipients missed the deeper significance; the majority of the 276 passengers were probably not believers. More likely, Luke was paralleling the way Jesus broke bread with his disciples (Luke 9:16; 24:30). Thus, Luke was portraying how Christ was present with them and would bring them through this disaster.

27:36-38 Then everyone was encouraged, and all 276 of us began eating—for that is the number we had aboard. After eating, the crew lightened the ship further by throwing the cargo of wheat overboard.NLT Some critics have argued that this is too high a number of people on the ship. However, the historian Josephus wrote of being on a vessel bound for Italy with six hundred fellow passengers. Ships of this size were common.

The passengers and crew were *encouraged* and *began eating.* There was no need to ration what was left or save it for later, for they knew they would soon be on land. Had they not eaten, they might not have had the strength to swim to shore.

In the first instance of jettisoning (see 27:18), some of the cargo had to be kept for ballast, lest the ship become completely unmaneuverable. Now, by lightening the load even more, the ship would ride higher in the water and be able to get closer to shore before running aground.

27:39-41 In the morning they did not recognize the land, but they noticed a bay with a beach, on which they planned to run the ship ashore, if they could. So they cast off the anchors and left them in the sea. At the same time they loosened the ropes that

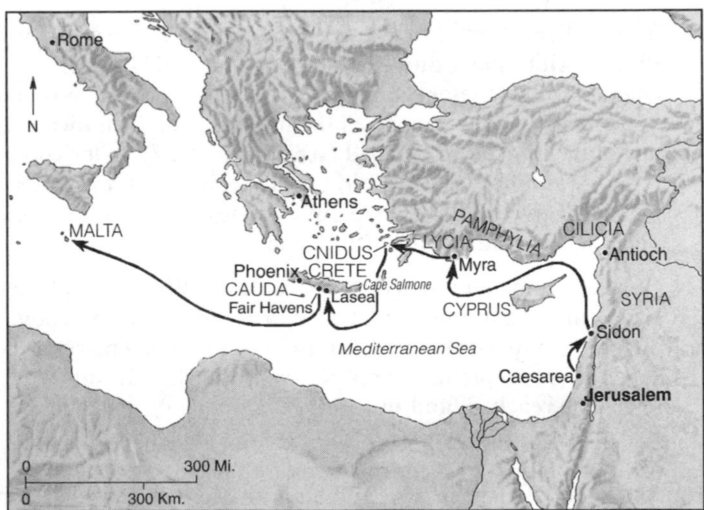

THE TRIP TOWARD ROME

Paul began his two-thousand-mile trip to Rome at Caesarea. To avoid the open seas, the ship followed the coastline. At Myra, Paul was put on a vessel bound for Italy. It arrived with difficulty at Cnidus, then went to Crete, landing at the port of Fair Havens. The next stop was Phoenix, but the ship was blown south around the island of Cauda, then was storm-driven for two weeks until it was shipwrecked on the island of Malta.

tied the steering-oars; then hoisting the foresail to the wind, they made for the beach. But striking a reef, they ran the ship aground; the bow stuck and remained immovable, but the stern was being broken up by the force of the waves.NRSV The disoriented sailors had no idea where they were. The geography and topography of what is now known as St. Paul's Bay on the northeast shore of modern Malta fits this description. They prepared *to run the ship ashore.*

The sailors *cast off the anchors,* thus eliminating any kind of "braking action." They *loosened the ropes* that held the *steering-oars* in place (these long wooden paddles served as a primitive kind of rudder). *Hoisting* a small sail *(the foresail)* would let the wind drive the ship ashore.

Before reaching land, however, the ship became wedged on a sandbar (modern research has confirmed between St. Paul's Bay and the island of Salmonetta the existence of a shallow channel only one to three hundred yards wide). Striking this underwater barrier between the two seas, the ship could go no further. Fierce waves began to strike the exposed rear of the vessel. Already weakened from a two-week pounding on the open seas, the ship quickly began to fall apart.

27:42 The soldiers wanted to kill the prisoners to make sure they didn't swim ashore and escape.NLT Roman soldiers were charged with the safekeeping and safe delivery of any prisoners in their care. The law required them to pay with their own lives if any of their prisoners escaped (see 12:19; 16:27). In the certain chaos of a shipwreck, it would be relatively easy for prisoners to slip away. The soldiers' instinctive reaction was to *kill the prisoners* so as to prevent this from happening.

27:43-44 But the centurion wanted to spare Paul's life and kept them from carrying out their plan. He ordered those who could swim to jump overboard first and get to land. The rest were to get there on planks or on pieces of the ship. In this way everyone reached land in safety.NIV Despite the potential for risk, the *centurion* Julius was impressed enough with Paul to keep the soldiers *from carrying out their plan.* As the highest ranking official, he had the full authority to make this decision.

Some swam; others floated ashore on pieces of the collapsing ship. The evacuation plan worked, because *everyone reached land in safety.* No prisoners are recorded as having escaped. This sequence of events preserved Paul for his later ministry in Rome and fulfilled his prophetic utterance that everyone on the ship would be saved (27:22).

In the minds of both Greeks and Romans, surviving a disaster at sea was evidence of a person's innocence. The powerful sea gods were not believed to spare the guilty.

THE JOURNEY

Paul's arduous trip to Rome (chapters 27–28) provides us with at least four good tips for making the most of our own journey through life:

1. Recognize the presence of God (27:1–28:31)—understand that God is with you, even in the darkest times.
2. Rely on the people of God (27:1-3; 28:2, 7-10, 14-15, 30)—lean on the people whom God graciously puts in your life.
3. Rest on the promises of God (27:22-25; cf. 23:11)—know that what God has said, he will do.
4. Remember the purposes of God (28:8-9, 17-31)—keep your eyes on the destination and ultimate goal.

Acts 28

PAUL ON THE ISLAND OF MALTA / 28:1-10

Detailed plots on his life, angry mobs, storms at sea, shipwrecks—all the forces of hell seemed to have been intensifying their efforts to keep Paul from reaching Rome. Now, on the island of Malta, the attack continued—Paul was bitten by a poisonous snake. Paul not only survived the serpent's attack unharmed, but he turned around and healed a number of sick people on the island. During the three-month stay in Malta (see 28:11), Paul was showered with hospitality. What the devil intended for evil God turned into good.

28:1-2 **Once we were safe on shore, we learned that we were on the island of Malta. The people of the island were very kind to us. It was cold and rainy, so they built a fire on the shore to welcome us and warm us.**[NLT] In about two weeks, the storm had pushed Paul's ship some 470 miles west of Fair Havens, Crete. Only when the crew and passengers came ashore did they realize that they had reached *Malta,* an island 60 miles south of Sicily and 320 miles from Rome. The islanders there were of Phoeni-cian ancestry and had given the island its name (taken from the Canaanite word for "refuge"). Malta had excellent harbors and was ideally located for trade. Many Roman soldiers retired there.

Though the islanders were considered barbarians by the Greeks and Romans (because they spoke a Phoenician dialect), they demonstrated warmth and civility to Paul and the rest of the shipwreck survivors.

28:3-4 **As Paul gathered an armful of sticks and was laying them on the fire, a poisonous snake, driven out by the heat, fastened itself onto his hand. The people of the island saw it hanging there and said to each other, "A murderer, no doubt! Though he escaped the sea, justice will not permit him to live."**[NLT] In cold weather, reptiles become extremely lethargic. Lying in a bundle of twigs and brush, a snake might easily go unnoticed. Apparently, the jostling of

> *It is only the little man who refuses the little task.*
> *William Barclay*

Paul's walking combined with the warmth of the fire caused the *poisonous snake* to become roused. It struck Paul on the hand.

The Maltese people quickly tried to make sense of these events by using their pagan presuppositions. Steeped in Greek legends and stories of gods relentlessly bringing wrongdoers to justice, they concluded that Paul must have been guilty of murder. Though he had somehow escaped divine retribution in the shipwreck, Nemesis, the Greek goddess of retribution, must have orchestrated this additional means of punishing him.

BEING A NEIGHBOR
In the wake of this shipwreck, Paul and the rest of the voyagers bound for Rome found the Maltese people to be extremely warm and hospitable. Nothing is said about whether these islanders were Christians; nevertheless, they demonstrated great compassion. Often this is still the case when disasters strike—unbelievers rush to do what they can. And sometimes, unfortunately, the church is dragging behind, too absorbed in its programs and internal affairs to help. As those who do know Christ, we ought to be leaders in the business of neighboring. Make it your goal to honor Christ by being the first to help in times of need.

28:5-6 But Paul shook off the snake into the fire and was unharmed. The people waited for him to swell up or suddenly drop dead. But when they had waited a long time and saw no harm come to him, they changed their minds and decided he was a god.[NLT] To the amazement of the Maltese observers, Paul not only did not drop dead, he did not even exhibit any swelling or discomfort. Paul was unfazed by this experience with the snake. God had promised safe passage to him (27:23-25), and nothing could prohibit his reaching Rome.

When these superstitious pagans saw that Paul was unhurt by the poisonous viper, they did a complete about-face in their assessment of him. They had assumed that Paul was a murderer (28:4); now they decided he was a god. A similar appraisal is reported in 14:11-18 when Paul ministered at Lystra. It is reasonable to assume that Paul deflected any idolatrous comments in the same manner as he had done previously.

28:7 There was an estate nearby that belonged to Publius, the chief official of the island. He welcomed us to his home and for three days entertained us hospitably.[NIV] The *chief official of the island* is literally the "first man of the island" and was an official designation, probably referring to a kind of political authority, like a governor. Apparently wealthy, this governor, named

Publius, had a large *estate.* Whether he invited all 276 people to his home or whether he invited only Paul (and Luke) is unclear. In view of the miracle on the beach (the snakebite), Paul's "divine" reputation, and the illness afflicting Publius's father, it is likely that Publius entertained only Paul and his immediate entourage (perhaps also Julius and the ship's owner).

SAFE IN GOD'S HANDS

To Paul's long list of trials and tribulations (see 2 Corinthians 11:23-28) can be added this bizarre incident of a snakebite (28:3-6). Truly the forces of hell itself were arrayed in a desperate attempt to keep the apostle from reaching Rome. But God had given his assurance that Paul would have the opportunity to preach the gospel there (see 23:11; 27:24). Through Paul, the life-changing message of the risen Christ would spread through even the highest strata of Roman society. This episode is a strong reminder that when we walk with the Lord, nothing can stop us from doing his will.

28:8-10 It so happened that the father of Publius lay sick in bed with fever and dysentery. Paul visited him and cured him by praying and putting his hands on him. After this happened, the rest of the people on the island who had diseases also came and were cured. They bestowed many honors on us, and when we were about to sail, they put on board all the provisions we needed.[NRSV] Malta *fever* is now known to be caused by microbes in goats' milk. This illness, like dysentery, seems to have been common on the island. A person could be ill for a few months to two or three years. When Paul learned that *the father of Publius* was suffering from this disease, he visited him, laid hands on him, and prayed over him. This is the only reference in Acts that mentions both prayer and laying on of hands.

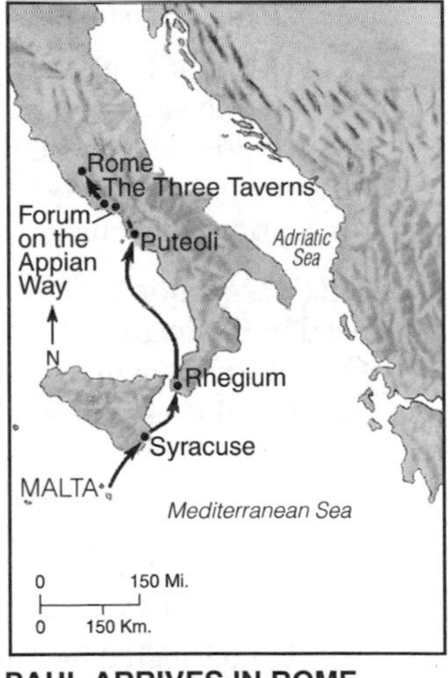

PAUL ARRIVES IN ROME

The shipwreck occurred on Malta, where the ship's company spent three months. Finally, another ship gave them passage for the one hundred miles to Syracuse, capital of Sicily, then sailed on to Rhegium, finally dropping anchor at Puteoli. Paul was taken to the Forum on the Appian Way and to The Three Taverns before arriving in Rome.

The man's complete healing followed. The news of this miracle spread quickly, and soon everyone with any kind of disease or ailment came to Paul to be cured. Perhaps Luke, a medical doctor by profession, used his skill and expertise as well, so that he and Paul were able to collaborate in a healing ministry. Paul probably also proclaimed the gospel in all its fullness during his stay; however, Luke does not state that here.

Three months passed (see 28:11), because the shipwreck survivors had to wait for the passing of winter and arrangements to complete their journey on another vessel. When at last the time came to leave the island, the grateful Maltese people inundated Paul and his friends with gifts and *provisions* for the remainder of their trip of 320 miles to Rome.

Even as a shipwrecked prisoner, Paul continued to minister to others. On this trip alone, Julius, Publius, the ship's passengers and crew, and all the Maltese people were affected. Because of one faithful witness, the gospel continued to spread.

PAUL ARRIVES AT ROME / 28:11-16

The last leg of Paul's journey to Rome was almost anticlimactic—smooth sailing, a warm reception by some Italian believers, his own private lodging (house arrest rather than imprisonment in a Roman penal facility). The stage was now set for Paul to begin ministering in the most influential city in the world.

28:11-12 **After three months we put out to sea in a ship that had wintered in the island. It was an Alexandrian ship with the figurehead of the twin gods Castor and Pollux. We put in at Syracuse and stayed there three days.**[NIV] Ships began sailing again between mid-February and mid-March, depending on the weather. Sailing vessels often would be named in honor of certain deities. These deities were thought to serve as protectors and would be called upon in times of trouble. *Castor and Pollux* were the twin sons of Zeus, the patrons of navigation. Their constellation (Gemini) was considered by sailors to be a sign of good luck. This Alexandrian ship was also likely a grain ship. It promptly (perhaps in one day's time) arrived in *Syracuse,* the chief city of Sicily.

28:13-14 **From there we sailed across to Rhegium. A day later a south wind began blowing, so the following day we sailed up the coast to Puteoli. There we found some believers, who invited us to stay with them seven days. And so we came to Rome.**[NLT] *Rhegium* is modern-day Reggio on the "toe" of Italy. *Puteoli* is now called Pozzuoli and is located some 150 miles south of Rome. Situated in the Bay of Naples, Puteoli was the preferred point of entry for Alexandrian wheat ships (prior to the building of larger port facilities at Portus, near Ostia, during the reign of Claudius).

At Puteoli, Paul and his colleagues met some fellow Christians and were allowed to stay with them for *seven days* (apparently while the ship was being unloaded or while the centurion, Julius, was conducting other official business).

How is it that a community of believers came to be in Puteoli? One possibility is that Jewish pilgrims from Rome to Jerusalem were among the first converts at Pentecost (2:1-10). Returning home, these zealous new followers of Christ began to evangelize their neighbors. From cosmopolitan Rome (with its many visitors), the gospel spread quickly to surrounding areas.

BEING MISSIONARY FRIENDLY

When Paul reached Italy, he and his entourage met some Christians who were delighted to host them. Imagine what that week must have been like. Imagine getting to sit and talk with the apostle Paul and hear story after story of God's power and faithfulness. What would such a visit do to your faith and for your family's spiritual health? Though we can't open our doors to Paul, we do have the opportunity to host modern-day missionaries home on furlough. In a similar manner, their presence in our midst can tremendously strengthen our own walks with God. Pray about hosting a missionary family home on leave.

28:15 The brothers and sisters in Rome had heard we were coming, and they came to meet us at the Forum on the Appian Way. Others joined us at The Three Taverns. When Paul saw them, he thanked God and took courage.[NLT] The *believers in Rome* heard about Paul's imminent arrival, probably due to messengers sent by the believers in Puteoli. Eager to meet and greet the great apostle, an entourage headed south and intercepted Paul's party *at the Forum on the Appian Way,* a town about forty-three miles from Rome. A second welcoming committee of Roman believers encountered Paul at *The Three Taverns,* thirty-five miles south of Rome. Paul's entrance to Rome was more like a victor's triumphal entry than a prisoner's march. A "tavern" was a shop or a place that provided food and lodging for travelers. The Appian Way, a main thoroughfare to Rome from the south, featured many such inns.

Paul was grateful for this warm Italian reception; he *thanked God and took courage.* Curiously, nothing more is said about Paul's interaction with the Roman church. Instead, Luke chose to focus on Paul's outreach efforts to the Jewish community in Rome and, after their rejection, to the Gentile population.

ENCOURAGING GOD'S LABORERS
When Paul was greeted by the Roman Christians he "took courage" (28:15). What exactly did they do? We're not told. Probably they prayed for him, surrounded him (literally), served him, and loved him. Maybe they even gave him little gifts or notes of welcome. After such a long, hard journey, Paul was thankful to see some friendly faces. We can perform a similar role in the lives of modern-day missionaries and pastors. Whether through a small gift, a pat on the back, a word of thanks, an E-mail note, or a card, you can show love and demonstrate appreciation to your spiritual leaders. It will help them take courage.

28:16 When we arrived in Rome, Paul was permitted to have his own private lodging, though he was guarded by a soldier.[NLT] At last Paul *arrived in Rome,* the most influential city on earth. This was the fulfillment of a long-term desire (Romans 1:10-16). Paul's *private lodging* was a rented house (see 28:30). Though *guarded* around the clock (in four-hour shifts) *by a soldier* (perhaps members of the Praetorian—or palace—guard, see Philippians 1:13), Paul had much more freedom than a typical prisoner.

PAUL PREACHES AT ROME UNDER GUARD / 28:17-31

Paul's first act in Rome was to call together the Jewish leaders. He wanted to declare his innocence of the charges brought against him in Jerusalem. But more than this, he wanted to proclaim the gospel to his Hebrew brothers.

A meeting was arranged in which Paul gave an all-day lecture on the kingdom of God and the Messiahship of Jesus. Only a few of the Jews accepted his message, but even those who rejected the gospel left quietly. Consequently, for two solid years, Paul was able to preach and minister unhindered to all who came to see him in his rented quarters—and the stream of visitors was apparently quite steady.

28:17 Three days after Paul's arrival, he called together the local Jewish leaders. He said to them, "Brothers, I was arrested in Jerusalem and handed over to the Roman government, even though I had done nothing against our people or the customs of our ancestors."[NLT] The decree of Claudius expelling Jews from Rome (18:2) happened eleven years previously (A.D. 49–60), so by the time of Paul's arrival, Jewish leaders were back in Rome. These Jews were likely an unofficial gathering of the leaders of various synagogues, not an official ruling body.

After *three days* (presumably to settle into his new accommodations), Paul *called together the local Jewish leaders* because he did not have the freedom to visit them in their synagogues. Beginning his presentation, Paul stated his innocence in the charge of violating Jewish laws or customs. Nevertheless, he had been *handed over to the Roman government.* This phrasing is similar to Christ's statements as found in Luke 9:44 and 18:32. The Jews in Rome were not hostile to Paul (see 28:21-22).

28:18-19 "The Romans tried me and wanted to release me, for they found no cause for the death sentence. But when the Jewish leaders protested the decision, I felt it necessary to appeal to Caesar, even though I had no desire to press charges against my own people."[NLT] Paul reiterated the Romans' inability or unwillingness to execute him. On three separate occasions, statements had been made to the effect that Paul had done nothing to deserve the *death sentence* (Claudias Lysias in 23:29; Festus in 25:25 and 26:31).

Paul emphasized that he had appealed to Caesar (25:11) because the Jewish leaders had adamantly and unjustly continued to pressure the authorities for a conviction. He felt he had no other recourse. And he further assured the Jews of his own motives in appealing to Caesar—not because he was trying to harm his own countrymen but solely to be declared innocent and set free.

28:20 "I asked you to come here today so we could get acquainted and so I could tell you that I am bound with this chain because I believe that the hope of Israel—the Messiah—has already come."[NLT] The phrase "the hope of Israel" has been mentioned several times by Paul (see 23:6; 24:15; 26:7; 28:20). For Paul, the messianic hope meant the fulfillment of God's messianic prophecies first given to the patriarch Abraham. For all of its history, the nation looked forward to a time when God's anointed one would rule over a heavenly kingdom. Because of his conviction that Jesus of Nazareth was that long-awaited *Messiah* and because of Christ's resurrection from the dead, Paul was adamant that his message and theology were consistent with Jewish hope through the ages. Paul wanted his countrymen to come to see (as he had) that this relatively new entity known as the Christian church was not a dangerous sect or departure from traditional orthodox Judaism but simply the next phase in the unfolding plan of God that had been first announced to Abraham.

28:21-22 **They replied, "We have not received any letters from Judea concerning you, and none of the brothers who have come from there has reported or said anything bad about you. But we want to hear what your views are, for we know that people everywhere are talking against this sect."**[NIV] The Jewish leaders had not heard specific allegations about Paul and his case, but they had heard a steady stream of negative comments about the *sect* of people who followed the one called Christ. There was a growing group of these people right there in Rome. The people *talking against* Christianity may have been Jews who kept up with events in Israel, together with skeptical Romans. Christians were denounced everywhere by the Romans because they were seen as a threat to the Roman establishment. They believed in one God, whereas the Romans had many gods, including Caesar. The Christians were committed to an authority higher than Caesar.

The Jewish leaders from Jerusalem probably had given up their attempt to have Paul prosecuted once his case came under the jurisdiction of the Roman emperor. Or perhaps they had heard about the shipwreck and presumed that Paul had been killed. In any case, they hadn't sent any word against Paul to the Jews in Rome. While Jews were allowed to practice their religion, they were viewed with some contempt by their "cosmopolitan" Roman neighbors. Whatever information the Jewish leaders had, they expressed an interest in hearing what Paul had to say.

MISSING HEAVEN BY INCHES
Paul quoted the prophet Isaiah to make the point that though the Jews knew all about God in an academic way, they didn't really know him personally (28:25-27). Though many of them had God's Word in their heads, it had never filtered down into their hearts and changed their lives. This is the great danger of being religious. Rich words and meaningful truth can turn into overused clichés and meaningless rituals. Years of going through the motions can cause our hearts to become numb to the truth. Even more sobering is the fact that in this deadened state, people often deceive themselves into thinking they are honoring God. Ask the Spirit of God to keep you open to the truth.

28:23-24 **After they had set a day to meet with him, they came to him at his lodgings in great numbers. From morning until evening he explained the matter to them, testifying to the kingdom of God and trying to convince them about Jesus both from the law of Moses and from the prophets. Some were convinced by**

what he had said, while others refused to believe.NRSV A meeting was arranged, and when the time for that appointment came, *great numbers* of Roman Jews came to hear from Paul. It was an all-day affair, during which Paul used the Old Testament to "explain" the gospel to the Jews. In essence, Paul reminded the Jews of the many Old Testament prophecies and references to the Messiah; then he skillfully demonstrated how Jesus, in his coming, living, dying, and rising, exactly fulfilled every divine promise and every Jewish hope.

The focus of Paul's message was the kingdom of God. This kingdom was a major preoccupation of Jewish thought and continues to be a major source of discussion. Some Christians believe the kingdom of God has already come in a spiritual sense because of the coming of the King (Luke 10:9-11; 17:20-21) and his bestowing of the Holy Spirit at Pentecost to dwell in the hearts of believers. Other followers of Christ believe the kingdom is yet future—a full, final, and physical reign of Jesus (after his return) over a perfect earthly kingdom where sin and evil no longer exist.

It is doubtful that Paul lectured all day or that this presentation was a monologue. As per Jewish custom, we can suppose this was an energetic and often heated dialogue, with much questioning back and forth. The effect of this long discourse and discussion was that some of the Jewish leaders *were convinced.* The verb is an imperfect, which probably conveys the idea that they were beginning to be convinced. This does not necessarily imply conversion, at least not as the result of this initial dialogue only. Others, however, *refused to believe,* demonstrating hard-heartedness (see 28:27) and spiritual blindness (Romans 11:10; 2 Corinthians 4:4).

28:25-27 They disagreed among themselves and began to leave after Paul had made this final statement: "The Holy Spirit spoke the truth to your forefathers when he said through Isaiah the prophet: 'Go to this people and say, "You will be ever hearing but never understanding; you will be ever seeing but never perceiving." For this people's heart has become calloused; they hardly hear with their ears, and they have closed their eyes. Otherwise they might see with their eyes, hear with their ears, understand with their hearts and turn, and I would heal them."'NIV In this interchange, Paul had the final word, and it was a strong rebuke. He compared the departing, arguing Jewish leaders to the long-ago audience of *Isaiah the prophet* (see Isaiah 6:9-10). Those Jews had heard the very word of God and had seen the spokesman of God, but because of stubbornness and pride, they had been unable to understand and perceive the deeper, life-changing implications of the divine revelation that was being extended to them. Rather than submitting to judgment by the truth, they had sat in judgment of truth. The great irony is that these Jews viewed themselves as religiously successful and slated for divine commendation, when in truth they were spiritually blind, deaf, and under divine condemnation! However, we must not generalize an anti-Semitic attitude in Paul's words; 28:24 says that some were convinced and believed.

28:28 **"So I want you to realize that this salvation from God is also available to the Gentiles, and they will accept it."**NLT As he had done on several prior occasions (see 13:46; 18:6; and 19:8-10), Paul announced a turning from the unresponsive, hard-hearted Jews to the receptive *Gentiles.* From that point on, the non-Jews would be given priority when it came to evangelical witness. At some future point, Paul apparently expected a change of heart by his countrymen (see Romans 11:25-32), but for the immediate future Paul would direct his ministry to those who were eager to embrace the truth about Christ.

MAKING THE MOST OF A BAD SITUATION

Paul remained in Rome under guard (28:16) in a rented house for two years (28:30). There sat the greatest apostle and spokesman for Christianity—unable to move freely and minister as he desired. However, Paul didn't complain or despair. He simply did what he could. Able to receive visitors, he taught, preached, and counseled even while he was confined to quarters. According to Philippians 4:22, he had a fruitful ministry. He also used the occasion to write epistles (Ephesians, Philippians, Colossians, and Philemon) that have impacted millions of believers down through the centuries. If you find yourself in a "negative" or unpleasant situation, look for ways to redeem the circumstances. There is never a time or place in which you can't glorify and serve God.

28:29 **And when he had said these words, the Jews departed and had a great dispute among themselves.**NKJV This verse is not included in most of the ancient manuscripts. It was most likely a scribal addition, but it adds nothing new. The fact that the Jews were arguing among themselves is a point previously made in 28:25.

28:30-31 **For the next two years, Paul lived in his own rented house. He welcomed all who visited him, proclaiming the Kingdom of God with all boldness and teaching about the Lord Jesus**

Christ. And no one tried to stop him.[NLT] Luke's record ends abruptly, but this was common. A number of ancient works have sudden endings. While Paul was under house arrest, he did more than speak to the Jews. He wrote letters, commonly called his Prison Epistles, to the Ephesians, Colossians, and Philippians. He also wrote personal letters, such as the one to Philemon. This ending shows the gospel going forward to Rome, as the great commission had directed. It had now reached the international capital of the Gentiles.

He *welcomed all who visited him,* and that list was surely long. Luke was with Paul in Rome (2 Timothy 4:11). Timothy often visited him (Philippians 1:1; Colossians 1:1; Philemon 1:1), as did Tychicus (Ephesians 6:21), Epaphroditus (Philippians 4:18), and Mark (Colossians 4:10). Paul witnessed to the whole Roman guard (Philippians 1:13) and was involved with the Roman believers.

Tradition says that Paul was released after two years of house arrest in Rome and then set off on a fourth missionary journey. Five reasons for this tradition are as follows: (1) Luke does not give us an account of his trial before Caesar—and Luke was a detailed chronicler; (2) the prosecution had two years to bring the case to trial, and time may have run out; (3) in his letter to the Philippians, written during his imprisonment in Rome, Paul implied that he would soon be released and would do further traveling; (4) Paul mentions several places where he intended to take the gospel, but he never visited those places in his first three journeys; (5) early Christian literature talks plainly about other travels by Paul.

During Paul's time of freedom, he may have continued to travel extensively, even going to Spain (see Romans 15:24, 28) and back to the churches in Greece. The books of 1 Timothy and Titus were written during this time. Later, Paul was imprisoned again, probably in Rome, where he wrote his last letter (2 Timothy). During this first Roman imprisonment, he spoke *with all boldness . . . and no one tried to stop him.* The Greek word *akolutos* ("without hindrance") is the last word of Acts, thus ending the book on a triumphal note.

Why does Acts end here and so abruptly? The book is not about the life of Paul but about the spread of the gospel, and that had been clearly presented by Luke. God apparently thought it was not necessary for someone to write an additional book describing the continuing history of the early church. Now that the gospel had been preached and established at the center of trade and government, it would spread across the world.

THE ADVENTURE CONTINUES

The book of Acts deals with the history of the Christian church and its expansion in ever-widening circles touching Jerusalem, Antioch, Ephesus, and Rome—the most influential cities in the western world. Acts also shows the mighty miracles and testimonies of the heroes and martyrs of the early church—Peter, Stephen, James, Paul. All the ministry was prompted and held together by the Holy Spirit, working in the lives of ordinary people—merchants, travelers, slaves, jailers, church leaders, males, females, Gentiles, Jews, rich, and poor. The book of Acts ends abruptly, showing that the history of the church was not yet complete. Many unsung heroes of the faith would continue the work, through the Holy Spirit, in succeeding generations, changing the world with a changeless message—that Jesus Christ is Savior and Lord for all who call on him. Today we are called to be a part of the sequel, to be the unsung heroes in the continuing story of the spread of the gospel. It is that same message that we Christians are to take to our world so that many more may hear and believe.

BIBLIOGRAPHY

Bruce, F. F. *The Book of Acts.* Grand Rapids: William B. Eerdmans Publishing Company, 1976.

———. *The Acts of the Apostles.* Grand Rapids: William B. Eerdmans Publishing Company; third edition, 1990.

Calvin, John. "Acts." In the Crossway Classic Commentaries. Edited by Alister McGrath and J. I. Packer. Wheaton, Ill.: Crossway Books, 1995.

Harrison, Everett. *Acts: The Expanding Church.* Chicago: Moody Press, 1975.

Longenecker, Richard. "Acts." In *The Expositor's Bible Commentary.* Vol. 9. Edited by Frank E. Gaebelein. Grand Rapids: Zondervan Publishing House, 1981.

Marshall, I. Howard. "Acts." In the Tyndale New Testament Commentaries. Grand Rapids: William B. Eerdmans Publishing Company, 1986.

Polhill, John B. "Acts." in the New American Commentary. Vol. 26. Nashville: Broadman Press, 1992.

Ryrie, Charles. *The Acts of the Apostles.* Chicago, Ill.: Moody Press, 1961.

Walvoord, John F., and Roy B. Zuck. *Bible Knowledge Commentary: New Testament Edition.* Wheaton, Ill.: Victor Books, 1983.

INDEX